Law, Governance and Technology Series

Volume 78

The *Law, Governance and Technology Series* is intended to attract manuscripts arising from an interdisciplinary approach in law, artificial intelligence and information technologies. The idea is to bridge the gap between research in IT law and IT-applications for lawyers developing a unifying techno-legal perspective. The series will welcome proposals that have a fairly specific focus on problems or projects that will lead to innovative research charting the course for new interdisciplinary developments in law, legal theory, and law and society research as well as in computer technologies, artificial intelligence and cognitive sciences. In broad strokes, manuscripts for this series may be mainly located in the fields of the Internet law (data protection, intellectual property, Internet rights, etc.), Computational models of the legal contents and legal reasoning, Legal Information Retrieval, Electronic Data Discovery, Collaborative Tools (e.g. Online Dispute Resolution platforms), Metadata and XML Technologies (for Semantic Web Services), Technologies in Courtrooms and Judicial Offices (E-Court), Technologies for Governments and Administrations (E-Government), Legal Multimedia, and Legal Electronic Institutions (Multi-Agent Systems and Artificial Societies).

Vera Lúcia Raposo
Editor

The European Artificial Intelligence Act

Promises and Perils?

Springer

Editor
Vera Lúcia Raposo
NOVA School of Law
NOVA University
Lisbon, Portugal

CEDIS (Research & Development Centre on Law and Society)
NOVA School of Law
NOVA University
Lisbon, Portugal

ISSN 2352-1902 ISSN 2352-1910 (electronic)
Law, Governance and Technology Series
ISBN 978-3-031-98405-1 ISBN 978-3-031-98406-8 (eBook)
https://doi.org/10.1007/978-3-031-98406-8

This work was supported by Instituto Juridico, University of Coimbra

This Springer imprint is published by the registered company Springer Nature Switzerland AG
The registered company address is: Gewerbestrasse 11, 6330 Cham, Switzerland

Preface

The advent of AI has introduced unprecedented opportunities, enhanced productivity and efficiency, and transformed virtually every area of our lives. However, these advancements come with significant risks, particularly in terms of privacy, security, and ethical considerations. At its core, human dignity might be at stake.

I do not invoke 'human dignity' lightly. I often tell my students that law students tend to rely too heavily on the concept of 'human dignity' in their exams and arguments, frequently without fully understanding or substantiating it. Yet, when it comes to AI, I truly think this concern applies. I write the preface of this book with full candour: I openly acknowledge that I know very little about AI, its true nature, its far-reaching implications, and what it might mean for the future of humankind. I invoke human dignity here because I genuinely believe that if AI is misused, it will ultimately affect our very existence, shaping our way of life and impacting our inherent dignity. In light of this belief, it is crucial to consider the responsible and ethical use of AI, ensuring that its deployment upholds and respects what makes us human. These considerations help explain the global momentum for some form of AI regulatory intervention, especially in the European Union (EU).

No jurisdiction has approached this with the same level of detail and stringency as the European lawmakers. This is not surprising, given the EU's recent history of pioneering digital regulatory frameworks. The 'Digital Europe' initiative underscores the EU's commitment to comprehensively addressing all aspects of the digital field, and AI is no exception. The so-called 'AI Act' is a direct outcome of this commitment.

The AI Act seeks to regulate AI (or AI systems, as it refers to them) with a focus on product safety, characterised by an extremely detailed and exhaustive approach. The Act's level of intricacy, its rigorous demands, and the often opaque nature of its provisions make it a natural focal point of attention and inquiry. Additionally, the AI Act carries the potential to exert a global influence akin to that of the General Data Protection Regulation—a phenomenon widely recognised as the 'Brussels Effect'—which amplifies its significance on an almost universal scale. This is the 'raison d'être' of this book.

The book features contributions from some of the most reputable experts in the field. While they come from diverse backgrounds and various disciplines, they all share a common passion for the subject and possess deep knowledge in their respective areas.

Part I focuses on the AIA, its history, and its general framework. It begins with an exploration of the events that led to the creation of the AI Act, narrated by Anton Vedder, Maja Nisevic, and Sofie Fleerackers (chapter 'Ethics First? On the EU Approach to AI Governance'). Following this, Markus Frischhut discusses how the AI Act incorporates and develops the so-called 'EU values' and examines the recognition and integration of these values within the Act (chapter 'The EU's Common Values (Art 2 EU-Treaty) as the Underlying Philosophy of the AI Act') and Sofia Palmieri and Tom Goffin delve into how the AI Act upholds respect for fundamental rights (chapter 'Artificial Intelligence and Fundamental Rights: Under the European Legal Eye').

Part II of the book dives into the specific content of the AIA. Opening this section, Denis Steckelmacher and Bart Bogaerts provide a critical examination of the concept of 'AI' as defined by the AI Act (chapter 'Definition of AI'). This sets the stage for the subsequent exploration of various segments of the AI Act, starting with the analysis of the institutional framework established by it, in a chapter authored by Abeer Malik and Barry Solaiman (chapter 'Appraising the Institutional Framework of the EU's Artificial Intelligence Act (AI Act)'). Subsequently, Rostam J. Neuwirth addresses forbidden AI systems (chapter 'Prohibited Artificial Intelligence Practices Revisited'), while Dariusz Szostek and Rafał Tomasz Prabucki analyse high-risk AI systems (chapter 'High-Risk AI Systems'), and Lee Andrew Bygrave and Rebecca Schmidt focus on non-high-risk AI systems (chapter 'Regulating Non-High-Risk AI Systems Under the EU's Artificial Intelligence Act, with Special Focus on the Role of Soft Law'). Tina van der Linden and Jorge Constantino, in turn, examine AI applications that fall outside the scope of the AI Act (chapter 'Artificial Intelligence (AI) Systems Not Covered by the AI Regulation'). Following this, Santa Slokenberga investigates issues related to non-compliance with the AI Act (chapter 'Enforcing the AI Act in a Composite EU Administration') and Gauthier Chassang discusses innovation and the model for regulatory sandboxes incorporated in the AI Act (chapter 'Regulatory Sandboxes for Trustworthy AI: An EU Framework for Experimenting AI Systems and Fostering Agile Regulation').

Building on this in-depth exploration of the AI Act's content, Part III of the book contextualises it within existing legal frameworks. Pin Lean Lau examines the AI Act and the GDPR relationship, addressing data protection issues (chapter 'The AI Act and Data Protection- The Interplay Between Artificial Intelligence and Data: the AI Act and the GDPR'), Matthew Dacoronias-Marina and Mateja Durovic discuss the role of consumer protection within the AI Act (chapter 'Consumer Protection in Light of the New AI Act: Behind the Smiles—Emotional AI, Consumer Trust, and the EU's Regulatory Response'), while Sofia Palmieri explores the intersection between the AI Act and the regulations governing medical devices (chapter

'AI Act and MDR: Investigating Regulatory Overlaps, Influences, and Joint Application Issues').

Part IV shifts the focus to other jurisdictions that are also working to establish legal frameworks for AI. The selected jurisdictions include the UK (analysed by Andrew Charlesworth in the chapter 'AI Regulation in the UK'), China (discussed by Meng Wang and Li Du, in the chapter 'Regulatory Issues Related to AI Development and Use: A Comparative Analysis of Chinese and EU Laws'), Singapore (examined by Mark Findlay and Jane Loo in the chapter 'Juxtaposing Approaches to Risk-Based AI Governance in Different 'Rights' Contexts: A Comparative Analysis Between Singapore and the EU'), Taiwan (covered by Chih-Hsiung Chen in the chapter 'Taiwan's AI Regulatory Approach: A Sector-Based Regulatory Approach'), and the US (explored by James X. Dempsey, in the chapter 'Artificial Intelligence Regulation in the United States: A Patchwork of Laws').

Finally, Part V presents concluding reflections authored by myself, offering a comprehensive and critical overview of the AI Act (chapter 'Reflections on the AI Act: Brussels, Do We Have a Problem?'). These concluding notes engage in an ongoing dialogue with the contributions of the various authors who participated in this challenging and insightful project.

This was not an easy endeavour. Invitations started to be sent right after the European Commission released its initial proposal, in April 2021, but the proposal was systematically subject to continuous changes, the final outcomes remained unclear until the very end and no one could know how delayed or how fast the approval procedure would be. The AI Act—Regulation (EU) 2024/1689—was finally approved on 13 June 2024 and published in the Official Journal of the European Union on 12 July 2024. To write about a moving target as the AI Act proposal is one of the most difficult tasks for any scholar. I can but praise the patience and resilience of 'my' authors.

I also want to thank the reviewers, who kindly made themselves available to assist the authors in writing the best possible chapters. In this vein, I sincerely appreciate their time and dedication: Andreas Kotsios, Hannah van Kolfschooten, Griet Verhenneman, João Leite, Peter Davies, Huixin (Elsa) Zhong, Jacek Gołaczyński, Tobias Mahler, Katja de Vries, Mahsa Shabani, Jonida Milaj-Weishaar, Asress Gikay, Maja Nisevic, Anastasiya Kiseleva, Uta Kohl, Jiyu Zhang, Siddharth Peter de Souza, Chung-Hsi Lee, Catherine Sharkey, and Iñigo de Miguel Beríain.

This book is an invitation to engage critically with the regulation that will define AI's trajectory in the EU and beyond. It is my hope that these pages not only illuminate the complexities of this landmark legislation but also inspire deeper reflection on the evolving relationship between law, technology, and society. The future of AI is not predetermined; it is a path we will shape together as a society.

Lisbon, Portugal Vera Lúcia Raposo

Contents

Contributors

Bart Bogaerts Vrije Universiteit Brussels, Brussels, Belgium

Lee A. Bygrave Norwegian Research Center for Computers and Law, Department of Private Law, University of Oslo, Oslo, Norway

Andrew Charlesworth University of Bristol, The Law School, Bristol, UK

Gauthier Chassang CERPOP, Inserm, UMR1295, University of Toulouse Paul Sabatier, Toulouse, France

Genotoul Societal Platform, GIS Genotoul Occitanie, Toulouse, France

Unesco Chair Ethics, Science and Society (E2S), Federal University of Toulouse, Toulouse, France

Chih-Hsiung Chen National Yang Ming Chiao Tung University School of Law, HsinChu City, Taiwan

Jorge Constantino TU Delft, Faculty of Technology, Policy and Management, Delft, The Netherlands

Matthew Dacoronias-Marina National and Kapodistrian University of Athens, Athens, Greece

James X. Dempsey Stanford University, Program on Geopolitics, Technology and Governance, Stanford, CA, USA

University of California, Berkeley School of Law, Berkeley, CA, USA

Li Du Faculty of Law, Asia-Pacific Academy of Economics and Management, University of Macau, Macau, China

Mateja Durovic King's College London, London, UK

Mark Findlay British Institute of International and Comparative Law, London, UK

Law School, University of Edinburgh, Edinburgh, UK

Sofie Fleerackers University of Amsterdam, Faculty of Law, Amsterdam, The Netherlands

Markus Frischhut MCI Management Center Innsbruck, Innsbruck, Austria

Tom Goffin Metamedica Unit, Department of Public Health and Primary Care, Faculty of Medicine and Health Science, Ghent University, Ghent, Belgium

Pin Lean Lau Brunel Law School | Centre for Artificial Intelligence: Social & Digital Innovations, Brunel, UK

University of London, Kingston Lane, Middlesex, Uxbridge, UK

Tina van der Linden Hogeschool Utrecht, Utrecht, The Netherlands

Jane Loo Centre for Digital Law, Singapore Management University, Singapore, Singapore

Abeer Malik Harvard Law School, Cambridge, US

Rostam J. Neuwirth Global Legal Studies, Faculty of Law, University of Macau, Macau, China

Maja Nisevic KU Leuven, Centre for IT & IP Law, Leuven, Belgium

Sofia Palmieri Metamedica Unit, Department of Public Health and Primary Care, Faculty of Medicine and Health Science, Ghent University, Ghent, Belgium

Rafał Tomasz Prabucki University of Silesia in Katowice, Katowice, Poland

Vera Lúcia Raposo NOVA School of Law, NOVA University, Lisbon, Portugal

CEDIS (Research & Development Centre on Law and Society), NOVA School of Law, NOVA University, Lisbon, Portugal

Rebecca Schmidt Faculty of Social Sciences, Oslo Metropolitan University, Oslo, Norway

Santa Slokenberga Faculty of Law, Uppsala University, Uppsala, Sweden

Barry Solaiman HBKU College of Law, Doha, Qatar

Denis Steckelmacher Vrije Universiteit Brussels, Brussels, Belgium

Dariusz Szostek University of Silesia in Katowice, Katowice, Poland

Anton Vedder KU Leuven, Centre for IT & IP Law, Leuven, Belgium

Meng Wang Faculty of Law, University of Macau, Macau, China

General Framework of the AI Act

Ethics First? On the EU Approach to AI Governance

Anton Vedder, Maja Nisevic, and Sofie Fleerackers

Contents

Abstract In this chapter, we attempt to clarify the EU governance framework for Artificial Intelligence (AI) by describing its—still brief—history. We do this under the guidance of the question: what has and might in the future become of the typical approach in terms of ethics rather than of new legislation that characterised EU AI governance in its earliest stages? We do so not only because we believe this clarification will enable a better understanding of the developments in the EU governance of AI during the past years and the years to come, but also because this ethics

The authors of this chapter have received funding from the European Union's Horizon Europe 283 Framework Programme under Grant Agreement n. 101057695.

A. Vedder (✉) · M. Nisevic
KU Leuven, Centre for IT and IP Law, Leuven, Belgium
e-mail: anton.vedder@kuleuven.be; maja.nisevic@kuleuven.be

S. Fleerackers
University of Amsterdam, The Netherlands, Faculty of Law, Amsterdam, Netherlands
e-mail: s.h.h.fleerackers@uva.nl

V. L. Raposo (ed.), *The European Artificial Intelligence Act*, Law, Governance and Technology Series 78, https://doi.org/10.1007/978-3-031-98406-8_1

approach might harbour a surplus value that cannot be completely or efficiently replaced by new legislation alone. For this reason, we will go to some lengths to explain the relevant differences between the ethics-approach on the one hand, and new legislation as an alternative to it, on the other, and to reflect critically on them. In this manner, we hope to deliver relevant considerations for an evaluation of the adequacy of the AI Act and the EU's governance of AI in general.

1 Introduction: A Brief History of the EU Approach to AI Governance

Gradually more often, under the banner of the *Brussels Effect*, the European Union (EU) is hailed as an exemplary regulator of technology (and by the same token of big technology companies).[1] The EU indeed stands out with its self-confident and systematic regulatory initiatives regarding new technologies.[2] The Brussels Effect concerns the global 'harmonising' effect of EU legislation by leading-by-example, thus enabling the EU to extend its regulatory reach de facto internationally through market mechanisms, albeit not de jure. Building on the General Data Protection Regulation (GDPR)'s success as a global standard for personal data protection, the EU may now set the international standard for AI governance with its Artificial Intelligence Act (AI Act).

Against this backdrop, it may come as a surprise that exactly in the area of AI, the EU initially seemed to be somewhat reticent when it did not immediately put forward traditional hard law as the tool for AI governance in the first place but ethical guidelines instead. In the *Artificial Intelligence for Europe* Communication from April 2018, the European Commission (EC) adopted its European AI Strategy for the years to come, aiming 'to ensure an appropriate ethical and legal framework, based on the Union's values and in line with the Charter of Fundamental Rights of the EU'.[3] Here, the EC identified draft AI ethics guidelines as the first step to address ethical concerns. It stated that self-regulation would provide for a first set of

[1] Bradford (2020) Just to avoid confusion: the Europe referred to in these eulogies is the European Union of the 27 Member States, while the role of the 'Europe' of the Council of Europe (46 member states) should not be underestimated where the governance of innovative technologies is concerned. Examples: Council of Europe Convention 108 on data protection (ETS No. 108, 28.01.1981), Guidelines on the protection of health-related data, Council of Europe's initiatives on AI.

[2] For example, the GDPR, which came into effect in 2018, set global standards for data privacy, safeguarding individuals' personal data and holding companies accountable for breaches. Building on this success, the EU has moved forward with the AI Act, which aims to establish rules for the ethical and safe development, deployment, and use of AI technologies.

[3] European Commission (2018) Communication on Artificial Intelligence for Europe from the Commission to the European Parliament, the Council, the European Economic and Social Committee and the Committee of the Regions' COM (2018) 237 final.

benchmarks, while the EC would monitor developments and 'if necessary, review existing legal frameworks'.

In the early spring of 2019, the AI High-Level Expert Group (HLEG), appointed by the EC in 2018, published its '*Ethics Guidelines for Trustworthy AI*', hereafter referred to as the Guidelines.[4] Around the same time, the HLEG also presented its *Policy and Investment Recommendations*.[5] Both documents served a complementary purpose: the former provides AI practitioners with practical guidance on how to comply with ethical principles in addition to their already existing legal obligations, while the latter document goes beyond ethical guidance offering policy advice to European institutions and Member States on how to establish adequate regulatory frameworks.[6] Almost simultaneously, the EC itself published an important communication about the intended 'human-centric' governance of artificial intelligence, and it clarified the central position of the work conducted by the HLEG.[7] In its statement, the Commission that would conclude its term of office by the end of 2019 expressed explicit support for the key requirements for trustworthy AI, as stipulated by the HLEG, because they 'are based on European values'. The EC pointed out that the Guidelines should be considered as a key element in its AI strategy, evidently suggesting that ethics would be the way forward while the first comprehensive regulation on AI should not be expected any time soon.

Putting forward the guidelines as a 'first step' in the governance of AI received applause but also criticism. Often the criticism went hand in hand with a plea for legislation as an alternative to the ethics approach. What these critics really demanded was a switch to *new* legislation, as AI of course is just as any other IT subject to all existing relevant laws. *New* legislation is called for when legislation as such is deemed necessary and issues might occur for which there is no relevant and applicable legislation yet, because of an as yet lacking conceptual fit between the actually existing laws and for instance a new technology or problems in its wake. To address such issues, adaptations of existing legislation or new legislation are called for. This is the kind of laws that the critics called for.

Interestingly, in their Guidelines, the experts of the HLEG acknowledge the importance of the law. The document starts first and foremost with the explicit claim that AI does not operate in a lawless world. A lot of already existing laws, such as the EU legal frameworks concerning safety, liability or personal data protection, that were not originally made for AI are relevant and applicable to AI, both at horizontal as well as sectoral levels. It is exactly to acknowledge this existing legal landscape that the HLEG, when laying out the framework for the guidelines, puts

[4] European Commission High-Level Expert Group on AI (2019) Ethics Guidelines for Trustworthy AI.

[5] European Commission High-Level Expert Group on AI (2019) Policy and Investment Recommendations for Trustworthy AI.

[6] Smuha (2019), p. 98.

[7] European Commission (2019) Communication from the Commission to the European parliament, the Council, the European Economic and Social Committee and the Committee of the Regions Building Trust in Human-Centric Artificial Intelligence COM(2019) 168 final.

forward the notion of 'lawful AI' as the first component of 'Trustworthy AI' – 'ethical' and 'robust' being the other two components at the centre of the EU's governance approach. According to the Guidelines, AI systems must in the first place be in accordance with relevant applicable laws.[8]

The Guidelines as such, however, do not contain specific inducements to special legislation. The experts of the HLEG do not provide substantial guidance on this first component of Lawful AI. They limit their scope rather to the other two components. Only in their second deliverable, the *Policy and Investment Recommendations for Trustworthy AI*,[9] they additionally offer policy advice to the Guidelines. By emphasising that the Guidelines marked a crucial first step in defining the kind of AI Europe seeks, the HLEG experts provide a comprehensive set of policy and investment recommendations in this document aiming to ensure that Trustworthy AI is not only developed and deployed but also fostered and scaled across Europe. The goal was to maximise AI's benefits while minimising and preventing potential risks by outlining 33 concrete recommendations addressed to the European institutions and Member States, highlighting key takeaways from their report, including the adoption of a risk-based governance approach to AI.

Some months after the publication of the Guidelines in 2019, the then president-elect of the new EC (2019–2024), Ursula von der Leyen, already announced that the new EC would put forward legislation for a 'coordinated European approach on the human and ethical implications of artificial intelligence as well as a reflection on the better use of big data for innovation'.[10] On 19 February 2020, the new Commission published the White Paper on Artificial Intelligence.[11] It presented a view concerning policy options on how to promote the uptake of AI—an 'ecosystem of excellence'—while simultaneously addressing the risks associated with certain uses of AI, promoting an 'ecosystem of trust'—the latter section explicitly supporting a human-centric approach building on the Guidelines.

In the EC's public consultation on the White Paper on AI, a diverse range of stakeholders, including governments, businesses, academia, and civil society has emphasised the importance of a regulatory approach that not only mitigates the risks of AI but also promotes innovation and the adoption of AI across various sectors.[12] A similar message was voiced on the side of the co-legislators, the European

[8] European Commission High-Level Expert Group on AI (2019) Ethics Guidelines for Trustworthy AI, p 6.

[9] European Commission High-Level Expert Group on AI (2019) Policy and Investment Recommendations for Trustworthy AI.

[10] Communication from President of the European Commission von der Leyen (2019) A Union that strives for more, My agenda for Europe: Political Guidelines for the next European Commission 2019–2024.

[11] European Commission (2020) White Paper on Artificial Intelligence - A European approach to excellence and trust COM (2020) 65 final.

[12] European Commission (2020) Public consultation on the AI White Paper - Final report.

Parliament[13] and the Council of the EU,[14] as well as in the European Council, the political body consisting of the heads of state or government of the EU member states.[15]

In April 2021, the Commission launched its first legislative initiative on AI—the proposal for a regulation on AI[16]—laying out the design for a horizontal regulatory framework specific to AI. In August 2024, the AI Act came into force. In this chapter, we will first present the ethics approach of the EU in some more detail, and then discuss some of the major criticisms brought against it. We will, subsequently, zoom in on the EU's move to new legislation with the AI Act and look at the role of ethics in this recent governance approach. We will, finally discuss some first steps for an evaluation of the move to legislation.

2 The Ethics Approach

Until now, we have clarified what we refer to when we mention (special) legislation for AI. We have, however, not been very precise with regards to the 'ethics approach'. In doing so, we relied on an intuitive understanding or use of the term 'ethics' that seems to be also characteristic of most of the contributions of the debate so far on the issue of AI governance in the EU. All of these have played an important role in the discussion without clear distinction, while the discussion might have benefited from more discernment. We will discuss here the aspects of the indiscriminate use of 'ethics' in the debate on AI governance: (1) ethics being an alternative normative system, similar to the law, but allegedly decisively different from the law by the lack of specific institutionalisations, for enforcement in particular, (2) ethics being a normative system that does not merely take form as a theoretical construct but also as embodied in the actual practice of thinking, feeling, communicating of humans and

[13] European Parliament Resolution of 20 October 2020 with recommendations to the Commission on a framework of ethical aspects of artificial intelligence, robotics and related technologies 2020/2012(INL); European Parliament Resolution of 20 October 2020 with recommendations to the Commission on a civil liability regime for artificial intelligence 2020/2014(INL); European Parliament Resolution of 20 October 2020 on intellectual property rights for the development of artificial intelligence technologies 2020/2015(INI); European Parliament Draft Report on Artificial intelligence in criminal law and its use by the police and judicial authorities in criminal matters 2020/2016(INI); European Parliament Draft Report on Artificial intelligence in education, culture and the audiovisual sector 2020/2017(INI).

[14] Council of the European Union (2019) Artificial intelligence b) Conclusions on the coordinated plan on artificial intelligence 6177/19; Council of the European Union (2020) Presidency conclusions - The Charter of Fundamental Rights in the context of Artificial Intelligence and Digital Change 11481/20.

[15] European Council (2020) Special meeting of the European Council (1 and 2 October 2020) – Conclusions, EUCO 13/20, p 6.

[16] European Commission (2021) Proposal for a Regulation of the European Parliament and of the Council laying down harmonised rules on artificial intelligence (Artificial Intelligence Act) and amending certain Union legislative acts' COM (2021) 206 final.

in traditions and patterns of behaviour, and (3) ethics being conceived predominantly in a deontological[17] or legalistic[18] manner by being primarily identified as the operationalisation of ethical values and the production and application of principles in specific contexts. In brief, 'ethics' for advocates and critics could refer to different three things:

- lack of possibilities of enforcement,
- different types of self-regulation and professional or branch codes, and
- the specific conception of ethics that the Guidelines are claimed to bear witness to.

The latter aspect has played a minor role in primarily ethicist contributions to the debate, but its importance should not be overlooked. We will return to it in Sect. 5. Here, we will focus on the other two. We start with the first one: ethics being different from the law. In the debate on AI governance in the EU ethics stands for HLEG as well as for many of the critics not merely for morality but simultaneously connotes a relative distance or, rather, non-interference by legislators. Fundamental to the ethics approach that gradually arose from 2018 onward is the belief that certain issues are better not dealt with by legislators through rigid legal rules, but by various stakeholders with knowledge or experience of the technology at hand, and of the possible positive or negative impact thereof, directly on the basis of principles and values. Of course, these principles and values and their practical applications in specific contexts lack the binding nature of hard law. Their bindingness is of a primarily moral nature in the form of motivation by the contents of the norm but can—depending on its degree of institutionalisation—extend to possibilities of being enforced by non-legal forms of oversight. By mentioning this latter point we are already moving on to the clarification of the second aspect.

The second aspect refers to ethics being used as a notion not only for ethical theory but also for the practice of ethical reasoning, decisions, communications, and even ingrained patterns of action and rudimentary institutionalisations. This is not unique to the debate on AI governance, but a common characteristic of the day-to-day, and even the philosophical use of the term, especially where ethics is compared or contrasted with law. The aspect goes often unnoticed because it is rhetorically quite burdensome to specify time and again whether one is referring to ethics as theory or ethics as practice. However, that may be, the vantage point of presenting high-level guidelines that can be elaborated and applied in real practice and the emphasis on the involvement of stakeholders in the Guidelines bear witness to this use of the term. The Guidelines are clearly meant as starting points for ethics in practice, not as theoretical contributions. One of the main criticisms of the ethics approach to be discussed in Sect. 3 hinges even on it.

The authors of the Guidelines themselves use a variety of different but somehow familiar notions in order to refer to, and account for, the guidelines. They present them as guiding statements concerning *seven* key requirements, building on *four*

---

[17] Hagendorff (2020), pp. 99–120.

[18] Rességuier and Rodrigues (2020), pp. 1–5.

foundational ethical principles, with which AI systems must comply. Simultaneously, and somewhat confusingly, the authors claim that AI systems can be considered trustworthy when showing three characteristics: In order to be trustworthy AI should be *lawful*, complying with all applicable laws and regulations; *ethical*, ensuring adherence to ethical principles and values; and *robust*, being safe both from a technical and social perspective. The Guidelines have limited their remit to providing guidance on the concepts of ethical and robust AI, explicitly not tackling the element of 'lawful AI'—although the latter is presented as equally crucial. Notwithstanding this scope and the fact that the Guidelines as such are not legally binding, the ethical principles set out in the Guidelines are reflected in many existing binding EU law provisions, for example, safety, personal data protection, privacy, or environmental protection rules. Compliance with such legal provisions is, as highlighted by the Guidelines, required under the first component for Trustworthy AI, lawfulness. Moreover, the AI HLEG recommended the further translation into law of the ethical guidance and the concerns identified by the authors of the Guidelines.[19] These recommendations emphasise the importance of empowering, benefiting, and protecting human beings. The HLEG believed that EU institutions and Member States would play a crucial role in achieving these objectives, acting as pivotal players in the data economy, procurers of Trustworthy AI systems, and standard-setters of sound governance.[20]

Focusing on the two components of Ethical and Robust AI, the Guidelines first put forward four foundational ethical principles: (i) *respect for human autonomy*, (ii) *prevention of harm*, (iii) *fairness* and (iv) *explicability*. These ethical principles act as ethical imperatives in that AI practitioners should always strive to adhere to them, if only because they are grounded in fundamental rights law. The document continues by translating these ethical principles into seven key requirements for AI systems to be met throughout their life cycle. The seven requirements themselves are put forward by the HLEG as being based on—and being justified by—broadly shared ethical principles and values.

To start with, the AI systems ought to be technically robust and safe (a). They should allow for transparency (b) and accountability (c). Finally, they should support, respect and uphold human agency and oversight (d), privacy and data governance (e), diversity, non-discrimination, fairness (f), environmental and societal well-being (g).[21] In this list of requirements, technical robustness and safety (a) seems to be a more or less preliminary requirement. Transparency and accountability (b–c) are probably best referred to as procedural requirements, whereas agency (d), privacy (e), diversity (f) and well-being (g) might be called substantial requirements. The authors make quite an effort to specify the requirements and to provide instructions for their implementation. They emphasise that throughout their

[19] European Commission High-Level Expert Group on AI (2019) Policy and Investment Recommendations for Trustworthy AI, pp. 37–40.

[20] Ibid. p. 47.

[21] European Commission High-Level Expert Group on AI (2019) Ethics Guidelines for Trustworthy AI, pp. 14–24.

life-cycle, AI systems should be continuously evaluated on the basis of these requirements. The audience addressed by the Guidelines is all the possible stakeholders in any AI system: developers, producers, users, government agencies, enterprises, etc. Each of these might voluntarily apply the requirements in order to obtain trustworthy AI. As a follow-up step, the authors of the Guidelines published a non-exhaustive *Assessment List for Trustworthy AI* (ALTAI). After a piloting phase, the HLEG presented the last version of this operationalisation of the key requirements, as its third deliverable in 2020.[22]

3 Main Criticisms

The ethics approach—the EC's embrace of the Guidelines and the ALTAI—has been criticised in various ways. Apart from an almost general agreement among critics concerning the abstract, high-level character of the Guidelines, that is deemed too high, critical views are surprisingly often not concerned with the substance or contents of the guidelines or with the internal coherence or clarity of the Guidelines. The dusky ways in which the document places the justificatory basis for the requirements in European values and fundamental rights and the controversial and in part lacking definitions for some of the basic concepts in the requirements, for instance, do not seem to bother the critics much.

Most critics of the Ethics Guidelines have rather focused on two other issues: (i) the allegedly favoured position in the HLEG of stakeholders from science and technology and from commercial backgrounds, and (ii) the perceived lack of possibilities for enforcement. In what follows, we explain both arguments and critically reflect on them.

In order to clarify the first criticism, it is important to remember what was already pointed out in the previous section, i.e., that in the debate on the ethics approach, ethics is not meant to merely refer to the contents of the guidelines, but also to connote the idea of abstinence of legislators on the one hand, and self-governance or self-regulation by the parties involved in the development, production and use of AI systems, on the other. One of the first to criticise the Guidelines, drawing a lot of attention and becoming one of the most cited, was Thomas Metzinger, a German professor of theoretical philosophy, including (applied) ethics, and himself a member of HLEG. Metzinger drew attention to the fact that only four out of 52 members of the HLEG were actually ethicists by profession, while most of the remaining 48 members were representatives of industry. His main objection against the final version of the Guidelines is that the instructions are too vague and abstract, ready to be used for rhetorical purposes, but unable to communicate red lines and no-go's regarding AI. He warns emphatically against a new era of 'fake ethics' and 'ethics

[22] European Commission High-Level Expert Group on AI (2020) Assessment List for Trustworthy Artificial Intelligence (ALTAI) for self-assessment.

washing' by AI ethics experts who are funded by the AI industry.[23] Metzinger was only one in—what would soon become—a row of critics who started to identify the turn to ethics in the debate on AI as a move away from serious debate and regulation to rhetorical window dressing or even as an intricate strategy to ensure significant influence of stakeholders with scientific, technical and commercial backgrounds, and to safeguard the interests of the professional bodies and corporations involved.

In addition to similar fears of too much, and biased, involvement from the side of commerce, science and technology, many voiced the objection that ethics lacks formal procedures for enforcement, e.g. by the use of monitoring and sanctions. In combination with the first criticism concerning the excessive influence of science and industry, critics warned against the belief that self-governance by scientists and corporate actors might adequately deal with the possible drawbacks of AI.[24] According to Thilo Hagendorff, no research has been performed on the actual implementation (or lack of it) of ethics guidelines in AI systems with regards to AI ethics guidelines in general, so not exclusively concerning the HLEG Ethics Guidelines.[25] Probably many would interpret this as all the more reason for agreeing with the two main criticisms.

The objections, however, must be put into perspective. Firstly, against the contention that science, technology and commerce have an inappropriate preferred position with regards to the actual ethical assessment and ensuing governance of AI, one might refer to the document of the Guidelines itself which does not prioritise for instance scientists, developers and producers over any other stakeholders. The document expressly states that the audience addressed are all possible stakeholders: developers, producers, users, government agencies, enterprises, etc.[26] That the guidelines as such would favour the uptake of AI governance by scientists and corporate actors in the first place, is not a contention inherent to the Guidelines. Focusing on these actors seems rather to apply to the HLEG's Assessment Lists for Trustworthy AI since these relate primarily to the stages of design, development and production of AI. Addressing an audience of developers and producers in the first place, however, does not automatically entail prioritisation of their interests. People involved in the design, development and production of AI systems will of course have much more relevant expertise concerning AI than possible future users or authorities. When it comes to being able to observe or perceive possibly emerging ethical problems or opportunities related to AI, the first-hand expertise with regards to AI is a favourable asset. Most importantly, designers, developers and producers are the naturally eligible candidates for building (respect for) values into AI. We will return to this in Sect. 5.

---

[23] See Metzinger (2019).

[24] See Calo (2017).

[25] See Hagendorff (2020).

[26] European Commission High-Level Expert Group on Artificial Intelligence (2019) Ethics Guidelines for Trustworthy AI, p. 5.

The lack-of-enforcement criticism requires further consideration as well. Ethics cannot be enforced in exactly the same way as law—at least to the degree that ethics is not embodied in law. Ethics, of course, is deemed to enforce itself by the persuasiveness of its arguments, of which consistency, rationality, and being eventually rooted in broadly shared values, are important constituents, and ought to result in the ability to account for one's beliefs, decisions and actions. In addition to that, through incorporation into human practices and by institutionalisation, ethics has also informal manners of enforcement of its own, such as praise and blame, e.g. during education, or reputation gain or loss during adulthood. Moreover, formal but still not exactly legal enforcement can be thought of. By means of institutionalisation in established organisations or associations of professionals and other stakeholders organisations, oversight systems as well as non-legal forms of enforcement might arise, such as ethics committees or committees in professional branches seeing to the enforcement of professional codes. In addition to the non-legal enforcement impact that the *contents* of the Ethics Guidelines and the ALTAI might have, there might also be a *supervenient* enforcement effect which has to do with the there being these Guidelines at all. Actors in the international market for AI systems benefit from a level playing field for competitors in this market. A stable set of norms applicable in a considerable number of countries helps to avoid uncertainties with regards to possibly arising social problems in the wake of AI, and so contributes to this level playing field. This argument, however, seems to rest on the assumption that the desire for a stable set of norms in order to avoid unequal conditions for competition actually and automatically motivates compliance with those norms—an assumption that at least theoretically stands in need of justification against arguments on variants of the so-called free rider problem.[27]

Even regardless of that, as mentioned in Sect. 2, the authors of the Guidelines consider lawfulness to be the very first component of trustworthy AI,[28] and, although the authors emphasise the non-binding character of the Guidelines, they invest quite some effort in explaining that the Guidelines are based on the fundamental rights of citizens.[29] In addition to this, as we pointed out before, many of the key requirements are reflected in already existing (and often use- or domain-specific) relevant and applicable provisions of European Union law, and thus translate such guidance into law and the accompanying legal enforcement procedures. The assumption that the ethics guidelines cannot be enforced—informally or formally, albeit indirectly, by their embodiment in the law—is therefore incorrect. Equally incorrect is the

[27] Baumol (1952).

[28] European Commission High-Level Expert Group on Artificial Intelligence (2019) Ethics Guidelines for Trustworthy AI, p. 6.

[29] See European Commission High-Level Expert Group on Artificial Intelligence (2019) Ethics Guidelines for Trustworthy AI, p 10: 'Understood as legally enforceable rights, fundamental rights therefore fall under the first component of Trustworthy AI (lawful AI), which safeguards compliance with the law. Understood as the rights of everyone, rooted in the inherent moral status of human beings, they also underpin the second component of Trustworthy AI (ethical AI), dealing with ethical norms that are not necessarily legally binding yet crucial to ensure trustworthiness'.

often heard suggestion that until the AI Act becomes applicable, AI is developed and applied in a legal vacuum. The ethics guidelines are in the first place meant for those AI related issues for which relevant and applicable laws do not yet exist, complementing the existing regulatory framework.

4 The EU's Artificial Intelligence Act

In the *White Paper on 'Artificial Intelligence: A European Approach to Excellence and Trust'*[30] (2020), the EC laid the groundwork for its legislative work on AI explicitly building further on the principles specified in the Ethics Guidelines. To fulfil the EC's purpose to promote the uptake of AI while addressing the associated risks, the White Paper on AI provided a blueprint for potential regulation of AI which consisted of two building blocks, each containing proposed policy options: an ecosystem of excellence and an ecosystem of trust. In this second building block, the EC argued that in addition to non-binding Ethics Guidelines, a clear European regulatory framework is required specifically on AI complementing the existing applicable legislation (such as consumer protection, data protection and the privacy regime).

In April 2021, the European Union took a significant step by introducing the first comprehensive legislation for AI. This move was marked by the EC's release of the AI Package, which included a Communication on Fostering a European Approach to Artificial Intelligence,[31] the 2021 Revised Coordinated Plan on AI, and the legislative proposal for an AI Regulation known as the AI Act.[32] The legislative proposal of the AI Act represents the EU's first attempt to establish a comprehensive EU legal horizontal framework for AI that applies to all AI systems placed on the market within the EU. After extensive negotiations and discussions, the AI Act was adopted in March 2023.[33] Although the AI Act entered into force on August, 1st, 2024, it will become fully applicable two years later, on August, 2nd, 2026, but there are a few

[30] European Commission (2020) White Paper on Artificial Intelligence COM (2020) 65 final, p. 1.

[31] European Commission (2021) Coordinated Plan on Artificial Intelligence 2021 Review (Annexes to the Communication from the Commission to the European Parliament, the European Council, the Council, the European Economic and Social Committee and the Committee of the Regions - Fostering a European approach to Artificial Intelligence) COM (2021) 205 final.

[32] European Commission (2021) Proposal for a Regulation of the European Parliament and of the Council laying down harmonised rules on artificial intelligence (Artificial Intelligence Act) and amending certain Union legislative acts COM (2021) 206 final.

[33] Regulation (EU) of the European Parliament and the Council of 13 March laying down harmonised rules on artificial intelligence and amending Regulations (EC) No 300/2008, (EU) No 167/2013, (EU) No 168/2013, (EU) 2018/858, (EU) 2018/1139 and (EU) 2019/2144 and Directives 2014/90/EU, (EU) 2016/797 and (EU) 2020/1828 (Artificial Intelligence Act).

exceptions: the prohibitions and obligations regarding AI litteracy do already apply from February, 2nd, 2025.[34]

The EC's regulatory approach aimed to establish stricter legal requirements on AI applications with significant implications for individuals and society, particularly in sensitive areas such as healthcare, finance, and law enforcement. Thus, the EC considered the key elements in the AI Act—a legal framework characterised by a risk-based approach specifically targeting AI systems classified as 'high-risk' based on the sector they operate in and their intended use. These high-risk systems are subject to mandatory obligations, including rigorous standards for 'training data', 'data and record-keeping', 'information provision', 'robustness and accuracy', 'specific requirements for remote biometric identification' and 'human oversight'. Additionally, the EC emphasised the importance of integrating the Guidelines into its regulatory framework to ensure that these principles become legally enforceable.[35]

The AI Act highlights several key principles in line with the Guidelines. Accordingly, the AI Act emphasises: (a) Fundamental rights, asserting that AI systems must be designed and used in ways that uphold human dignity and respect individual human rights, ensuring that AI does not undermine personal autonomy or lead to unjust discrimination, (b) Fairness, ensuring that AI systems are designed to prevent bias and ensure fairness, with the AI Act including provisions to address and mitigate risks of discrimination and unfair treatment resulting from AI applications, (c) Accountability, requiring that AI systems are subject to rigorous oversight and that mechanisms are in place to hold developers and users accountable for any adverse outcomes, with clear lines of responsibility for the design, implementation, and use of AI systems, (d) Transparency, clarifying that high-risk AI systems must be transparent, meaning users should be informed when interacting with an AI system, and the system's decisions should be explainable, as transparency helps build trust and accountability in AI systems.

Specifically, the AI Act integrates these ethical principles into legally enforceable requirements across several key Articles and non-binding Recitals, including the explanatory memorandum.

The explanatory memorandum first clarifies its basis in European values and fundamental rights and explains its aim to implement the second objective: developing an ecosystem of trust by proposing a legal framework for trustworthy AI, which is 'human-centric', so that people can trust that the technology is used in a way that is safe and compliant with the law, including the respect of fundamental rights. The memorandum moreover underlines that it 'ensures the protection of ethical principles as specifically requested by the European Parliament' in its Resolution on a Framework of Ethical Aspects of Artificial Intelligence, Robotics and Related

---

[34] EU Commission (2024) - AI Act enters into force - available at https://commission.europa.eu/news/ai-act-enters-force-2024-08-01_en; European Union, Rules for Trustworthy Artificial Intelligence in the EU, https://eur-lex.europa.eu/legal-content/EN/TXT/?/uri=legissum:4762484

[35] Ibid.

Technologies[36] and identifies the respect for fundamental rights as part of its objectives, i.e. to 'ensure that AI systems placed on the Union market and used are safe and respect existing law on fundamental rights and Union values' and to 'enhance governance and effective enforcement of existing law on fundamental rights and safety requirements applicable to AI systems'. Also throughout its (non-binding) recitals,[37] this ambition to protect citizen's rights is expressis verbis mentioned as a core aim in the AI Act, whereby fundamental rights are repeatedly referred to as a benchmark for AI regulation in the EU. More specifically, **Recital 25** identifies that AI technology can be misused to create powerful tools for manipulation, exploitation, and social control. Such practices are particularly harmful and should be prohibited, as they contradict fundamental EU values like respect for human dignity, freedom, equality, democracy, and the rule of law, as well as fundamental rights including non-discrimination, data protection, privacy, and the rights of the child. Furthermore, **Recital 29** clarifies the significant adverse impacts that AI systems can have on fundamental rights.

The AI Act lays down a classification for AI systems with different requirements and obligations tailored on a 'risk-based approach'—assigning AI systems to four classifications: unacceptable risk (prohibited), high-risk (permitted but subject to compliance with a set of requirements), limited risk (permitted but subject to information and transparency obligations), and minimal or no risk.[38] Accordingly, legally binding **Article 5** of the AI Act prohibits certain AI practices that pose serious risks to these rights.

The AI Act further establishes a robust framework for regulating high-risk AI systems, with a strong emphasis on principles such as transparency, accountability, and fairness. **Article 6** of the Act identifies high-risk AI systems, recognising their significant impact on individuals and society and the need for stricter regulation. Transparency is a foundational element of the AI regulatory framework, highlighted in **Article 13**, which mandates that high-risk AI systems be designed and developed with sufficient transparency. This requirement allows deployers to interpret the system's output and use it appropriately, ensuring clear and comprehensible operation. The emphasis on transparency aims to facilitate accountability and trust, enabling users to fully understand and manage the implications of AI system use and comply with ethical and legal standards within the regulatory framework. Additionally, **Article 10** addresses fairness by requiring rigorous data governance to prevent

---

[36] European Parliament Resolution of 20 October 2020 with recommendations to the Commission on a framework of ethical aspects of artificial intelligence, robotics and related technologies 2020/2012(INL).

[37] With mentions of fundamental rights protection notable in recitals (1), (5), (13), (15), (18), (27)-(28) (32), (37)-(39), (43), (47), (50), (58), (72) and (79). Recital 5 includes a reference to the protection of ethical principles.

[38] This hierarchy of risks is often referred to as 'the risk pyramid'. It might have been inspired by the 'Kritikalitätspyramide und risikoadaptiertes Regulierungssystem für den Einsatz algorithmischer Systeme' introduced in the Gutachten der Datenethikkommission (Oktober 2019) for the German Federal Government.

biases and ensure equitable operation of AI systems. Furthermore, **Article 11** of the AI Act strengthens accountability by mandating that providers of high-risk AI systems maintain comprehensive documentation and records. This ensures that these systems are subject to rigorous audits and can be held accountable for their operations. **Article 14** emphasises the necessity of designing and developing high-risk AI systems with human-machine interface tools that facilitate effective oversight by natural persons during the system's usage while human oversight is specifically aimed at preventing or minimising risks to health, safety, and fundamental rights, particularly in cases where these risks persist despite other protective measures. **Article 15** complements accountability requiring that AI systems are designed and developed in such a way that they achieve an appropriate level of accuracy, robustness, and cybersecurity and that they perform consistently in those respects throughout their lifecycle. Continuous post-market surveillance, mandated by **Article 72**, ensures that high-risk AI systems remain compliant with legal standards and maintain safety and effectiveness throughout their lifecycle. Finally, **Article 21** establishes a comprehensive compliance and enforcement mechanism by requesting cooperation with relevant authorities.

Although the process of having a new and comprehensive legislation on AI such as the AI Act had a clear aim to regulate AI in a way that would ensure its development and deployment in alignment with European values, some academic scholars criticised the proposal on the AI Act for the lack of sufficient protection of fundamental rights.[39] Additional critics refer to the risk-based approach that has been criticised for treating fundamental rights protection as a technical and administrative matter rather than a comprehensive, rights-based concern. The critics contended that this approach lacked the necessary systematic scrutiny and oversight, ultimately transforming fundamental rights into a set of technical requirements that might not fully align with the AI Act's intended legal framework. Furthermore, the authors warned against the oversimplification of the risk categorisation of AI systems into four classifications, which they argued was insufficient for ensuring the robust fundamental rights protection that the AI Act aspired to achieve.[40] Do these criticisms still apply to the AI Act as they have now been adopted?

5 Looking Forward

In the previous sections, we outlined and clarified the move in the EU governance from ethics to legislation. In the discussion in this section, we will present some preliminary thoughts on this transition.

Upon examining the AI Act, it becomes evident that the legislation heavily draws from the logic and various aspects of the European product safety and liability

[39] See also Smuha et al. (2021), p. 5.

[40] Ibid.

regime, focusing on specific AI use cases rather than outcomes-based harms, long-term effects, and the impact on intangible values such as human dignity.[41] While the AI Act often reminds the reader of elements of existing safety and liability frameworks, such as risk classification, certification and notified bodies, it does not comprehensively address broader ethical concerns and the nuanced impacts on fundamental rights. Notably, the ethics seem to be mainly and merely traceable in the AI Act's (non-binding) recitals and a limited number of articles. Concepts such as bias, transparency, explainability, and fundamental rights that are key notions in the Guidelines initially appear to serve as normative guides throughout the text, whereas the precise interpretation and the individual rights to be derived from them is left open in many respects.

Following the release of the AI Act proposal, critics raised concerns that it failed to establish a robust framework for 'legally' Trustworthy AI in accordance with the Guidelines set by the High-Level Expert Group on AI. For example, scholars argued that the proposal did not adequately provide fundamental rights protection or sufficient safeguards to maintain the rule of law and democracy. Notably, the analysis highlighted by Smuha et al. regarding the AI Act's approach to safeguarding fundamental rights remains applicable even after the Act's adoption, although the final text may have addressed some of these concerns.[42] Thus, while the finalised version of the AI Act may have implemented improvements and clarifications, the foundational concerns related to the risk-based approach, the confusion of safety and rights standards, and the potential oversimplification of risk categorisation continue to be relevant. These issues emphasise the ongoing need for caution to ensure that the implementation of the AI Act does not jeopardise the protection of fundamental rights. Currently, the EU legislator seems to be divided, with one side advocating for increased fundamental rights protection and the other favouring innovation. One solution could involve continuous stakeholder engagement and consultation to address the concerns raised. Additionally, ongoing reviews and assessments of the AI Act's impact on fundamental rights could be conducted to identify and rectify any potential weaknesses. This would help ensure that the AI Act's implementation upholds fundamental rights while promoting innovation and technological advancement.

The successful transition from an ethics-first approach to a legislative framework may largely depend on how prominently EU institutions position the Guidelines within the broader governance framework for AI. The European Commission has consistently acknowledged the necessity of both ethical and regulatory frameworks to address the complexities of AI. It is imperative for the EU to guide stakeholders through the evolving landscape of AI governance, offering a clear drawing of the purpose and limits of these frameworks. As AI technology develops rapidly, the

[41] For exampe see the opinion of scholars, such as Almada, Petit (2023); Heikkilä (2024); Kop (2021).

[42] Smuha et al. (2021).

provision of clarity and coherent guidance by the EU becomes crucial in ensuring that ethical considerations remain a central component of regulatory practices.

Now, since we know the outcome of the legislative process, attempting to provide for a more substantial portion of the ethics approach in the law itself does not make much sense anymore. The complementarity of both governance modalities might nevertheless still offer a promising way out. We believe that in any regulatory framework on AI, the ethics approach harbours a surplus value that cannot be completely or efficiently replaced by specific legislation alone. Voluntary ethical (and technical) standards and legal standards can and should form a symbiotic relationship where both have their role to play.

In the EU, as explicitly mentioned in the EC's AI strategy, a first start to ensuring an appropriate governance framework on AI actually was made with ethics. The prominent role of the open norms of the Ethics Guidelines has been approached with distrust. It might however also be interpreted as a sign of an—initial—conscious reluctance of EU legislators to put forward specific norms already then. An important reason for leaving special AI issues and drawbacks first to the realm of ethics rather than that of law might be that ethics for the time being leaves more opportunities for reflection and debate by a plurality of stakeholders than legislation, while nevertheless being useful for the preparation of possible legislation. Governance issues with regard to technology can of course be caused by the technological developments themselves; but many more issues are apt to arise in the wake of the transformations that technological developments bring to societal practices, routines and patterns of interaction. These are mostly not immediately evident but may take time and effort to become observed and appreciated. Well-considered normative or even regulatory responses to such transformations may take time. From this perspective, it is understandable that back in 2019 the erstwhile European Commission thought it better to deploy AI governance first with ethical guidelines. Given the dynamic development of AI and its applications complete abandonment of the ethics approach is not advisable.

As explained previously, the Guidelines consist of a set of relatively abstract and open norms, both procedural and substantial. The abstractness and openness make the Guidelines suitable to be applied to relatively new transformations of practices and behaviour patterns. Simultaneously, the abstractness and openness of the norms have been a source of concern regarding the implementation of the Guidelines. Some have therefore suggested supplementing the guidelines with detailed technical information so that they could become much more specific and articulate.[43] The HLEG itself included in its Guidelines a pilot version of an assessment list with the aim to operationalise the abstractness of the norms underpinning Trustworthy AI. The Group then initiated surveys and sharing of best practices with stakeholders in order to flesh out a final 'Assessment List for Trustworthy Artificial Intelligence

[43] Hagendorff (2020), pp. 111–112.

(ALTAI) for self-assessment to offer a useful concretisation of its Ethics Guidelines'.[44]

The inclusion of such additional technical information might also help to motivate the developers and producers of AI systems to take into account the guidelines. Some have claimed that unlike professional branches such as the medical ones, professions and organisations involved in AI are not yet characterised by common purposes, history, or legal and professional accountability mechanisms.[45] This may make it relatively difficult to obtain a common understanding of the norms in the Guidelines and hinder their dissemination; it does, however, not make it impossible to make a start with building such a common framework that could also foster motivation and compliance on professional and organisational levels. Establishing special committees and assessment procedures within organisations and professional sectors may contribute in this respect.[46] Again, one could approach these initiatives with distrust; but one could also consider them open-mindedly as good and honest attempts to assign to the critical process of ethical deliberation a more or less natural or obvious place in the organisation or professional association.

Of course, motivation and compliance are not merely matters of organisations and professions but also of individuals, with their own personalities, characters and intellectual horizons. One might therefore think not merely of supplementing the Guidelines with organisational measures, such as the establishment of ethics committees and assessment procedures, but also to direct the attention to individual professionals, researchers and students, and to provide them with formation in order to educate them about the technological aspects as well as the ethical and societal aspects of AI.[47] With regards to the role of individuals, Hagendorff suggests that the approach of the Guidelines in terms of principles (requirements), which ethicists would refer to as being of a rather deontologist kind, be at least supplemented by one in terms of virtues, of good human character dispositions combined with practical intelligence.[48] And indeed, the High Level Expert Group's follow-up actions after the publication of the Guidelines—the involvement of stake-holders for input in the Assessment List for Trustworthy AI, and the procedures coming along with this as a bottom-up approach—seem to sit better with a virtue ethical framework than with the deontological one of the Guidelines taken on their own.

---

[44] High-Level Expert Group on Artificial Intelligence (2020) Assessment List for Trustworthy Artificial Intelligence (ALTAI). European Commission, Brussels.

[45] See for instance Mittelstadt (2019).

[46] See for example the ways in which ethics assessment committees and procedures for scientific research are organised at a Belgian university (and universities elsewhere): https://www.kuleuven.be/english/research/ethics/committees.

[47] Leonelli (2016), pp. 1–128.

[48] Hagendorff (2020), p 112.

6 Conclusion

In this chapter, we hope to have delivered some basic considerations and qualifications for an evaluation of the transition in the EU governance approach of AI from a primarily ethical to a primarily legislative one. We have succinctly discussed the Guidelines and the main criticisms they received. The criticisms concerned the allegedly too great roles assigned to science and corporations and their representatives on the one hand and the presupposed lack of enforcement potential of the Guidelines on the other. We nuanced both of these claims and drew attention to the possibility that the EU legislators might have chosen positively for the ethics approach in order to avoid rash assessments and premature legislation. We also suggested that the Guidelines might inspire flanking measures in order to create a rich environment for organisational measures and personal formation.

For the critics, the move to legislation might make sense, at least at first glance. The process of legislation comes with democratic control, which may be considered a counterbalance against the alleged influence of science and corporations. Law also seems to offer more opportunities for enforcement. For the advocates of the ethics approach it might be discomforting, however, to see that although important elements of the Guidelines are returning in the recitals of the proposed AI Act, they are not similarly evidently present in the specific provisions of the regulation. In the future, a system of co-existence of the two governance mechanisms, as complementary tools in society's toolbox, each with its own scope and purpose, might offer a fruitful perspective.

References

Almada M, Petit N (2023) The EU AI Act: A medley of product safety and fundamental rights? EUI, RSC, Working Paper, 2023/59. https://hdl.handle.net/1814/75982

Baumol W (1952) Welfare economics and the theory of the state. Harvard University Press, Cambridge

Bradford A (2020) The Brussels effect. How the European Union rules the world. Oxford University Press. https://doi.org/10.1093/oso/9780190088583.001.0001

Calo R (2017) Artificial intelligence policy: a primer and roadmap. SSRN Journal:1–28

Datenethikkommission (2019) Gutachten der Datenethikkommission. https://www.bmi.bund.de/SharedDocs/downloads/DE/publikationen/themen/it-digitalpolitik/gutachten-datenethikkommission.pdf;jsessionid=4D61B402543A5707C15EFB123FC8DAC1.2_cid350?__blob=publicationFile&v=7

Hagendorff T (2020) The ethics of AI ethics. An evaluation of guidelines. Minds Mach 30:99–120. https://doi.org/10.1007/s11023-020-09517-8

Heikkilä M (2024) The AI Act is done. Here's what will (and won't) change: the hard work starts now. MIT Technology Review. https://www.technologyreview.com/2024/03/19/1089919/the-ai-act-is-done-heres-what-will-and-wont-change/

Kop M (2021). EU artificial intelligence act: the European approach to AI. Stanford-Vienna Transatlantic Technology Law Forum, Transatlantic Antitrust and IPR Developments, Stanford University, September Issue

Leonelli S (2016) Locating ethics in data science: responsibility and accountability in global and distributed knowledge production systems. Philosoph Transact Series A Math Phys Eng Sci 374(2083):1–128

Metzinger T (2019) Ethik-Waschmachinen made in Europe. Der Tagesspeigel, 4 August 2019. https://background.tagesspiegel.de/ethik-waschmaschinen-made-in-europe

Mittelstadt B (2019) AI ethics – too principled to fail? SSRN Electr J https://doi.org/10.2139/ssrn.3391293

Rességuier A, Rodrigues R (2020) AI ethics should not remain toothless! A call to bring back the teeth of ethics. Big Data Soc 7(2):1–5

Smuha NA (2019) The EU approach to ethics guidelines for trustworthy artificial intelligence. Comput Law Rev Int 20(4):97–106

Smuha NA, Ahmed-Rengers E, Harkens A, Li W, MacLaren J, Piselli R, Yeung K (2021). How the EU can achieve legally trustworthy AI: a response to the European Commission's Proposal for an Artificial Intelligence Act. https://doi.org/10.2139/ssrn.3899991

The EU's Common Values (Art 2 EU-Treaty) as the Underlying Philosophy of the AI Act

Markus Frischhut

Contents

The author would like to thank Vera Raposo for the invitation to join this book project, as well as Hannah van Kolfschooten for valuable feedback. The author would also like to thank his students at Management Center Innsbruck and at the University of Bologna, as well as the participants of the following events (seminars, conferences, round table discussions) for valuable questions and feedback: Lancaster University (3 November 2021), Uppsala University (17 February 2022), Ghent University (21 April 2022), Universidad Internacional Menéndez Pelayo, Santander (30 June 2022), NOVA University of Lisbon (20 February 2024 & 1 October 2024), University of Salerno (16 April 2024), the Permanent Representation of Austria to the EU, Brussels (16 May 2024), and the Université Côte-d'Azur (20 June 2024). The author would also like to thank Dean Harris and Brad Glosserman for additional feedback on U.S. 'executive orders'. All remaining mistakes are those of the author. This contribution was finished in July 2024.

M. Frischhut (✉)
MCI Management Center Innsbruck, Innsbruck, Austria
e-mail: markus.frischhut@mci.edu

V. L. Raposo (ed.), *The European Artificial Intelligence Act*, Law, Governance and Technology Series 78, https://doi.org/10.1007/978-3-031-98406-8_2

Abstract As the impact of artificial intelligence (AI) can include benefit and harm, the AI Act (AIA) takes a risk-based approach, putting an emphasis on the development of secure, trustworthy and ethical AI. In terms of the various categories of the AIA, EU values play an important role in 'prohibited' AI, fundamental rights in 'high-risk' AI, and soft-law (and ethical principles) in 'low-risk' AI, referring to voluntary 'codes of conduct'. Relying on values is an obvious approach in the EU, being a 'Union of values' since the Lisbon Treaty. While the hierarchy of EU law results in the legal obligation for EU secondary law to be in line with EU primary law (i.e., the values enshrined in Art 2 TEU), it is convincing in a particularly sensitive and impactful field, as in the case of AI, to put a special emphasis on values and fundamental rights. Values rather occur in the preamble, hardly in the binding text of the AIA. An exception is the keyword of 'fundamental rights' that occurs 44 times in the articles, due to the importance for 'high-risk' AI, followed by other values and principles. Some EU values do not occur at all (e.g., pluralism and tolerance). Rather abstract values can be combined with more concrete legal principles, where the latter are legally binding, have legal addressees and can have legal consequences. Hence, it is not very surprising that the principle (and value) of non-discrimination plays an important role in the AIA. Consequently, the overall-approach of the AIA can be summarised as 'human-centric', hence related to 'human well-being' and based on the ideas of 'humanism'.

1 Point of Departure: Challenges, Research Question and Methodology

Artificial intelligence (AI), machine learning[1] or the more specific field of deep learning,[2] including so-called neural networks,[3] are disruptive technologies.[4] AI has advantages (such as the ability of processing big quantity of information), but also comes with various challenges. AI can be biased because of biased data (e.g. medical data only based on male participants), bad quality algorithms (e.g. because of the programmers' biases) and can lack transparency due to the general 'black box'-phenomenon.[5] This can lead to challenges in various sectors (e.g. ChatGPT[6] in education[7] or in legaltech[8]), including particular sensitive ones such as healthcare. In

---

[1] On this concept, see, for instance, The Royal Society (2017).

[2] Algorithms 'designed to learn, meaning to modify their programming to account for new data'; Buiten (2019), p. 49. On this concept, see also LeCun et al. (2015).

[3] On a technological overview of these new technologies, see Buiten (2019), pp. 49–50; Zerilli and Weller (2021).

[4] In the following, I will refer to the overall term of AI. See also the contribution of Steckelmacher and Bogaerts in this book.

[5] Durán and Jongsma (2021); von Eschenbach (2021); Martini (2019).

[6] Ebers and Quarch (2024).

[7] Zuber and Gogoll (2024).

[8] Ebers and Quarch (2024).

the latter sector, this can result in problems for both physical health (e.g. in case of surgeries),[9] but also for mental health.[10] Besides the health sector, 'subliminal AI'[11] systems can subconsciously influence our decisions, for example, to buy certain products or services.

AI systems, the companies providing such systems and the data required for its training inevitably lead to the regulatory necessity to provide for normative solutions beyond a single nation state. The United States of America (U.S.)[12] and China[13] are more technically advanced than the European Union (EU).[14] In the U.S., President Biden has issued an 'Executive Order',[15] on 'safe, secure, and trustworthy development and use of Artificial Intelligence'. While the EU might not be able to compete with the U.S. or China on a technical level, the European Commission and the EU at large strive to provide 'secure, trustworthy and ethical artificial intelligence'.[16] This focus on trustworthy AI in the U.S. (end of October 2023) came two and a half years after the EU (April 2021). Trust shall be achieved by putting an emphasis on values and ethics. As I will show later,[17] ethical rules in the EU are strongly linked to EU values and related principles.

Why are the AI Act (AIA)[18] and its underlying philosophy of relevance both for the EU, but also beyond?[19] First, in 'its relations with the wider world, the Union

---

[9] Kowalewski et al. (2019); Sahm (2019).

[10] Roa and Biller-Andorno (2023).

[11] Neuwirth (2022).

[12] On the U.S., see the contribution of Dempsey in this book.

[13] On China, see the contribution of Li in this book.

[14] For an overview in economic terms, see Bryson and Malikova (2021).

[15] The White House (2023), then repealed in 2025 by the next administration. 'Most executive orders, significant and insignificant alike, involved (if foreign policy orders are placed to the side) the administration of public lands, the public workforce, or other public operations - although they also sometimes affected, and indeed were intended to affect, nongovernmental actors.[] The President in these cases, whether claiming authorisation from a federal statute delegating him power or from the Constitution itself, asserted his right as head of the executive branch to determine how its internal processes and constituent units were to function', Kagan (2001), pp. 2291–2292. Such executive orders can have 'force and effect of law', Newland (2015).

[16] European Commission (EC), 'Proposal for a regulation laying down harmonised rules on Artificial Intelligence (Artificial Intelligence Act [AIA]) and amending certain union legislative acts', COM(2021) 206 final 21 April 2021 [Proposal AIA].

[17] *Infra*, Sect. 2.

[18] Regulation (EU) 2024/1689 of the European Parliament and of the Council of 13 June 2024 *laying down harmonised rules on artificial intelligence and amending Regulations (EC) No 300/2008, (EU) No 167/2013, (EU) No 168/2013, (EU) 2018/858, (EU) 2018/1139 and (EU) 2019/2144 and Directives 2014/90/EU, (EU) 2016/797 and (EU) 2020/1828 (Artificial Intelligence Act)*, OJ L, 2024/1689 (2024) [AIA]. An EU regulation has 'general application' and is 'binding in its entirety and directly applicable in all Member State' (Art 288(2) TFEU). In other words, it does not have to be implemented into national law, like an EU directive.

[19] Presumably, the AIA will not only apply to the EU27, but also to the European Economic Area (EEA), i.e. also in relation to Norway, Iceland and Liechtenstein, subject to a decision of the EEA Joint Committee.

shall uphold and promote its values' (Art 3(5) TEU).[20] The values-based approach (see below) can be seen as one explanation for the **extraterritorial** application of the AIA (recitals 21 and 22).[21] This extraterritorial scope of the AIA can also be understood as an 'anti-circumvention mechanism'.[22] In the context of cross-border health care, we know the phenomenon of 'circumvention tourism'[23] and in the global digital world of AI, it is an appropriate move by the EU to exclude rather obvious **circumvention** possibilities. Second, it remains to be seen some years after the adoption and application of the AIA, whether we will observe an application of EU rules outside the EU by private companies or third-countries, apart from this extraterritorial application. This 'ability to influence global dynamics'[24] has been referred to as the 'Brussels effect'.[25] As in the case of the data protection,[26] this should not be interpreted as 'a mere goal of extraterritoriality or imperialism', but rather 'shows that the Union aims to ensure that formal territorial limitations do not undermine the protection of fundamental rights [...] and the related democratic values in the Union'.[27] Both the extraterritorial application and a possible 'Brussels-effect' showcase the importance of the AIA as the first binding regulatory approach at international level.

This focus on EU values and related principles leads to the **research question**, in which way the EU's values, as enshrined in Art 2 TEU,[28] can be seen as the underlying philosophy of the AIA. While some of these values can also be found beyond the EU in the Council of Europe,[29] the focus of this contribution will be on the EU and its AIA.

In terms of **methodology**, this contribution will take both a quantitative and qualitative approach. The quantitative approach will depict the references in both the Commission's proposal (see Table 2) and the finally adopted AIA (see Table 1). This will include both references of the AIA to the EU's 'values' as such, but also references to particular values (e.g. 'non-discrimination') that can be found in Art 2 TEU. Besides a quantitative methodology, this contribution will also apply a qualitative methodology, and analyse how the EU's values of Art 2 TEU can be seen as the underlying philosophy of the AIA and have shaped its structure and content. It

[20] See also Floridi (2021), p. 220.

[21] Asking for more clarification in this regard in the binding articles of the Proposal AIA, Ebers et al. (2021), p. 591.

[22] de Gregorio (2022), p. 301.

[23] Cohen (2012).

[24] de Gregorio (2022), p. 299.

[25] Bradford (2012, 2021).

[26] Regulation (EU) 2016/679 of the European Parliament and of the Council *on the protection of natural persons with regard to the processing of personal data and on the free movement of such data, and repealing Directive 95/46/EC (General Data Protection Regulation)*, O.J. L 119/1 (2016) [GDPR].

[27] de Gregorio (2022), p. 301.

[28] Consolidated version of the Treaty on European Union, O.J. C 202/13 (2016).

[29] See, for example, van Kolfschooten and Shachar (2023).

Table 1 Quantitative analysis concerning AI Act

Value	Articles	Recitals	Annexes	Total
Values	1	8	0	**9**
Human dignity	0	6	0	**6**
Freedom	7	22	1	**30**[a]
Democracy	2	8 + 1[b]+6 (DP[c]) + 1(DC)[d]	1 (DP)	**19**
Equality	0	3	0	**3**
Rule of law	1	7	0	**8**
Human rights	0	1	0	**1**
… of minorities	0	0	0	**0**[e]
… fundamental rights	44	54	2	**100**
Pluralism	0	0	0	**0**
Non-discrimination	2	20	1	**23**[f]
Tolerance	0	0	0	**0**
Justice	0	1	0	**1**[g]
Solidarity	0	0	0	**0**
Gender equality	1	2	0	**3**
Total	**58**	**140**	**5**	**203/203**

[a]Frischhut (2022), pp. 83–92

[b]The hits concerning freedom include various forms (with hits indicated in square brackets): as part of the 'Area of Freedom, Security and Justice' (AFSJ, Title V TFEU) [2], as certain freedoms enshrined in the CFR (i.e., freedom of expression [2], freedom of assembly [2], freedom of [the arts and] science[s] [2], freedom of strike [1]), as 'rights and freedoms' [20, comprising 10 hits for 'fundamental rights and freedoms'] and explicitly as value (recital 28) [1]

[c]'[D]emoctratic values', in recital 110

[d]'[D]emocratic processes'

[e]'[D]emocratic control'

[f]A national minority is addressed in recital 16 and ethnic or religious minorities are addressed in recital 29, but not as values.

[g]Both non-discrimination, as well as discrimination as an illegal pattern

[h]Justice also occurs as 'AFSJ' (recital 40 and Annex X), justice as a sector (like healthcare, agriculture, etc.; in recital 4, Art 74 para 8), and as 'administration of justice (4 hits in recitals, 1 hit in Annex III). Justice also occurs as 'Court of Justice of the EU' (recital 169, Art 74 and Art 101)

also makes a difference whether values (etc.) are covered in the (binding) **articles** or only in the **recitals**, which play a role in the interpretation of the binding text.[30] In case of the Commission's proposal (see Table 2), the **main text** (recitals and articles) also has to be differentiated from the 'explanatory memorandum', introducing this proposal, respectively, has to be differentiated from the 'legislative financial statement' (LFS) and the Annexes. This contribution will focus on **explicit**

[30] 'While the preamble to a Union act may explain the content of the provisions of that act and provides elements of interpretation which are likely to shed light on the intention of the author of that act, it has no binding legal value and cannot be relied upon to derogate from the provisions of the act itself or to interpret those provisions in a manner contrary to their wording'; ECJ judgement of 25 March 2021, *Balgarska Narodna Banka*, C-501/18, EU:C:2021:249, para 90. See also ECJ judgement of 5 March 2024, *Kočner v EUROPOL*, C-755/21 P, EU:C:2024:202, para 59.

Table 2 Quantitative analysis concerning Commission proposal

Value	Articles	Recitals	*Explan. Mem.*[a]	*LFS*[b]	Annexes	Total
Values	0	3	*7*	*3*	0	**13**
Human dignity	0	4	*1*	*0*	0	**5**
Freedom	5	10	*6*	*0*	1	**22**[c]
Democracy	0	2 + 1 (DP[d])	*0*	*0*	1 (DP)	**4**
Equality	0	3	*1*[e]	*0*	0	**4**
Rule of law	0	2	*0*	*0*	0	**2**
Human rights	0	0	*0*	*0*	0	**0**
… of minorities	0	0	*0*	*0*	0	**0**
… fundamental rights	19	21	30	*7*	1	**78**[f]
Pluralism	0	0	*0*	*0*	0	**0**
Non-discrimination	0	12	*4*	*0*	1	**17**
Tolerance	0	0	0	0	0	**0**
Justice	0	4	0	0	1	**5**[g]
Solidarity	0	0	*0*	*0*	0	**0**
Gender equality	0	0	*1*	*0*	0	**1**
Total	**24**	**62**	***50***	***10***	**5**	**151/151**

[a]Explanatory memorandum
[b]Legislative financial statement
[c]Freedom occurs in various forms as follows (with hits indicated in square brackets): as part of the 'AFSJ' [3], as certain freedoms enshrined in the CFR (i.e., freedom of expression [4], freedom of assembly [3], freedom to conduct business [1], freedom of art and science [2]), as 'rights and freedoms' [7], and two times explicitly as values (recitals 15 and 40 Proposal AIA)
[d]'[D]emocratic processes'
[e]Not including the one hit on 'gender equality'
[f]This number does not include the five hits for the CFR, which occurs three times in the explanatory memorandum (including once in footnote 8 of Proposal AIA), once in the preamble, once in Art 52 para 3
[g]The AFSJ also occurs once in the preamble, once in the explanatory memorandum, and once in the annex

references to values, not on implicit[31] references. It will cover both a collective reference to the EU's (common) values, as well as to particular values, as enshrined in Art 2 TEU (comprising both the first and the second sentence). As the list of values of Art 2 TEU also comprises 'human rights', this analysis will also include 'fundamental rights', as covered in Art 2 TEU and the Charter of Fundamental Rights of the EU (CFR).[32] Without going into details at this stage,[33] most 'fundamental rights'[34] of the CFR can be qualified as 'human rights'.

[31] For instance, in the context of regulatory sandboxes, recital 140 refers to participants' requirement to act 'in good faith', which can be seen as values-related.

[32] Consolidated version, O.J. C 202/389 (2016).

[33] For further details, see *infra* Sect. 2.

[34] On fundamental rights, see the contribution of Goffin and Palmieri in this book.

In the following, Sect. 2 will lay out the normative framework of EU values, principles and ethics. Section 3 will then place the AIA within this normative framework. Section 4 will analyse in which way EU values influence both the structure of the AIA, as well as its underlying philosophy. Besides EU values as such, Sect. 5 will analyse some selected particular values (e.g. non-discrimination) and their role in the AIA.

2 Normative Framework: Law, Ethics, Values and Principles

In the following, the normative framework on which this contribution is based will be briefly presented in an **overview**, to be followed by further details. A normative framework can be provided by the discipline of law, but also by norms outside the legal sphere. In the first case, this can be the law of a nation state or, for example, of the EU. Ethics, as a branch of practical philosophy, pertains to a different discipline but can equally provide guidance. These two disciplines touch base, if, for example, one refers to the other. For instance, there are various examples where EU law refers to ethics.[35] As I have argued elsewhere, values can be seen as a bridge between the two disciplines of law and philosophy (i.e. ethics).[36] While values cannot only have a legal or philosophical, but also a social, political, artistic or economic connotation,[37] I will focus on the legal values that have been enshrined by the Lisbon Treaty in Art 2 TEU. This Art 2 TEU also names 'human rights', which provides an important link to the rights enshrined in the CFR. Besides more abstract values, also more concrete (legal and/or ethical) principles can pertain to this normative framework, which will be described in more detail below.

The AIA offers a horizontal (not a sectoral) approach.[38] Therefore, its relationship with other EU secondary law is key.[39] In **EU law**, various EU directives and regulations are of relevance for AI, robotics and related topics. They include the

[35] See, for further details, Frischhut (2015, 2019).

[36] Frischhut (2019, 2022).

[37] Frischhut (2022), pp. 11–15.

[38] Cf.: 'this proposal presents a balanced and proportionate horizontal regulatory approach to AI that is limited to the minimum necessary requirements to address the risks and problems linked to AI' (Proposal AIA, p. 3). Horizontal, as opposed to various sectoral approaches (e.g., the Machinery Products [note 43], General Product Safety Rules [note 44]) (cf. Proposal AIA, p. 5).

[39] For example, the AIA applies in parallel to Regulation (EU) 2017/745 of the European Parliament and of the Council *on medical devices* [...], O.J. L 117/1 (2017), as amended by O.J. L, 2024/1860 [Regulation Medical Devices]. For further details, see Palmieri et al. (2021); van Kolfschooten (2023).

topics of product liability,[40] data protection,[41] machinery products,[42] or product safety.[43] While this contribution will not cover the normative framework provided by these (and other) legal documents, in its application the AIA will have to be read together with them, for example, Art 22 GDPR on 'automated individual decision-making'.[44]

'Ethics' and 'morality' can provide similar answers to the above-mentioned challenges brought by AI. However, these two concepts must be differentiated. **Ethics** is a branch of practical (as opposed to theoretical) philosophy, which deals with what is morally right or wrong. According to the Oxford Dictionary, ethics is 'the branch of knowledge that deals with moral principles', respectively, 'moral principles that govern a person's behaviour of the conducting of an activity'.[45] This includes normative ethics (as opposed to meta-ethics), which can be sub-divided into applied ethics and normative theories; the latter comprise deontology, consequentialism, and virtue ethics.[46] Ethics must be distinguished from **morality**, which reflects the attitudes of people what is right or wrong, relative to culture, region and time. According to the Oxford Dictionary, morality is about 'principles concerning the distinction between right or wrong or good and bad behaviour', respectively, 'a particular system of values and principles of conduct'.[47] Hence, morality refers to factual rules ('mores') and codes of conduct in a specific (cultural, territorial and temporal) social system.[48] According to the CJEU,[49] (public)[50] morality has a cultural, a regional and a temporal component. While morality changes over the years

[40] Council Directive 85/374/EEC *on the approximation of the laws, regulations and administrative provisions of the Member States concerning liability for defective products*, O.J. L 210/29 (1985), as repealed by O.J. L, 2024/2853 [Directive Product Liability].

[41] GDPR (see note 27).

[42] Regulation (EU) 2023/1230 of the European Parliament and of the Council *on machinery* [...], O.J. L 165/1 (2023), as amended by O.J. L, 2024/2748 (2023) [Regulation Machinery Products].

[43] Regulation (EU) 2023/988 of the European Parliament and of the Council *on general product safety* [...], O.J. L 135/1 (2023), as amended by O.J. L, 2024/3171 [Regulation general product safety].

[44] See ECJ judgement of 7 December 2023, *SCHUFA Holding (Scoring)*, C-634/21, EU:C:2023:957.

[45] Stevenson (2010), pp. 600–601.

[46] See, Frischhut (2019), p. 9. Deontology focuses on the action, consequentialism on the outcomes of this action, and virtue ethics on the (character traits of the) actor.

[47] Stevenson (2010), p. 1150.

[48] Frischhut (2015), pp. 536–537.

[49] This abbreviation refers to the Court of Justice of the EU in the sense of Art 19(1) TEU, which comprises not only the Court of Justice (ECJ), but also the General Court (GC).

[50] 'Public morality' is a so-called 'reason of justification' in the context of the free movement of goods (Art 36 Treaty on the Functioning of the European Union [TFEU]; consolidated version: O.J. C 202/47 [2016]). In this context, 'in principle it is for each Member State to determine in accordance with its own scale of values and in the form selected by it the requirements of public morality in its territory', as long as a country does not follow a principle of double morality. See ECJ judgement of 11 March 1986, *Conegate*, C-121/85, EU:C:1986:114, paras 14–15. For further details, see Frischhut (2015), pp. 541–545.

(evolutionary character), it is different from country to country and is based on certain values.[51]

Various papers have approached the topic of AI more from an ethical,[52] or more from a moral[53] perspective.[54] Various stakeholders (e.g., European Commission [EC] Coordinated Plan on Artificial Intelligence,[55] European Declaration on Digital rights[56]) and expert groups have contributed to discussion what should be the underlying philosophy of the AIA, amongst them the Ethics Advisory Group,[57] the High-level Expert Group on Artificial Intelligence[58] (HLEG-AI),[59] or the European Group on Ethics in Science and New Technologies[60] (EGE),[61] to name but a few.

Law tends to lag behind technological developments. This might be one reason for the increasing **references** of EU law to ethics, however less so to morality.[62] However, in case of these references it is not always clear, what the content of the legal norm referring to ethics should be in the end.[63] Not only for these cases have I argued that EU values and EU human (or fundamental) rights should play an important role.[64]

Since the entry into force of the Lisbon Treaty, Art 2 TEU has turned the EU into a '**Union of values**'. Art 2 TEU consists of two sentences, where the first one is based on the idea of pre-existing values, on which the 'Union is founded'. These values comprise 'respect for human dignity, freedom, democracy, equality, the rule of law and respect for human rights, including the rights of persons belonging to

---

[51] ECJ judgement of 11 March 1986, *Conegate*, C-121/85, EU:C:1986:114, para 14; see also Frischhut (2015), p. 544.

[52] Bartneck et al. (2019); Beck (2012); Coeckelbergh (2020); Dignum (2019); Dubber et al. (2020); Hansson (2017); Hengstschläger and Austrian Council for Research and Technology Development (2020); Ienca et al. (2022); Jobin et al. (2019); Kirchschläger (2021); Lammert (2019); Liao (2020); Lin et al. (2017); Mantelero (2022); Rath et al. (2019); Sartor (2020); Spiekermann (2019); Stix (2021); Tasioulas (2019); Thaler (2021); Vallor (2022); Walz and Firth-Butterfield (2019).

[53] Hilgendorf (2013); Klenk (2021); Neuhäuser (2012); Neuhäuser (2013); Shaw (2021); Tigard (2021).

[54] Of course, one should be aware of the fact that there are obviously some overlaps.

[55] European Commission (2018).

[56] European Commission (2022b); European Commission (2022a).

[57] Ethics Advisory Group (2018).

[58] High-level Expert Group on Artificial Intelligence (HLEG-AI) (2019a); HLEG-AI (2019b); HLEG-AI (2020).

[59] The Commission has 'appointed a group of experts to provide advice on its artificial intelligence strategy'; cf. European Commission (2022c).

[60] Cf. Commission Decision (EU) 2021/156 *renewing the mandate of the European Group on Ethics in Science and New Technologies*, O.J. L 46/34 (2021). On this new mandate, see Frischhut (2021b).

[61] European Group on Ethics in Science and New Technologies (EGE) (2012).

[62] Frischhut (2019).

[63] Such a reference of EU law to ethics with an unclear outcome can be especially problematic, as legal certainty is one element of the 'rule of law', one of the EU's values.

[64] Frischhut (2019, 2022).

minorities'. Human dignity is the first value and the first human right mentioned in the CFR. The second sentence[65] of Art 2 TEU mentions that these 'values are common to the Member States in a society in which pluralism, non-discrimination, tolerance, justice, solidarity and equality between women and men prevail'. Having argued that both values and **human rights** shall play a role in the EU's relationship towards ethics, two clarifications have to be made. First, while for reasons of clarity I have referred to values and human rights, the latter are also 'values' themselves. Second, as already mentioned above, not only human dignity (Art 1 CFR[66]), but also most (other) rights covered in the CFR are fundamental rights[67] entitling not only EU citizens,[68] but all human beings. Values are more abstract comparted to principles (see below) and to detailed legal provisions, as the above-mentioned GDPR. Despite their abstract character, they are part of EU primary law and in terms of legal hierarchy stand above EU secondary law, which also has to be interpreted in a value-conform[69] way. As it would go beyond the scope of this article, the individual values cannot be presented in detail, but can be found elsewhere (available open access[70]).

Human dignity can be seen as the 'corner-stone' of the EU's values.[71] In the field of AI systems used to evaluate the creditworthiness of natural persons, AI systems can be used to determine whether certain 'benefits and services should be granted, denied, reduced, revoked or reclaimed by authorities' (recital 58); as those AI systems might have a significant impact on human dignity, they consequently have been classified as high-risk. Art 14 on '**human oversight**' can also be related to human dignity. As analysed in the context of data protection law, 'human oversight typically relates to human dignity'.[72] Finally, yet importantly, the 'human centric' approach of the AIA is also strongly related to human dignity. Human dignity is often equated with the respectful treatment of human beings.[73] While the content of this value has not changed, now not only do other human beings have to respect this value, but equally AI systems. Besides this corner-stone of human dignity, also

[65] As I have argued elsewhere, the concepts mentioned in this second sentence should not necessarily be seen as 'less', but are also 'values', although with some differences. For instance, 'tolerance' and 'pluralism' are less determined in comparison to 'non-discrimination', and unlike the latter concept cannot be legally enforced. For further details, see Frischhut (2022).

[66] 'Human dignity is inviolable. It must be respected and protected'.

[67] 'Fundamental rights' as basic rights that can be asserted against a state or, for example, against the EU (as a supranational organisation); see also Pache (2020), p. 129.

[68] 'While human rights are the rights of all individuals regardless of their nationality, citizenship rights are fundamental rights that belong only to nationals of a particular country'; Benedek (2017), p. 44; translation.

[69] Bogdandy and Spieker (2019, 2020); Potacs (2016).

[70] Frischhut (2022).

[71] Frischhut (2019), p. 14.

[72] Veale and Zuiderveen Borgesius (2021), p. 103.

[73] Frischhut (2022).

other values (e.g. non-discrimination) play a role for AI systems, as to be shown below (Sect. 5).

Besides these general values of Art 2 TEU, we can also find more **specific** values.[74] That is, for example, the case for health. Here the health ministers in 2006 have defined health values (for health systems) that are more abstract and underlying principles that are more concrete.[75] These health values comprise 'universality, access to good quality care, equity, and solidarity', where '[b]eneath [!] these overarching values, there is also a set of operating principles', which cover quality, safety, care that is based on evidence and ethics, patient involvement, redress, privacy and confidentiality.[76] For AI in the context of physical or mental health, these health values might also need to be adhered to (on 'soft-law',[77] see below).

On the one hand the abstract character of EU values might be a challenge when applying them to a particular situation, on the other hand this makes abstract values more timeless and better suited to new circumstances. Abstract values can complement more concrete principles. These **principles** can pertain to the legal and or the ethical realm. **Legal principles** can have certain addressees and can be legally enforceable. For instance, if a Member State sets up unproportioned barriers to the economic fundamental freedoms, under EU law these barriers may not be applied because of the primacy of EU law and its 'principle' of proportionality. Proportionality, precaution and responsibility are just a few examples of principles that can be traced to both disciplines, ethics and the law.

Besides legal principles, also **ethical principles** are of relevance for AI and other topics of digitalisation. In their seminal book 'Principles of biomedical ethics', Beauchamp and Childress have identified the following four **ethical** principles: respect for autonomy, non-maleficence, beneficence and justice.[78] This so-called 'principlism' approach has the advantage of being more 'user-friendly' and more 'hands on', compared to the three (above-mentioned) normative theories of deontology, consequentialism and virtue ethics. The fact that in this field well-established and long-standing standards exist, has led to some arguing that these standards of bioethics shall also be transferred to the digital world.[79] Floridi and colleagues have opted for an approach of applying these four principles, plus adding a new one that is specific to and essential for the field of digitalisation, i.e., 'explicability'.[80] This approach of the four principles of medical ethics has been seen as 'a good starting

---

[74] For further details, see Frischhut (2022).

[75] Council conclusions *on Common values and principles in European Union Health Systems*, O.J. C 146/1 (2006).

[76] Ibid.

[77] While this health values are not legally binding (i.e. soft-law), they can become legally binding if hard-law, for example, an EU directive refers to them: Directive 2011/24/EU of the European Parliament and of the Council *on the application of patients' rights in cross-border healthcare*, O.J. L 88/45 (2011), as amended by O.J. L, 2025/327 [Directive patient mobility].

[78] Beauchamp and Childress (2019).

[79] While this is obvious for AI in the field of health, this approach goes beyond health-related AI.

[80] Floridi et al. (2018).

point but insufficient in addressing all the ethical issues that arise in AI-based systems'.[81] This analogous application has also[82] been criticised by Mittelstadt, who argued that AI and medicine are fundamentally different, and that therefore these medical principles could not be adopted by analogy.[83]

Turning back to the legal field, the above-mentioned documents (Product Liability Directive, General Data Protection Regulation) pertain to the legal field, are binding and legally enforceable, i.e. 'hard-law'. As opposed to 'hard-law', '**soft-law**' is not legally binding. While soft-law[84] is not legally binding, it should not be underestimated. It can have a self-binding effect on the entity issuing such a document, it can also become legally binding if referenced by a legally binding document. The above-mentioned reference of the legally binding 'Directive patient mobility' to the soft-law document of health values is an example for the latter category. 'Soft-law' can be understood in a narrower sense, where only the documents of entities that could also issue hard-law (e.g., the European Parliament [EP], together with the Council of the EU) would be covered. However, the author suggests to follow a broader understanding, according to which also non-binding documents of other entities shall be included. Hence, also an AI related 'code of conduct'[85] of a private company falls under this broad understanding of soft-law.

To summarise, the normative framework on which this contribution is based comprises law, including values (e.g., human dignity) and legal principles (e.g., proportionality, transparency[86]), and besides hard- also soft-law. As mentioned above, values can be seen as a bridge between law and philosophy (ethics). In the latter field, we can identify ethics as another normative approach, referring either to normative theories (deontology, consequentialism, and virtue ethics) or to ethical principles, where 'principlism' offers a well-established approach that can also be transferred to the digital field.

---

[81] Dolic, Zrinjka et al. (2019), p. 15.

[82] Hagendorff (2022) has suggested a virtue-based framework. While the author supports the role of virtues (i.e., character traits that also need to be practised) for a democratic society, in the field of applied ethics in AI, (legal and) ethical principles might be more useful, as the character traits of the humans involved might rather be an additional element, which cannot replace the substantive requirements.

[83] Mittelstadt (2019). While his concerns might be valid ('AI development lacks (1) common aims and fiduciary duties, (2) professional history and norms, (3) proven methods to translate principles into practice, and (4) robust legal and professional accountability mechanisms'), they should not be seen as insurmountable obstacles. Rather they can serve as valuable hints that must be taken into account in analogous application of these biomedical ethics principles. See, already Frischhut (2021a), p. 73.

[84] See, for further details, Weismann (2023).

[85] See, *infra*, Sect. 4.3.

[86] On AI and transparency, see Wulf and Seizov (2020); Rotenberg (2022).

3 The AIA within this Normative Framework

Before turning to the finally adopted AIA, it is worth taking a brief look at its **genesis**. In a controversially[87] discussed resolution of 2017, the EP has emphasised the importance of the 'underlying principles and values of the Union law, such as non-stigmatisation, transparency, autonomy, individual responsibility and social responsibility, and on existing ethical practices and codes'.[88] In the 'code of ethical conduct for robotics engineers', annexed to this resolution, the EP has referred to the above-mentioned four principles of the 'principlism'-approach.[89] Already in 2018, the Commission emphasised that the 'Union's values and fundamental rights [shall be] at the forefront of the AI landscape'.[90] Likewise, in its AI White Paper of 2020, the Commission has emphasised the importance of excellence and trust; hence, AI has to be 'human-centric, ethical, sustainable and respects fundamental rights and values'.[91] Similarly, also other important stakeholders, such as the Commission's ethics advisory body, the EGE,[92] or the HLEG-AI[93] have emphasised the importance of ethics and values. In its 2019 'Ethics Guidelines for Trustworthy AI',[94] the HLEG-AI has proposed AI that is lawful, (technically) robust and ethical, in order to establish a 'framework for trustworthy (!) AI'. It has identified four ethical principles. Hence, reminiscent of, but also different to the four of the above-mentioned 'principlism' approach: respect for human autonomy, prevention of harm, fairness, and explicability.[95] This can be seen as a condensed version of the above-mentioned approach of Floridi,[96] combining non-maleficence and beneficence to 'prevention of harm' and referring to fairness instead of justice.[97] Besides hard- and soft-law (top-down approach), also society has to be included in the debate of such an important issue

---

[87] The question (not a demand), whether there should be a 'specific legal status for robots in the long run'; European Parliament resolution *with recommendations to the Commission on Civil Law Rules on Robotics (2015/2103(INL))*, O.J. C 252/239 (2018) [EP resolution robotics], pt. 59 lit. f, has been rejected by many (cf. Dvorsky (2018)).

[88] EP resolution robotics pt. 13.

[89] *Supra*, at note 79.

[90] EC, 'Artificial Intelligence for Europe', COM(2018) 237 final 25 April 2018, p. 19.

[91] EC, 'White Paper on Artificial Intelligence - A European approach to excellence and trust', COM(2020) 65 final 19 February 2020, p. 25.

[92] The EGE has proposed 'a set of fundamental ethical principles, based on the values laid down in the EU Treaties and the [CFR]'; EGE (2018), p. 5.

[93] HLEG-AI (2019a).

[94] For the other three deliverables, see European Commission (2022c).

[95] HLEG-AI (2019a), p. 8. Based on that, they have developed seven 'key requirements', including human agency and oversight, technical robustness and safety, privacy and data governance, transparency, diversity, non-discrimination and fairness, societal and environmental wellbeing, and accountability.

[96] See *supra* note 80.

[97] Justice and fairness are often used interchangeably. However, the notion of 'unjust' is often perceived to carry a stronger way of condemnation compared to 'unfair'; see Frischhut (2022).

(bottom-up approach). That is why the EP has demanded a 'public debate on how to explore the enormous potential of AI based on fundamental European values, the principles of transparency, explainability, fairness, accountability, responsibility and trustworthiness, as well as the principle that AI and robotics should be human-centred and developed to complement humans'.[98]

These various preliminary steps then let to the Commission's **proposal** for an AIA in April 2021, which has been assessed differently in literature: it has been seen more critical[99] or more positive[100] in general, or was also seen critically as not taking enough into account the specific requirements of one sector, for instance health care.[101] After this short genesis, let us turn to the finally adopted AIA.

Part of the **underlying philosophy** of the finally adopted AIA is to ensure a 'high level of protection of health, safety [and] fundamental rights' (recital 1). The **high-level** approach is not new in EU law and can be found in the fields of environmental protection,[102] human health,[103] employment[104] and consumer protection,[105] to name but a few. Art 114 TFEU and Art 16 TFEU (data protection) are the legal bases for the AIA. This high-level approach can also be found in Art 114(3) TFEU as a requirement for the Commission to take into account 'a high level of protection' in the fields of 'health, safety, environmental protection and consumer protection', when drafting new proposals for EU legislation. This high-level approach resonates well with EU values, which also comprise fundamental rights.

Based on ideas already addressed at European[106] and at national[107] level, the AIA takes a **risk-based** approach, which can be seen as an expression of the above-mentioned legal principle of proportionality. This underlying approach of focusing on values and fundamental rights and the resulting risk-based approach can be summarised as follows: The higher the risk, the stricter the rules. This risk-based approach strongly also influences the structure of the AIA. At the top of the pyramid of this risk-based approach stands 'prohibited AI' (see Sect. 4.1). According to recital 28 practices that 'are particularly harmful and abusive [...] should be prohibited because they contradict Union values of respect for human dignity, freedom, equality, democracy and the rule of law and fundamental rights'.

The AIA also supports the other elements of the above-mentioned normative framework (Sect. 2). Recital 8 is key in this regard and refers to 'secure, trustworthy

---

[98] European Parliament resolution *on artificial intelligence in a digital age (2020/2266(INI))*, O.J. C 465/65 (2022).

[99] Valta and Vasel (2021); Veale and Zuiderveen Borgesius (2021).

[100] Burri and von Bothmer (2021); Ebers et al. (2021), p. 601; Heil (2022).

[101] van Kolfschooten (2022).

[102] Art 3(3) TEU, Art 191(2) TFEU, Art 37 CFR.

[103] Art 9 TFEU, Art 168(1) TFEU, Art 35 CFR.

[104] Art 9 TFEU, Art 147 TFEU.

[105] Art 169(1) TFEU, Art 38 CFR. On AI and consumer law, see Ebers (2021).

[106] The HLEG-AI (2019a, p. 2) has referred to the necessity to '[a]dopt adequate measures to mitigate these risks when appropriate, and proportionately to the magnitude of the risk'.

[107] Datenethikkommission (2019), p. 177.

and ethical AI' as well as to 'the protection of ethical principles', as requested by the EP.[108] However, ethics mainly occurs in the preamble of the AIA referencing some of the above-mentioned documents (HLEG-AI, etc.) and only occurs in Art 60(3) AIA[109] on testing of high-risk AI systems in real world conditions outside AI regulatory sandboxes,[110] as well as in case of codes of conduct in case of the voluntary[111] application of the AIA (Art 95(2)(a)).

4 AIA and EU Values as Such

Based on the **hierarchy of EU law**, EU secondary law (e.g., a regulation) has to be in conformity with EU primary law.[112] The latter does not only comprise the EU's common values (Art 2 TEU),[113] but also the afore-mentioned high-level of protection in the fields of health, consumer protection, etc. Because of this hierarchy, EU secondary law has to be interpreted in a value-conform[114] way. Nonetheless, it should be welcomed that the AIA goes beyond this general impact of EU values. Hence, references of the AIA to values (and related concepts) are not formally necessary, but can have a clear substantive meaning. In a similar way to the afore-mentioned approach of fulfilling certain ethical requirements beyond the mandatory legal minimum level, references to EU values substantially shape the underlying philosophy of the AIA.[115]

After having placed the AI within the normative framework of this contribution and before turning to prohibited (Sect. 4.1), high-risk (Sect. 4.2) and low-risk (Sect. 4.3) AI, let us also take a quantitative approach and see, how often both the keyword of 'values' as well as particular values occur in the AIA (Table 1) and the Commission's proposal (Table 2). The combination of a qualitative approach (i.e. the normative framework as the underlying philosophy shaping the structure and the content) and a quantitative approach shall provide a more holistic view of the AIA.

---

[108] European Parliament resolution *with recommendations to the Commission on a framework of ethical aspects of artificial intelligence, robotics and related technologies (2020/2012(INL))*, O.J. C 404/63 (2021).

[109] 'The testing of high-risk AI systems in real world conditions under this Article shall be without prejudice to any ethical review that is required by Union or national law'.

[110] On regulatory sandboxes, see the contribution of Chassang in this book.

[111] See Sect. 4.3.

[112] 'The Court has consistently held that, if the wording of secondary law is open to more than one interpretation, preference should be given to the interpretation which renders the provision consistent with the Treaty rather than to the interpretation which leads to its being incompatible with the Treaty […]'; ECJ judgement of 4 May 2016, *Philip Morris Brands and Others*, C-547/14, EU:C:2016:325, para 70.

[113] Bogdandy and Spieker (2020).

[114] Bogdandy and Spieker (2019, 2020); Potacs (2016).

[115] Therefore, the AIA is in conformity with the afore-mentioned documents of EU institutions and other important stakeholders (EGE, HLEG-AI, etc.).

As mentioned above, Art 2 TEU refers to 'human rights' and the CFR comprises 'fundamental rights'. These two terms largely overlap, as most fundamental rights can be qualified as human rights.[116] Therefore, also the search term of 'fundamental rights' has been included in this quantitative analysis. This analysis (Table 1) reveals that values (including both the keyword of 'values', as well as particular values) occur less in the binding[117] text of the AIA, i.e. in the articles, with 58 hits. Within the articles, 'fundamental rights' take the biggest share with 44 hits, due to their importance for 'high-risk' AI (see below Sect. 4.2). Values (both as a keyword and particular values) do occur more often (140 hits) in the recitals, which are of relevance for the interpretation of the AIA, as reflecting the wording of the binding text of the articles.[118]

Looking at **particular EU values**, the keyword of 'fundamental rights' ranks first (100 hits in total), with an almost equal representation in the binding articles (44 hits) and in the recitals (54 hits). Four values[119] do not occur at all in the AIA. This might not be so surprising for pluralism and tolerance, two concepts that are hardly enforceable.[120] This analysis is not true for solidarity, which besides being an EU value can also be qualified as a legal principle.[121]

In comparison to a quantitative analysis of the Commission proposal (see Table 2),[122] the references to particular EU values in the finally adopted AIA have increased. From 24 to 58 in the articles and from 62 to 140 in the recitals. The general reference to the keyword of 'values' has decreased from 13 to 9, whereas the hits for individual values have almost all increased. A general increase of hits in the finally adopted AIA is not surprising, as it is a common pattern that dossiers become more complex and comprehensive during a legislative procedure.

[116] These rights are fundamental in the sense of their importance and basic function, but at the same time are human rights as most of these rights entitle all human beings.

[117] Likewise, the annexes to the AIA are binding, covering five hits (with no value standing out significantly in terms of hits).

[118] See *supra* note 30.

[119] Human rights of minorities, pluralism, tolerance and solidarity.

[120] *Supra* note 65.

[121] Frischhut (2022), pp. 83–92.

[122] Because of the structure of the Commissions' proposal, this Table comprises two additional columns, printed in Italics.

4.1 Prohibited AI: An EU Values Based Approach

Values and fundamental rights are the AIA's underlying philosophy, as they do not only determine the risk-based approach, but also result in certain AI being prohibited.[123] Following the above-mentioned research question, this section shall answer the question in which way values and fundamental rights have determined the AIA.[124]

As mentioned in the introduction, AI has pros and cons. Likewise, the AIA, apart from mentioning 'many beneficial uses of AI' also highlights that this technology 'can also be misused and provide novel and powerful tools for manipulative, exploitative and social control practices' (recital 28). The arguments for prohibiting these practices are **based on** the following **values**: 'Such practices [i.e., 'manipulative, exploitative and social control practices'] are particularly harmful and abusive and should be **prohibited** because they contradict **Union values** of respect for **human dignity**, **freedom**, **equality**, **democracy** and the **rule of law** and **fundamental rights** enshrined in the Charter, including the right to **non-discrimination**, to data protection and to privacy and the rights of the child' (recital 22; emphases added).

Art 5(1) AIA prohibits the following AI practices: subliminal, manipulative or deceptive techniques (lit. a), exploitative AI systems (lit. b), social scoring (lit. c), certain AI systems for making risk assessments concerning criminal offences (lit. d), facial recognition[125] databases (lit. e), certain detection of emotions at workplace and at educational institutions (lit. f), certain biometric categorisation systems (lit. g), and the use of certain 'real-time' remote biometric identification systems in publicly accessible spaces (lit. h).

Subliminal, manipulative or deceptive AI systems (see also recital 29) contravene human dignity, the freedom of the person (against these influences) and their fundamental rights.[126] While manipulation clearly conflicts with the value of freedom, it also contravenes treating a dignified human with respect and goes against many fundamental rights (mental integrity, freedom of thought, and freedom of expression, to name but a few).

Andorno has convincingly argued that human dignity is the basis of human rights, not vulnerability. Nonetheless, (as he has also emphasised) **vulnerability** plays an important role in human dignity, human rights and non-discrimination.[127] Therefore, the AIA is right in prohibiting 'an AI system that **exploits** any of the vulnerabilities of a natural person or a specific group of persons due to their age, disability or a specific social or economic situation' (Art 5(1) lit. b, emphasis added;

---

[123] For further details on 'prohibited' AI, see Veale and Zuiderveen Borgesius (2021), pp. 98–102.

[124] This section only addresses some selected questions of prohibited AI systems from the angle of EU values and fundamental rights. For more details, see the contribution of Neuwirth in this book.

[125] See, for example, Raposo (2023a, 2023b).

[126] Obviously, also other values can be affected.

[127] Andorno (2016).

see also recital 29). Such AI is also prohibited because it infringes the 'do no harm' principle (ibid).[128]

Whether referring to George Orwell' dystopian book 1984 and its key slogan of 'Big Brother is watching you',[129] or to contemporary practice in China,[130] **social scoring**[131] is problematic and 'may lead to discriminatory outcomes and the exclusion of certain groups' (recital 31). More precisely, recital 31 emphasises that AI systems used for social scoring 'may violate the right to **dignity** and **non-discrimination** and the values of **equality** and **justice**' (emphases added). Likewise, the value of freedom can also be negatively affected.

The same concern ('Big Brother is watching you') also applies to **'real-time' remote biometric identification** systems in publicly accessible spaces. As emphasised in recital 32, such AI may 'evoke a feeling of **constant surveillance** and indirectly **dissuade** the exercise of the freedom of assembly and other **fundamental rights**' (emphases added). Hence, here values and fundamental rights are invoked as arguments to prohibit these forms of AI. Likewise, constant surveillance can infringe human dignity, freedom, but also other values and fundamental rights (privacy, data protection, etc.).[132]

Before moving on to fundamental rights and their role in 'high-risk' AI, it shall be briefly mentioned that in case of prohibited AI, the AIA foresees **higher penalties**, including administrative fines to be imposed by the Member States (Art 99(3)).

4.2 High-Risk: The Triple Protection Approach

The EU's **values** enshrined in Art 2 TEU[133] are **human-centric** and the **AIA**'s approach concerning 'high-risk'[134] AI reflects this approach by following the philosophy of protecting the health and safety of humans. Besides this health-related aspect, also the fundamental rights of humans have to be safeguarded and pertain to the AIA's underlying philosophy. In this regard, the AIA is in line with the so-called

[128] That is also the reason, why research conducted for legitimate reasons and doing no harm is not prohibited (recital 25).

[129] Orwell (1949), p. 5, et passim.

[130] Kostka (2019); Jiang (2020); Zeng and Wong (2022).

[131] While in human rights' issues one should always consider both natural and legal persons, the prohibition of social scoring only addresses 'natural persons'.

[132] Space precludes a detailed analysis.

[133] Outside Art 2 TEU, the ECJ has developed 'animal welfare' as an additional value, not addressing humans. ECJ judgement of 17 December 2020, *Centraal Israëlitisch Consistorie van België and Others*, C-336/19, EU:C:2020:1031, para 41: '[…] EU value, namely animal welfare, as now enshrined in Article 13 TFEU, according to which the European Union and the Member States must pay full regard to the welfare requirements of animals, when formulating and implementing animal welfare policy'.

[134] On the high-risk AI, see the contribution of Szostek and Prabucki in this book.

'New Legislative Framework' (NLF),[135] which strives for a 'comprehensive regulatory framework to operate effectively for the safety [!] and compliance of industrial products with the requirements adopted to protect the various public interests [!] and for the proper functioning of the single market'.[136] The 'human centric' approach does not only aim at protecting humans, it also gives them (e.g., 'stop button', see below) the last word ('**human oversight**'). As emphasised by recital 7, in order to 'ensure a consistent and **high** [!] level of protection of public interests as regards **health, safety and fundamental rights**, common rules for high-risk AI systems should be established'.[137] Human oversight is essential and showcases this values-based philosophy of the AIA, as humans shall have the last word. This shall also guarantee that humans are treated as subjects and not as objects, thereby respecting the Kantian[138] inspired value of human dignity.

The main reason for classifying AI systems as 'high-risk'[139] is the fact that they 'pose a risk of harm to **health** and **safety**, or an adverse impact on **fundamental rights**'[140] (Art[141] 7(1)(b)). As also known from the medical devices regulation,[142] the AIA refers to the 'intended purpose'[143] of the system (e.g. Articles 7 to 14). For these 'high-risk' AI systems, the AIA foresees a risk management system (Art 9), and requirements as regards data and data governance (Art 10), technical documentation (Art 11) and record-keeping (Art 12), transparency and the provision of information to deployers (Art 13), human oversight (Art 14), and accuracy, robustness and cybersecurity (Art 15) (see also recital 66).

The question, not a demand (!), of the EP in 2017 to address the possible 'specific legal status for robots',[144] has produced a huge outcry.[145] Besides the question of whether the EU has the legal competence[146] to legislate on the question of also

---

[135] Cf. also Veale and Zuiderveen Borgesius (2021), p. 102.

[136] EC, *'The 'Blue Guide' on the implementation of EU product rules 2022'*, O.J. C 247/1(10) (2022).

[137] Emphases added. Besides human or fundamental rights, this recital also refers to another value, i.e., non-discrimination, as well as to the CFR.

[138] Kant (2014).

[139] On risk regulation in the EU (values, internal market, etc.), see Weimer (2019); Fraser and Bello y Villarino (2023).

[140] Emphases added.

[141] All articles or recitals without further indication refer to the AIA.

[142] Regulation Medical Devices, Art 5, et passim. On medical devices, see the contribution of Van Roijen in this book.

[143] Defined in Art 3(12) AIA. On intended versus actual use, see Yu (2022).

[144] The EP called on the Commission to reflect, amongst others, on the question of: 'creating a specific legal status for robots in the long run, so that at least the most sophisticated autonomous robots could be established as having the status of electronic persons responsible for making good any damage they may cause, and possibly applying electronic personality to cases where robots make autonomous decisions or otherwise interact with third parties independently'; EP resolution robotics pt. 59 lit. f. See also *supra* at note 88.

[145] Dvorsky (2018).

[146] Art 345 TFEU: 'The Treaties shall in no way prejudice the rules in Member States governing the system of property ownership'. While 'property ownership' is not the same as the question of a

providing ('AI driven')[147] robots with a **legal personhood** besides natural and legal persons, this addresses the relationship between human beings and AI/robots in a very fundamental way. Liability issues[148] could be outsourced to AI/robots, to name just one possible concern. The relationship between human beings and robots has already been addressed in Asimov's laws[149] for requirements directed at robots[150] and in 'robotic ethics'[151] for requirements directed at humans.

Against this background, the '**human centric**'[152] approach of the AIA can, amongst others, be seen in Art 14 on 'human oversight'.[153] According to this concept, 'high-risk' AI systems 'shall be designed and developed in such a way, including with appropriate human-machine interface tools, that they can be effectively overseen by natural persons' (Art 14(1)) and it shall 'aim to prevent or minimise the risks to health, safety or fundamental rights that may emerge [from] a high-risk AI system'[154] (Art 14(2)). One practical and also symbolically important element in this regard is the requirement that humans shall be able 'to intervene in the operation of the high-risk AI system or interrupt the system through a "stop" button or a similar procedure that allows the system to come to a halt in a safe state' (Art 14(4) lit. e). Human oversight is explicitly linked to human dignity in recital 27 AIA: 'human agency and oversight means that AI systems are developed and used as a tool that serves people, respects human dignity and personal autonomy, and that is functioning in a way that can be appropriately controlled and overseen by humans'.

After 'prohibited' AI and 'high-risk' AI, let us now turn to 'low-risk' AI systems.

'legal status', the competence is not one of the EU, especially if Art 345 TFEU is interpreted broadly; see Kühling (2018).

[147] While the resolution (note 159) refers to robots, the reference to 'the most sophisticated autonomous robots' and 'cases where robots make autonomous decisions' can be seen as an implicit reference to 'AI driven' robots.

[148] After the AIA, a next issue would have been the question of AI liability. See EC, Proposal for a Directive on adapting non-contractual civil liability rules to artificial intelligence (AI Liability Directive), COM(2022) 496 final 28 September 2022. In February 2025, the Commission announced to withdraw this proposal; EC, Commission work programme 2025, COM(2025) 45 final 11 February 2025, Annex IV, p. 26.

[149] Asimov (1950).

[150] While these three laws are addressed at the robot (not injure a human being, obey human orders, etc.), they nonetheless concern the relationship of robots and humans.

[151] 'Robo-ethics is of course not an ethics developed for robots, as in Asimov's famous principles', it is 'rather an ethics designed for humans to interact with robots'; Hilgendorf (2017), pp. 26–27.

[152] Proposal AIA, p. 1.

[153] Cf. Koulu (2020).

[154] Emphases added.

4.3 Low-Risk: A Soft-Law Ethical Approach

Under this meta-term of 'low-risk'[155] AI, we can identify two sub-categories, 'limited-risk' AI (referred to as 'certain' AI systems[156]), and 'minimal-risk' AI (referred to as, 'other than high-risk AI systems'[157]).

The AIA foresees transparency obligations for '**limited**-risk' AI (Art 50). Transparency is a legal principle,[158] not an EU value (Art 2 TEU) and will consequently not be further covered in this contribution.[159]

In case of '**minimal**-risk', the AIA takes a 'soft-law' approach, by not foreseeing binding legal obligations (e.g., as in Chap. III AIA for 'high-risk' AI) based on certain values, including fundamental rights, but allows for a **voluntary** approach. Recital 27 refers to the seven non-binding ethical principles for AI that have been developed by the AI HLEG-AI,[160] which should 'serve as a basis for the drafting of codes of conduct'.

Art 95(**1**) tasks the AI Office[161] and the Member States to 'encourage and facilitate the drawing up of codes of conduct, including related governance mechanisms, intended to foster the voluntary application' of the requirements for high-risk AI systems to 'minimal-risk' AI systems. Hence, in this case the AIA foresees a voluntary opt-in possibility. Art 95(**2**) tasks the AI Office and the Member States in a similar way to encourage the voluntary application 'of specific requirements to all AI systems'. These codes shall be based on clear objectives and key performance indicators (KPIs). Besides the already mentioned ethical guidelines for trustworthy AI, Art 95(**2**) mentions the following elements in this regard: the impact of AI systems on environmental sustainability, AI literacy, an inclusive and diverse design of AI system, as well as the negative impact of AI systems on vulnerable persons or groups of vulnerable persons.

According to recital 48, the '**fundamental right** to a high level of **environmental protection** enshrined in the Charter and implemented in Union policies should also be considered when assessing the severity of the harm that an AI system can

[155] On 'low-risk' AI, see the contribution of Bygrave and Schmidt in this book.

[156] Title of Art 50 AIA, the only article of Chapter IV.

[157] Art 95 AIA.

[158] 'The principle of transparency is stated in Articles 1 TEU and 10 TEU and in Article 15 TFEU. It enables citizens to participate more closely in the decision-making process and guarantees that the administration enjoys greater legitimacy and is more effective and more accountable to the citizen in a democratic system'; ECJ judgement of 9 November 2010, *Schecke*, C-92/09, EU:C:2010:662, para 68.

[159] The AIA emphasises the following 'safety net': 'It is important that AI systems related to products that are not high-risk in accordance with [the AIA] and thus are not required to comply with the requirements set out for high-risk AI systems are nevertheless safe when placed on the market or put into service. To contribute to this objective, Regulation (EU) 2023/988 [Regulation general product safety, see *supra* note 43 would apply as a safety net' (recital 166).

[160] See notes 58 and 95.

[161] Cf. Art 3(47) AIA.

cause, including in relation to the health and safety of persons'.[162] **Sustainability** is a strongly anchored principle in EU law,[163] which has already been addressed in 1979 by Hans Jonas coining his 'ecological imperative',[164] and which has recently received increasing attention, for instance by the German Constitutional Court[165] addressing the legal situation of 'future generations', or by the EU's 'Green Deal'.[166]

Considering the situation of **vulnerable** people is well in conformity with a human rights-based approach as well as the value of human dignity. As mentioned above, Andorno emphasised that 'human vulnerability' has played a key role in the context of human rights, although it is not vulnerability but 'human dignity' (Art 2 TEU, Art 1 CFR) that can be seen as the 'normative foundation' for human rights.[167]

In the different fields of 'prohibited' AI, 'high-risk' and 'low-risk' AI we have seen various approaches. Sometimes an approach of referring more to values, to human rights, and/or principles. In the following, let us now turn to particular values and the role they play in the AIA.

5 AIA and Particular EU Values (Excerpt)

For reasons of scope, it is not possible to analyse all of the values listed in Art 2 TEU in detail here. Therefore, a few selected statements that are of central importance for the AIA will be briefly repeated, and the very frequently mentioned value of non-discrimination will be discussed.

The 'Union values of respect for human dignity, freedom, equality, democracy and the rule of law and fundamental rights enshrined in the Charter, including the right to non-discrimination' (recital 28) have been named as reasons for **prohibiting** certain forms of AI. Likewise, AI systems providing **social scoring**[168] 'lead to **discriminatory** outcomes and the exclusion of certain groups' and they 'may violate the right to **dignity** and **non-discrimination** and the values of **equality** and **justice**' and consequently should be prohibited (recital 31).[169] While non-discrimination and equality might often be at stake in case of applying AI to various fields, they are especially affected when a human's key situation in society is at

[162] Emphases added.

[163] Recital 9 TEU, Art 3(3) and (5) TEU, recital 3 CFR; see also Art 11 TFEU and Art 37 CFR.

[164] 'Act so that the effects of your action are compatible with the permanence of real human life on earth' (translation); Jonas (1979), p. 36. This 'ecological imperative' is reminiscent of Kant's 'categorical imperative'; Kant (2014), pp. 71, 87, 97, 105.

[165] BVerfG order of 24 March 2021, *Constitutional complaints against the Climate Protection Act partially successful*, 1 BvR 2656/18, 1 BvR 96/20, 1 BvR 78/20, 1 BvR 288/20, 1 BvR 96/20, 1 BvR 78/20, para 146 (et passim).

[166] EC, 'The European Green Deal', COM(2019) 640 final 11 December 2019.

[167] Andorno (2016).

[168] More precisely, 'of natural persons by public or private actors'.

[169] Emphases added.

stake. Finally, in the field of the **administration of justice and democratic processes**, certain AI systems 'should be classified as high-risk, considering their potentially significant impact on **democracy**, the **rule of law**, individual **freedoms** as well as the right to an effective remedy and to a fair trial',[170] especially concerning 'risks of potential biases, errors and opacity' (recital 61). The AIA is aptly stating these values, which would be affected in these key fields of legal and democratic processes.

After these three examples of addressing several values, let us turn to the value of **non-discrimination**, which can also be qualified as a legal principle. Non-discrimination can be qualified as a value (Art 2 TEU) and in addition also as a legal principle[171] that can be enforced against individuals.[172] In the context of AI, a main problem concerning justice[173] or fairness[174] has always been seen in the possible discrimination concerning algorithms,[175] especially because of the so-called 'black box-effect'.[176] Discriminatory practices can be aggravated by AI, as existing discrimination in real life can be the basis of training data for AI, which would perceive this discriminatory status-quo as 'normal' or even 'desirable'. AI would then have to be truly intelligent, to sort out such a bias. Such a possible prolongation of existing biases is addressed in the context of educational and vocational training (recital 56), recruitment (recital 57) or in the field of evaluating the creditworthiness of people (recital 58). In the employment context, this recital 57 (on recruitment) refers to the criteria of gender, age, disabilities, racial or ethnic origin and sexual orientation. Those are almost all of the criteria mentioned in Art 19(1) TFEU (religion or belief is missing), and also from Art 21 CFR some criteria are missing (i.e., colour, ethnic or social origin, genetic features, language, religion or belief, political or any other opinion, membership of a national minority, property, and birth). Non-discrimination is also addressed in the context of law-enforcement (recital 59) or migration (recital 60), to name but a few.

A way to overcome discrimination is via '**high data quality**', which requires high quality for training, validation and testing data sets plus implementation of

---

[170] Emphases added.

[171] ECJ judgement of 16 February 2022, *Poland v Parliament and Council*, C-157/21, EU:C:2022:98, para 324 ('principles of equality and non-discrimination'). Non-discrimination is also a general principle of EU law; cf. Tridimas (2006), pp. 59–135 on equality and non-discrimination; Klamert and Kochenov (2019); Tobler (2022).

[172] Non-discrimination is a cross-sectional issue (Art 10 TFEU) and various EU directives have been adopted based on what today is Art 19 TFEU (discrimination based on sex, racial or ethnic origin, religion or belief, disability, age or sexual orientation). Besides this, non-discrimination is human right enshrined in Art 21 CFR. Discrimination based on nationality is mainly addressed at Member States and can be found in Art 18 TFEU, respectively in the economic fundamental freedoms.

[173] One of the EU's values. According to Morelli (2002), p. 301, the terms just/unjust 'often carry a stronger tone of condemnation than fair/unfair'.

[174] See, for instance, Franke (2021).

[175] Cf. Orwat (2019).

[176] Cf. Martini (2019), concerning Proposal AIA.

appropriate data governance and management practices (recital 67). As the AIA states, '[t]raining, validation and testing data sets shall be relevant, sufficiently representative, and to the best extent possible, free of errors and complete in view of the intended purpose' (Art 10(3)), a requirement that might help avoid discrimination but has been criticised as practically challenging.[177]

Finally, non-discrimination also plays an important role in the context of the **geographical application** of the AIA. For the objective of guaranteeing 'an effective protection of rights and freedoms of individuals across the Union', the AIA states that the 'the rules established by this Regulation should apply to providers of AI systems in a non-discriminatory manner'; to achieve this aim of non-discrimination, the AIA applies in an **extraterritorial** way (recital 21). As mentioned above, this extraterritorial application has to be seen against the background of the EU's obligation to 'uphold and promote its values' in 'its relations with the wider world' (Art 3(5) TEU).

6 Analysis and Summary

The AIA strives to lay down 'a uniform legal framework in particular for the development, the placing on the market, the putting into service and the use of [AI systems] in the Union, in accordance with Union values' (recital 1).[178] Likewise, also ethics is part of the underlying philosophy of the AIA.

In terms of the various **categories of the AIA**, values play an important role for 'prohibited' AI, fundamental rights (besides health and safety) for 'high-risk' AI, and ethical principles (as part of soft-law codes of conduct) for 'low-risk' AI. The goal of the AIA and its 'risk-based approach' then is to provide rules for 'trustworthy' AI.

As we have seen, in the AIA **values** rather **occur** in the preamble, hardly in the binding text of the AIA. An exception are 'fundamental rights' that occur 44 times in the articles, due to their importance for 'high-risk' AI, followed by the value and principle of non-discrimination. Some EU values do not occur at all (e.g., pluralism and tolerance), most likely due to their rather undetermined content and lack of justiciability. Likewise, solidarity is a value that does not occur in the AIA and could have received a more prominent role.

Referring to values is an obvious approach in a 'Union of values'. While the **hierarchy of EU law** results in the legal obligation for EU secondary law to be in conformity with EU primary law (i.e., the values enshrined in Art 2 TEU), it is convincing in a particularly sensitive and impactful field, as in the case of AI, to put a

---

[177] Such a requirement can be seen as 'practically impossible', Heil (2022), p. 9, respectively as 'utopian', Raposo (2022), p. 108; both with regard to Proposal AIA.

[178] According to the explanatory memorandum, the 'proposal is **based on** EU values and fundamental rights' (Proposal AIA, p. 1; emphasis added). Values are also used as an argument in the context of subsidiarity (Proposal AIA, p. 6).

special emphasis on values and fundamental rights. As the AIA takes a **horizontal** approach, it is not very surprising that it refers to the EU's general values, not to the 2006 health values, etc. Similarly, the AI Act has been criticised as 'not do[ing] justice to the vulnerability of patients'.[179] This statement is reminiscent of a similar discussion some years ago where it was debated whether health services[180] shall be excluded from the general services[181] directive. While AI users might struggle with the parallel application of the medical devices regulation and the AIA,[182] adding a distinct AIA for health might be overcomplicating.

As I have argued elsewhere (in the field of 'robotic medicine'), especially in quickly developing fields, **law** (binding *per se*) shall be **complemented** by (rather abstract) values and (more concrete) legal and ethical principles.[183] This has the advantage of not only offering guidelines in case the legislative process is too slow to respond to new challenges, it can also be seen as a more ambitious approach, going beyond[184] what the existing law already requires. By doing so, the idea is to (re-)gain citizens' (and other individuals') **trust** in a more and more complex world.[185]

The AIA does not refer to morality,[186] but to ethics, where it, amongst others, 'supports the objective of promoting the European **human-centric** approach to AI and being a global leader in the development of secure, **trustworthy and ethical** AI [and] ensures the protection of **ethical principles**' (recital 8; emphases added). A reference to ethics can in the end leave unclear, what the precise outcome in law shall be. Similarly, as I have argued in 'The Ethical Spirit of EU law',[187] the AIA does not refer to normative theories (deontology, consequentialism or virtue ethics), but to **values and human (or fundamental) rights**. Apart from these normative theories, the AIA does also not explicitly refer to the above-mentioned 'principlism' approach, as developed in bioethics and transferred to the digital world.[188] However, in the field of voluntary codes of conduct, the AIA suggests to take into account the

[179] van Kolfschooten (2022), p. 110. On AI and healthcare, see also Lekadir et al. (2022); Solaiman and Bloom (2022).

[180] Directive patient mobility.

[181] Directive 2006/123/EC of the European Parliament and of the Council *on services in the internal market*, O.J. L 376/36 (2006).

[182] Palmieri et al. (2021).

[183] Frischhut (2021a), p. 79.

[184] I.e., in terms of achieving a higher level of protection. See also (at) notes 102–106.

[185] I have argued for a similar approach in the field of EU decision-making and lobbying; Frischhut (2020).

[186] Also not to 'public morality'(*supra* notes 50–51), which is convincing given the fact that this concept is mainly used in EU law to allow Member States to deviate from obligations of EU law. On the other hand, ethics is rather used in a more ambitious way, i.e., to raise standards, not to lower them.

[187] Frischhut (2019).

[188] The risk-based approach, emphasising the 'health, safety and fundamental rights' can be seen as an implicit reference to the 'do no harm' idea (see also recital 29).

seven principles of the 'ethics guidelines for trustworthy AI', developed by the HLEG-AI (recital 27).

For a risk-based approach, it is also only logical to specifically consider the situation of **vulnerable** persons. Art 5 on 'prohibited' AI refers to certain vulnerabilities (e.g., age or disability). This should not be read as an exhaustive list,[189] as there is no close list of vulnerable persons.[190] Likewise, in the context of 'high-risk' AI, Art 7(2) lit. h also refers to vulnerable persons and their situations, 'imbalance of power, or the persons who are potentially harmed or suffer an adverse impact are in a vulnerable position in relation to the deployer of an AI system, in particular due to status, authority, knowledge, economic or social circumstances, or age'. Hence, accepting information and other asymmetries.[191]

When criticising this draft, one has to accept the fact that the EU legislator is following **various objectives**, i.e., EU values but also economic objectives, including innovation.[192] The EU was striving for a **balanced** approach[193] and while a certain outcome would always be criticised from the one or the other side (or eventually even by both), the AIA can be seen as a balanced approach between a more neoliberal scheme as in the U.S. and a more intervening approach as in China.[194] As aptly analysed by De Gregorio, 'the Union is defining a constitutional framework in between where it provides the values guiding private actors'.[195] This is remarkable because based on Art 2 TEU the (general) values of the EU are either binding on the EU (and its institutions) and/or the Member States. The AIA can be seen as an extension of EU values down the line (i.e., from a vertical perspective) as well as a mainstreaming of EU values.

The underlying philosophy of the AIA is not limited to Europe. As mentioned above, the EU's 'ability to influence global dynamics'[196] has been referred to as the 'Brussels effect'.[197] It remains to be seen if the AIA[198] will have a similar effect as the GDPR. As mentioned above, the **extraterritorial** scope of the AIA (recitals 21–22) can be seen as an 'anti-circumvention mechanism'.[199]

---

[189] Veale and Zuiderveen Borgesius (2021), p. 99.

[190] Cf. Andorno (2016).

[191] Cf. James (2008).

[192] One question that can be seen as an element of criticism is whether 'deep fakes' are correctly placed in Art 50(4), requiring only transparency measures. See also Ebers et al. (2021), p. 592.

[193] Cf. Proposal AIA, p. 1.

[194] Cf. de Gregorio (2022), p. 284.

[195] de Gregorio (2022), p. 295. On private vs. public stakeholders, see Georgieva et al. (2022).

[196] de Gregorio (2022), p. 299.

[197] Bradford (2012, 2021).

[198] On the 'Brussels effect' and the AIA, see Almada and Radu (2024).

[199] de Gregorio (2022), p. 301. With stricter rules for providers ('irrespective of whether they are established within the Union or in a third country') than for deployers ('established within the Union') of AI systems (recital 21).

In summary, the overall-approach[200] of the AIA can be summarised as **human-centric,**[201] hence related to 'human well-being'[202] and based on the ideas of 'humanism'.[203] In practical terms, this is also related to the question of who has the final word, that is to say humans[204] and not AI.[205]

References

Almada M, Radu A (2024) The Brussels side-effect: how the AI act can reduce the global reach of EU policy. German Law J 25:646–663. https://doi.org/10.1017/glj.2023.108

Andorno R (2016) Is vulnerability the foundation of human rights? In: Masferrer A, García-Sánchez E (eds) Human dignity of the vulnerable in the age of rights: interdisciplinary perspectives, vol 55. Springer International Publishing, Switzerland, pp 257–272

Asimov I (1950) I, Robot. Doubleday, Garden City

Bartneck C, Lütge C, Wagner AR, Welsh S (2019) Ethik in KI und Robotik. Hanser, München

Beauchamp TL, Childress JF (2019) Principles of biomedical ethics. Oxford University Press, New York

Beck S (ed) (2012) Jenseits von Mensch und Maschine: Ethische und rechtliche Fragen zum Umgang mit Robotern, Künstlicher Intelligenz und Cyborgs, Robotik und Recht, vol 1. Nomos Verlag, Baden-Baden

Benedek W (2017) Menschenrechte verstehen: Handbuch zur Menschenrechtsbildung, 3rd edn. Berliner Wissenschafts-Verlag; Neuer Wissenschaftlicher Verlag, Berlin, Wien

Bogdandy AV, Spieker LD (2019) Countering the judicial silencing of critics: article 2 TEU values, reverse Solange, and the responsibilities of National Judges. Eur Const Law Rev 15:391–426. https://doi.org/10.1017/S1574019619000324

Bogdandy AV, Spieker LD (2020) Reverse Solange 2.0: Die Durchsetzung europäischer Werte und die unions- und strafrechtliche Verantwortung nationaler Richter. Europarecht (EuR) 55:301–331

Bradford A (2012) The Brussels effect. Northwest Univ Law Rev 107:1–67

Bradford A (2021) The Brussels effect: how the European Union rules the world. Oxford University Press, New York

Bryson JJ, Malikova H (2021) Is there an AI cold war? Glob Persp 2. https://doi.org/10.1525/gp.2021.24803

[200] Proposal AIA, p. 1; cf. also Valta and Vasel (2021), p. 142.

[201] Cf. Pachl and Valenti (2019).

[202] 'AI should be a tool for people and be a force for good in society with the ultimate aim of increasing human well-being' (Proposal AIA, p. 1).

[203] The second recital of the TEU refers to the 'cultural, religious and humanist [!] inheritance of Europe, from which have developed the universal values of the inviolable and inalienable rights of the human person, freedom, democracy, equality and the rule of law'. See also Nida-Rümelin (2021).

[204] See in this context also the demand for additional five substantive and a procedural fundamental right for the CFR: von Schirach (2021). Article 3 of this document, on AI, reads as follows (translation): 'Every person has the right to have algorithms that burden him or her be transparent, verifiable and fair. Essential decisions must be made by a human being'.

[205] According to recital 73, there should be guarantees that the 'system is subject to in-built operational constraints that cannot be overridden by the system itself and is responsive to the human operator'. On the tricky question of 'machines learning values', see Petersen (2020).

Buiten MC (2019) Towards intelligent regulation of artificial intelligence. Eur J Risk Regul 10:41–59. https://doi.org/10.1017/err.2019.8
Burri T, von Bothmer F (2021) The new EU legislation on artificial intelligence: a primer. SSRN Journal. https://doi.org/10.2139/ssrn.3831424
Coeckelbergh M (2020) AI ethics. The MIT Press, Cambridge
Cohen IG (2012) Circumvention tourism. Cornell Law Rev 97:1309–1398
Datenethikkommission (2019) Gutachten der Datenethikkommission der Bundesregierung
de Gregorio G (2022) Digital constitutionalism in Europe: reframing rights and powers in the algorithmic society. Cambridge studies in European law and policy. Cambridge University Press, Cambridge
Dignum V (2019) Responsible artificial intelligence. Springer International Publishing, Cham
Dolic Z, Castro R, Moarcas A (2019) Robots in healthcare: A solution or a problem? In-depth analysis requested by the ENVI committee
Dubber MD, Pasquale F, Das S (eds) (2020) The Oxford handbook of ethics of AI. Oxford University Press, Oxford
Durán JM, Jongsma KR (2021) Who is afraid of black box algorithms? On the epistemological and ethical basis of trust in medical AI. J Med Ethics 47:329–335. https://doi.org/10.1136/medethics-2020-106820
Dvorsky G (2018) Experts Sign Open Letter Slamming Europe's Proposal to Recognize Robots as Legal Persons. https://gizmodo.com/experts-sign-open-letter-slamming-europe-s-proposal-to-1825240003
Ebers M (2021) Liability for artificial intelligence and EU consumer law. JIPITEC 12:204–220
Ebers M, Quarch BM (eds) (2024) Rechtshandbuch ChatGPT: KI-basierte Modelle in der Praxis, 1st edn. Nomos, Baden-Baden
Ebers M, Hoch VRS, Rosenkranz F, Ruschemeier H, Steinrötter B (2021) The European Commission's proposal for an artificial intelligence act—a critical assessment by members of the robotics and AI law society (RAILS). J 4:589–603. https://doi.org/10.3390/j4040043
Ethics Advisory Group (2018) Towards a digital ethics: Report by the Ethics Advisory Group established by the European Data Protection Supervisor, the EU's independent data protection authority. https://edps.europa.eu/sites/edp/files/publication/18-01-25_eag_report_en.pdf
European Commission (2018) Coordinated Plan on Artificial Intelligence: COM(2018) 795 final. https://eur-lex.europa.eu/legal-content/EN/TXT/?uri=CELEX:52018DC0795&qid=1544801589474
European Commission (2022a) Declaration on European Digital Rights and Principles: COM(2022) 28 final. https://digital-strategy.ec.europa.eu/en/library/declaration-european-digital-rights-and-principles#Declaration
European Commission (2022b) Establishing a European Declaration on Digital rights and principles for the Digital Decade: COM(2022) 27 final
European Commission (2022c) High-level expert group on artificial intelligence. https://digital--strategy.ec.europa.eu/en/policies/expert-group-ai
European Group on Ethics in Science and New Technologies (2012) Ethics of information and communication technologies: Opinion No 26. Publications Office of the European Union, Luxembourg
European Group on Ethics in Science and New Technologies (2018) Statement on Artificial Intelligence, Robotics and 'Autonomous' Systems. https://ec.europa.eu/research/ege/index.cfm
Floridi L (2021) The European legislation on AI: a brief analysis of its philosophical approach. Philos Technol 34:215–222. https://doi.org/10.1007/s13347-021-00460-9
Floridi L, Cowls J, Beltrametti M, Chatila R, Chazerand P, Dignum V, Luetge C, Madelin R, Pagallo U, Rossi F, Schafer B, Valcke P, Vayena E (2018) AI4People—an ethical framework for a good AI society: opportunities, risks, principles, and recommendations. Mind Mach 28:689–707. https://doi.org/10.1007/s11023-018-9482-5
Franke U (2021) Rawls's original position and algorithmic fairness. Philos Technol 34:1803–1817. https://doi.org/10.1007/s13347-021-00488-x

Fraser H, Bello y Villarino J-M (2023) Acceptable risks in Europe's proposed AI act: reasonableness and other principles for deciding how much risk management is enough. Eur J Risk Regul 15:431–446. https://doi.org/10.1017/err.2023.57

Frischhut M (2015) "EU": short for "ethical" union?: the role of ethics in European Union law. Heidelberg J Int Law (HJIL) 75:531–577

Frischhut M (2019) The ethical spirit of EU law. Springer International Publishing, Cham

Frischhut M (2020) Strengthening transparency and integrity via the new 'independent ethics body' (IEB). Study requested by the European Parliament's AFCO committee: PE 661.110, Brussels

Frischhut M (2021a) Robotic medicine in the EU: digital ethics and EU common values. In: Milapidou M (ed) New technologies in health: medical, legal and ethical issues. Nomiki Bibliothiki, Athens, pp 67–85

Frischhut M (2021b) The new mandate of the European Commission's ethics advisory body for science and new technologies. Further developments and larger context: EU Law Analysis blog contribution. http://eulawanalysis.blogspot.com/2021/04/the-new-mandate-of-european-commissions.html

Frischhut M (2022) The ethical spirit of EU values: status quo of the Union of values and future direction of travel. Springer International Publishing, Cham, Switzerland

Georgieva I, Timan T, Hoekstra M (2022) Regulatory divergences in the draft AI act: differences in public and private sector obligations. PE 729.507, Brussels

Hagendorff T (2022) A virtue-based framework to support putting AI ethics into practice. Philos Technol 35. https://doi.org/10.1007/s13347-022-00553-z

Hansson S-O (ed) (2017) The ethics of technology: methods and approaches. Philosophy, technology and society. Rowman & Littlefield International, London, New York

Heil M (2022) Die neue KI-Verordnung (E) - Regulatorische Herausforderungen für Kl-basierte Medizinprodukte-Software. MedizinProdukte-Recht:1–11

Hengstschläger M, Austrian Council for Research and Technology Development (eds) (2020) Digital transformation and ethics. Ecowin Verlag, Salzburg, München

High-level Expert Group on Artificial Intelligence (2019a) Ethics Guidelines for Trustworthy AI. https://digital-strategy.ec.europa.eu/en/library/ethics-guidelines-trustworthy-ai

High-level Expert Group on Artificial Intelligence (2019b) Policy and investment recommendations for trustworthy Artificial Intelligence. https://ec.europa.eu/digital-single-market/en/news/policy-and-investment-recommendations-trustworthy-artificial-intelligence

High-level Expert Group on Artificial Intelligence (2020) Assessment List for Trustworthy Artificial Intelligence (ALTAI) for self-assessment. https://digital-strategy.ec.europa.eu/en/library/assessment-list-trustworthy-artificial-intelligence-altai-self-assessment

Hilgendorf E (ed) (2013) Robotik im Kontext von Recht und Moral. Robotik und Recht, vol 3. Nomos Verlag, Baden-Baden

Hilgendorf E (2017) Modern technology and legal compliance. In: Hilgendorf E, Kaiafa-Gbandi M (eds) Compliance measures: and their role in German and Greek law. P.N. Sakkulas, Athēna, pp 21–35

Ienca M, Pollicino O, Liguori L, Andorno R, Stefanini E (eds) (2022) The Cambridge handbook of information technology, life sciences and human rights. Cambridge law handbooks. Cambridge University Press, Cambridge

James HS Jr (2008) Asymmetric information. In: Kolb RW (ed) Encyclopedia of business ethics and society. Sage Publications, Los Angeles, pp 123–125

Jiang M (2020) A brief prehistory of China's social credit system. Commun Public 5:93–98. https://doi.org/10.1177/2057047320959856

Jobin A, Ienca M, Vayena E (2019) The global landscape of AI ethics guidelines. Nat Mach Intell 1:389–399. https://doi.org/10.1038/s42256-019-0088-2

Jonas H (1979) Das Prinzip Verantwortung: Versuch einer Ethik für die technologische Zivilisation. Insel Verlag, Frankfurt am Main

Kagan E (2001) Presidential administration. Harv Law Rev 114:2245–2385

Kant I (2014) Groundwork of the metaphysics of morals: edited and translated by Mary Gregor and Jens Timmermann. Cambridge University Press, Cambridge

Kirchschläger PG (2021) Digital transformation and ethics: ethical considerations on the robotization and automatization of society and economy and the use of artifical intelligence. Nomos Verlag, Baden-Baden

Klamert M, Kochenov D (2019) Article 2 TEU. In: Kellerbauer M, Klamert M, Tomkin v (eds) Commentary on the EU treaties and the charter of fundamental rights. Oxford University Press, Oxford, pp. 22–30

Klenk M (2021) How do technological artefacts embody moral values? Philos Technol 34:525–544. https://doi.org/10.1007/s13347-020-00401-y

Kostka G (2019) China's social credit systems and public opinion: explaining high levels of approval. New Media Soc 21:1565–1593. https://doi.org/10.1177/1461444819826402

Koulu R (2020) Proceduralising control and discretion: human oversight in artificial intelligence policy. Maastricht J Eur Comp Law 27:720–735. https://doi.org/10.1177/1023263X20978649

Kowalewski K-F, Kriegmair MC, Michel M-S (2019) Kollaborative Automatisierung und Robotik in Medizin und Pflege – Die Prozesse im Operationssaal. Medizinrecht (MedR) 37:925–927. https://doi.org/10.1007/s00350-019-5394-5

Kühling J (2018) Art. 345 [Eigentumsordnung]. In: Streinz R (ed) EUV/AEUV, 3rd edn. C.H. Beck, München, pp 2621–2629

Lammert N (2019) Roboterethik: Zur Rolle der Politik. In: Woopen C, Jannes M (eds) Roboter in der Gesellschaft: Technische Möglichkeiten und menschliche Verantwortung. Springer, Berlin, Heidelberg, pp 111–114

LeCun Y, Bengio Y, Hinton G (2015) Deep learning. Nature 521:436–444. https://doi.org/10.1038/nature14539

Lekadir K, Quaglio G, Garmendia AT, Gallin C (2022) Artificial intelligence in healthcare: applications, risks, and ethical and societal impacts. PE 729:512

Liao SM (ed) (2020) Ethics of artificial intelligence. Oxford University Press, New York, NY

Lin P, Abney K, Jenkins R (eds) (2017) Robot ethics 2.0: from autonomous cars to artificial intelligence. Oxford University Press, New York, NY

Mantelero A (2022) Beyond data: human rights, ethical and social impact assessment in AI, vol 36, 1st edn. Information Technology and Law Series,. T.M.C. Asser Press, Den Haag

Martini M (2019) Blackbox Algorithmus: Grundfragen einer Regulierung Künstlicher Intelligenz. Springer, Cham

Mittelstadt B (2019) Principles alone cannot guarantee ethical AI. Nat Mach Intell 1:501–507. https://doi.org/10.1038/s42256-019-0114-4

Morelli MF (2002) Fairness. In: Roth JK (ed) International encyclopedia of ethics. Fitzroy Dearborn, London, Chicago, Illinois, pp 301–302

Neuhäuser C (2012) Künstliche Intelligenz und ihr moralischer Standpunkt. In: Beck S (ed) Jenseits von Mensch und Maschine: Ethische und rechtliche Fragen zum Umgang mit Robotern, Künstlicher Intelligenz und Cyborgs. Nomos Verlag, Baden-Baden, pp 23–42

Neuhäuser C (2013) Roboter und moralische Verantwortung. In: Hilgendorf E (ed) Robotik im Kontext von Recht und Moral. Nomos Verlag, Baden-Baden, pp 269–286

Neuwirth RJ (2022) The EU artificial intelligence act: regulating subliminal AI systems. Routledge, London

Newland E (2015) Executive orders in court. Yale Law J 124:1836–2201

Nida-Rümelin J (2021) A. Digitaler Humanismus - philosophische Aspekte Künstlicher Intelligenz. In: Chibanguza KJ, Kuß C, Steege H (eds) Künstliche Intelligenz: Recht und Praxis automatisierter und autonomer Systeme, 1st edn. Nomos Verlag, Baden-Baden, pp 29–40

Orwat C (2019) Diskriminierungsrisiken durch Verwendung von Algorithmen: Eine Studie, erstellt mit einer Zuwendung der Antidiskriminierungsstelle des Bundes. Nomos Verlag, Berlin

Orwell G (1949) Nineteen eighty-four: a novel. Penguin modern classics. Penguin Books, Harmondsworth

Pache E (2020) § 7 Begriff, Geltungsgrund und Rang der Grundrechte der EU. In: Heselhaus S, Nowak C (eds) Handbuch der Europäischen Grundrechte, 2nd edn. C.H. Beck, München, pp 122–180

Pachl U, Valenti P (eds) (2019) A human-centric digital manifesto for Europe: How the digital transformation can serve the public interest

Palmieri S, Walraet P, Goffin T (2021) Inevitable influences: AI-based medical devices at the intersection of medical devices regulation and the proposal for AI regulation. Eur J Health Law 28:341–358. https://doi.org/10.1163/15718093-bja10053

Petersen S (2020) Machines learning values. In: Liao SM (ed) Ethics of artificial intelligence. Oxford University Press, New York, NY, pp 413–434

Potacs M (2016) Wertkonforme Auslegung des Unionsrechts? Europarecht (EuR) 51:164–176. https://doi.org/10.5771/0531-2485-2016-2-164

Raposo VL (2022) Ex machina: preliminary critical assessment of the European draft act on artificial intelligence. Int J Law Inf Technol 30:88–109. https://doi.org/10.1093/ijlit/eaac007

Raposo VL (2023a) 'Look at the camera and say cheese': the existing European legal framework for facial recognition technology in criminal investigations. Inf Commun Technolgy Law 33:1–20. https://doi.org/10.1080/13600834.2023.2239621

Raposo VL (2023b) When facial recognition does not 'recognise': erroneous identifications and resulting liabilities. AI & Soc 39:1857–1869. https://doi.org/10.1007/s00146-023-01634-z

Rath M, Krotz F, Karmasin M (eds) (2019) Maschinenethik. Springer Fachmedien Wiesbaden, Wiesbaden

Roa TM, Biller-Andorno N (2023) Black box algorithms in mental health apps: an ethical reflection. Bioethics 37:790–797. https://doi.org/10.1111/bioe.13215

Rotenberg M (2022) Artificial intelligence and the right to algorithmic transparency. In: Ienca M, Pollicino O, Liguori L, Andorno R, Stefanini E (eds) The Cambridge handbook of information technology, life sciences and human rights. Cambridge University Press, Cambridge, pp 153–165

Sahm S (2019) Digitale Anthropologie: Ethische Probleme der Anwendung künstlicher Intelligenz und Robotik in der Pflege und Medizin. Medizinrecht (MedR) 37:927–933. https://doi.org/10.1007/s00350-019-5395-4

Sartor G (2020) Artificial intelligence and human rights: between law and ethics. Maastricht J Eur Comp Law 27:705–719. https://doi.org/10.1177/1023263X20981566

Shaw P (2021) "Context Matters": the law, Ethics and AI. In: Hervey M, Lavy M (eds) The law of artificial intelligence. Sweet & Maxwell, London, 3–001–3-062

Solaiman B, Bloom MG (2022) AI, explainability, and safeguarding patient safety in Europe: toward a science-focused regulatory model. In: Cohen IG, Minssen T, Price NW, Robertson C, Shachar C (eds) The future of medical device regulation: innovation and protection. Cambridge University Press, Cambridge, pp 91–102

Spiekermann S (2019) Digitale Ethik: Ein Wertesystem für das 21. Jahrhundert, Droemer, München

Stevenson A (ed) (2010) Oxford dictionary of English: first edition edited by Judy Pearsall, Patrick Hanks. Oxford University Press, Oxford

Stix C (2021) Actionable principles for artificial intelligence policy: three pathways. Sci Eng Ethics 27:15. https://doi.org/10.1007/s11948-020-00277-3

Tasioulas J (2019) First steps towards an ethics of robots and artificial intelligence. J Pract Ethics 7:49–83

Thaler A (2021) Values and ethical principles for AI and robotics: a qualitative content analysis of EU soft law initiatives. In: Schriften zur Rechts- und Staatsphilosophie, vol 26, 1st edn. Verlag Dr. Kovac, Hamburg

The Royal Society (2017) Machine learning: the power and promise of computers that learn by example

The White House (2023) Executive Order on the Safe, Secure, and Trustworthy Development and Use of Artificial Intelligence | The White House. https://www.whitehouse.gov/briefing-room/presidential-actions/2023/10/30/executive-order-on-the-safe-secure-and-trustworthy-development-and-use-of-artificial-intelligence/

Tigard DW (2021) Responsible AI and moral responsibility: a common appreciation. AI Ethics 1:113–117. https://doi.org/10.1007/s43681-020-00009-0
Tobler C (2022) General principles of equal treatment in EU non-discrimination law. In: Ziegler KS, Neuvonen PJ, Moreno-Lax V (eds) Research handbook on general principles in EU law: constructing legal orders in Europe. Edward Elgar Publishing, Cheltenham, pp 350–366
Tridimas T (2006) The general principles of EU law, 2nd edn. Oxford University Press, Oxford
Vallor S (ed) (2022) The Oxford handbook of philosophy of technology. Oxford University Press, Oxford
Valta M, Vasel JJ (2021) Kommissionsvorschlag für eine Verordnung über Künstliche Intelligenz: Mit viel Bürokratie und wenig Risiko zum KI-Standort? Zeitschrift für Rechtspolitik (ZRP):142–145
van Kolfschooten H (2022) EU regulation of artificial intelligence: challenges for patients' rights. Common Mark Law Rev 59:81–112
van Kolfschooten H (2023) The AI cycle of health inequity and digital ageism: mitigating biases through the EU regulatory framework on medical devices. J Law Biosci 10. https://doi.org/10.1093/jlb/lsad031
van Kolfschooten H, Shachar C (2023) The Council of Europe's AI convention (2023-2024): promises and pitfalls for health protection. Health Policy 138:104935. https://doi.org/10.1016/j.healthpol.2023.104935
Veale M, Zuiderveen Borgesius F (2021) Demystifying the draft EU artificial intelligence act — analysing the good, the bad, and the unclear elements of the proposed approach. Comput Law Rev Int 22:97–112. https://doi.org/10.9785/cri-2021-220402
von Eschenbach WJ (2021) Transparency and the black box problem: why we do not trust AI. Philos Technol 34:1607–1622. https://doi.org/10.1007/s13347-021-00477-0
von Schirach F (2021) Jeder Mensch. Luchterhand, München
Walz A, Firth-Butterfield K (2019) Implementing ethics into artificial intelligence: a contribution, from a legal perspective, to the development of an AI governance regime. Duke Law Technol Rev 18:180–231
Weimer M (2019) Risk regulation in the EU internal market. In: Weimer M (ed) Risk regulation in the internal market. Oxford University Press, Oxford, pp 47–85
Weismann P (2023) Soft law and its importance in ensuring member states' compliance with union law, 1st edn. Beiträge zum ausländischen öffentlichen Recht und Völkerrecht, vol 321. Nomos, Baden-Baden
Wulf AJ, Seizov O (2020) Artificial intelligence and transparency: a blueprint for improving the regulation of AI applications in the EU. Eur Bus Law Rev 31:611–640
Yu H (2022) Regulation of digital health Technologies in the European Union: intended versus actual use. In: Cohen IG, Minssen T, Price NW, Robertson C, Shachar C (eds) The future of medical device regulation: innovation and protection. Cambridge University Press, Cambridge, pp 103–114
Zeng Y, Wong SH (2022) Social media, fear, and support for state surveillance: the case of China's social credit system. China Inf 0920203X2210881. https://doi.org/10.1177/0920203X221088141
Zerilli J, Weller A (2021) The technology. In: Hervey M, Lavy M (eds) The law of artificial intelligence. Sweet & Maxwell, London, p 2-001-2-0044
Zuber N, Gogoll J (2024) Vox Populi, Vox ChatGPT: large language models. Educ Democr Philos 9:13. https://doi.org/10.3390/philosophies9010013

Artificial Intelligence and Fundamental Rights: Under the European Legal Eye

Sofia Palmieri and Tom Goffin

Contents

Abstract Artificial Intelligence (AI) is transforming various sectors, presenting both opportunities and risks to fundamental rights, democracy, and the rule of law. AI systems can infringe on rights such as privacy, non-discrimination, and freedom of expression, necessitating a robust regulatory framework. The European Union's AI Act addresses these challenges through a risk-based approach to AI governance. This chapter examines the AI Act's effectiveness in protecting fundamental rights. It explores risk classification, risk mitigation strategies, and the Fundamental Rights Impact Assessment (FRIA) as a compliance tool. Additionally, it questions whether

S. Palmieri · T. Goffin (✉)
Metamedica Unit, Department of Public Health and Primary Care, Faculty of Medicine and Health Science, Ghent University, Ghent, Belgium
e-mail: Tom.Goffin@UGent.be

V. L. Raposo (ed.), *The European Artificial Intelligence Act*, Law, Governance and Technology Series 78, https://doi.org/10.1007/978-3-031-98406-8_3

the AI Act's framework is sufficient or if additional rights and regulations are needed. A critical analysis of the Act's product safety approach highlights potential shortcomings in addressing broader human rights concerns. The chapter also introduces the Council of Europe's AI Convention, outlining its human rights-centric framework and assessing how it complements the AI Act. The interplay between the two instruments is analysed to determine whether their combined framework sufficiently protects fundamental rights. The chapter concludes by evaluating whether the EU and Council of Europe's regulatory efforts provide comprehensive protection or if further legal developments are necessary to address AI-related risks.

1 Introduction

Although Artificial Intelligence (AI) is revolutionising multiple sectors globally, from healthcare and education to finance and security, it also poses significant implications for fundamental rights, democracy and the rule of law. AI systems can potentially infringe upon fundamental rights such as privacy, non-discrimination, equality and freedom of expression. For instance, AI-driven surveillance technologies can lead to mass data collection and breach privacy rights. Similarly, algorithmic biases can perpetuate discrimination in various domains, including hiring practices and law enforcement. These concerns necessitate a robust regulatory framework to mitigate risks and safeguard fundamental rights. Europe, both the European Union and the Council of Europe, has been at the forefront of regulating AI to ensure its alignment with human rights and democratic values. This chapter primarily focuses on the AI Act and is poised to explore the European approach to AI and fundamental rights. After analysing whether and how the AI Act contributes to the protection of fundamental rights about AI use and development, the chapter also takes incidentally into consideration the Council of Europe Framework Convention on artificial intelligence, human rights, democracy, and the rule of law (hereafter: AI Convention). The reason for such additional focus is to assess how the two pieces of regulation, the AI Act and the AI Convention, merge and enhance one another, allowing for broad fundamental rights protection from the risks posed by AI.

In this chapter, we first focus on the AI Act and discuss how far it has succeeded in protecting fundamental rights. We thereby link fundamental rights protection to the product safety risk-based approach taken in the AI Act. We analyse the fundamental rights impact assessment tool of the AI Act and question whether the fundamental rights framework of the AI Act is a sufficient base or whether it is necessary to add additional rights and frameworks and also focus on the potential pitfalls of the AI Act within the scope of this chapter. In the second part of this chapter, we introduce the AI Convention without making an in-depth analysis and link the AI Convention with the AI Act. We round up this chapter with a conclusion assessing the question of whether the combined framework of the EU and the Council of Europe is sufficient to guarantee the protection of fundamental rights.

As a note to the reader, both ‘fundamental rights’ and ‘human rights’ will be used in this chapter. The authors are aware that there are legal differences between them. The term ‘fundamental rights’ is mostly used explicitly in national constitutions of EU Member States, whereas the term ‘human rights’ is used in international law. The EU has come to use fundamental rights to describe the obligations of the EU and its Member States towards everyone in the EU.[1] Nevertheless, also many cross-overs exist between human rights and fundamental rights. According to the European Union Agency for Fundamental Rights, both fundamental rights and human rights entitle individuals to expect and receive certain levels of treatment.[2] Both terms refer to the same content and are often used interchangeably. The links between the two notions can be seen in the similarities between the Charter of Fundamental Rights of the European Union, the European Convention on Human Rights and the Universal Declaration of Human Rights.[3]

2 The AI Act of the European Union

3 Introduction

Recognising the fundamental rights (FR) issues associated with the deployment and use of AI, the European Commission perceived the need to create a human-centric approach to AI grounded in fundamental rights. A pivotal moment in the development of this approach of the EU AI Act was the April 2018 Communication from the European Commission titled ‘Artificial Intelligence for Europe’. This document outlined a European AI Strategy with the ambitious goal of ‘making the EU a world-class hub for AI and ensuring that AI is human-centric and trustworthy’. As highlighted extensively in other chapters, trustworthy AI from the European perspective is an AI that respects fundamental rights and European values. Given the EU Commission’s commitment to this vision, the AI Act was reasonably expected to take the form of a fundamental rights instrument. However, the EU lacks competence in directly regulating fundamental rights. According to Article 5(1) of the

[1] European Union Agency for Fundamental Rights, ‘What are fundamental rights?’, https://fra.europa.eu/en/content/what-are-fundamental-rights.

[2] European Parliament, Fact sheet: Respect for fundamental rights in the European Union, 29 September 2020.

[3] Charter of Fundamental Rights of the European Union, N° 2000/C, 364/1, Official Journal of the European Communities 18 December 2000; Council of Europe. ‘Convention for the Protection of Human Rights and Fundamental Freedoms’. Council of Europe Treaty Series 005, Council of Europe, 1950.United Nations General Assembly. The Universal Declaration of Human Rights (UDHR). New York: United Nations General Assembly, 1948.

Treaty on European Union (TEU), the Union's system of competencies is based on the principle of conferral.[4] As detailed in paragraph 2 of the same article, this principle restricts the EU's actions to the boundaries established by the Treaties, which delineate both the areas in which the European institutions can intervene and the objectives they must pursue. The competencies assigned to the EU do not encompass the authority to legislate directly on fundamental rights, thus precluding the possibility of the EU enacting legislation specifically in this domain.[5] Moreover, while the Charter of Fundamental Rights of the European Union exists as part of the Lisbon Treaty, Article 52 of the Charter explicitly states that none of its provisions extend the EU's competencies beyond those conferred by the Treaties. Consequently, the EU, while steadfast in its goal of safeguarding fundamental rights through a human-centric approach to AI, had to operate within the confines of its established competencies. To achieve this, the EU has opted for a dual approach in balancing internal market objectives with the safeguarding of fundamental rights the AI legal framework: product safety legislation (based on Article 114 of the Treaty on the Functioning of the European Union), utilising the legal tools available within its jurisdiction, and data protection (based on Article 16 of the Treaty on the Functioning of the European Union).[6]

Therefore, the AI Act presents important features that recall action that combines implicitly or explicitly two repertoires of EU law. While presenting the nature of a product safety regulation, the AI Act presents important features that recall the nature of a fundamental rights instrument. Fundamental Rights are mentioned multiple times throughout the AI Act, so much so that Article 3(2) extends the definition of product risks to include fundamental rights. The result is a product safety regulation that heavily relies on a language closer to the domain of fundamental rights. The AI Act in itself cannot be considered as a fundamental rights framework for AI, it only aims to guarantee 'a contrario' that the existing fundamental rights, as inter alia described in the Charter, are protected. With a set of requirements and obligations for all value chain participants, the AI Act seeks to enhance and promote the protection of the diverse rights protected by the Charter, guaranteeing a direct human-centric approach towards AI. Additionally, it is made clear that the reasoning behind the AI Act can be attributed to the protection of fundamental rights and to cast light upon the possible risks that accompany AI.[7]

The accompanying memorandum for the AI Act illustrates that 'the use of AI with its specific characteristics (e.g., opacity, complexity, dependency on data, autonomous behaviour) can adversely affect a number of fundamental rights enshrined in the EU Charter of Fundamental Rights ('the Charter')'. Among the diverse fundamental rights, the AI Act's memorandum explicitly mentions the right to human dignity (Article 1), respect for private life and protection of personal data

[4] Lenaerts (2019), pp. 779–93, https://doi.org/10.1017/GLJ.2019.62.

[5] Scheppele et al. (2021), pp. 3–121, https://doi.org/10.1093/yel/yeaa012.

[6] Treaty on the Functioning of the European Union, OJ 26 October 2012.

[7] Husman (2023).

(Articles 7 and 8), non-discrimination (Article 21) and equality between women and men (Article 23), the rights to freedom of expression (Article 11) the right to an effective remedy and to a fair trial, the rights of defence and the presumption of innocence (Articles 47 and 48).[8] Against this background, the Commission's AI Act seeks to ensure a high level of protection for fundamental rights and aims to address various sources of risks through a clearly defined risk-based approach.[9]

It should be emphasised that it is not strange that regulations dedicated to product safety refer heavily to fundamental rights. Moreover, as noted by Almada and Petit, the domain of consumer protection law to which product safety regulations relate, is deeply entwined with fundamental rights, consumer protection itself being a fundamental right, mentioned in article 38 of the Charter.[10] Also, other product safety regulations explicitly refer to the protection of fundamental rights in both a general and a specific manner. This, for example, is the case with the Medical Device Regulation that explicitly refers both to fundamental rights generally and specifies personal data protection (article 8 of the Charter) among its objectives. Nevertheless, compared to other product safety regulations, the AI Act shows a higher level of commitment to fundamental rights, at least in its desiderata.[11] And we see this commitment in several passages of the text of the regulation and also in its essence. This hybrid nature, as we will see later on might cause some issues when assessing the suitability of the AI Act to fulfil its desiderata in terms of fundamental right protection. Or, as worded by Almada and Petit, this hybrid nature causes a mismatch between regulatory means and ends.[12]

To analyse the AI Act's contribution to fundamental rights protection, we must first understand the nature of this risk-based legal instrument. The following paragraphs aim to evaluate the AI Act's impact on fundamental rights through the lens of a product safety regulation. Given the hybrid nature of the AI Act, we also address the significant challenges this approach presents. This ambitious effort to create comprehensive and effective regulation has resulted in inconsistencies and loopholes within the AI regulatory framework. Below, we highlight some of these issues concerning the fundamental rights aspects identified in the AI Act and discussed earlier.

---

[8] Kusche (2024), pp. 1–14, https://doi.org/10.1080/13669877.2024.2350720.

[9] Ibid.

[10] Almada and Petit (2022), https://doi.org/10.2139/ssrn.4308072.

[11] See Article 114(3) TFEU.

[12] Almada and Petit (2022).

3.1 Conflicting Perspectives on Risk

The AI Act's double nature in presenting both product safety regulation features and fundamental rights nuances starts from its definition of risk. The AI Act characterises risk as '…the combination of the probability of an occurrence of a hazard causing harm and the degree of severity of that harm'.[13] This definition aligns with a product safety perspective on risk, where harm is quantitatively assessed and is defined as a fusion of its likelihood and impact. This rather traditional regulatory approach to risk aims to adjust one or both factors to reach an acceptable level.[14] This approach, typical of a product safety perspective, is based on four features that characterise risk as also intended in this regulation. First, risks are *actuarial*, meaning the negative outcome is measurable harm to an individual, group, or the environment.[15] Second, risks are *probabilistic*, allowing for reliable predictions of event likelihood.[16] Third, risks are *discrete*, each associated with a specific potential event.[17] Fourth, risks are *unidimensional*, meaning they can be uniformly measured by their harm metric. Two risks are comparable if they share the same combined probability and severity.[18]

However, these features are not readily applicable in scenarios where AI systems might negatively impact fundamental rights. The first feature—the actuarial approach—fails in contexts where the severity of harm is not easily quantified.[19] The actuarial approach fails in contexts like autonomous vehicle safety where the severity of potential harms is not easily quantifiable, such as unpredictable accident outcomes and complex ethical dilemmas in decision-making, which are challenging to measure and predict accurately.[20] Probabilistic risk assessment is less practical in complex systems, where it is difficult to predict all possible events, such as in the relatively uncharted territory of human-machine interactions.[21] An example of unpredictability in human-machine interaction can be seen in the deployment of AI-powered chatbots as social companions. These chatbots are designed to provide companionship through chat and meaningful conversation.[22] However, in theory, the AI system should be based on the predictability of their behaviour. Chatbots like Replika reacted in unpredictable ways, causing mental and physical harm to their users. The univocal relation between risk and specific causal events might be inadequate for many AI applications, where harmful outcomes may result from cumula-

[13] Art 3(2) AI Act.

[14] Luzak (2020), pp. 630–649, https://doi.org/10.1017/err.2020.13.

[15] Battistelli and Grazia Galantino (2019), pp. 64–78, https://doi.org/10.1177/0011392118793675.

[16] Garnett and Parsons (2017), pp. 502–16, https://doi.org/10.1111/risa.12633.

[17] OECD (2021).

[18] OECD (2021).

[19] Hildebrandt (2017), https://doi.org/10.2139/ssrn.3081776.

[20] Katherine Evans et al. (2020), pp. 3285–3312, https://doi.org/10.1007/s11948-020-00272-8.

[21] Kostogryzov et al. (2023), https://doi.org/10.5772/intechopen.106869.

[22] Skjuve et al. (2021), p. 102601, https://doi.org/10.1016/j.ijhcs.2021.102601.

tive rather than isolated events.[23] An example illustrating the inadequacy of a univocal relation between risk and specific causal events in AI applications can be found in algorithmic bias within hiring processes. Rather than stemming from isolated incidents, bias often results from cumulative factors embedded within the data used to train AI models. For instance, if historical hiring data reflects biased decisions against certain demographics, AI algorithms trained on this data may perpetuate discriminatory practices by recommending candidates based on skewed criteria. This cumulative effect of biased data can lead to systemic inequalities in employment opportunities, disadvantaging marginalised groups and perpetuating societal biases. Addressing these challenges requires not only identifying and mitigating biases within AI algorithms but also reevaluating how data is collected, curated, and used to ensure fairness and equal opportunity in automated decision-making processes.[24] Lastly, the feature of unidimensionality falls short when dealing with value incommensurability, where competing values cannot be reduced to a single metric.[25] An example of the limitation of risk unidimensionality in the context of AI involves autonomous vehicles and the ethical dilemma of decision-making in potential accident scenarios. Autonomous vehicles are designed to prioritise safety and efficiency, often relying on algorithms to make split-second decisions on the road. However, when faced with a situation where harm is unavoidable (e.g., a choice between hitting pedestrians or swerving into another vehicle), the values of minimising harm to different parties (pedestrians versus passengers versus other drivers) cannot be easily reduced to a single metric. Traditional risk assessments may quantify the likelihood of accidents but struggle to account for the incommensurability of these competing human values—such as the right to life, fairness, and individual autonomy—when translated into algorithmic decision-making.[26]

3.2 *Fundamental Rights Justified Risk Classes*

The engagement of the AI Act with fundamental rights is seen in the definition of risk classes, where fundamental rights are put on the same level as risks to health and safety, more traditionally included and considered in product safety regulations.[27]

The centrality of fundamental rights for the risk classes leads the AI Act to make an ex-ante assessment, we can say by default, of the AI systems to be considered too risky for, inter alia, fundamental rights to be placed on the European market. The AI Act gives no justification regarding the selection of forbidden AI systems listed in

[23] Schafer (2021), pp. 385–390, https://doi.org/10.1007/s11623-021-1456-8.

[24] Ferrara (2023), p. 3, https://doi.org/10.3390/sci6010003.

[25] Sieckmann (2021), pp. 113–134, https://doi.org/10.1007/978-3-030-77321-2_5.

[26] Green and Chen (2021), pp. 1–33, https://doi.org/10.1145/3479562.

[27] Almada and Petit (2022).

Annex III.[28] The general areas, which are further specified in terms of types of application, are biometrics insofar as their specific use is not completely banned by Art. 5, critical infrastructure, education and vocational training, employment and workers management, access to essential private and public services, law enforcement, migration and asylum, and the administration of justice and democratic processes.

None of the items in Annex III is implausible, but there is no rule from which their inclusion can be derived, which is also why negotiations between EU Commission, Parliament and member states revolved around this list.[29] Moreover, Article 7(1) of the AI Act permits amendments to Annex III by the Commission if the AI systems to be added are intended to be used in any of the areas of application listed in the Annex and if they pose a risk that is 'equivalent to or greater than the risk of harm or of adverse impact posed by the high-risk AI systems already referred to in Annex III.' There is no indication of a method for determining the equivalence of risk, and there is certainly no rule that would specify the link between fundamental rights and the items on the list in Annex III.

Over this imaginary and not particularly well-defined limit between acceptable and unacceptable risk for fundamental rights, the focus of the AI Act shifts to those systems more likely to cause breaches of fundamental rights. For these high-risk AI systems, the AI Act imposes a series of security requirements, already discussed in the various chapters of this book, and not least proposes a fundamental rights impact assessment analysed in the next paragraph. In the AI Act, the formulation of safety requirements imposed on AI systems often aligns more closely with the language and principles of fundamental rights than traditional product safety laws. For example, Article 10 of the AI Act addresses 'data and data governance', stipulating that high-risk AI systems must ensure the quality and integrity of datasets used, as well as compliance with data governance and management practices. This requirement emphasises the protection of individuals' rights to privacy and data protection, reflecting the values inherent in fundamental rights frameworks rather than focusing solely on product safety.

Such provisions are designed to safeguard against biases and inaccuracies that could lead to discrimination, thus protecting the fundamental rights of individuals affected by AI systems. This approach demonstrates the AI Act's commitment to embedding fundamental rights considerations into its regulatory structure beyond the typical scope of product safety law.

The risk to fundamental rights becomes, in fact, the main criterion for more stringent obligations, thus, for example, the fundamental rights impact assessment or, the need to provide for human oversight.[30] Similarly, compliance with these safety requirements is also assessed in terms of the extent to which the manufacturer is able to minimise or eliminate the risks to fundamental rights identified in the

[28] Kusche (2024).

[29] Bertuzzi, Luca 'MEPs seal the deal on Artificial Intelligence Act' Euractive, 2023.

[30] Cirone (2024).

fundamental rights impact assessment. In this sense, fundamental rights are not an afterthought of the AI Act but rather its backbone.

3.3 *Diverse Strategies for Risk Mitigation*

The conflicting and somehow confusing nature of the AI Act in between product safety regulation and fundamental right instrument is noticeable also in how the regulation calls to the mitigation or elimination of risks.

In product safety, risk is managed through a satisficing approach—as long as an AI system meets the established safety criteria, it is deemed acceptable, whether it barely meets the standard or significantly exceeds it. Fundamental rights protection, however, follows a different logic within the EU legal system. Each fundamental right has an 'essence' that must be preserved, and beyond this essence, their protection is not merely about compliance but about continuous enhancement.[31] This approach follows an optimisation logic, meaning that fundamental rights must be safeguarded and promoted to the fullest extent possible. The principle of proportionality plays a key role in achieving this, ensuring that only measures that least restrict fundamental rights are acceptable. When integrating fundamental rights protection into a product safety framework, this difference in approach becomes crucial. Ideally, such a transition requires moving beyond the satisficing logic of minimum compliance and towards an optimising logic, where AI systems are designed not just to meet fundamental rights standards but to actively uphold and enhance them.

This change is not smooth. On the one hand, as noted by some authors, the 'satisfacing approach' might be more pragmatic in the face of technological uncertainty, such as with AI systems.[32] When the capabilities of AI are not fully understood, setting clear boundaries that AI systems must not cross is simpler than evaluating whether an AI system best realises the underlying principles. On the other hand, the AI Act might end up prioritising the protection of fundamental rights that are more easily defined in a 'satisficing optic', like economic rights, over those that are less quantifiable, such as rights related to political participation.[33]

Almada et al. proposed one way out of this conundrum, which is to impose a logic of optimisation on product safety processes when it comes to fundamental rights protection.[34] The problem, this time, is practical. Frequent and ongoing updates of technical standards would be required under a norm of optimisation of fundamental rights protection. Such updates, in turn, would deprive the product safety regime of the stability associated with standardisation processes. Additionally,

[31] Brkan (2018), pp. 332–368, https://doi.org/10.1017/S1574019618000159.

[32] Artinger et al. (2022), pp. 598–635, https://doi.org/10.1257/jel.20201396.

[33] Almada and Petit (2022).

[34] Almada and Petit (2022).

changing a technical standard is not just a document revision. Drastic consequences might follow when existing compliant products are no longer compatible with new requirements. In particular, updating a standard is of little use if the actual systems are not updated to match the new specifications. Yet, changes to the system might not be feasible or, even if they are, might take a long time. In that case, technology would lag behind the demands of the law,[35] even the highest standards would fall short of achieving the desired optimisation level. Consequently, safeguarding fundamental rights through product safety measures is unlikely to adequately meet the objectives of either branch of the law, much less optimising their fulfilment.

3.4 Fundamental Rights Impact Assessment

With the intention of giving more attention to fundamental rights, the AI Act introduces a fundamental rights impact assessment (FRIA) for high-risk AI systems. The introduction of the FRIA has been firmly sustained by the European Parliament, which considered this amendment as an important contribution to the realisation of a human-centric AI through the respect of fundamental rights.[36] According to the Act Act, to efficiently ensure that fundamental rights are protected, deployers of high-risk specified AI systems should carry out an FRIA to use them. Article 27 states that deployers that are bodies governed by public law or are private entities providing public services, and deployers (in disregard of their public or private nature) of high-risk AI systems referred to in points 5 (b) and (c) of Annex III, except those identified in point 2 of annex III, shall perform an assessment of the impact on fundamental rights that the use of such system may produce.

The aim of the FRIA is for the deployer to identify the specific risks to the rights of individuals or groups of individuals likely to be affected and identify measures to be taken in the case of materialisation of those risks. The impact assessment should identify the deployer's relevant processes in which the high-risk AI system will be used in line with its intended purpose and should include a description of the period of time and frequency in which the system is intended to be used as well as of specific categories of natural persons and groups who are likely to be affected in the specific context of use. While performing this assessment, the deployer should consider information relevant to a proper assessment of the impact, including, but not limited to, the information given by the provider of the high-risk AI system in the instructions for use. In light of the risks identified, deployers should determine measures to be taken in the case of a materialisation of those risks. These measures might include governance arrangements specific to the context of use, such as human oversight according to the instructions of use or complaint handling and

[35] Bennett Moses and Zalnieriute (2020), https://doi.org/10.5040/9781509930968.

[36] Cirone, 'L'AI Act e l'obiettivo (Mancato?) Di Promuovere Uno Standard Globale per La Tutela Dei Diritti Fondamentali'.

redress procedures, as they could be instrumental in mitigating risks to fundamental rights in concrete use cases. The impact assessment should be performed prior to deploying the high-risk AI system and should be updated when the deployer considers that any of the relevant factors have changed. For that purpose, deployers shall perform an assessment consisting of multiple, partially already mentioned information: (a) a description of the deployer's processes in which the high-risk AI system will be used in line with its intended purpose; (b) a description of the period of time within which, and the frequency with which, each high-risk AI system is intended to be used; (c) the categories of natural persons and groups likely to be affected by its use in the specific context; (d) the specific risks of harm likely to have an impact on the categories of natural persons or groups of persons identified pursuant to point (c) taking into account the information given by the provider pursuant to Article 13; (e) a description of the implementation of human oversight measures, according to the instructions for use; (f) the measures to be taken in the case of the materialisation of those risks, including the arrangements for internal governance and complaint mechanisms. Therefore, we see that the deployers must tackle four main points in their FRIA, consisting of: (1) identification of risks, (2) analysis of the potential impact of these risks, (3) selection and adoption of the measures to prevent or mitigate the risks, (4) periodic review of the effectiveness of these measures.[37]

The obligation to carry out the FRIA applies to the first use of the high-risk AI system. In similar cases, the deployer may rely on previously conducted FRIA's or existing impact assessments carried out by the provider. However, the FRIA is not a on-off process. On the contrary, the acceptability of the impact of AI systems on fundamental rights must always be monitored throughout the lifecycle of the system.[38] Therefore, if during the high-risk AI system lifecycle, the deployer considers any of the elements listed above has changed or is no longer up to date, the deployer shall take the necessary steps to update the information. Failure to do so, or if the system is found to no longer comply with the applicable requirements, may result in the suspension or withdrawal of its certification, in accordance with Article 44 of the AI Act.

Once the assessment has been performed, the deployer shall notify the market surveillance authority of its results, submitting the filled-out template (still to be developed by the the European Artificial Intelligence Office: the AI office) as part of the notification.[39] In the case referred to in Article 46(1),[40] deployers may be exempt

[37] Mantelero (2022), pp. 1–43, https://doi.org/10.1007/978-94-6265-531-7_1.

[38] European Commission, Study to Support an Impact Assessment of Regulatory Requirements for Artificial Intelligence in Europe, (2021) available at https://artificialintelligenceact.eu/wp-content/uploads/2022/06/AIA-COM-Impact-Assessment-3-21-April.pdf.

[39] Art. 26 (5) AI Act.

[40] For reference, Article 46(1): By way of derogation from Article 43 and upon a duly justified request, any market surveillance authority may authorise the placing on the market or the putting into service of specific high-risk AI systems within the territory of the Member State concerned, for exceptional reasons of public security or the protection of life and health of persons, environmental protection or the protection of key industrial and infrastructural assets. That authorisation

from that obligation to notify. The summarised findings of the impact assessment also have to be included in the information to be submitted by deployers of high-risk AI systems in accordance with Article 49(3) of the AI Act. It should be noted that the FRIA does not further protect fundamental rights but rather helps to apply security requirements, redress and control mechanisms in a more measured and appropriate manner to the protection of the fundamental rights that those AI systems are most likely to impact.

However, despite these good intentions, an initial analysis of the relevant provisions reveals that the FRIA does not appear to have been fully integrated into the regulatory framework. This observation further underscores that this integration was the result of a political compromise.[41] The implementation of the FRIA has to take into account at least two different dynamics that risk to jeopardise its noble intention.

Firstly, this implementation must consider the range of existing fundamental rights and their complementarity with other non-fundamental rights legislation. The Charter of Fundamental Rights of the EU is divided into six chapters covering different fundamental rights on dignity, freedoms, equality, solidarity, citizens' rights, and justice. Each fundamental right has a different focus, ranging from freedom of business and the right to non-discrimination to the right to asylum. Therefore, an in-depth knowledge of fundamental rights is needed to assess the impact of high-risk AI systems on these rights. Moreover, certain legislative frameworks may contain provisions that safeguard specific dimensions of fundamental rights. For example, media regulation laws may include aspects relevant to freedom of expression and information, while medical treatment laws may address principles related to individual autonomy, privacy, or bodily integrity. While the AI Act functions as a horizontal framework applicable across various sectors, its implementation does not always require an in-depth understanding of each sector-specific legal framework. However, in some cases, sectoral legislation may provide relevant context for assessing fundamental rights considerations in AI applications. In many cases, such legislation might include special requirements or criteria that must be complied with where there is a restriction of fundamental rights. Secondly, EU Member States may have different fundamental rights in addition to the Charter or different nuances in interpreting these fundamental rights.[42]

Considering these two dynamics, the implementation of the FRIA as a solid instrument for protecting fundamental rights might be in danger. To address the misalignment between the end of the FRIA and its actual implementation, one possibility is to limit the FRIAs to fundamental rights most likely to be affected by the

shall be for a limited period while the necessary conformity assessment procedures are being carried out, taking into account the exceptional reasons justifying the derogation. The completion of those procedures shall be undertaken without undue delay.

[41] Cirone, 'L'AI Act e l'obiettivo (Mancato?) Di Promuovere Uno Standard Globale per La Tutela Dei Diritti Fondamentali'.

[42] Pirker (2018), p. 133156, https://doi.org/10.15166/2499-8249/203.

deployment of high-risk AI systems.[43] This approach avoids the presumption of mapping *all* fundamental rights impacted by AI deployment. However, it remains to be seen whether deployers will be capable of appropriately 'selecting' the relevant fundamental rights. Therefore, the recently established European AI Office must tackle these challenges in its Future FRIA Template Questionnaire and will need to elaborate clearer guidelines to implement the FRIA.

On a different note, organisations may already have compliance governance mechanisms in place to bring legal, IT and business professionals together for impact assessments such as a DPIA. Organisations may be able to leverage these mechanisms in relation to FRIAs. The first step will consist of a pre-FRIA screening to detect high-risk AI systems (therefore requiring a FRIA to be completed, among other requirements arising from the EU AI Act). If an up-to-date and easy-to-understand list of high-risk AI systems is provided by legal professionals, such pre-FRIA screening may be completed by relevant business departments that are most informed about the features of the specific high-risk AI systems. However, given the potential risk involved in relation to incorrect classifications, this pre-FRIA screening will likely still require validation from legal professionals. After establishing that a FRIA will be needed, relevant input relating to the technical and business context of the deployment can be collected from IT and business professionals. Legal professionals, using the explanations provided by their colleagues, can assess the effects of the deployment on fundamental rights, internally or with the help of specialised external counsels. However, in-house legal teams may not be fully armed with the necessary knowledge to analyse the effects of AI systems on human rights. Therefore, they may need further training or external counsel's help that provides different sets of know-how (e.g. IT, data protection and human rights laws). Additionally, there might be a need to involve the providers of high-risk AI systems for additional technical information or for accessing the 'provider' FRIAs on the specific AI system. Ensuring access to this knowledge, either internal or via consultancy, could therefore be a part of a company's legal responsibility.

The governance mechanism will also depend on the granularity of the analysis to be conducted. The Future FRIA Template Questionnaire will likely indicate the required level of detail and how organisations shall prepare for this new assessment.

Establishing a solid governance framework for pre-FRIA screening and completing the Future FRIA Template Questionnaire are crucial as market surveillance authorities will need to be notified of the results of the FRIAs. This means that organisations may fall under regulatory scrutiny in the event that they do not comply with the FRIA-related obligations.

[43] Cf. Recital 48 that sums up all fundamental rights: he right to human dignity, respect for private and family life, protection of personal data, freedom of expression and information, freedom of assembly and of association, the right to non-discrimination, the right to education, consumer protection, workers' rights, the rights of persons with disabilities, gender equality, intellectual property rights, the right to an effective remedy and to a fair trial, the right of defence and the presumption of innocence, and the right to good administration.

3.5 *Creation (or Extension) of a Right*

One of the main criticisms moved to the initial Commission's proposal was that, while focusing on establishing requirements and safeguards applicable to the various operators of AI systems, the AI Act lacked individual rights and remedies for persons on the receiving end of such systems.[44]

In contrast, the AI Act, as approved by the European Parliament on 14th March 2024, includes some rights and remedies available to natural and legal persons interacting with or impacted by AI systems, making the nature of this piece of legislation even more controversial. The AI Act contains an explicit 'right to request from the deployer clear and meaningful explanations of the role of the AI system in the decision-making procedure and the main elements of the decision taken'.[45] Article 86 has been perceived as a welcome addition to ensure the protection of fundamental rights. The practical impact of the AI Act's right to explanation may be limited, as it applies only to high-risk AI systems that could negatively affect health, safety, or fundamental rights. Its added value is also constrained by significant overlap with the GDPR, which is often interpreted as granting a similar right—though this remains a matter of debate. Despite these limitations, the AI Act's right to explanation still holds meaningful value, particularly in reinforcing transparency obligations in high-risk AI applications.[46] When applicable, the new provision grants the affected person a right to receive clear and meaningful information about a decision directly from the decision-maker; exercising this right does not presume entering legal proceedings. Hence, there are conceivable circumstances in which this right to explanation could serve its purpose of 'providing a basis on which the affected persons are able to exercise their rights', as specified in Recital 171 of the AI Act.[47] This addition to Article 86 has caused a shift in the legal basis on which the AI Act is built. In this sense, this addition would have exceeded the purview of Article 114 TFEU and led to the modification of the legal basis of the AI Act by adding to Article 114 TFEU and Article 16 TFEU, which is known to confer competence on the EU in matters of data protection.[48]

[44] Smuha et al. (2021), https://doi.org/10.2139/ssrn.3899991.

[45] Article 86 AI Act.

[46] Kelder (2024).

[47] Kelder (2024).

[48] Recital 3 AI Act.

4 The Product Safety Approach: A Risk for Fundamental Rights

While academic literature is still rather uncertain on whether and how the AI Act protects fundamental rights sufficiently, its attempt to contribute to the fundamental rights protection is undeniable. However, it must not be forgotten that the AI Act does so within the European market competence of the EU. It, therefore, seems reductive to say that the AI Act does not pay attention to fundamental rights when it would rather appear that the AI Act does pay attention, but in a manner consistent with the European competence from which it originates.

In this sense, the AI Act moves on the first level of fundamental rights risks identified beforehand, offering *ex-ante* protection through security requirements applicable to high-risk AI that ultimately aim to protect fundamental rights. Take, for instance, the case of AI, which offers discriminatory outputs due to a biased dataset. To this, the AI Act attempts to provide solutions by offering data governance requirements that aim to ascertain the quality of the dataset with which the AI is trained, implicitly ensuring the right to non-discrimination.[49]

However, it could be argued that the AI Act also clumsily attempts to act on the second level of fundamental rights infringement, this is by attempting to offer protection to fundamental rights also extended to behaviour carried out through the use of AI systems and in certain contexts of use by operating a presumption of risk. The AI Act acts on this second level of infringement in two different ways. Firstly, the AI Act identifies forbidden uses of AI systems, which by definition are forbidden because they carry out uses that are not in line with fundamental rights. On the other hand, for high-risk AI, Annex III of the AI Act identifies specific contexts of use and intended use to be considered high risk, to which the requirements inherent in the design of the AI, therefore, apply. Thus, for example if point 5 of Annex III opened the door to appropriate regulation of the AI Act in the medical sphere, in reality, the uses indicated below to restrict the scope, closes it almost completely.

Moreover, although the AI Act in Annex I does not explicitly speak of a context of use, it does refer to regulations that implicitly delineate a context of use in certain cases. This is, for example, the case with the reference to the Medical Device Regulation (hereafter: MDR).[50] By referring to this regulation, the AI Act implies that AI systems whose use is intended to be one of those indicated in Article 2 of the MDR may be considered high-risk AI, but only insofar as they are subject to a third-party conformity assessment. This applies primarily to those classified as higher than risk class I according to the MDR, as the latter are generally exempt from such assessment. Consequently, these AI systems must comply with the relevant

[49] Gerybaite et al. (2022), pp. 385–409.

[50] Regulation (EU) 2017/745 of the European Parliament and of the Council of 5 April 2017 on medical devices, amending Directive 2001/83/EC, Regulation (EC) No 178/2002 and Regulation (EC) No 1223/2009 and repealing Council Directives 90/385/EEC and 93/42/EEC.

requirements, which, as already mentioned, ultimately contribute to protecting human rights.[51]

However, in this way, everything that according to the MDR does not intend to be a proper use of a medical device will not be included among the high risk medical devices, leaving such AI systems without adequate protection for fundamental rights. Case in point, certain mHealth apps, such as AI-powered diagnostic assistants that analyse symptoms and medical history or provide tailored well-being recommendations, which, while not falling within the purview of the MDR, could still fall within the purview of the AI Act as high-risk AI systems or under other relevant classifications and thereby would need security requirements to address the possible risks they pose to fundamental rights.[52]

It could be said that in trying to pay attention to the second level of fundamental rights issues, i.e., also paying attention to the uses and contexts of AI systems, the AI Act ultimately narrows rather than broadens the scope of its security requirements. In this sense, if the AI system cannot fit into the uses or contexts deemed as high risk, no safety requirements will apply. This would *de facto* leave the AI system without fundamental rights protection at the first level, which is compliance by design with the fundamental rights ensured by the requirements of the AI Act.

In a general sense, therefore, it should be said that the second level of fundamental rights protection can and must find protection in the traditional fundamental rights protection instruments. When faced with unlawful uses of AI systems that violate fundamental rights as enshrined in the ECHR and Charter of Fundamental Rights, as well as other international, European and national declarations of rights, recourse will be had to ordinary justice at all levels.[53]

On another note, since the AI Act does not cover all AI systems, nor AI systems, through their entire lifecycle, the question remains whether the protection of the fundamental rights by the AI Act does the job sufficiently. Although we can be quite sure that sufficient fundamental rights protection is in place for the development of high-risk AI systems, the protection for its use, as just mentioned, is less satisfying, and all AI systems that are not considered high-risk are not even covered at all. The product safety/risk-based approach of the AI Act consequently protects against high-risk infringements of fundamental rights but does not cope with the risks of infringements of other AI systems with a lower risk level. One can only hope that the additional legal framework that are simultaneously applicable, do cover this issue as well.

---

[51] Palmieri and Goffin (2023), pp. 406–427.

[52] Hauglid and Mahler (2023), pp. 1–23.

[53] Ziller (2024).

5 Council of Europe's Framework Convention

On 17 May 2024, the Committee of Ministers for the Council of Europe adopted the Framework Convention on Artificial Intelligence and Human Rights, Democracy and the Rule of Law. After the paper on the 'Possible elements of a legal framework and the Rule of law' commissioned by the *ad hoc* Committee on Artificial Intelligence (CAHAI), later succeeded by the Committee on Artificial Intelligence (CAI), was adopted in December 2021, the Committee of Ministers of the Council of Europe instructed the CAI to elaborate a Framework Convention on the activities within the lifecycle of artificial intelligence systems, based on the Council of Europe's standards on human rights, democracy and the rule of law and conductive to innovation, which can be composed of a binding legal instrument of a transversal character, including notably general common principles.[54]

The Committee of Ministers also decided to allow for the inclusion in the negotiations of the European Union and interested non-European States sharing the values and aims of the Council of Europe.

The Framework Convention focuses on the protection and furtherance of human rights, democracy, and the rule of law, and it does, unlike the AI Act, not expressly regulate the economic and market aspects of AI systems. The Council of Europe is not competent to regulate the latter. Taken as a whole, it provides a common legal framework at the general level in order to apply the existing international and domestic legal obligations that are applicable to each Party in the sphere of human rights, democracy and the rule of law of each Party and aims to ensure that the activities within the lifecycle of AI systems by both public and private actors comply with these obligations, standards and commitments.[55]

The Council of Europe has chosen a Framework Convention. Whilst the Framework Convention is a legally binding instrument under international law, the word 'Framework' highlights the scope for Contracting Parties to translate the Convention's provisions to their specific country situation through national legislation and appropriate governmental policies.[56] The Framework Convention, therefore, ensures that each Party's existing applicable obligations on human rights, democracy and the rule of law, including within the EU Member States the Charter of Fundamental Rights of the EU, are also applied to activities within the lifecycle of AI systems. In this sense, the Framework Convention is aligned with the applicable human rights protection systems and mechanisms of each Party, including their international law obligations and other international commitments and their applicable domestic law. As such, no provision of the Convention is intended to

[54] Recital 2, Explanatory report to the Council of Europe Framework Convention on Artificial Intelligence and Human Rights, Democracy and the Rule of Law.

[55] Recital 2 and 4, Explanatory report to the Council of Europe Framework Convention on Artificial Intelligence and Human Rights, Democracy and the Rule of Law.

[56] Framework Convention of the Council of Europe for the Protection of National Minorities (ETS No. 157), entry into force 1 February 1998.

create new human rights or human rights obligations or undermine the scope and content of the existing applicable protections, but rather, by setting out various legally binding obligations contained in its Chapters II to VI, to facilitate the effective implementation of the applicable human rights obligations of each Party in the context of the new challenges raised by AI. Despite the Convention not creating new rights or human rights obligations, its importance remains clear. It rather designs more specific provisions to apply the existing standards of the Council of Europe on human rights to the AI context.[57]

The Convention not only has a symbolic and meta-legal value but is also a normative instrument, with the capacity for quasi-constitutional integration into the legal systems of the Contracting Parties and great interpretative potential. As stated by Cotino, 'Although in general the AI Convention is not characterised by clear-cut specific obligations and rights, there are several reasons to take it normatively into account. (…) It is worth recalling that for years, among dozens of declarations and documents, some essential ethical principles of AI have been made visible and distilled. (…) The future Convention is positive in that it goes beyond declarations in the real of soft law and regulates these principles'.[58] Article 1 of the Convention describes this responsibility of the Contracting Parties as follows: 'Each Party shall adopt or maintain appropriate legislative, administrative or other measures to give effect to the provisions set out in this Convention. These measures shall be graduated and differentiated as may be necessary in view of the severity and probability of the occurrence of adverse impacts on human rights, democracy and the rule of law throughout the lifecycle of artificial intelligence systems. This may include specific or horizontal measures that apply irrespective of the type of technology used'. As indicated in the Explanatory Report, its implementation is an obligation of result and not an obligation of means. In this respect, the principle of subsidiarity is essential, putting upon the Parties the main responsibility to ensure respect for human rights and to provide for redress for violations of human rights.[59]

Throughout its text the Convention creates various obligations in relation to the activities within the lifecycle of AI systems—(1) planning and design, (2) data collection and processing, (3) development of artificial intelligence systems, including model building and/or fine-tuning existing models for specific tasks, (4) testing, verification and validation, (5) supply/making the systems available for use, (6) deployment, (7) operation and monitoring, and (8) retirement.[60] This reference to the lifecycle ensures a comprehensive approach towards addressing AI-related risks and adverse impacts on human rights, democracy and the rule of law by capturing

[57] Van Kolfschooten and Shachar (2023), pp. 2–3, https://doi.org/10.1016/j.healthpol.2023.104935.

Explanatory report to the Council of Europe Framework Convention on Artificial Intelligence and Human Rights, Democracy and the Rule of Law, 9.

[58] Cotino Hueso (2024); Ziller (2024), p. 205, referring to the CoE news of 12 October 2023.

[59] Explanatory report to the Council of Europe Framework Convention on Artificial Intelligence and Human Rights, Democracy and the Rule of Law, 9.

[60] Art. 1 of the Convention.

all stages of activities relevant to all AI systems. Applying these obligations to the entirety of the lifecycle ensures that the Convention can cover not only current but future risks in view of rapid and often unpredictable technological developments. It applies horizontally across all sectors, both public and private, with limited exceptions for protection of national security interests, research and development activities unless they have the potential to interfere with human rights, democracy and the rule of law, and an exclusion for national defence. (Article 3). The field of application of the AI Convention, thereby, is much wider than the AI Act.

Within the Convention, AI is different than in the AI Act, defined as 'a machine-based system that for explicit or implicit objectives, infers, from the input it receives, how to generate outputs such as predictions, content, recommendations or decisions that may influence physical or virtual environments. Different artificial intelligence systems vary in their levels of autonomy and adaptiveness after deployment'. (Article 2). The field of application of the AI Convention, therefore, is broader than the AI Act.

The Convention stipulates general obligations—protection of human rights and integrity of democratic processes and respect for the rule of law—and general principles related to activities within the lifecycle of AI systems—respect for human dignity and individual autonomy, transparency and oversight, accountability and responsibility, equality and non-discrimination, privacy and personal data protection, reliability and safe innovation - for actors applying AI systems (Chapter II and III). It thereby formalises fundamental AI principles to underpin concrete individual rights.[61] Each party shall, to the extent remedies are required by its international obligations and consistent with its domestic legal system, adopt and maintain measures to ensure the availability of accessible and effective remedies for violations of human rights (Article 14) and ensure that where an AI system—any AI system - significantly impacts upon the enjoyment of human rights, effective procedural guarantees, safeguards and rights, in accordance with international and domestic law, are available to persons affected thereby (Article 15).

In order to guarantee that AI systems do not infringe on human rights, similarly to the AI Act, the Convention puts forward a risk and impact management framework. Article 16 puts an obligation on the Contracting Parties to adopt measures for the identification, assessment, prevention and mitigation of risks posed by AI systems by considering actual and potential impacts on human rights, democracy and the rule of law. These measures should also ensure that adverse impacts of AI systems are adequately addressed and documented. However, since its field of application is wider than that of the AI Act, just applying the FRIA will not be sufficient for the Contracting Parties to comply with this obligation.

The measures shall be graduated and differentiated and take due account of the context and intended use of AI systems, in particular as concerns risks to human rights, democracy, and the rule of law; take due account of the severity and

[61] Van Kolfschooten and Shachar (2023), pp. 2–3, https://doi.org/10.1016/j.healthpol.2023.104935.

probability of potential impacts; consider, where appropriate, the perspectives of relevant stakeholders, in particular persons whose rights may be impacted; apply iteratively throughout the activities within the lifecycle of the artificial intelligence system; include monitoring for risks and adverse impacts to human rights, democracy, and the rule of law; include documentation of risks, actual and potential impacts, and the risk management approach; and require, where appropriate, testing of artificial intelligence systems before making them available for first use and when they are significantly modified (Article 16)

The Convention also stipulates some specific obligations for Member States implementing the Convention, such as ensuring non-discrimination (Article 17), providing for public consultation (Article 19), and investing in digital literacy and skills (Article 20). Finaly the Convention requires States to report to the Conference of Parties with details of activities undertaken to give effect to the implementation of the Convention (Article 24), the exchange relevant and useful information between Contracting Parties (Article 25) and to establish effective oversight mechanisms (Article 26).

The Convention opened for signature on the occasion of the Conference of Ministers of Justice in Vilnius (Lithuania) on 5 September 2024. It will enter into force on the first date of the month following the expiration of a period of three months after the date on which five signatories, including at least three member states of the Council of Europe, have expressed their consent to be bound to the Convention (Article 30).

6 Interplay Between the AI Act and the Framework Convention

Although the AI Act was created under the competency of the European Union and the Framework Convention under the competency of the Council of Europe, they are, for the biggest part, complementary in their goals and their limitations. The European Union participated in the negotiations represented by the European Commission, including in its delegation also representatives from the European Union Agency for Fundamental Rights (FRA) and the European Data Protection Supervisor (EDPS) and the AI Act was explicitly taken into account when developing the Convention.[62] This intention for a close collaboration between the EU and the Council of Europe can also be found in other provisions. The existing human rights framework on which the Contracting Parties need to evaluate the AI systems explicitly mentions the Charter of Fundamental Rights of the EU as well.[63] Also, when dealing with the Parties' obligation on data protection, the GDPR is

[62] Recital 4 and Preamble of Explanatory report to the Council of Europe Framework Convention on Artificial Intelligence and Human Rights, Democracy and the Rule of Law.

[63] F.e. *Ibid.* p. 12.

mentioned.[64] The EU will implement the Convention through the AI Act.[65] It will be implemented alongside other relevant EU laws when needed. Since the AI Act and the AI Convention apply to slightly different areas, it is important to assess the adequacy of the EU's implementation of the Convention in the AI Act.

As mentioned by van Kolfschooten and Shachar, the AI Convention will not override the AI Act but instead aims to complement it. 'The AI Convention and the AI Act exist within different legal frameworks, although they regulate the same object (AI systems) and apply to overlapping actors (27 EU Member States). The AI Act focuses on streamlining products using AI within the EU internal market, while the AI Convention centres on protecting fundamental rights of people affected by AI systems'.[66] It is therefore wrong to say that the two organisations have worked in parallel. There is a great deal of interaction between the institutions of the two European organisations.[67]

Or to quote Contino (as translated by Ziller): 'the Convention puts the lyrics to the prose that is the AI Act. The AI Act establishes the foundations and structures of a safe and trusted AI ecosystem; the Convention focuses on its impact on people and democratic society. The AI Act is methodological, detailed, and precise, charting a clear path through technical and legal complexity and setting firm standards and concrete obligations for providers, users, and implementers of AI systems. In contrast, on the lyrical side, the Convention rises to normatively integrate the fundamental values, ethical principles and human rights that should guide the evolution of AI'.[68]

Nevertheless, the field of application of the AI Act and the Framework Convention is different. The Convention applies to the entire lifecycle of the AI system, as when the AI system evolves over time and applies to all AI systems. AI Act, on the contrary, focuses mainly on regulating the development phase. Even more, it only sets strict rules for 'high-risk' AI systems. This said, when applying concrete rules to AI systems within Europe, there remains a clear preference for the rules of the AI Act. Article 27 of the AI Convention thereby stipulates that the Parties which are members of the European Union shall, in their mutual relations, apply European Union rules governing the matters within the scope of the Convention, without prejudice to the object and purpose of the Convention and without prejudice to its full

[64] *Ibid.* p. 18.

[65] Press release of the European Commission, 5 September 2024, 'Commission sings Council of Europe framework Convention on Artificial Intelligence', https://digital-strategy.ec.europa.eu/en/news/commission-signs-council-europe-framework-convention-artificial-intelligence#:~:text=The%20Commission%20has%20signed%20the,on%20behalf%20of%20the%20EU.&text=The%20Convention%20is%20the%20first,AI%20regulation%20in%20the%20world.

[66] Van Kolfschooten and Shachar (2023), pp. 2–3, https://doi.org/10.1016/j.healthpol.2023.104935.

[67] Ziller (2024), p. 205, referring to the CoE news of 12 October 2023 'Secretary General 10. Marija Pejčinović Burić met with European Commissioner for Justice Didier Reynders. The meeting focused on the cooperation between the Council of Europe and the European Union and on the ongoing preparations for the Convention on Artificial Intelligence'.

[68] Cotino Hueso (2024).

application with other Parties. According to the Explanatory Report, the Drafters of the Convention intended to include European Union law measures, principles, and procedures provided for in the European Union legal order, particularly laws, regulations, administrative provisions, and other requirements, including court decisions. The question, however, still remains how this will be accomplished, knowing that the field of application of both regulatory frameworks is not the same. For those AI systems that are not covered by the AI Act, it will remain the Contracting Parties' sole responsibility under the Convention, to guarantee sufficient protection of human rights, i.e. to carry out a sufficient impact assessment. Taking into account that the Convention is a convention, it is, therefore, up to the States themselves to decide whether or not to sign and ratify the Convention. Taking into account that the Convention is only a Framework Convention, and thereby only limited directly enforceable obligations will be put on the Contracting Parties, it remains questionable whether we really can state that fundamental/human rights are sufficiently protected within all AI systems through the AI Act of the EU and the AI Framework Convention of the Council of Europe.

7 Conclusion

We can, therefore, conclude that the gaps left open by the EU AI Act, due to its 'product safety' character, rather than a 'fundamental rights protection' and limiting itself to mainly regulating high-risk AI systems in their development phase, are somehow completed by the CoE AI Framework Convention, including mutual respect. Both legal frameworks tend to work together to form a general framework creating responsibilities for both Member States, as developers and users of AI systems, in order to guarantee to be human-centric and thereby respect the existing fundamental/human rights frameworks.

However, many questions remain: How will the Contracting Parties of the AI Convention deal with the human rights protection of AI systems that are not covered by the AI Act? Can the systems, such as the FRIA, developed within the AI Act specifically for high-risk AI systems also be used for other AI systems? Is the provided framework of both regulations enough to fully guarantee human/fundamental rights protection? For example, as briefly mentioned in this chapter, except for a right to request from the deployer clear and meaningful explanations of the role of the AI system in the decision-making procedure and the main elements of the decision taken, as stipulated in the AI Act—a right that in Article 15.2 has a twin brother in the AI Convention -, no AI specific human rights have been created. Let us hope that the AI Act and the AI Convention are only the starting point of the discussion of AI systems and the respect for human/fundamental rights based on the already existing international and domestic rights frameworks. This discussion further fills the gaps that were identified in this chapter but also tackles the question of whether we need to create additional – perhaps context-specific - rights in order to deal with the risks AI systems pose to human beings.

References

Almada M, Petit N (2022) The EU AI Act: between product safety and fundamental rights. SSRN Electr J. https://doi.org/10.2139/ssrn.4308072

Artinger FM, Gigerenzer G, Jacobs P (2022) Satisficing: integrating two traditions. J Econ Literat 60(2):598–635. https://doi.org/10.1257/jel.20201396

Battistelli F, Grazia Galantino M (2019) Dangers, risks and threats: an alternative conceptualization to the catch-all concept of risk. Curr Sociol 67(1):64–78. https://doi.org/10.1177/0011392118793675

Bennett Moses L, Zalnieriute M (2020) Law and technology in the dimension of time. In: Ranchordás S, Roznai Y (eds) *Time, law, and change: an interdisciplinary study*. Hart Publishing. https://doi.org/10.5040/9781509930968

Brkan M (2018) The concept of essence of fundamental rights in the EU legal order: peeling the onion to its core. Eur Const Law Rev 14(2):332–368. https://doi.org/10.1017/S1574019618000159

Cirone E (2024) L'AI Act e l'obiettivo (Mancato?) Di Promuovere Uno Standard Globale per La Tutela Dei Diritti Fondamentali. Quaderni AISDUE, no. 2

Cotino Hueso L (2024) El Convenio Sobre Inteligencia Artificial, Derechis Humanos, Democracia y Estado de Derecho Del Consejo de Europa. Administración & Cidadanía, EGAP

Evans K, De Moura N, Chauvier S, Chatila R, Dogan E (2020) Ethical decision making in autonomous vehicles: the AV ethics project. Sci Eng Ethics 26(6):3285–3312. https://doi.org/10.1007/s11948-020-00272-8

Ferrara E (2023) Fairness and bias in artificial intelligence: a brief survey of sources, impacts, and mitigation strategies. Science 6(1):3. https://doi.org/10.3390/sci6010003.

Garnett K, Parsons DJ (2017) Multi-case review of the application of the precautionary principle in European Union law and case law. Risk Anal 37(3):502–516. https://doi.org/10.1111/risa.12633

Gerybaite A, Sofia P, Francesco V (2022) Equality in healthcare AI: did anyone mention data quality? Biolaw Journal- Rivista Di BioDiritto 4:385–409

Green B, Chen Y (2021) Algorithmic risk assessments can alter human decision-making processes in high-stakes government contexts. Proc ACM Human-Comput Interact 5(CSCW2):1–33. https://doi.org/10.1145/3479562.

Hauglid MK, Mahler T (2023) Doctor Chatbot: the EU's regulatory prescription for generative medical AI. Oslo Law Rev 1:1–23

Hildebrandt M (2017) Privacy as protection of the incomputable self: agonistic machine learning. SSRN Electr J. https://doi.org/10.2139/ssrn.3081776

Husman H (2023) Regulating artificial intelligence – is it possible? An evaluation of the proposed European artificial intelligence act in light of the European Charter of Fundamental Rights. Örebro University

Kelder K (2024) On the Relative Importance of the AI Act Right to Explenation. The Digital Constitutionalist (blog) Accessed July 4, 2024

Kostogryzov A, Makhutov N, Nistratov A, Reznikov G (2023) Probabilistic predictive modelling for complex system risk assessments. In: Abdalla R, El-Diasty M, Kostogryzov A, Makhutov N (eds) Time series analysis - new insights. IntechOpen. https://doi.org/10.5772/intechopen.106869

Kusche I (2024) Possible harms of artificial intelligence and the EU AI Act: Fundamental Rights and Risk. J Risk Res:1–14. https://doi.org/10.1080/13669877.2024.2350720

Lenaerts K (2019) Limits on limitations: the essence of fundamental rights in the EU. Germ Law J 20(6):779–793. https://doi.org/10.1017/GLJ.2019.62

Luzak J (2020) A broken notion: impact of modern technologies on product liability. Eur J Risk Regul 11(3):630–649. https://doi.org/10.1017/err.2020.13

Mantelero A (2022) Beyond data. In: Beyond data, by Alessandro Mantelero (ed) Information technology and law series. T.M.C. Asser Press, The Hague, pp 1–43. https://doi.org/10.1007/978-94-6265-531-7_1

OECD (2021). OECD Regulatory Policy Outlook 2021. https://www.oecd.org/en/publications/2021/10/oecd-regulatory-policy-outlook-2021_c5274577.html
Palmieri S, Goffin T (2023) A blanket that leaves the feet cold: exploring the AI act safety framework for medical AI. Eur J Health Law 30(4):406–427
Pirker B (2018) Mapping the scope of application of EU fundamental rights: a typology. Text/html,PDF. Eur Pap A J Law Integr 2018(3): 133156. https://doi.org/10.15166/2499-8249/203
Schafer B (2021) Death by a thousand cuts: cumulative data effects and the corbyn affair. Datenschutz und Datensicherheit - DuD 45(6):385–390. https://doi.org/10.1007/s11623-021-1456-8
Scheppele KL, Vladimirovich KD, Grabowska-Moroz B (2021) EU values are law, after all: enforcing EU values through systemic infringement actions by the European Commission and the Member States of the European Union. Yearb Eur Law 39:3–121. https://doi.org/10.1093/yel/yeaa012
Sieckmann J-R (2021) To balance or not to balance: the quest for the essence of rights. In: Sieckmann J-R (ed) Proportionality, balancing, and rights, Law and Philosophy Library, vol. 136. Springer International Publishing, Cham, pp 113–134. https://doi.org/10.1007/978-3-030-77321-2_5.
Skjuve M, Følstad A, Inge FK, Bae Brandtzaeg P (2021) My Chatbot companion - a study of human-chatbot relationships. Int J Human-Comput Stud 149:102601. https://doi.org/10.1016/j.ijhcs.2021.102601
Smuha NA, Ahmed-Rengers E, Harkens A, Li W, MacLaren J, Piselli R, Yeung K (2021) How the EU can achieve legally trustworthy AI: a response to the European Commission's proposal for an artificial intelligence act. SSRN Electr J. https://doi.org/10.2139/ssrn.3899991
van Kolfschooten H, Shachar C (2023) The Council of Europe's AI Convention (2023–2024): promises and pitfalls for health protection. Health Policy 138:104935. https://doi.org/10.1016/j.healthpol.2023.104935
Ziller J (2024) The Council of Europe Framework Convention on Artificial Intelligence vs. the EU Regulation: Two Quite Different Legal Instruments. *CERIDAP* - Rivista Interdisciplinare Sul Diritto Delle Amministrazioni Pubbliche, no. 2

The AI Act's Content

Definition of AI

Denis Steckelmacher and Bart Bogaerts

Contents

Abstract Artificial Intelligence is present in human imagination since Antiquity but is considered to have been founded as a research field only in 1956 during the Darthmouth Summer Research Project on Artificial Intelligence. While this workshop identified a set of tasks and approaches that are Artificial Intelligence, a strong definition, that maintains its accuracy over decades, has always remained elusive. In this chapter, we will explore the area of Artificial Intelligence Research, how AI is often defined, and then discuss possible other definitions.

D. Steckelmacher (✉) · B. Bogaerts
Vrije Universiteit Brussels, Brussels, Belgium
e-mail: denis.steckelmacher@vub.be; bart.bogaerts@vub.be

V. L. Raposo (ed.), *The European Artificial Intelligence Act*, Law, Governance and Technology Series 78, https://doi.org/10.1007/978-3-031-98406-8_4

1 Computer Science

Artificial Intelligence is part of the broader field of Computer Science, the science of designing and working with computers. We provide a general introduction to Computer Science in this section, to better position Artificial Intelligence in the world, and its relation with technology in general. In the next section, we deeply explore Artificial Intelligence Research, before, in Sects. 3 and 4, discussing how to precisely define AI.

The computers, phones, smart appliances and machines that we use every day, or that make the world run, are not harvested from nature but are man-made machines. These machines have two essences that closely interact with each other:

1. The hardware, the physical realisation and existence of the machine. The hardware encompasses the silicon used to manufacture microprocessors, plastics used for the keyboard, the chemistry of screens, the metal of cables, etc. Improving hardware requires research and development in electronics, chemistry, physics and engineering in general. Computer Science usually does not try to make hardware better.
2. The software, that runs on the hardware. Software is made of algorithms and data, and we discuss in the next section what an algorithm is. The same hardware can run an infinite variety of software, which explains why we can update the software on a computer, or install a new program, without having to buy a new computer. Computer Science is the science of software, and mainly revolves around making better software, or using software to tackle the problems of the world.

1.1 Algorithms

Algorithms are not limited to computers. The word algorithm itself is more than a millennium old and originates from the name and work of *al-Khwārizmī,* a well-respected Persian mathematician from the ninth century.[1]

An algorithm is the description of a step-by-step process that allows a person, a machine or a computer to perform some tasks, by combining smaller and easier tasks that the person, machine or computer is already able to perform.

1.1.1 Example of an Algorithm

The best-known algorithm, that almost everyone learns in high school, is the algorithm that allows to find the roots of a second-degree equation. We briefly review this algorithm in this section, because it is a clear example of an algorithm that can be performed both by a person, and by a computer.

[1] Van der Waerden (2013).

We consider the equation below:

$ax^2 + bx + c = 0$with a, b and c given (we assume that we know these numbers by the time we want to perform the algorithm). The purpose of the algorithm is, given a, b and c, to find the x values for which the equation above holds, so for which $ax^2 + bx + c$ is equal to zero.

The algorithm that we learn in high-school assumes a person (or a computer) that is able to add numbers, multiply numbers, divide numbers, and compute the square root of a number. This last requirement is in practice challenging to obtain in the real world, and people usually defer to a calculator for computing the square root, while computers implement an additional algorithm, that allows them to compute a square root by only performing additions, multiplications and divisions. The algorithm is as follows:

1. We compute a number which we call 'delta' and is equal to $b^2 - 4$ ac. Because we know a, b and c, it is possible to compute delta exactly and to write it on a piece of paper.
2. If delta is negative, it is impossible to find a value of x that satisfies the equation, so we simply write 'no root' on the piece of paper.
3. If delta is positive, it allows us to compute the two roots of the equation: $\frac{-b+\sqrt{delta}}{2a}$ and $\frac{-b-\sqrt{delta}}{2a}$.
4. If the two roots are the same (which happens when delta is exactly zero), we usually consider that there is only a single root for the equation.

1.1.2 Algorithms and Computer Science

The above algorithm is expressed in a human readable form, in English. Computer Science mainly revolves in designing and expressing algorithms:

- How can a given problem, that matters in the real world, be expressed as an algorithm that uses simple-enough constructs to be performed by a computer?
- How can an algorithm be expressed in a computer language in a way that is correct and fast?

Computers do not understand English, but, over the decades, a variety of tools have been designed to allow humans (programmers) to express algorithms in a language that is understandable both by trained experts (the programmers) and a machine. These languages are called 'programming languages', and more than a thousand of them exist, with varied properties, ease of use, acceptance by the field, and speed considerations.

The algorithm is the mathematical concept of what has to be done (and can be expressed in English like the example above). A program is the expression of an algorithm in some programming language, also called the *implementation* of the algorithm. That expression is usually stored in a computer file, akin to a Word document but much simpler. Programmers can open the file to modify it and improve it.

The computer itself can also open the program to run it, to perform the algorithm it describes. Programs, both readable and modifiable by a person and runnable by a computer, are at the core of Computer Science. They are the tangible expression of an algorithm and are being referred to when some regulation mentions something like 'the implementation of an AI system'.

1.2 Research Areas in Computer Science

Artificial Intelligence is one of the research areas in Computer Science, but not the only one. Other research areas either consider how to improve the computers themselves, or how to use computers for the improvement of the world. Focusing on the areas that aim at improving how computers work, we start with:

- Cryptography and Security in Computing in general: algorithms that allow to transfer or store information securely between two people or pieces of software, even if they are separated by a potentially-hostile network or other equipment. Cryptography also considers the problem of authentication (asserting that some is who they pretend to be). Password management and 2-factor authentication are also in the realm of Security in Computing.
- Compiler Technology and High-Performance Computing: improved algorithms that make specific computing devices (small or big computers, computers in cars, calculators, or big computers in datacenters) faster and more energy-efficient at running programs.
- Software Engineering and Programming Languages: this area lies at the border between Human Sciences (programmers are people) and Computer Science and considers methods and processes that make writing good programs, that work and do what the end-users want, easier and cheaper. This area encompasses the design of new programming languages, but also testing methodologies, managing the history of ever-changing pieces of software, delivering updates to the users, efficiently collecting and representing the users' requirements, and analysing programs to identify and locate problems.

Computer Science also considers the use of computers for running algorithms that produce knowledge in other domains, such as:

- Computational Biology applies computers to biology, for instance to simulate how medicines interact with molecules in our body, or to detect variants of viruses, establish phylogenetic trees between species, etc.
- Computer-Aided Design, for managing, designing and simulating various physical and engineering processes, such as heat transfer in structures, the load-bearing capacity of bridges, or how electricity may flow in a particular grid.
- Weather forecasts, something that almost everyone uses on a daily basis, and requires some of the most advanced and multidisciplinary knowledge in human history. Good weather forecasts mix accurate simulation of large-scale physical

processes, along with advanced data engineering and various forms of Artificial Intelligence (Machine Learning, Optimisation and Constraint Solving).
- Graphics and Multimedia consider the use of computers for the production of human-consumed text, images, videos and audio. This field encompasses algorithms for drawing text, curves and 3D shapes, but also research on audio and video compression, critical in our current age of video streaming and videoconferencing, where every little bit of data is paid for in transfer time and energy expenditure.

Artificial Intelligence is a special area of Computer Science, in the sense that it relates and touches many of the other areas and is not clearly categorised as 'Computer Science for Computers' or 'Computer Science for the World'. We now focus on Artificial Intelligence and present its subfields, each accompanied with a brief review of the current scientific literature on the topic.

2 Subfields of Artificial Intelligence Research

Later in this chapter, we discuss how to succinctly define Artificial Intelligence, aiming for a definition that considers what an AI system does, as opposed to the technical means it uses to do it. Before doing so, this section reviews the different research areas of Artificial Intelligence. AI researchers all over the world want to solve as many problems requiring AI as possible, while avoiding losing their time on problems that cannot or should not be solved with AI. As such, we consider that a review of scientific research in AI closely captures the set of real-world problems that require AI and thus gives the reader an overview of what is 'being artificially intelligent'.

2.1 Search & Function Optimisation

Search and Function Optimisation are two different families of problems, but are solved by similar (or even identical) algorithms. We therefore present these two families together.

Search consists of finding a specific solution in a large problem space, with as little compute time as possible. The best-known example of a Search problem is the Sudoku game: given a grid of numbers (and missing numbers), and the set of rules of the game, the player has to find what numbers to put in every empty cell. Mazes are another example of search problems, where only one specific path leads to the exit.

Function Optimisation can be seen as a variant of Search, in which not only *any* solution is required, but *the best one*. Function optimisation considers a mathematical function, something that computes an output value given some input, and tries to produce the input that leads to the highest-possible output value.

Two kinds of functions are generally considered: black-box functions, for which the actual computations are not known to the optimisation algorithm, and white-box functions, for which the computations are known. An example of a black-box function is an industrial process that is too complicated to analyse with known physics equations. We can see the process as producing some output, for instance how efficiently some product can be manufactured, given how the production machines are configured, but we don't know exactly how the machine configurations influence the output.An example of a white-box function is some quadratic function, $y = -8x^2 + 2x + 3$, for which it is possible to analytically find the value of x that maximises y.

Both Search and Function Optimisation are highly general and abstract. In practice, the 'problem space' and 'input' can be anything that can be represented on a computer, such as graphs (road networks, machines on the Internet), descriptions of manufacturing machines, text, photos, etc. We provide more details below.

2.1.1 Real-World Applications

We first note that 'Search' does not have the same definition in AI research than in the general society. While most people consider 'searching' looking for some piece of text, file or video, Search in AI means 'creating a solution that meets constraints'.

The Search application most people use on a daily basis is route planning,[2] used primarily for GPS navigation. Given a map of localities connected by roads, a start point, and an end point, the algorithm has to find a path between the start and end points that is feasible (does not jump nor teleports) and maximises some objective, such as speed or economy. A more general approach does not consider roads and localities, but the mathematical objects of edges and nodes in a graph. Many real-world objects can be mapped to edges and nodes in a graph, which allows the same algorithms to compute short routes for delivery trucks, but also efficient routing of data on the Internet,[3] or manufacturing objects with as little machine movement as possible.[4]

A difficult Search problem is the Boolean Satisfiability Problem (SAT). Given a large set of statements such as 'A or B', 'not A or B or C' or just 'D', a true/false value has to be assigned to every variable (A to D in our example) such that *every* statement is true. Finding solutions to SAT problems, in reasonable time, is so difficult that there is an ongoing world-wide competition of SAT algorithms.[5] SAT is

---

[2] Huang (2018), pp. 3513–3525.

[3] Dantzig (1960), pp. 187–190.

[4] Cantor and Gerla (1974), pp. 1062–1069.

[5] Heule et al. (2024), The International SAT Competition Web Page, http://www.satcompetition.org/.

used to find how to update a Linux system,[6] prove that two logic circuits perform the same operation (used in silicon manufacturing), or detect the impact of DNA mutations in the occurrence of diseases.[7]

Finally, Search is often used in games to produce artificial opponents, such as in chess,[8] make virtual opponents move in an intelligent way,[9] or play the game itself.[10] This last point has more of an academic purpose than a real-world use.

2.1.2 Algorithms

The best-known algorithm for Search is A*.[11] If we introduce a concept of quality of the solution, Optimisation algorithms are numerous and include Iterated Local Search,[12] the nature-inspired Ant-Colony Optimisation algorithm[13]—that considers virtual ants that depose virtual pheromones that evaporate over time, so that the shortest path automatically contains the most pheromones - genetic algorithms[14] and the cross-entropy method.[15]

The above algorithms are compatible with black-box function, for which no knowledge is available. White-box functions are known to the algorithm, that is able to perform operations on it. With white-box functions, approaches such as Gradient Descent are available.[16] Gradient descent needs to compute the gradient (derivative) of the function, hence its need to know the equations of the function. Gradient Descent is presented in more details later in this chapter, as it is the core of how Neural Networks (part of Machine Learning) are trained.

2.2 Natural Language Processing

Natural language processing considers every operation performed by a computer on human-understandable or human-produced language, in all its forms. This broad research field includes, for instance, translation, voice recognition, sentiment analysis (from a piece of text, inferring the mood of the writer), text to speech (having a

---

[6] Libzypp library, https://en.opensuse.org/Portal:Libzypp.

[7] Haworth and Hernandez (2021), pp. 62–73.

[8] Maharaj et al. (2022), p. 550.

[9] Marques-Silva (2008), pp. 74–80.

[10] Haworth and Hernandez (2021), pp. 62–73.

[11] Cui and Shi (2011), pp. 125–130.

[12] Lourenço et al. (2003), pp. 320–353.

[13] Dorigo et al. (2006), pp. 28–39.

[14] Sivanandam and Deepa (2008), pp. 15–37.

[15] De Boer et al. (2005), pp. 19–67.

[16] Ruder (2016). arXiv preprint arXiv:1609.04747.

machine pronounce words), or text understanding (having a machine follow natural language instructions, for instance).

The two main aims of Natural Language Processing are:

- Proposing a user interface that is intuitive for as many people as possible. NLP algorithms are used here to produce natural language text or speech, and/or to understand natural language text or speech. Chatbots and automatic voicemails are examples of user-facing NLP systems. For this point, the user that interacts with the NLP system does it in real-time. The user is in front of the system.
- Extracting knowledge from human discourse produced some significant time in the past (not a user in front of a machine). Text summarisation, voice recognition on archive data, and optical character recognition (turning photos of old documents to real text, searchable by a computer) are examples of NLP used to human-produced text or voice to digital data on which further processing can be done.

Some tasks, such as Machine Translation (translating between two natural languages) can be performed either in real-time or on historical data.

2.2.1 Real-World Applications

Natural Language processing has been used to propose user-friendly human-machine interfaces, such as voice-based automatic answering machines[17] and chatbots that people interact with using natural language. Producing speech with a machine also helps accessibility, with tools such as Read Aloud[18] that transform text on webpages and documents to speech, to help blind people navigate the Internet.

Going in the other direction, understanding human speech leads to easy-to-use dictation devices[19] and automatic video subtitling, used, for instance, by the Czech Parliament to offer subtitled meetings.[20] That last application is particularly interesting when combined with Machine Translation, which allows someone to understand a foreigner in real time.[21]

Reading human script is also often considered Natural Language Processing (some people consider that it is part of Computer Vision) and is used in note-taking applications[22] and to automatically read addresses on paper mail.[23]

[17] McCarthy et al. (2017), p. e7817.

[18] LSD Software, Read Aloud: A Text to Speech Voice Reader, https://addons.mozilla.org/en-US/firefox/addon/read-aloud/.

[19] Nuance, Dragon Speech Recognition, https://www.nuance.com/dragon.html.

[20] Pražák et al. (2006), pp. 501–508.

[21] Zhang and Huang (2016).

[22] Grahame (2016), pp. 47–50.

[23] Rosenbaum et al. (1993).

Finally, sentiment analysis allows to give an overall score or quality to a piece of text (or speech). It is used to flag customers that need special attention, complains that are worth looking at, mis-information on the Internet,[24] detect suicidal people,[25] detect possible child abuse,[26] etc.

2.2.2 Algorithms

Understanding written human text requires methods such as classical parsing[27] (that looks at the words, and knows the grammar of the language, to analyse sentences) or Machine Learning approaches such as Sequence-to-Sequence neural networks.[28] Machine Learning is explored in more details later in this chapter.

Understanding speech requires signal processing such as Fourier Transforms, that map an audio signal to a description of the frequencies (high, medium, low pitches) in it.[29] Then, phoneme detection identifies sounds like vowels and consonants, before grouping them in words.[30] As is often the case in Natural Language Processing, where the tasks to be performed (understanding speech, understanding text, translation, etc.) are complicated, but data abundant, Machine Learning approaches often compete or outperform hand-written algorithms based on expect linguistic knowledge. For instance, speech recognition can also be performed from sound directly to text by a neural network.[31]

Optical Character Recognition can be performed by matching the shape of letters to images of characters, or by training a neural network to do the task.[32] Sentiment analysis can be performed in various ways, from the simplest (looking for specific keywords, or counting occurrences of some words) to Machine Learning approaches,[33] some of them able to infer that sentences such as 'This movie is as pleasant as an ice-cream by a cold winter day' is a negative review.

---

[24] Bhutani et al. (2019), pp. 1–5.

[25] Christensen et al. (2014), pp. 8193–8212.

[26] Lyu et al. (2020), p. 105250.

[27] Collins (2003), pp. 589–637.

[28] Lewis et al. (2019). arXiv preprint arXiv:1910.13461.

[29] Liu et al. (2019), pp. 4727–4739.

[30] Ostendorf and Roukos (1989), pp. 1857–1869.

[31] Chorowski et al. (2015), p. 28.

[32] Charles et al. (2012), pp. 659–662.

[33] Yadollahi et al. (2017), pp. 1–33.

2.3 Knowledge Representation and Reasoning

One of the most valuable resources of mankind is knowledge. We collect vast amounts of it in different places (libraries, or digital archives), we build institutions with the sole purpose of transferring this knowledge (schools), and most of our current welfare is obtained thanks to applications of this knowledge. In order to transfer this knowledge, we typically use natural language. However, to transfer this knowledge to a computer, or some other artificially intelligent agent, for it to use this knowledge intelligently, natural language no longer suffices. Natural language is often ambiguous, and computers are (still) far from close to humans in resolving these ambiguities. For this reason, *logics* are developed. They are formal languages (and hence, without ambiguities, and perfectly interpretable by a machine), often designed to not just be readable by machines, but also by humans. For instance, the sentence 'All men are human' can be expressed as $\forall m : Man(m) \rightarrow Human(m)$ in typed first-order logic. With the knowledge that '$\forall$' is read '*for all*', and '$\rightarrow$' is 'implies', we can recognise the original natural language sentence and interpret the formula as 'for any object or idea "m", if m is a man, then m is a human'.

Once knowledge has been represented in a formal way, it can be used in several to perform several tasks. For instance, deducing conclusions from a set of statements, proving whether something is true or false, or explaining something by producing the smallest amount possible of statements that will cause some recipient of these statements to deduce what we want it to deduce.

2.3.1 Real-World Applications

Databases constitute the most-used application of logic in computer science. All communication with databases happens through logic. Somewhat more recently, the *semantic web* has surged in popularity. The idea underlying the semantic web is that any agent (human or artificial) on the internet can publish not just textual webpages, but also logical elements, such as information about themselves or others online.[34] Publishing this knowledge openly makes it reusable for other agents. Moreover, each agent can publish this knowledge using their own ontology, for instance while one might use the symbol 'marriedTo' to represent the relation between two people, someone else might use 'spouse'. How these different ontologies relate can then again be represented in a suitable logic. Other applications of logic and knowledge include: *certifying correctness of hardware design* (see the description of Boolean satisfiability above), *configuration tools*, where a complex system needs to be configured, either automatically, or in interaction with a human, *verifying correctness of other systems,* or even *explaining decisions made by other AI methods.*

[34] Hitzler (2021), pp. 76–83.

2.4 Machine Learning

Machine Learning is the last big subfield of Artificial Intelligence that we consider in this chapter, on purpose, to emphasise that despite the hype for Machine Learning, Artificial Intelligence is much broader than that. Regulators must therefore pay extra attention to whether they want to regulate Machine Learning (and its fundamental aspect, the fact that a machine learns) or something bigger in AI (for its close interaction with people for instance).

Machine Learning considers problems in which an algorithm has to extract knowledge from inputs presented to it. The extracted knowledge is what the algorithm 'learns' and is a summary of the inputs that have been presented to the algorithm.

Three families of Machine Learning algorithms exist:

- Supervised Learning, the best known by the general public. The algorithm is presented a large set of input-output pairs, called the training set (sometimes also the dataset, but training set is more precise). An example of such set is a large list of photos along with the name of the person in the photo. The goal of the algorithm is to learn a mapping from input to output, that correctly maps the inputs seen during training to their respective outputs, and also, hopefully, correctly maps new inputs (not seen during training) to the outputs they should have. The knowledge extracted by the algorithm is the mapping, some computer data that can have many different forms depending on the exact algorithm, such as the description of a decision tree, or the weights of a neural network. The important aspect is that the mapping is somewhat tangible, as it can be represented as a computer file, and is most of the times orders of magnitude smaller than the training set used to produce it.
- Unsupervised Learning has no output. The algorithm is presented a large amount of inputs and learns the structure of it. The knowledge it extracts can then be used for a computer to answer questions such as 'have I already seen something similar?' or 'is this significantly different from what I've seen when training?'.
- Reinforcement Learning sits somewhat in-between. It considers a setting in which the learning algorithm (here called the 'agent') has to learn how to perform a sequential task, such as assembling something, guiding a user on a website, managing the heating and cooling of a building, bidding on an energy market, etc. The agent is provided inputs (called 'states'), such as images acquired through a camera, and executes actions, such as moving a robot arm or turning on a machine in an industrial plant. After every action, the agent is provided with a reward, a single number that can be anything, positive or negative. The objective of the agent is, by trying actions and observing rewards, to progressively learn what action leads to the best-possible sum of future rewards in any particular state. Reinforcement Learning is used when the designer of a system knows what has to be done (and hence can produce rewards) but not how to do it (in which case Supervised Learning would have been more efficient).

- Reinforcement Learning is not Supervised Learning because the agent is not told what to do in every state, it only observes rewards and has to guess, try and learn what to do. Reinforcement Learning is not Unsupervised either, because the rewards are there, the agent is fully alone doing its task.

2.4.1 Real-World Applications

Machine Learning can be applied to so many real-world domains that it sometimes feels like anything can be done with Machine Learning. Because listing these applications is not possible in a book chapter, we instead choose to only succinctly present some applications of Machine Learning and dedicate more pages later to explaining how these algorithms work and how they can potentially impact society.

Supervised Learning is used whenever some annotated data is available, and an automated way of generalising that annotated data is desirable. Supervised learning can be used in biology to count cells, detect cancerous cells and predict the structure or function of proteins.[35] It also excels in Computer Vision, where it can be used to recognise handwriting,[36] producing a textual description of the contents of images,[37] detecting corrosion on public infrastructure,[38] or analysing satellite images for signs of human activity and needs.[39] Supervised Learning also achieved great success in Machine Translation,[40] a task on which human knowledge (knowing vocabulary lists, grammar rules, etc) was thought to be necessary.

Unsupervised Learning is mainly used for fraud detection,[41] and generative modelling,[42] a task in which 'things' are shown to the algorithm, that learns to produce new (original) 'things' that look like the algorithm saw during training, such as new images in the pointillist style. Obstacle detection can also be performed with Unsupervised Learning[43]: if the algorithm has seen obstacle-free routes during training, and it does not recognise what it sees, then there is most probably an obstacle somewhere.

Reinforcement Learning first attracted wide attention in the AI field when it allowed a computer program to beat the human champion at Go,[44] a board game previously thought to be 50 years ahead of what AI can do. Outside of game playing, Reinforcement Learning is used whenever we know what has to be done, but

[35] Larranaga et al. (2006), pp. 86–112.

[36] Dutta et al. (2018). pp. 80–85.

[37] Hossain et al. (2019), pp. 1–36.

[38] Atha and Jahanshahi (2018), pp. 1110–1128.

[39] Yeh et al. (2020), pp. 1–11.

[40] Popel et al. (2020), pp. 1–15.

[41] Hilas and Mastorocostas (2008), pp. 721–726.

[42] Salakhutdinov (2015), pp. 361–385.

[43] Wellington et al. (2006), pp. 1287–1304.

[44] Silver et al. (2017), pp. 354–359.

not how to do it, such as optimising the cooling of large datacenters,[45] designing efficient prevention strategies for infectious diseases.[46]

2.4.2 Biases in Data and in Algorithms

Machine Learning considers mathematical approaches that extract knowledge from the data presented to them, using formulas and algorithms. No part of them has a consciousness or knows the rules of society. This means that Machine Learning algorithms are inherently unbiased but are also completely unable to correct the bias in the data they receive, to detect that they are tricked, or that their output is improper or impolite.

Several events have sparked interest towards biases in Machine Learning, and how to avoid them. Microsoft Corporation once design at chatbot that could learn from the interactions it had with people, and that was quickly turned to a racist and nazi propaganda machine by Twitter users.[47] Microsoft disabled the chatbot shortly after deploying it. Google developed an image recognition engine that worked very well but never saw dark-skinned people in its training set (probably because nobody designing it thought of that). It was however presented with numerous images of gorillas, annotated as 'gorilla', and over-generalised in a way that some Black people were classified as gorillas.[48] The system was taken offline and Google apologised profusely.

There are two takeaways in the examples listed above: first, even big tech companies had biases in their datasets, and damaged their public image due to it. Second, the problem always comes from the dataset. A very simple example of a Machine Learning algorithm could be the simple computation of an average, for which an exact mathematical formula exists. There is no bias in the formula. But if only the height of tall people is given to the average function, then it will predict that the average height of humans is much larger than what it actually is.

Correcting biases in Machine Learning systems is therefore a human problem, not an algorithmic one. People gathering data for Machine Learning should be well aware of their own possible biases, and on how to collect balanced datasets.[49]

---

[45] Li et al. (2019), pp. 2002–2013.

[46] Libin et al. (2020), pp. 155–170.

[47] Schwartz (2019), In 2016, Microsoft's Racist Chatbot Revealed the Dangers of Online Conversation, https://spectrum.ieee.org/in-2016-microsofts-racist-chatbot-revealed-the-dangers-of-online-conversation.

[48] Barr (2015), Google Mistakenly Tags Black People as 'Gorillas,' Showing Limits of Algorithms, https://www.wsj.com/articles/BL-DGB-42522.

[49] Mehrabi et al. (2021), pp. 1–35.

2.4.3 Explainable Machine Learning

Explainable Machine Learning, also sometimes referred to as Explainable AI (Machine Learning is sometimes confused with the wider field of AI), focuses on the interaction between an algorithm, and the people who use it. Contrary to biases discussed above, that consider the data presented to the algorithm, Explainability is purely an algorithmic issue. Most modern Machine Learning methods, such as neural networks, are perfectly grounded, use exact algorithms for which every formula is known, but the formulas are so far from how the human brain works that it is impossible, given a prediction or decision output by the algorithm, to know *why* it produced that prediction.

An illustration of that problem is a neural network based method for predicting whether someone could pay back a loan. The description of a person comes in (age, salary, household size, etc), and a yes or no answer is produced by the algorithm. Neural networks are built on matrix multiplications and simple operations such as sinuses. However, nobody, given the description of a person and the numerical value of every cell of a dozen of matrices, could explain why the loan was rejected.

Explainable Machine Learning considers technical approaches that allow to link inputs to outputs of algorithms in a way that makes more sense for humans. It is closely related to psychology and human-computer interface design. The field is still in its early days, but some results are already available, such as knowledge that people well-versed in a domain (banking, medicine, etc) are usually able to make sense of decision rules, decision trees, and simple regressions.[50] Several approaches therefore exist that first train an algorithm using an easily trainable but not-explainable method, such as neural networks, then *distills* the resulting knowledge to a set of rules or a decision tree, much harder to train but somewhat explainable.

2.4.4 Algorithms

Supervised Learning methods include decision trees, learned with algorithms such as ID3 and C4.5,[51] random forests,[52] support vector machines,[53] Gaussian mixture models[54] and neural networks. Because, for most people, AI is synonym with Machine Learning, that in turn is synonym with Neural Networks, we take the opportunity to briefly present them and explain how they work in the next section.

Unsupervised Learning methods include k-Nearest Neighbors,[55] algorithms that aim at quickly finding which data points look like some other data point, Gaussian

[50] Arrieta et al. (2020), pp. 82–115.

[51] Singh and Gupta (2014), pp. 97–103.

[52] Biau and Scornet (2016), pp. 197–227.

[53] Hearst et al. (1998), pp. 18–28.

[54] Rasmussen (1999), p. 12.

[55] Friedman et al. (1975), pp. 1000–1006.

mixture models referenced above, and special kinds of neural networks used for generative modelling. Generative modelling consists of observing a dataset, learning its structure and inherent properties, and be able to generate new data points that look like what was in the dataset. The first main generative modelling approaches is Generative Adversarial Neural networks,[56] in which two neural networks, the generator and the discriminator, are trained together. The generator is rewarded for producing outputs that the discriminator is unable to differentiate from the original dataset. The discriminator is rewarded for being able to tell apart generated and original data points. The second Generative Modelling approach is Variational Autoencoders,[57] in which a single neural network learns to map an original datapoint to something that looks as close as possible to it, with some randomness in the network that allows to 'vary' the output and produce new data points that look like the ones in the dataset.

Reinforcement Learning methods are divided in two families, depending on whether they learn how good doing something in a particular situation is (value-based methods), or how often they should perform an action in a particular situation (policy-based methods). Both approaches have strengths and weaknesses on different domains, and none dominates the other. Value-based methods include DQN,[58] known to play Atari games at human level, its modern variants such as Rainbow,[59] and the MuZero algorithm[60] that combines value-based Reinforcement Learning with a Search algorithm (Monte-Carlo Tree Search) to achieve super-human level on the game of Go. Policy-based methods usually perform better than value-based methods on robotic tasks, with the two dominant approaches being PPO[61] and, the current state-of-the-art, the Soft Actor-Critic.[62]

2.4.5 Neural Networks

The term 'neural network' originates from the work of Rosenblatt et al. in 1958 on the Perceptron, a proposed computer model of how the brain stores data.[63] Since that visionary paper, the same architecture (simple components connected in layers, like the neurons in the brain) has been used for progressively more advanced methods, such as the multi-layer perceptron,[64] backpropagation,[65] convolutional neural

---

[56] Goodfellow et al. (2020), pp. 139–144.

[57] Kingma and Welling (2013), arXiv preprint arXiv:1312.6114.

[58] Mnih et al. (2015), pp. 529–533.

[59] Hessel et al. (2018).

[60] Schrittwieser et al. (2021), pp. 27580–27591.

[61] Schulman et al. (2017). arXiv preprint arXiv:1707.06347.

[62] Haarnoja et al. (2018). arXiv preprint arXiv:1812.05905.

[63] Rosenblatt (1958), p. 386.

[64] Ruck et al. (1990), pp. 40–48.

[65] Almeida (1989), pp. 199–208.

networks[66] and recurrent neural networks.[67] These methods continued to be called 'neural networks', even though they are now very far from how neurons and the brain work.

In the modern literature, a neural network is any kind of differentiable parametric function. A function 'f' computes an output 'y' given some input 'x', which is usually denoted 'y = f(x)'. The computation done by f can be anything, from a simple addition to a large sequence of mathematical operations. A parametric function adds another input, θ (theta), the parameter, to form 'y = f(x, θ)'.

Using a parametric function for supervised learning is straightforward: given examples of inputs 'x' and outputs 'y', the learning algorithm has to find θ such that the outputs predicted by 'f' are as close as possible to the true outputs presented to the algorithms. Gradient descent[68] does this by assuming that 'f' is differentiable, hence has a gradient, a mathematical concept that answers the question 'how should I change θ for the output of f(x, θ) to be a bit closer to the true output y'. Explaining how it is done is outside the scope of this chapter, but the Gradient Descent review referenced above can easily be followed by an interested reader with (good) high-school mathematical literacy.

The most important take-away of this section is that a neural network is therefore not magical. It is a piece of computer code that computes an output given some input and a parameter θ (usually by performing a number of matrix multiplications and some additions), and the Gradient Descent algorithm, that allows to find θ such that the outputs produced by the function are close to what can be found in some dataset. Everything in these algorithms has exact implementations, readable by any programmer, and devoid of incantations, dark magic or randomness.

3 Defining Artificial Intelligence

The first part of this chapter focused on exploring and detailing several areas of Artificial Intelligence system. By listing what is, at the time of writing this chapter, done on a regular basis by Artificial Intelligence researchers, we aim at helping the reader grasping the scope of current AI research, but also how big it is, how varied it is, and how difficult to succinctly define it is.

[66] LeCun and Bengio (1995), p. 1995.

[67] Hochreiter and Schmidhuber (1997), pp. 1735–1780.

[68] Ruder (2016). arXiv preprint arXiv:1609.04747.

3.1 Artificially-Intelligent Nature or Behavior

Artificial Intelligence may refer to the research field of AI, intelligent systems (AI systems), and Artificial Intelligence tasks such as text translation, speech recognition, or image captioning:

1. The research field of Computer Science that focuses on defining Intelligence, studying it in natural systems, and replicating it in computer programs and algorithms. Artificial Intelligence research also encompasses mathematics concepts such as proofs, formal logic and numerical analysis. Artificial Intelligence research is usually self-defined: researchers claim that they do, or do not do, Artificial Intelligence research.
2. Artificial Intelligence systems, such as robots, computer software, or web platforms, that have a particular hardware or software realisation (e.g. it uses Machine Learning and this particular Planning algorithm). This definition focuses on *how* a system performs a task, its *technical means*. It is possible to use Machine Learning to propose holiday trips to people on a website (which would fall under this definition of an Artificial Intelligence system), but it is also possible to propose holiday trips at random, which would then not be considered being Artificially Intelligent by most people.
3. An Artificial Intelligence task or problem. This is a specific outcome that has to be reached, such as 'finding the shortest path from A to B'. This definition focuses on *what* task has to be performed, the *overall objective* (as opposed to the technical means above). As in mathematics, the set of Artificial Intelligence tasks is assumed to be timeless and perpetual, part of the Universe. We, humans, discover the existence of these problems as society evolves.

Schuett et al. study in more detail the difference between defining Artificial Intelligence according to what a system does, or how it does it.[69]

Interestingly, while non-AI experts focus on the Point 2 above approach to recognising and defining AI (focusing on the tools and means used to achieve an objective), AI researchers follow Point 3, and systematically wonder whether a particular task is Artificial Intelligence by nature, or could be solved without Artificial Intelligence.

In the remaining of this chapter, we argue that we should focus on Point 3: is a particular task an Artificial Intelligence task? A system is then an AI system if it solves an AI task, regardless of the means used. We believe that a definition built on *what it does* is longer-term, and more robust to future technological developments.

We also hope that defining AI according to what a system does, not how it does it, will avoid some of the early criticism that was received by the AI Act early in its inception[70]: an AI system is regulated or forbidden based on what it does, its particu-

[69] Schuett (2019). arXiv preprint arXiv:1909.01095.

[70] MacCarthy and Propp (2021), https://www.brookings.edu/blog/techtank/2021/05/04/machines-learn-that-brussels-writes-the-rules-the-eus-new-ai-regulation/.

lar use or deployment in the real world. A malevolent entity thus cannot pretend not to be using AI. It is also clearer that the use of the tool is forbidden, not the making of the tool itself.

Focusing on the what, the task performed by a system, instead of how it does it, also nicely reflects the general rule of Law that someone should be judged on their actions and not their nature.

3.2 *Definitions Used in the Artificial Intelligence Act*

The Artificial Intelligence Act refers to AI systems and tasks in various places, and tries to define AI in a succinct yet general enough way. A complete review of the Act is outside the scope of this chapter, but we provide some snippets of the Act with comments on the definitions they contain.

In this section, we refer to Articles and Annexes from a pre-approval version of the AI Act[71] of April 2024.

Article 3 contains a very brief definition of AI:

> 'AI system' is a machine-based system designed to operate with varying levels of autonomy and that may exhibit adaptiveness after deployment and that, for explicit or implicit objectives, infers, from the input it receives, how to generate outputs such as predictions, content, recommendations, or decisions that can influence physical or virtual environments;

This definition focuses on what the system does, with a mention that it is machine-based (man-made may have been clearer). We note that a succinct list of AI tasks, such as prediction and recommendation, are listed. These tasks appear to focus mostly on Machine Learning, and tasks such as logic reasoning, planning, function optimisation, or translation, are not mentioned. The 'may' in the definition ensures that it is not a closed list, and allows for any machine-based system to be considered an AI system. This links to Article 5 that we discuss now:

> (a) the placing on the market, putting into service or use of an AI system that deploys subliminal techniques beyond a person's consciousness or purposefully manipulative or deceptive techniques, with the objective to or the effect of materially distorting a person's or a group of persons' behaviour by appreciably impairing the person's ability to make an informed decision, thereby causing the person to take a decision that that person would not have otherwise taken in a manner that causes or is likely to cause that person, another person or group of persons significant harm;

Article 5 provides a description of actions a system cannot perform, which completely focuses on the *what* a system does. Combined with Article 3, that has a very open definition of an AI system, it seems that the regulators tried to rephrase the AI Act to actually not care about whether a system is an AI system or not.

[71] The AI Act (pre-approval version from April 2024), EUR-Lex document 52021PC0206, https://www.europarl.europa.eu/meetdocs/2014_2019/plmrep/COMMITTEES/CJ40/AG/2024/02-13/1296003EN.pdf.

Earlier versions of the draft, consulted by the author in 2020 and 2021, had a definition of 'AI System' that was less open and explicitly listed AI methods (focusing on the how). Criticism about allowing forbidden tasks if they are done by a non-AI system seems to have been addressed by making it impossible to say that a system is not AI.

The analysis of the definitions of AI in the AI Act already stop here, because the Act does not try to provide further definitions of AI. The rest of the Act focuses on forbidden or regulated activities (what, not how), mentioning the term 'AI' often, but always ensuring that the 'AI' in 'AI System' is wide enough that any man-made machine, algorithm or device falls into the definition. The authors of this chapter welcome this phrasing in the AI Act and draw the parallel with how the legal system aims for, and should, judge persons according to their actions and not their nature.

3.3 Tentative Definition Focusing on the What

While Sect. 2 provides a detailed list of fields in Artificial Intelligence research, which gives an intuition of what AI is through examples, we propose in this section a short discussion on how to concisely define AI, in a way that is broad enough to cover current and futures applications of AI, yet simple enough to be understandable by the general public. We don't aim at providing a legal definition of AI, and strive to focus on what a system does, not how it does it.

3.3.1 Artificial System

For most people, the Artificial part of Artificial Intelligence is important, and a person is not an AI system. It is however an open question of whether some Artificial Intelligence forbidden activities (such as tricking a person or causing harm to them) remain forbidden if they are performed by something that is not an AI system, such as a person or an animal. In case it is important to distinguish a person from a 'system' in 'AI system', we propose the following definition of *system*:

> A man-made artifact that is not a legal person, such as, but not limited to, a robot, a website, a computer program or a physical object.

This definition aims at considering everything possible, except for natural elements (animals, plants, the Earth) and people. We consider that a trained dog is not an AI System. We also consider that, if, in the future, some advanced computer programs or robots act such that that society recognises them as people and makes them legal persons, these 'persons' are not systems anymore and should be judged on their own.

The definition above provides a brief list of systems, that includes websites and physical objects. We believe that it is important to note that AI may be deployed on many physical devices, not only computers or robots. A website is usually not considered a robot, but, because it presents information to a person and is dynamic (it can react to clicks), a website may still have significant psychological impact on the human being visiting it and is not just a nice-looking sheet of paper.

3.3.2 Artificial Intelligence System

We aim at defining an Artificial Intelligence System as:

> A system that performs an Artificial Intelligence task.

We therefore purely focus on *what* the system does and do not mention any possible technical mean of achieving the task. This simple definition builds on the definition of what an AI task is.

3.3.3 Artificial Intelligence Task

Defining what is an Artificial Intelligence Task is the most difficult aspect of the definition. We observe in the literature several directions being followed to define an AI task:

- Approaches that focus on *intelligence*: an AI task is a task that requires intelligence. This then allows to move to philosophy and thousands of years of thinking about what *intelligence* is. In his book The Quest for Artificial Intelligence,[72] Niels J. Nielsson defines intelligence as: 'intelligence is that quality that enables an entity to function appropriately and with foresight in its environment'.
- Approaches that focus on the effect of the task: an AI task is a task that requires interacting directly or indirectly with people, or computing something based on data generated by people, or producing data or decisions that will be used by people or will influence people. The aim of this approach is to avoid falling into 'everything is AI', because, following the definition of intelligence by Nielsson, any useful computer program or algorithm is intelligent (and therefore AI). This approach tries to make the distinction between algorithms that interact with people (websites, loan decisions, chatbots) and algorithms that don't (motion planning in a factory, packet routing on the Internet).
- Approaches based on lists: the approach followed by the AI Act, that sometimes refers to an AI task as any task *listed in some Annex*. This approach is the most precise, but also the most anchored in current times. Creative people come up with new tasks to artificially solve every day, and identifying which ones are AI, to update a legal document, would require significant work.

If the aim of a definition of AI is to select what tools or products fall under a regulation, we propose to adopt the widest-possible definition, to avoid missing a tool or product. We therefore suggest following the *intelligence* approach, even though it

[72] Nilsson (2009).

encompasses most if not all computer programs and algorithms. Over-simplifying things a bit, we therefore propose that everything artificial and that performs something (so, every robot even the simplest one, every dynamic website, every computer program) is an Artificial Intelligence System.

4 Conclusion

In this chapter, we aimed at providing a definition of Artificial Intelligence. The first section started with an overview of Computer Science, and gave an intuition of what an algorithm is, and how tangible it is. The second section explored the area of Artificial Intelligence research, and described a selection of tasks tackled by AI. Finally, the third section took a step back and discussed how Artificial Intelligence can be defined based on what an AI system does, to finally propose a succinct definition.

References

Almeida LB (1989) Backpropagation in perceptrons with feedback. In: Neural computers. Springer, Berlin, Heidelberg, pp 199–208

Arrieta AB, Díaz-Rodríguez N, Del Ser J, Bennetot A, Tabik S, Barbado A et al (2020) Explainable artificial intelligence (XAI): concepts, taxonomies, opportunities and challenges toward responsible AI. Inf Fusion 58:82–115

Atha DJ, Jahanshahi MR (2018) Evaluation of deep learning approaches based on convolutional neural networks for corrosion detection. Struct Health Monit 17(5):1110–1128

Bhutani B, Rastogi N, Sehgal P, Purwar A (2019, August) Fake news detection using sentiment analysis. In: In 2019 twelfth international conference on contemporary computing (IC3). IEEE, pp 1–5

Biau G, Scornet E (2016) A random forest guided tour. Test 25(2):197–227

Cantor DG, Gerla M (1974) Optimal routing in a packet-switched computer network. IEEE Trans Comput 23(10):1062–1069

Charles PK, Harish V, Swathi M, Deepthi CH (2012) A review on the various techniques used for optical character recognition. Int J Eng Res Appl 2(1):659–662

Chorowski JK, Bahdanau D, Serdyuk D, Cho K, Bengio Y (2015) Attention-based models for speech recognition. Adv Neural Inf Process Syst 28

Christensen H, Batterham PJ, O'Dea B (2014) E-health interventions for suicide prevention. Int J Environ Res Public Health 11(8):8193–8212

Collins M (2003) Head-driven statistical models for natural language parsing. Comput Linguist 29(4):589–637

Cui X, Shi H (2011) A*-based pathfinding in modern computer games. Int J Comput Sci Netw Secur 11(1):125–130

Dantzig GB (1960) On the shortest route through a network. Manag Sci 6(2):187–190

De Boer PT, Kroese DP, Mannor S, Rubinstein RY (2005) A tutorial on the cross-entropy method. Ann Oper Res 134(1):19–67

Dorigo M, Birattari M, Stutzle T (2006) Ant colony optimization. IEEE Comput Intell Mag 1(4):28–39

Dutta K, Krishnan P, Mathew M, Jawahar CV (2018) Improving CNN-RNN hybrid networks for handwriting recognition. In: In 2018 16th international conference on frontiers in handwriting recognition (ICFHR). IEEE, pp 80–85
Friedman JH, Baskett F, Shustek LJ (1975) An algorithm for finding nearest neighbors. IEEE Trans Comput 100(10):1000–1006
Goodfellow I, Pouget-Abadie J, Mirza M, Xu B, Warde-Farley D, Ozair S et al (2020) Generative adversarial networks. Commun ACM 63(11):139–144
Grahame JA (2016) Digital note-taking: discussion of evidence and best practices. J Physician Assist Educ 27(1):47–50
Haarnoja T, Zhou A, Hartikainen K, Tucker G, Ha S, Tan J et al. (2018) Soft actor-critic algorithms and applications. arXiv preprint arXiv:1812.05905
Haworth G, Hernandez N (2021) The 20th top chess engine championship, TCEC20. J Int Comput Games Assoc 43(1):62–73
Hearst MA, Dumais ST, Osuna E, Platt J, Scholkopf B (1998) Support vector machines. IEEE Intell Syst Their Appl 13(4):18–28
Hessel, M., Modayil, J., Van Hasselt, H., Schaul, T., Ostrovski, G., Dabney, W., et al. (2018). Rainbow: Combining improvements in deep reinforcement learning. In Thirty-second AAAI conference on artificial intelligence
Heule M et al. (2024) The international SAT competition web page, http://www.satcompetition.org/
Hilas CS, Mastorocostas PA (2008) An application of supervised and unsupervised learning approaches to telecommunications fraud detection. Knowl-Based Syst 21(7):721–726
Hitzler P (2021) A review of the semantic web field. Commun ACM 64(2):76–83
Hochreiter S, Schmidhuber J (1997) Long short-term memory. Neural Comput 9(8):1735–1780
Hossain MZ, Sohel F, Shiratuddin MF, Laga H (2019) A comprehensive survey of deep learning for image captioning. ACM Comput Surv (CsUR) 51(6):1–36
Huang H, Bucher D, Kissling J, Weibel R, Raubal M (2018) Multimodal route planning with public transport and carpooling. IEEE Trans Intell Transp Syst 20(9):3513–3525
Kingma DP, Welling M (2013) Auto-encoding variational bayes. arXiv preprint arXiv:1312.6114
Larranaga P, Calvo B, Santana R, Bielza C, Galdiano J, Inza I et al (2006) Machine learning in bioinformatics. Brief Bioinform 7(1):86–112
LeCun Y, Bengio Y (1995). Convolutional networks for images, speech, and time series. In: The handbook of brain theory and neural networks. MIT Press, 3361(10), 1995
Lewis M, Liu Y, Goyal N, Ghazvininejad M, Mohamed A, Levy O et al. (2019). Bart: Denoising sequence-to-sequence pre-training for natural language generation, translation, and comprehension. arXiv preprint arXiv:1910.13461
Li Y, Wen Y, Tao D, Guan K (2019) Transforming cooling optimization for green data center via deep reinforcement learning. IEEE Transact Cybernet 50(5):2002–2013
Libin PJ, Moonens A, Verstraeten T, Perez-Sanjines F, Hens N, Lemey P, Nowé A (2020) Deep reinforcement learning for large-scale epidemic control. In: Joint European conference on machine learning and knowledge discovery in databases. Springer, Cham, pp 155–170
Liu W, Liao Q, Qiao F, Xia W, Wang C, Lombardi F (2019) Approximate designs for fast Fourier transform (FFT) with application to speech recognition. IEEE Transact Circuits Syst I Regul Pap 66(12):4727–4739
Lourenço HR, Martin OC, Stützle T (2003) Iterated local search. In: Handbook of metaheuristics. Springer, Boston, MA, pp 320–353
Lyu Y, Chow JCC, Hwang JJ (2020) Exploring public attitudes of child abuse in mainland China: a sentiment analysis of China's social media Weibo. Child Youth Serv Rev 116:105250
MacCarthy and Propp (2021) Machines learn that Brussels writes the rules: The EU's new AI regulation, https://www.brookings.edu/blog/techtank/2021/05/04/machines-learn-that-brussels-writes-the-rules-the-eus-new-ai-regulation/
Maharaj S, Polson N, Turk A (2022) Chess AI: competing paradigms for machine intelligence. Entropy 24(4):550

Marques-Silva J (2008) Practical applications of boolean satisfiability. In: In 2008 9th international workshop on discrete event systems. IEEE, pp 74–80
McCarthy IO, Wojno AE, Joseph HA, Teesdale S (2017) Check and report Ebola (CARE) hotline: the user perspective of an innovative tool for postarrival monitoring of Ebola in the United States. JMIR Public Health Surveill 3(4):e7817
Mehrabi N, Morstatter F, Saxena N, Lerman K, Galstyan A (2021) A survey on bias and fairness in machine learning. ACM Comput Surv (CSUR) 54(6):1–35
Mnih V, Kavukcuoglu K, Silver D, Rusu AA, Veness J, Bellemare MG et al (2015) Human-level control through deep reinforcement learning. Nature 518(7540):529–533
Nilsson NJ (2009) The quest for artificial intelligence. Cambridge University Press
Ostendorf M, Roukos S (1989) A stochastic segment model for phoneme-based continuous speech recognition. IEEE Trans Acoust Speech Signal Process 37(12):1857–1869
Popel M, Tomkova M, Tomek J, Kaiser Ł, Uszkoreit J, Bojar O, Žabokrtský Z (2020) Transforming machine translation: a deep learning system reaches news translation quality comparable to human professionals. Nat Commun 11(1):1–15
Pražák A, Psutka JV, Hoidekr J, Kanis J, Müller L, Psutka J (2006, September) Automatic online subtitling of the Czech parliament meetings. In: International conference on text, speech and dialogue. Springer, Berlin, Heidelberg, pp 501–508
Rasmussen C (1999) The infinite Gaussian mixture model. Adv Neural Inf Proces Syst 12
Rosenbaum WS, Carris BT, Ankerstjerne A (1993) U.S. Patent No. 5,249,687. U.S. Patent and Trademark Office, Washington, DC
Rosenblatt F (1958) The perceptron: a probabilistic model for information storage and organization in the brain. Psychol Rev 65(6):386–408
Ruck DW, Rogers SK, Kabrisky M (1990) Feature selection using a multilayer perceptron. J Neural Netw Comput 2(2):40–48
Ruder S (2016) An overview of gradient descent optimization algorithms. arXiv preprint arXiv:1609.04747
Salakhutdinov R (2015) Learning deep generative models. Ann Rev Statist Its Appl 2:361–385
Schrittwieser J, Hubert T, Mandhane A, Barekatain M, Antonoglou I, Silver D (2021) Online and offline reinforcement learning by planning with a learned model. Adv Neural Inf Proces Syst 34:27580–27591
Schuett J (2019) A legal definition of AI. arXiv preprint arXiv:1909.01095
Schulman J, Wolski F, Dhariwal P, Radford A, Klimov O (2017) Proximal policy optimization algorithms. arXiv preprint arXiv:1707.06347
Silver D, Schrittwieser J, Simonyan K, Antonoglou I, Huang A, Guez A et al (2017) Mastering the game of go without human knowledge. Nature 550(7676):354–359
Singh S, Gupta P (2014) Comparative study ID3, cart and C4.5 decision tree algorithm: a survey. Int J Adv Inf Sci Technol (IJAIST) 27(27):97–103
Sivanandam SN, Deepa SN (2008) Genetic algorithms. In: Introduction to genetic algorithms. Springer, Berlin, Heidelberg, pp 15–37
The AI Act (pre-approval version from April 2024), EUR-Lex document 52021PC0206, https://www.europarl.europa.eu/meetdocs/2014_2019/plmrep/COMMITTEES/CJ40/AG/2024/02-13/1296003EN.pdf
Van der Waerden BL (2013) A history of algebra: from al-Khwārizmī to Emmy Noether. Springer Science & Business Media
Wellington C, Courville A, Stentz A (2006) A generative model of terrain for autonomous navigation in vegetation. Int J Robot Res 25(12):1287–1304
Yadollahi A, Shahraki AG, Zaiane OR (2017) Current state of text sentiment analysis from opinion to emotion mining. ACM Comput Surv (CSUR) 50(2):1–33
Yeh C, Perez A, Driscoll A et al (2020) Using publicly available satellite imagery and deep learning to understand economic well-being in Africa. Nat Commun 11(1):1–11
Zhang G, Huang J (2016) U.S. Patent No. 9,477,657. U.S. Patent and Trademark Office, Washington, DC

Appraising the Institutional Framework of the EU's Artificial Intelligence Act (AI Act)

Abeer Malik and Barry Solaiman

Contents

Abstract This chapter critiques the institutional framework of the European Union's Artificial Intelligence Act (AI Act), the first comprehensive law to regulate AI globally. While the Act adopts a product safety model to leverage existing EU regulatory structures, it risks inheriting their limitations, raising questions about its ability to address AI's unique challenges. The analysis identifies several concerns, including overlapping roles and unclear mandates among key institutions, such as the European Commission and the newly established AI Office. These inefficiencies are compounded by the Act's integration into a broader, complex web of EU regulations, such as data and sector-specific laws, creating enforcement ambiguities and potential gaps in oversight. The chapter concludes by recommending clearer institutional delineations, streamlined governance mechanisms, and targeted reforms to align regulatory structures with the Act's goals. By addressing these issues, the EU can strengthen its capacity to ensure effective AI governance.

A. Malik (✉)
Harvard Law School, Cambridge, US

B. Solaiman
HBKU College of Law, Doha, Qatar

V. L. Raposo (ed.), *The European Artificial Intelligence Act*, Law, Governance and Technology Series 78, https://doi.org/10.1007/978-3-031-98406-8_5

1 Introduction

There has been an escalating demand from international bodies, industry leaders, and academic scholars for a unified global framework for AI governance. Notably, the UN Secretary-General and his Envoy on Technology have emphasised the necessity of internationally coordinated AI regulation, contending it is the only viable strategy to harness the benefits of AI for humanity while mitigating its risks and uncertainties.[1] The European Union's (EU) Artificial Intelligence Act (AI Act) is a landmark effort in this regard, marking the world's first significant attempt by a government body to regulate AI technologies across a region.[2] With its European AI Office (a central coordinating institution created under the AI Act) as 'the first body globally that enforces binding rules on AI', the AI Act positions itself as an international reference point.[3] The institutional governance framework of the AI Act is, thus, a pivotal element in the regulation of AI within the EU that merits thorough examination.

The AI Act follows a product safety regulatory approach—with the European Commission's (EC) 'Blue Guide' offering crucial soft law guidance—building upon decades of EU experience concerning product safety regulations.[4] From an institutional governance perspective, it has been posited that this approach may help circumvent enforcement issues that have arisen in the data protection sphere by leveraging existing mechanisms for EU coordination in product risks.[5] However, this approach brings with it a distinct set of problems. By grafting AI regulation onto legacy product safety structures, the Act risks emulating the very weaknesses that exist within those frameworks, potentially undermining its effectiveness. There are also concerns regarding the fundamental suitability of the governance architecture itself in achieving the aims of the AI Act.[6] Indeed, one must question whether

[1] Coeckelbergh (2024), p. 1; Section 2.3 of OECD (2024) Recommendation of the Council on Artificial Intelligence. https://legalinstruments.oecd.org/en/instruments/OECD-LEGAL-0449. For an analysis contrasting regulatory approaches to AI across key regions—the US, the EU, Asia, Africa, and the Americas—and a proposed general institutional network, see Walter (2024).

[2] Wörsdörfer (2023), p. 1.

[3] European Commission (2023) Commission Welcomes Political Agreement on Artificial Intelligence Act. https://ec.europa.eu/commission/presscorner/detail/en/ip_23_6473.

[4] Almada and Radu (2024), p. 3; Commission Notice – The 'Blue Guide' on the implementation of EU product rules 2022 (Text with EEA relevance) 2022/C 247/01 (Blue Guide) OJ C 247; Recitals 46 and 64 of Regulation of the European Parliament and of the Council on Laying Down Harmonised Rules on Artificial Intelligence and Amending Regulations (EC) No 300/2008, (EU) No 167/2013, (EU) No 168/2013, (EU) 2018/858, (EU) 2018/1139 and (EU) 2019/2144 and Directives 2014/90/EU, (EU) 2016/797 and (EU) 2020/1828 (Artificial Intelligence Act) OJ L, 2024/1689 (AI Act); the move from soft law to hard law has been described in the 'AI to Law' framework, see Solaiman (2023).

[5] Almada and Radu (2024), p. 3.

[6] See Solaiman and Malik (2024) for related critiques of how the AI Act's risk-based framework may empower private actors at the expense of end-users, particularly in healthcare context.

the AI Act is a 'castle built on sand'—a governance structure ill-suited to the unique complexities of AI technologies, threatening the very goals it seeks to achieve.

This chapter critically examines the institutional framework of the AI Act arguing that the Act lays out a complex, bureaucratic, and convoluted governance system and that its provisions lack precision. The chapter proceeds as follows. First, it examines the governance structures established under the AI Act, outlining the roles and responsibilities of the various institutions established at the Union and national levels, identifying drafting ambiguities and overlapping functions that blur their mandates. Second, it highlights how this already complex paradigm is further complicated when situating the AI Act within the broader and still developing regulatory ecosystem for AI the EU. Finally, the chapter concludes with recommendations for clarifying institutional roles to ensure effective AI governance.

One theme arising out of the analysis is that of excessive complexity. While convened for a different purpose, we posit that the findings of the Advisory Scientific Committee of the European Systemic Risk Board are apt in the context of the AI Act: 'Regulatory frameworks that are excessively complex can create the illusion of a well-controlled system, while creating incentives for players to game the system, possibly leading to additional risks'.[7] We do not make normative claims regarding the complexity of the Regulation but identify problematic areas that merit closer examination in future research. Indeed, the consequences of such complexity are amplified in the context of fundamental rights. A complex risk-based regulatory approach potentially restricts the EU's ambitions under the AI Act to effectively safeguard those rights and other values because the existing product safety framework is not designed to enhance those principles.[8]

2 Overview of Key Institutions

This section examines the various institutions with responsibility for governance under the AI Act created at the EU and national level. The AI Act adopts a tiered institutional model, centralising AI oversight in the new EU-level regulatory bodies, while assigning front-line responsibilities to the national regulators designated by individual Member States.[9] The legislative architecture has been outlined by Novelli et al., with institutions at the supranational (EU) level, the national level and the corporate level.[10] At the EU level, there is the European Commission (EC) under which the AI Office falls. The EC appoints an Advisory Forum and Scientific Panel of Independent Experts (Scientific Panel) that advise and support the other institu-

[7] Gai et al. (2019), p. 20.

[8] Almada and Radu (2024), p. 3.

[9] Ernst & Young Global Limited (2024) The European Union Artificial Intelligence Act. https://assets.ey.com/content/dam/ey-sites/ey-com/en_gl/topics/ai/ey-eu-AI Act-political-agreement-overview-february-2024.pdf.

[10] Novelli et al. (2024), p. 20.

Table 1 Composition, Appointment and Role of the Key Institutions

Institution	Composition	Appointed by	Role
AI Office	–	EC	Monitor and supervise compliance of GPAI models and ensure harmonised implementation and enforcement of the AI Act
AI Board	Representatives from each Member State	Member States	Advise and assist the EC and the Member States
Advisory Forum	Stakeholders from various sectors with expertise in AI—industry, start-ups, SMEs, civil society, and academia	EC	Provide technical expertise and advise the EC and the AI Board
Scientific Panel of Independent Experts	Independent experts from scientific community with technical expertise in AI	EC, in consultation with the AI Board	Provide expert scientific advice to assist the AI Office and the Member States
Notifying Authorities	Any public entity that meets their specific national organisational characteristics and needs.	Member States	Assess, designate and notify third-party conformity assessment bodies (CABs) and monitor their activities
Market Surveillance Authorities		Member States	Act as a single point of contact and conduct market surveillance to ensure that AI systems on the market conform to the applicable laws and regulations and comply with the existing EU health and safety requirements.[a]

[a] For a detailed examination of the implications of AI in healthcare, see Solaiman and Cohen (2024)
[b] Table inspired by Novelli et al. (2024), p. 11–12

tions. There is also the AI Board that stands separately at the EU level.[11] At the national level, the AI Act creates ‘national competent authorities’ (NCAs) consisting of at least one notifying authority and at least one market surveillance authority (MSA).[12] These NCAs provide advice and guidance on the implementation of the AI Act to SMEs in particular.[13] The entities at the Union and national levels monitor and assess conformity of institutions at the corporate level, such as AI providers.[14] Table 1 provides a brief snapshot of the specific composition, appointing entity and respective roles of each institution. The sections below examine the institutions in more detail.

[11] Recital 148 AI Act; EU Artificial Intelligence Act (2024) The AI Office: What is it, and how does it work?. https://artificialintelligenceact.eu/the-ai-office-summary/. European Commission (2024) European AI Office. https://digital-strategy.ec.europa.eu/en/policies/ai-office.

[12] Article 70(1) AI Act.

[13] Article 70(8) AI Act.

[14] Articles 53(3), 75(1), 16(k) and 34 AI Act.

2.1 *EU Level Institutions*

At the EU level, the AI Act establishes the AI Office, which is a conduit for the EC to develop expertise and capabilities in AI (facilitated by Member States).[15] The AI Act also establishes the AI Board to advise and facilitate the EC and Member States on the consistent and effective application of the AI Act.[16] An Advisory Forum and a Scientific Panel are further established to provide technical expertise, and support enforcement activities under the Regulation.[17]

2.1.1 The European Commission and the AI Office

The EC and the AI Office play distinct yet interrelated roles within the governance framework of the AI Act. The EC oversees compliance and enforcement of the AI Act, particularly through the AI Office which is tasked with monitoring and supervising AI systems. This section highlights the specific responsibilities assigned to each entity under the Act, and the potential challenges in delineating their functions that leave governance within the AI regulatory framework rather ambiguous.

2.1.1.1 Roles and Responsibilities of the EC

At the apex of the institutional structure is the EC, tasked with monitoring the effects of the AI Act by supervising compliance of general purpose AI (GPAI) models and ensuring enforcement of the Regulation through its AI Office.[18] The AI Act entrusts the EC with extensive responsibilities, including reporting on the use of real-time biometric identification systems,[19] setting standards for technical documentation of high-risk AI systems, developing benchmarks for the systems placed on the market to ensure they are accurate, robust and secure,[20] and developing guidelines for the implementation of the Act, the classification of high-risk AI systems as well as for the quality management systems.[21] To ensure the Regulation keeps pace with the technological advancements, the EC must assess the effectiveness of the Act and functioning of the AI Office at specified intervals, and submit reports to the European Parliament and the Council addressing any limitations.[22] To

[15] Article 64 AI Act.

[16] Articles 65 and 66 AI Act.

[17] Articles 67 and 68 AI Act.

[18] Article 88 AI Act.

[19] Article 5(7) AI Act.

[20] Articles 11(1) and 15(2) AI Act. For a discussion of how technical standards and conformity assessments may struggle to address opacity and explainability challenges in complex AI systems, see Solaiman and Bloom (2022).

[21] Articles 6, 63(1) and 96 AI Act.

[22] Article 112 AI Act.

this end, while the EC is empowered to adopt delegated acts to amend and update the AI Act—for example, by adding or modifying high-risk AI use cases in Annex III or updating EU declaration of conformity contents listed in Annex V[23]—the European Parliament or the Council may revoke this authority at any point.[24]

Additionally, the EC may issue standardisation requests to assist AI providers in demonstrating conformity with the AI Act. Where such a standardisation request is not accepted by the European Standardisation Organisation (ESO) or technical complexity of a harmonised standard delays its adoption, the EC is authorised to adopt common specifications after consultation with the Advisory Forum to aid compliance with the requirements.[25] Common specifications are akin to harmonised standards; however, unlike harmonised standards, which are developed by organisations independent of the EU, the development process of these specifications remains exclusively within the purview of EU institutions.[26] The AI Act further empowers the EC to request documentation from the AI providers, conduct evaluations of the GPAI models, request providers to take appropriate measures to effectively implement the Regulation, and impose fines for non-compliance.[27]

Some roles of the EC are dictated by data protection requirements. Thus, providers of high-risk AI systems are required to register information about their AI system in the EU database that is established and managed by the EC.[28] The database will have public and non-public sections. The EC is designated as the 'controller' for the purposes of Regulation (EU) 2018/1725, which applies to the processing of data by EU bodies.[29] Thus, the EC must comply with cybersecurity requirements, and ensure that access to non-public sections of the database is strictly limited.[30]

The EC's mandate also extends to assistance at the national level. In addition to supporting the NCAs with operating AI regulatory sandboxes, their post-market monitoring plan and serious incident reporting,[31] the EC is tasked with maintaining and updating lists of notified bodies, coordinating their activities and investigating their competence.[32]

[23] Articles 7(1), 43(5) and 47(5) AI Act.

[24] Article 97 AI Act.

[25] Articles 40-41 AI Act.

[26] Pouget (2024) Institutional Context. https://artificialintelligenceact.eu/context/.

[27] Articles 91-93 and 101 AI Act.

[28] Recital 131 and Article 71(1) AI Act.

[29] Recital 131 and Article 71(4)(6) AI Act.

[30] Recital 131 AI Act.

[31] Articles 57(1)(17), 58, 72(3) and 73 AI Act.

[32] Articles 35, 37 and 38 AI Act.

2.1.1.2 Roles and Responsibilities of the AI Office

The EC has established the AI Office as the central coordinating body to develop EU expertise and capabilities in AI and to enforce the AI Act through 'implementation, monitoring and supervision of AI systems and AI governance'.[33] The AI Office sits within the Commission as part of the Directorate-General for Communication Networks, Content and Technology (the 'Directorate General'), with a pivotal role in developing tools, methodologies and benchmarks to evaluate model capabilities; analysing systemic risks stemming from GPAI models; investigating potential infringement and non-compliance of the Regulation upon request from MSAs or on its own initiative; and ensuring uniform application of the AI Act.[34]

Notably, where an AI system is based on a GPAI model and both the model and system are developed by the same provider, the AI Office holds the powers of an MSA to monitor and supervise compliance of that AI system with the Regulation.[35] These powers, thus, grant the Office significant investigatory and enforcement capabilities within the Act's governance framework. The AI Office further has the authority to request technical documentation and any other relevant information from AI providers to assess compliance and conduct model evaluations. If an AI model potentially poses 'serious and substantiated concern of systemic risk', the AI Office may require AI providers to implement mitigation measures or restrict, withdraw or recall the model from the market, where it deems appropriate.[36] The AI Office is also mandated to provide standardised templates for areas under the AI Act upon the AI Board's request, create information platforms and central databases, support enforcing rules on banned and high-risk AI by coordinating with the sectoral bodies and national authorities, organise communication campaigns on AI Act obligations, and promote best practices in AI-related public procurement procedures.[37]

An integral part of the AI Office's role is to encourage collaboration, owing to which the Office will also assist other institutions under the AI Act. This includes supporting the MSAs in conducting joint investigations by providing them access to information on GPAI;[38] serving as the Secretariat for the AI Board; providing administrative support to the Advisory Forum and the Scientific Panel; supporting NCAs in establishing and operating AI regulatory sandboxes to promote interaction and cross-border cooperation; assisting the EC in preparing decisions, implementing and delegated acts, guidelines documents, and standardisation requests; ensuring supervisory coordination with other EU regulations such as the Digital Services

[33] Articles 64 and 3(47) AI Act.

[34] Article 92(1) and Recital 162 AI Act; Article 3 of the Commission Decision of 24.1.2024 Establishing the European Artificial Intelligence Office C(2024) 390 final (Commission Decision Establishing the AI Office).

[35] Article 75 AI Act.

[36] Articles 92, 92 and 93 AI Act.

[37] Article 62(3) AI Act; Article 3 Commission Decision Establishing the AI Office.

[38] Articles 75(3) and 74(11) AI Act.

Act and the Digital Markets Act; and coordinating establishment of governance systems at both EU and national levels.[39] The Office will additionally facilitate cooperation within the EC and with the stakeholders at the inter-institutional and international levels.[40]

The AI Office and the AI Board are also jointly tasked with supporting development of codes of practice by collaborating with NCAs and consulting civil society organisations, stakeholders, and experts, including the Scientific Panel, where necessary.[41] While the EC ultimately holds the authority to approve these codes, if the codes cannot be finalised or the AI Office deems them inadequate, the EC may specify common rules for their implementation.[42] The AI Office and the AI Board will also evaluate the codes' achievements and contributions to the AI Act, review and adapt the codes, assist in assessing available standards, and monitor compliance with the Regulation, including adherence to the approved codes.[43] Additionally, the AI Office (and the Member States) will facilitate developing codes of conduct and governance mechanisms for voluntary application to AI systems not classified as high-risk.[44]

2.1.1.3 Drafting Infelicities

One of the drawbacks of the AI Act is that the role of the AI Office cannot easily be disentangled from the mandate of the EC given that the tasks of the EC are conducted through the AI Office.[45] One must examine other sources (explored below) to piece together the functions of the AI Office more clearly because the AI Act itself lacks clarity. The AI Act states that:

> 'AI Office' means the Commission's function of contributing to the implementation, monitoring and supervision of AI systems and general-purpose AI models, and AI governance, provided for in Commission Decision of 24 January 2024; references in this Regulation to the AI Office shall be construed as references to the Commission.[46]

This approach of referring to two entities results in an unclear delineation (at least textually) of these institutions. Despite the Act stating that one shall be construed as the other, it remains unclear where the responsibilities of each entity begin and end. There are provisions on the EC without reference to the AI Office despite explicit provisions to the AI Office existing elsewhere. For example, as noted above, there

---

[39] Article 3 Commission Decision Establishing the AI Office; See also Articles 65(8) and 57(15) AI Act.

[40] Articles 4-7 Commission Decision Establishing the AI Office.

[41] Recital 116 AI Act.

[42] Article 50(7) AI Act.

[43] Articles 56(6)(7) and 89(1) AI Act.

[44] Article 95(1) AI Act.

[45] Article 64 AI Act.

[46] Article 3(47) AI Act.

are provisions requiring the EC to oversee reports on real-time biometric identification systems, issue guidelines for AI system conditions, and cooperate with ENISA (the European Union Agency for Cybersecurity) on cybersecurity matters.[47] In some cases, the EC retains unilateral decision-making authority, such as in systemic risk assessment (Article 52(3)), conformity assessments (Articles 46(5) and 30(5)), and validation of national measures against non-compliant or otherwise compliant, but risky, AI systems (Articles 81 and 82).

At the same time, Recital 96 introduces the AI Office as a separate actor responsible for facilitating compliance through developing impact assessment questionnaire templates.[48] Yet, there are instances where both entities are referenced jointly, further blurring the distinction between their respective functions. For example, Recital 162 assigns the EC supervisory and enforcement powers over the obligations of GPAI providers, while also empowering the AI Office to 'carry out all necessary actions to monitor the effective implementation of this Regulation as regards general-purpose AI models'.[49] This overlapping structure invites uncertainty as to the functional independence of the AI Office. Is it a subsidiary entity operating under the EC's broader authority, or does it possess distinct, autonomous roles?

This entangled drafting of the AI Act results in a lack of clarity about the delineation of roles, and true intent behind the governance arrangements underlying the provisions. Consequently, one must examine other sources to determine the placement of the institutional foundations. Primarily, the Commission Decision on establishing the AI Office, which explicitly outlines the Office's mission and tasks, and emphasises cooperation with the stakeholders, national authorities, and other EU bodies as well as the importance of cross-sectoral collaboration within the EC and international partnerships.[50]

The Commission Decision establishes the AI Office as 'part of the administrative structure of the Directorate-General for Communication Networks, Content and Technology (the 'Directorate-General')'.[51] This integration, however, introduces its own complexities. Firstly, The Directorate-General comprises multiple units, with the AI Office engaging with several of them depending on the relevant issues. Yet, neither the AI Act nor the Commission Decision delineates the composition of the AI Office or its collaborative engagement with these various units within the Directorate-General, leaving its precise organisational structure and its method for ensuring expertise ambiguous.[52] Secondly, the extent of the AI Office's operational independence remains unclear. Unlike other EU agencies, the AI Office lacks a legal personality and is bound by the Directorate-General's management plan, which dictates the strategic priorities and resource allocation for the AI Office, directly

[47] Recitals 36, 53 and 78 AI Act.

[48] Recital 96 AI Act.

[49] Recital 162 AI Act.

[50] Articles 1-7 Commission Decision Establishing the AI Office.

[51] Article 1 Commission Decision Establishing the AI Office.

[52] Novelli et al. (2024), p. 10.

influencing its scope and direction. Moreover, the Office's autonomy is curtailed by the predefined competencies of other EU entities and national authorities.[53] Although the Commission Decision mandates the AI Office to avoid duplicating the efforts of other EU bodies under sector-specific legislation (particularly when issuing guidance),[54] its ambiguous coordination mechanisms render achieving this objective rather difficult. This ambiguity further extends to managing potential conflicts or overlaps in competencies.[55]

Adding another layer to these complexities is the prospect of the European Parliament or the Council revoking the EC's authority to adopt delegated acts.[56] While this could be a safeguard against potential overreach, it could also be perceived as a challenge to the AI Act's adaptability. On one hand, this might be beneficial from an accountability standpoint, ensuring oversight and preventing unchecked modifications to the regulatory framework.[57] As some academics suggest:

> the revocation should not be viewed as a sanction against the [EC] for exceeding its powers but rather, as a response to a change in the political situation where one of the two co-legislators believes that the matter at hand would be best resolved directly through a legislative act rather than an executive one.[58]

On the other hand, the power to adopt delegated acts enables the EC 'to react quickly and flexibly'.[59] Consequently, a revocation might impede the timely updates necessary to address emerging AI-related risks and developments, potentially hindering the Act's ability to effectively regulate AI technologies.

Thus, the intertwined roles of the EC and the AI Office, coupled with ambiguities in their operational structures and the potential limitation of the EC's delegated powers, result in a governance framework that lacks clarity and may struggle with adaptability and effective oversight. These drafting infelicities highlight the need for a clearer delineation of roles and responsibilities to ensure efficient implementation and enforcement of the AI Act.

2.1.2 AI Board

The AI Board is an advisory body created under the AI Act to ensure cohesive implementation of the AI Act.[60] The AI Board comprises a representative from each Member State, appointed for 3-year term, with one of the representatives as the

[53] Novelli et al. (2024), p. 12.

[54] Article 7 Commission Decision Establishing the AI Office.

[55] Novelli et al. (2024), p. 12.

[56] Article 97 AI Act.

[57] See Peers and Costa (2012), p. 453.

[58] Mańko (2022), p. 2.

[59] Council of the European Union (2024) Implementing and Delegated Acts. https://www.consilium.europa.eu/en/council-eu/decision-making/implementing-and-delegated-acts/.

[60] Article 65(1) and Recital 149 AI Act.

chair.[61] The Member State representatives must possess the required expertise and authority within their countries to effectively contribute to achieving the Board's tasks, be empowered to gather pertinent information to promote coherence and cooperation among their NCAs, and act as the primary contact point between the AI Board and their Member States.[62] The European Data Protection Supervisor and the AI Office participate in the AI Board's meetings but merely as observers and without any voting privileges, with the latter also serving as the Secretariat.[63] The AI Board also creates two permanent sub-groups to promote collaboration and information exchange among MSAs and notifying authorities, and reserves the right to establish temporary sub-groups to address specific issues. Representative of the Advisory Forum may be invited to the latter as observers.[64]

The AI Board is tasked with advising and assisting the EC and the Member States, which includes advising the EC on international AI matters, facilitating coordination among NCAs, supporting joint activities of MSAs, and sharing technical expertise and best practices among Member States. The AI Board additionally advises on the enforcement rules concerning the GPAI models, contributes to harmonising administrative practices, issues recommendations and opinions on relevant matters, and supports the EC in promoting AI literacy. Like the AI Office, the AI Board must cooperate with other EU institutions and international organisations, which involves providing consultations to the EC when updating the functional specification of the EU database, assisting the NCAs and the EC in developing organisational and technical expertise required for the AI Act's implementation, supporting the AI Office and the NCAs with the operation of regulatory sandboxes, advising on guidance documents, and facilitating development of benchmarks, codes of practice and codes of conduct. The Board's mandate also involves obtaining feedback from the Member States on qualified alerts regarding GPAI models and offering related opinions to the EC, reflecting its multifaceted role in overseeing AI regulation and implementation.[65]

The drafting of the AI Act presents further ambiguities in this area given the apparent overlapping roles and unclear delineations between the AI Office and the AI Board. Both entities are entrusted with a broad array of parallel and intersecting duties.[66] For instance, advising the EC on AI-related matters, cultivating technical prowess and best practices, harmonising administrative practices, and providing guidance on enforcement rules, implementation, monitoring, and supervision of AI systems in accordance with the AI Act. Both institutions are also jointly responsible for developing codes of practice, supporting NCAs with regulatory sandboxes and joint investigations.

[61] Article 65(2)(3)(8) AI Act.

[62] Article 65(4) AI Act.

[63] Article 65(2)(8) AI Act.

[64] Article 65(6) AI Act.

[65] Articles 66 and 71(1) AI Act.

[66] Novelli et al. (2024), p. 14.

Such entwinement raises concerns regarding the imperative and efficacy of sustaining two distinct entities with somewhat analogous functions. Novelli et al posit that merging these institutions might be imprudent considering the need for political representation of Member States at the EU level.[67] However, the potential redundancy or the lack of clear demarcation could result in duplication of efforts, operational inefficiencies, and stakeholder confusion regarding which body holds definitive authority over specific matters—thus, undermining the coherence of the institutional framework, and potentially weakening the enforcement and uniform application of the AI Act across the EU.

Further exacerbating this limitation is the AI Board's predominantly advisory role within the AI Act. The potential for Member States to construe the provisions of the AI Act disparately, without a robust mechanism for revising or harmonising decisions at the EU level, amplifies these issues. Unlike the European Data Protection Board under the GDPR, the AI Board lacks binding authority to resolve disputes or revise decisions by national authorities, which could lead to fragmented enforcement and regulatory practices across the EU. This fragmentation poses risks, particularly concerning the use of AI for surveillance and other sensitive applications, where uniform oversight is crucial to prevent abuses and safeguard fundamental rights.[68] Therefore, the ambiguous and overlapping roles of the AI Office and the AI Board, coupled with the latter's deficiency in enforcement prerogatives, underscore potential limitations within the AI Act's drafting, which raises questions about how effectively and efficiently institutions will operate.

2.1.3 Scientific Panel of Independent Experts and Advisory Forum

The AI Act requires forming a panel of independent experts (Scientific Panel) to integrate the scientific community and facilitate enforcement of the Regulation.[69] The EC, in coordination with the AI Board, will determine the Scientific Panel's size and appoint experts who must be independent from any AI provider, possess expertise in AI, maintain confidentiality and demonstrate impartiality and objectivity in their work.[70] The Scientific Panel's role is to advise and assist the AI Office in various tasks, including in implementing and enforcing the AI Act, particularly with regard to GPAI models. This involves identifying concrete or systemic risks that a GPAI model might pose at the EU level and alerting the AI Office; developing evaluation tools; advising on model classification; and aiding in the creation of tools and templates. Additionally, the Scientific Panel extends support to the Member States

[67] Novelli et al. (2024), p. 16.

[68] Novelli et al. (2024), p. 16, 23.

[69] Article 68(1) AI Act.

[70] Article 68(2)(4) AI Act.

in enforcement of the AI Act upon their request (and at times for a fee), while also assisting cross-border market surveillance activities.[71]

The final EU level institution created under the AI Act is the Advisory Forum, designated to provide technical expertise and advice to the EC and the AI Board.[72] Aiming for a diverse composition, the Forum will encompass stakeholders from various sectors such as industry, start-ups, SMEs, civil society, and academia—ensuring a balanced representation of both commercial and non-commercial interests. Much like the Scientific Panel, the EC selects the Advisory Forum's members based on their specialised knowledge in AI, who will serve for a period of 2 years with the Fundamental Rights Agency, ENISA, the European Committee for Standardization (CEN), the European Committee for Electrotechnical Standardization (CENELEC), and the European Telecommunications Standards Institute (ETSI) serving as permanent members.[73] The Advisory Forum is empowered to issue opinions, recommendations, and written contributions upon request of the AI Board and the EC. Like the Board, the Forum may form sub-groups to address specific issues related to the AI Act's objectives and is required to publish an annual report detailing its activities.[74]

While an in-depth examination of the structural and organisational framework of European Standardisation Organisation (ESO) is outside the scope of this chapter, it remains imperative to briefly underscore that organisations like CEN and CENELEC are private bodies, lacking adequate stakeholder participation and democratic control. Their potential to wield disproportionate influence could potentially undermine the authority of states and democratic accountability.[75] These concerns are pertinent in the context of their integration into the institutional architecture of the AI Act, particularly as permanent members of the Advisory Forum tasked with advising the EC and the AI Board. This incorporation raises questions about the inclusivity, transparency, and democratic legitimacy of the advisory process within the AI Act framework. Moreover, should these challenges persist, they could hinder effective stakeholder engagement, compromise the quality of advice provided to the EC and the AI Board, and undermine the overall integrity of the regulatory framework for AI governance.

Furthermore, the delineation between the roles of the Scientific Panel and the Advisory Forum also lacks clarity. Where the Scientific Panel provides expert scientific advice to the AI Office and the Member States, the Advisory Forum assists the EC and the AI Board. This raises ambiguity regarding the exclusivity of each institution's support. Is the Scientific Panel's expert advice solely for the AI Office and the Member States? Should it be accessible to other institutional bodies

---

[71] Articles 68(3), 69 and 90 AI Act.

[72] Article 67(1) AI Act.

[73] Article 67(2)-(5) AI Act.

[74] Article 67(8)-(10) AI Act.

[75] Ebers (2022), pp. 340–344; For further details on the outlook of European standardisation under the AI Act, see Laux et al. (2024).

considering the AI Act's overarching effort to secure impartial and external feedback for its comprehensive implementation? While the Panel's advice may indirectly make its way to the EC and the AI Board through the Office's participation in the Board's meetings, its effective impact is questionable, given the AI Office's lack of voting power and its presence as a mere observer. This might diminish the impact of the specialised opinions and further raises questions on the rationale behind the separation of the two institutions when one's mandate appears to indirectly overlap with the other.[76]

2.2 *National Level Institutions*

While the AI Office oversees cases where the same provider supplies both the GPAI model and the AI system built on it, supervisory responsibilities are delegated to national authorities when different entities provide the model and the system. Nevertheless, where GPAI systems can be directly used for high-risk purposes, the national authorities are mandated to cooperate with the AI Office to ensure adherence to the AI Act.[77] Thus, at the national level, national competent authorities (NCAs) are instituted to ensure effective enforcement of the Regulation within their respective jurisdictions.

2.2.1 National Competent Authorities

Under the AI Act, the NCAs, including notifying authority and MSA (examined in detail below), must operate in an independent, impartial and unbiased manner, and provide guidance on the implementation of the AI Act, particularly for the SMEs.[78] For NCAs to perform their tasks effectively, the Member States must ensure they have adequate technical and financial resources, including sufficient personnel with 'an in-depth understanding of AI technologies, data and data computing, personal data protection, cybersecurity, fundamental rights, health and safety risks and knowledge of existing standards and legal requirements'.[79]

If AI systems are developed or deployed by EU institutions, bodies, offices, or agencies within the scope of the Regulation, the European Data Protection Supervisor (EDPS) will act as the competent authority for their supervision.[80] The EDPS is the independent data protection authority responsible for monitoring the processing of personal data by the EU institutions and bodies, counselling on

[76] Novelli et al. (2024), pp. 16–17.

[77] Recital 161 and Article 75 AI Act.

[78] Article 70(8) AI Act.

[79] Article 70(3) AI Act.

[80] Article 70(9) AI Act.

legislation, agreements and act affecting data privacy, and cooperating with national authorities to ensure uniform data protection.[81] While there are extensive provisions on the roles and responsibilities of other institutions created under the Act, the roles, tasks and powers of the EDPS, in relation to the those institutions (especially its role as a MSA) are not as robustly articulated and hence require further clarification.[82]

In addition to the specific responsibilities examined in the following sections, NCAs are required to establish and operate AI regulatory sandboxes within Member States. These sandboxes are controlled environments that foster innovation and facilitate the development, testing, and validation of innovative AI systems before they are placed on the market. NCAs must establish at least one national-level sandbox and provide guidance, supervision, and support within these sandboxes to identify and mitigate risks related to fundamental rights, health, safety, and compliance with regulatory obligations. NCAs must also allocate sufficient resources and may cooperate with other relevant authorities and actors within the AI ecosystem. Additionally, they must coordinate their activities and submit annual reports to the AI Office and the AI Board, providing information on the progress, results, incidents, and recommendations related to the operation of AI regulatory sandboxes.[83]

2.2.2 Notifying Authority and (Conformity Assessment Bodies/Notified Bodies)

Notifying authorities are national authorities designated by each Member State, tasked with establishing and managing 'assessment, designation and notification' procedures of third-party conformity assessment bodies (CABs) and monitoring their activities.[84] The AI Act requires notifying authorities to operate independently and impartially, maintain confidentiality and to strictly refrain from engaging in activities carried out by the CABs to avoid any conflicts of interest.[85] CABs, in turn, must submit applications to these authorities, providing details of their activities, modules and accreditation certificates where applicable. Notifying authorities will subsequently verify whether these bodies meet the criteria listed in Article 31 of the AI Act, which includes fulfilling organisational, quality management, resource, and cybersecurity requirements; ensuring independence from AI system providers or any other parties with economic interests, and avoiding any direct involvement in

[81] European Data Protection Supervisor (n.d.) About Us. https://www.edps.europa.eu/about/about-us_en.

[82] EDPS Press Release (2023) EDPS' Final Recommendations on the AI Act. https://www.edps.europa.eu/system/files/2023-10/EDPS-2023-12-Own-Initiative-Opinion-AI-ACT_EN.pdf. European Data Protection Board (2021), p. 13.

[83] Article 57 AI Act.

[84] Article 28(1) AI Act. All high-risk AI systems must undergo conformity assessment before they are placed on the market. For further details on conformity assessment procedures under the AI Act, see Thelisson and Verma (2023).

[85] Article 28(3)-(6) AI Act.

the design, development, or marketing of such systems; maintaining objectivity and confidentiality; accommodating AI providers of different sizes and sectors; ensuring the highest professional integrity and competence; among others.[86] If met, the notifying authorities will notify the relevant CABs—recognising them as notified bodies[87]—along with a notification to the EC and the Member States. However, the notified CABs may only begin their activities as notified bodies if no objections are raised by the EC or other Member States within specified timelines. Where such objections arise, the EC will consult the relevant Member States and the CABs before making a final decision.[88] In the absence of such objections, the CABs may officially conduct activities as notified bodies—i.e. verifying the conformity of high-risk AI systems, assessing its quality management system and technical documentation, while balancing the need for thorough assessment with minimising administrative burdens, especially for SMEs.[89] Where the conformity of the AI system is established, the notified body issues Union technical documentation assessment certificate and informs the notifying authorities and other notified bodies.[90] Additionally, they must provide relevant documentation to the notifying authorities as part of their oversight responsibilities.[91]

Although these provisions collectively strive to establish a robust and transparent framework for ensuring the safety and compliance of AI systems within the EU, the AI Act may fall short of actualising this vision for several reasons. Despite these extensive provisions in the AI Act outlining a framework for notified bodies, an open question remains as to how often their services will be required. In most cases involving standalone high-risk systems, AI providers can certify conformity based on internal control—i.e. through self-assessment alone—and are encouraged to do so as a 'general rule' under the AI Act. The exception to this is high-risk AI systems intended for biometric use, which are required to undergo certification by notified bodies.[92] However, once harmonised standards or common specifications for these systems are established, self-assessment would suffice, potentially rendering notified bodies unnecessary even for biometric systems.[93]

Even where the AI Act mandates conformity assessment by these bodies, issues of impartiality arise. The Regulation requires notified bodies to operate independently and ensure objectivity.[94] However, in practice, notified bodies may struggle to maintain complete independence as they are typically private sector firms

---

[86] Articles 29 and 31 AI Act.

[87] Article 3(22) AI Act.

[88] Article 30 AI Act.

[89] Article 34 AI Act.

[90] Articles 44, 45 and Annex VII AI Act.

[91] Article 34 AI Act.

[92] Recital 125 AI Act; See also Cefaliello and Kullmann (2022), pp. 552-553 and Ebers et al. (2021), p. 595.

[93] Article 43(1) AI Act; Veale and Borgesius (2021), p. 106.

[94] Article 31 AI Act.

providing certification services.[95] Although such bodies are listed online and are subject to certain standards, their day-to-day activities or actual working procedures remain largely opaque, with the frequent subcontracting practices compounding the concern.[96] This governance model risks creating a 'privatised compliance industry' if the burden of oversight shifts from public authorities, such as data protection authorities or similar entities, to commercial firms.[97] The potential consequence is a regulatory regime marred with fragmented accountability, conflicts of interest, diminished transparency, and market incentives that may influence the very assessments meant to safeguard public interest.[98]

Another issue pertains to the insufficient guidance for the institutions to effectively oversee compliance of the AI Act. Consider, for instance, the requirement of independence of the notifying authorities from the CABs. While the AI Act emphasises the avoidance of conflict of interests, it lacks detailed instructions on how to implement oversight mechanisms. The current supervision controls by accreditation bodies provide some oversight but tend to concentrate more on technical abilities and quality management systems rather than addressing broader impartiality concerns.[99] Similarly, while the AI Act mandates notified bodies to conduct periodic audits to ensure the AI systems maintain conformity, it does not specify the frequency of these audits nor the criteria for triggering them.[100]

2.2.3 Market Surveillance Authority

The AI Act requires each Member State to designate a MSA to act as a single point of contact.[101] The Act's convoluted definitional approach arises again in this context. An MSA (or a notifying authority) is a 'national competent authority' for the purposes of the Regulation.[102] At the same time, the references in the AI Act to MSAs (and notifying authorities) 'shall be construed as references to the European Data Protection Supervisor [for] AI systems put into service or used by Union institutions, agencies, offices and bodies'.[103]

MSAs have several roles under the Regulation, including monitoring and control of the market, imposing corrective measures and penalties, collaborating with other

---

[95] Veale and Borgesius (2021), p. 106.

[96] Veale and Borgesius (2021), p. 106; Galland (2013), p. 369; Article 33 AI Act.

[97] Skelton (2021) Europe's Proposed AI Regulation Falls Short on Protecting Rights. https://www.computerweekly.com/feature/Europes-proposed-AI-regulation-falls-short-on-protecting-rights.

[98] See Laux et al. (2023), p. 27; Wörsdörfer (2023), p. 5; For a general understanding of risks of reliance on private sector in the context of algorithmic impact assessment, see Selbst (2021).

[99] Novelli et al. (2024), p. 18.

[100] Annex VII AI Act; Mökander et al. (2021), p. 260.

[101] Article 70(2) AI Act.

[102] Article 3(48) AI Act.

[103] Article 3(48) AI Act.

institutions, and being notified of certain matters, among others.[104] For example, where AI systems present a risk to the health or safety, or to fundamental rights, of persons (and the provider is aware of that risk), the provider must inform the MSA competent for the high-risk system concerned.[105] Moreover, recognising that they may lack specialised expertise in fundamental rights, the Act requires MSAs to collaborate with public authorities tasked with supervising and enforcing compliance with fundamental rights.[106] While this cooperation may strengthen oversight, it also adds to the complex enforcement framework. As part of their reporting obligations, MSAs shall also report annually to the EC and relevant NCAs regarding relevant matters of Union law on competition rules.[107] Additionally, there should be an annual report concerning the use of prohibited practices and what measures were taken.[108] MSAs may also receive mandates from authorised representatives (those appointed to represent providers established in third countries) of high-risk AI systems.[109] Adding to this plethora of obligations, Regulation on Market Surveillance and Compliance of Products further delineates the tasks of MSAs and clarifies the rights and duties of economic operators in relation to market surveillance.[110]

It was noted above that the definitional approach under the AI Act is convoluted. The same is true with the interwoven design of institutional authority. Article 75 designates monitoring and supervisory authority for GPAI systems to the AI Office. However, to carry out those functions, the AI Office shall have the powers of an MSA.[111] Yet, the AI Office must cooperate with an MSA where an MSA has sufficient reason to consider that one of the purposes of an AI system is non-compliant with the provisions of the AI Act.[112] The text is ambiguous on the effect of this crossover but it exists to avoid overlapping competencies.[113] The Regulation also requires that an MSA is established as a single point of contact for the public and other counterparts, but the obvious inference is that there would be two points of contact if the AI Office assumes the functional role of an MSA, which one would assume is not the intention of the AI Act.[114] This arrangement raises questions about

---

[104] European Commission (n.d.) Product Safety and Market Surveillance. https://commission.europa.eu/business-economy-euro/product-safety-and-requirements/product-safety/product-safety-and-market-surveillance_en.

[105] Articles 20(2) and 79(1) AI Act.

[106] Article 77 AI Act.

[107] Article 22(3) AI Act.

[108] Article 74(2) AI Act.

[109] Article 72(2) AI Act.

[110] Regulation (EU) 2019/1020 of the European Parliament and of the Council of 20 June 2019 on market surveillance and compliance of products and amending Directive 2004/42/EC and Regulations (EC) No 765/2008 and (EU) No 305/2011 (Regulation on Market Surveillance and Compliance of Products).

[111] Article 75(1) AI Act.

[112] Article 75(2) AI Act.

[113] Recital 161 AI Act

[114] Recital 153 AI Act.

the design of the governance structure. Rather than creating a simple structure, exceptions are created to sidestep the overlap of roles of two institutions, creating ambiguities about the scope of authority.

One study has examined considerations of transparency under the AI Act. It criticises the Regulation for lacking independent oversight mechanisms ('fire alarms'), which results in accountability gaps.[115] Post-market monitoring is the responsibility of providers which creates a closed information loop that restricts access to important data. This is problematic because MSAs rely on providers for incident reporting and while individuals have the right to lodge a complaint with the MSAs, the authorities are not mandated to investigate them.[116] Instead the AI Act grants discretionary leeway to MSAs, allowing them to manage such complaints in accordance with their established procedures.[117] In practice, this discretion could result in significant enforcement disparities across Member States and imbalances in protection levels throughout the EU—potentially mirroring the fragmentation observed among data protection authorities (DPAs) under the GDPR. Just as variations in financial resources and technical expertise among DPAs have led to inconsistent enforcement across the Union,[118] differences in 'resources, coordination mechanisms, [and] powers with regard to non-compliant products' among MSAs may also result in more rigorous market surveillance in some Member States than in others.[119] There are also resource and expertise shortages and coordination complexities within MSAs, which will struggle to manage the complex and vast regulatory landscape.[120] Furthermore, the ability of such institutions to bring about transparency will be limited by confidentiality clauses.[121] Ultimately, there is an absence of independent feedback mechanisms, and this can exacerbate the risks associated with provider-dominated monitoring, especially in areas where state secrecy might hinder effective oversight.[122]

[115] Busuioc et al. (2023), pp. 100–102.

[116] Busuioc et al. (2023), pp. 100–102; Siegmann and Anderljung (2022), p. 38.

[117] Article 85 AI Act.

[118] Sivan-Sevilla (2021) Trends in Privacy Enforcement: A Comparative Analysis of post-GDPR Enforcement Styles. https://il.boell.org/en/2021/11/18/trends-privacy-enforcement-comparative-analysis-post-gdpr-enforcement-styles.

[119] Recital 33 Regulation on Market Surveillance and Compliance of Products.

[120] See Gstrein (2022), p. 764.

[121] Busuioc et al. (2023), pp. 100–102.

[122] Busuioc et al. (2023), pp. 100–102.

3 Interaction with Other Legislation

The governance structures outlined above should also be understood as operating within a broader regulatory sphere in the EU that encompasses many regulations, directives, and legal regimes.[123] It is beyond the scope of this chapter to examine that sphere in detail, but it is worth highlighting those interactions to elucidate the multilayered complexity of the governance ecosystem given that each regulation and directive establishes separate entities and institutions. The governance arrangements under the AI Act are already complex. Contemplating those arrangements as part of a much larger matrix raises questions about whether arrangements are excessively complex for all stakeholders.

For example, where AI systems are safety components of products falling under other EU regulations, then institutions falling under other regulations will also be involved.[124] Those products include 'machinery, toys, lifts, equipment and protective systems intended for use in potentially explosive atmospheres, radio equipment, pressure equipment, recreational craft equipment, cableway installations, appliances burning gaseous fuels, medical devices, in vitro diagnostic medical devices, automotive and aviation'.[125] The AI Act refers to the relevant directives and regulations in its annexes, such as the Medical Device Regulation (MDR) and the Regulation on in-vitro diagnostic medical devices (IVD).[126] Each regulation has its own requirements and institutions. Thus, the AI Act explicitly connects into that broader institutional matrix by referring to such regulations.

Data laws are of particular significance in the AI context given that data is used to train AI and is processed by it. The General Data Protection Regulation (GDPR), the Data Governance Act (DGA), the Digital Services Act (DSA), the Digital Markets Act (DMA), and the Data Act (DA) are all relevant in this regard. There are also sector specific regulations such as the European Health Data Space (EHDS). The inclusion of these regulations into considerations about AI necessarily brings the relevant institutions established under those laws into the fold when examining the governance and institutional matrix.

Forthcoming directives will further increase the number of institutions with responsibilities for governing AI. The Artificial Intelligence Liability Directive

[123] A helpful overview is provided by Neuwirth (2024), p. 94; See also European Parliamentary Research Service (2022), pp. 56–59. See, for e.g., Minssen et al. (2024) on the interconnections between the AI Act, liability directives, and other laws creating an emerging regulatory ecosystem in the healthcare sector.

[124] Recital 50 AI Act.

[125] Recital 50 AI Act.

[126] Regulation (EU) 2017/745 of the European Parliament and of the Council of 5 April 2017 on Medical Devices, Amending Directive 2001/83/EC, Regulation (EC) No 178/2002 and Regulation (EC) No 1223/2009 and Repealing Council Directives 90/385/EEC and 93/42/EEC [2017] OJ L117/1 (MDR); Regulation (EU) 2017/746 of the European Parliament and of the Council of 5 April 2017 on In Vitro Diagnostic Medical Devices and Repealing Directive 98/79/EC and Commission Decision 2010/227/EU [2017] OJ L117 (IVD).

(AILD) and the revised Product Liability Directive (revised PLD) are proposed directives that will further complicate the landscape.[127] The former will seek to protect individuals from harms caused by AI systems. The latter will be amended to bring AI within the definition of the directive. The EC, EU courts, national authorities, and other institutions will likely have some governance role for these directives. Again, this will increase the number of institutions governing AI, and the AI Act should be understood as only one part of that matrix.

Finally, there are also queries about how the AI Act will set alongside initiatives of other EU institutions. For example, there has been concern that the AI Act will 'crowd out' other AI policy efforts in the EU, such as the Council of Europe's Framework Convention.[128] It is beyond the scope of this chapter to examine this Convention but it illustrates how more institutions are entering the governance era, which tends towards our note of caution earlier in this chapter about 'excessive complexity' in the governance arrangements for AI.

4 Conclusion and Recommendations

The AI Act signifies a significant step in regulating AI technologies within the EU, but its institutional framework requires refinement to effectively achieve its objectives. The excessive complexity and overlapping functions of the EU entities created under the Act introduce ambiguities that could hinder effective governance. At the national level, the responsibilities of NCAs are similarly convoluted, and their interaction with EU-level bodies lacks clarity, which could lead to potential enforcement gaps.

To address these concerns, there is a pressing need to clearly delineate the roles of the EC, the AI Office and the AI Board by assigning distinct, non-overlapping mandates to each entity. For example, the AI Office should be granted legal personhood to ensure its operational autonomy, empowering it to execute its functions independently from the EC. This status might also enhance its legitimacy in overseeing AI systems without undue influence from the Directorate-General and ensuring coherence with other European regulatory bodies possessing analogous responsibilities.[129] The AI Board's task remit should also be expanded to enhance effective implementation and enforcement of the AI Act.[130] This involves strength-

[127] Proposal for a Directive of the European Parliament and the Council on Adapting Non-Contractual Civil Liability Rules to Artificial Intelligence (AI Liability Directive) COM (2022) 496 final (AILD); Proposal for a Directive of the European Parliament and of the Council on Liability for Defective Products COM (2022) 495 final (Revised PLD).

[128] Feldstein (2023), p. 9; Committee on Artificial Intelligence (CAI) Council of Europe Framework Convention on Artificial Intelligence and Human Rights, Democracy and the Rule of Law CM(2024)52-final (133rd Session of the Committee of Ministers, 17 May 2024).

[129] Curtis et al. (2023), p. 56.

[130] Stahl et al. (2022), p. 13.

ening its advisory role with binding decision-making powers, akin to the role of European Data Protection Board under the GDPR, to avoid risking potential misuse of AI by some Member States and ensure uniform enforcement across the EU.[131]

The separation of the Scientific Panel and the Advisory Forum also merits reconsideration. Consolidating the two into a single entity could mitigate duplication and enhance decision-making processes by combining the Advisory Forum's broad stakeholder engagement with the Scientific Panel's specialised expertise—potentially elevating the quality of advice provided to EU and national entities by addressing both technical complexities and societal implications of AI. If a merger is infeasible, improved coordination through clear delineation of scopes, roles, and tasks, accompanied by unified reporting, could still streamline processes and present a cohesive advisory voice.[132]

The existing institutional governance framework at the national level is also flawed, hinging on voluntary ex-ante product assessments and mandatory ex-post market surveillance.[133] To ensure rigorous and impartial risk assessments and certifications, current self-assessment regime by AI providers—prone to conflicts of interest and regulatory capture—should be replaced with legally mandated oversight by independent third-party notified bodies endowed with investigatory and enforcement powers.[134] Furthermore, clear guidelines on their interactions with EU-level entities, detailed instructions on implementing oversight mechanisms and ensuring that these bodies have adequate resources and expertise for these bodies are essential for effective enforcement.[135]

Harmonising the AI Act's interaction with other EU regulations and ensuring the institutions established by the AI Act complement rather than conflict with entities created under other legislative instruments, is imperative and robust coordination mechanisms among various EU and national entities should be established to manage the multi-regulatory environment effectively.

Ultimately, a streamlined, transparent, and well-defined institutional framework is essential for the AI Act to fulfil its promise of safeguarding fundamental rights while promoting innovation.[136] By addressing the identified ambiguities and complexities, the EU can set a global benchmark for AI regulation, ensuring responsible and ethical development and deployment of AI technologies. This chapter serves as a technical resource for other research, indicating where future analyses may arise.

---

[131] Novelli et al. (2024), p. 23.

[132] Novelli et al. (2024), p. 22.

[133] Wörsdörfer (2023), p. 17.

[134] Kop (2021), p. 8; Yeung et al. (2020), p. 79; Wörsdörfer (2023), p. 18.

[135] AlgorithmWatch (2021), p. 7.

[136] For a broader analysis of the role of the AI Act in cultivating public trust and safeguarding fundamental rights in sectoral settings, see Solaiman (2025).

References

AlgorithmWatch (2021) Draft AI Act: EU Needs to Live Up to its Own Ambitions in Terms of Governance and Enforcement. https://algorithmwatch.org/en/wp-content/uploads/2021/08/EU-AI-Act-Consultation-Submission-by-AlgorithmWatch-August-2021.pdf

Almada M, Radu A (2024) The Brussels side-effect: how the AI Act can reduce the global reach of EU policy. German Law J 1–18. https://doi.org/10.1017/glj.2023.108

Busuioc M, Curtin D, Almada M (2023) Reclaiming transparency: contesting the logics of secrecy within the AI act. Eur Law Open 2:79–105. https://doi.org/10.1017/elo.2022.47

Cefaliello A, Kullmann M (2022) Offering false security: how the draft artificial intelligence act undermines fundamental workers rights. Eur Labour Law J 13:542–562. https://doi.org/10.1177/20319525221114474

Coeckelbergh M (2024) The case for global governance of AI: arguments, counter-arguments, and challenges ahead. AI Soc 1–4. https://doi.org/10.1007/s00146-024-01949-5

Commission Notice – The 'Blue Guide' on the Implementation of EU Product Rules 2022 (Text with EEA relevance) 2022/C 247/01 OJ C 247

Committee on Artificial Intelligence (CAI) Council of Europe Framework Convention on Artificial Intelligence and Human Rights, Democracy and the Rule of Law CM(2024)52-final (133rd Session of the Committee of Ministers, 17 May 2024)

Council of the European Union (2024) Implementing and Delegated Acts. https://www.consilium.europa.eu/en/council-eu/decision-making/implementing-and-delegated-acts/

Curtis S, Reddel R, Moës N (2023) A Blueprint for the European AI Office. The Future Society. https://thefuturesociety.org/wp-content/uploads/2023/10/a-blueprint-for-the-european-ai-office.pdf

Ebers M (2022) Standardizing AI – the case of the European Commission's proposal for an artificial intelligence act. In: DiMatteo L, Poncibo C, Cannarsa M (eds) The Cambridge handbook of artificial intelligence: global perspectives on law and ethics. Cambridge University Press, Cambridge, pp 321–344

Ebers M, Hoch V, Rosenkranz F et al (2021) The European Commission's proposal for an artificial intelligence act – a critical assessment by members of the robotics and AI law society (RAILS). J Multidiscip Sci J 4:589–603. https://doi.org/10.3390/j4040043

EDPS Press Release (2023) EDPS' Final Recommendations on the AI Act. https://www.edps.europa.eu/system/files/2023-10/EDPS-2023-12-Own-Initiative-Opinion-AI-ACT_EN.pdf

Ernst & Young Global Limited (2024) The European Union Artificial Intelligence Act. https://assets.ey.com/content/dam/ey-sites/ey-com/en_gl/topics/ai/ey-eu-AI Act-political-agreement-overview-february-2024.pdf

EU Artificial Intelligence Act (2024) The AI Office: what is it, and how does it work?. https://artificialintelligenceact.eu/the-ai-office-summary/

European Commission (2023) Commission Welcomes Political Agreement on Artificial Intelligence Act. https://ec.europa.eu/commission/presscorner/detail/en/ip_23_6473

European Commission (2024) European AI Office. https://digital-strategy.ec.europa.eu/en/policies/ai-office

European Commission (n.d.) Product Safety and Market Surveillance. https://commission.europa.eu/business-economy-euro/product-safety-and-requirements/product-safety/product-safety-and-market-surveillance_en

European Data Protection Board (2021) EDPB-EDPS Joint Opinion 5/2021 on the Proposal for a Regulation of the European Parliament and of the Council Laying Down Harmonised Rules on Artificial Intelligence (Artificial Intelligence Act). https://artificialintelligenceact.eu/wp-content/uploads/2022/05/AIA-EDPBEDPS-Opinion-18-June-21.pdf

European Data Protection Supervisor (n.d.) About Us. https://www.edps.europa.eu/about/about-us_en

European Parliamentary Research Service (2022) AI and Digital Tools in Workplace Management and Evaluation: An Assessment of the EU's Legal Framework. https://www.europarl.europa.eu/RegData/etudes/STUD/2022/729516/EPRS_STU(2022)729516_EN.pdf
Feldstein S (2023) Evaluating Europe's push to enact AI regulations: how will this influence global norms? Democratization 1–18. https://doi.org/10.1080/13510347.2023.2196068
Gai P, Kemp M, Serrano AS et al (2019). Reports of the Advisory Scientific Committee No 8/June 2019: Regulatory Complexity and the Quest for Robust Regulation. European Systemic Risk Board. https://www.esrb.europa.eu/pub/pdf/asc/esrb.asc190604_8_regulatorycomplexityquestrobustregulation~e63a7136c7.en.pdf
Galland JP (2013) The difficulties of regulating markets and risks in europe through notified bodies. Eur J Risk Reg 4:365–373. https://doi.org/10.1017/S1867299X00002634
Gstrein OJ (2022) European AI Regulation: Brussels effect versus human dignity? Zeitschrift für Europarechtliche Studien (ZEuS) 4:755–772. https://doi.org/10.5771/1435-439X-2022-4-755
Kop M (2021) EU Artificial Intelligence Act: The European Approach to AI. Transatlantic Antitrust and IPR Developments 1–11. https://law.stanford.edu/wp-content/uploads/2021/09/2021-09-28-EU-Artificial-Intelligence-Act-The-European-Approach-to-AI.pdf
Laux J, Wachter S, Mittelstadt B (2023) Trustworthy artificial intelligence and the European Union AI act: on the conflation of trustworthiness and acceptability of risk. Reg Gov 18:3–32. https://doi.org/10.1111/rego.12512
Laux J, Wachter S, Mittelstadt B (2024) Three pathways for standardisation and ethical disclosure by default under the European Union artificial intelligence act. Comput Law Secur Rev 53:1–11. https://doi.org/10.1016/j.clsr.2024.105957
Mańko R (2022) The European Parliament's right to challenge commission delegated acts. European Parliamentary Research Service. https://www.europarl.europa.eu/RegData/etudes/BRIE/2022/739257/EPRS_BRI(2022)739257_EN.pdf
Minssen T, Solaiman B, Köttering L et al (2024) Governing AI in the European Union: Emerging Infrastructures and Regulatory Ecosystems in Health. In: Solaiman B, Cohen IG (eds) Research handbook on health, AI and the Law. Edward Elgar Publishing p. 311–331. https://doi.org/10.4337/9781802205657.ch18
Mökander J, Axente M, Casolari F et al (2021) Conformity assessments and post-market monitoring: a guide to the role of auditing in the proposed European AI regulation. Minds Mach 32:241–268. https://doi.org/10.1007/s11023-021-09577-4
Neuwirth RJ (2024) The EU artificial intelligence act: regulating subliminal AI systems. Routledge
Novelli C, Hacker P, Morley J et al (2024) A Robust governance for the AI Act: AI Office, AI board, scientific panel, and national authorities. Eur J Risk Reg 2024:1–25. https://doi.org/10.1017/err.2024.57
OECD (2024) Recommendation of the Council on Artificial Intelligence. https://legalinstruments.oecd.org/en/instruments/oecd-legal-0449
Peers S, Costa M (2012) Accountability for delegated and implementing acts after the treaty of lisbon. Eur Law J 18:427–460. https://doi.org/10.1111/j.1468-0386.2012.00607.x
Pouget H (2024) Institutional Context. https://artificialintelligenceact.eu/context/
Selbst A (2021) An institutional view of algorithmic impact assessment. Harv J Law Technol 35:117–191
Siegmann C, Anderljung M (2022) The Brussels effect and artificial intelligence: how EU regulation will impact the global AI market. Centre for the Governance of AI. https://doi.org/10.48550/arXiv.2208.12645
Sivan-Sevilla I (2021) Trends in privacy enforcement: a comparative analysis of post-GDPR enforcement styles. https://il.boell.org/en/2021/11/18/trends-privacy-enforcement-comparative-analysis-post-gdpr-enforcement-styles
Skelton SJ (2021) Europe's proposed AI regulation falls short on protecting rights. https://www.computerweekly.com/feature/Europes-proposed-AI-regulation-falls-short-on-protecting-rights
Solaiman B (2023) From 'AI to Law' in healthcare: the proliferation of global guidelines in a void of legal uncertainty. *Med Law 42*(2):391–406. https://doi.org/10.31235/osf.io/4zf97

Solaiman B (2025) The European Union's artificial intelligence act and trust: towards an AI Bill of rights in Healthcare? Law, Innovation and Tech 17(1):318–334. https://doi.org/10.1080/17579961.2025.2469986

Solaiman B, Bloom M (2022) AI, Explainability, and Safeguarding Patient Safety in Europe: Toward a Science-Focused Regulatory Model. Cambridge University Press 91–102. https://doi.org/10.1017/9781108975452.008

Solaiman B, Cohen IG (eds) (2024) Research handbook on health, AI and the law. Edward Elgar Publishing. https://doi.org/10.4337/9781802205657

Solaiman B, Malik A (2024) Regulating Algorithmic Care in the European Union: Evolving Doctor–Patient Models Through the Artificial Intelligence Act (AI-Act) and the Liability Directives. *Med L Rev 33*:1–22. https://doi.org/10.1093/medlaw/fwae033

Stahl BC, Rodrigues R, Santiago N et al (2022) A European agency for artificial intelligence: protecting fundamental rights and ethical values. Comput Law Secur Rev 45:1–25. https://doi.org/10.1016/j.clsr.2022.105661

Thelisson E, Verma H (2023) Conformity assessment under the EU AI act general approach. AI Ethics 4:113–121. https://doi.org/10.1007/s43681-023-00402-5

Veale M, Borgesius FZ (2021) Demystifying the draft EU artificial intelligence act: analysing the good, the bad, and the unclear elements of the proposed approach. Comput Law Rev Intl 4:97–112. https://doi.org/10.9785/cri-2021-220402

Walter Y (2024) Managing the race to the moon: global policy and governance in artificial intelligence regulation—a contemporary overview and an analysis of socioeconomic consequences. Discov Artif Intell 4(14):1–24. https://doi.org/10.1007/s44163-024-00109-4

Wörsdörfer M (2023) The E.U.'s artificial intelligence act: an ordoliberal assessment. AI and Ethics 1–30. https://doi.org/10.1007/s43681-023-00337-x

Yeung K, Howes A, Pogrebna G (2020) AI governance by human rights-centered design, deliberation, and oversight: an end to ethics washing. In: Dubber MD, Pasquale P, Das S (eds) The Oxford handbook of ethics of AI. Oxford University Press, Oxford, pp 76–106

Prohibited Artificial Intelligence Practices Revisited

Rostam J. Neuwirth

Contents

Abstract In April 2021, the European Commission launched its initial proposal for an Artificial Intelligence Act (AIA). More than three years later, on 1 August 2024, the Act finally entered into force. This chapter revisits the category of 'prohibited AI practices' enshrined in Article 5 AIA, which are banned because they are deemed to pose unacceptable risks to the European Union's values and fundamental rights. After several amendments, the prohibition now covers eight different but interre-

The author would like to thank Huixin Zhong for her constructive feedback on an earlier version of this chapter and gratefully acknowledges the financial support for a research project entitled 'Legal Synaesthesia: A Semiotic Approach to the Global Regulation of Artificial Intelligence' [MYRG2022-00075-FLL] provided by the University of Macau.

R. J. Neuwirth (✉)
Global Legal Studies, Faculty of Law, University of Macau, Macau, China
e-mail: rjn@um.edu.mo

V. L. Raposo (ed.), *The European Artificial Intelligence Act*, Law, Governance and Technology Series 78, https://doi.org/10.1007/978-3-031-98406-8_6

lated categories of artificial intelligence (AI) practices, namely AI systems that deploy subliminal or purposefully manipulative or deceptive techniques, AI systems that exploit vulnerabilities, AI systems that predict the risk of committing a criminal offence, the creation of facial recognition databases, emotion recognition systems, social scoring systems, biometric categorisation systems and remote real-time biometric identification systems used for the purpose of law enforcement. The chapter examines each of these categories in isolation and critically contrasts the respective changes introduced during the negotiation phase. Last, it undertakes a brief outlook on the interplay between each of these categories and future regulatory challenges in this rapidly evolving field of technology.

1 Introduction

> The first is that for the individual citizen, everything which is not forbidden is allowed. The second is that for public bodies, and notably government, everything which is not allowed is forbidden.[1]

The original proposal by the European Commission for a draft Artificial Intelligence Act (DAIA), otherwise known as the 'EU AI Regulation', was released on 21 April 2021.[2] The final version of the Artificial Intelligence Act (AIA) was eventually agreed upon in December 2023 and was endorsed by the Members of the European Parliament (MEPs) on 13 March 2024 with 523 votes in favour, 46 against and 49 abstentions. Following the so-called corrigendum procedure that added hundreds of amendments, the text of the AIA was published in the European Union's (EU) Official Journal and finally entered into force on 1 August 2024.[3] In accordance with the relevant provision of Article 113 AIA, it unfolds its applicability in gradual stages and will not be fully enforceable until 24 months after 1 August 2024, except for: bans on prohibited practices (applicable six months after its entry into force); codes of practice (nine months); general purpose AI rules, including governance (12 months); and obligations for high-risk systems (36 months).

This chapter aims to critically revisit an earlier discussion of the so-called 'prohibited AI practices' enshrined in Article 5 DAIA by comparing the wording and scope of the original draft proposal with the final version of the law.[4] The DAIA's version included the four categories of 'subliminal AI systems (lit. a)), 'AI systems exploiting vulnerabilities' (lit. b)), so-called 'social scoring systems' (lit. c)) and 'real-time' remote biometric identification systems' (old lit d./new lit. h)). The text

---

[1] Laws (2000), p. 256.

[2] European Commission, *Proposal for a Regulation Laying Down Harmonised Rules on Artificial Intelligence (Artificial Intelligence Act)*, COM (2021) 206 final (21 April 2021) [DAIA].

[3] Regulation (EU) 2024/1689 laying down harmonised rules on artificial intelligence (Artificial Intelligence Act), OJ L 2024/1689 (12 July 2024) [AIA].

[4] Neuwirth (2023a, b).

of each of these categories was subject to numerous amendments that both clarified some of the concepts and added new categories, such as AI systems used to predict the commission of a criminal offence (new lit. d), to create a facial recognition database (lit. e.)), to infer the emotions of a natural person in the workplace or in educational institutions (lit. f.)) and to categorise persons based on their biometric data to deduce or infer their race, political opinions, trade union membership, religious or philosophical beliefs and sex life or sexual orientation (lit. g)).[5]

The chapter's primary purpose is to cover the years of the genesis of the EU's AIA and to gain further insights into the regulation of not only prohibited AI systems but also AI and disruptive technologies altogether. To this end, Sect. 2 briefly discusses the wider context of the present global debates about AI governance and regulation. Section 3 briefly presents each of the four categories of prohibited AI systems and identifies their principal regulatory challenges. Each subsection is concluded with a critical evaluation of the individual amendments to the original text. Section 4 summarises the findings, evaluates the AIA's contribution to the global regulation of AI and formulates the contributions as general lessons to be learned for future tasks, with the chapter then concluding in Sect. 5 with a serious warning for a dystopian future.

2 The Rise of Artificial Intelligence: From Ethical Concerns to Binding Norms

Before assessing the current status of the AIA's prohibited AI practices, it is helpful to provide a short overview of the wider context of the global debate on the regulation of AI. This is relevant in view of the divergent approaches to AI regulation across the globe and the possible conflicts that arise due to the extraterritorial effects of such regulation.[6] This particularly matters for the specific issue of 'prohibited AI practices', which requires a common understanding of the core AI values that may face unacceptable risks from AI and leads to the conclusion that such practices ought to be banned.

To begin with, the origin of the recent rise of AI and the trend towards intense legal and sociopolitical debates on the subject at the national, regional and global levels is difficult to precisely date. From an historical perspective, AI has been the dream of many since the darkness of time.[7] From a technological point of view, AI has constantly evolved in line with related fields and gone through different stages, broadly covering three stages since the 1950s.[8] However, such classifications also vary as they depend on the terminology used and by which scientific discipline. The

[5] Cf. Article 5(1) lit. a) to h) AIA, *supra* note 3.

[6] Wang (2024).

[7] Nilsson (2010), pp. 3–9.

[8] Raximov et al. (2021), pp. 1–3.

origin of AI, or at least its establishment as a research discipline,[9] is often dated to the 1956 Dartmouth Conference.[10] This conference proposed to study AI, assuming that 'every aspect of learning or any other feature of intelligence can in principle be so precisely described that a machine can be made to simulate it'.[11] However, a lawyer is recorded as having already invoked the exact notion of AI in writings dating back to 1764.[12] The fascination of humans to create artificial devices to replace humans or as artificial life has been recorded since time immemorial 'in religion, folklore, mythology, science fiction, popular science, and futurist projections'.[13]

The difficulties in tracking the origins of AI only confirm the relevance of Kranzberg's fifth law, according to which '[A]ll history is relevant, but the history of technology is the most relevant'.[14] At the same time, it also proves that the evolution of technology can neither be contained to a single scientific or technological field nor separated from the evolution of humanity. The same is true for AI and law, which also intersect at numerous levels.[15] From the perspective of the comprehensive regulation of AI, the beginnings can be traced to the first release by the European Commission of the proposal for an AI Act in April 2024.[16] The same proposal can be credited for having set the ball rolling for not only a debate about the regulation of AI but also for engendering global awareness about the serious risks and dangers potentially associated with AI. This was the latest then that the so-called 'race to the development of AI' officially turned into a 'global race of the regulation of AI'.[17]

This shift is also reflected in the adoption of the United Nations Educational, Scientific and Cultural Organization (UNESCO) Recommendation on the Ethics of AI in November 2021.[18] This document firmly established AI as a global issue given that UNESCO has wide membership that includes 193 states. The 'pervasive, far-reaching and global implications' of AI had previously been regionally recognised in the 2019 Principles of AI issued by the Organisation for Economic Co-operation and Development.[19] Most importantly for the prohibited AI Practices, the UNESCO Recommendation recognised in Recital 1 'the profound and dynamic positive and negative impacts of artificial intelligence (AI) on societies, environment, ecosystems and human lives, *including the human mind*'. The final report by the United Nations (UN) Advisory Body also mentions the evolving risks posed by AI that manifest themselves differently for different people and societies and offers an

[9] Moor (2006), p. 87.

[10] Cordeschi (2007).

[11] McCarthy et al. (2006).

[12] Hutcheson (1764), p. 107.

[13] Belk et al. (2020), p. 221.

[14] Kranzberg (1986), p. 553.

[15] Krausová (2017), p. 61.

[16] DAIA, *supra* note 2.

[17] Smuha (2022), p. 59.

[18] United Nations Educational, Scientific and Cultural Organization (UNESCO; 2022).

[19] Organisation for Economic Co-operation and Development (2019), p. 6.

'open-ended framework for focusing on those who could be harmed by AI'.[20] Most recently, the UN General Assembly also followed up with a resolution on the safety of AI, which calls upon all Member States and, when applicable, other stakeholders, to 'refrain from or cease the use of artificial intelligence systems that are impossible to operate in compliance with international human rights law or that pose undue risks to the enjoyment of human rights'.[21]

While the EU was negotiating the final version of the AIA, the global race towards the regulation of AI fuelled national efforts to regulate AI across the globe. The People's Republic of China (PRC) is already emerging as a leading global player in the development of AI, and it is also playing a pioneering role in the regulation of AI. Following several ethical recommendations related to AI, the PRC adopted a few sectoral laws that are parallel to several related laws, such as the 2017 Cybersecurity Law, the 2021 Data Security Law and the 2021 Personal Information Protection Law. For the time being, the PRC has opted for a more sectoral rather than a comprehensive approach to AI regulation, as was chosen by the EU. It has adopted specific AI regulations on recommender algorithm-generated suggestions, deep synthesis technology and generative AI.[22]

Even the United States (US), as another global leader in AI development, reflects this trend as it has moved from an emphasis on the development to the parallel consideration of the regulation of AI. This is reflected in the adoption of an executive order on 'Maintaining American Leadership' in AI in 2019 to one aiming for the 'Safe, Secure, and Trustworthy Development and Use of' AI in 2023.[23]

While many regulators in other countries around the world are also preparing AI-related laws and regulations, the regional and global component has also gained momentum. Also testifying to this trend are the PRC's Global Initiative formulated in October 2023 and the Bletchley Declaration by countries that attended the AI Safety Summit convened by the UK government in November 2023.[24] The initiative

---

[20] United Nations High-Level AI Advisory Board (2024), p. 31.

[21] United Nations General Assembly (2024), p. 5 (para 5).

[22] Cyberspace Administration of China (CAC), *Provisions on the Administration of Algorithm-generated Recommendations for Internet Information Services* (entry into force 1 March 2022), https://www.pkulaw.com/en_law/faf51f90a44d31adbdfb.html; *Provisions on the Administration of Deep Synthesis of Internet-Based Information Services* (entry into force: 1 January 2023), https://www.pkulaw.com/en_law/90cff392df74a3ebbdfb.html?keyword=Provisions%20on%20the%20Administration%20of%20Deep%20Synthesis; Cyberspace Administration of China (CAC), *Interim Measures for the Administration of Generative Artificial Intelligence Services* (entry into force: 15 August 2023), https://www.pkulaw.com/en_law/6dc227b9153496c2bdfb.html?keyword=Interim%20Measures%20for%20the%20Administration%20of%20Generative%20Artificial%20Intelligence%20Services.

[23] Executive Order No. 13859, 84 Fed. Reg. 3967 (14 February 2019), https://www.govinfo.gov/content/pkg/FR-2019-02-14/pdf/2019-02544.pdf; Executive Order 14110 of October 30, 2023, 88 Fed Reg, 210 (1 November 2023), https://www.govinfo.gov/content/pkg/FR-2023-11-01/pdf/2023-24283.pdf.

[24] Ministry of Foreign Affairs of the PRC, *Global AI Governance Initiative* (20 October 2023), https://www.mfa.gov.cn/eng/wjdt_665385/2649_665393/202310/t20231020_11164834.html; Ministry of Foreign Affairs of the PRC, Global AI Governance Initiative (20 October 2023),

by the Council of Europe to negotiate a Framework Convention on Artificial Intelligence is more advanced in the process as is the Human Rights, Democracy, and the Rule of Law instrument, which was adopted on 17 May 2024 as the first legally binding global instrument to address the risks posed by AI and is now open for signature and ratification from states all around the world.[25] On the question of prohibited AI practices that pose unacceptable risks, it is unfortunate that in contrast to the initial draft, the final version of the Framework Convention no longer contains a prohibition similar to that of Article 5 DAIA (Art. 14 of the Framework Convention).[26]

As a last step, the narrative of the debate on the global race to regulate AI has been criticised—due to its antecedents of a nuclear arms race and space race—for its negative impact on future developments.[27] What was termed the 'global race to regulate AI' should be reformulated as a 'cooperation for global AI regulation', and the debate about the substantive regulation of AI should be linked to institutional aspects and a reform of the international system.[28] The crucial role of institutional aspects of global AI governance are also mirrored in related questions regarding the institutional oversight of the AIA with the recent creation of an EU AI Office.[29] Similar debates are also taking place in the PRC.[30] Institutional aspects are particularly important in the context of the monitoring and enforcement of unacceptable risks posed by AI and, therefore, should form, as mentioned from the outset, a central part of the debate about the regulation of AI.[31]

---

https://www.mfa.gov.cn/eng/wjdt_665385/2649_665393/202310/t20231020_11164834.html; Government of the United Kingdom, *The Bletchley Declaration by Countries Attending the AI Safety Summit, 1-2 November 2023* (1 November 2023), https://www.gov.uk/government/publications/ai-safety-summit-2023-the-bletchley-declaration/the-bletchley-declaration-by-countries-attending-the-ai-safety-summit-1-2-november-2023.

[25] Council of Europe Committee on Artificial Intelligence, *Framework Convention on Artificial Intelligence, Human Rights, Democracy and the Rule of Law* (9 May 2024), https://www.coe.int/en/web/artificial-intelligence/cai.

[26] Council of Europe Committee on Artificial Intelligence, *Zero Draft [Framework] Convention on Artificial Intelligence, Human Rights, Democracy and the Rule of Law*, CAI(2022)07 (20 June 2022); Council of Europe Committee on Artificial Intelligence (CAI), *Draft Framework Convention on Artificial Intelligence, Human Rights, Democracy and the Rule of Law*, CM(2024)52-prov1 (15 March 2024).

[27] Ulnicane (2023); Armstrong et al. (2016).

[28] Neuwirth (2024), p. 39.

[29] European Commission, *Commission Decision of 24.1.2024 establishing the European Artificial Intelligence Office*, C(2024) 390 final (24 January 2024).

[30] Parasol (2021).

[31] Neuwirth (2023a), pp. 47–49, 88, 120.

3 'Prohibited AI Practices' Posing Unacceptable Risks

The rapid pace of innovation in the field of technology makes it difficult to predict the future risks associated with AI. While regulation must not hamper innovation altogether, it must also be used to safeguard the safe and sustainable development of technologies. It is especially important that potential existential AI risks, which are unknown now but may arise from technological advances in the future, are closely monitored and possibly regulated.[32] In this regard, security and development are not a pair of opposites that are in conflict but a reminder of the need to seek solutions in the spirit of their complementarity. Against this backdrop, the list of prohibited practices enshrined in Article 5 or Title II of the AIA assumes the greatest relevance. According to the original proposal, this section 'comprises all those AI systems whose use is considered unacceptable as contravening Union values, for instance by violating fundamental rights'.[33]

Broadly speaking, the following four categories of AI practices were listed in Article 5 of the DAIA:

1. An AI system that deploys subliminal techniques (Art. 5 lit. a).
2. An AI system that exploits any of the vulnerabilities (Art. 5 lit. b).
3. AI systems for the evaluation or classification of natural persons or groups of persons (social scoring systems; Art. 5 lit. c).
4. 'Real-time' remote biometric identification systems in publicly accessible spaces for the purposes of law enforcement (Art. 5 lit. d).

The text of each of these paragraphs was the subject of a profound analysis and received critical comments upon the publication of the initial proposal of the AIA.[34] Although they have been found to be closely related to each other, they shall be briefly individually revisited in the following sections.

3.1 Subliminal, Manipulative or Deceptive AI Systems

The first category of prohibited AI practices listed in Art. 5 lit. a) DAIA comprised the kind of AI system that 'deploys subliminal techniques beyond a person's consciousness in order to materially distort a person's behaviour in a manner that causes or is likely to cause that person or another person physical or psychological harm'. Both the wording and the scope of this category gave rise to multiple interdisciplinary questions of legal, scientific and technological kinds. Right after the release of the proposal, critical comments were voiced regarding the meaning of the term 'subliminal', which was nowhere defined or explained in the proposal.

[32] Hendrycks et al. (2023).

[33] Explanatory Memorandum of the AIA, *supra* note 2, at 12.

[34] Neuwirth (2023a, b).

In fact, an entire book published in August 2022 was dedicated to this paragraph alone.[35] It found, for instance, that humans are generally only aware of 5% or less of their entire cognitive functions, whereas the remaining percentage lies beyond their awareness but still exerts an important influence on their lives.[36] This means that if AI systems can reach out to the subliminal levels of perception, they will be far more effective than those that only target the supraliminal levels of perception, that is, those of which humans are aware. It also found that there is no absolute threshold that distinguishes between subliminal and supraliminal thresholds of perception.[37] Instead, scientific studies have shown that 'thresholds for a given stimulus vary both intra and interpersonally'.[38] In other words, not only does every person differ from every other person but also that the same person's ability to perceive stimuli constantly changes. This effectively means that it would be impossible to enforce this particular prohibition because it would be impossible to establish an objective criterion for determining whether an AI system fell inside or outside the provision. For this reason, the concept of '*transliminal*' was proposed to better encompass the ability of AI systems to exert an influence upon cognition both above (supraliminal) and below (subliminal) the threshold of perception.[39]

A third major finding was that certain doubts have existed across the history of scientific experiments on subliminal perceptions regarding the effectiveness of subliminal techniques, even given the scientific experiments carried out in the early twentieth century.[40] As of 2005, it was still reported that in spite of 'numerous findings demonstrating effects of subliminal perception, some people still maintain that the phenomenon itself does not even exist'.[41] More recent experiments, however, can now be regarded to have confirmed the overall effectiveness of subliminal techniques and to put an end to the myth of the complete ineffectiveness of subliminal methods of manipulation.[42]

For instance, it was found in 2011 in the field of nonconscious consumer psychology that research in this area is no longer concerned with whether, but exactly how, the related methods change consumer behaviour.[43] Put simply, it may not (yet) be possible to remotely control or manipulate a person into adopting a specific behaviour, but subliminal cues were found effective in altering a person's behaviour. This may only be a matter of time, since it has already been predicted that 'the collection of big data, profiling, targeted advertisements and other 'immersive' and neuromarketing-based applications can be expected to enhance the overall effi-

[35] Neuwirth (2023a).

[36] Mlodinow (2012), p. 34; Wehling (2016), p. 43.

[37] Neuwirth (2023a), p. 67.

[38] Smith and McCulloch (2012), p. 551 [*Italics* added].

[39] Neuwirth (2023a), pp. 88–89; Quackenbos (1906).

[40] Pötzl (1960).

[41] Dijksterhuis et al. (2024), p. 77.

[42] Neuwirth (2023a), p. 43.

[43] Chartrand and Fitzsimons (2011), p. 3.

ciency of subliminal stimuli'.[44] Another study stated that AI may render the use of subliminal techniques more effective on a large scale based on 'micro-targeting, large-scale application, and the relentless collection of feedback and dissemination of tailored information'.[45] Related to this, the recent advances in the field of AI and its combination with other technologies were summarised by stating that they allow for a move from 'programming computers to programming people'.[46]

Testifying to this dark prediction, manipulative practices exist in the form of so-called 'dark patterns', which were initially defined as 'deceptive elements that are intentionally crafted to make the users do actions that they wouldn't do otherwise'.[47] These practices were also included in the Digital Services Act (DSA), which defined them as practices on the online interfaces of online platforms 'that materially distort or impair, either on purpose or in effect, the ability of recipients of the service to make autonomous and informed choices or decisions'.[48] Additionally, it was confirmed that dark patterns use cognitive mechanisms to influence the consumer, which can also be exercised in subliminal ways.[49] This example confirms that most manipulative practices will rely on stimuli received both subliminally and supraliminally, which is the reason the notion of 'transliminal' has been said to better embrace the danger of manipulation.

The distinction between harmful forms of subliminal manipulation and those deemed helpful, such as nudging, is equally problematic. A nudge is defined as 'any aspect of the choice architecture that alters people's behaviour in a predictable way without forbidding any options or significantly changing their economic incentives',[50] and it is also related to subliminal methods.

The book also found that even though the exact classification of an AI system as subliminal is scientifically impossible, there already exists ample evidence of the possibility of using subliminal stimuli in combination with AI and other technologies.[51] One such example is the so-called 'brain spyware', which is a term to describe 'software intentionally designed to detect private information'.[52] Such software has been used in a lab in combination with brain–computer interfaces to conduct experiments aimed at hacking a person's brain to 'deduce private information such as banking information, recognised faces, PIN numbers, location of residency and month of birth from the brains of BCI users by showing them visual stimuli and using a machine learning model to detect familiar information based on the brain's

[44] Reitberger et al. (2011), pp. 310, 233.

[45] Zhong et al. (2024), p. 20003 [reference omitted].

[46] Helbing et al. (2019), p. 76.

[47] Cara (2019), p. 105.

[48] Recital 67 Regulation (EU) 2022/2065 on a Single Market for Digital Services and amending Directive 2000/31/EC (Digital Services Act), OJ L 277/1 (27 October 2022).

[49] Organisation for Economic Co-operation and Development (2022), p. 9.

[50] Thaler and Sunstein (2008), pp. 6, 244.

[51] Neuwirth (2023a), pp. 25–31.

[52] Martinovic et al. (2012), p. 145.

response'.[53] Most importantly, such attacks on the privacy of thoughts in the brain can also be carried out subliminally.[54]

Overall, the mind-reading abilities of technologies are advancing at a rapid speed, even allowing for the need to reconstruct visual experiences from the human brain.[55] The recent rise of large language models and generative AI in combination with neurotechnologies and profiling further enhances the possibility of subliminally manipulating the human mind. Generative AI had already been qualified as a 'potential tool in the hands of malicious actors' because of its ability 'to create deepfakes, provide plausible deniability, and spread subliminal messages or deceiving content'.[56]

However, it is not only the technical progress that poses regulatory challenges. Even within the field of law, new challenges arise. For instance, concerns were voiced related to the definition and scope of the phrase 'physical or psychological harm'. In this regard, the DAIA was described as 'under protective'.[57] The reason is that it fails, in particular, to take into account possible cultural, social or political harms caused, such as by a manipulated election, algorithmic bias or other collective harms to society.[58] It will also be necessary to broaden the scope of harms to better encompass not only collective but also cumulative harms, that is, damage caused by the repeated consumption of a product.[59] It must also consider the possibility of harm being caused by the combined consumption of two different products at the same time, even though each of them in isolation would cause no harm.[60]

Further legal challenges will arise from the future relationship between the AIA and other relevant laws or even entire fields of law. This includes the consistent application of the AIA in line with other acts, such as the Digital Services Act (DSA), which also addresses 'dark patterns'.[61] In addition, subliminal algorithmic activity that manipulates a user will potentially 'fall under the transparency provision of the G if data processing is involved'.[62] This equally relates to and challenges the entire set of fundamental rights, with the right to freedom of thought at the forefront. In this context, the adoption of new laws or the creation of new rights,

[53] Steinhagen and Kettani (2020), p. 78.

[54] Frank et al. (2017), p. 133.

[55] Takagi and Nishimoto (2023), p. 14453.

[56] Ferrara (2024), p. 6.

[57] Smuha et al. (2021), p. 21 [footnote omitted]; Ebers et al. (2021), p. 592 [footnote omitted]; Uuk (2022).

[58] Cupać and Sienknecht (2024), p. 1.

[59] Veale and Borgesius (2021), p. 102.

[60] Neuwirth and Migliorini (2023).

[61] Recital 67 Digital Services Act; Regulation (EU) 2022/2065 on a Single Market For Digital Services and amending Directive 2000/31/EC (Digital Services Act), OJ L L 277/1 (27 October 2022).

[62] Herman (2024), p. 11.

such as neuro rights, should be carefully balanced against the possibility to interpret and apply existing norms in a new way.[63]

As far as the amendments to the originally proposed text are concerned, the phrase 'purposefully manipulative or deceptive techniques' was added to AI systems deploying subliminal techniques. This certainly expanded the scope to more kinds of manipulative practices, including those that operate transliminally, that is, above and below the threshold of awareness, such as dark patterns. As a second element, the final version added a clarification to the issue of the distortion of human behaviour by adding the possibility of 'appreciably impairing the ability to make an informed decision'. Last, it deleted the formulation of 'physical or psychological harm' and replaced it with the concept of 'significant harm'. These amendments can be deemed to expand the scope to some manipulative practices by AI systems that were not covered by the original version, notably those systems operating supraliminally. However, other changes, such as the use of 'significant harm' have done little to address new forms of collective or cumulative harms.

3.2 AI Systems Exploiting Vulnerabilities

The second category of prohibited AI practices listed in Art. 5 lit. b) DAIA was related to 'an AI system that exploits any of the vulnerabilities of a specific group of persons due to their age, physical or mental disability'. The wording of this provision is similar to the one covering subliminal AI systems, and it did not further explain the concept of 'vulnerability'. Instead, it defined vulnerability by singling out specific groups, such as children or persons with disabilities, who are deemed especially vulnerable based on their 'age, physical or mental disability'.[64] The problem with such an approach is that it overlooks the fact that both digital technologies and, in particular, AI not only exploit existing vulnerabilities but also create new ones. Thus, every person is actually vulnerable, which is the reason the stigmatisation of a specific group may create a false sense of safety.[65] In this context, combinations of different technologies (e.g., wearable health devices, Radio Frequency Identification devices to track movements, real-time target advertising or recommender systems) as well as different drivers of vulnerabilities may reinforce each other, as interactions 'between vulnerabilities can be compounded, as they intersect and influence each other'.[66] This observation also underscores the need to step up the joint study of law and the senses as captured by the concept of legal synaesthesia.[67]

---

[63] Bublitz (2014), p. 12; Neuwirth (2023c).

[64] Explanatory Memorandum of the AIA, *supra* note 2, at 13.

[65] Neuwirth (2023b), p. 6.

[66] Novelli et al. (2024), p. 3.

[67] Neuwirth (2022), p. 1.

Overall, this provision was also qualified as too narrow because not only age and physical or mental disability should be covered but also many other characteristics protected in EU law.[68] Therefore, it was suggested that the protection of vulnerabilities be expanded to all characteristics protected under EU equality law as laid down in Article 21 of the EU Charter on Fundamental Rights.[69]

The amendments to the category of AI systems exploiting vulnerabilities are equally limited and are mainly of a stylistic character. They eliminate 'physical or mental' before disability but add another element of vulnerability with the wording of 'a specific social or economic situation'. Finally, the phrase 'physical or psychological harm' is replaced with 'significant harm' as in the previous category. Overall, the amendments are of minor significance but at least help to diffuse the stigmatisation of certain groups of people by a little bit. This and the category of subliminal systems could have been merged and been drafted in a more concise and consistent way by merely emphasising the manipulative and exploitative nature of some AI systems and the serious harms they can cause. It has been argued that in the current version, there may still be a need to enhance the protection of the general public and, specifically, vulnerable groups.[70]

3.3 *Social Scoring Systems*

The third category of prohibited AI practices listed in Art. 5 (1) lit. c) DAIA targeted the 'use of AI systems by public authorities or on their behalf for the evaluation or classification of the trustworthiness of natural persons over a certain period of time based on their social behaviour or known or predicted personal or personality characteristics'. The condition for such a ban is that the practices prove detrimental or provide unfavourable treatment for certain natural persons or whole groups in particular situations. Unfortunately, the meaning of 'social scoring systems' was not further clarified in the DAIA. This would have been desirable as the use of AI for scoring is, in general, increasing. Moreover, it may be difficult to distinguish social scoring from other forms of scoring, such as the use of AI for polygenic risk scoring that 'provide a measure of individual disease risk based on one's genome-wide information'. It was argued that polygenic risk scores should also be outlawed because of the risk of too quickly drawing conclusions about causal relationships between genetics and behaviour.[71]

Another more general problem with social scoring is that it is part of a dichotomous system of 'rewards and punishments' or 'sticks and carrots', which shapes us

[68] Uuk (2022), p. 4.

[69] Smuha et al. (2021), p. 22.

[70] Zhong et al. (2024), p. 20006.

[71] Raz and Minari (2023), p. 2.

all and is widely regarded as universal.[72] Similar to the question of AI for good or for bad, it is hard to distinguish between legitimate forms of the evaluation of behaviour and illegitimate ones. As in the case of subliminal manipulation and nudging, dichotomies and dualistic thinking are likely to meet their limitations in this rapidly evolving and complex field of automated scoring systems. This is the reason that the mere use of binary methods or regulations, such as prohibitions or recommendations, has generally been found problematic in the regulation of technologies, in particular, and law, in general.[73]

Another wide misperception is that social scoring systems are exclusively used in countries outside the EU, notably in China or India.[74] The fact is that such systems are increasingly being used in the United States and Europe as well.[75]

As for the future, new technologies and their increasing interconnection create further possibilities and risks for the use of social scoring systems by both public and private authorities. Therefore, in this context, too, it was found that the scope of protection against social scoring systems should be clarified and, notably, extended to include private actors.[76]

In the case of social scoring systems, the amendments were broader. They first eliminated the limitation of their use to only public authorities by extending their use to everyone. The other requirement of leading to 'detrimental or unfavourable treatment' was left in place. However, the draft added four new categories to social scoring systems or that were at least closely related to social scoring systems, which is likely to cause some confusion as they are organised in separate paragraphs (i.e., lit. d) to g)) rather than in subparagraphs. Each of these paragraphs adds 'the placing on the market, the putting into service for *this specific purpose*', although to exactly what this refers remains unclear.

The first new category added by way of lit. d) refers to an AI system used 'for making risk assessments of natural persons in order to assess or predict the risk of a natural person committing a criminal offence'. In particular, this refers to profiling practices or the assessment of personality traits and characteristics of persons with the help of AI. This marks a very wide field of application, the usages and implications of which will have to be assessed by deeper analyses of the existing and future technologies and their possibilities.[77] This paragraph will most likely have to be considered in closer connection with the future of the justice systems in each Member State and the EU as a whole.

The second new category listed in lit. e) is AI systems used 'to create or expand facial recognition databases through the untargeted scraping of facial images from the internet or CCTV footage'. This addition is important as there have been

[72] Kinderman (2019), pp. 91–92.

[73] Eisenberger (2016), pp. 156–157; Neuwirth (2018), p. 14.

[74] Schroeder (2022).

[75] Citron and Pasquale (2014); Pasquale (2015); Loefflad and Grossklags (2024), p. 1516.

[76] Smuha et al. (2021), p. 23.

[77] Dakalbab et al. (2022).

numerous voices raised regarding facial recognition technology, which is being applied in a wide range of fields that are not limited to public authorities or the justice system. Moreover, it is a field that—despite technological limitations—evolves very quickly, which is why its future use needs to be closely monitored.[78] Despite its rapid evolution, there also remain important ethical concerns, notably with regard to privacy of the image data used, bias with regards to discrimination against certain segments of the population and safety due to potential malicious use of the technology.[79] This addition certainly marks an important step against excessive surveillance and data collection, but it will also require a closer systemic observation in order to secure consistency between the AIA and the General Data Protection Regulation (GDPR) as well as other relevant acts.

The third new category of lit. f) is most closely related to the kind of biometric scoring systems regarding emotion recognition systems or 'AI systems to infer emotions of a natural person'. The recognition of emotions is a complex procedure and includes various aspects, such as 'subjective experience, cognitive processes, behavioural influences, physiological responses, and communication', which can be used in many areas, such as 'marketing, human–robot interaction, healthcare, mental health monitoring, and security'.[80] Despite some conceptual clarifications on 'emotions' that are provided in Recital 18 by way of an illustrative list including 'happiness, sadness, anger, surprise, disgust etc', the exact delimitation of emotions from physical states, such as 'pain or fatigue', will prove as difficult as drawing a line between subliminal and supraliminal perception.[81] It is already difficult to classify emotions on their own, let alone to automatically mine opinions and sentiments from natural language and perhaps other sources.[82] The scope of the provision is also limited to its use in the workplace and educational institutions unless it is used for 'medical or safety reasons'. Last, the role of emotional recognition systems in connection with other applications, such as in support of subliminal AI systems, will also require further study and close observation.[83]

The last new category added in lit g) relates more to the former fourth category of biometric identification systems and shall be discussed in the next subsection.

---

[78] Hamann and Smith (2019); Raposo (2022).

[79] Wen and Holweg (2023), p. 2.

[80] Khare et al. (2024), p. 1.

[81] Lumley et al. (2011), p. 942 ('Thus, pain is partially an emotional experience, and the correspondence between pain and bodily damage is variable'.).

[82] Chafale and Pimpalkar (2014), p. 14.

[83] Neuwirth (2023b), p. 11; Bulgakova (2023), p. 95.

3.4 'Real-Time' Remote Biometric Identification Systems

The last category of prohibited AI practices concerns biometric identification systems provided that they operate remotely and in real time (Art. 5 (1) lit. d) DAIA). This prohibition, however, is limited and only applies to the use of these systems for the purpose of law enforcement and not in other contexts. Generally, biometrics can be described as 'a rapidly evolving field which – with the assistance of AI – allows for a wider use of data today and tomorrow'.[84]

Unlike the concepts invoked in previous categories, the DAIA offers additional interpretative guidance as to the meaning of the notion of a remote biometric identification system, which 'should be defined functionally, as an AI system intended for the identification of natural persons at a distance through the comparison of a person's biometric data with the biometric data contained in a reference database, and without prior knowledge whether the targeted person will be present and can be identified, irrespectively of the particular technology, processes or types of biometric data used'.[85]

Among biometric identification systems, fingerprint biometrics, facial recognition technology and iris recognition are likely the best known ways to identify a person. These traditional technologies have already raised concerns under existing law, such as under the GDPR, the EU Charter of Fundamental Rights and the Law Enforcement Directive.[86] However, the problems do not end there. The rapid advances in biometrics, the increased use of biometric technologies and the combination of two or more factors means that the taxonomy of biometric technologies is constantly changing, which brings problems for their consistent and future-proof regulation.[87] There are already a variety of combinations of biometric systems in use, such as retinas, hand geometry, voices, signatures, palm-print features and ears.[88] Additionally, biometrics increasingly relies on both biological and behavioural characteristics. Behavioural biometrics refers to methods to identify persons based on their behaviour, such as keystroke dynamics, graphical authentication systems, mouse dynamics, gait (i.e., the way a person walks), smile or lip movements and even odour as well as biological signals, such as those measured by the electrocardiogram (recording of the beating of the heart) and the electroencephalogram (recording of the activity of the brain).[89]

Given that no single system is accurate or safe as it can also be circumvented, a general trend is to combine features into 'multimodal biometric systems', such as voice and face recognition similar to the two-factor authentication for accessing

---

[84] Neuwirth (2023b), p. 11.

[85] Art. 3(35) DAIA, *supra* note 2.

[86] Raposo (2022), p. 46.

[87] Ramos (2023), p. 1.

[88] de Luis-García et al. (2003), p. 2539.

[89] Revett (2008), pp. 2–12.

bank or email accounts.[90] The trend towards the multimodal combination of biometric identification systems also confirms the wider trend of the possibility of the creative combination of different technologies for different purposes. For instance, various biometric systems can now be used to infer important personal information about the emotional state of a person from various biometric data, such as respiratory rhythm, gait or speech.[91] This information can not only be used to identify a person but also to subliminally manipulate and even intentionally create and exploit personal vulnerabilities.

The text of the former fourth category discussed here was largely left untouched in terms of its principal scope as it still remains limited to use for the purpose of law enforcement. Most changes merely clarified or added a few concepts, such as the use of such systems in the case of a targeted search for 'missing children' or the criteria in the context of 'a terrorist attack'. Another major change was the introduction of the requirement of the notification of the relevant market surveillance authority and national data protection authority when such systems are being used by law enforcement authorities (Paragraph 4).

A fourth new category of prohibited AI systems was added in the course of the negotiations about this category of biometric identification systems. This new category is listed in lit g) and covers 'the use of biometric categorisation systems that categorise individually natural persons based on their biometric data to deduce or infer their race, political opinions, trade union membership, religious or philosophical beliefs, sex life or sexual orientation'. Many difficulties will also arise in this context regarding the interpretation of some these concepts, which must be deemed to be essentially contested concepts and even involve a large number of contradictions expressed through oxymora.[92] For instance, it would be interesting how a philosophical belief might be established and by whom, particularly as the entire question of the identity of a person is subject to philosophical debates.[93]

In view of the amendments and additions introduced to Article 5 AIA, the final evaluation is mixed. While some concepts were clarified, the introduction of new ones raises new concerns; and while the scope of some provisions was enlarged, the more casuistic and descriptive nature of some additions may result in once more narrowing the scope. What is safe to say is that at this stage, putting some urgently needed regulatory limits on the perceived total freedom of both public authorities and private actors in the digital space marks an immensely important step.

---

[90] de Luis-García et al. (2003), p. 2552; De Cristofaro et al. (2014), p. 1.

[91] Feldman et al. (2019); Jerath and Beveridge (2020).

[92] Gallie (1956); Neuwirth (2013).

[93] Kind (2023).

4 The EU AI Act Revisited

While the original proposal for an AIA was launched on 21 April 2021, the AIA finally entered into force on 1 August 2024. The AIA will, however, only become fully effective after 24 months (i.e., from 1 August 2026), considering the specific provisions listed in Article 113 AIA featuring scaled periods of implementation for different chapters. As for the prohibited AI practices listed in Article 5 AIA, the prohibition will apply six months from the date of entry into force of the AIA, which means from 1 February 2025.

Overall, the years from the original proposal of the AIA to its final adoption provide useful lessons for the current and future debates about the optimal regulatory approaches to the regulation of AI. On the positive side, it was certainly an achievement of the Draft AIA to inspire a constructive global politico–legal debate about this immensely important matter for the future of humanity. The nature of AI as a global commons has since then been recognised and confirmed, as can be seen in the adoption of the UNESCO Recommendation on the Ethics of AI in November 2021 and the 2024 United Nations General Assembly Resolution on safe AI.[94] Due to its comprehensive scope, its persuasive authority certainly also inspired regulators in other jurisdictions, such as in the PRC and in the US, both of which adopted specific regulations on AI before the entry into force of the AIA.

On the negative side, it also provided important lessons regarding the optimal focus of the debate. First, the framing of the debate as a 'global race to regulate AI' has been found to be misguided and potentially harmful.[95] The goal to be the first to regulate AI was especially misguided and misplaced.[96] The subsequent delays to the AIA, which were also caused by the emergence of large language models in the form of AI chatbots (i.e., Chat-GPT) during that period, proved that it is better to aim for the best rather than the fastest regulatory strategy because it is particularly important to future proof laws in the regulation of technologies. Other difficulties also confirmed that AI is a subject matter that requires global coordination to complement the various national and regional regulatory initiatives and to envisage a radical reform of the institutional framework of global governance. A more profound failure that is common to most approaches to the governance of AI is the exclusion of AI systems used for military purposes.[97]

---

[94] UNESCO (2022) Recommendation on the Ethics of Artificial Intelligence. UNESCO, Paris, https://unesdoc.unesco.org/©ark:/48223/pf0000381137 and United Nations General Assembly (2024) *Seizing the Opportunities of Safe, Secure and Trustworthy Artificial Intelligence Systems for Sustainable Development*, A/78/L.49 (11 March 2024), https://documents.un.org/doc/undoc/ltd/n24/065/92/pdf/n2406592.pdf?token=G7NNCJ6Tit6a2ELlw0&fe=true.

[95] Armstrong et al. (2016); Ulnicane (2023); Neuwirth (2024), p. 39.

[96] European Parliament (2023), 'EU AI Act: First Regulation on Artificial Intelligence' (8 June 2023), https://www.europarl.europa.eu/topics/en/article/20230601STO93804/eu-ai-act-first-regulation-on-artificial-intelligence.

[97] Art. 2(3) DAIA, *supra* note 3.

The genesis of the AIA, however, revealed further specific deficiencies and future serious regulatory challenges. These were exemplified by the comparison of the original with the final version of Article 5 AIA on 'prohibited AI practices', which now covers a few more categories than those of subliminal AI systems, exploitative AI systems, social scoring systems and real-time remote biometric identification systems. The new additions include AI systems used to make predictions about persons committing a criminal offence, to create facial recognition databases, to infer emotions of persons in the workplace or educational institutions and the use of biometric categorisation systems to infer different traits or characteristics of a person. In spite of these extensions, the years between the initial formulation of the proposal and final adoption of the AIA could have been used to repair some of the principal problems, as indicated in the following paragraphs.

First of all, each of the essentially contested concepts, such as those of 'subliminal perception', 'exploitation', 'vulnerability' or 'harm', should have been further clarified after consultation with experts in the different scientific fields concerned. For the sake of future proofing the law, it would also have been useful to consider existing AI systems and to make more concrete projections about their future path of development in light of the trend for their convergence and systemic risks arising from them, which are those 'characterised by high complexity, multiple uncertainties, major ambiguities, and transgressive effects on other systems outside of the system of origin'.[98] In this regard, it would also have been helpful if some of the many concerns expressed through constructive criticism or concrete examples in academic writings would have been seriously considered and adequately addressed as a consequence. Generally, it is important that any future regulatory effort must be based on a more interdisciplinary and novel scientific understanding of the matter involved.

However, if the legislature intended to keep the meaning of some of these contested concepts vague, then the multiple rounds of amendments should not have added other vague concepts that not only unnecessarily increased the length of the document but also created further confusion.[99] For instance, it is unclear what added value the replacement of 'psychological and physical harm' with 'significant harm' has brought. Further problems will likely arise from the distinction between emotions and the physical states of a person.

The tendency to opt for too detailed, too lengthy and too specific regulatory approaches is further aggravated by the lack of general systemic oversight. This becomes visible with regard to both the mutual relationship between each of the now eight prohibited categories within Article 5 AIA and the relationship of the AIA to other acts, notably the Digital Services Act and Digital Markets Act. to mention but two of many more regulatory acts adopted by the EU on digital technologies in recent years.[100] Such lack of systemic oversight and the resulting fragmentation is

---

[98] Renn et al. (2022), p. 1902.

[99] Endicott (2001), p. 379.

[100] Papakonstantinou and De Hert (2022), p. 48.

frequent and can be highlighted by the example of vulnerable AI systems, which in a way contravenes the spirit of the EU Charter as it might stigmatise specific groups and create a false sense of safety for the rest of the population.

Specifically, too, the scope of Article 5 AIA and, notably, its division now into eight different but closely interrelated categories should have been reconsidered in light of the ongoing trend of the convergence of technologies. In the regulation of technologies, there should generally be fewer but more inclusive and consistent approaches to avoid a greater fragmentation in the law and overregulation leading to internal contradictions and frequent conflicts. For Article 5 AIA, this should have meant to prepare for the actual case in which the use of an AI system, such as a recommender or biometric identification system, may not be covered by any of the four separate listed categories but rather violates the spirit of all eight categories in their practical effect. Overall, the scope of prohibited AI practices should be regularly reviewed in light of new scientific insights of their overall impact on human wellbeing. In this regard, it seems that even 'older' technologies, such as smartphones, have not been duly regulated in proportion to their negative impacts.[101]

The debate should also not be confused by the traditional separation of public and private law. This particularly applies to the case of social scoring systems, which have been put in place by both public authorities and private actors. The elimination of the limitation of their use by 'public authorities or on their behalf' was the correct step and marks a rare positive example of an improvement in the final version of the AIA.

As for the ban on biometric identification systems, it has fortunately now been extended beyond the sole use by law enforcement authorities. It was important to widen the scope to prepare for and protect against their unwanted use in other contexts, such as emotion recognition systems, given that the rapid advances in biometrics already allow for the detection of the emotional state of a person based on a variety of factors, such as facial expressions, gait or the rhythm of the heartbeat. However, some gaps between these categories remain, as the information gained from biometric systems can also be used to enhance the accuracy and efficiency of systems aiming at the subliminal manipulation or exploitation of the vulnerabilities of persons or entire groups of persons.[102]

Much of the future success of the AIA will depend on the enforcement of the law. It was only in early 2024 that the European Commission set up the AI Office 'within the Commission as part of the administrative structure of the Directorate-General for Communication Networks, Content and Technology'.[103] It is a positive sign that no separate external agency was created, as this may be more conducive to a coherent and consistent application of the law. However, considerations of the feasibility of the enforcement of the AIA and, notably, the prohibitions listed in Art. 5

---

[101] Cytowic (2024).

[102] Miotto and Chen (2022), p. 405.

[103] Recitals 5 and 6 of the EC Decision establishing the EU AI Office; European Commission, *Commission Decision of 24.1.2024 establishing the European Artificial Intelligence Office*, C(2024) 390 final (24 January 2024).

AIA should have been given greater importance from the beginning as important precedents exist from the enforcement of the prohibition of subliminal advertising in the Television Without Frontiers Directive.[104]

Paradoxically, and against the traditional mode of thinking, the final evaluation of the AIA must be that the glass is both half full and half empty. It is similar to the question of technology neutrality, according to which AI must be regarded to be 'neither good nor bad; nor is it neutral'.[105] Therefore, important challenges for the future regulation of AI remain, challenges that include issues regarding the future proofing of regulations, which ultimately will also require novel thinking about life and the role of law in future societies.[106]

5 Conclusion

> [...] everything is allowed, especially when it is forbidden.[107]

Once the AIA will have resumed its full legal force, the focus will shift from the regulation to the enforcement of prohibited AI practices. There will be further serious difficulties encountered, such as the paradoxical question of how to detect subliminal forms of manipulation if they occur below the threshold of a person's awareness. Most likely, answers to this question will need to be sought in the development and use of the technologies themselves. Against the backdrop of the global and pervasive nature of AI, its cross-boundary nature and its close relationship to other related technologies, it will be necessary to closely observe the impact it has and the risks it bears over time.

More than that, AI is not a mere technology. It provides an unprecedented opportunity for a deeper understanding of the human brain and its mysterious workings. This means, however, that we should not just focus on the search for good AI; we should also critically reflect on and update the scientific understanding of human intelligence. The ultimate goal of the development of AI must not only be to improve artificial forms of intelligence but also to cultivate human intelligence accordingly. This task also entails the development of new visions for societies that are based on novel modes of legal reasoning and the newfound role of law.

In these various endeavours, the category of prohibited AI systems marks a key concept for the future search for the proper legal treatment of those digital and other technologies that pose unacceptable and possibly existential risks to each

---

[104] Neuwirth (2023a), p. 17.

[105] Kranzberg (1986), p. 545.

[106] Neuwirth (2024), pp. 22 and 33.

[107] See the jocular saying: 'In Germany everything is forbidden, unless something is specifically allowed, whereas in Britain everything which is not specifically forbidden, is allowed. In France everything is allowed, even if it is forbidden; and in Italy everything is allowed, especially when it is forbidden,' reprinted in Schütze (2012), p. 88 (FN 24).

individual, to groups of people and to humanity as a whole. This is the reason it is also a topic for international cooperation aiming for a global consensus regarding the safe use of AI. If no such consensus on AI, including the law's foundations such as the role of the right to freedom in the age of neuroscience, can be found and agreed upon, there is a risk of the Orwellian scenario not to fulfil itself but deteriorate even further. To recall, it was in 1948 that Orwell predicted that the invention of new forms of mass media carried the process of manipulating public opinion further, which meant that 'private life came to an end'. Several decades after 1984, the risk is now that private thought has become an oxymoron and come to an end at the same time.[108]

References

Armstrong S, Bostrom N, Shulman C (2016) Racing to the precipice: a model of artificial intelligence development. AI Soc 31:201–206. https://doi.org/10.1007/s00146-015-0590-y

Belk R, Humayun M, Gopaldas A (2020) Artificial life. J Macromarket 40(2):221–236. https://doi.org/10.1177/0276146719897361

Bublitz JC (2014) Freedom of thought in the age of neuroscience: a plea and a proposal for the renaissance of a forgotten fundamental right. Archiv für Rechts- und Sozialphilosophie 100(1):1–25

Bulgakova D (2023) The prohibited artificial intelligence practice. Theory Pract Forensic Sci Crim 32(3):89–112. https://khrife-journal.org/index.php/journal/article/view/574

Cara C (2019) Dark patterns in the media: a systematic review. Netw Intell Stud 7(14):105–113

Chafale D, Pimpalkar A (2014) Review on developing corpora for sentiment analysis using Plutchik's wheel of emotions with fuzzy logic. Int J Comput Sci Eng 2(10):14–18

Chartrand TL, Fitzsimons GJ (2011) Nonconscious consumer psychology. J Consum Psychol 21:1–3. https://doi.org/10.1016/j.jcps.2010.12.001

Citron DK, Pasquale F (2014) The scored society: due process for automated predictions. Wash Law Rev 89(1):1–34

Cordeschi R (2007) AI turns fifty: revisiting its origins. Appl Artif Intell 21(4–5):259–279. https://doi.org/10.1080/08839510701252304

Cupać J, Sienknecht M (2024) Regulate against the machine: how the EU mitigates AI harm to democracy. Democratization 00:1–24. https://doi.org/10.1080/13510347.2024.2353706

Cytowic RE (2024) Your stone age brain in the screen age: coping with digital distraction and sensory overload. The MIT Press, Cambridge

Dakalbab F, Abu Talib M, Abu Waraga O, Bou Nassif A, Abbas S, Nasir Q (2022) Artificial intelligence & crime prediction: a systematic literature review. Soc Sci Humanit Open 6(1):1–23. https://doi.org/10.1016/j.ssaho.2022.100342

De Cristofaro E, Du H, Freudiger J, Norcie G (2014) A comparative usability study of two-factor authentication. arXiv:1309.5344 99:1–10. https://doi.org/10.48550/arXiv.1309.5344

de Luis-García R, Alberola-López C, Aghzout O, Ruiz-Alzola J (2003) Biometric identification systems. Signal Process 83:2539–2557. https://doi.org/10.1016/j.sigpro.2003.08.001

Dijksterhuis A, Aarts H, Smith PK (2024) The power of the subliminal: on subliminal persuasion and other potential applications. In: Hassin RR, Uleman JS, Bargh JA (eds) The new unconscious. Oxford University Press, Oxford, pp 77–106

[108] Neuwirth (2023a), p. 121.

Ebers M, Hoch VRS, Rosenkranz F, Ruschemeier H, Steinrötter B (2021) The European Commission's Proposal for an Artificial Intelligence Act—a critical assessment by members of the Robotics and AI Law Society (RAILS). J 4:589–603. https://doi.org/10.3390/j4040043
Eisenberger I (2016) Innovation im Recht. Verlag Österreich, Vienna
Endicott T (2001) Law is necessarily vague. Leg Theory 7(4):379–385
Feldman BL, Adolphs R, Marsella S, Martinez AM, Polla SD (2019) Emotional expressions reconsidered: challenges to inferring emotion from human facial movements. Psychol Sci Public Interest 20:1–68. https://doi.org/10.1177/1529100619832930
Ferrara E (2024) GenAI against humanity: nefarious applications of generative artificial intelligence and large language models. J Comput Soc Sci 00:1–21. https://doi.org/10.1007/s42001-024-00250-1
Frank M, Hwu T, Jain D, Knight RT, Martinovic I, Mittal P, Perito D, Sluganovic I, Song D (2017) Using EEG-based BCI devices to subliminally probe for private information. Proceedings of the 2017 workshop on privacy in the electronic society (WPES'17) 00:133–136. https://doi.org/10.1145/3139550.3139559
Gallie WB (1956) Essentially contested concepts. Proc Aristot Soc 56:167–198
Hamann K, Smith R (2019). Facial recognition technology: where will it take us. Crim Just 34(1):9–13
Helbing D, Frey BS, Gigerenzer G, Hafen E, Hagner M, Hofstetter Y, van den Hoven J, Zicari RV, Zwitter A (2019) Will democracy survive big data and artificial intelligence? In: Helbing D (ed) Towards digital enlightenment: essays on the dark and light sides of the digital revolution. Springer, Cham, pp 73–98
Hendrycks D, Mazeika M, Woodside T (2023) An overview of catastrophic AI risks. rXiv:2306.12001 [cs.CY] 1–54. https://doi.org/10.48550/arXiv.2306.12001
Herman J (2024) Dark patterns: EU's regulatory efforts. Secur Priv 7(6):1–14. https://doi.org/10.1002/spy2.441
Hutcheson F (1764) A short introduction to moral philosophy. Robert & Andrew Foulis, Glasgow
Jerath R, Beveridge C (2020) Respiratory rhythm, autonomic modulation, and the spectrum of emotions: the future of emotion recognition and modulation. Front Psychol 11(1980):1–7. https://doi.org/10.3389/fpsyg.2020.01980
Khare SK, Blanes-Vidal V, Nadimi ES, Rajendra Acharya U (2024) Emotion recognition and artificial intelligence: a systematic review (2014–2023) and research recommendations. Inf Fusion 102(102019):1–36. https://doi.org/10.1016/j.inffus.2023.102019
Kind A (2023) Biometrics and the metaphysics of personal identity. IET Biometrics 12(3):129–182, https://doi.org/10.1049/bme2.12062
Kinderman P (2019) A manifesto for mental health: why we need a revolution in mental health care. Springer Nature, Cham
Kranzberg M (1986) Technology and history: 'Kranzberg's Laws'. Technol Cult 27(3):544–560
Krausová A (2017) Intersections between law and artificial intelligence. Int J Comput 27(1):55–68
Laws J (2000) The rule of reason – an international heritage. In: Andenas M (ed) Judicial review in international perspective. Kluwer Law International, The Hague, pp 247–258
Loefflad C, Grossklags J (2024) How the types of consequences in social scoring systems shape people's perceptions and behavioral reactions. FAccT '24: Proceedings of the 2024 ACM Conference on Fairness, Accountability, and Transparency 00:1515–1530. https://doi.org/10.1145/3630106.3658986 at 1516
Lumley MA, Cohen JL, Borszcz GS, Cano A, Radcliffe AM, Porter LS, Schubiner H, Keefe FJ (2011) Pain and emotion: a biopsychosocial review of recent research. J Clin Psychol 67(9):942–968. https://doi.org/10.1002/jclp.20816
Martinovic I, Davies D, Frank M, Perito D, Ros T, Song D (2012) On the feasibility of side-channel attacks with brain-computer interfaces. Proceedings of the 21st USENIX Security Symposium 00:143–158. https://www.usenix.org/conference/usenixsecurity12/technical-sessions/presentation/martinovic

McCarthy J, Minsky ML, Rochester N, Shannon CE (2006) A proposal for the Dartmouth Summer Research Project on Artificial Intelligence, August 31, 1955. AI Mag 27(4):12–14. file:///C:/Users/rjn/Downloads/1904-Article%20Text-1900-1-10-20080129.pdf

Miotto L, Chen J (2022) Manipulation, real-time profiling, and their wrongs. In: Klenk M, Jongepier F (eds) The philosophy of online manipulation. Routledge, London, pp 392–409. https://doi.org/10.4324/9781003205425

Mlodinow L (2012) Subliminal: how your unconscious mind rules your behaviour. Vintage Books, New York, NY

Moor J (2006) The Dartmouth College Artificial Intelligence Conference: the next fifty years. AI Mag 27(4):87–91. file:///C:/Users/rjn/Downloads/1911-Article%20Text-1907-1-10-20080129.pdf

Neuwirth RJ (2013) Essentially oxymoronic concepts. Global J Comp Law 2(2):147–166. https://doi.org/10.1163/2211906X-00202002

Neuwirth RJ (2018) Law in the time of oxymora: a synaesthesia of language, logic and law. Routledge, London

Neuwirth RJ (2022) Law, artificial intelligence, and synaesthesia. AI Soc 00:1–12. https://doi.org/10.1007/s00146-022-01615-8

Neuwirth RJ (2023a) The EU's Artificial Intelligence Act: regulating subliminal AI systems. Routledge, London

Neuwirth RJ (2023b) Prohibited artificial intelligence practices in the proposed EU Artificial Intelligence Act (AIA). Comput Law Secur Rev 48(105798):1–14. https://doi.org/10.1016/j.clsr.2023.105798

Neuwirth RJ (2023c) Das Gehirn im Spannungsfeld von Recht und Neurotechnologien: dargestellt am Beispiel subliminaler KI-Systeme. In: Symposion Dürnstein (eds) Das Gehirn und seine Gesellschaft: Tagungsband zum Symposion Dürnstein 2023. Tredition, Hamburg, pp 135–148

Neuwirth RJ (2024) The global institutional governance of AI: a four-dimensional perspective. Int J Digital Law Gov 00:1–41. https://doi.org/10.1515/ijdlg-2024-0004

Neuwirth RJ, Migliorini S (2023) Unacceptable risks in Human-AI Collaboration: legal prohibitions in light of cognition, trust and harm. EUR Workshop Proceedings (CEUR-WS.org) 00:1–7. https://ceur-ws.org/Vol-3547/paper4.pdf

Nilsson NJ (2010) The quest for artificial intelligence: a history of ideas and achievements. Cambridge University Press, Cambridge

Novelli C, Casolari F, Rotolo A, Taddeo M, Floridi L (2024) Taking AI risks seriously: a new assessment model for the AI Act. AI Soc 00:1–5. https://doi.org/10.1007/s00146-023-01723-z

Organisation for Economic Co-operation and Development (2019) Recommendation on artificial intelligence. OECD, Paris

Organisation for Economic Co-operation and Development (2022) Dark commercial patterns. OECD, Paris

Papakonstantinou V, De Hert P (2022) The regulation of digital technologies in the EU: the law-making phenomena of 'Act-ification', 'GDPR Mimesis' and 'EU Law Brutality'. Technol Regul 2022:48–60. https://doi.org/10.26116/techreg.2022.005

Parasol M (2021) AI development and the 'Fuzzy Logic' of Chinese cyber security and data laws. Cambridge University Press, Cambridge

Pasquale F (2015) The Black Box Society: the secret algorithms that control money and information. Harvard University Press, Cambridge, MA

Pötzl O (1960) The relationship between experimentally induced dream images and indirect vision. Psychol Issues 2(3):41–120

Quackenbos JD (1906) The transliminal. North Am Rev 183(597):237–249

Ramos LFM (2023) Biometric technologies and the law: developing a taxonomy for guiding policymakers. arXiv:2312.00013 [cs.CY] 00:1–11. https://doi.org/10.48550/arXiv.2312.00013

Raposo VL (2022) (Do not) remember my face: uses of facial recognition technology in light of the general data protection regulation. Inf Commun Technol Law 32(1):45–63. https://doi.org/10.1080/13600834.2022.2054076

Raximov N, Primqulov O, Daminova B (2021) Basic concepts and stages of research development on artificial intelligence. 2021 International Conference on Information Science and Communications Technologies (ICISCT):1–4, https://doi.org/10.1109/ICISCT52966.2021.9670085
Raz A, Minari J (2023) AI-driven risk scores: should social scoring and polygenic scores based on ethnicity be equally prohibited? Front Genet 14:1–4. https://doi.org/10.3389/fgene.2023.1169580
Reitberger W, Meschtscherjakov A, Mirlacher T, Tscheligi M (2011) Ambient persuasion in the shopping context. In: Müller J, Alt F, Michelis D (eds) Pervasive advertising. Springer, London, pp 309–323
Renn O, Laubichler M, Lucas K, Kröger W, Schanze J, Scholz RW, Schweizer P-J (2022) Systemic risks from different perspectives. Risk Anal 42(9):1902–1920. https://doi.org/10.1111/risa.13657
Revett K (2008) Behavioural biometrics: a remote access approach. John Wiley & Sons, Hoboken, NJ
Schroeder R (2022) Aadhaar and the social credit system: personal data governance in India and China. Int J Commun 16:2370–2386. https://ijoc.org/index.php/ijoc/article/view/19059
Schütze R (2012) An introduction to European law. Cambridge University Press, Cambridge
Smith PK, McCulloch K (2012) Subliminal perception. In: Ramachandran VS (ed) Encyclopedia of human behavior, vol 1, 2nd edn. Academic Press, London, pp 551–557
Smuha NA (2022) From a 'Race to AI' to a 'Race to AI Regulation': regulatory competition for artificial intelligence. Law Innov Technol 13(1):57–84
Smuha NA, Ahmed-Rengers E, Harkens A, Li W, MacLaren J, Piselli R, Yeung L (2021) How the EU can achieve legally trustworthy AI: a response to the European Commission's Proposal for an Artificial Intelligence Act. SSRN 00:1–64. https://papers.ssrn.com/sol3/papers.cfm?abstract_id=3899991
Steinhagen D, Kettani H (2020) An inventory of existing neuroprivacy controls. ICISDM 2020: Proceedings of the 2020 the 4th International Conference on Information System and Data Mining 00:77–83. https://doi.org/10.1145/3404663.3404664
Takagi Y, Nishimoto S (2023) High-resolution image reconstruction with latent diffusion models from human brain activity. Proceedings of the IEEE/CVF Conference on Computer Vision and Pattern Recognition (CVPR) 00:14453–14463
Thaler RH, Sunstein CR (2008) Nudge: improving decisions about health, wealth, and happiness. Yale University Press, New Haven, CT
Ulnicane I (2023) Against the new space race: global AI competition and cooperation for people. AI Soc 38:681–683. https://doi.org/10.1007/s00146-022-01423-0
United Nations Educational, Scientific and Cultural Organization (2022) Recommendation on the Ethics of Artificial Intelligence. UNESCO, Paris. https://unesdoc.unesco.org/©ark:/48223/pf0000381137
United Nations General Assembly (2024) Seizing the Opportunities of Safe, Secure and Trustworthy Artificial Intelligence Systems for Sustainable Development, A/78/L.49 (11 March 2024). file:///C:/Users/rjn/Downloads/A_78_L.49-EN.pdf
United Nations High-Level AI Advisory Body (2024) Governing AI for Humanity: Final Report. United Nations, New York, NY. https://www.un.org/sites/un2.un.org/files/governing_ai_for_humanity_final_report_en.pdf
Uuk R (2022) Manipulation and the AI Act. The Future of Life Institute (18 January 2022). https://futureoflife.org/wp-content/uploads/2022/01/FLI-Manipulation_AI_Act.pdf?x49432
Veale M, Borgesius FZ (2021) Demystifying the Draft EU Artificial Intelligence Act. Comput Law Rev Int 22(4):97–112
Wang Y (2024) Do not go gentle into that good night: The European Union's and China's different approaches to the extraterritorial application of artificial intelligence laws and regulations. Comput Law Secur Rev 53:1–13. https://doi.org/10.1016/j.clsr.2024.105965

Wehling E (2016) Politisches Framing. Wie eine Nation sich ihr Denken einredet und daraus Politik gemacht wird. Halem Verlag, Köln

Wen Y, Holweg M (2023) A phenomenological perspective on AI ethical failures: the case of facial recognition technology. AI Soc 00:1–18. https://doi.org/10.1007/s00146-023-01648-7

Zhong H, O'Neill E, Hoffmann JA (2024) Regulating AI: applying insights from behavioural economics and psychology to the application of Article 5 of the EU AI Act. Proceedings of the AAAI Conference on Artificial Intelligence 38(18):20001–20009. https://doi.org/10.1609/aaai.v38i18.29977

High-Risk AI Systems

Dariusz Szostek and Rafał Tomasz Prabucki

Contents

Abstract The chapter delves into the complexities of regulating artificial intelligence (AI) systems classified as high-risk under the European Union's Artificial Intelligence Act (AI Act). The authors explore the challenges of defining and categorising high-risk AI systems, highlighting the dynamic evolution of legislative proposals and amendments. The text provides an in-depth analysis of key provisions, such as Article 6, which outlines the criteria for high-risk classification, and Annex III, detailing specific use cases and risk scenarios. The chapter emphasises the importance of implementing robust risk management systems, as required by Article 9 of the AI Act, and ensuring compliance with evolving cybersecurity, transparency, and accountability standards. It also examines the interplay between existing EU regulations, such as GDPR and NIS, and the requirements introduced by the AI Act. By addressing the responsibilities of AI providers, stakeholders, and regula-

D. Szostek · R. T. Prabucki (✉)
University of Silesia in Katowice, Katowice, Poland
e-mail: dariusz.szostek@us.edu.pl; rafal.prabucki@us.edu.pl

V. L. Raposo (ed.), *The European Artificial Intelligence Act*, Law, Governance and Technology Series 78, https://doi.org/10.1007/978-3-031-98406-8_7

tors, the authors underline the need for a balanced and flexible regulatory framework. This work serves as a critical resource for understanding the intricacies of high-risk AI regulation, offering valuable insights for legislators, AI developers, and industry professionals.

1 Introduction

The issue of regulating Artificial Intelligence (AI), as the previous chapters have already shown, is extremely complex. It is not straightforward to determine the scope of regulation, but also the definition of terms relating to AI. All the more so as there is no uniform artificial intelligence or method of its training. After all, we have machine learning, genetic algorithms, neural networks, fuzzy logic, Ant colony optimisation algorithms, swarm intelligence and, on the other hand, automated theorem proving and expert systems,[1] AI is understood differently by lawyers, by business, and by IT or Industry 4.0 specialists. There are many definitions of AI in non-EU government documents (more on this in the previous chapter), and even more types in journalism, ranging from weak and strong AI, through AGI (Artificial General Intelligence), to the concept of ASI (Artificial Super Intelligence). There have also been various concepts of a method of regulating AI based solely on legal regulation, or the creation of a new directive on the responsibility of algorithms, complementing existing legislation, to the concept of creating an algorithm as a regulator of AI (as a law or as a RegTech tool).[2] Most of the studies pointed to the need to take into account the dynamics of algorithm liability including AI, technology neutrality and also to take into account the existing body of law.

Ultimately, the concept regarding liability for AI, including the singling out of AI high risks, pursued by the European Commission in the AI Act is to a large extent based on the concept presented by Wendehorst in the document 'Safety and Liability Related Aspects of Software' developed for the European Commission and is horizontal in nature however scattered across multiple pieces of legislation.[3]

Both the Report and the studies produced by Wendehorst point out that the responsibility for algorithms is very complex and involves a number of elements, including infrastructure. For the proper, secure functioning of algorithms, including AI systems as referred to in Article 3(1) of the draft regulation of the European Parliament and of the Council laying down harmonised rules on artificial intelligence (Artificial Intelligence Act) and amending certain legislative acts of the

[1] See Barfield and Pagallo (2020), pp. 19–23.

[2] By which the authors mean various activities using already existing technical solutions, e.g. learning frameworks based on experiences using Blockchain. See Su et al. (2024), pp. 1–8.

[3] See Wendehorst (2021), pp. 40–44.

union,[4] it is necessary to secure but also to control not only the AI algorithm itself but also the Internet connectivity services, the IoT terminal tools (including sensors, collecting, transmitting data feeding AI), the 'purity' and transparency of the data acquired and used, the security of the 'cloud' used and the security and vulnerability (in the sense of cyber threats) of the algorithms used. Only together do all these elements constitute the security of an AI system, or algorithms more broadly. A consequence of the above is the need to separate the responsibilities of the various actors involved in the 'chain' used by the algorithms including AI. Significantly, the different actors may fall under different, often distant, regulations in terms of liability, whether already in force or yet to be designed. Consequently, a flaw in one component of the 'chain' can have a cascading impact on the other elements.[5]

The horizontal approach to high-risk AI systems is important in determining liability for AI. Whether legislation is broad in scope, covering all or a very wide range of products or activities (often referred to as 'horizontal' legislation), or narrow in scope, covering only specific types of products and activities (often referred to as 'sectoral' legislation), is determined by a number of factors, including whether the safety requirements or liability imposed are appropriate necessary and proportionate for a broad or only a narrow range of products or activities, taking into account that any requirements or liability may increase overall safety and user confidence, but also add costs and make it more difficult for small and medium-sized enterprises to enter the market; and considerations of clarity, consistency and practicality of the law. In the area of high-risk AI systems, a broad and therefore horizontal scope of liability was rightly adopted.

2 High-Risk AI Definition

2.1 Evolution of Legislation

The issue of the definition of AI, including high-risk AI has been an issue since the very beginning of the debate on AI regulation, very intense, as evidenced by the more than 3000 amendments to the AI Act.[6] Since the publication of the draft AI Act, each presidency, in particular the Czech Republic, have put forward compromise proposals for regulation, including high-risk AI. Over the course of various presidencies, the proposed regulations related to defining high-risk AI have dynamically evolved. These changes range from emphasising the need to establish a definition for 'general purpose AI system' as a main goal (Broad Scope), to

[4] Article 3(1) in European commission: proposal for a regulation of the European parliament and of the council: laying down harmonised rules on artificial intelligence (artificial intelligence act) and amending certain union legislative acts, https://eurlex.europa.eu/legal-content/EN/TXT/?uri=CELEX%3A52021PC0206.

[5] See Wendehorst (2020), pp. 150–180.

[6] See Bracy (2022).

rejecting this direction in favour of adding a definition for 'AI systems' and ultimately to including an additional definition for 'risk' at the beginning of Article 3 (Risk Scenarios).[7] According to AI Act, the definition of an AI system is:

> (…) a machine-based system that is designed to operate with varying levels of autonomy and that may exhibit adaptiveness after deployment, and that, for explicit or implicit objectives, infers, from the input it receives, how to generate outputs such as predictions, content, recommendations, or decisions that can influence physical or virtual environments.

The specified additional definition of risk is as follows:

> (…) the combination of the probability of an occurrence of harm and the severity of that harm.

This approach to establishing the foundation for an appropriate understanding of high-risk AI is a result of discussions that took place during the Czech Presidency. Due to concerns from several member states that the AI regulation might encompass systems that do not pose a serious risk of violating fundamental rights, the Czech Presidency suggested adding a horizontal layer to the high-risk classification. This approach draws inspiration from the AI high-level expert group and the OECD classification framework.[8] The above definitions are intended to build a flexible framework, also for operating high-risk AI problems. However, the definition of AI systems proves to be a problem right from the start. In the opinion of Professor Philip Hacker, it has an unqualified form and corresponds to the definition of a software.[9]

2.2 *Definition*

The European legislator in defining high-risk AI, has used a descriptive method in the definition. Interestingly, the very definition of high-risk AI is not found in the glossary defined in Article 3 (Definitions) as much as it is regulated descriptively in a number of provisions, starting with Article 3 (1)—high-risk AI is primarily an AI system with a 'risk' (describe in Article 3(2)) through Article 6 as well as Annex I and III to the AI Act. Of particular relevance to the classification of a given AI system as high risk is Article 6 which distinguishes, in principle, three situations when we have a high-risk AI.

A safety component of a product or a product itself: Article 6(1) distinguishes two conditions whose fulfilment determines the recognition of an AI system as high-risk AI:[10] The first condition (a):

[7] See Article 3(1) and 3(2) in Regulation laying down harmonised rules on artificial intelligence (artificial intelligence act) from 21 May 2024, pp. 158–159, https://data.consilium.europa.eu/doc/document/PE-24-2024-INIT/en/pdf.

[8] See Bertuzzi (2022).

[9] See Hacker (2024).

[10] See Article 6(1) in Regulation laying down harmonised rules on AI Act, pp. 178–179.

> the AI system is intended to be used as a safety component of a product, or the AI system is itself a product, covered by the Union harmonisation legislation listed in Annex I

The second condition (b):

> the product whose safety component pursuant to point (a) is the AI system, or the AI system itself as a product, is required to undergo a third-party conformity assessment, with a view to the placing on the market or the putting into service of that product pursuant to the Union harmonisation legislation listed in Annex I

The first condition can be met if we answer two questions that can be reconstructed from the regulation. A positive answer to one or both questions means that the first condition (a) is fulfilled. This model can be called the 'product test':

(1) Is the AI system intended to be used as a safety component of a product (the product itself is also covered by AI Act)[11]?
(2) Is the AI system itself a product covered by the Union harmonisation legislation listed in Annex I?

This test can be presented graphically, as the complexity of the second question requires checking 19 Regulations and Directives—see Fig. 1. Obtaining a positive answer in the product test allows us to move on to the second mandatory part of the condition (b). At this point, we receive further instructions. The goal is to place high-risk AI on the market or the putting into service. The requirement is a conformity assessment conducted by a third party.

A description of listed AI systems: Thus, the above presents the issue of recognising a certain AI system as high-risk AI based on Article 6(1). However, as indicated at the beginning of this subsection, it is also important to analyse Article 6(2), which states that the AI systems listed in Annex III are also considered high-risk AI.[12] The wording of this provision is as follows:

> In addition to the high-risk AI systems referred to in paragraph 1, AI systems referred to in Annex III shall be considered to be high-risk.

The mentioned Annex III contains eight areas, along with specific details about the circumstances in which the application of an AI system will cause it to be considered high-risk AI or not (use-cases).[13] Additionally, Article 6(3) provides an exclusion, adding important elements that, if not met, allow the AI system to be treated as not high-risk AI.[14] However, within the same article, reservations are added about when the first paragraph applies to specific situations, as well as a final paragraph that always causes the system to be considered high-risk AI according to Annex III. Considering Article 6(4),[15] which indicates that the responsibility to

[11] Hense and Mustać (2025), pp. 53–56.

[12] See Article 6(2) on Regulation laying down harmonised rules on AI Act, p. 179.

[13] See Annex III in Regulation laying down harmonised rules on AI Act.

[14] See Article 6(3) in Regulation laying down harmonised rules on AI Act, pp. 179–180.

[15] See Article 6(4) in Regulation laying down harmonised rules on AI Act, p. 180.

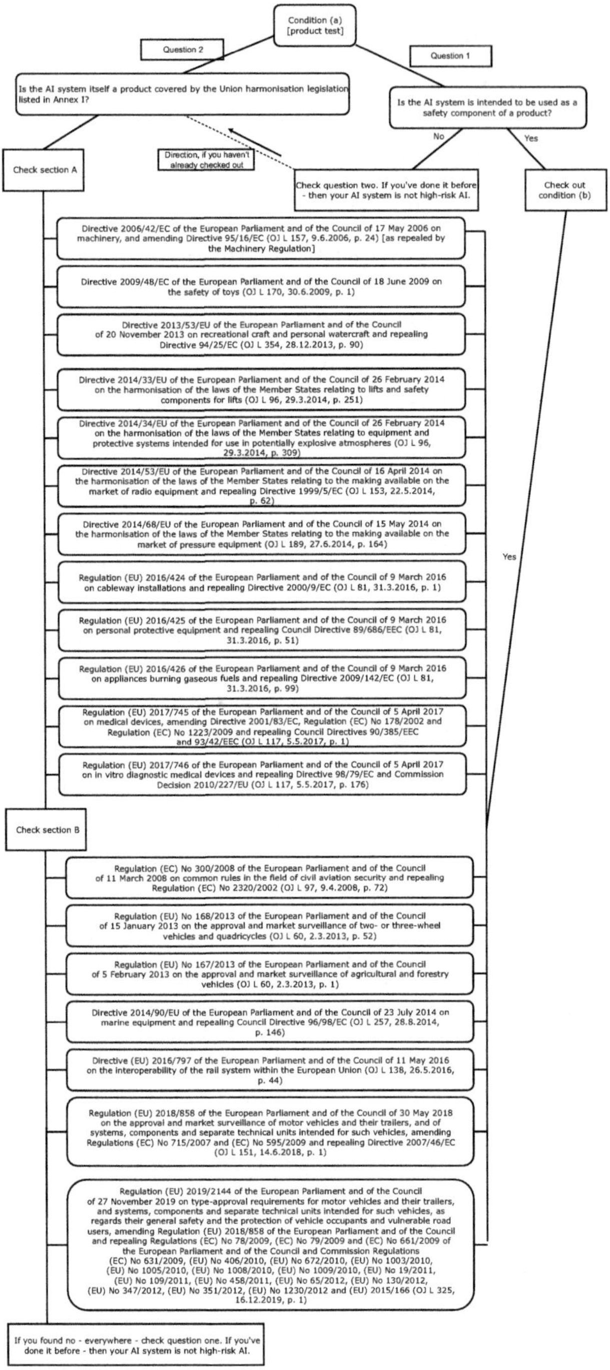

Fig. 1 Product test—based on Article 6(1)

Fig. 2 Areas and uses-cases from Annex III

demonstrate that a certain AI system from Annex III is not high-risk AI lies with the provider, the following analysis plan can be reconstructed:

1. Check Annex III for the areas and use-cases indicated therein (see Fig. 2);
2. If so, a decision will be made on whether to undertake actions aimed at verifying, through the collection of documentation, that a certain AI system is not high-risk AI;
3. The exclusion that the system performs profiling of natural persons;
4. Implementation of the 'filter provision'. Fulfilment of the conditions that entitle an investigation into whether an AI system is not a high-risk AI system. If any of

the conditions from the second paragraph of Article 6(3) are met, one or more, the solution is not considered a high-risk AI system. These conditions are:

(a) the AI system is intended to perform a narrow procedural task;
(b) the AI system is intended to improve the result of a previously completed human activity;
(c) the AI system is intended to detect decision-making patternsor deviations from prior decision-making patterns and is not meant to replace or influence the previously completed human assessment, without proper human review; or
(d) the AI system is intended to perform a preparatory task to an assessment relevant for the purposes of the use cases listed in Annex III.

5. Exclusion of the risks indicated in Article 6(3) in the first paragraph:[16]

> (…) it does not pose a significant risk of harm to the health, safety or fundamental rights of natural persons, including by not materially influencing the outcome of decision making.

Although Articles 6(3) and 6(4) refer to AI systems, according to the authors, the reconstructed model is actually a 'practice test.' An important element of this test is the 'filter provisions'. These provisions serve as an alternative path by which one can seek to exclude an AI solution from being classified as high-risk. This 'door' is likely to be exploited, particularly in the context of defining terms such as 'perform a preparatory task'. Only the implementation of a certain use of an AI system in a specific area will cause it to be considered high-risk AI. This also follows from the very definition of 'provider,' whose activities according to Article 3(3) include:[17]

> (…) puts the AI system into service under its own name or trademark, whether for payment or free of charge.

Case studies: For example, if I create my own chat using a provided solution for creating 'custom' chats, I will be the 'provider' who will need to document that my solution, which falls within one of the areas in Annex III, is not high-risk AI. It should also be noted that according to Articles 6(6), 6(7), and 6(8), Article 6(3) is essentially a flexible framework that can be amended under the principles outlined in these paragraphs.[18] According to the provision in Article 6(8), the first paragraph of Article 6(3) is—with regard to the protected values mentioned therein—unchangeable. However, additional rules allow for adjustments to the points listed in the second paragraph of Article 6(3), with the reservation that no deviations can be made that would undermine the first paragraph. This is not the only aspect that is maintained in a 'flexible', i.e., modifiable system for this type of high-risk AI. Article 7 defines the framework issues, which is Annex III. As a result, under appropriate conditions and specified rules, the scope derived from Article 6(2) can change.

[16] This, too, is an important part of the filter provision. See Madiega (2024), p. 9.
[17] See Article 3(3) in Regulation laying down harmonised rules on AI Act, p. 159.
[18] See Article 6(6–8) in Regulation laying down harmonised rules on AI Act, pp. 180–181.

In the context of the issues related to high-risk AI, it is important to note that, unlike other countries such as China or the USA, the implementation of certain innovations, for example in law enforcement, will always be subject to more stringent operational rules (high-risk AI), if not outright prohibition. It is worth mentioning that Annex III includes an entire section (point 6) titled 'Law enforcement'. This point is also a consequence of Recital 59. Privacy and data protection have always been important values in EU countries, whether considered in terms of ethical principles or specific legal provisions. Therefore, it should come as no surprise that this impacts critical societal issues such as law enforcement.[19]

On the other hand, an interesting aspect is the development of AI-based innovations within the judiciary, which does not seem to be threatened. That is, even in this case, point 8(a) in Annex III indicates such applications as high-risk AI, but not in the category of unacceptable risk. According to Veressa, a researcher in this field, this is a mistake. However, the authors view it as an opportunity to support the judiciary, which can benefit from such possibilities. After all, strict high-risk AI rules must be met to use such a system. This will not hinder the development of so-called LegalTech.[20]

Summary: Section 1: Classification of AI Systems as High-Risk, identifies three types of high-risk AI as defined in Article 6:

1. A safety component of a product (based on Annex I);
2. A product itself (based on Annex I);
3. A description of listed AI systems (based on Annex III).

It should be noted, however, that in the case of the last situation, there are modifiable frameworks established in Article 7 for Annex III, as well as in Article 6(6) for the second paragraph of Article 6(3). It should also be added that the layer of exceptions from the second paragraph of Article 6(3) is a new solution that has already been commented on by P. Hacker, with whom the authors agree:[21]

> While this does provide companies with a way out of the AI Act, the risk of misclassification is significant, which should act as a deterrent to companies simply claiming not to pose significant risks with their AI systems. Overall, in my view, this constitutes a balanced and necessary provision within a risk-based framework.

Such complexity has led to the emergence of the first methodologies that would allow the assessment of the risk of being classified as 'high-risk AI', which would be helpful for AI system providers.[22] Furthermore, summarising this topic, it should be emphasised that Article 6(5) refers to Article 96, indicating that the emerging guidelines will provide examples of both high-risk AI and non-high-risk AI.[23] Such

[19] Wielki (2024), pp. 174–178. See Mantelero (2022), pp. 60–83.

[20] Cf. Veress (2024), pp. 80–83. See Dymitruk (2021), pp. 67–80.

[21] Hacker (2024).

[22] See Novelli et al. (2024).

[23] See Article 6(5) and 96 in Regulation laying down harmonised rules on AI Act, pp. 180 and 347–348.

actions should help providers in the future to determine whether their AI system is or is not high-risk AI.

3 Principles of Market Admissibility for High-Risk AI

The fundamental principle is the admissibility of using high-risk AI systems. However, it is necessary to fulfil a number of obligations specified in the AI Act, and consequently to accept responsibility for such systems and accountability in terms of their training, operation, etc. They must meet the requirements of Chapter 2 of the AI Act, which, it should be emphasised, are based on the generally accepted state of knowledge. This means that, due to the exceptionally rapid development of AI, including the increasingly frequent use of quantum computers, the requirements that entrepreneurs, administration, or other entities introducing high-risk AI systems to the market will have to meet will increase year by year and will be subject to continuous verification.[24]

3.1 Risk Management System

As indicated in Article 9(1):[25]

> A risk management system shall be established, implemented, documented and maintained in relation to high-risk AI systems.

This system should consist of a continuous, iterative process that runs throughout the entire lifecycle of a high-risk AI system, requiring regular and systematic updates. It should include the steps from Article 9(2)- with the identifying and analysing known and foreseeable risks most likely to affect health, safety, and fundamental rights based on the intended purpose of the high-risk AI system and evaluating other potential risks based on data gathered from the post-market monitoring system referred to in Article 72 and adopting appropriate risk management measures per the provisions of the Article 9(2)—[26] see Fig. 3.

The risk management requirements are not a new, unknown solution in EU regulations. Similar obligations were introduced some time ago by the GDPR regulations and the NIS Directive concerning the assessment of cybersecurity risks. Thus, the EU has already proposed a well-functioning system, but this time relating to AI systems rather than personal data or cybersecurity risks. The measures to meet the risk management requirements must take into account the generally accepted state

---

[24] Issues related to the need for discussion on quantum engineering have been raised before—also in correlation with the development of AI. See Kop (2021).

[25] See Article 9(1) in Regulation laying down harmonised rules on AI Act, p. 185.

[26] See Article 9(2) and 72 in Regulation laying down harmonised rules on AI Act, pp. 185–186 and 311–312.

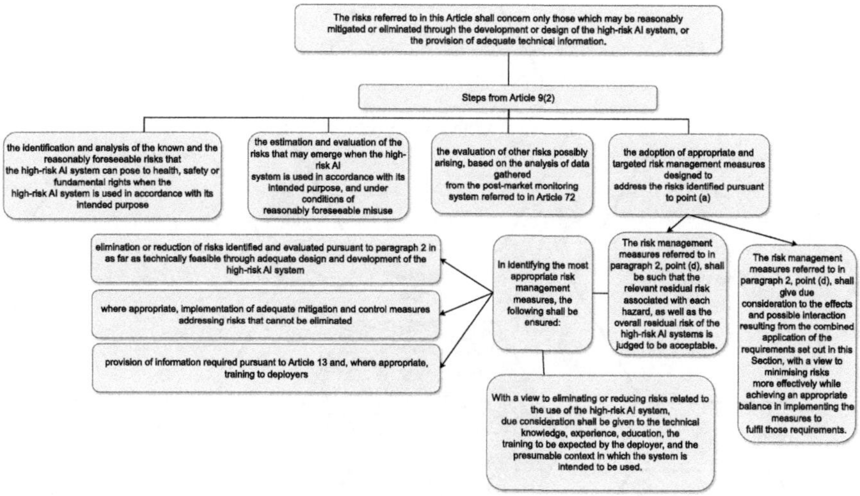

Fig. 3 Risk management in AI Act

of technical knowledge and common specifications. According to the authors, we are once again dealing with a solution that is consistent with information security risk management. A close reading of the proposed regulations reveals a reference to the principles outlined in the ISO 27001 standard, which originate from ISO technical reports. The work on risk management developed at that time remains the foundation for similar models to this day (see Fig. 4).[27] It should be emphasised that the role of ISO standards in the entire process of building systems that comply with the AI Act is very important. The initial work on mapping legal requirements to technical standards already indicates that an important element and challenge will be aligning ISO standards with AI Act requirements.[28]

3.2 *Testing High-Risk AI Systems*

AI Act regulations foresee the obligation to test and document such testing for high-risk systems. Here, it is necessary to refer again to Article 9(6):[29]

> High-risk AI systems shall be tested for the purpose of identifying the most appropriate and targeted risk management measures. Testing shall ensure that high-risk AI systems perform

---

[27] The figure refers to the standard PN-EN 13335-1:1999, which in Poland was published by PKN (Polish Committee for Standardisation) in 1999, based on the technical report TR 13335-1 issued in 1996 in Poland.

[28] The justification for such further work has been indicated by: Golpayegani et al. (2023), pp. 189–200.

[29] See Article 9(6) in Regulation laying down harmonised rules on AI ACT, p. 187.

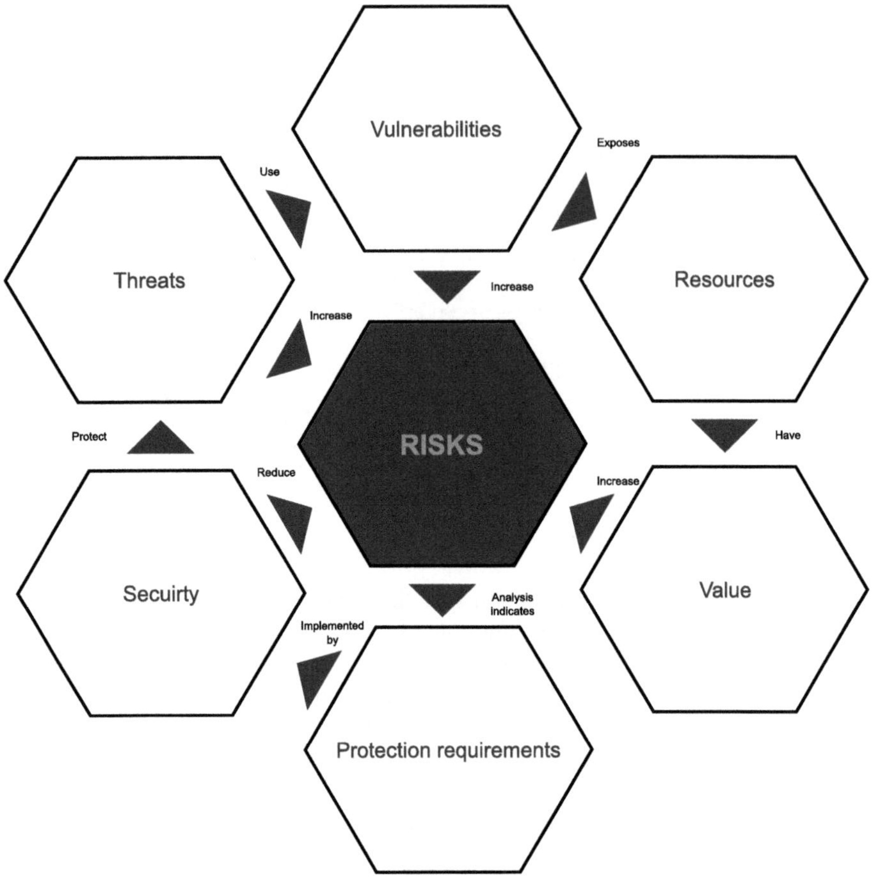

Fig. 4 Based on risk management from PN-I-13335:1999

> consistently for their intended purpose and that they are in compliance with the requirements set out in this Section.

The subsequent paragraphs also refer to testing issues, with Article 9(7) referring to Article 60 regarding real-world testing, and Article 9(8) further specifying issues related to testing:[30]

> The testing of high-risk AI systems shall be performed, as appropriate, at any time throughout the development process, and, in any event, prior to their being placed on the market or put into service. Testing shall be carried out against prior defined metrics and probabilistic thresholds that are appropriate to the intended purpose of the high-risk AI system.

It should be added, in terms of the closure of Article 9, that the last two paragraphs are related to the issue of deployers.

[30] See Article 9(7–8) and 60 in Regulation laying down harmonised rules on AI Act, pp. 187–188 and 285–290.

3.3 *Data and Data Governance*

One of the most important elements of any AI system is data. In the case of high-risk AI, an entire Article 10 is dedicated to this issue. Data governance is one of the most crucial aspects of high-risk AI. According to Article 10, activities such as 'training, validation, testing' must be conducted on datasets that are properly managed. The second paragraph highlights the following best practices in data management:[31]

(a) the relevant design choices;
(b) data collection processes and the origin of data, and in the case of personal data, the original purpose of the data collection;
(c) relevant data-preparation processing operations, such as annotation, labelling, cleaning, updating, enrichment and aggregation;
(d) the formulation of assumptions, in particular with respect to the information that the data are supposed to measure and represent;
(e) an assessment of the availability, quantity and suitability of the data sets that are needed;
(f) (examination in view of possible biases that are likely to affect the health and safety of persons, have a negative impact on fundamental rights or lead to discrimination prohibited under Union law, especially where data outputs influence inputs for future operations;
(g) appropriate measures to detect, prevent and mitigate possible biases identified according to point (f);
(h) the identification of relevant data gaps or shortcomings that prevent compliance with this Regulation, and how those gaps and shortcomings can be addressed.

Training, validation, and testing data sets must be relevant, sufficiently representative, and as error-free and complete as possible for their intended purpose. They should have appropriate statistical properties, especially regarding the people or groups the high-risk AI system is designed for. These characteristics can be met by individual data sets or their combination. Additionally, data sets should consider geographical, contextual, behavioural or functional elements specific to the intended use of the high-risk AI system.

To ensure bias detection and correction in high-risk AI systems, providers may exceptionally process special categories of personal data, with appropriate safeguards for fundamental rights and freedoms. This processing must comply with Regulations (EU) 2016/679 and (EU) 2018/1725, and Directive (EU) 2016/680, and meet all the following conditions:[32]

---

[31] See Article 10 in Regulation laying down harmonised rules on AI Act, pp. 188–191.

[32] See Article 10 in Regulation laying down harmonised rules on AI Act, pp. 190–191.

(a) the bias detection and correction cannot be effectively fulfilled by processing other data, including synthetic or anonymised data;
(b) the special categories of personal data are subject to technical limitations on the re-use of the personal data, and state-of-the-art security and privacy-preserving measures, including pseudonymisation;
(c) the special categories of personal data are subject to measures to ensure that the personal data processed are secured, protected, subject to suitable safeguards, including strict controls and documentation of the access, to avoid misuse and ensure that only authorised persons have access to those personal data with appropriate confidentiality obligations;
(d) the special categories of personal data are not to be transmitted, transferred or otherwise accessed by other parties;
(e) the special categories of personal data are deleted once the bias has been corrected or the personal data has reached the end of its retention period, whichever comes first;
(f) the records of processing activities pursuant to Regulations (EU) 2016/679 and (EU) 2018/1725 and Directive (EU) 2016/680 include the reasons why the processing of special categories of personal data was strictly necessary to detect and correct biases, and why that objective could not be achieved by processing other data.

In the authors' opinion, it should be emphasised that the AI Act is another legal act that draws attention to data. GDPR, NIS2, and now the AI Act highlight that the importance of data protection and management is becoming an increasingly significant priority. It should be emphasised that the importance of data is also highlighted by other acts that consistently expand the branch of EU law related to digital data, such as the Data Act and the Data Governance Act.

3.4 *Documentation and Other Information*

According to the study, when deciding on AI high-risk we have to reckon with the strictest documentation obligations.[33] Documentation issues arise from Article 11. The technical documentation for a high-risk AI system must be prepared before the system is placed on the market or put into service and must be kept up to date. It should demonstrate compliance with the requirements of this section and provide necessary information to national authorities and notified bodies for compliance assessment. The documentation must include at least the elements specified in Annex IV. SMEs, including start-ups, may provide these elements in a simplified manner using a form established by the Commission. This form will be accepted for conformity assessment purposes.[34]

[33] Hupont et al. (2023).
[34] See Article 11 in Regulation laying down harmonised rules on AI Act, p. 192.

If a high-risk AI system is related to a product covered by Union harmonisation legislation listed in Annex I, Section A, a single set of technical documentation must be prepared, containing all required information. The Commission may adopt delegated acts to amend Annex IV to ensure the documentation includes all necessary information for compliance assessment in light of technical progress.[35]

Equally important is the collection of digital data, especially logs, as mentioned in Article 12. High-risk AI systems must allow for the automatic recording of events (logs) throughout their lifetime. Logging capabilities should enable the recording of events relevant to:[36]

(a) identifying situations that may result in the high-risk AI system presenting a risk within the meaning of Article 79(1) or in a substantial modification;
(b) facilitating the post-market monitoring referred to in Article 72;
(c) and monitoring the operation of high-risk AI systems referred to in Article 26(5).

It should be noted that for high-risk AI operating in the area, or based on the case study described in Annex III, the following minimum is provided. See Article 11 in Regulation laying down harmonised rules on AI Act, p. 194.:

(a) recording of the period of each use of the system (start date and time and end date and time of each use);
(b) the reference database against which input data has been checked by the system;
(c) the input data for which the search has led to a match;
(d) the identification of the natural persons involved in the verification of the results, as referred to in Article 14(5).

The final element concluding the documentation and information part in section 2 is the issue of instructions specified in Article 13. High-risk AI systems must be designed and developed to ensure sufficient transparency, enabling deployers to interpret and use the system's output appropriately. This transparency must comply with the obligations of the provider and deployer as outlined in Section 3.

High-risk AI systems should include instructions for use in an appropriate digital or other format, providing concise, complete, correct, and clear information that is relevant, accessible, and understandable to deployers. Article 13 contains specific indications of what information should be included in the instructions.[37]

It should be emphasised that the issues indicated in Section 2 are further developed in Section 3—Obligations of providers and deployers of high-risk AI systems and other parties. In matters such as documentation keeping (Article 18), automatic logging (Article 19), or the important issue mentioned in Article 20—Corrective actions and duty of information.[38]

[35] See Article 11 in Regulation laying down harmonised rules on AI Act, pp. 192–193.

[36] See Article 12 in Regulation laying down harmonised rules on AI Act, p. 193.

[37] See Article 12 in Regulation laying down harmonised rules on AI Act, pp. 194–196.

[38] See Article 18–20 in Regulation laying down harmonised rules on AI Act, pp. 205–207.

The last mentioned article particularly highlights an important issue. Providers of high-risk AI systems must take immediate corrective actions if they find or suspect that their system does not comply with the Regulation. These actions may include bringing the system into conformity, withdrawing, disabling, or recalling it. Providers must inform distributors, deployers, authorised representatives, and importers as appropriate. If the system presents a risk as defined in Article 79(1), the provider must investigate the causes, collaborate with the reporting deployer if applicable, and inform the relevant market surveillance authorities and, if applicable, the notified body that issued the certificate.[39]

3.5 *Human Role in High-Risk AI*

One of the elements that distinguishes the AI Act from other regulations concerning algorithms is its human-centred approach, placing humans and human rights as paramount. Thus, the EU has determined that the development of AI cannot deviate from the fundamental values defined in human rights. It also imposes the obligation to create high-risk AI in such a way that there is always and at every moment of the AI system's operation the possibility of effective human oversight.[40] The role of humans in high-risk AI is strongly emphasised for understandable reasons—legal regulations are addressed to people, not algorithms. The final effect of AI's operation is related to how humans approach its construction. Furthermore, Article 14(4) outlines the objectives that can be achieved by complying with the indications in this article:[41]

(a) to properly understand the relevant capacities and limitations of the high-risk AI system and be able to duly monitor its operation, including in view of detecting and addressing anomalies, dysfunctions and unexpected performance;
(b) to remain aware of the possible tendency of automatically relying or over-relying on the output produced by a high-risk AI system (automation bias), in particular for high-risk AI systems used to provide information or recommendations for decisions to be taken by natural persons;
(c) to correctly interpret the high-risk AI system's output, taking into account, for example, the interpretation tools and methods available;
(d) to decide, in any particular situation, not to use the high-risk AI system or to otherwise disregard, override or reverse the output of the high-risk AI system;

[39] See Article 20 in Regulation laying down harmonised rules on AI Act, p. 207.

[40] This should not be unexpected, as the role of the human being and humanity's position in the various aspects was very much underlined in the European Parliament resolution of 20 October 2020 with recommendations to the Commission on a framework of ethical aspects of artificial intelligence, robotics and related technologies (2020/2012(INL)).

[41] See Article 14 in Regulation laying down harmonised rules on AI Act, pp. 196–198.

(e) to intervene in the operation of the high-risk AI system or interrupt the system through a 'stop' button or a similar procedure that allows the system to come to a halt in a safe state.

In the authors' opinion, the control and supervision of AI systems is one of the most critical issues. The appropriate fitting of human resources into this issue is a guarantee that there will be those who are designated responsible for the correct, i.e. AI ACT-compliant, operation of high-risk AI. However, it should be noted that there were many expectations regarding the discussed provision. For example, J. Walter identified the following de lege ferenda proposals.[42] First, the AI Act should acknowledge that human oversight is not always reliable. Article 14 could thus be amended to include a clause about the risks of human oversight. Second, tests assessing the feasibility and efficacy of human oversight in preventing harm should be mandatory for high-risk AI applications. The test requirements could be included under the conformity assessments in Article 19 of the proposed AI Act. Specifically, the tests should determine whether humans are capable of accurately assessing the quality of algorithmic advice and whether they are able to overrule it when necessary. In their most elementary form, such tests would compare actual outcomes under human oversight with the hypothetical outcomes that would have resulted without human intervention. Third, when feasible and appropriate, these tests should include information intended to improve the human decision-makers' ability to assess and correct algorithmic recommendations. To that end, feedback about the outcomes of past decisions seems to be a promising intervention. Finally, if the tests reveal that human oversight does not prevent harm, that it exacerbates harmful decisions or that it introduces new types of bias, it should not be relied upon. In these cases, the AI Act should include a mechanism that limits or prohibits human oversight.

The European Union's AI Act has addressed some, but not all, of the concerns outlined in the suggestions of J. Walter. Regarding Article 14, which the authors previously commented on, the Act acknowledges the necessity of human oversight, particularly in high-risk AI systems. However, it does not go as far as explicitly recognising the potential unreliability of human oversight. Instead, it mandates that systems be designed to allow for effective human oversight to minimise risks, but the depth of addressing human oversight's limitations may not fully meet the concerns about its reliability. Also, concerning Article 19, it is important to take note of the current situation. The Act requires conformity assessments for high-risk AI applications, which include some level of testing for human oversight. These tests are aimed at ensuring compliance with the Act's requirements, including the ability of human overseers to manage and mitigate risks. However, the Act does not explicitly require tests that assess the feasibility and efficacy of human oversight in preventing harm in the manner suggested. It focuses more on ensuring oversight mechanisms are in place rather than rigorously testing their effectiveness.

---

[42] Walter (2023).

Similarly, the issue is the same in the case of Enhancing Decision-Making Capabilities. In this field, certain aspects are also considered, but not all. While the Act does encourage transparency and the provision of information to users, it does not specifically mandate feedback mechanisms that would directly enhance the ability of human overseers to assess and correct AI recommendations. The focus is more on ensuring that oversight mechanisms exist and are functional. Furthermore, the Act does not include a mechanism for limiting or prohibiting human oversight in cases where it is found to be ineffective or harmful. The emphasis remains on ensuring human involvement, even though empirical evidence might suggest that in some scenarios, this involvement could exacerbate biases or other issues.

In conclusion, while the AI Act incorporates provisions for human oversight and testing in high-risk AI systems, it does not fully address the more nuanced concerns about the limitations of human oversight and the need for rigorous testing and potential prohibition where oversight is found to be ineffective. The Act leans more towards ensuring the presence of oversight mechanisms rather than questioning their efficacy or implementing stronger corrective measures where oversight fails. In this context, the authors propose that the solution for general requirements should be the application of ISO standards. The very first paragraph already contains the phrase 'effectively overseen by natural persons during the period in which they are in use', which raises concerns about issues such as the quality of oversight and the competence of the person carrying it out (besides the fact that they should be appropriate).

3.6 Accuracy, Robustness and Cybersecurity

High-risk AI systems must be designed and developed to achieve an appropriate level of accuracy, robustness, and cybersecurity, maintaining consistent performance throughout their lifecycle -5. To measure these appropriate levels of accuracy and robustness, the Commission, in cooperation with relevant stakeholders and organisations like metrology and benchmarking authorities, will encourage the development of benchmarks and measurement methodologies. The accuracy levels and relevant accuracy metrics of high-risk AI systems must be declared in the accompanying instructions for use. High-risk AI systems should be as resilient as possible to errors, faults, or inconsistencies that may occur within the system or its operating environment, particularly due to interactions with humans or other systems. Technical and organisational measures must be taken to ensure this. Robustness may be achieved through technical redundancy solutions, which can include backup or fail-safe plans. High-risk AI systems must also be resilient against unauthorised third-party attempts to alter their use, outputs, or performance by exploiting system vulnerabilities. Technical solutions to ensure cybersecurity must be appropriate to the circumstances and risks. These solutions should include measures to prevent, detect, respond to, and control attacks aimed at manipulating the training dataset (data poisoning) or pre-trained components (model poisoning), inputs designed to

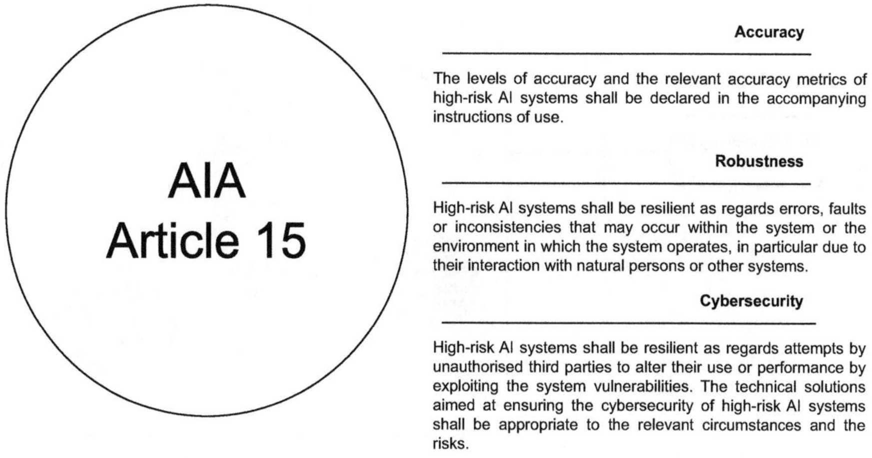

Fig. 5 Article 15 of the AI ACT

cause errors (adversarial examples or model evasion), confidentiality attacks, or model flaws.[43] It should be emphasised that issues related to the dangers of AI systems are already addressed in the matrix prepared by MITRE in the special Atlas.[44] This is not the only example of such a study. Equally important is the standardisation of attacks on artificial intelligence systems undertaken by NIST in the document 'Adversarial Machine Learning: A Taxonomy and Terminology of Attacks and Mitigations.'[45] Standardising these dangers makes it easier to defend against them, following the principle of 'know your enemy'. Additionally, the authors would like to highlight that, in their opinion, the issue of cybersecurity is addressed sufficiently.[46] Accordingly, both legal and technical standards are crucial in the context of threats. In the authors' opinion, it should be emphasised that these threats pertain to all three values mentioned in this subsection, not just cybersecurity. For high-risk AI systems, they gain particular significance, and these include (Fig. 5):[47]

Nefarious activity/abuse (NAA): 'intended actions that target ICT systems, infrastructure, and networks by means of malicious acts with the aim to either steal, alter, or destroy a specified target'.

Eavesdropping/Interception/ Hijacking (EIH): 'actions aiming to listen, interrupt, or seize control of a third party communication without consent'.

[43] See Article 15 in Regulation laying down harmonised rules on AI Act, pp. 199–200; ENISA (2020), p. 7.

[44] Atlas has been expanding since 2021, with the last update in 2024, which shows how dynamic the threats to AI systems are. See Mitre (2021).

[45] NIST (2024).

[46] Build links between the AI ACTand other regulations was one of ENISA's requests. See ENISA (2023).

[47] ENISA (2020), p. 27.

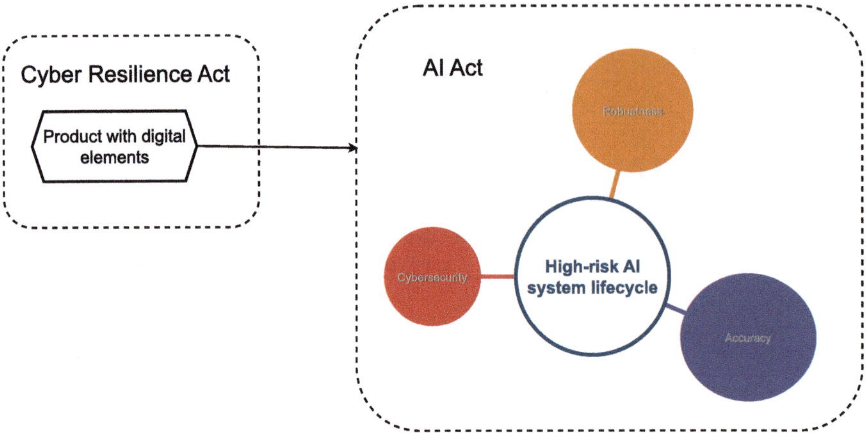

Fig. 6 A link on cyber security in the AI ACT and CRA

Physical attacks (PA): 'actions which aim to destroy, expose, alter, disable, steal or gain unauthorised access to physical assets such as infrastructure, hardware, or interconnection'.

Unintentional Damage (UD): unintentional actions causing 'destruction, harm, or injury of property or persons and results in a failure or reduction in usefulness'. Failures or malfunctions (FM): 'Partial or full insufficient functioning of an asset (hardware or software)'.

Outages (OUT): 'unexpected disruptions of service or decrease in quality falling below a required level'.

Disaster (DIS): 'a sudden accident or a natural catastrophe that causes great damage or loss of life'.

Legal (LEG): 'legal actions of third parties (contracting or otherwise), in order to prohibit actions or compensate for loss based on applicable law'.

According to other regulations, an AI system is a product with digital elements. Therefore, based on other legal frameworks, it must meet the security requirements addressed in the Cyber Resilience Act.[48] In the authors' opinion, this is one of the key issues that needs to be mapped in the context of other regulations related to cybersecurity, particularly with regard to Annex I and III. The outlined exemplary linkage highlights how the AI Act is also linked (or should be linked) to other regulations and directives of this type. See Fig. 6. It should be emphasised that this is just the beginning of the mapping process, as acts such as the DSA and GDPR will also be significant in many aspects.[49] It should also be noted that the 'cybersecurity'

[48] See article 3(1) in Proposal for a Regulation of the European Parliament and of the Council on horizontal cybersecurity requirements for products with digital elements and amending Regulation (EU) 2019/1020.

[49] This was suggested by Philipp Hacker in a 2023 press article in TechMonitor, indicating that existing acts should be linked to the AI Act. Noone (2023).

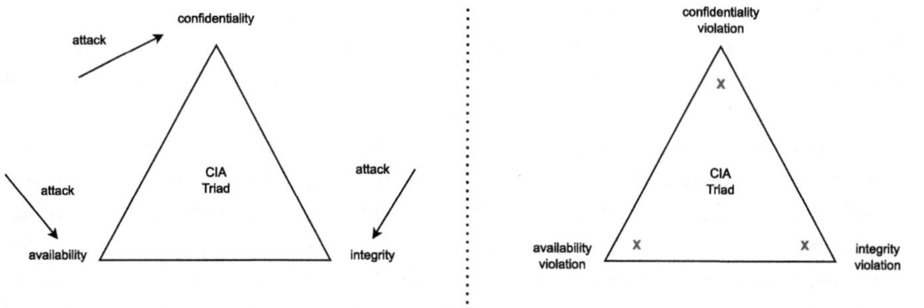

Fig. 7 CIA triad under and after attack

approach in the AI Act should be directly related to the elements of the CIA triad, but in the context of AI systems (7). This is a different approach than in other acts, as it takes into account specific AI systems, such as learning systems. According to the authors, this is interestingly presented in the NIST 800-30 document. According to it, an attack is executed on a specific target, and its consequences depend on the adopted defence procedures. The consequences are mapped onto the CIA triad, and it is worth noting that, according to NIST, the confidentiality criterion also includes the issue of privacy.[50] This makes it possible to present the following taxonomy of attacks on learning systems, based on the work of Surma:[51]

1. Confidentiality violation—involves obtaining information related to the learning, updating, testing, and usage processes of the system.
2. Integrity violation—involves disrupting the learning, updating, or testing process according to the attacker's objectives.
3. Availability violation—involves slowing down or stopping the system's operation, which hinders its practical use.

However, this is a concise highlight of the issue, but the entire Article 15, along with its individual elements, requires further work and academic development (Fig. 7).

3.7 *Obligations of Providers and Deployers of High-Risk AI Systems and Other Parties*

Section 3 of the AI Act consists of specific obligations for entities involved with high-risk AI, such as through their preparation or import. Some articles from this section have already been mentioned earlier. The individual articles introduce additional obligations for specific entities. Article 16 outlines the obligations for providers, while Article 23 does so for importers and Article 24 for distributors. Article 26

[50] NIST (2012).

[51] Surma (2020).

specifies the obligations for deployers. This way, additional obligations are defined based on the role a certain entity assumes in the AI systems market if it deals with high-risk AI. Articles 25 and 27 add additional requirements for everyone based on the AI value chain and fundamental rights.[52]

An interesting solution in Section 3 is the reference to the 'AI value chain' concerning high-risk AI. The AI Act itself does not define the term. In their work, Angler and Renda point out that 'the AI value chain can be defined as the organisational process through which an AI system is developed and deployed'. They also emphasise that 'it is important to identify which organisations are responsible for different parts of this process to ensure regulatory compliance and the safe and responsible functioning of AI systems'. In their view, 'this organisational focus distinguishes the AI value chain from algorithmic development, which concentrates on the technological steps of building an AI system'. The AI value chain varies depending on the type of algorithmic development (e.g., expert rules, search, supervised machine learning) and the environments (e.g., products, applications, websites) where the AI system is integrated.[53]

This also provides an appropriate transition to Article 27, which refers to fundamental rights. Both articles complement the obligations of entities that wish to operate in the AI market and must meet additional obligations due to high-risk AI.[54]

4 Summary

In the authors' opinion, the AI Act introduces new issues related to data, which create additional obligations for organisations implementing AI systems. In the context of high-risk AI, it is necessary to pay attention to the issue of AI Governance. As shown in the Fig. 8, these are essentially all the obligations and frameworks constructed by Sections 2 and 3. This is a significant and comprehensive area that will need to be managed by organisations, especially by the so-called 'business'.

According to the authors, it is important to continue the process of mapping the AI ACT with ISO standards. These standards enable the credibility of AI systems (as well as their ethical and technical compliance). This does not exclude abuses, but mechanisms based on a reporting system, measurement and monitoring methods enabled by technical standards can be addressed to businesses and thus appropriately implemented. The role of standards like ISO/IEC 42001, as emphasised in the text, is to support the AI Act. Analysis through the framework of the standard allows organisations to improve their effectiveness and efficiency in risk management. This is undoubtedly an advantage in this context.[55]

---

[52] See Section 3 in Regulation laying down harmonised rules on AI Act, pp. 201–223.

[53] Engler and Renda (2022), p. 2.

[54] See Article 27 in Regulation laying down harmonised rules on AI Act, pp. 221–223.

[55] See ISO (2023).

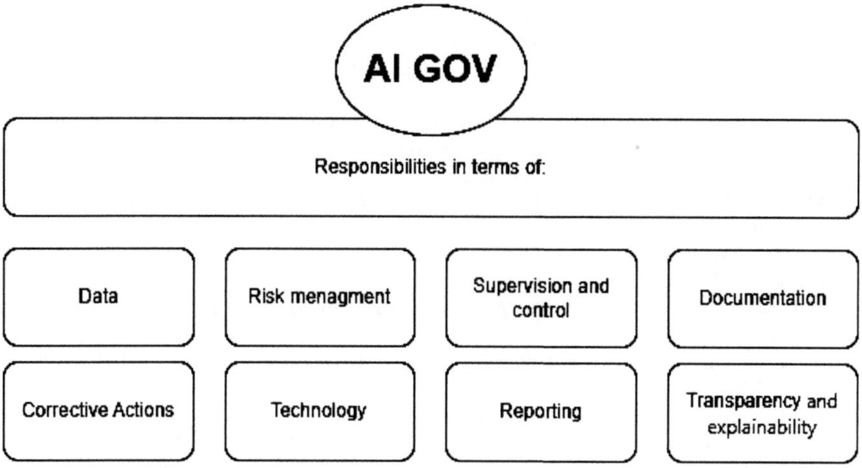

Fig. 8 AI Governance in AI ACT

Additionally, the authors recognise that new regulations will lead to a dynamic development of Data Governance, meaning that the role of such departments and experts on data security and their use in AI systems will increase. Furthermore, the AI ACT indicates that the relationships and dependencies between different regulations and directives are evolving so dynamically that the connections between legal acts are becoming increasingly complex. In this context, it is necessary to continue mapping these processes in the area that, according to the authors, can already be called digital law. Additionally, it seems reasonable to verify over the years whether the objectives of the regulation have been achieved.

References

Barfield B, Pagallo U (2020) Law and artificial intelligence. https://doi.org/10.4337/9781786439055.00011

Bertuzzi (2022) https://www.euractiv.com/section/tech/news/ai-act-czech-presidency-pushes-narrower-aidefinition-shorter-high-risk-list

Bracy J (2022) A look at European Parliament's AI Act negotiations. https://iapp.org/news/a/a-look-at-european-parliaments-ai-act-negotiations

Dymitruk M (2021) Borderlands of the law and technology: from digital machines to LegalTech. In: Szostek D, Załucki M (eds) Legal Tech. Information technology tools in the administration of justice. https://doi.org/10.1007/978-946265-531-7

Engler AC, Renda A (2022) Reconciling the AI value chain with the EU's Artificial Intelligence Act. https://openfuture.eu/wpcontent/uploads/2024/03/220930CEPS-In-depth-analysis-AI-act-value-chain.pdf

ENISA (2020) Artificial intelligence cybersecurity challenges. Threat landscapefor Artificial Intelligence. https://www.enisa.europa.eu/publications/artificialintelligence-cybersecurity-challenges20

ENISA (2023) Cybersecurity of AI and Standardisation. https://doi.org/10.2824/277479

European Parliament (2020) Resolution of 20 October 2020 with recommendations to the Commission on a framework of ethical aspects of artificial intelligence, robotics and related technologies (2020/2012(INL). https://www.europarl.europa.eu/doceo/document/TA-92020-0275EN.pdf

Golpayegani D, Pandit JH, Lewis D (2023) Comparison and analysis of 3 key AI documents: EU's Proposed AI Act, Assessment List for Trustworthy AI (ALTAI), and ISO/IEC 42001 AI Management System, Artificial Intelligence and Cognitive Science, 30th Irish Conference, AICS 2022, Munster, Ireland, December 8–9, 2022, Revised Selected Papers. https://doi.org/10.1007/978-3-031-26438-2_15

Hacker P (2024) Comments on the Final Trilogue Version of the AI Act. https://doi.org/10.2139/ssrn.4757603

Hense P, Mustać T (2025) AI Act Compact. Compliance, management & use cases in corporate practice

https://www.europarl.europa.eu/RegData/etudes/BRIE/2021/698792/EPRSBRI(2021)698792EN.pdf

Hupont I, Micheli M, Delipetrev B, Gómez E, Garrido JS (2023) Documenting high-risk AI: a European regulatory perspective. Computer 56. https://doi.org/10.1109/MC.2023.3235712

ISO (2023) Information technology — Artificial intelligence — Management system, ISO/IEC 42001:2023. https://www.iso.org/standard/81230.html

Kop M (2021) Establishing a legal-ethical framework for quantum technology. https://yjolt.org/blog/establishing-legal-ethical-framework-quantumtechnology

Madiega T (2024) Artificial intelligence act, PE 698.792

Mantelero A (2022) Beyond data. Human rights, ethical and social impact assessment in AI, information technology and law series, vol 36. https://doi.org/10.1007/978-94-6265-531-7

Mitre (2021) ATLAS Matrix. https://atlas.mitre.org/matrices/ATLAS

NIST (2012) Guide for conducting risk assessments, NIST SP 800-30 Rev. 1. https://doi.org/10.6028/NIST.SP.800-30r1

NIST (2024) Adversarial machine learning: a taxonomy and terminology of attacks and mitigations, NIST AI 100-2 E2023. https://doi.org/10.6028/NIST.AI.100-2e2023

Noone G (2023) This is how GPT-4 will be regulated. https://www.techmonitor.ai/digital-economy/ai-and-automation/this-is-howgpt-4-will-be-regulated?cf-view

Novelli C, Casolari F, Rotolo A, Taddeo M, Floridi L (2024) AI risk assessment: a scenario-based, proportional methodology for the AI Act. Digit Soc 3:13. https://doi.org/10.1007/s44206-024-00095-1

Polski Komitet Normalizacyjny (1999) ISO/IEC TR 13335-1 (PN-I-13335-1:1999)

Su H, Xiang C, Ramesh B (2024) Towards confidential chatbot conversations: a decentralised federated learning framework. The JBBA. https://doi.org/10.31585/jbba-7-1-(3)2024

Surma J (2020) Hacking machine learning: towards the comprehensive taxonomy of attacks against machine learning systems, ICIAI 2020: Proceedings of the 2020 the 4th International Conference on Innovation in Artificial Intelligence. https://doi.org/10.1145/3390557.3394126

Veress E (2024) Artificial intelligence as a legal or technological person, and as a judge? In: Gryszczynska A (ed) Legal aspects of artificial intelligence. https://doi.org/10.32041/9788367149372/2

Walter J (2023) Human oversight done right: the AI Act should use humans to monitor ai only when effective. https://ftp.zew.de/pub/zewdocs/policybrief/en/pb02-23.pdf. Last

Wendehorst C (2020) Strict liability for AI and other emerging technologies. JETL. https://doi.org/10.1515/jetl-2020-0140

Wendehorst C (2021) Safety and liability related aspects of software. European Commision, Brussels

Wielki R (2024) Use of artificial intelligence in law enforcement and criminal justice. In: Gryszczynska A (ed) Legal aspects of artificial intelligence. https://doi.org/10.32041/9788367149372/5

Regulating Non-High-Risk AI Systems Under the EU's Artificial Intelligence Act, with Special Focus on the Role of Soft Law

Lee A. Bygrave and Rebecca Schmidt

Contents

Abstract The remit of this chapter is twofold. First, it provides a concise overview of how the EU's Artificial Intelligence Act regulates non-high-risk AI systems—that is, systems deemed by the Act as not presenting a high or unacceptable risk. Second, the chapter elucidates the role that the Act assigns to codes of practice and codes of

L. A. Bygrave (✉)
Norwegian Research Center for Computers and Law, Department of Private Law, University of Oslo, Oslo, Norway
e-mail: lee@uio.no

R. Schmidt
Faculty of Social Sciences, Oslo Metropolitan University, Oslo, Norway
e-mail: rebecca.schmidt@oslomet.no

V. L. Raposo (ed.), *The European Artificial Intelligence Act*, Law, Governance and Technology Series 78, https://doi.org/10.1007/978-3-031-98406-8_8

conduct for governing these systems. In tackling the first-mentioned task, the chapter draws up a typology consisting of four types of non-high-risk AI systems: (1) those that appear to be high-risk systems but are actually not high-risk (type 1 systems); (2) those presenting limited risk due to their potential for deceiving or manipulating humans (type 2 systems); (3) general-purpose AI systems (type 3 systems); and (4) those that are otherwise low risk (type 4 systems). Regarding the role of codes of practice and codes of conduct, the chapter highlights how the Act assigns the former type of code different fields of application and different degrees of legal effect than the latter type of code. Whereas codes of practice are reserved for governing type 2 and type 3 systems, and are probably compulsory for type 3 systems (at least as a 'stop-gap' measure in advance of the adoption of harmonised standards), codes of conduct are purely voluntary and capable of governing all non-high-risk systems (i.e. types 1 to 4). Additionally, codes of conduct are envisaged as governing all AI systems (also high-risk systems) in respect of certain matters specified in the Act. A key argument advanced in the chapter is that codes of practice may be regarded as instruments of meta-regulation that are truly embedded in the Act, whereas codes of conduct are simply instruments for potential meta-regulation. As such, codes of practice will likely play a much more crucial role under the Act than will codes of conduct. Extending this argument, the chapter predicts that the meta-regulatory potential of codes of conduct will likely be undercut by the Act's failure to provide a compelling incentive structure for their creation. This will weaken, in turn, the Act's ability to promote various considerations that are relatively peripheral to its central thrust yet societally important—such as AI literacy, participatory design, gender equality and environmental sustainability. Hence, the chapter rounds off with several suggestions for strengthening the traction of codes of conduct under the Act.

1 Introduction

The Act on Artificial Intelligence (AIA)[1] adopted by the European Union (EU) in June 2024 has rightly attracted considerable attention for being the hitherto most comprehensive legislative attempt anywhere in the world to regulate artificial intelligence (AI). Most of the attention has been directed at the ways in which the Act regulates AI systems that it deems to present a high or unacceptable risk. Concomitantly, there is relatively little scholarship dealing extensively with how the Act applies to AI systems that are deemed to present a lower level of

[1] Regulation (EU) 2024/1689 of the European Parliament and of the Council of 13 June 2024 laying down harmonised rules on artificial intelligence and amending Regulations (EC) No 300/2008, (EU) No 167/2013, (EU) No 168/2013, (EU) 2018/858, (EU) 2018/1139 and (EU) 2019/2144 and Directives 2014/90/EU, (EU) 2016/797 and (EU) 2020/1828 (Artificial Intelligence Act) [2024] OJ L, 12.7.2024, pp. 1–144.

risk—hereinafter termed 'non-high-risk' systems. The paucity of scholarship is particularly troubling given that the latter category encompasses the vast majority of AI systems that are currently deployed or in the process of being developed. It is also troubling given that the Act's governance of these systems is complex, multifaceted and challenging to navigate. An aim with this chapter is to help correct the scholarly imbalance and bring greater clarity to this area of regulation.

The primary research questions addressed herein are: what AI systems does the AIA deem, directly or indirectly, as being non-high-risk systems, and what role does the Act envisage codes of practice and codes of conduct playing in the regulation of such systems? The answers provided are necessarily brief and, in some respects, superficial or conjectural. This is due largely to the AIA only recently entering into force, with many dimensions of its governance regime—including codes of practice and codes of conduct—just beginning to be operationalised. Nonetheless, it is important to seek answers to these questions already now. This is particularly so with the question concerning codes of practice and codes of conduct as these are envisaged by the legislator as providing many if not most of the 'rules of the road' for development and deployment of numerous non-high-risk AI systems. Yet, the mechanics of both sets of codes remain hazy in crucial respects.

The chapter first describes the various categories of non-high-risk systems and the main ways in which the Act addresses the risks they represent (Sect. 2). Thereafter, it proceeds to lay out the respective roles of codes of conduct, codes of practice and, to a lesser degree, harmonised standards (Sect. 3). It then compares and critically discusses the respective reach and traction of each type of code under the Act (Sect. 4). Finally, the chapter sums up its findings and conclusions (Sect. 5).

2 What Are Non-High-Risk AI Systems for AIA Purposes?

2.1 General Remarks

Non-high-risk AI systems for the purposes of the AIA (and this chapter) are AI systems other than those that the Act deems to be prohibited or high-risk. Note, though, that the AIA employs the term 'non-high-risk' (or a variation of it—i.e. 'not high-risk') more narrowly, this being predominantly as a qualification for AI systems that seemingly fall within the high-risk category but that the system providers deem to present a lower level of risk (see e.g. Article 6(4) and recital 53).[2] Thus, employing the qualification 'non-high-risk' (or 'not high-risk') to *all* systems that are neither prohibited nor high risk, is not entirely consistent with the Act's nomenclature. However, it is entirely consistent with the Act's logic.[3] By contrast,

---

[2] These are 'type 1' systems in our categorisation scheme laid out further below.

[3] It is also consistent with the European Commission's use of the qualification 'non-high-risk' in its proposal for the AIA. See European Commission (2021). Proposal for a Regulation of the European

using the adjective 'low-risk' to describe all such systems would be inappropriate given that some of the risk levels of this category of systems go beyond the adjective's ordinary connotations.

A related introductory point on nomenclature is that the Act largely avoids expressly grading the risk levels of the AI systems that fall outside the prohibited or high-risk categories. Thus, it eschews use of labels, such as 'low-risk', 'minimal risk' or 'mid-level risk'. However, one may still gainfully employ these labels as part of bringing an external analytical perspective to the Act.

Non-high-risk AI systems under the AIA vary considerably in the level and kind of risk they represent. At the same time, the Act's description of many of these systems is nebulous, partly because the Act is primarily concerned with delineating requirements for AI systems deemed to present high-risk or unacceptable risk, leaving the characteristics of other systems relatively underdetermined. The focus of the preparatory works to the AIA, along with most attendant scholarship and other expert commentary, is also directed at high-risk and prohibited systems.

The core distinctions turn on both the level of risk and the intended purpose of the systems concerned. The latter parameter is defined as 'the use for which an AI system is intended by the provider, including the specific context and conditions of use, as specified in the information supplied by the provider in the instructions for use, promotional or sales materials and statements, as well as in the technical documentation' (Article 3(12) AIA). As for risk, this represents a combination of 'the probability of an occurrence of harm and the severity of that harm' (Article 3(2)). Harm is primarily measured in terms of a system's 'impact on the health, safety and fundamental rights of persons in the Union' (recital 46), including impact on 'democracy, the rule of law and environmental protection' (recital 2), and extends across multiple dimensions: 'material or immaterial, including physical, psychological, societal or economic harm' (recital 5). This conception of harm reflects a central aspect of the Act's stated overarching purpose, which is to ensure 'a high level of protection of health, safety, fundamental rights enshrined in the Charter, including democracy, the rule of law and environmental protection, against the harmful effects of AI systems in the Union' (Article 1(1)). It bears emphasis that the Act's focus on AI systems' deleterious impact on persons and society differs from the thrust of preexisting AI risk management standards developed by the International Organization for Standardization (ISO) and International Electrotechnical Commission (IEC) which tend to conceive risk in a more value-neutral manner—that is, primarily in terms of positive or negative outcomes for organisations, including AI systems themselves.[4]

Parliament and of the Council laying down Harmonised Rules on Artificial Intelligence (Artificial Intelligence Act) and amending certain Union Legislative Acts (COM(2021) 206 final (12 April 2021), recital 81. See also European Commission (2020). White Paper: On Artificial Intelligence – A European approach to excellence and trust COM(2020) 65 final (19 February 2020), p. 24 (referring to 'no-high-risk' systems).

[4] See ISO/IEC 23894 standard on AI risk management. See also Soler Garrido et al. (2023), p. 7.

For AIA purposes, a high-risk system is deemed to have a 'significant harmful impact' in respect of people's health, safety etc. (recital 46). Thus, by implication, a non-high-risk system could be deemed as not having such an impact. This is, however, simply a point of departure from which there may be some deviation. For instance, certain non-high-risk systems—particularly those involving general-purpose AI (GPAI)—may pose considerable de facto risk, as made clear below.

Taking a broad perspective, we can discern four main types of non-high-risk systems covered by the AIA:

(1) those falling *prima facie* within the categories of high-risk systems listed in Annex III AIA but that are, actually and exceptionally, not high risk (hereinafter termed 'type 1 systems' or 'Article 6(3) systems');
(2) those intended to interact directly with humans or to generate content, and that in large part present a significant potential for deceiving or manipulating humans (hereinafter termed 'type 2 systems' or 'Article 50 systems');
(3) general-purpose AI (GPAI) systems and models (hereinafter termed 'type 3 systems' or 'Chapter V systems'); and
(4) those that are otherwise non-high-risk (hereinafter termed 'type 4 systems' or 'Article 95 systems').

Type 2 and 3 systems break down, in turn, into sub-categories, as expounded in the following.

It bears emphasis that the AIA foresees movement between risk categories. For example, GPAI systems or models could be employed in high-risk applications (see also recital 85 to this effect), while systems that are first assessed by providers as type 1 could end up being subsequently deemed high risk by market surveillance authorities (see Article 80(2)).

Regardless of the afore-mentioned typology, *all* non-high-risk AI systems deployed in the EU will have to comply with the General Product Safety Regulation (GPSR).[5] The latter constitutes a regulatory floor applying independently of the AIA (see also recital 166 AIA to this effect). Other legislation will also play a role. For example, AI systems that are integrated within intermediary services falling under the scope of the Digital Services Act (DSA)[6] will have to conform with that Act's requirements (see also recitals 118–119 AIA to this effect). At the same time, some of those requirements will also help fulfil the requirements of the AIA (see also recitals 120 and 136 AIA to this effect).

[5] Regulation (EU) 2023/988 of the European Parliament and of the Council of 10 May 2023 on general product safety, amending Regulation (EU) No 1025/2012 of the European Parliament and of the Council and Directive (EU) 2020/1828 of the European Parliament and the Council, and repealing Directive 2001/95/EC of the European Parliament and of the Council and Council Directive 87/357/EEC [2023] OJ L 135, 23.5.2023, pp. 1–51.

[6] Regulation (EU) 2022/2065 of the European Parliament and of the Council of 19 October 2022 on a Single Market for Digital Services and amending Directive 2000/31/EC (Digital Services Act) [2022] OJ L 277, 27.10.2022, pp. 1–102.

2.2 *Type 1 Systems/Article 6(3) Systems*

As noted in the previous section, type 1 systems comprise those that initially seem to be high-risk as they *prima facie* fall within the categories listed in Annex III of the Act but are, actually and exceptionally, not high risk because they do not 'pose a significant risk of harm to the health, safety or fundamental rights of natural persons, including by not materially influencing the outcome of decision making' (Article 6(3) AIA). They are, as it were, sheep that might look like wolves, at least from afar. Since they are dealt with primarily in Article 6(3) of the Act, they can also be termed 'Article 6(3) systems'.

A non-exhaustive list of type 1 systems is set out in the recitals to the Act. The list includes:

- identity check systems employed by law enforcement agencies (LEAs) in the presence of the person concerned (recital 33);
- systems for biometric verification and authentication (as opposed to *identification*: on the difference, see recital 15) employed by a person 'for the sole purpose of having access to a service, unlocking a device or having secure access to premises' (recital 54);
- other biometric systems 'intended to be used solely for the purpose of enabling cybersecurity and personal data protection measures' (recital 54);
- 'AI systems provided for by Union law for the purpose of detecting fraud in the offering of financial services and for prudential purposes to calculate credit institutions' and insurances undertakings' capital requirements' (recital 58);
- 'AI systems specifically intended to be used for administrative proceedings by tax and customs authorities as well as by financial intelligence units carrying out administrative tasks analysing information pursuant to Union anti-money laundering law' (recital 59);
- 'AI systems intended for purely ancillary administrative activities that do not affect the actual administration of justice in individual cases, such as anonymisation or pseudonymisation of judicial decisions, documents or data, communication between personnel, administrative tasks' (recital 61).

Also included are decisional support systems that do not materially influence the outcome of decision-making, do not perform profiling of natural persons, and that satisfy one or more of the following four criteria: (i) they perform a narrow procedural task; (ii) they improve the result of previously completed human activity; (iii) they detect anomalies; (iv) they do preparatory work (Article 6(3); see also recital 53). At the risk of spelling out the obvious, this list of criteria is not to be construed as exemplificatory, but as a *numerus clausus*.

Further elaboration of type 1 systems will take place in due course since the Commission is required to provide guidelines setting out, *inter alia*, 'a comprehensive list of practical examples of use cases of AI systems that are high-risk and not high-risk' in accordance with Article 96 (Article 6(5)).

Providers of type 1 systems must document their assessment of why the systems are not high-risk, and they must register their systems in a public database in accordance with Article 49(2) (Article 6(4)). Note, though, that they do not need to wait for external vetting of their assessment before placing their systems on the market or putting them into service. Further, documentation of their assessment need not be publicly disclosed; rather, such documentation shall be provided to the relevant market surveillance authority (MSA) upon the latter's request (Article 6(4)). Thus, the Act places a great deal of trust on the providers to carry out an honest assessment, at least initially. However, the relevant MSA may later review the assessment and overturn it, thereby compelling the provider to comply with the Act's requirements for high-risk systems (Article 80(2)). Failure to comply may lead to the imposition of a fine pursuant to Article 99 (Article 80(7)). How well this compliance scheme will function, remains to be seen, but it certainly has weak points.[7]

Whether type 1 systems deserve being singled out as a separate category of non-high-risk AI systems is questionable. If a provider's risk assessment is not overturned by a MSA, the system becomes, in effect, a sub-category of one or more of the other three types—most typically type 4—and it must then comply with the requirements for that type. However, we choose to treat them as a category in their own right because of the special measures they attract.

2.3 *Type 2 Systems/Article 50 Systems*

Type 2 systems are intended to interact directly with humans or to generate content, and include a variety of systems that pose risks of deception, manipulation, or discrimination. Examples are chatbots, emotion recognition systems (as defined in Article 3(39)), biometric categorisation systems (as defined in Article 3(40)), systems for generating 'deep fakes' (as defined in Article 3(60)), and GPAI systems. Some of the risks such systems give rise to are outlined in recitals 132–134.

These systems are subject to a qualified set of transparency obligations set out in Article 50; hence, an alternative nomenclature for type 2 systems could be 'Article 50 systems'. Three categories of transparency obligations apply. Each is attached to a particular kind of AI system.

The first is for AI systems intended to interact directly with humans. Providers of such systems must ensure that they are 'designed and developed in such a way that the natural persons concerned are informed that they are interacting with an AI system, unless this is obvious from the point of view of a natural person who is reasonably well-informed, observant and circumspect, taking into account the circumstances and the context of use' (Article 50(1)). Part of the latter criterion is the degree of vulnerability of the people with whom the systems interact (recital 132).

[7] Cf. Wachter (2024), p. 686 (noting the enforcement burden for MSAs 'that may have neither the time nor the resources to test provider claims and systematically audit systems').

The second category of transparency obligation pertains to AI systems generating synthetic content. Providers of such systems 'shall ensure that the outputs of the AI system are marked in a machine-readable format and detectable as artificially generated or manipulated' (Article 50(2)). This extends expressly to GPAI systems (also those without systemic risk).

The third category applies to emotion recognition systems and biometric categorisation systems. In this case, deployers (not providers) of such systems 'shall inform the natural persons exposed thereto of the operation of the system, and shall process the personal data in accordance with Regulations (EU) 2016/679 and (EU) 2018/1725 and Directive (EU) 2016/680, as applicable' (Article 50(3)).

These obligations—particularly the first two categories—can be seen as manifestations of a principle of 'transparency by design' in that they attempt to ensure that transparency is hardwired, as it were, into the system from the start and not just added as an afterthought. This intention comes through also in the preamble: 'it is appropriate to require providers of those systems to *embed* technical solutions that enable marking in a machine readable format and detection that the output has been generated or manipulated by an AI system and not a human' (recital 133; emphasis added). The 'by design' approach resonates with those parts of the Act dealing with high-risk AI systems where design mandates also apply, not just in relation to transparency (Article 13) but a range of other properties, including accuracy, robustness and cybersecurity (Article 15), oversight and understandability (Article 14), and accessibility, particularly for persons with disabilities (recital 80). The approach fits in with a broader pattern of design-oriented principles originating outside the AIA framework.[8]

However, the transparency requirements under Article 50 are modest. Whereas '[h]igh-risk AI systems should be designed in a manner to enable deployers to understand how the AI system works, evaluate its functionality, and comprehend its strengths and limitations' (recital 72), the transparency requirements under Article 50 simply concern the mere demarcation or flagging of the artificial nature of the system or its product, not the understanding of the system's functionality. Additionally, the requirements are blunted by exemptions, primarily for law enforcement. Further, in respect of systems generating synthetic data (including deep fakes), the preamble emphasises that the transparency obligation must be tempered by regard for other fundamental rights.[9] More generally, one may question whether

[8] See e.g. Bygrave (2021).

[9] 'Compliance with this transparency obligation should not be interpreted as indicating that the use of the system or its output impedes the right to freedom of expression and the right to freedom of the arts and sciences guaranteed in the [CFREU], in particular where the content is part of an evidently creative, satirical, artistic or fictional work or programme, subject to appropriate safeguards for the rights and freedoms of third parties. In those cases, the transparency obligation for deep fakes … is limited to disclosure of the existence of such generated or manipulated content in an appropriate manner that does not hamper the display or enjoyment of the work, including its normal exploitation and use, while maintaining the utility and quality of the work' (recital 134).

the limited form of transparency advanced in Article 50 will adequately mitigate the considerable risks posed by type 2 systems.[10]

Further specification on the meaning and reach of the transparency requirements is left for future codes of practice (Article 50(7)). These codes may subsequently be approved by the Commission through implementing acts pursuant to the procedure laid down in Article 56 paragraphs 6–8 (Article 50(7)). The nature and function of these codes is dealt with in more detail in Sect. 3.2.2 below.

2.4 Type 3 Systems/Chapter V Systems

Type 3 systems comprise so-called general-purpose AI (GPAI) systems and models. As these are chiefly dealt with in Chapter V of the Act, they can also be labelled 'Chapter V systems'. Such systems are based on GPAI models and have 'the capability to serve a variety of purposes, both for direct use as well as for integration in other AI systems' (Article 3(66)). A GPAI model is an 'AI model, including where such an AI model is trained with a large amount of data using self-supervision at scale, that displays significant generality and is capable of competently performing a wide range of distinct tasks regardless of the way the model is placed on the market and that can be integrated into a variety of downstream systems or applications' (Article 3(63)), but does not include an AI model 'used for research, development or prototyping activities before [being] … released on the market' (Article 3(63)).[11]

GPAI models 'are typically trained on large amounts of data, through various methods, such as self-supervised, unsupervised or reinforcement learning' (recital 97), with 'large generative AI models' being 'a typical example … given that they allow for flexible generation of content, such as in the form of text, audio, images or video, that can readily accommodate a wide range of distinctive tasks' (recital 99). A GPAI model as such is not a system until other components, such as a user-interface, are added to it, but 'AI models are typically integrated into and form part of AI systems' (recital 97).

The AIA operates with two classes of GPAI models: those involving systemic risk and those not involving such risk. The systemic risk category forms a special risk level situated between the low- and high-risk categories. The concept of 'systemic risk' is a legal transplant imported from the European System for Financial Supervision (ESFS) via the Digital Services Act.[12] In the ESFS, the European

[10] Cf. Wachter (2024), p. 684 ('Transparency alone is insufficient to address these issues').

[11] In AI scholarship, the term 'foundation models' is often used instead of GPAI models. For a seminal exposition and critique of foundation models, see Bommasani et al. (2021). Note, though, that conceptualisations of foundation models are not necessarily fully commensurate with the AIA's conceptualisation of GPAI models, particularly because of the Act's carve-out for models 'used for research, development or prototyping activities before [being] … released on the market'.

[12] Article 34 DSA requires Very Large Online Platforms (VLOPs) and Very Large Online Search Engines (VLOSEs)—i.e. platforms and search engines with more than 45 million monthly users in

Systemic Risk Board is tasked with macroprudential oversight and risk-mitigation to preserve financial stability. In that context, systemic risk refers to 'the type of risk that, once triggered, can propagate throughout the financial system, threaten the functionality of the system as a whole and, in the worst case scenario, lead to financial crisis'.[13] More generally, the concept of systemic risk is now used to denote potential dangers to the functionality of any societally important system where their impact typically creates emergent, interacting, non-linear, stochastic ripple effects across the system or on other systems in ways that are challenging for conventional risk management strategies to capture.[14]

In the context of the AIA, 'systemic risk' denotes 'a risk that is specific to the high-impact capabilities of general-purpose AI models, having a significant impact on the Union market due to their reach, or due to actual or reasonably foreseeable negative effects on public health, safety, public security, fundamental rights, or the society as a whole, that can be propagated at scale across the value chain' (Article 3(65)). Initial classificatory criteria for determining which GPAI models involve systemic risk are set out in Article 51 paragraphs 1 and 2 (see also recitals 110–111), with an assumption that systemic risk is present when the cumulative amount of computation used for a model's training is greater than 10^{25} floating point operations (Article 51(2)).[15] The degree to which FLOPs may properly be regarded as a reliable proxy for systemic risk—particularly in light of its broad definition in Article 3(65) AIA—is debatable.[16] However, the Commission is empowered to adjust these criteria 'in light of evolving technological developments' (Article 51(3)). It is also given extensive power to determine which models involve systemic risk (Article 52), according to criteria laid out in Annex XIII. These criteria include the amount of data and computation for training the model, its input and output modalities, its degree of autonomy and scalability, and its number of end-users, with a presumption of high impact once that number reaches 'at least 10 000 registered business users established in the Union'. Arguably, the AIA's conception of systemic risk does not, on its face, capture all of the facets of such risk that are highlighted in scholarship—particularly the elements of emergence and non-linearity—but these can probably be read into the provisions. Overall, the AIA currently leaves a great

the EU—to undertake assessments of 'systemic risk' in respect of four sets of risk areas: dissemination of illegal content; negative effects on the exercise of fundamental rights; negative effects on democratic processes, civic discourse, electoral processes and public security; and negative effects on minors, public health, gender-based violence and individuals' physical and mental well-being. However, the DSA neither expressly defines 'systemic risk' nor explains in detail how it is to be assessed, so it provides little help for understanding the concept for AIA purposes.

[13] Myklebust (2023), p. 92.

[14] See further Renn et al. (2022).

[15] Put somewhat simplistically, a floating point operation (FLOP) in this context is basically a measure of computing capacity for training AI models. The AIA defines it more precisely as 'any mathematical operation or assignment involving floating-point numbers, which are a subset of the real numbers normally represented in computers by an integer of fixed precision scaled by an integer exponent of a fixed base' (Article 3(67)).

[16] Cf. Wachter (2024), p. 698 ('Using FLOPs as a proxy for danger or capability is unworkable').

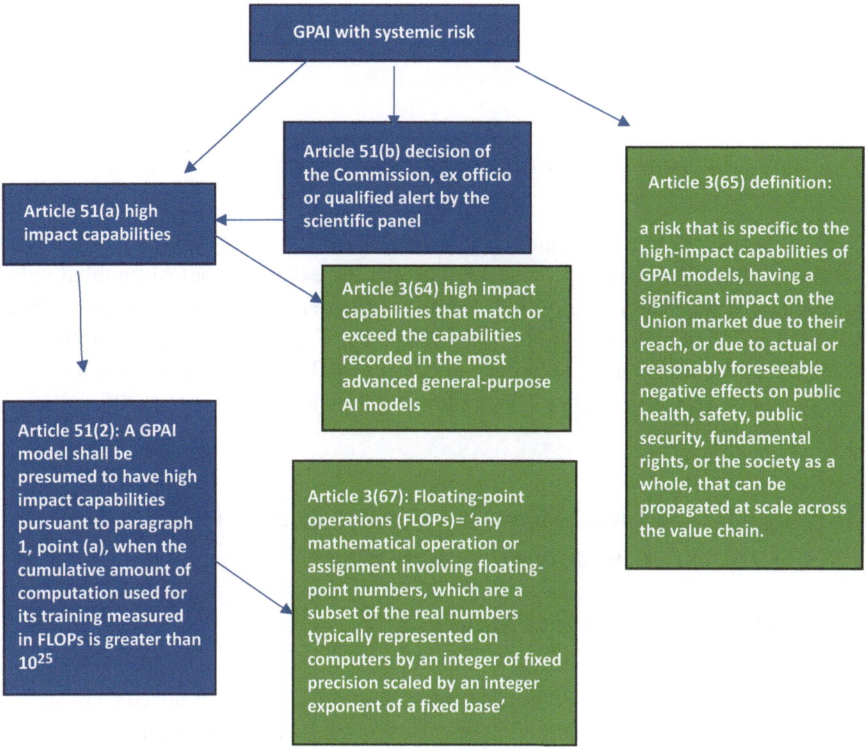

Fig. 1 Definition of AI with systemic risk

deal of uncertainty about what could constitute a systemic risk beyond the presumption in Article 52(2). At the same time, the Act confers on the Commission considerable discretion in elaborating this risk category, particularly given that the Act provides little indication as to how the various Annex XIII criteria shall be weighed against each other (Fig. 1).

With one exception, all GPAI models are subject to transparency and other risk mitigation requirements (Article 53; see also Article 50(2)). The requirements for models involving systemic risk are more stringent (Article 55), including model evaluations, risk assessment and mitigation, documentation and reporting obligations, as well as ensuring adequate cybersecurity (Article 55(1)(a)–(d)). The exception is for GPAI models 'released under a free and open source license, and whose parameters, including the weights, the information on the model architecture, and the information on model usage, are made publicly available' (recital 104) and that do not present a systemic risk (Article 53(2)).

As with type 2 (Article 50) systems, the AIA foresees the drafting of EU codes of practice to promote adherence to the risk mitigation measures for type 3 systems laid out in Articles 53 and 55 (Article 56)). The Commission can give these codes its official stamp of approval through adopting implementing acts (Article 56 paragraphs 6–8). The nature and function of these codes is dealt with in more detail in Sect. 3.2.2 below.

2.5 *Type 4 Systems/Article 95 Systems*

Type 4 systems form a large, amorphous category of relatively benign products and services. The AIA does not provide a list of specific examples, but AI-enabled video games and spam filters would likely qualify. Providers of such systems are subject to the lightest regulatory burden under the AIA. They are merely encouraged to draw up and comply with voluntary codes of conduct pursuant to Article 95, as elaborated in Sect. 3.2.3 below. Thus, they may also be termed 'Article 95 systems'.

3 Not All Soft Law Is Equal: Codes of Conduct, Codes of Practice, Harmonised Standards

3.1 *What Are Codes and Standards?*

The AIA envisages codes of conduct, codes of practice and harmonised standards to play a significant role in the governance of non-high-risk AI systems. This is particularly the case with codes of practice for GPAI models: such codes 'should represent a central tool for the proper compliance with the obligations provided for under this Regulation for providers of general-purpose AI models' (recital 117).

As a point of departure, codes of practice, codes of conduct and harmonised standards can be considered soft law in that they are not initially set down as statutory instruments, but as legally non-binding tools developed by private actors, often in support of legislation or contract. However, the description 'soft law' can be confusing when we look at the actual function of these instruments because, in many contexts, they may become integrated in hard law.[17] An important instance of such integration is as tools of meta-regulation—i.e. mechanisms by which the state (or, in this case, the EU) as regulator makes regulatees responsible and accountable for their own efforts to self-regulate.[18] Within this regulatory framework, codes as well as standards have three principal overlapping functions: (i) enhancing the accountability of regulatees; (ii) filling in gaps in the attendant legislative frameworks (sometimes in contexts where the authority to fill in the gaps through

---

[17] See e.g. Case C-588/21 P, *PublicResourceOrg, Inc and Right to Know CLG v. European Commission*, judgement of 5 March 2024 (Grand Chamber) (ECLI:EU:C:2024:201), para. 89 (recognising that harmonised standards may 'form part of EU law owing to their legal effects').

[18] Parker (2007). See also e.g. Coglianese and Mendelson (2010), p. 148 (defining meta-regulation as 'ways that outside regulators deliberately—rather than unintentionally—seek to induce targets to develop their own internal, self-regulatory responses to public problems').

legislation does not exist or is weak);[19] and (iii) broadening the traction of ethical and legal values beyond the formal bounds of these frameworks.

Amongst the assumed strengths of codes and standards are their ability to provide regulatory flexibility, increase regulatory certainty and promote the 'buy in' of regulatees. They are also seen as enhancing regulatory cost-efficiency. For example, the Unfair Commercial Practices Directive (UCPD)[20] states that '[t]he control exercised by code owners at national or Community level to eliminate unfair commercial practices may avoid the need for recourse to administrative or judicial action and should therefore be encouraged' (recital 20). Unsurprisingly, codes of conduct and codes of practice are promoted by the EU as key constituents of its 'Better Regulation Agenda',[21] and figure evermore saliently in technology regulation,[22] while harmonised standards feature centrally in the 'New Legislative Framework'.[23]

Nonetheless, the increasing use of codes and standards has facets that bring their legitimacy into question. A primary issue in this regard is that they involve an outsourcing of normative power from democratic institutions to private bodies that do not always act in the public interest nor possess 'the necessary institutional, procedural, and substantive governance structure to answer hard normative questions'.[24] Further, while the drafting of standards and codes may be formally framed as committed to multistakeholderism, the process is frequently arcane, requiring considerable domain-specific expertise to participate in meaningfully. This accentuates the likelihood of particular well-resourced actors dominating negotiations.[25]

It is important to note that the AIA maintains a distinction between codes of practice and codes of conduct, in the sense that each are assigned different fields of application and are intended to differ in their respective degrees of legal effect. Codes of practice are reserved for use in governing type 2 and type 3 systems. Moreover, they are probably compulsory for type 3 systems, at least as a 'stop-gap' measure prior to the adoption of harmonised standards. In contrast, codes of conduct are, as a point of departure, not compulsory and are reserved for governing all non-high-risk systems (i.e. types 1 to 4). Additionally, codes of conduct are

[19] See further e.g. Micklitz (2023a) (noting the EU's resort to encouragement of technical standards as a way of offsetting its weakness in bringing about further harmonisation of national private law, especially in the face of EU Member State resistance).

[20] Directive 2005/29/EC of the European Parliament and of the Council of 11 May 2005 concerning unfair business-to-consumer commercial practices in the internal market and amending Council Directive 84/450/EEC, Directives 97/7/EC, 98/27/EC and 2002/65/EC of the European Parliament and of the Council and Regulation (EC) No 2006/2004 of the European Parliament and of the Council ('Unfair Commercial Practices Directive') [2005] OJ L 149, 11.6.2005, pp. 22–39.

[21] See generally Garben and Govaere (2018).

[22] See generally Vander Maelen (2022); Griffin (2024a).

[23] See further e.g. Colombo and Eliantonio (2017). See also Sect. 4.2 below.

[24] Micklitz (2023b), p. 16. For problematisation in respect of the AIA, see e.g. Wachter (2024), p. 690ff and references cited therein.

[25] Further on these problems in respect of the codes-of-conduct regime for the DSA, see Griffin (2024b).

envisaged as governing *all* AI systems (also high-risk systems) in respect of certain matters specified in the Act, as elaborated further on in this chapter.

These differences are especially noteworthy for running against the grain of broader regulatory discourse. As such, they can engender initial confusion. Outside the context of the AIA, academic and entrepreneurial literature often does not distinguish between the two forms of code, or, if it does, the distinction is not stringently applied. For example, Vrielink and Montfort state:

> Some scholars distinguish a code of practice from a code of conduct. A code of conduct is defined as a practical document of standards governing client relationship [*sic*], and a code of practice as a technical document setting standards for the members of a profession. The definition of a code of practice used in this entry encompasses both types of documents.[26]

Both types of code are also sometimes referenced (again, outside the context of the AIA) interchangeably with other terms, such as 'codes of ethics', 'business codes', 'integrity codes' and 'industry guides'. This blending of nomenclature is understandable given the content and heritage of the norms concerned. For instance, codes of conduct often build on and express ethical principles, so, in practice, such codes are typically intertwined or merged with codes of ethics.

However, it is common to distinguish, on the one hand, codes of conduct and codes of practice from standards on the other, especially technical standards (less so with managerial or organisational standards). Whereas the purpose of codes of conduct and codes of practice is to delineate the expected behaviour and ethical principles with which individuals or members of a profession, industry sector or other community should comply, standards are typically aimed at delineating more concrete measurable benchmarks and technical specifications for the quality of products, services or organisational processes.

Often, codes of practice and codes of conduct are drafted by those later applying them; at the very least organisations implementing them have signed up to them. Standards, in contrast, are usually developed by standard-setting organisations (which may also consist of relevant industry actors) and can be implemented by a whole range of actors and organisations usually going beyond those involved in the drafting process. Signing up to a standard is also usually not necessary. Rather, standards are bought and then implemented in the respective organisations' structures.

Although typically drafted by non-state actors, codes of practice and codes of conduct are not just creatures of the private sector. They may be developed by a broad array of actors from both public and private sector, including civil society. A pertinent example of a public sector code is the 'Guide to Good Practice for Digital and Data-Driven Health Technologies', published by the UK Department of Health and Social Care (DHSC) in 2021. This sets out 12 principles for the safe and ethical development, use and procurement of AI and data-driven technologies for use within the UK National Health Service (NHS). The guide's purpose is to inform

[26] Vrielink and Montfort (2010), p. 492.

digital service providers about what the NHS expects when it procures digital and data-driven technology for use in healthcare.

The AIA also envisages public sector bodies—in addition to private sector entities—playing a significant role in code development, as described further on in this chapter.

Traditionally, adherence to a code of conduct or code of practice is voluntary, although violations may result in disciplinary actions within the relevant community and sometimes have legal consequences. The potential for such consequences is exemplified by Article 6(2)(b) UCPD which provides for the possibility that breach of a code of conduct by a trader who has undertaken to comply with the code may amount to a misleading commercial practice if the breach, first, 'in its factual context, taking account of all its features and circumstances, [...] causes or is likely to cause the average consumer to take a transactional decision that he would not have taken otherwise', and, second, involves non-compliance with a commitment that 'is not aspirational but ... firm and ... capable of being verified'. As pointed out further below, the AIA does not operate on its face with this sort of remedial regime, although non-compliance with a code under the Act—especially a code of practice—may bring potentially detrimental consequences and could, if the code is used in marketing, amount to a misleading commercial practice under the UCPD in particular circumstances.

Standards may also be subject to a more stringent compliance regime. This is particularly the case when the standards are intended to implement or supplement the requirements of framework legislation—a function increasingly baked into EU regulation, particularly the 'New Approach' and 'New Legislative Framework' initiatives. At the same time, codes of conduct and codes of practice may refer to standards and vice-versa so, in practice, these types of instruments will often be intertwined. The close interaction between codes and standards is exemplified in the AIA, which, as detailed in Sect. 3.2.2, envisages use of codes of practice to govern GPAI models in advance of the adoption of harmonised standards for such models (see Articles 50(4) and 55(2)).

3.2 *Codes in the AIA: Definition and Application*

3.2.1 General Remarks

Although the AIA distinguishes between codes of conduct and codes of practice, it omits specific definitions of both forms of instrument. This is unlike, say, the UCPD which defines (in Article 2(f)) a code of conduct as follows:

> an agreement or set of rules not imposed by law, regulation or administrative provision of a Member State which defines the behaviour of traders who undertake to be bound by the code in relation to one or more particular commercial practices or business sectors.

This definition would appear to provide a fairly accurate depiction of both codes of conduct and codes of practice for AIA purposes, although the 'trader' category should not be treated as fully commensurate with the categories 'provider' or 'deployer' of AI systems (the principal actors subject to code governance under the AIA).

A more AI-specific (but non-legal) description of codes of conduct is provided by d'Angelo and others:

> Broadly, these can be characterised as statements that set out and define certain requirements or principles that should be followed by organisations developing or procuring AI applications to ensure the safe and ethical development and use of these systems. These generally do not define measurable criteria or include an audit process. This category includes codes of conduct and codes of ethics, which are often used interchangeably in the literature reviewed.[27]

While the first sentence of this quote appears to describe reasonably accurately how the AIA envisages both codes of conduct and codes of practice, the second sentence does not. As detailed below, the AIA provides that its codes shall contain key performance indicators and similar criteria for the purposes of measuring the degree to which the codes achieve their objectives.

In the absence of a conclusive definition of either codes of practice or codes of conduct, we must turn to their envisaged application in the AIA in order to enhance our understanding of these instruments for the purposes of the Act. Table 1 provides an overview of meta-regulatory elements (including also harmonised standards) used for the different types of AI, including high-risk AI.

Table 1 Overview of meta-regulatory elements in AIA

	High risk AI	Type 2	Type 3	Type 1 and 4
Primary Meta-Regulatory Instrument	**Harmonised standards:** see Art. 40(2) for Ch. 3 Sec. 2 requirements.	**Codes of Practice:** see Art. 50(7); can be approved by Commission through implementing acts	**Codes of Practice:** see Art. 56(1); can be approved by Commission through implementing acts (Art. 56(6)). Harmonised standards (see Art. 40(2)) which replace codes of practice (Art. 55(2)).	**Codes of Conduct:** see Art. 95(1) for voluntary application of high-risk AI requirements; and Art. 95(2) for the list of requirements.
Subsidiary Meta-Regulatory Instrument	Implementing acts containing common specifications (Art. 41) if adequate harmonised standards do not emerge.	Implementing acts containing common specifications if code of practice deemed inadequate (Art. 50(7)).	Implementing acts containing common specification if code of practice deemed inadequate (Art. 56(9)).	None.

[27] d'Angelo et al. (2022), p. 10.

Harmonised standards are the primary meta-regulatory tool for high-risk AI, whereas codes of practice and codes of conduct are the primary tools for non-high-risk AI. In the following, we describe more closely the Act's framework for codes of practice and codes of conduct, highlighting their respective regulatory functions.

3.2.2 Codes of *Practice* Under the AIA

As highlighted in the table above, codes of practice play three roles under the AIA. First, they may help to govern type 2 systems. More specifically in this regard, they may 'facilitate the effective implementation of the obligations regarding the detection and labelling of artificially generated or manipulated content' as set out in Article 50, paragraphs 1 to 5 (Article 50(7)). Second, they may help govern the development and use of GPAI models (i.e. type 3 systems), at least up until harmonised standards are published (Article 53(4)). Third, they may help govern the development and use of GPAI models with systemic risk, again at least up until the adoption of harmonised standards for such models (Article 55(2)). Part of the function of the latter governance application is to 'help to establish a risk taxonomy of the type and nature of the systemic risks at Union level, including their sources' and to elaborate 'specific risk assessment and mitigation measures' (recital 116). Another function, applying to all GPAI models, is that of demonstrating compliance—i.e. GPAI model providers may use the codes as evidence that they comply with their obligations under the AIA (Articles 53(4) and 55(2)).

The Act requires the AI Office to 'encourage and facilitate the drawing up of codes of practice at Union level ...' (Articles 50(7) and 56(1)). In doing so, the AI Office shall take into account 'international approaches' (Article 56(1)), which suggests that the codes ought to be aligned, where appropriate, with conceptions of good AI governance existing beyond Europe. On its face, the use of the phrasing 'encourage and facilitate' suggests that the codes are not compulsory. This impression is reinforced by the fact that the Act envisages situations where providers of the AI systems/models concerned do not adhere to a code of practice, in which case they must 'demonstrate alternative adequate means of compliance for approval by the Commission' (Articles 53(4) and 55(2)). However, the lack of mandatory adherence to a code does not necessarily mean that drawing up a code is purely voluntary, and the Act's operationalisation seems to assume the drafting of codes is the normal procedure, at least for GPAI systems and models as a 'stop-gap' measure in advance of, or in combination with, the adoption of harmonised standards. Moreover, Article 56(9) is ambiguous on point: it first stipulates a date by when codes of practice 'shall be ready at the latest', yet then provides rules to cover the situation when codes 'cannot be finalised' or are not able to be deemed 'adequate'—in such a situation, the Commission may step in and fill the gap with 'implementing acts'.

Regardless, once a code of practice is drawn up, it becomes subject to a relatively stringent governance regime under Article 56, as detailed below. Moreover, a code of practice may have an impact when regulators set the level of fines for non-compliance with the Act (see particularly Article 101(1) in respect of GPAI models and, less obviously, Article 99(4)(g) in respect of type 2 systems).

The AIA envisages a wide array of entities as potential architects of codes of practice, with the AI Office and the European Artificial Intelligence Board (EAIB) charged with taking a central role in code formation. Providers of GPAI models and relevant national regulatory authorities shall be invited as participants in the drafting process, with 'other relevant stakeholders' (including civil society organisations, industry, academia, 'downstream providers' and 'independent experts') in a 'support' role (Article 56(3)). By casting some of the listed participants in a 'support' role, the code development framework formally privileges certain institutional and corporate stakeholders over others. It remains to be seen how much this privilege will undercut the pretensions of multistakeholderism manifest both in Article 56(3) and in the policy descriptions of the framework.[28]

While the Act refers to the need to take account of 'international approaches' (Article 56(1)), it omits explicit reference to the need to take account of other pertinent factors, such as the 'state of the art' in terms of technical solutions and industry best practices. This is surprising and differs from the provisions on codes of conduct, as elaborated in Sect. 3.2.3 below. However, these sorts of factors may be read into the overarching reference to 'international approaches'.

The AI Office and EAIB are also charged with overseeing and evaluating code development and deployment. Especially noteworthy here is the stipulation that they 'shall aim to ensure' that codes 'clearly set out their specific objectives and contain commitments or measures, including key performance indicators as appropriate, to ensure the achievement of those objectives' (Article 56(4)). Additionally, they 'shall regularly monitor and evaluate the achievement of the objectives of the codes' and publish assessments of the codes' adequacy (Article 56(6)). These stipulations ought, in principle, to bring about a disciplining effect in respect of code compliance and 'riskwashing'.[29]

The Commission may subsequently approve codes through implementing acts, thereby giving the codes 'a general validity within the Union' (Articles 50(7) and 56(6)). This is yet another area in which the Commission is accorded a privileged norm-determining status under the Act.

---

[28] The AI Office has framed at least the initial stages of developing the code of practice for GPAI as a 'multi-stakeholder' consultation: see https://digital-strategy.ec.europa.eu/en/consultations/ai-act-have-your-say-trustworthy-general-purpose-ai and https://digital-strategy.ec.europa.eu/en/news/ai-act-participate-drawing-first-general-purpose-ai-code-practice.

[29] We use the term 'riskwashing' to denote a situation in which a company gives the impression of managing risk properly when it does not. The term was first coined to describe this sort of practice in relation to companies' use of regulatory sandboxes in the financial sector. See further Brown and Piroska (2021).

3.2.3 Codes of *Conduct* Under the AIA

Article 95(1) encourages the drawing up of codes of conduct for voluntary application to non-high-risk AI systems of 'some or all of' the requirements for high-risk systems, 'taking into account', in effect, the state of the art. The provision reads in full as follows:

> The AI Office and the Member States shall encourage and facilitate the drawing up of codes of conduct, including related governance mechanisms, intended to foster the voluntary application to AI systems, other than high-risk AI systems, of some or all of the requirements set out in Chapter III, Section 2 taking into account the available technical solutions and industry best practices allowing for the application of such requirements.

In doing so, the AI Office and Member States shall also take into account 'the specific interests and needs of SMEs, including start-ups' (Article 95(4)).

The wording of Article 95(1) differs in several notable respects from the formulations used for codes of practice. First, the voluntary character of code application is made explicit. Second, besides the AI Office, Member States are accorded a role in code formation, whereas the EAIB is formally not. Third, there is no reference to 'international approaches' having to be taken into account, but there is reference to 'available technological solutions and industry best practices'. Fourth, codes of conduct are implicitly envisaged as capable of operating exclusively at national level, not just as Union-wide instruments, reflecting their more flexible and spontaneous nature relative to codes of practice, which are much more intended as an instrument to implement the AIA's primary obligations.

The omission of any reference to the need to consider 'international approaches' is surprising, and the Act does not provide a clear explanation for this absence. It would seem beneficial to acknowledge the importance of aligning codes of conduct with international standards of good governance where appropriate. The fact that this alignment is not emphasised—unlike in the case of codes of practice—could be attributed to the perception that codes of conduct have less regulatory impact and scope. However, in practice, addressing what constitutes the 'state of the art' may still require consideration of solutions and practices beyond Europe, even though these may not consistently meet the high standards typically expected from EU-based industries.

Article 95(1) covers *all* non-high-risk AI systems—i.e. types 1 to 4. Thus, a type 2 or type 3 system might be covered by both a code of practice and a code of conduct, with the latter being potentially more wide-ranging than the former as it could extend to numerous requirements that are ordinarily reserved for high-risk systems.

A second category of codes of conduct is provided for in Article 95(2), which requires the AI Office and Member States to

> facilitate the drawing up of codes of conduct concerning the voluntary application, including by deployers, of specific requirements to all AI systems, on the basis of clear objectives and key performance indicators to measure the achievement of those objectives ....

The provision continues by laying down a non-exhaustive list of 'elements' for inclusion in such codes. These include 'applicable elements provided for in Union ethical guidelines for trustworthy AI' (Article 95(2)(a)), environmental sustainability (Article 95(2)(b)), AI literacy (Article 95(2)(c)), participatory design (Article 95(2)(d)), and gender equality (Article 95(2)(e)).

Article 95(2) is significant for four reasons. First, it extends to all AI systems. Second, it brings in matters that are otherwise not dealt with extensively by the AIA. Third, by referring to 'clear objectives' and KPIs, it attempts to peg codes of conduct to concrete goals so that they do not remain simply aspirational (see also recital 165).[30] The latter ambition must be seen in light of the riskwashing threat and empirical evidence indicating that pre-existing codes have tended to lack operationalising measures.[31] The ambition is backed up by Article 112(7) requiring the Commission to assess regularly the impact and effectiveness of codes of conduct.

The fourth reason is that Article 95(2) seeks to operationalise the role of ethics within a hard-law framework for AI regulation. The ethical guidelines to which it refers are those published in 2019 by the High-Level Expert Group (HLEG) appointed by the European Commission to consider the ethical implications of AI and propose principles for its governance. The guidelines' special status within the AIA is further underlined in recital 27:

> Without prejudice to the legally binding requirements of this Regulation and any other applicable Union law, those guidelines contribute to the design of a coherent, trustworthy and human-centric AI, in line with the Charter and with the values on which the Union is founded.

The recital goes on to state that the seven principles proposed by the HLEG (human agency and oversight; technical robustness and safety; privacy and data governance; transparency; diversity, non-discrimination and fairness; societal and environmental well-being and accountability) 'should be translated, when possible, in the design and use of AI models' and 'should in any case serve as a basis for the drafting of codes of conduct under this Regulation'.

Recital 165 provides additional context regarding the development of codes of conduct. It states that such codes shall be developed in an inclusive fashion, involving relevant stakeholders from the business sector, civil society, academia and research, trade unions and consumer organisations. This is reflected in Article 95(3), which permits a diverse range of actors to participate in code formation, extending to 'any interested stakeholders and their representatives, including civil society organisations and academia'. On the face of the Act, these stakeholders are not restricted to playing a mere 'support role'—unlike the situation with codes of practice. In this respect, the Act goes further here in embracing a form of 'multistakeholderism', but the embracement is soft: Article 95(3) does not require this governance form; it is simply allowed.

---

[30] The phrasing emulates the thrust of the DSA provisions on codes of conduct for VLOPs and VLOSEs (Article 45(3) DSA; see also recital 103 DSA).

[31] d'Angelo et al. (2022), p. 43 ('A notable feature of the examined codes of conduct, with the exception of the NHS's 'A Guide to Good Practice for Digital and Data-Driven Health Technologies' (UK DHSC 2021), is the marked lack of tangible steps to meet requirements which are invariably presented in general terms').

As a sidenote, recital 165 also states that the 'Commission may develop initiatives, including of a sectorial nature, to facilitate the lowering of technical barriers hindering cross-border exchange of data for AI development, including on data access infrastructure, semantic and technical interoperability of different types of data'. It is unclear whether these initiatives are intended as being manifest in codes of conduct.

3.3 *The AIA's Regulatory Approach for Non-High-Risk AI: Embedded v. Potential Meta-Regulation*

In the preceding section, we observed marked distinctions between codes of practice and codes of conduct. The former appear to align more closely with harmonised standards, while the latter adopt a distinctly softer regulatory approach. Table 2 summarises the primary differences among these three instruments.

Table 2 Differences between harmonised standards, codes of practice and codes of conduct in AIA

	Harmonised standards	Codes of practice	Codes of conduct
Standard Setting	Commission issues standardisation requests (Art. 40(2)). European Standardisation organisations draft standards (Regulation (EU) 1025/2012).	AI Office may invite all providers of GPAI models, relevant national competent authorities, to participate in drawing-up of codes of practice. Additional stakeholders (civil society organisations, industry, academia and others) in support role (Art. 56(3)).	AI Office and Member States initiate (Art. 95(1)). Drafted by individual providers or deployers, or by organisations representing them. Involvement of deployers and any interested stakeholders (Art. 95(3)).
Monitoring	Conformity assessment through internal control or external control via notified bodies (Art. 43(1)).	Regular reports to AI Office on implementation (Art. 56(5)). Commission can request documentation and information (Art. 91) and conduct evaluations (Art. 92). AI Board can issue recommendations (Art. 66(1)(e)).	No provisions
Regulatory Effect	Presumption of conformity with requirements of Chapter III section 2 and Chapter V sections 2 and 3 (Art. 40(1)).	Providers may rely on codes of practice to demonstrate compliance with AIA obligations; otherwise need to demonstrate alternative measures (Arts. 53(4) and 55(2)).	Voluntary application (Art. 95(1) and 95(2)).

(continued)

Table 2 (continued)

	Harmonised standards	Codes of practice	Codes of conduct
Enforcement	Not directly enforced but play crucial role in demonstrating compliance (Art. 43(1)). Penalties (Art. 99(4)).	AI Office may invite all providers of GPAI models to adhere to codes of practice (Art. 56(7)). Power to request measures (Art. 93). Fines for providers who intentionally or negligently infringed relevant provisions of AIA, whereby commitments made in relevant codes of practice in accordance with Art. 56 shall be taken into account (Art. 101(1)).	AI Board can issue recommendations (Art. 66(1)(e)); otherwise no provisions.
Oversight	Implementing Acts by the Commission outlining common specifications if no standards or non-compliance with legal requirements (Art. 41(1); recital 121).	Monitoring of codes of practice (AI Office and Board) (Art. 56(6)). If code of practice not realised within 12 months after AIA entered into force or is inadequate, the Commission is empowered to adopt implementing acts with common specifications (Art. 56(9)). Implementing acts in case of insufficient codes of practice regarding type 2 systems (Art. 50(7)).	Four years after entry into force then every three years, evaluation (by Commission) of impact and effectiveness of codes of conduct for Chapt. II obligations as well as possibly other requirements (Art. 112(7)).
Type of Meta-Regulation	Embedded	Embedded	Potential

We discern two distinct approaches to meta-regulation: embedded meta-regulation (pursued with codes of practice and harmonised standards) and potential meta-regulation (pursued with codes of conduct). What does this terminology denote?

By 'embedded meta-regulation', we mean that the envisaged regulatory instrument constitutes a quasi-obligatory tool to achieve a defined legislative purpose or, as phrased by the AIA itself, 'a central tool for the proper compliance with the obligations provided for under this Regulation' (recital 117). Embedded meta-regulation is further defined by the fact that the legislation mandates the development of the regulatory instruments and, as with codes of practice and harmonised standards, sets a timeline for their creation. If the instruments do not meet expectations, the regulator can intervene and potentially even replace them. In the AIA, this aspect is particularly evident, as the Commission has been granted considerable authority to 'correct' both harmonised standards (Article 41(1)) and codes of practice (Article 56(9)) through implementing acts. While this approach is not unusual in the context of product safety regulation, it reflects a notable consolidation of regulatory power within the Commission, especially when viewed alongside the other assigned powers as outlined above.

Finally, enforcement measures back the instruments because they address obligations emerging directly from the legislative text.

In contrast, potential meta-regulation uses tools that, although foreseen in the legislative framework, are optional. When describing codes of conduct, the AIA uses terminology such as 'shall encourage and facilitate the drawing up of codes of conduct' (Article 95(1)). There are only few specifications of their nature (e.g. recital 165), monitoring is more limited, and there are no specific remedies for the legislator to resort to should the applied meta-regulatory tools not live up to expectations.

4 Regulating Non-High-Risk AI Through Embedded and Potential Meta-Regulation: Challenges and Opportunities

At the time of finalising this chapter, the AIA has only been in in force for ten months. Presently, standards have been mandated solely for the obligations of high-risk AI systems described in Chapter III. A Code of practice for GPAI is close to finalisation, whereas an equivalent process has not yet started for codes of conduct. This analysis accordingly underscores certain emerging trends and anticipated developments concerning the application of soft-law instruments in regulating non-high-risk AI. Our observations are based on the afore-mentioned characteristics of the codes, coupled with insights from other regulatory frameworks, such as the General Data Protection Regulation (GDPR)[32] and the Digital Services Act (DSA).

4.1 Codes of Practice

As elaborated above, codes of practice constitute a form of embedded meta-regulation. The AIA envisages their drafting and even provides a clear deadline: 12 months after the entry into force of the AIA (Article 56(9)). At the time of writing,

[32] Regulation (EU) 2016/679 of the European Parliament and of the Council of 27 April 2016 on the protection of natural persons with regard to the processing of personal data and on the free movement of such data, and repealing Directive 95/46/EC (General Data Protection Regulation) [2016] OJ L 119, 4.5.2016, pp. 1–88.

the drafting process for a GPAI code of practice is nearing completion, with a final version expected in July 2025. Thus, codes of practice will likely play a role in regulating the requirements imposed on GPAI models in Chapter V AIA.[33] How they will interact with harmonised standards, though, remains unclear. They might indeed be a placeholder until harmonised standards are drafted, or they might form the basis of the latter. Much will depend on the quality of both the drafting process and the codes of practice themselves. In respect of GPAI especially (and, to a lesser degree, type 2 systems), the AIA has developed a comprehensive and thorough regulatory framework for codes of practice—one that covers their drafting, adequacy, oversight and enforcement. In this regard, they resemble harmonised standards more than what one normally associates with other types of codes such as codes of conduct.

The CJEU in *James Elliot* clarified that harmonised standards can be considered being part of EU law.[34] In *Mitnitsa Varna*, the Court subsequently outlined that this can be the case 'when that standard was conceived, managed and monitored by the Commission and when it produces binding legal effects following publication of its references in the Official Journal of the European Union'.[35]

From these judgments, two essential requirements have crystallised.[36] First, the Commission must participate in the development of the standard (conceived, managed and monitored). In the case of codes of practice, these steps are not executed by the Commission but by the AI Office and Board. Thus, public involvement takes place at a slightly lower level. Yet, it is still there, and ultimately the Commission is involved at the end of the process by either approving or overwriting codes of practice through implementing acts. Thus, even though there are differences in the process, both instruments have in common that they have significant public involvement in their development. The second requirement is the publication in the Official Journal (OJ) and here specifically the effect of 'creating conformity to essential requirements established in the legislative act'.[37] Codes of practice are not published in the OJ, yet they de facto have the same effect as described in *Mitnitsa Varna*: Articles 53(4) and 55(2) establish that providers may rely on codes of practice to demonstrate compliance with the obligations set out in the AIA, and otherwise need to demonstrate alternative measures. The wording is slightly different compared to harmonised standards where Article 40(1) speaks of a presumption of conformity,

[33] European Commission, AI Act: Participate in the drawing-up of the first General-Purpose AI Code of Practice, 30 July 2024, https://digital-strategy.ec.europa.eu/en/news/ai-act-participate-drawing-first-general-purpose-ai-code-practice.

[34] Case C-613/14, *James Elliott Construction Limited v Irish Asphalt Limited*, judgement of 27 October 2016 (ECLI:EU:C:2016:821), para. 40.

[35] Case C-185/17, *Mitnitsa Varna*, judgement of 22 February 2018 (ECLI:EU:C:2018:108), para. 39.

[36] Eliantonio and Volpato (2022).

[37] Ibid.

rather than 'may rely on', but the effect seems to be very similar. This raises the question of how voluntary these codes really are.[38]

Another distinction that might be of importance is that codes of practice appear to have more of a self-regulatory nature because those later applying them are also involved in the drafting process. Thus, Article 56(3) states that 'all providers of general-purpose AI models, as well as relevant national competent authorities, [shall be invited] to participate in the drawing-up of codes of practice'. Other actors from civil society, industry or academia only support the process. Whereas standards are drafted by standard setters and are later applied by a whole range of actors not necessarily involved in the drafting process, here those applying the codes seem to be also those who have drafted it. Still, there are two arguments against declaring this process entirely self-regulatory. The first concerns public involvement which, as outlined above, is fairly evolved. The other is that it is unclear what happens if a GPAI provider emerges after a code of practice was drafted. There will not be a new drafting round so this actor must then sign up to the existing document without having been involved in its drafting process.

The afore-mentioned parallel to harmonised standards also points to some of the problems that emerge from relying on codes to specify often vague legislative requirements. Questions around legitimacy[39] and particularly legal certainty arise. Harmonised standards are far from being a perfect regulatory tool and their nature was contested throughout their application as embedded regulatory tools in European legislation. Particularly, their current use in the AIA has received considerable critical attention.[40] Yet they are tightly regulated, markedly through Regulation 1025/2012. Member states and the Parliament have, for example, a means to formally object to standards (Article 11 Regulation 1025/2012). Such a regulation is missing for codes of practice, and the provisions in Article 56 do not fully make up for the framework provided by Regulation 1025/2012. The lack of an equivalent background regulatory environment for codes of practice is arguably problematic given that they fulfil a very similar role to harmonised standards in the AIA. It is at the very least questionable whether the mostly formal differences between the two types of instruments are sufficient to justify this much looser framework for codes of practice, or whether considering their similarities to standards, such codes also need more stringent processes and regulation surrounding this potentially newest part of EU Law. The answer is in large part dependent on the success of the drafting process, which is still ongoing, and whether it can meet the upcoming legitimacy requirements and offer meaningful guidance for Articles 53 and 55.

[38] See for codes in the context of the DSA: Griffin and Vander Maelen (2023a) and Griffin and Vander Maelen (2023b).

[39] Vander Maelen (2022), p. 770.

[40] Laux et al. (2024).

4.2 Codes of Conduct

As noted above, codes of conduct are instruments for potential meta-regulation. Their actual application is much more uncertain, and experience from other fields suggests they could play only a minor role.

The governance regime for Article 95 codes is very light touch, indeed almost non-existent. This is a radical contrast to the regimes set up under, say, the GDPR and DSA. There is no system of code approval by an independent regulatory authority (cf. Article 40(5) GDPR). There is no system of code registration (cf. Article 40(6) GDPR). There is no system for monitoring or control of codes of conduct (cf. Article 10 UCPD and Articles 41(3)(f) and 45(4) DSA) and thus no provisions dealing with monitoring bodies and their accreditation (cf. Article 41 GDPR). There is no system for Commission approval of codes of conduct (cf. Article 40(9) GDPR which empowers the Commission to deem a code of conduct as having 'general validity' within the EU). Furthermore, the existence of a code of conduct or adherence to it has no obvious effect on the level of sanctions (cf. Article 83(2)(j) GDPR which permits the level of administrative fines to be adjusted in light of codes of conduct; Article 75(3) DSA which requires the Commission, when deciding how to handle certain infringements of the DSA by VLOPs and VLOSEs, to take into account 'possible commitment to adhere to relevant codes of conduct'). The only quasi-compliance mechanism is the AI Board's power to issue recommendations on the operation and application of codes of conduct (along with codes of practice) (Article 66(1)(e)), but this is patently weak.

One reason for this light touch approach might be fear of overloading the AI industry with more red tape, thus stymying innovation and production processes. In the data protection field, there were complaints from industry long ago about the lengthy and even 'tortuous' process of obtaining approval of codes of conduct from data protection authorities.[41] So the fear has some justification.

A major problem, however, is that the AIA does not provide a compelling incentive structure for creating codes of conduct beyond a general moral incentive. The problem is exacerbated by the fact that drafting *useful* codes of conduct (i.e. codes that are not simply the equivalent of floral wallpaper) requires considerable expertise, time and other resources. Thus, there is a cost involved. Hence, the question must be asked: what is the benefit? Under the AIA, there is no tangible reward in the form of, say, more regulatory lenience. There may be, however, extra-legal benefits, such as creating public goodwill by playing the 'responsible actor' role. Nonetheless, experience from the data protection sector (where there is a more developed legal incentive structure) suggests that code of conduct uptake pursuant to the AIA is unlikely to be significant.[42]

---

[41] See Korff (2002), p. 187.

[42] See Kamara (2020), p. 720 ('Despite the encouragement and guidance, the numbers of approved codes of conduct in Member States are negligible'). See also Vander Maelen (2020); Vander Maelen (2024).

This is unfortunate as codes of conduct are envisaged by the AIA as a major vehicle for operationalising a range of considerations that are relatively peripheral to the Act's central thrust yet societally important—such as AI literacy, participatory design and environmental sustainability. In this regard, the weakness of the code of conduct regime will hardly help efforts to make these relatively 'soft' values more than simply aspirational. Moreover, it is clear that there is a real need for tailored rules for particular AI systems that fall outside the high-risk or type 2 and 3 categories—the case, for instance, with automated speech recognition systems used by law enforcement agencies in the course of transcribing investigative interviews.[43]

This then raises the question whether the code of conduct regime ought to be hardened. Hacker, for example, has pushed for codes of conduct to be made potentially binding, using Article 40 GDPR as a model. He argues for a regime in which a proposed code of conduct may be approved by the relevant regulatory authority, thus offering developers and providers a safe harbour from challenging liability situations. Not all proposals would be eligible for approval; only those 'endorsed by at least one trade association acting in the specific sector, or by a minimum number of AI companies operating in a specific area (e.g., 20)'.[44] This is a sensible avenue of reform.

Other possible measures for hardening the AIA's code of conduct regime could be modelled on the DSA's equivalent regime. While codes of conduct under the DSA are also voluntary, their bite is hardened in several minor but potentially significant ways once adopted. First, VLOPs and VLOSEs must undergo, 'at their own expense and at least once a year', independent auditing of the commitments they make under these codes (Article 37(1)(b) DSA). Second, if they refuse to implement the recommendations of the auditors, they must justify their refusal (Article 37(6) DSA). Third, they must appoint internal yet independent officers to monitor compliance with the code commitments (Article 41(3)(f) DSA). Fourth, the Commission and the European Board for Digital Services must regularly monitor and evaluate whether the codes meet their stated objectives, and the evaluation results must be published (Article 45(4) DSA). Fifth, the Commission and the Board must 'encourage and facilitate regular review and adaptation of the codes of conduct', and, in cases of 'systematic failure to comply with the codes of conduct, the Commission and the Board may invite the signatories to the codes of conduct to take the necessary action' (Article 45(4) DSA). Finally, in deciding how to handle certain infringements of the DSA by VLOPs and VLOSEs, the Commission shall take into account 'possible commitment to adhere to relevant codes of conduct' (Article 75(3) DSA). We are not suggesting that all of these elements of the DSA regime be replicated in a revamped AIA, but they provide a smorgasbord of possible reform alternatives on top of those offered by the GDPR.

[43] Stoykova et al. (2024).

[44] Hacker (2024).

5 Summing Up and Conclusions

This chapter has outlined the emerging regulatory framework for non-high-risk AI systems under the AIA. Four categories of non-high-risk AI are identified: AI systems that would *prima facie* be considered high-risk but are actually not (type 1); AI systems interacting with humans that must adhere to certain transparency obligations (some of which overlap with high-risk AI) (type 2/Article 50 systems); GPAI systems and GPAI models that involve systemic risks (type 3); and finally the large amorphous group of systems that fall neither in the high nor prohibited risk category nor in types 1–3 (type 4/Article 95 systems).

Moving to the regulatory mechanisms employed for these systems, with a particular focus on codes of practice and codes of conduct, the chapter finds the former category of code to function as an embedded meta-regulation tool that is expected to play a key role in ensuring compliance with transparency requirements and obligations for GPAI. Although codes of practice are intended to function as an interim solution for GPAI until harmonised standards are established, it remains to be seen whether and how this progression will occur, depending on the quality and effectiveness of the codes. While codes of practice share similarities with harmonised standards, they lack the comprehensive regulatory framework provided by Regulation 1025/2012, raising concerns regarding legal certainty and legitimacy. In contrast, codes of conduct are described as potential meta-regulation instruments that are less likely to have a significant impact, relative to codes of practice. Further, the chapter concludes that major uptake of codes of conduct is unlikely due to the lack of incentives provided by the AIA to adopt such codes, and this will hinder efforts to operationalise important societal values such as AI literacy and sustainability.

Acknowledgements Work on this chapter was conducted under the aegis of the project 'Vulnerability in the Robot Society' (VIROS) funded by the Research Council of Norway (project number 288285). Special thanks are due to Tobias Mahler for useful commentary on a previous draft of the text. Thanks go also to Live Sunniva Hjort for assistance in drawing up the tables and figure. The usual disclaimer still applies.

References

Bommasani R et al (2021) On the opportunities and risks of foundation models. https://arxiv.org/abs/2108.07258

Brown E, Piroska D (2021) Governing Fintech and Fintech as governance: the regulatory sandbox, riskwashing, and disruptive social classification. New Polit Econ 27:19–32. https://doi.org/10.1080/13563467.2021.1910645

Bygrave LA (2021) Security by design: aspirations and realities in a regulatory context. Oslo Law Rev 8:126–177. https://doi.org/10.18261/olr.8.3.2

Coglianese C, Mendelson E (2010) Meta-regulation and self-regulation. In: Baldwin R, Cave M, Lodge M (eds) Understanding regulation: theory, strategy, and practice, 2nd edn. Oxford University Press, Oxford, pp 146–168

Colombo C, Eliantonio M (2017) Harmonized technical standards as part of EU law: Juridification with a number of unresolved legitimacy concerns?: Case C-613/14 James Elliot Construction Limited v. Irish Asphalt Limited, EU:C:2016:821. MJECL 24(2):323–340. https://doi.org/10.1177/1023263X17709753

d'Angelo C, Flanagan I, Dadiso Motsi-Omoijiade I, Virdee M, Gunashekar S (2022) Labelling initiatives, codes of conduct and other self-regulatory mechanisms for artificial intelligence applications: from principles to practice and considerations for the future. RAND Corporation, Santa Monica. https://www.rand.org/pubs/research_reports/RRA1773-1.html

Eliantonio M, Volpato A (2022) The European System of Harmonised Standards, Legal Opinion for ECOS. https://ssrn.com/abstract=4055292

Garben S, Govaere I (2018) The EU better regulation agenda: a critical assessment. Hart Publishing, Oxford

Griffin R (2024a) Codes of conduct in the Digital Services Act: functions, benefits & concerns. Technol Regul: 167–187. https://doi.org/10.26116/techreg.2024.016

Griffin R (2024b) Codes of conduct in EU digital regulation and AI policy: the potential and risks of soft law tools. In: Prifti K et al (eds) Digital governance: confronting the challenges posed by artificial intelligence. TMC Asser Press, The Hague. ch. 12

Griffin R, Vander Maelen C (2023a) Codes of conduct in the Digital Services Act: exploring the opportunities and challenges. https://doi.org/10.2139/ssrn.4463874

Griffin R, Vander Maelen C (2023b) Twitter's retreat from the code of practice on disinformation raises a crucial question: are DSA codes of conduct really voluntary? https://dsa-observatory.eu/2023/06/12/twitters-retreat-from-the-code-of-practice-on-disinformation-raises-a-crucial-question-are-dsa-codes-of-conduct-really-voluntary/

Hacker P (2024) AI regulation in Europe: from the AI Act to future regulatory challenges. In: Ajunwa I, Adams-Prassl J (eds) Oxford handbook of algorithmic governance and the law. Oxford University Press, Oxford, pp _ (forthcoming)

Kamara I (2020) Article 40. In: Kuner C, Bygrave LA, Docksey C (eds) The EU General Data Protection Regulation: a commentary. Oxford University Press, Oxford, pp 716–724

Korff D (2002) EC study on the implementation of data protection directive – report on the findings of the study. European Commission, Brussels

Laux J, Wachter S, Mittelstadt B (2024) Three pathways for standardization and ethical disclosure by default under the European Union Artificial Intelligence Act. Comput Law Secur Rev 53:1–13. https://doi.org/10.1016/j.clsr.2024.105957

Micklitz H-W (2023a) Soft law, technical standards and European private law. In: Eliantonio M, Korkea-aho E, Mörth U (eds) Research handbook on soft law. Edward Elgar Publishing, Cheltenham, pp 145–161

Micklitz, H-W (2023b) The Role of Standards in Future EU Digital Policy Legislation: A Consumer Perspective. Brussels: ANEC/BEUC

Myklebust T (2023) The legitimacy of the European Systemic Risk Board in respect of its performance, roles and contributions to the financial regulatory system. Oslo Law Rev 9:92–109. https://doi.org/10.18261/olr.9.2.2

Parker C (2007) Meta-regulation: legal accountability for corporate social responsibility. In: McBarnet D, Voiculescu A, Campbell T (eds) The new corporate accountability: corporate social responsibility and the law. Cambridge University Press, Cambridge. ch 7

Renn O, Laubichler M, Lucas K, Kröger W, Schanze J, Scholz RW, Schweizer P-J (2022) Systemic risks from different perspectives. Risk Anal 42:1902–1920. https://doi.org/10.1111/risa.13657

Soler Garrido J, Fano Yela D, Panigutti C, Junklewitz H, Hamon R, Evas T, André A, Scalzo S (2023) Analysis of the preliminary AI standardisation work plan in support of the AI Act. Publications Office of the European Union, Luxembourg. https://doi.org/10.2760/5847

Stoykova R, Porter K, Beka T (2024) The AI Act in a law enforcement context: the case of automatic speech recognition for transcribing investigative interviews. Forensic Sci Int: Synergy 9:100563. https://doi.org/10.1016/j.fsisyn.2024.100563

Vander Maelen C (2020) Codes of (mis)conduct? An appraisal of Articles 40-41 GDPR in view of the 1995 Data Protection Directive and its shortcomings. Eur Data Prot Law Rev 6:231–242

Vander Maelen C (2022) Hardly law or hard law? Investigating the dimensions of functionality and legalisation of codes of conduct in recent EU legislation and the normative repercussions thereof. Eur Law Rev 47:752–772

Vander Maelen C (2024) Don't count your codes before they hatch: a theoretical and empirical analysis of Codes of Conduct under the General Data Protection Regulation. University of Ghent: PhD thesis

Vrielink MO, Montfort Cv (2010) Codes of ethics and codes of practice. In: Anheier HK, Toepler S (eds) International encyclopedia of civil society. Springer, New York, pp 492–497. https://doi.org/10.1007/978-0-387-93996-4_165

Wachter S (2024) Limitations and loopholes in the EU AI Act and AI liability directives: what this means for the European Union, the United States, and Beyond. Yale J Law Technol 26(3):671–718

Artificial Intelligence (AI) Systems Not Covered by the AI Regulation

Jorge Constantino and Tina van der Linden

Contents

Abstract The AI Act brands itself as the first-ever legislation that uniformly regulates the use of AI systems in European society across all sectors. However, this branding from the AI Act appears not to be one hundred per cent accurate. Rather, the AI Act has brought exemptions to its 'uniformed' rules on the use of AI systems in the European Union. This chapter analyses the exemptions of certain AI systems from the EU AI Act, particularly focusing on national security, military, interna-

---

J. Constantino
TU Delft, Faculty of Technology, Policy and Management, Delft, The Netherlands

T. van der Linden (✉)
Hogeschool Utrecht, Utrecht, The Netherlands
e-mail: tina.vanderlinden@hu.nl

V. L. Raposo (ed.), *The European Artificial Intelligence Act*, Law, Governance and Technology Series 78, https://doi.org/10.1007/978-3-031-98406-8_9

tional cooperation, research, and personal use, and discusses the implications for fundamental rights and legal accountability.

1 Introduction

For various reasons, the AI Act does not cover some categories of Artificial Intelligence (AI) systems. In this chapter, we provide an overview of these categories of AI systems and mention one or more examples of each of them. For each category, we discuss the reason why they are not covered, and review other rules that might apply to them. Next, studying the legal doctrine, we investigate if these AI systems pose any risks to fundamental rights and European values, and whether the rules that do apply to them sufficiently address such risks.

As we have no less than seven categories of AI systems to discuss, and the topic is still quite new, we have chosen to reflect on the limitations of the AI Act and the challenges that these limitations may represent to a democratic society. By our legal analysis, we hope to contribute to the legal doctrine and other scholars interested in the European AI Act's legal, societal, and technological impact. This chapter starts by looking into the exemptions for AI systems used for national security, military, and international cooperation in the context of fighting crime. AI systems used in the context of national security are excluded from the domain of the AI Act to avoid interference with Member States in matters of national security. Moreover, excluding military AI systems may be based on the specificities of the Member States' and the common Union defence policies found under the Treaty of the European Union and public international law. Lastly, AI systems deployed in the context of international arrangements with foreign authorities and international organisations are also excluded to promote cooperation in exchanging information and evidence to combat crime.

This chapter also analyses AI systems used or deployed in society, such as AI systems in the context of transportation, personal non-professional activities, research, and under free and open source licences. The AI Act is ambiguous regarding excluding AI systems in transportation. We argue that, in essence, transportation is not an exemption but rather a different way of putting the requirements for these high-risk AI systems in dedicated legislation that is already in place. We note that AI systems for personal non-professional activity are not covered by the AI Act provided the deployer is a natural person. However, these AI systems may (depending on their functionality) be covered by other rules in order to safeguard fundamental rights at stake. To support innovation, AI used in the research context is also excluded from the scope of the AI Act. Similarly, AI systems used under 'free and open source licences' are excluded to avoid hampering innovation. However, it is not really clear what is meant by the term 'free and open source licences'. In both cases, we note that these exemptions pose further challenges, loopholes, and legal uncertainty because the exemptions may be misused. We offer conclusions outlining that while the introduction of AI is good for society's development, the AI Act may have missed the opportunity to present a coherent approach to minimising the risks of AI in critical aspects where fundamental rights are at stake due to current loopholes (intentionally or unintentionally) provided by the AI Act.

2 National Security, Military & International Cooperation

2.1 National Security and Intelligence Agencies

In this section, we note that AI systems used within the context of national security, military, and international cooperation are part of the exempted categories as expressly stated in Art. 2(3) AI Act, establishing that this legal instrument *'does not apply to areas outside the scope of Union law, and shall not, in any event, affect the competences of the Member States concerning national security, regardless of the type of entity entrusted by the Member States with carrying out tasks in relation to those competences.'*

The AI Act has justified the exclusion of AI systems for national security purposes on the basis that national security *'remains the sole responsibility of Member States in accordance with Article 4(2) TEU [Treaty of the European Union] and by the specific nature and operational needs of national security activities and specific national rules applicable to those activities*'.[1] The background provided by the European legislator suggests that the AI Act is mindful not to intrude in matters of national security, military, and international cooperation in the context of fighting crime and threats to the stability of the region, democracy, and European values. It appears that the European Commission tried to avoid legal challenges by Member States regarding the lack of competence of Union law in matters of national security. However, in *La Quadrature du Net and Others v Premier ministre and Others*,[2] a court case involving telecommunication service providers storing and processing personal data (allegedly) to comply with national security purposes, the CJEU ruled that the TEU does not render 'EU law [such as the AI Act] inapplicable'.[3] Thus, the ruling from the CJEU may serve as an argument that although State Members have the right to establish their own national security frameworks, the TEU does not require the AI Act to exempt AI systems in the context of national security or defence.

Furthermore, the AI Act justifies exempting AI systems used for national security under the premise that security and intelligence units, namely secret services and national defence, are governed under their own national frameworks.[4] Can this be a

[1] Consideration 24 AI Act.

[2] CJEU 6 October 2020, Joined Cases C-511/18, C-512/18 and C-520/18, ECLI:EU:C:2020:791.

[3] CJEU 6 October 2020, Joined Cases C-511/18, C-512/18 and C-520/18, ECLI:EU:C:2020:791, § 99.

[4] Consideration 24 AI Act.

sufficient explanation for the unwillingness of the AI Act to regulate AI systems in the context of defence and national security? Maybe, the legislators' intention was not to overregulate certain sectors. For example, in the Netherlands,[5] the Dutch National Intelligence and Secret Services (AIVD) is bound by its legal framework, the Intelligence and Security Services Act 2017 ('*Wiv*' 2017). Under this legal framework, the AIVD is allowed to use (and request) data and algorithmic tools (arguably AI) for the sole purpose of protecting national security and the democratic legal order.[6] Similarly, the AIVD must implement technological and human components respecting legal requirements such as data accuracy, completeness, data quality, and deploying trustworthy algorithmic models.[7] Thus, one may argue that these unique requirements applicable exclusively to the Dutch military, intelligence and secret services may be the same or similar requirements as the ones stated under Articles 14 (human oversight) and 15 (trustworthiness of AI technologies) of the AI Act; therefore, in the Dutch example, there is no need to further regulate AI in the context of national security and defence.

The previous example may advocate for the exemption of AI systems in the context of national security among democratic states that adhere to the rule of law. However, what about states that may have a record or are being challenged for questionable practices in their intelligence units?[8] The unwillingness of the AI Act to provide a coherent uniform framework across all Member States has left unattended accountability gaps regarding legal and moral responsibility for the development and deployment of AI tools for national security purposes.[9] The decision of the AI Act not to regulate AI systems in the context of defence and national security neglects fundamental rights issues and undermines the AI Act's human-centred approach. The current gap in the AI Act allows room for an environment where AI for national security purposes may be developed under disharmonious legal and ethical frameworks in the European zone. Thus, it is plausible that exemptions on AI systems used in the context of national security might bring future challenges to democratic values and fundamental rights.[10]

The Committee on Artificial Intelligence (CAI) from the Council of Europe (CoE) proposes a different approach, only exempting AI systems that protect 'essential' national security interests,[11] inevitably sparking discussion on what can be considered 'essential'. In any case, the CAI stresses that the exemptions for national security purposes need to be consistent with international law, including human rights law obligations and the democratic order.

[5] The jurisdiction the authors are most familiar with.

[6] Articles 8, 9 *Intelligence and Security Services Act* 2017 ('*Wiv*' 2017).

[7] Article 24 *Wiv* 2017.

[8] Omtzigt (2023); In 't Veld (2022); Sartor and Loreggia (2022).

[9] Smuha et al. (2021), p. 19.

[10] ECNL (2024).

[11] Art. 3 of the 18 December 2023 Draft Framework Convention on Artificial Intelligence, Human Rights, Democracy and the Rule of Law, 1680ade043 (coe.int). An earlier alternative draft proposed to allow the signatory Parties to choose for themselves: 1680abde66 (coe.int).

AI systems used in intelligence and security domains undoubtedly offer advantages to fight threats to national security. For example, it is claimed that traditional Open Source Intelligence (OSINT) search techniques are being replaced by AI-powered OSINT to provide more efficiency national security and cyber defence.[12,13] Similarly, the AIVD is building up knowledge and skills regarding resilient AI tools,[14] to be able to advise key decision-makers. The AIVD is also investigating AI from an academic research approach by collaborating with different Dutch universities.[15]

Despite the good intentions and efforts to deploy AI for a good cause, we must stay alert regarding the risks of AI systems (e.g., bias, cyber-attacks, inaccuracy, etc.). In particular, AI systems used in intelligence and security domains that have not been properly tested or scrutinised against cyber vulnerabilities due to different secrecy policies. Moreover, there is not assurance that AI systems used under this context do not violate citizens' fundamental rights.[16] For example, using OSINT powered by AI models will bring legal, ethical, and organisational challenges to intelligence and security agencies.[17] The rise of ChatGPT, deep fakes, and unfiltered data and information present a risk to national security operations and citizens' fundamental rights.[18] Suppose that an OSINT AI-powered provides inaccurate information to intelligence practitioners, flagging the wrong person. A warrant will be requested to deploy surveillance and build a profile against this person. In the worse case scenario, he or she may subsequently be wrongfully prosecuted for a crime never committed and paying legal expenses as well as suffering emotional harm.[19] This extreme example, shows that some fundamental rights may be at stake: for example, privacy, health, or a fair trial (including the right to an explanation for algorithmic outputs). How can the AI Act, seeking to protect fundamental rights, include such a blanket exemption for everything falling under 'national security'?[20]

The national security exemption umbrella can also be problematic because national security does not have a uniform meaning and is broadly used to indicate different agencies such as national secret services, military intelligence, and even police enforcement intelligence units.[21]

In summary, the AI Act should have followed a more coherent and holistic approach to protect fundamental rights in the context of national security

---

[12] Eijkman and Weggemans (2013), p. 285. CTIVD (2021).

[13] Summary of Report Automated OSINT: tools and sources for open source investigation, CTIVD No. 74 (2021). Virginia Commonwealth University (2023).

[14] Dutch government (2024), p. 41.

[15] Strategisch Actieplan voor Artificiële Intelligentie (2019), p. 50. See also: NWO (2022).

[16] Virginia Commonwealth University (2023).

[17] Smuha et al. (2021), p. 19.

[18] Intelligence College in Europe (2023); el Rahwan (2023).

[19] Dias (2020); Safi (2018).

[20] See for instance, Recitals 43, 59 AI Act.

[21] Smuha et al. (2021), p. 19.

exemptions.[22] Uniformity and specific guidance -or harmonised rules- are needed in the intelligence and security domains to assess the use of algorithms and AI tools in the light of accountability principles such as necessity and proportionality, as well as continuous oversight.[23] If the stability of the international legal order is one of the bases for international intelligence and security cooperation, harmonised rules across all Member States should apply to intelligence and security domains. The AI Act would have been an excellent opportunity to regulate the use of AI in intelligence and security domains to establish clear boundaries to protect the international legal order and fundamental rights.

2.2 *Military Purposes*

Sadly, war is again everyday's business. Where only a few years ago, from a European perspective, we discussed use of AI for military purposes in a hypothetical, detached way,[24] it is now a very harsh reality close to home. Both in Gaza[25] and in Ukraine[26] AI is used for military purposes, as we speak (write).

The AI Act '*does not apply to AI systems where and in so far they are placed on the market, put into service, or used with or without modification exclusively for military, defence or national security purposes, regardless of the type of entity carrying out those activities*', art. 3(3) AI Act. It should be noted that general purpose AI (in particular: large language models) can also be very useful for military purposes.[27]

It is not just Hollywood-style 'killer robots' that we are talking about here, although autonomous drone swarms resemble them.[28] It is also facial recognition software,[29] and software for generating targets for military strikes on the basis of massive amounts of data,[30] all deeply worrying.[31]

The reasons for excluding military AI systems from the scope of the AI Act are explained by Consideration 24: '*As regards military and defence purposes, such exclusion is justified both by Article 4(2) TEU and by the specificities of the Member States' and the common Union defence policy covered by Chapter 2 of Title V TEU*

[22] ECNL (2024).

[23] Constantino and Wagner (2024).

[24] See for example Hallaq et al. (2017).

[25] McKarnan and Davies (2024).

[26] Bergengruen (2024).

[27] Roscoe (2024).

[28] Weber (2024).

[29] Bergengruen (2023).

[30] The 'Lavender' AI application, as described by Abraham (2024). See also McKarnan and Davies (2024).

[31] Gault (2023).

that are subject to public international law, which is therefore the more appropriate legal framework for the regulation of AI systems in the context of the use of lethal force and other AI systems in the context of military and defence activities. As regards national security purposes, the exclusion is justified both by the fact that national security remains the sole responsibility of Member States in accordance with Article 4(2) TEU and by the specific nature and operational needs of national security activities and specific national rules applicable to those activities'.

So, AI for military purposes should be regulated by public international law, in particular international humanitarian law, that has indeed a number of regulations in place that would apply to such AI:[32]

- 1907 Hague Regulations (Convention (IV) respecting the Laws and Customs of War on Land and its annex: Regulations concerning the Laws and Customs of War on Land. The Hague, 18 October 1907)
- Convention (I) for the Amelioration of the Condition of the Wounded and Sick in Armed Forces in the Field, Geneva, 12 August 1949
- Convention (II) for the Amelioration of the Condition of Wounded, Sick and Shipwrecked Members of Armed Forces at Sea. Geneva, 12 August 1949
- Convention (III) relative to the Treatment of Prisoners of War. Geneva, 12 August 1949
- Convention (IV) relative to the Protection of Civilian Persons in Time of War. Geneva, 12 August 1949
- Protocol Additional to the Geneva Conventions of 12 August 1949, and relating to the Protection of Victims of International Armed Conflicts (Protocol I), 8 June 1977
- Protocol Additional to the Geneva Conventions of 12 August 1949, and relating to the Protection of Victims of Non-International Armed Conflicts (Protocol II), 8 June 1977
- Protocol additional to the Geneva Conventions of 12 August 1949, and relating to the Adoption of an Additional Distinctive Emblem (Protocol III), 8 December 2005.

There are also some non-binding documents, specifically on AI for military purposes.[33]

Use of AI in a military context literally comes with threats, not just for human rights and European values. Human life, and human 'well-being' in an almost cynical sense (seeing the immense suffering from news footage in Ukraine and Gaza) are at stake, regardless of whether or not AI is used. AI has the potential to make things worse: more victims, more casualties, more destruction—but it depends of course on how it is used. A case can also be made for the position that use of AI

[32] Overview copied from International Humanitarian Law – International Justice Resource Center (ijrcenter.org).

[33] Stanley-Lockman and Christie (2021); AI Task Force (2019).

potentially leads to better military decision making—and therefore it would be irresponsible not to use it.[34]

In general, there are worries about the extent to which an AI could comply with IHR. Can it correctly distinguish between combattants and non-combattants?[35] Can it adequately deal with notions like proportionality?[36] Who is accountable for decisions and actions taken by military AIs?[37] Is there a risk of them going rogue (as we see in films), getting out of control?[38]

Then there is the risk of AI developed for military purposes (so outside of the purview of the AI Act) being repurposed for non-military use, e.g. by the (military) police, in prisons, during riots. Consideration 24 tries to address these worries: '*if an AI system developed, placed on the market, put into service or used for military, defence or national security purposes is used outside those temporarily or permanently for other purposes, for example, civilian or humanitarian purposes, law enforcement or public security purposes, such a system would fall within the scope of this Regulation*'.

It is probable that a repurposed military AI system would be used then as a high-risk system, meaning that it would need to comply with all the requirements for high-risk AI systems and it would need to get a CE marking. Are there any guarantees that these obligations will indeed be complied with? What happens if not?

In general, enforcement of international humanitarian law is problematic if it is not complied with by the states engaged in a military conflict.[39] If it is enforced at all, it is (years) after the fact, and not in a way that is of any use to the people suffering from violations. We are not confident at all that the deterrent effect of the possibility of maybe, later, having to face an international tribunal to be held accountable for war-crimes (committed with or without the help of AI) is strong enough to keep warriors from committing them. And use of AI does make it harder to determine who is responsible for certain actions.

A lot still needs to be done in this field. Time is running out, as can be seen in the news every day. The 'Stop killer robots'-initiative is still active.[40] The REAIM conference[41] concluded with a Call to Action:[42] '*We encourage multi-stakeholder dialogue on best practices to guide the development, deployment and use of AI in the military domain to ensure an interdisciplinary discussion throughout of good practices and policies on responsible use of AI in the military domain*'. Well, yes. In

[34] Meerveld et al. (2023), p. 13.

[35] Winter (2022), pp. 9–10.

[36] Winter (2022), pp. 15–17.

[37] Boutin (2023).

[38] Gadek (2024), pp. 119–121.

[39] Zyberi (2018).

[40] Stop Killer Robots started as an initiative in 2012—but the discussion on killer robots was sparked by a warning published in 2007: Sharkey (2007). See Stop Killer Robots - Less Autonomy, More humanity.

[41] Held in The Hague on 15–16 February 2023, both authors attended.

[42] REAIM (2023).

November 2023 the UN General Assembly adopted the first ever resolution on autonomous weapons, stressing the '*urgent need for the international community to address the challenges and concerns raised by autonomous weapons systems*'.[43] This is rather a job for politicians involving negotiations, diplomacy, power-play and so on, than for us lawyers. At the end of the day, in international law (and especially in cases where an armed conflict is at stake) we reach the limits of what law can do. But we should never stop trying!

2.3 Foreign Authorities and International Organisations

The AI Act also provides exemptions regarding the use of AI systems in the context of international agreements for law enforcement and judicial cooperation with the Union or with Member States. This exemption covers third countries and international organisations engaged by the Union or Member States to carry out an activity in the context of international cooperation for law enforcement or administration of justice purposes. For example, under this umbrella we may situate cooperation with international organisations or third countries such as Europol, Interpol, Eurojust, The European Public Prosecutor's Office (EPPO), and providers of surveillance and espionage tools such as the case of Israel (Pegasus Spyware).[44]

The AI Act has justified this exemption based on the need for future cooperation with foreign partners in the exchange of information and evidence to basically prosecute crime, whether in the context of law enforcement or administration of justice.[45]

Unlike AI exemptions for national security and military purposes, exemptions regarding the cooperation with international organisations in the context of law enforcement and judicial cooperation require that the third country or international organisation, engaged in such cooperation, provides adequate safeguards regarding the protection of fundamental rights and freedoms of individuals.[46]

The exemption is accompanied by the caveat that the third country or international organisation must be compliant with the protection of fundamental rights and freedoms of individuals. It may be inferred that the AI Act allows law enforcement or judicial agencies, which ever has jurisdiction, to 'police' the fulfilment of this caveat by the third country or the international organisation providing AI systems. In other words, the agency that engages a third country or international organisation to develop an AI system for them has also the power to decide if this third country or international organisation, working with them, complies with the protection of

[43] United Nations General Assembly (2023).

[44] Marzocchi and Mazzini (2022); In 't Veld (2022). 2022 https://www.europarl.europa.eu/RegData/etudes/IDAN/2022/732268/IPOL_IDA(2022)732268_EN.pdf; https://www.sophieintveld.eu/nl/pega-draft-report.

[45] Consideration 22 AI Act.

[46] Art. 2 (4) AI Act.

fundamental rights and freedoms of individuals.[47] Strange situation to be judge and party in one's own case.

However, contrary to the provisions of the AI Act, Article 82 of The Treaty on the functioning of the European Union (TEU) outlines that, for instance, judicial cooperation in criminal matters is within the jurisdiction of the European Parliament and the Council. The Article invokes the European Parliament and the Council to introduce measures that support the rights of individuals in criminal proceedings in a way that supports the maximum protection for individuals (victims and perpetrators). Thus, it is strange that the AI Act has decided to exclude the regulation of AI systems in the context of judicial cooperation. It seems inconsistent with the mandate of the European Parliament and the Council. On the other hand, the Committee on Artificial Intelligence (CAI) appears to be more concerned than the AI Act regarding the deployment of AI systems in the context of international cooperation. The CAI has proposed to regulate the use of AI systems commissioned by public authorities -for instance, law enforcement and judicial agencies- to third parties to develop systems in accordance with the CAI framework.[48]

The fact that third-countries or international organisations are granted special treatment raises concerns whether they may be shielded under a blanket of impunity for illegal deployment of AI systems in the European Union.[49] These exceptions could give rise to clever or subtle ways to implement high-risk AI systems in the European Union through third countries or international organisations under the excuse that they are systems for law enforcement or judicial cooperation within the context of Article 2(4) of the AI Act.[50] Of course, this circumvention to allow the use of high-risk AI systems in the context of law enforcement or judicial cooperation from public authorities in third countries or international organisations brings great risk to conflict with Union laws that, for instance, protect the right to privacy or the right to a fair trial.

The exclusion of AI systems under Article 2(4) also raises questions whether the European Union, its Member States, and crime-control organisations are measured under the same rule which requires public authorities and public organisations to be accountable and transparent in their decisions.[51] Particularly, this exception from Article 2(4) appears to be inconsistent with Consideration 38 which acknowledges that the actions of law enforcement authorities using AI systems are characterised by a degree of power imbalance which impacts a person's fundamental rights.[52]

The exemptions to AI systems in the context of international cooperation for law enforcement and administration of justice represent a threat to fundamental rights and European values. For instance, core fundamental rights contained in the EU

---

[47] Consideration 22 AI Act.

[48] Article 3 Committee on Artificial Intelligence (CAI).

[49] Raposo (2022), p. 101.

[50] EDPB-EDPS (2021), p. 8.

[51] Docksey and Propp (2023), p. 12; Naarttijärvi (2019), p. 35.

[52] Consideration 38.

Charter of Fundamental Rights are likely to be affected: human dignity (art. 1); respect for private life and protection of personal data (art. 7 and 8); right to equal treatment (art. 21) right to a fair trial, defence and presumption of innocence (art. 47, 48).

Similarly, in the international context, the Council of Europe has warned about the introduction of AI systems for law enforcement and judicial purposes, affecting the fundamental rights of people caught in the criminal justice system. In this vein, it is worth acknowledging UNESCO's assessment regarding countries lacking an adequate understanding of the societal risks of AI systems used to administer justice.[53] Based on these international authorities it can be argued that the deployment of AI systems for law enforcement and administration of justice, whether in the European Union or outside, needs to have appropriate and effective regulation because of the imminent risks to fundamental rights.[54]

Similarly, we need to take into account the 'supply chain' effect in this exception. Third countries and or international organisations can also engage industry suppliers to provide cutting edge technology.[55] In this scenario, it is unclear whether suppliers of AI technologies would also be covered under the foreign authorities and or international organisations exemption. The issue with this exemption is that the line becomes blurry when third countries or international organisations engage or hire private suppliers to develop AI systems for law enforcement or judicial cooperation purposes. Where do these suppliers of AI systems to foreign authorities fall under? Would the Brussels effect apply to them? Are they covered under the 'immunity' blanket of the AI exceptions? Or is it open to future legal challenges and further legal uncertainty in these domains? These loopholes of course represent more legal uncertainty to providers and users of AI systems. Similarly, these loopholes can seriously undermine the adequate protection of fundamental rights.

The Act does not question whether high-risk AI systems used by third countries or international organisations in the course of international cooperation or law enforcement, have measures in place to combat, or at least minimise, the irresponsible or inappropriate use of AI systems to collect biometric data.[56] For instance, there is no guarantee, or at least evidence, that third countries or international organisations have the same standards for respect to the right to a fair trial, a fair defence, and presumption of innocence, cherished by the EU Charter of Fundamental Rights.[57] One may rightfully question whether in the course of a fair trial, the information gathered through AI systems used by third countries and provided to the European Union or its Member States or its European agencies, qualifies as information that is free from bias or inaccuracies.[58] And one may question whether the

53 UNESCO (2023).

54 Cilevics (2020).

55 Powell and Oswald (2024).

56 Compare with Consideration 20.

57 EU Charter of Fundamental Rights Articles 47, 48.

58 Consideration 38.

AI products used in third party countries and international organisations are robust AI systems that can assure compliance with fundamental rights.

A way to overcome the shortcoming of article 2(4) may be by allowing the use of information within the meaning of Article 2(4), provided that there is a judicial authorisation that would warrant the deployment of high-risk AI systems against EU citizens.[59] For example, in extreme cases where there has been previous criminal history and plausible likelihood of re-offending in scenarios where the imminent re-offending would endanger the life of another.

In summary, the current exemption for AI systems in the context of international cooperation with law enforcement and the administration of justice does not look promising because the information or evidence collected by these high-risk AI systems used in third countries or international organisations could lead to false criminal accusations against innocent people.[60] Arguably, the AI Act could also be misleading in terms of protecting people's rights because on one hand, it says that its core purpose is to protect citizens in the Union from harmful use of AI. However, on the other hand, it opens a secret door to deploy information within the course of law enforcement and judicial cooperation against people in the Union, and perhaps many of these people are unaware that they are innocent targets of wrecked surveillance tools used by public authorities in third countries.[61] The exemptions provided for military, national security, law enforcement purposes, judicial cooperation, or foreign authorities, and the loopholes that these exemptions may bring seem to be incompatible with the aim of the AI Act which is to provide a harmonised horizontal legal framework to ensure a minimum standard across all Member States to protect citizens from harmful AI systems.[62]

3 Society

3.1 Transportation

After large language models, transportation may be one of the first fields in which the general public will see AI in action on a big scale. Self driving cars have been a tech-dream of decades, and after many years of development and testing under real life circumstances, they seem to be on the edge of being introduced on our public roads—except that that has also been true for quite a few years.[63] Anyway, self driving taxis are already being used on public roads in the US.[64] In addition to all the

[59] Human Rights Watch (2021).

[60] Human Rights Watch (2021).

[61] Dambly and Beelen (2022).

[62] Compare with Considerations 1, 2, and 3.

[63] Badue et al. (2021).

[64] Lu (2023).

technical challenges (in particular in the transitional period with still large numbers of human driven cars), there are serious open questions about their regulation, in particular regarding the assignment of liability for the accidents that will still happen[65] (even if self driving cars appear to be much safer than human driven cars).[66] Civil liability is mostly a matter for member states. There is however the proposed Artificial Intelligence Liability Directive, introducing a rebuttable presumption of causality in order to help victims harmed by AI (art. 4 AILD). Also, the AILD will help victims getting access to relevant evidence (art. 3 AILD).

At first glance, art. 2(2) AI Act seems to exclude all AI systems used in means of transportation from the AI Act. This provision is formulated in a very difficult to read and ambiguous way. High-risk AI systems already covered by the eight 'legislations' (six Regulations and two Directives) mentioned explicitly in Section B of Annex I,[67] all addressing means of transportation,[68] are not covered by the AI Act. Except that: such high-risk AI systems are required to undergo a third-party conformity assessment (art. 6(1)), and sandboxes only apply if all the requirements for high-risk AI systems have been integrated under that particular applicable Union harmonisation legislation (art. 57).

The other articles that do apply concern amendments to those legislations (art. 102–109 AI Act), basically inserting the requirements for high-risk AI (Chapter III section 2) into those legislations. And evaluation and review by the Commission of the list set out in Annex III and of the list of prohibited AI practices laid down in Article 5 (art. 112 AI Act).

So, in essence, this is not really an exemption, just a different way of putting the requirements for these high-risk AI systems in the dedicated legislation that is already in place.

The reason for this is explained in Consideration 49: '*As regards high-risk AI systems that are safety components of products or systems, or which are themselves products or systems falling within the scope of (…) it is appropriate to amend those acts to ensure that the Commission takes into account, on the basis of the technical and regulatory specificities of each sector, and without interfering with existing governance, conformity assessment and enforcement mechanisms and authorities established therein, the mandatory requirements for high-risk AI systems laid down*

[65] van Wees (2022).

[66] Nees (2019) proving that the 'safer than human' standard is not tenable.

[67] Under the heading of 'other Union harmonisation legislation' meaning not based on the New Legislative Framework in contrast to the legislations mentioned under Section A of Annex I.

[68] Civil aviation security; the approval and market surveillance of two- or three-wheel vehicles and quadricycles; the approval and market surveillance of agricultural and forestry vehicles; marine equipment; the interoperability of the rail system; on the approval and market surveillance of motor vehicles and their trailers, and of systems, components and separate technical units intended for such vehicles; type-approval requirements for motor vehicles and their trailers, and systems, components and separate technical units intended for such vehicles, as regards their general safety and the protection of vehicle occupants and vulnerable road users; and finally common rules in the field of civil aviation.

in this Regulation when adopting any relevant delegated or implementing acts on the basis of those acts'.

So, the other rules that apply to high-risk AI systems in this field are the eight legislations mentioned (as amended by articles 102–108 of the AI Act), and all the delegated and implementing acts based upon them.[69]

Which threats to fundamental rights and European values might result from using such systems? One could think of a support system (be it for pilots, tractor-drivers or someone else) having been designed for the typical, standard user (a white male?), and not working optimally with other kinds of users. Or one could think of the violation of driver and passenger privacy resulting from the mandatory installation of eCall systems in motor vehicles which allows locating and hearing the people involved in the accident.[70] Finally, fundamental rights and European values may be compromised by whatever approach to the unsolvable ethical trolley-problem is implemented.[71] Or even by who decides which approach will be implemented.[72]

It is not really clear how such threats are addressed in these regulations—one of the main reasons being that the rules are created in a very obscure way, lacking democratic accountability e.g. by standardisation organisations.[73] It is not clear that the assessment of the risks for fundamental rights can be entrusted to, basically, the industry itself.

As the AI Act itself, the regulations do '*not appear to ensure that fundamental rights interferences by AI are subjected to demanding tests of necessity and proportionality for narrowly defined purposes, nor to consistently allocate legal responsibility for the wrongs and harms of AI in an appropriate manner*'.[74]

So, it cannot really be assessed if there is a gap here. Many things are unclear—which in itself may be considered a gap.

[69] For an overview of all EU legislation on transport, see EUR-Lex: https://eur-lex.europa.eu/summary/chapter/32.html.

[70] Wisman (2019), p. 183 ff. See the proposed Commission Delegated Regulation of 14.2.2024 amending Regulation (EU) 2015/758 of the European Parliament and of the Council as regards the standards relating to eCall, C(2024) 823 final.

[71] The trolley problem forces an actor to choose between victims, thereby exposing the inconsistency of our moral intuitions. Feffer et al. (2023), p. 5980.

[72] Interestingly, German legislation already contains a provision saying that in case of an inevitable accident, no distinctions between humans shall be made (except in the number of human lives at stake). See Straßenverkehrsgesetz, § 1e, 2(2)(c), § 1e StVG - Betrieb von Kraftfahrzeugen mit autonomer... - dejure.org.

[73] Wisman (2019), p. 217 ff.

[74] Smuha et al. (2021), p. iii.

3.2 Personal Non-professional Activity

We do not want the law to intrude too much in what we do in our private sphere: in our homes, not in any professional capacity. Enforcement would severely violate privacy, probably disproportionate to the harm or risk caused by such activity (serious crime excepted of course). The GDPR allows us to keep our own address book (art. 2(2)(c) GDPR), copyright law allows us to make home-copies of copyrighted material (art. 2(2)(b) Copyright Directive). In the same vein, the AI Act does not apply to deployers who are natural persons using AI systems in the course of a purely personal non-professional activity (art. 2(10) AI Act.[75] Obligations of providers of these systems are unaffected.

Such personal AI systems may well involve or affect other people or society at large, in addition to the user him- or herself. We use four brief examples: having intelligent personal home assistants (IPHAs) in one's house,[76] posting content on social media to amplify an urban myth, using Personal AI[77] to answer private emails and chat-messages, and finally using social robots for company and sex.

Of course, these AI systems may (depending on their functionality) be covered by other rules, both addressing the provider of such systems and/or the private person using the system for their own purposes. If personal data are processed by an IPHA, the GDPR may still apply.[78] IPHAs and social robots are required to meet certain cybersecurity standards. The DSA addresses providers of social media platforms, obliging them (to some extent) to police their end-users' behaviour.[79] Criminal law, and the upcoming CSAM Regulation, may be relevant for social media and other online communication providers and for providers of sex robots. Social media have, for their users, an ambiguous relation to freedom of expression (art. 10 ECHR).[80] On the one hand they offer great opportunities for people to express themselves, and also for receiving tons of information. However, social media also offer opportunities to abuse this freedom, by insulting, harming, threatening others, doxing, incitement to hatred, etc. So, both criminal law and tort law may cover some uses of social media.

Use of AI by natural persons in the course of a purely personal non-professional activity may cause risks; both for other natural persons and for society at large. For instance, a visitor may not be aware of the fact that the host has an IPHA in his home, and that any conversation is potentially recorded and listened into by its

[75] The literal wording is: 'This Regulation does not apply to obligations of deployers who are natural persons using AI systems in the course of a purely personal non-professional activity'. But how can a regulation (not) apply to obligations?

[76] De Conca (2021a).

[77] Such as Personal AI | AI Digital Twins.

[78] De Conca (2021b), pp. 237–238.

[79] Art. 34–36 DSA.

[80] Helberger et al. (2020).

provider, resulting in potentially grave privacy data protection violations.[81] In turn, it is foreseeable that the consequences of these breaches may pose chilling effects to society because one's private home may no longer be regarded as private.

On a societal scale, our freedom of thought may be at stake, if we are under constant surveillance and if our data exhaust is used to manipulate us, for commercial or political purposes.[82] Fake news can be used to cause polarisation in societies, to manipulate election results.[83] Personal use of social media can contribute to such effects. Chatbots that continue to 'learn' from their use can be poisoned with such fake content—really hard to trace and to get rid of. Societal harm (such as: reduced social cohesion) can also be the result of addictive AI: again, social media.[84] Private use of sex robots may lead to misogyny, to lower thresholds for sexual violence towards and abuse of humans including children.[85]

All of these dangers are not really effectively addressed by the other rules that are applicable to such personal AIs. With the DSA, Europe tries to bridle the spread of fake news by social media. Criminal law tries to deter rape, sexual violence and sexual child abuse.

In our view, the fact that for use of personal AI in communication with others, not even transparency (art. 52 AI Act) is required is a serious gap in the regulation. Also, the fact that, for instance, guests in a house are not necessarily informed of data-collection by IPHAs. The law is struggling with the systemic risk that fake news filter bubbles created by social media pose to democratic societies.

Of course, including AI used by natural persons for private purposes in the AI Act would not by itself solve all of these issues. Maybe we need to admit that law can only do so much. Not every challenge presented by use of technology can be dealt with by law, or by law alone.

3.3 Research

The purpose of the AI Act is, among other things, to '*improve the functioning of the internal market and promote the uptake of human-centric and trustworthy artificial intelligence (AI) ... and supporting innovation*'.[86] AI is good, for citizens, for business and for the public interest,[87] and we need to make sure that Europe reaps its benefits. At the same time, we want to ensure '*a high level of protection of health,*

[81] De Conca (2021a), pp. 257–273.

[82] Alegre (2022).

[83] Stachofsky et al. (2023).

[84] González-Bailón and Lelkes (2023), pp. 174–175.

[85] Sterri and Earp (2021).

[86] Art. 1 and Consideration 25 and 97 AI Act.

[87] According to the sheets used by Lucilla Sioli, Director for Artificial Intelligence and Digital Industry DG CNECT, European Commission in her presentation introducing the proposal for the AI Act in a CEPS webinar on 23 April 2021, AI-Presentation-CEPS-Webinar-L.-Sioli-23.4.21.pdf.

safety, fundamental rights enshrined in the Charter, including democracy, the rule of law and environmental protection, against the harmful effects of AI systems in the Union'.[88] Innovation shall not be stifled.[89]

That is why AI used for research (art. 2(6) AI Act)[90] and research to develop AI (art. 2(8) AI Act)[91] are not covered by the AI Act. Art 2(8) AI Act is quick to add that '*testing in real world conditions shall not be covered by that exclusion*'. Also, AI tools that may be used in research but that can also be used for other purposes than research, will fall under the AI Act.[92] Academic research is typically covered by specific rules, such as codes of conduct for research integrity.[93]However, in practice it may be hard to distinguish between research and early stages of product development (which would not be covered by the research exemption). Research may be intended to lead to product development and commercialisation of such a product—where do we draw the line? This legal uncertainty might actually hamper innovation.[94]

There is also the risk that very harmful AI is actually used under the disguise of research. If this is done in internal processes of an organisation, e.g. in the use of their discretionary power, if only to see what the results would be (which could be called 'research'), how could such use ever come to light and be challenged by people harmed by such use? Use of risk-assessment models to decide who to investigate comes to mind here.

So: the lack of a definition to clarify what is meant by research, and how it can be distinguished from other activities, can be seen as gaps.

3.4 *Free and Open Source Licences*

AI systems released under free and open source licences are not covered by the provisions of the AI Act, unless they are placed on the market or put into service as high-risk AI systems or as an AI system that falls under article 5 (prohibited AI practices) or article 50 (transparency obligations for chatbots, deepfakes and the like), says article 2 (12) AI Act. It is not really clear what is meant by 'free and open

[88] Art. 1 AI Act.

[89] Davies (2023).

[90] Stapleton (2024).

[91] Just a random example: Wang and Aouf (2024).

[92] Consideration 25 AI Act.

[93] Such as, among others: Netherlands Code of Conduct for Research Integrity, Netherlands+Code+of+Conduct+for+Research+Integrity_2018_UK.pdf (nwo.nl), supplemented by rules on use of generative AI: NWO's preliminary position on generative AI in the application and review process | NWO.

[94] Panteli et al. (2024).

source licences'.[95] It is striking that Consideration 89 refers to 'free and open-source tools, services, processes, or AI components other than general-purpose AI models', while this restriction to non-general-purpose AI models does not appear in art. 2(12). So, an open-source general-purpose AI model is not covered by art. 51–55 AI Act, even if it comes with a (potential) systemic risk.

An example (admittedly a general-purpose AI model) is Cohere Aya, a massively multilingual generative language model that follows instructions in 101 languages.[96] Other examples can be found on Hugging Face.[97]

Such systems are excluded from applicability of the AI Act in order not to hamper innovation.[98] Depending on how open source is understood (does it include the datasets used for training and testing?) transparency seems to be covered to some extent. And maybe the assumption is that for 'serious', professional and/or commercial applications that are not 'high risk' but that can nevertheless have serious consequences, no free and open-source software would be used?

Of course, all other law applies to whatever these open source systems are used for, such as: administrative law for use by government agencies, consumer protection law for use by commercial enterprises, non-discrimination law, contract law, tort law, data protection law (in particular art. 22 GDPR), law of criminal procedure, etc.

Threats to fundamental rights by use of these systems include everything the AI Act aims to protect against: '*ensuring a high level of protection of health, safety, fundamental rights (…), including democracy, the rule of law and environmental protection, against the harmful effects of AI systems*'.[99]

To some extent these threats are indeed addressed by existing (pre-AI Act) legislation such as the GDPR—except that enforcing such legislation is particularly challenging when AI is used, which is why the AI Act was proposed in the first place. For instance, as a social media user, how do you know how the content that is presented to you was selected by an open source algorithm? How could you ever challenge this selection? As a lookalike of a blacklisted shoplifter: how do you know that you are mistakenly being 'recognised' by open source facial recognition software, and therefore under increased surveillance while strolling through the shopping mall? And that therefore you were 'randomly' (not) chosen for inspection by shop security personnel? As someone who is put on a list of potential insurance fraudsters due to a high-risk score calculated by an open source model: even if you can find out that you are actually on that list, how can you ever challenge that, or disprove your risk score?

---

[95] See Downing (2024), who renames them 'mystery licenses'. On the legal aspects of open source AI see Riddiough (2023), and the discussion on open source AI on the Open Source Initiative at Open Source AI Deep Dive – Open Source Initiative.

[96] See Üstün et al. (2024), pp. 25–36 (their approach to safety, toxicity and bias).

[97] Hugging Face, The AI community building the future, at Hugging Face – The AI community building the future.

[98] See Castro (2024).

[99] Art. 1 AI Act.

This is a gap: natural persons subjected to decisions by AI systems released under free and open source licences are not entitled to the right to explanation of individual decision making given by art. 86 (however limited that right may be, see subsections 2 and 3).[100] And this is an inconsistency: for an affected person, what is the difference between being harmed by a 'normal' AI or by an AI system released under a free and open source licence? You are harmed, maybe you do not (or cannot) even know that an AI system was used to harm you, and even if you do know this, you have no right to an explanation under the AI Act.[101]

4 Conclusion

We can conclude that the AI Act has purposely or inadvertently left some gaps in regulating AI systems in the context of national security, military, foreign authorities, transportation, personal non-professional activity, research, and free and open source licences.

For instance, in the realm of the AI Act, AI systems for national security are excluded on the basis that national security remains the sole responsibility of Member States.[102] However, the complexities of technologies such as AI systems used for national security and intelligence purposes are not strangers to the common risks that AI may pose to society. In particular, if AI systems have not been properly tested or scrutinised against flaws that may well jeopardise citizens' fundamental rights. In this context, the AI Act undermines the whole human-centred AI approach. The AI Act missed the opportunity to provide a more coherent and holistic approach to protecting fundamental rights in the context of AI systems deployed by intelligence and security sectors.

Similarly, AI tools are currently being deployed for military purposes, such as the case in Ukraine[103] and Gaza.[104] Nonetheless, the AI Act does not apply to AI systems deployed exclusively for military, defence or national security purposes. The reasons for excluding military AI systems from the scope of the AI Act are also based on Article 4(2) TEU and the common Union defence policy that are subject to public international law.[105] Like AI systems for national security and intelligence purposes, AI in a military comes with threats, not just for human rights and European values, but in essence for human life. This gap provided by the AI Act could best be filled by international humanitarian law. However, unfortunately it is true that enforcement of international humanitarian law is problematic if it is not complied

[100] Depending on the situation, art. 12–22 GDPR may still be of help.

[101] But again maybe under art. 22 GDPR.

[102] Art. 4(2) TEU.

[103] Bergengruen (2024).

[104] McKarnan and Davies (2024).

[105] Chapter 2 of Title V TEU.

with by states engaged in a military conflict.[106] Thus, we need to start with multi-stakeholder engagement to find best practices to guide the development and deployment of AI systems for military purposes.

AI systems in the context of international agreements with third countries or international organisations for law enforcement and judicial cooperation with the Union or with Member States are also covered under the exemption umbrella. The exemption finds its justification in the need for future cooperation with foreign partners in the exchange of information and evidence to fight crime. The AI Act has established that third countries or international organisations need to provide adequate safeguards regarding the protection of fundamental rights and freedoms of individuals. However, there is no guarantee or evidence, that third countries or international organisations have the same standards in regard to safeguards for fundamental rights and core values. Thus, the exemption in this category presents risks to fundamental rights and European values such as human dignity, respect for private life and protection of personal data and right to a fair trial.

Self driving cars have been a tech-dream for decades, which is why the transportation sector may be one of the first fields in which the general public will see AI in action on a big scale. Despite the technological excitement about self driving there are serious matters to be addressed. One of them is the assignment of liability for motor-vehicle accidents. Hence, the AI Act appears to have left civil liability matters to be taken care of by member states.[107] However, transportation appears not to be an exemption, instead it is a different way of putting the requirements for these high-risk AI systems in legislation that is already in place.[108] At first glance, the threats to fundamental rights and European values that these technologies may bring is for instance the violation of driver and passenger privacy resulting from the mandatory installation of eCall systems in motor vehicles.[109] Similar to the previous categories, it is not really clear how such threats are addressed in the AI Act or other regulations referred by the AI Act,thus, creating a lack of democratic accountability. Many things remind unclear, which in itself may be considered a gap.

The AI Act is not applicable to natural persons deploying or using AI systems, as long as it for purely personal non-professional activity.[110] The exemption may find a solid ground on the basis that 'my home my castle', therefore, the state cannot or should not interfere in the intimate sphere. However, AI systems that are used in the context of purely personal non-professional activity still have the means to affect other people or society at large. For instance, the use of intelligent personal home assistants (IPHAs) presents issues of consent and privacy regarding home guests being unaware of the fact that the host has IPHAs in their home, and that any

[106] Zyberi (2018).

[107] Art. 2(2) AI Act.

[108] Consideration 49.

[109] Wisman (2019), p. 183 ff.

[110] Art. 2(10) AI Act.

conversation is potentially recorded and listened into.[111] Subsequently, we may be victims of surveillance, exposing our data without our consent, at the risk of being manipulated or used for commercial or political purposes.[112] The effects regarding the use of these technologies are in some cases regulated by other legal frameworks such as the GDPR or criminal law. Nonetheless, the AI Act -a uniform legal instrument- has left a significant gap in this area. Of course, including AI used by natural persons for private purposes in the AI Act would not by itself solve all of these issues. Perhaps, we may face reality that not every challenge presented by the use of technology can be dealt with by law alone.

Of course, AI is good, for citizens, for business and for the public interest.[113] That is why AI systems used for research purposes are not covered by the AI Act.[114] However, in practice it may not be easy to distinguish between purely academic or scientific research and early stages of product development for future commercialisation -which should not benefit from this exemption. Where do we draw the line? There is lack of a definition in the AI Act to ascertain what is meant by research, and how it can be distinguished from other activities. Thus, it is wise to not to let the innovation hype take over from our freedoms, our democracy, and what it means to be a human.

Lastly, in broad terms, AI systems deployed under free and open source licences are not governed by the provisions of the AI Act. It is unclear what is meant by 'free and open source licences'.[115] However, this exemption excludes high-risk AI systems or AI systems falling under prohibited practices.[116] This category exemption is not free from threats to democratic values, the rule of law, and of course fundamental rights.[117] For instance, natural persons subjected to decisions by AI systems under the free and open source licences umbrella may not entitled to the right to explanation.

The above gaps found in the AI Act pose questions about whether the Act itself undermines all the work and effort it put into preparing a framework to protect humans from harmful (untrustworthy) AI. We have exposed some potential risks to fundamental rights, democratic values, and the rule of law. These gaps and risks need to be urgently re-addressed in order to ensure 'a high level of protection of health, safety, fundamental rights as enshrined in the Charter of Fundamental Rights of the European Union (the "Charter"), including democracy, the rule of law and

[111] De Conca (2021a), pp. 257–273.

[112] Alegre (2022).

[113] According to the sheets used by Lucilla Sioli, Director for Artificial Intelligence and Digital Industry DG CNECT, European Commission in her presentation introducing the proposal for the AI Act in a CEPS webinar on 23 April 2021, AI-Presentation-CEPS-Webinar-L.-Sioli-23.4.21.pdf.

[114] Art. 2(6)(8) AI Act.

[115] See Downing (2024), who renames them 'mystery licenses'. On the legal aspects of open source AI see Riddiough (2023), and the discussion on open source AI on Open Source AI Deep Dive – Open Source Initiative.

[116] Art. 5 AI Act.

[117] Art. 1 AI Act.

environmental protection, to protect against the harmful effects of AI systems in the Union, and to support innovation' in the course of 'the development, the placing on the market, the putting into service and the use of artificial intelligence systems' (Consideration 1)—in other words, to achieve the very purpose of the AI Act.

References

Abraham Y (2024) 'Lavender': the AI machine directing Israel's bombing spree in Gaza, 972 Magazine 3 April 2024, 'Lavender': The AI machine directing Israel's bombing spree in Gaza (972mag.com)

AI Task Force (2019) Artificial Intelligence in Support of Defence, September 2019, Report of the AI Task Force September 2019.pdf (defense.gouv.fr)

Alegre S (2022) Freedom to think: protecting a fundamental human right in the digital age. Atlantic Books

Badue C, Guidolini R, Carneiro RV, Azevedo P, Cardoso VB, Forechi A, Jesus L, Berriel R, Paixao TM, Mutz F, de Paula Veronese L (2021) Self-driving cars: a survey. Expert Syst Appl 165:113816. https://www.sciencedirect.com/science/article/pii/S095741742030628X

Bergengruen V (2023) Ukraine's 'Secret Weapon' against Russia is a controversial U.S. Tech Company, Time, 14 November 2023, Ukraine's 'Secret Weapon' Against Russia Is Clearview AI | TIME

Bergengruen V (2024) How tech giants turned Ukraine into an AI War Lab, Time, 8 february 2024, Tech Companies Turned Ukraine Into an AI War Lab | TIME

Boutin B (2023) State responsibility in relation to military applications of artificial intelligence. Leiden J Int Law 36(1):133–150. https://doi.org/10.1017/S0922156522000607

Castro D (2024) The EU's AI Act creates regulatory complexity for open-source AI, Center for Data Innovation 4 March 2024, The EU's AI Act Creates Regulatory Complexity for Open-Source AI – Center for Data Innovation

Cilevics B (2020) Justice by algorithm–the role of artificial intelligence in policing and criminal justice systems. Report of Committee on Legal Affairs and Human Rights, Council of Europe. https://pace.coe.int/en/files/28723/pdf

Constantino J, Wagner B (2024) Accountability and oversight in the Dutch intelligence and security domains in the digital age. Front Polit Sci 6:1383026. https://doi.org/10.3389/fpos.2024.1383026

CTIVD (2021) Toezichtsrapport nr. 72 over de inzet van bijzondere bevoegdheden ter ondersteuning van een goede taakuitvoering van de AIVD en de MIVD, https://www.ctivd.nl/binaries/ctivd/documenten/rapporten/2021/04/15/rapport-72/CTIVD+NR72+Toezichtsrapport.pdf

Dambly P, Beelen A (2022) Europe: Analysis of the Proposal for an AI Regulation, (MAIEI, 2022), https://montrealethics.ai/europe-analysis-of-the-proposal-for-an-ai-regulation/

Davies P (2023) 'Potentially disastrous' for innovation: Tech sector reacts to the EU AI Act saying it goes too far. Euronews.next, 15 December 2023, 'Potentially disastrous' for innovation: Tech sector reacts to the EU AI Act saying it goes too far | Euronews

De Conca S (2021a) The enchanted house: An analysis of the interaction of intelligent personal home assistants (IPHAs) with the private sphere and its legal protection. PhD Tilburg University, online available at Microsoft Word - Enchanted House printer copy.docx (uvt.nl)

De Conca S (2021b) Smart home for lawyers: IoT in the home and its implications for the GDPR. Tijdschrift voor Internetrecht 2021(6):231–241. Article UDH:IR/17009. https://denhollander.info/artikel/17009

Dias A (2020) The colleague, the girl, the police: Student framed and imprisoned over terror offences tells whole story for the first time, 21 April 2020, ABC.net, The colleague, the girl, the police: Student framed and imprisoned over terror offences tells whole story for the first time - triple j (abc.net.au)

Docksey C, Propp K (2023) Government access to personal data and transnational interoperability: an accountability perspective. Oslo Law Rev (1):1–34

Downing K (2024) Choose your own adventure, the EU AI Act and Openish AI, at choose your own adventure: the EU AI Act and Openish AI – Law Offices of Kate Downing (katedowninglaw.com), 6 February 2024

Dutch government (2024) The Government-wide vision on generative AI of the Netherlands, 17 January 2024, at Government-wide vision on generative AI of the Netherlands | Parliamentary document | Government.nl

ECNL (2024) Packed with Loopholes: why the AI Act fails to protect civic space and the rule of law, European Center for Non-for-profit Law, 2024, Packed with loopholes: why the AI Act fails to protect civic space and the rule of law | ECNL

EDPB-EDPS (2021) Joint Opinion 5/2021 on the proposal for a Regulation of the European Parliament and of the Council laying down harmonised rules on artificial intelligence (Artificial Intelligence Act), edpb-edps_joint_opinion_ai_regulation_en.pdf (europa.eu)

Eijkman Q, Weggemans D (2013) Open source intelligence and privacy dilemmas: is it time to reassess state accountability? Secur Hum Rights 23(4):285–296, online available at Microsoft Word - 03 Eijkman Weggemans v2.doc (cyberwar.nl)

el Rahwan A (2023) European research about using Artificial Intelligence and Interoperability for Solving Challenges of OSINT and Cross-Border Investigations, Border Security Report 10 February 2023, European research about using Artificial Intelligence and Interoperability for Solving Challenges of OSINT and Cross-Border Investigations - Border Security Report (border-security-report.com)

Feffer M, Heidari H, Lipton ZC (2023) June. Moral machine or tyranny of the majority? In: Proceedings of the AAAI Conference on Artificial Intelligence, vol 37, no 5, pp 5974–5982

Gadek G (2024) Unreliable AIs for the military. In: Schraagen JM (ed) Responsible use of AI in military systems. Chapman and Hall/CRC, pp 101–123. https://doi.org/10.1201/9781003410379

Gault M (2023) Palantir Demos AI to fight wars but says it will be totally ethical don't worry about it, 26 April 2023, Palantir Demos AI to Fight Wars But Says It Will Be Totally Ethical Don't Worry About It (vice.com)

González-Bailón S, Lelkes Y (2023) Do social media undermine social cohesion? A critical review. Soc Issues Policy Rev 17(1):155–180. Do social media undermine social cohesion? A critical review - González-Bailón - 2023 - Social Issues and Policy Review - Wiley Online Library

Hallaq B, Somer T, Osula A-M, Ngo K, Mitchener-Nissen T (2017) Artificial intelligence within the military domain and cyber warfare. In: 16th European Conference on Cyber Warfare and Security (ECCWS 2017), Dublin, Ireland, 29–30 June 2017. Published in: Proceedings of 16th European Conference on Cyber Warfare and Security. The Title of the Paper Goes Here, in Title Case and Title Style (warwick.ac.uk)

Helberger N, Van Drunen M, Eskens S, Bastian M, Moeller J (2020) A freedom of expression perspective on AI in the media–with a special focus on editorial decision making on social media platforms and in the news media. Eur J Law Technol 11(3). A freedom of expression perspective on AI in the media – with a special focus on editorial decision making on social media platforms and in the news media | European Journal of Law and Technology (ejlt.org)

Human Rights Watch (2021) How the EU's Flawed Artificial Intelligence Regulation endangers the Social Safety Net: Questions and Answers, https://www.hrw.org/news/2021/11/10/how-eus-flawed-artificial-intelligence-regulation-endangers-social-safety-net

in 't Veld S (2022) Draft Report Committee of Inquiry to investigate the use of Pegasus and equivalent surveillance spyware. European Parliament, https://www.sophieintveld.eu/download/getFile/5073

Intelligence College in Europe (2023) French seminar on open-source intelligence (OSINT), March 2023, Intelligence College in Europe (intelligence-college-europe.org)

Lu Y (2023) 'Lost Time for No Reason': how driverless taxis are stressing cities. The New York Times, 20 November 2023, 'Lost Time for No Reason': How Driverless Taxis Are Stressing Cities - The New York Times (nytimes.com)

Marzocchi E, Mazzini M (2022) Pegasus and surveillance spyware. Policy Department for Citizens' Rights and Constitutional Affairs, Directorate-General for Internal Policies PE 732.268, Pegasus and surveillance spyware (europa.eu)

McKarnan B, Davies H (2024) 'The machine did it coldly': Israel used AI to identify 37,000 Hamas targets. The Guardian, https://www.theguardian.com/world/2024/apr/03/israel-gaza-ai-database-hamas-airstrikes

Meerveld HW, Lindelauf RHA, Postma EO, Postma M (2023) The irresponsibility of not using AI in the military. Ethics Inf Technol 25(1):14

Naarttijärvi M (2019) Legality and democratic deliberation in black box policing. Technol Regul 35–48. http://urn.kb.se/resolve?urn=urn:nbn:se:umu:diva-164827

Nees MA (2019) Safer than the average human driver (who is less safe than me)? Examining a popular safety benchmark for self-driving cars. J Safety Res 69:61–68. https://www.sciencedirect.com/science/article/pii/S0022437518304511

NWO (2022) Two grants awarded within the KIC call for 'Data and Intelligence', 16 May 2022, Two grants awarded within the KIC call for 'Data and Intelligence' | NWO

Omtzigt P (2023) Pegasus and similar spyware and secret state surveillance, Report 15825, Council of Euorpe, (20 September 2023), https://pace.coe.int/en/files/29415 or https://pace.coe.int/pdf/aa984c36c6453ff2f5ae7a2079f90285ffeb19690007cea2c849692eaf5d7ef5?title=Doc.%2015825.pdf

Panteli T, Hommerson S, van de Weijer C (2024) Why the AI act is a huge triumph and how we can make it work. Research Professional News 21 March 2024, Why the AI act is a huge triumph and how we can make it work - Research Professional News

Powell R, Oswald M (2024) Assurance of Third-Party AI Systems for UK National Security. Centre for Emerging Technology and Security Research Report, 01.17.2024_assurance_report.pdf (turing.ac.uk)

Raposo VL (2022) Ex machina: preliminary critical assessment of the European Draft Act on artificial intelligence. Int J Law Inf Technol 30(1):88–109

REAIM (2023) Call to Action, https://www.government.nl/binaries/government/documenten/publications/2023/02/16/reaim-2023-call-to-action/REAIM+2023+Call+to+Action.pdf

Riddiough J (2023) Licensing and Legal Considerations for Open-Source AI, 7 March 2023, Licensing and Legal Considerations for Open-Source AI - AI Models

Roscoe J (2024) Russia, China, North Korea, and Iran Used GPT for 'Malicious Cyber Activities', OpenAI Says, Vice.com February 15, 2024, Russia, China, North Korea, and Iran Used GPT for 'Malicious Cyber Activities', OpenAI Says (vice.com)

Safi M (2018) University of NSW student wrongly accused of terrorism offences plans to sue police and media, The Guardian, 23 November 2018, University of NSW student wrongly accused of terrorism offences plans to sue police and media | Australia news | The Guardian

Sartor G, Loreggia A (2022) The impact of Pegasus on fundamental rights and democratic processes. European Parliament, (December, 2022), https://www.europarl.europa.eu/RegData/etudes/STUD/2022/740514/IPOL_STU(2022)740514_EN.pdf

Sharkey N (2007) Robot wars are a reality. In: The Guardian, 18 August 2007, Robot wars are a reality | Noel Sharkey | The Guardian

Smuha NA, Ahmed-Rengers E, Harkens A, Li W, MacLaren J, Piselli R, Yeung K (2021) How the EU can achieve legally trustworthy AI: a response to the European Commission's Proposal for an Artificial Intelligence Act (August 5, 2021). Available at SSRN: https://ssrn.com/abstract=3899991 or https://doi.org/10.2139/ssrn.3899991

Stachofsky J, Schaupp LC, Crossler RE (2023) Measuring the effect of political alignment, platforms, and fake news consumption on voter concern for election processes. Gov Inf Q 40(3):101810

Stanley-Lockman Z, Christie EH (2021) An Artificial Intelligence Strategy for NATO, 25 October 2021, NATO Review - An Artificial Intelligence Strategy for NATO
Stapleton A (2024) The best AI tools for research papers and academic research (Literature review, grants, PDFs and more), Academia Insider, The best AI tools for research papers and academic research (Literature review, grants, PDFs and more) – Academia Insider
Sterri AB, Earp BD (2021) The ethics of sex robots. In: The Oxford handbook of digital ethics, pp 1–22
Strategisch Actieplan voor Artificiële Intelligentie 2019, Rapport SAPAI (overheid.nl)
UNESCO (2023) Global Toolkit on AI and the Rule of Law for the Judiciary, CI/DIT/2023/AIRoL/01, https://unesdoc.unesco.org/ark:/48223/pf0000387331
United Nations General Assembly (2023) Seventy-eighth session, First Committee, Agenda item 99, General and complete disarmament, L56.pdf (reachingcriticalwill.org)
Üstün A, Aryabumi V, Yong ZX, Ko WY, D'souza D, Onilude G, Bhandari N, Singh S, Ooi HL, Kayid A, Vargus F (2024) Aya model: an instruction finetuned open-access multilingual language model. arXiv preprint arXiv:2402.07827
van Wees KAPC (2022) Civil liability for autonomous vehicles in the Netherlands. In: Netherlands Reports to the Twenty-first International Congress of Comparative Law, 23–28 October 2022, Asunción (Paraguay). In press
Virginia Commonwealth University (2023) Artificial Intelligence (AI) Challenges and Advantages in National Security, 6 December 2023, Artificial Intelligence (AI) Challenges and Opportunities in National Security (vcu.edu)
Wang C, Aouf N (2024) Explainable deep adversarial reinforcement learning approach for robust autonomous driving. IEEE Transactions on Intelligent Vehicles
Weber J (2024) Autonomous drone swarms and the contested imaginaries of artificial intelligence. Digital War, pp 1–4. Autonomous drone swarms and the contested imaginaries of artificial intelligence | Digital War (springer.com)
Winter E (2022) The compatibility of autonomous weapons with the principles of international humanitarian law. J Conflict Secur Law 27(1):1–20. https://doi.org/10.1093/jcsl/krac001
Wisman THA (2019) The quest for the effective protection of the right to privacy: on the policy and rulemaking concerning mandatory Internet of Things systems in the European Union, PhD-Thesis, Vrije Universiteit Amsterdam. complete+dissertation.pdf (vu.nl)
Zyberi G (2018) Enforcement of international humanitarian law. Human Rights Institutions, Tribunals and Courts: Legacy and Promise (Springer, 2018), pp 377–400, https://www.duo.uio.no/bitstream/handle/10852/66318/zyberi.pdf

Enforcing the AI Act in a Composite EU Administration

Santa Slokenberga

Contents

Santa Slokenberga's work has been supported by WASP HS 'AI and Automated Systems and the Right to Health – Revisiting Law Accounting for the Exploitation of Users Preferences and Values', 2021–2025.

S. Slokenberga (✉)
Faculty of Law, Uppsala University, Uppsala, Sweden
e-mail: santa.slokenberga@jur.uu.se

V. L. Raposo (ed.), *The European Artificial Intelligence Act*, Law, Governance and Technology Series 78, https://doi.org/10.1007/978-3-031-98406-8_10

Abstract To achieve the EU's ambitions in the field of AI, the AI Act sets out a number of compliance requirements for placing artificial intelligence systems (AI) on the market, putting them into service, and deploying them within the Union, adresses general-purpose AI models, and also prohibits certain AI practices. Complex mechanisms for furthering compliance and dealing with non-compliance are envisaged to support adherence to the rules. These involve the existing administrative actors and newly created or designated ones at the Union and Member State levels.

This chapter studies how the AI Act responds to the necessity to ensure that the prescribed legal requirements in the AI Act are followed and violations are addressed in a complex administrative landscape. It shows that the AI Act, being a horizontal framework, is highly dependent on the existing structures in the fields AI will relate to. Therefore, focusing on the consistency of the rules is a key facet of enforcement governance. Even though an ambition is to have a multi-level governance structure, precisely the need for consistency and dispute resolution risks creating a hierarchy where the Commission will hold the top position in enforcement. This might be a step towards greater integration of administrative law in the EU system.

1 Introduction

The Artificial Intelligence Act (AI Act)[1] is a market regulatory tool with an important human rights facet. It is anchored in Article 114 and Article 16 Treaty on the Functioning of the European Union (TFEU) and is crafted with a vision to take the EU to new heights in the field of AI.[2] At its core are several ambitions, including furthering the development and availability of the technology and its uptake among commercial actors and individuals.[3] To achieve that, human centricity and trustworthiness, along with an aspiration for a high level of protection of health, safety, and fundamental rights, have an essential role to play.[4] These ambitions relate to the

[1] Regulation (EU) 2024/1689 of the European Parliament and of the Council of 13 June 2024 laying down harmonised rules on artificial intelligence and amending Regulations (EC) No 300/2008, (EU) No 167/2013, (EU) No 168/2013, (EU) 2018/858, (EU) 2018/1139 and (EU) 2019/2144 and Directives 2014/90/EU, (EU) 2016/797 and (EU) 2020/1828 (Artificial Intelligence Act) (Text with EEA relevance) PE/24/2024/REV/1 OJ L, 2024/1689, 12.7.2024, ELI: http://data.europa.eu/eli/reg/2024/1689/oj.

[2] See Proposal for a Regulation of the European Parliament and of the Council Laying Down Harmonised Rules on Artificial Intelligence (Artificial Intelligence Act) and Amending Certain Union Legislative Acts COM/2021/206 final, Explanatory Memorandum.

[3] See Recital 1 AI Act.

[4] See Article 1(1) AI Act.

EU's broader objectives, including realising the digital decade and creating the digital single market.[5]

The AI Act provides a series of compliance requirements for placing artificial intelligence (AI) systems on the market, putting them into service, and deploying them within the Union, addresses general-purpose AI models, and prohibits certain AI practices. In particular, the AI Act details requirements pertaining to high-risk AI systems and operators of such systems, sets transparency rules for some systems, prescribes harmonised rules for placing general-purpose AI models on the market, and envisages measures to support innovation. To support adherence to the rules, mechanisms for furthering compliance and dealing with non-compliance are envisaged. They include rules for market monitoring, enforcement of the obligations that the AI Act prescribes, sanctions for violations, and affords some remedies to individuals. For the enforcement of these rules, a composite administrative framework is established, involving both the existing administrative actors and newly created or designated ones at the EU and Member State levels.[6]

This chapter seeks to analyse the enforcement of the AI Act within the framework of composite administration. In particular, it studies how the AI Act responds to the necessity to ensure that the prescribed legal requirements are followed and violations are addressed in a complex administrative landscape. This chapter begins by setting out central compliance requirements set out in the AI Act and explores how these are enforced through coordinated EU and Member State regulatory structures. Thereafter, it examines the distribution of enforcement responsibilities between the EU and the Member States in regard to ensuring consistent application of the AI Act and managing non-compliance. Finally, it assesses the AI Act's sanctions regime and remedies available to individuals. By building on the AI Act's composite administrative framework, this chapter provides an insight into the balance between the need for effective enforcement of the EU regulatory standards with the flexibility needed for accommodating diverse national administrative law mechanisms, and multiple AI contexts.

2 What to Comply with? A Brief Insight into the Central Requirements Under the AI Act

The AI Act is built on a risk-based approach to AI systems.[7] AI systems that are deemed to have an unacceptable risk within the EU legal order pursuant to Article 5 are prohibited in accordance with rules set out in that provision. High-risk AI sys-

[5] See Proposal for a Regulation of the European Parliament and of the Council Laying Down Harmonised Rules on Artificial Intelligence (Artificial Intelligence Act) and Amending Certain Union Legislative Acts COM/2021/206 final, Explanatory Memorandum.

[6] See Article 1(2) AI Act.

[7] See Article 2(1) AI Act for a definition.

tems—AI systems that are classified as such following a test set out in Article 6 of the AI Act—are subject to a comprehensive set of rules prescribed within the AI Act. For other than high-risk AI systems, voluntary compliance is encouraged with a view to enhancing trust in these systems, and furthering larger uptake, and transparency measures are prescribed.[8] Furthermore, also general-purpose AI models are subject to some requirements of the AI Act,[9] along with systems containing such models, the so-called general-purpose AI systems.[10]

In line with the market regulatory approach that the EU pursues in regard to products, the AI Act sets out principles and requirements that need to be ensured for a specific high-risk AI system. These requirements include data and data governance rules,[11] automatic recording of events (logs) over the lifetime of the system,[12] sufficient transparency so that the deployers can interpret a system's output and use it appropriately,[13] and information provision,[14] as well as the design of a system so that an effective oversight by natural persons can be ensured when the high-risk AI system is in use.[15] Furthermore, the high-risk AI system is required to be accurate, robust, and cybersecure and have consistent performance throughout the lifecycle.[16] Although the AI Act provides specifications under each of these requirements, the application of these requirements is commonly left to the respective actors, with due regard to a particular high-risk AI system, as well as the generally acknowledged state of the art on AI and AI-related technologies. A key tool to demonstrate compliance with applicable requirements is technical documentation, which also enables the national competent authorities and notified bodies to assess the compliance of the AI system with the applicable requirements.[17] When ensuring compliance with the applicable requirements, a risk management system—a continuous iterative process that is planned and run throughout the entire lifecycle of a high-risk system, requiring a regular, systematic review and updating[18]—shall also be taken into account.[19]

Providers of high-risk AI systems are required to implement and document quality management system and ensure document keeping for a period ending ten years after the high-risk system has been placed on the market and put into service,[20] keep

[8] See Recital 165 AI Act.

[9] See Article 2(63) AI Act for a definition.

[10] See Article 2(66) AI Act for a definition.

[11] See Article 10 AI Act for those requiremnts.

[12] See Article 12, in particular 12(1) AI Act.

[13] Article 13, in particular 13(1) AI Act.

[14] Article 13, in particular 13(2) AI Act.

[15] Article 14, in particular 14(1) AI Act.

[16] See Article 15 AI Act.

[17] Article 11(1) AI Act.

[18] Article 9(2) AI Act.

[19] See Article 8(1) AI Act.

[20] Article 18(1) AI Act.

the automatically generated logs to the extent that the logs are under their control,[21] take corrective actions to bring the high-risk system in conformity with the AI Act when they consider or have reasons to consider that the AI system is not in conformity with the AI Act,[22] and cooperate with the competent authorities.[23] Furthermore, import,[24] distribution,[25] representation in connection with high-risk AI system providers established in third countries[26] and use are also regulated.[27] The obligations placed on the authorised representatives, importers, and distributors are crafted in a way to prevent a third-country establishment as a means to circumvent the requirements that the AI Act prescribes.

AI systems that are not regarded as high-risk are subject to traceability and transparency requirements. Furthermore, voluntary compliance with some or all of the relevant mandatory requirements applicable to high-risk AI systems is also encouraged,[28] as well as adherence to ethical standards.[29] This is to be achieved, in particular, by voluntary codes of conduct.[30] Disregarding that such systems are not comprehensively regulated under the AI Act,[31] they should nonetheless be expected always to be safe, but this general requirement stems from the General Product Safety Regulation.[32]

Finally, regarding general-purpose AI models and the obligations of providers of such models, a distinction can be drawn between models that present systemic risk and models that do not. Providers of general-purpose AI models must comply with the technical documentation requirements, information, and documentation obligations vis-à-vis providers of AI systems who intend to integrate the general-purpose AI model into their AI system. They shall also put into place a policy to comply with the Union law on copyright and related rights and make available a sufficiently detailed summary of the content used for training of the general-purpose AI

[21] Article 19(1) AI Act.

[22] Article 20(1) AI Act.

[23] Article 21 AI Act.

[24] Article 23 AI Act.

[25] Article 24 AI Act.

[26] Article 22 AI Act.

[27] Deployers of the AI systems, such as healthcare actors, are under particular responsibilities, too. For examples, see Articles 26 and 27 AI Act.

[28] Recital 165 AI Act.

[29] See Recital 165 AI Act.

[30] Recital 165 AI Act.

[31] Recital 165 AI Act.

[32] Recital 166 AI Act. See Regulation (EU) 2023/988 of the European Parliament and of the Council of 10 May 2023 on general product safety, amending Regulation (EU) No 1025/2012 of the European Parliament and of the Council and Directive (EU) 2020/1828 of the European Parliament and the Council, and repealing Directive 2001/95/EC of the European Parliament and of the Council and Council Directive 87/357/EEC (Text with EEA relevance) PE/79/2022/REV/1 OJ L 135, 23.5.2023, pp. 1–51.

model.[33] Additional obligations apply when a general-purpose AI model is regarded as presenting a systemic risk. These obligations include performing model evaluation in accordance with standardised protocols and tools reflecting state of the art, assessing and mitigating possible systemic risks at the Union level, as well as keeping track of and reporting serious incidents and corrective measures to address them and ensuring an adequate level of cybersecurity for the model, as well as the physical infrastructure of the model.[34]

3 Division of Responsibilities in the Enforcement of the AI Act

3.1 Mapping Out the Competent Actors

Providers, along with other actors involved in bringing an AI system to the market, as well as deployers, are responsible for complying with the requirements prescribed to them. To facilitate the consistent and effective application of the regulation, an AI Board is created.[35] Its work is supported by an advisory forum,[36] which is tasked with providing technical expertise and advising the Board and the Commission, and contributing to fulfilling the tasks of the Board and the Commission.[37] Furthermore, the AI Act envisages a complex institutional setup to support effective compliance and to deal with non-compliance. In regard to high-risk AI systems, central actors include two national authorities—a notifying authority and a market surveillance authority. In regard to the general-purpose AI models, the central actors include the Commission, a European AI Office, and a scientific panel of independent experts. Further to these key actors, as the AI Act applies without prejudice to other Union laws, information access empowerment to human rights authorities is also envisaged.[38]

[33] See Article 53 AI Act.

[34] See Article 51(1) AI Act.

[35] Article 65(1) AI Act.

[36] See Article 67 AI Act.

[37] See Article 67(1) AI Act.

[38] See, in particular, Articles 77(2) and 77(3) AI Act.

3.2 AI Systems and Competent Actors

Each Member State is required to have at least two national competent authorities, namely, a notifying authority and a market surveillance authority.[39] Notifying authorities are responsible for setting up and carrying out the necessary procedures for the assessment, designation, and notification of conformity assessment bodies and for their monitoring.[40] Conformity assessment bodies are subject to the notification procedure to be able to carry out the tasks prescribed to them under the AI Act,[41] in particular, the verification of the conformity of high-risk AI systems in accordance with the conformity assessment procedures.[42]

Market surveillance authorities are key in overseeing the market. Whereas the AI Act requires at least one market surveillance authority,[43] in reality, and rather naturally, it means a large number of market surveillance authorities across the EU, considering the landscape that exists for ensuring market surveillance in diverse fields under the Market Surveillance Regulation. For high-risk AI systems related to products covered by the Union harmonisation legislation listed in Section A of Annex I, namely, Union harmonisation legislation based on the New Legislative Framework, the market surveillance authority for the purposes of the AI Act is the authority responsible for market surveillance activities designated under those legal acts.[44] The Member States may derogate from this, in appropriate circumstances, and designate another authority.[45] For financial services, a different authority applies.[46] There, too, in appropriate circumstances, a deviation is possible.[47] Whereas multiple authorities can be involved to ensure the effective application of the AI Act, one authority shall be designed as a single point of contact, and its identity shall be communicated to the Commission.[48]

Other tasks of these authorities in furthering compliance are not easily traceable in the AI Act, and to the extent they are, deep interrelatedness with the Union level can be noted. For example, they may provide guidance and advice on implementing the AI Act, particularly regarding SMEs. In doing so, however, they are obliged to consider the guidance and advice of the Board and Commission. Where this guidance concerns systems covered by other EU laws, relevant competent authorities

---

[39] Article 70(1) AI Act.

[40] Article 28(1) AI Act.

[41] See Article 30 for the notification procedure, Article 31 for the requirements relating to notified bodies, and Article 32 setting out the rule for presumption of conformity with requirements relating to notified bodies.

[42] Article 34(1) AI Act. The conformity assessment is set out in Article 43 AI Act.

[43] See Article 70(1) AI Act.

[44] Under Article 74(3) AI Act.

[45] Article 74(3) AI Act.

[46] See Article 74(6) AI Act.

[47] Article 74(7) AI Act.

[48] Article 70(2) AI Act.

need to be consulted[49] so that competencies are minded. The detailed competencies are subject to annual review and update of each member state,[50] so that the authorities are equipped to handle the assigned tasks.

3.3 General-Purpose AI Models and Competent Actors

Supervising and enforcing the obligations of general-purpose AI model providers is a prerogative of the Commission. To realise that, the AI Act creates a particular—and rather comprehensive—institutional mechanism. A central role is assigned to the AI Office. It is the platform through which the Union's expertise and capabilities in the field are ensured,[51] and it has been assigned responsibility for carrying out all necessary actions to monitor the effective implementation of the AI Act regarding general-purpose AI models. Whereas some central tasks are set out in the AI Act, a full set of competencies is prescribed in the decision that establishes the AI Office. Secondly, a scientific panel of independent experts is crafted to support enforcing the AI Act and, in particular, support the fulfillment of the technical tasks of relevance to enforcement.[52]

4 Enforcement of Obligations Pertaining to AI Systems in the Union

4.1 Market Surveillance

The AI Act envisages market surveillance of AI systems, delineates Member States' responsibilities in designating relevant market surveillance actors, and prescribes certain market surveillance modalities.[53] These are examined in detail below. However, the general market surveillance measures and powers assigned to the

---

[49] Article 70(8) AI Act.

[50] Article 70(3) AI Act.

[51] Article 64(1) AI Act. According to Article 64(1), the AI Office is the means through which the Union's expertise and capabilities in the field are ensured. It is 'part of the administrative structure of the Directorate-General for Communication Networks, Content and Technology (the "Directorate-General")'

Commission Decision of 24 January 2024 establishing the European Artificial Intelligence Office C/2024/390 OJ C, C/2024/1459, 14.2.2024, ELI: http://data.europa.eu/eli/C/2024/1459/oj Article 1.

[52] See Article 68(3) and Recital 164 AI Act.

[53] The AI Act merely provides some clarifications of relevance for the effective enforcement of the AI Act and sets out some additional obligations and specifications. See Article 74 AI Act.

market surveillance authorities[54] are set out in the Union law on market surveillance.[55] It sets out a market surveillance mechanism to ensure that only compliant products that meet the applicable requirements prescribed in applicable Union law are made available on the Union market. In that regard, it lists a range of powers to ensure access to the necessary information so that market surveillance can be carried out. The AI Act adds to it by specifying a power to carry out unannounced on-site inspections and physical checks of the products, as well as a power to acquire product samples, including under a cover identity, to inspect those samples and to reverse-engineer them in order to identify non-compliance and to obtain evidence may be performed remotely.[56] Moreover, it provides conditions for accessing the source code for high-risk AI systems.[57]

The specific procedures for market surveillance set out in the AI Act are not applicable to AI systems related to products covered by the Union harmonised legislation listed in section A of Annex I, which contains a list of Union harmonisation legislation based on the New Legislative Framework, in the case where the legal acts already provide for procedures ensuring an equivalent level of protection and have the same objective. In those cases, the relevant sectorial procedures apply instead.[58] In its original version adopted by the EU legislator, it includes 12 legislations, namely, on machinery, on the safety of toys, on recreational craft and personal watercraft, relating to lifts and safety components for lifts, relating to equipment and protective systems intended for use in potentially explosive atmospheres, relating to the making available on the market of radio equipment, on cableway installations, on personal protective equipment, on appliances burning gaseous fuels, in regard to medical devices and in vitro diagnostic medical devices.

4.2 *Dealing with AI Systems Presenting Risk*

The procedure for dealing with AI systems presenting risk is targeted at AI systems presenting risks to the health or safety, or to fundamental rights, of persons.[59] Where a market surveillance authority has sufficient reasons to consider that an AI system

[54] See, in particular, Chapter V of Regulation (EU) 2019/1020 of the European Parliament and of the Council of 20 June 2019 on market surveillance and compliance of products and amending Directive 2004/42/EC and Regulations (EC) No 765/2008 and (EU) No 305/2011 (Text with EEA relevance) PE/45/2019/REV/1 OJ L 169, 25.6.2019, pp. 1–44.

[55] Article 74(1) AI Act. Regulation (EU) 2019/1020 of the European Parliament and of the Council of 20 June 2019 on market surveillance and compliance of products and amending Directive 2004/42/EC and Regulations (EC) No 765/2008 and (EU) No 305/2011 (Text with EEA relevance) PE/45/2019/REV/1 OJ L 169, 25.6.2019, pp. 1–44.

[56] See Article 74(5) AI Act and Article 14(4)(d) and (j) AI Act.

[57] See Article 74(13) AI Act.

[58] Article 74(4) AI Act.

[59] Article 79(1) AI Act.

presents such a risk, it is under an obligation to carry out an evaluation to assess compliance with all the requirements that are applicable to the system concerned under the AI Act. In this evaluation, the market surveillance authority is obliged to cooperate with relevant human rights authorities and other public authorities or bodies of relevance to a particular AI system.[60]

In case of a found non-compliance, the market surveillance authority shall, without undue delay, require that the relevant operator within the prescribed time[61] takes the necessary corrective actions to bring the AI system into compliance, withdraw, or recall it.[62]

What actions may be requested is not a straightforward question. One aspect to consider is the choice between various possible solutions, at times, even co-existing ones for achieving the aim. Another aspect to consider is a question of how specified corrective actions a market surveillance authority may request. Whereas it could be regarded as sufficient to impose a requirement of compliance, one could question whether more concrete measures could also be requested, indicating how to comply with the AI Act. Whereas nothing in the AI Act seems to set explicit limitations for specific actions, it could in some cases be regarded as problematic in light of the spirit of the AI Act. For example, it is for the providers to find a way to ensure that a particular system complies with the AI Act. Nonetheless, where compliance requests are made, the providers are obliged to take 'all appropriate corrective actions'.[63] It could be argued that where a specific solution is requested, a comparable alternative is likely an acceptable option, too. Furthermore, where a general request for compliance is made, the obligation vested in the operator means that the operator can choose the necessary actions to ensure compliance.

In case the operator does not take adequate corrective action within the prescribed period, the market surveillance authority shall take all appropriate provisional measures to restrict the AI system from being made available on its national market or put into service to withdraw the product or the standalone AI system from that market or recall it.[64]

Regarding non-compliance, a relevant notified body shall be informed. Where the case is considered not to be limited to that member state only, the Commission and other Member States shall be informed of the results of the evaluation and actions required of the operator.[65] In cases where the operator has not complied with the required measures, the Commission, as well as other Member States, shall be informed of the relevant measures.[66] Market surveillance authorities of other

[60] See Article 79(2) AI Act.

[61] See Article 79(2) AI Act.

[62] Article 79(4) AI Act.

[63] Article 79(2) AI Act.

[64] Article 79(5) AI Act.

[65] See Article 79(2) and (3) AI Act.

[66] See Article 79(5) AI Act.

member states are expected to take relevant action and inform the Commission accordingly.[67]

Market surveillance authorities and the Commission are positioned to assist each other in dealing with systems presenting a risk. Pursuant to Article 79(7), a disagreement with the notified national measure could emerge. In such a case, objections shall be communicated to the Commission, along with their objections to this measure. This has to be done within the period of 3 months of the notification unless it concerns non-compliance with the prohibited AI practices. In such a case, the prescribed period is 30 days. Where no objection has been raised provisional measure taken by a market surveillance authority of another Member State, that measure shall be deemed justified.[68]

A question could emerge about actions by other Member States once objections are communicated to the Commission and other Member States. Article 79(7) seems to be constructed in a way that requires immediate action. However, it does not limit the autonomy of the market surveillance authorities to investigate and call into question the decision of the market surveillance authority initiating the procedure. Therefore, it could well be so that they arrive at a conclusion that a particular action is not required. Such reasoning is supported not only by the construction of the provision, where the Commission shall be notified regarding the adopted measures, but also by the institutional autonomy of the national administrative authorities.

In dealing with AI systems presenting risk, the procedural rights of the concerned operator in accordance with Article 18 of Regulation (EU) 2019/102 apply. In particular, before any measure, decision, or order is taken, the operator concerned shall be given the opportunity to be heard within a particular period unless it is not possible to give the operator that opportunity because of the urgency. In such a case, the operator shall be given that opportunity as soon as possible thereafter, and the measure, decision, or order shall be promptly reviewed. The measure, decision or order in question shall not only be transparent regarding the grounds on which it is based, but also be communicated without delay to the operator concerned, informing simultaneously of the remedies available to it under the law of the Member State concerned and of the time limits to which those remedies are subject.

4.3 Union Safeguard Procedure

Disagreements regarding a decision of the Member State trigger the Union safeguard procedure. Whereas each Member State is in the position to raise objections regarding situations that could affect their territory, the Commission has powers to consider compliance with the Union law regarding all decisions taken by the market surveillance authorities, including those confined to one Member State. Where

[67] Article 79(7) AI Act.

[68] Article 79(8) AI Act.

either of the situations has occurred, a consultation procedure with the market surveillance authority of the relevant member state and the operator or operators shall be started, and the evaluation of the national measure shall be initiated.[69]

On the basis of this evaluation, the Commission shall make a decision on the justification of the market surveillance authority's decision and inform the market surveillance authorities concerned and other market surveillance authorities. The Commission shall do this within 6 months unless it is a question of prohibited AI practices, in which case it is 60 days.[70]

Where the Commission finds that the measure is not justified, the Member State concerned is required to withdraw the measure and inform the Commission of the action.[71] Where the Commission finds that the decision is justified, all Member States are expected to engage so that the AI system is removed from the market. The Commission is to be informed immediately. It remains to be seen whether the Member States will report on any action or inaction or merely respond with an action when specifically requested by the Commission. Likely, regarding all decisions, an assessment of the necessity to take action needs to be made.[72] In this administrative setup, the Commission becomes in a way a higher administrative instance, even though all actions are taken subsequently by the national authorities, and access to the judicial review is ensured through the national judicial systems.

4.4 Compliant AI Systems Which Present a Risk

There could be cases where a particular system complies with the AI Act but it nonetheless presents a risk to the health or safety of persons, to fundamental rights, or to other aspects of public interest protection. In that case, not only does the evaluation need to be performed, but consultation with an authority in the field of human rights shall also be conducted. Where this is the case, the Member State shall request the relevant operator to take the necessary actions so that the risk is no longer present,[73] and inform the Commission and other Member States accordingly.[74] The provider must take the corrective action within the timeline the market supervisory authority prescribes.[75] After receiving this information, the Commission is obliged to initiate a consultation procedure with the concerned Member States and the relevant operators and evaluate the measures taken. The Commission is in the position

[69] Article 81(1) AI Act.
[70] Article 81(1) AI Act.
[71] Article 81(2) AI Act.
[72] Article 81(2) AI Act.
[73] Article 82(1) AI Act.
[74] See Article 82(3) AI Act.
[75] Article 82(2) AI Act.

to assess the justification of the requested national measures, and, where necessary, propose other appropriate measures for action.[76]

4.5 Enforcing Compliance

4.5.1 An Overview of Enforcement Measures

Member States are under a general duty to 'take all necessary measures to ensure that the provisions of the AI Act are implemented'.[77] The AI Act envisages penalties and other enforcement measures to enforce compliance, and Member States are entrusted to lay down relevant rules.[78] For some selected non-compliances, penalties and rules for their application are set out in the AI Act. However, it does not preclude Member States from prescribing penalties for other violations in so far as they are in line with the AI Act. This discretion could apply, for example, in setting penalties for inadequate operation of high-risk devices in the healthcare context. In regard to other enforcement measures, many details are not provided in the AI Act. It merely guides that other enforcement measures may include 'warnings and non-monetary measures, applicable to infringements by operators'.[79] These are to be adopted by the Member states.

4.5.2 Formal Non-Compliance

Formal non-compliance is non-compliance with some specified rules of the AI Act that do not lead to the AI system being regarded as such, which presents a level of risk incompatible with the AI Act. It captures a set of different non-compliances with the requirements set out in the AI Act. First, non-compliance with rules on the affixation of the CE marking,[80] or failure to affix the CE. Second, it captures the failure to draw up the EU declaration of conformity,[81] or incorrect drawing up of the EU declaration of conformity. Third, failure to register a system in the EU database for high-risk AI systems listed in Annex III. Fourth, failure to appoint an authorised representative when that is required under the AI Act. Finally, if the technical documentation required pursuant to the AI Act is not available.

Unlike risk management, formal non-compliance is a domain within which the Member States dominate and neither the other Member States nor the Commission is involved. The AI Act leaves it to the Member States to prescribe periods for

[76] Article 82(4) AI Act.

[77] See Article 99(1) in conjunction with Recital 168 AI Act.

[78] Article 99(1) AI Act.

[79] Article 99(1) AI Act.

[80] See Article 48 AI Act for relevant requirements.

[81] See Article 47 AI Act for relevant requirements.

compliance.[82] However, where the compliance 'persists', the Member States are instructed to act on restricting or prohibiting the high-risk AI system from being made available in the market or recalled or withdrawn without delay.[83]

4.5.3 Fines

The AI Act prescribes three levels of administrative fines, accepting that in some states, these fines may also be imposed by competent national courts or other bodies.[84] The AI Act sets out the maximum level of fines expressed in EUR and the percentage of the total worldwide annual turnover for the preceding financial year of the entity concerned, which shall be applied in a manner to ensure effectiveness, proportionality and dissuasiveness.[85] Generally, whichever is higher, the amount provided in EUR or the percentage shall be applied for undertakings. However, in the case of the SME's, the rule is the opposite, whichever is lower.[86]

Non-compliance with the prohibited AI practices as set out in Article 5 is subject to administrative fines of up to EUR 35 000 000 or, if the offender is an undertaking, up to 7% of its total worldwide annual turnover for the preceding financial year.[87] Non-compliance with a list of obligations related to operators or notified bodies is subject to administrative fines of up to EUR 15 000 000 or, if the offender is an undertaking, up to 3% of its total worldwide annual turnover for the preceding financial year, whichever is higher.[88] In the case of SMEs, whichever is lower.[89] This applies to the failure to comply with the obligations of providers of high-risk AI systems,[90] failure to comply with rules pertaining to the authorised representatives,[91] importers,[92] or deployers.[93] Moreover, sanctions are also envisaged for failing to comply with the requirements and obligations of notified bodies.[94] Finally, sanctions are also envisaged for failing to comply with the transparency obligations for providers and deployers of certain AI systems.[95]

---

[82] Article 83(1) AI Act.

[83] Article 83(2) AI Act.

[84] Article 99(9) AI Act.

[85] Article 99(1) AI Act.

[86] Article 99(6) AI Act.

[87] Article 99(3) AI Act.

[88] Article 99(3) AI Act.

[89] Article 99(6) AI Act.

[90] See Article 16 AI Act for relevant rules.

[91] See Article 22 AI Act for relevant rules.

[92] See Article 23 AI Act for relevant rules.

[93] See Article 26 AI Act for relevant rules.

[94] See Article 31, Article 33(1), (3) and (4) or Article 34 AI Act for relevant obligations.

[95] See Article 50 AI Act for relevant obligations.

The supply of incorrect, incomplete or misleading information to notified bodies or national competent authorities in reply to a request shall be subject to administrative fines of up to EUR 7 500 000 or, if the offender is an undertaking, up to 1% of its total worldwide annual turnover for the preceding financial year.[96]

5 General Purpose AI Models

5.1 On the Surveillance and Investigations

Supervising and enforcing the obligations of providers of general-purpose AI models is a competence of the Commission.[97] However, the Commission is required to entrust the carrying out of these tasks to the AI Office.[98] Whereas the Commission and the AI Office have a range of powers in regard to actions aimed at the providers of the general-purpose AI models, these are often to be exercised, standing shoulder to shoulder with the Board.

The AI Office is empowered to take the necessary actions in the field,[99] without the AI Act providing much specification regarding what these are. These could, however, be expected to be rather general observational actions, as any interaction with the providers of the general-purpose AI models is regulated in detail in the AI Act. One concrete guidance, nonetheless, is given, namely the reception of the complaints from the downstream providers regarding infringements of the AI Act.[100] As a general rule, when taking action, the rights of economic operators are safeguarded under Article 18 of Regulation (EU) 2019/1020, without prejudice to more specific procedural rights provided for in the AI Act.[101]

The AI Office is supported by the scientific panel in carrying out the monitoring activities.[102]

The scientific panel has the power to issue *qualified alerts* to the AI Office, where the scientific panel has reason to suspect that a general-purpose AI model poses a concrete and identifiable risk at the Union level, or where it has reason to suspect that a general-purpose AI model meets the criteria that would lead to a classification as general-purpose AI model with systemic risk.[103] This alert may trigger follow-ups, such as investigations; therefore, a qualified alert shall be duly reasoned, and—

[96] Article 99(5) AI Act.

[97] See Article 88(1) and Recital 162 AI Act.

[98] Article 88(1) and Recital 164 AI Act.

[99] The AI Office's mandate also captures AI systems based on a general-purpose AI model, where the model and the system are developed by the same provider, see Article 75(1) AI Act.

[100] See Article 89(1) AI Act.

[101] Article 94 AI Act.

[102] Article 89(1) AI Act.

[103] Article 90 and Recital 163 AI Act.

at least—the following shall be indicated: First, information regarding the point of contact of the provider of the general purpose AI model with systemic risk concerned. Second, a description of relevant facts and reasons for the alert. Third, other relevant information, including that which the panel has gathered on its own initiative.[104] To enable the scientific panel to fulfil their functions, they may, through the Commission, acquire information from a provider that is necessary for performing their tasks.[105] Once the scientific channel has issued a qualified alert, the Commission, through the AI Office, and after having informed the Board, may take measures to get access to documentation and information, conduct the evaluations, and request any measures taken by the operators.[106]

The AI Office is tasked with investigating possible infringements of the rules prescribed to the providers of general-purpose AI models. The investigations may be initiated on its own initiative, following the results of its monitoring activities, or upon request from market surveillance authorities.[107] The investigation powers include the following central steps aimed at bringing clarity regarding compliance with the obligations that the AI Act prescribes for general-purpose AI models. First, documentation request. Second, evaluations of the general-purpose AI models.

The documentation request is the prerogative of the Commission. Pursuant to Article 91(1), the Commission may request the provider of the general-purpose AI model concerned to provide the documentation drawn up by the provider in accordance with Articles 53 and 55 or any additional information necessary to assess the provider's compliance with the AI Act. This request[108] shall be made in line with the requirements set out in the AI Act. In particular, it shall state the legal basis and the purpose of the request, as well as specify what information is required, and set a period within which the information is to be provided. Moreover, as non-compliance with the information request is sanctioned (see the section below), it shall indicate the fines that the AI Act sets out for supplying incorrect, incomplete, or misleading information.[109]

The AI Act enables evaluations of the general-purpose AI models in two cases, followed by a consultation with a Board in two situations. First, to assess compliance of the provider with obligations under the AI Act if the information gathered following the documentation request is deemed insufficient to assess compliance with the AI Act. Second, to investigate systemic risks at the Union level of general-purpose AI models with systemic risk.[110] These evaluations may be preceded by a structured dialogue. If the Commission proceeds with an evaluation, it may *inter*

[104] See Article 90(3) AI Act.

[105] Article 91(3) and Recital163 AI Act.

[106] See Article 90(2) AI Act. These measures shall be notified to the Board pursuant to Article 90(2) AI Act.

[107] Recital 162 AI Act.

[108] Including that made following the request from the scientific panel.

[109] Article 91(4) AI Act.

[110] This is, in particular, following a qualified alert from the scientific panel. See Article 92(1)(b) AI Act.

alia access the source code of the general-purpose AI model concerned,[111] and the providers of the general-purpose AI model concerned or its representative shall supply the requested information.[112] Such a request for access shall state the legal basis, the purpose, and reasons for the request. It shall also set the period within which the access is to be provided and inform of the fines or failure to provide access.[113] These evaluations may be carried out by the Commission or by independent experts.

Where necessary and appropriate, the Commission may request providers to act on the following three issues. First, to take appropriate measures to comply with the obligations set out in Articles 53 and 54. Second, to implement mitigation measures, where the evaluation carried out in accordance with Article 92 has given rise to serious and substantiated concerns of systemic risk at the Union level. Third, to restrict the making available on the market, withdraw or recall the model.[114] Before these measures, the AI Office may initiate a structured dialogue with the provider of the general-purpose AI model.[115] If, during the structured dialogue, the provider of the general-purpose AI model with systemic risk offers commitments to implement mitigation measures to address a systemic risk at the Union level, the Commission may, by decision, make those commitments binding and declare that there are no further grounds for action.[116]

5.2 *Sanctioning the Non-Compliance*

Compliance with the obligations that are set out for the providers of general-purpose AI models is enforceable also through fines[117] in the amount 3% of the annual total worldwide turnover in the preceding financial year or EUR 15 000 000 of the actor concerned, whichever is higher.[118] In particular, failure to comply with 'the relevant provisions of this Regulation', as well as failure to collaborate with regard to the following three measures. First, a request for a document or information pursuant to Article 91 or the supply of incorrect, incomplete, or misleading information.[119] Second, failure to comply with a measure that has been requested under Article

[111] Article 92(3) AI Act.
[112] Article 92(5) AI Act.
[113] Article 92(4) AI Act.
[114] Article 93(1) AI Act.
[115] Article 93(2) AI Act.
[116] Article 93(3) AI Act.
[117] See Recital 169 AI Act.
[118] Article 101(1) AI Act.
[119] Article 101(1)(b) AI Act.

93.[120] Third, failure to provide access to the general-purpose AI model or general-purpose AI model with systemic risk for the evaluation.[121]

Although the sanctions capture a range of obligations, only wrongdoings committed intentionally or negligently may be sanctioned.[122] Similarly as in regard to the AI systems, before the Commission takes a decision regarding a fine,[123] the actor concerned shall be given an opportunity to be informed of the preliminary findings and be given an opportunity to be heard.[124] In fixing the amount of the fine or periodic penalty payment, regard shall be had to the nature, gravity and duration of the infringement, taking due account of the principles of proportionality and appropriateness, as well as any commitments made under the structured dialogue and decision of the commission or relevant codes of practice.[125] Nonetheless, any fine imposed shall be effective, proportionate and dissuasive,[126] and it should be communicated to the Board as appropriate.[127] These decisions are decisions within the meaning of Article 263 TFEU, and therefore, subject to the juridical review of the Court of Justice of the European Union (CJEU). Article 101(5) indicates that the CJEU may cancel, reduce or increase the fine imposed.

6 Sanctioning National Authorities, Union Institutions, Bodies, Offices, and Agencies

6.1 On the Violations and Fines

Unlike for Member State authorities, where the Member States have discretion in putting forward rules for determining the extent to which administrative fines may be imposed in public authorities and bodies established in the respective Member State,[128] the AI Act sets out clear rules for Union institutions, bodies, offices, and agencies in Article 100. Those is the prerogative of the European Data Protection Supervisor (EDPS), which, before taking any decisions in that regard, shall give the Union institution, body, office or agency which is the subject of the proceedings

[120] Article 101(1)(c) AI Act.

[121] Article 101(1)(d) AI Act.

[122] See Article 101(1) AI Act.

[123] See Article 101(2) AI Act.

[124] Article 101(1) AI Act. Detailed arrangements and procedural safeguards for proceedings remain to be specified by the Commission with implementing acts. See Article 101(6) AI Act.

[125] Article 101(1). On codes, see Article 56 AI Act.

[126] Article 101(3) AI Act.

[127] Article 101(4) AI Act.

[128] See Article 99(8) AI Act.

conducted by the EDPS the opportunity of being heard on the matter regarding the possible infringement.[129]

These actors are subject to two administrative fine thresholds, significantly lower than those set for the market actors. In particular, non-compliance with the prohibition of the AI practices referred to in Article 5 is subject to administrative fines of up to EUR 1 500 000.[130] Whereas non-compliance of the AI system with any other requirements or obligations under the AI Act, is subject to administrative fines of up to EUR 750 000.[131] Although the sanctions are rather limited, they have to be seen in light of where the fine is paid from and where it is paid to. The fine is paid by the Union actors from their budget resources, and they are intended to contribute to the general budget of the Union.[132]

6.2 *Application of Fines*

The power to impose fines on the Union institutions, bodies, offices, and agencies is vested with the EDPS.[133] The EDPS when deciding whether to impose an administrative fine and when deciding on the amount of the administrative fine in each individual case, shall take into account all relevant circumstances of the specific situation, and give due regard to seven considerations set out in the AI Act.[134] First, the infringement's nature, gravity, and duration and its consequences. Second, the degree of responsibility of the actor concerned, considering the technical and organisational measures they have implemented. Thirdly, any action taken by the respective actor to mitigate the damage suffered by affected persons. Fourthly, the degree of cooperation with EDPS to remedy the infringement and mitigate the possible adverse effects of the infringement. Fifth, any similar previous infringements by the respective actor. Sixth, the manner in which the infringement became known to the EDPS, in particular whether, and if so to what extent, the actor concerned notified the infringement. Finally, the annual budget of the Union institution, body, office, or agency. Although, unlike in regard to other actors, effectiveness, dissuasiveness and proportionality are not prescribed as a consideration when setting a fine, further guidance regarding the provision of fines is nonetheless provided in the AI Act. Pursuant to Article 100(6), the fines shall not affect the effective operation of the Union institution, body, office, or agency fined.

---

[129] Article 100(4) AI Act.

[130] Article 100(2) AI Act.

[131] Article 100(3) AI Act.

[132] Article 100(6) AI Act.

[133] Article 100(1) AI Act.

[134] Article 100(1) AI Act.

The Union actor, who is subject to proceedings conducted by the EDPS, shall be given an opportunity to be heard on the matter regarding the possible infringement,[135] and among the defense rights, also access the proceedings.[136] The EDPS is not permitted to base decisions on elements and circumstances on which the parties concerned have not been able to comment on.[137]

7 Remedies

The AI Act, as a market surveillance measure, aims at establishing a well-functioning internal market in the field of AI, finding a balance between market objectives and other rights and interests it aims to safeguard. As such, it is not overly forthcoming on the rights of individuals subject to the use of AI systems. That is despite the claim to have fundamental rights in its backbone, balanced against the market objectives, and in a situation where the use of AI can undoubtedly trigger a range of rights of individuals. For example, in emergency care, life is often at stake. Nonetheless, the AI Act is rather scarce in providing remedies. Against the background that 'Union and national law already provide effective remedies to natural and legal persons whose rights and freedoms are adversely affected by the use of AI systems',[138] it sets out two principal actions. Firstly, a right to lodge a complaint with the market supervisory authority.[139] Secondly, a right to an explanation of individual decision-making.[140] Further remedies are to be adopted, e.g., as part of the non-contractual liability directive, but the legislative process for that has not been completed yet,[141] or their effectiveness is yet to be seen, e.g., under the revised product liability framework.[142]

Pursuant to Article 85, any natural or legal person holds a right to lodge a complaint with a market surveillance authority if they have grounds to consider that there has been an infringement of the AI Act.[143] The Act does not elaborate on how well-founded these grounds should be. Nonetheless, from the wording of the provi-

[135] Article 100(4) AI Act.

[136] See Article 100(5) AI Act.

[137] Article 100(4) AI Act.

[138] Recital 170 AI Act.

[139] Article 85 AI Act.

[140] Article 86 AI Act.

[141] European Parliament (2024) Legislative Observatory. https://oeil.secure.europarl.europa.eu/oeil/popups/ficheprocedure.do?reference=2022/0303(COD)&l=en.

[142] See Directive (EU) 2024/2853 of the European Parliament and of the Council of 23 October 2024 on liability for defective products and repealing Council Directive 85/374/EEC (Text with EEA relevance)

PE/7/2024/REV/1 OJ L, 2024/2853, 18.11.2024; transposition must be completed by 9 December 2026. See Article 22(1) AI Act.

[143] Article 85(1) AI Act.

sion, it is clear that to lodge a complaint, one does not need to be directly affected by the respective AI system.[144] The submitted complaint also does not directly enable the person submitting it to enjoy particular rights under the AI Act, such as the right to receive a reply. Instead, the AI Act requires that the complaints be considered for the purpose of conducting market surveillance activities and handled in accordance with the dedicated procedures established by the market surveillance authorities.[145] In reality, following the doctrine of institutional autonomy, each Member State is expected to establish a procedure for managing these complaints—or, accounting for the existing reality, to rely on the existing ones for that purpose in connection with the existing market surveillance mechanisms, and national rules could prescribe some rights to the individuals, such as a right to reply.[146]

Article 86 envisages a right to an explanation of individual decision-making regarding a decision taken by a deployer that is taken by deployer based on the output from a high-risk AI system. This right applies only if four conditions are met. First, it applies only as far as the Union law does not otherwise provide this right.[147] Second, there is no Union law or national law providing for an exemption from this right.[148] Third, the decision has to relate to be based on an output from a high-risk AI system listed in Annex III, except for AI systems intended to be used as safety components in the management and operation of critical digital infrastructure, road traffic, or in the supply of water, gas, heating or electricity. Fourth, the decision has to produce legal effects or similarly significantly affect that person in a way that they consider to have an adverse impact on their health, safety, or fundamental rights.[149] Only when these conditions are met does an individual have a right to obtain clear and meaningful explanations from the deployer of the role of the AI system in the decision-making procedure and the main elements of the decision taken.

8 Concluding Discussion

The AI Act sets up a new framework for the governance of AI in the EU legal order, putting forward a regulation-by-design approach for certain AI.[150] AI that is subject to the AI Act but is in the market without compliance with the AI Act is subject to sanctions.

---

[144] The person lodging a complaint benefits from a wisthleblowing framework protection. See Article 87 and Recital 172 AI Act.

[145] See Article 85 AI Act.

[146] See e.g., existing in Latvia, Law on Submissions Latvijas Vēstnesis, 164, 11.10.2007, Sect. 5.

[147] Article 86(3) AI Act.

[148] Article 86(2) AI Act.

[149] Article 86(1) AI Act.

[150] On this approach, see Almada (2023), pp. 697–709.

To make the new framework work, a complex multi-level governance structure is envisaged, allocating central responsibilities for the Member States and the EU. In line with an early philosophy of multi-level governance in the EU, and adhering to the principle of sincere cooperation, each actor contributes in line with his or her capabilities or knowledge to the success of the overall exercise.[151] The responsibilities of the Member States are constrained to their jurisdiction, including, as relevant, collaborations with other Member States and the EU. Much responsibility lies at the Union level, both regarding high-risk AI systems and general-purpose AI models. Especially regarding the high-risk AI systems, and the power dynamics between the Union and the Member States, the mechanism leans heavily towards the EU level. Whereas, in regard to the work done to ensure compliance, it is the other way around, and the centre of gravity remains at the Member State level. This approach, however, can be said to be a natural outcome in steering the Union matters in a fragmented legal landscape and balancing the need to ensure effective enforcement whilst being highly dependent on the national administrative structures.

Whereas the pros and cons of such an approach can be discussed, one can also wonder whether there were any viable alternatives. The EU has opted for a horizontal approach to regulate AI systems, building on the existing regulatory approaches and relating to frameworks in different fields. This strategic choice has left rather limited options for different solutions than embracing all of the existing structures. Thinkable alternatives would for example risk creating AI-niched administrative structures that would be dependent on the existing actors in diverse fields, and create complex competence questions, as already now in regard to the fundamental rights actors. One could argue that the approach taken by the legislator responds to the need for flexibility for diverse fields and national adaptations, but it creates need for considerable work on consistency to make the approach function.

Whereas some of the features set forward in the AI Act resemble other legal frameworks, others are rather new. This approach goes well with a previous observation that when it comes to the EU, '[a] one-size-fits-all solution to effective policy implementation does not exist'.[152] The Commission, under its legislative initiative competencies, and ultimately the Union legislator are placed to find a strategy that can be expected to serve the purposes in a particular policy area.

Overall, the AI Act builds on, at least on the surface, the idea of a competence split between the Union and the Member State level, and synergies between these two, in particular, through the union safeguard procedure. However, as the union safeguard procedure is rather scarcely regulated, it is difficult to foresee how it will function in practice. Also, whereas in the AI Act, much of the measures to ensure effective enforcement remain to be specified at the national level, whether and how these rules are to be applied is a matter that may engage other Member States and the Union. These considerations are such that they are directly targeted at addressing one of the main multi-level enforcement challenges—clarity of rules on

---

[151] See the European Commission (2001) White Paper on Governance, pp. 34–35.

[152] Thomann and Sager (2017), pp. 1385–1407.

competence sharing.[153] Under the AI Act's approach, however, multi-level governance is not necessarily easy to be seen as an alternative to a hierarchical approach.[154] That is as if ultimately, in the name of consistency and dispute resolution, a hierarchy between the EU and Member States emerges, placing the Commission at the top of the administrative structure. This is a considerable transformative step taken by the EU, with implications for the infrastructure for implementing the EU law. This could potentially be argued to bring the enforcement system higher up to the EU level, with access to CJEU, carefully safeguarded under early case law.[155]

The AI Act is a brand-new framework, albeit following well-established approaches within the governance of the EU internal market and technology, including personal data. Generally, the effectiveness of new policies largely depends on their enforcement, particularly the investigation and sanctioning of violations of the prescribed requirements.[156] Whereas it is clear that the AI Act sets forth preconditions for furthering compliance and enforcing the requirements through other means, how that will turn out in practice remains to be seen. First appraisals could possibly be made when relevant Member State laws are in place, whereas the success of the mechanism can only be judged once it is fully functioning. In line with the polycentric governance theory, which supports the idea that multiple levels of governance are conducive to effective implementation, points of departure can be said to be promising,[157] however, not necessarily, challenge free.[158]

References

Almada M (2023) Regulation by design and the governance of technological futures. Eur J Risk Regul 14(4):697–709. https://doi.org/10.1017/err.2023.37

European Commission (2001) White Paper on Governance. COM(2001) 248 final. https://eur-lex.europa.eu/legal-content/EN/TXT/?uri=legissum:l10109

European Commission (2021) Explanatory Memorandum, Proposal for a Regulation of the European Parliament and of the Council Laying Down Harmonised Rules on Artificial Intelligence (Artificial Intelligence Act) and Amending Certain Union Legislative Acts. COM/2021/206 final. https://eur-lex.europa.eu/legal-content/EN/TXT/HTML/?uri=CELEX:52021PC0206

European Commission (2024) Commission Decision of 24 January 2024 establishing the European Artificial Intelligence Office. C/2024/390 OJ C, C/2024/1459, 14.2.2024. https://eur-lex.europa.eu/eli/C/2024/1459/oj

[153] See the European Commission (2001) White Paper on Governance, pp. 34–35.

[154] Hooghe and Marks (2003), pp. 233–243.

[155] See Plaumann line of cases. Case 25-62, Plaumann & Co. v Commission of the European Economic Community, English special edition 1963 00095 ECLI identifier: ECLI:EU:C:1963:17.

[156] Joerges (1999), pp. 311–338.

[157] Hooghe and Marks (2003), pp. 233–243.

[158] Söderlund and Larsson (2024), p. 41.

European Parliament (2024) 2022/0303(COD) Adapting non-contractual civil liability rules to artificial intelligence (AI Liability Directive). In: Legislative Observatory. https://oeil.secure.europarl.europa.eu/oeil/en/procedure-file?reference=2022/0303(COD)
Hooghe L, Marks G (2003) Unraveling the Central State, but how? Types of multi-level governance. Am Polit Sci Rev 97(2):233–243. https://doi.org/10.1017/S0003055403000649
Joerges C (1999) "Good Governance" through comitology? In: Joerges C, Vos E (eds) EU committees: social regulation, law and politics. Hart Publishing, Oxford, pp 311–338
Söderlund K, Larsson S (2024) Enforcement design patterns in EU law: an analysis of the AI Act. DISO 3(2) 41. https://doi.org/10.1007/s44206-024-00129-8
Thomann E, Sager F (2017) Toward a better understanding of implementation performance in the EU multilevel system. J Eur Public Policy 24(9):1385–1407. https://doi.org/10.1080/13501763.2017.1314542

Regulatory Sandboxes for Trustworthy AI: An EU Framework for Experimenting AI Systems and Fostering Agile Regulation

Gauthier Chassang

Contents

Abstract The Artificial Intelligence Act (AIA) introduces the mechanism of a regulatory sandbox in the AI field. This chapter analyses the provisions of the AIA and explores the concept, the attached rules and challenges regarding the setting up of, and the participation in AI regulatory sandboxes. It highlights the expected added value of AI regulatory sandboxes and identifies some of the remaining uncertainties, which should deserve further clarification in the future to maximise their benefits for innovators and regulators while supporting a dynamic and competitive AI industry in the EU.

G. Chassang (✉)
CERPOP, Inserm, UMR1295, University of Toulouse Paul Sabatier, Toulouse, France

Genotoul Societal Platform, GIS Genotoul Occitanie, Toulouse, France

Unesco Chair Ethics, Science and Society (E2S), Federal University of Toulouse, Toulouse, France
e-mail: gauthier.chassang@inserm.fr

V. L. Raposo (ed.), *The European Artificial Intelligence Act*, Law, Governance and Technology Series 78, https://doi.org/10.1007/978-3-031-98406-8_11

1 Introduction

Building upon the initial proposal of the European Commission (EC),[1] the concept of AI regulatory sandbox is introduced within Chapter VI of the AI Act[2] (AIA) as specific measures designed to support EU innovation. Regulatory sandboxes represent a novel approach to facilitating the development of new technologies wherein competent public authorities play a direct role in supporting innovative initiatives in AI and compliance with relevant regulations. The AI regulatory sandbox scheme facilitates coordinated efforts by authorities to support experimentation processes for the development of robust, ethical and safe AI systems (AIS) in Europe, particularly where such systems may pose a high risk to individuals' rights and freedoms. While the term 'sandbox' may evoke images of childhood, as Ranchordas rightly observed about regulatory sandboxes, 'playing with sandboxes is no child's play'.[3] This chapter introduces the concept of regulatory sandbox and analyses the provisions of the AIA concerning AI regulatory sandboxes and the attached legal mechanisms for their establishment and participation. It also highlights remaining uncertainties or complexities for implementation. The chapter is not focusing on the regulatory framework applicable to EU institutions and bodies, although it will be referenced on occasion.

2 The Concept of AI Regulatory Sandbox

2.1 Origins of the Concept

The first sandbox-like initiative was created in 2012 and the term 'regulatory sandbox' was not coined until 2015.[4] Since 2016, the sandboxing approach to digital innovation has been essentially developed in the context of financial technologies (FinTech). Regulatory sandboxes are now developed in other sectors such as health, legal services, aviation, transport, logistics and energy including the use of new, emerging technologies, such as AI, or the innovative use of existing technologies.[5]

---

[1] Proposal for a Regulation of the European Parliament and of the Council *laying down harmonised rules on Artificial Intelligence (Artificial Intelligence Act)* and amending certain Union legislative acts, COM(2021) 206 final, 21 April 2021. Referred to in footnotes as 'Draft AIA'.

[2] Regulation (EU) 2024/1689 of the European Parliament and of the Council *laying down harmonised rules on artificial intelligence* and amending Regulations (EC) No 300/2008, (EU) No 167/2013, (EU) No 168/2013, (EU) 2018/858, (EU) 2018/1139 and (EU) 2019/2144 and Directives 2014/90/EU, (EU) 2016/797 and (EU) 2020/1828 (Artificial Intelligence Act - AIA), OJ L 2024/1689, 14 May 2024.

[3] Ranchordas (2021), p. 3.

[4] Attrey et al. (2020), Jeník and Lauer (2017).

[5] Council Conclusions *on Regulatory sandboxes and experimentation clauses as tools for an innovation-friendly, future-proof and resilient regulatory framework that masters disruptive challenges*

In 2019, the EU institutions adopted the 'innovation principle' as a key driver of policies and regulatory initiatives in the field of research and development (R&D). This principle promotes 'smart, future-oriented regulation and policies designed to encourage innovation activities that can deliver socially and environmentally beneficial progress'[6] including in AI.[7] According to this principle, any EU regulatory initiative on new or emerging technologies and on the innovative use of existing technologies must consider the impact of the rules on innovation and ensure that they do not negatively affect the EU's ability to innovate and lead in science and technology. Therefore, in addition to supporting competition, ensuring coherence, predictability, effectiveness and efficiency, EU legislation should ensure that it is 'innovation-friendly' (i.e. technologically neutral and open to innovation), 'future-proof' (i.e. proactive, forward-looking and providing maximum legal clarity and certainty for a given sector), evidence-based, flexible (i.e. balanced in terms of stringency and, where possible, not too detailed to allow room for innovation), sustainable and resilient.[8] The innovation principle calls to pay particular attention to business and to the needs of small and medium-sized enterprises[9] (SMEs). In line with this principle, the EC and the Council of the EU consider regulatory sandboxes as tools to leverage the potential of innovation and to reduce potential negative impacts of regulations by improving the 'design software' of legislation at Member States and EU level.

Legally, regulatory sandboxes are based on experimentation clauses inserted within national or EU laws. Experimentation clauses are 'legal provisions which enable the authorities tasked with implementing and enforcing the legislation to exercise on a case-by-case basis a degree of flexibility in relation to testing innovative technologies, products, services or approaches'.[10] These clauses allow for temporary derogations to applicable rules under specific testing conditions and controls. The AIA Chapter VI (Articles 57–63) establishes an experimentation clause for AI regulatory sandboxes whether in-lab or in real-world conditions.[11] In-lab regulatory sandboxes have a specific nature. They do not involve early deployment of technologies in public physical or digital spaces nor potential lay individuals' testers

in the digital age, BETREG 27, 13,023/20, 16 November 2020, p. 3. Referred to in footnotes as 'Council Conclusions on Regulatory sandboxes'.

[6] EC FactSheet, The Innovation Principle, 13 December 2019.

[7] Communication from the Commission to the European Parliament, the European Council, the Council, the European Economic and Social Committee and the Committee of the Regions, *Artificial Intelligence for Europe*, COM/2018/237 final, 25 April 2018.

[8] Council Conclusions on Regulatory sandboxes, p.3; EC (2021) Better Regulation Toolbox. Chap. 3, Tool #22: Research & Innovation. https://ec.europa.eu/info/sites/default/files/br_toolbox_-_nov_2021_-_chapter_3.pdf

[9] See Art.2 EC Recommendation 2003/361/EC of 6 May 2003 *concerning the definition of micro, small and medium-sized enterprises*, OJ L 124/36, 20 May 2003.

[10] Rec.9 Council Conclusions on Regulatory sandboxes.

[11] Art.53(1a) Council of the EU, Consolidated compromise version of the draft AIA, Institutional Document: 2021/0106(COD), 13955/22, Brussels, 3 November 2022.

and more control is expected, by default, to manage risks. Complementary legal provisions will be necessary to ground the establishment of sectoral AI regulatory sandboxes at the EU and/or national level. These experimentation clauses shall specify the sandboxing context, purposes, boundaries, procedures and derogations granted to existing rules to allow testing innovative technologies in a regulatory favourable environment. They could make exceptions to a prohibition to deploy a certain technology, to certain requirements to obtain approval, to provide documentation, or consist in a catch-all clause.[12]

While regulatory sandboxes are relatively new policy instruments, several examples existed in different Member States and sectors, which, since 2019, allowed the identification of shared characteristics and differences which have been considered throughout the AIA drafting.[13]

2.2 *Purposes of AI Regulatory Sandboxes*

The EU aims to take the global lead in the AI market and to be attractive for innovators (AIS providers or prospective providers) without neglecting the conditions derived from shared values and fundamental rights protection.

A specific objective of the AIA is to ‘enhance governance and effective enforcement of existing law on fundamental rights and safety requirements’ applicable to AIS. In relation to this latter, the EC proposed: (a) the AI regulatory sandboxing scheme, and (b) other measures to reduce the regulatory burden and support SMEs and start-ups innovation.[14] Both aspects are complementary. The AI regulatory sandbox mechanism is envisaged as an additional measure to the setting up of a ‘governance system at Member States level, building on already existing structures, and a cooperation mechanism at Union level with the establishment of a European Artificial Intelligence Board’ (EAIB) intended to enforce the rules of the AIA.[15] Since the draft AIA, this approach has been supported by several stakeholders through consultations, especially by the Business Associations,[16] and has been welcomed by the European Parliament (EP) as an important tool to ‘introduce, in

[12] BMWK and Reallabore (2019) Making space for innovation. The Handbook for regulatory sandboxes, point 3.1.

[13] EC (2021) Better Regulation Toolbox, Tool #69, op. cit; Attrey et al. (2020) provide an international analysis of non-AIS specific sandbox examples; EC (2023), Directorate-General for Energy, Efthymiou V, Hartz N, McGranaghan M et al. Regulatory sandboxes – Policy report drafted by WG5’s regulatory sandboxes task force, Publications Office of the European Union, p. 28.

[14] EC (2021) Commission Staff Working Document Impact Assessment Accompanying the Proposal for a Regulation of the European Parliament and of the Council *laying down harmonised rules on Artificial Intelligence* (Artificial Intelligence Act) and amending certain Union legislative acts, Annexes, Part 1 and 2, SWD(2021) 84 final, 21 April 2021. Annexes, Part 1/2; see also Art.1(2)(g) AIA.

[15] Point 1.1 Explanatory Memorandum, Draft AIA.

[16] Point 3.1 Explanatory Memorandum, Draft AIA.

cooperation with regulators, innovative new ideas, allowing safeguards to be built into the technology from the start, thus facilitating and encouraging its market entry'.[17] In particular, SMEs face significant challenges when trying to access the EU internal market and the AIA could discourage talented innovators from investing, developing or deploying their products in the EU due to a high level of constraints. SMEs should not be left behind, even if they aim to be 'small-scale providers'.[18] SMEs have great innovative ideas, but they often lack the resources for legal advice and face difficulties accessing highly secured experimental environments and appropriate experimental data. AI regulatory sandboxes should temporarily solution these issues. In addition, they are also expected to decrease compliance costs for innovators, in particular for SMEs,[19] what necessitates a certain paradigm shift. For the EC, the adverse effects of compliance costs could 'divert resources from other purposes, potentially including research and innovation' and 'may also discourage innovation [...]' by serving 'defensive' R&D 'as opposed to R&D that itself aims to develop new technologies, processes or products'.[20] Therefore, AI regulatory sandboxes shall support SMEs in the development of their AIS at no or limited cost.

Regulatory sandboxes should not be seen as a way to desensitise innovators or to reduce the need for them to build internal capacity to monitor AIS compliance with legal, ethical and technical requirements. On the contrary, sandboxes empower innovators on the path of responsible research and innovation.

The AIA defines AI regulatory sandbox as a controlled framework set up by a competent authority, which offers providers or prospective providers of AIS the possibility to develop, train, validate and test, where appropriate in real-world conditions, an innovative AIS, pursuant to a sandbox plan for a limited time under regulatory supervision.[21] Sandboxes could be established in physical, digital or hybrid form and may accommodate physical as well as digital products.[22] None of the intermediary AIA versions qualified these activities as premarketing R&D in AI. Inscribing sandboxes as a specific framework for the conduct of AI R&D would have clarified the interplay between the sandbox legal regime and Articles 2(6), 2(8) and the related Recital 25 AIA exempting AIS or models developed and put into service solely for R&D purposes from the AIA application, prior to being placed on the market. Read as a whole, it appears that this exemption does not cover the provisions on AI regulatory sandboxes and testing in real-world conditions. On this latter, the AIA provides that 'testing in real-world conditions' means the temporary testing of an AIS for its intended purpose in real-world conditions outside a laboratory or

[17] EP Resolution of 12 February 2019 *on a comprehensive European industrial policy on artificial intelligence and robotics*, 2018/2088(INI).

[18] Art.3(3) Draft AIA. This term is not used anymore in the AIA.

[19] Art.62(2) AIA.

[20] EC (2021) Better Regulation Toolbox, Tool #22, op.cit. p. 175.

[21] Art.3(55) AIA.

[22] Rec.138, Art.3(55) AIA.

otherwise simulated environment, with a view to gathering reliable and robust data and to assessing and verifying the conformity of the AIS with the AIA requirements. This shall not qualify as placing the AIS on the market or putting it into service provided that all the conditions laid down in Article 57 or 60 are fulfilled.[23] This definition raises the question of whether AI-based clinical trials or investigation should be considered as testing in real-world conditions. That said, Recital 25 explicitly reminds that 'in any event, any research and development activity should be carried out in accordance with recognised ethical and professional standards for scientific research and should be conducted in accordance with applicable Union law', including both EU guidelines on AI ethics[24] and the applicability of the specific provisions for research in other regulations such as the EU General Data Protection Regulation (GDPR),[25] or of specific acts such as the EU Clinical Trial Regulation[26] or the Medical Device Regulations.[27] The validation objective pursued within sandboxes seems underdeveloped in the AIA while this specific purpose raises important issues, in particular for distinguishing AIS validation in a sandbox and other legal procedures necessary for getting AIS marketing authorisation, such as certification.

The AIA indicates that AI regulatory sandboxes shall aim at (**a**) improving legal certainty to achieve regulatory compliance with this Regulation or, where relevant, other applicable Union and national law; (**b**) supporting the sharing of best practices through cooperation with the authorities involved in the sandbox; (**c**) fostering innovation and competitiveness and facilitating the development of an AI ecosystem; (**d**) contributing to evidence-based regulatory learning; (**e**) facilitating and accelerating access to the Union market for AIS, in particular when provided by SMEs, including start-ups.[28] Regulatory sandboxes are tools for practicing regulatory fitness and simplification aiming to accommodate regulations to the recent market trends and product evolutions while safeguarding EU values, ethics and fundamental rights.[29]

---

[23] Art.3(57) AIA.

[24] AIHLEG (2019) Ethics Guidelines for Trustworthy AI; AIHLEG (2020) Assessment List for Trustworthy Artificial Intelligence (ALTAI) for self-assessment.

[25] Regulation (EU) 2016/679 of the European Parliament and of the Council of 27 April 2016 *on the protection of natural persons with regard to the processing of personal data and on the free movement of such data*, and repealing Directive 95/46/EC (General Data Protection Regulation), OJEU L 119/1, 4 May 2016.

[26] Regulation (EU) 536/2014 of the European Parliament and of the Council of 16 April 2014 *on clinical trials on medicinal products for human use*, and repealing Directive 2001/20/EC, OJEU L 158/1, 27 May 2014.

[27] Regulation (EU) 2017/745 of the European Parliament and of the Council of 5 April 2017 *on medical devices*, amending Directive 2001/83/EC, Regulation (EC) No 178/2002 and Regulation (EC) No 1223/2009 and repealing Council Directives 90/385/EEC and 93/42/EEC, OJEU L 117, 5 May 2017; Regulation (EU) 2017/746 of the European Parliament and of the Council of 5 April 2017 *on in vitro diagnostic medical devices* and repealing Directive 98/79/EC and Commission Decision 2010/227/EU, OJEU L 117/176, 5 May 2017.

[28] Art.57(9), Rec. 139 AIA.

[29] Frischhut (2022).

In no case, the purpose of sandboxes is full deregulation, but agile governance. They pursue a policy learning purpose in a context where, as summarised by Brynjolfsson in 2018, 'technologies are advancing rapidly and decision-makers are out of date.'[30] Regulatory sandboxes shall help reduce this gap through transparent and good faith collaborations between innovators and authorities in support of a novel approach to regulation of highly complex, emerging and often disruptive technologies. Authorities should be able to better understand the current technology developments, the underlying business models, risks and regulatory challenges in order to design appropriate legal, and perhaps ethical, requirements. By fostering confidence, synergies, incremental and dynamic regulatory construction, sandboxes serve an 'anticipatory innovation governance' model providing authorities with the ability 'to consistently perceive, understand and act on the future as it emerges in the present',[31] based on 'constant feedback loops between innovation and regulation'.[32] This shall enhance regulatory developments at national and EU level and ultimately boost the AI internal market development.

3 The Setting Up of AI Regulatory Sandbox

3.1 Organise Sandboxing

The setting up of at least one AI regulatory sandboxes per Member State is made mandatory by Article 57(1) AIA. The preliminary versions of the AIA allowed Member States to determine the establishment of an AI regulatory sandbox, which prompted criticism regarding the potential for fragmentation and the likelihood of counterproductive sandbox-shopping practices. Additionally, there were concerns about the scope and validity of the regulatory assessments performed by foreign authorities.[33] By considering the costs that could likely be important and that could not be afforded by all Member States, the AIA established a minimal obligation associated with facilitation measures. Firstly, a State may fulfil this obligation by participating in an existing sandbox, provided that participation provides an equivalent level of national coverage for the participating Member States. Secondly, the Commission may provide technical support, advice and tools for the establishment and operation of sandboxes.[34]

[30] Le Monde (2018). Hors Série – Dans la tête des robots. Entretien avec Erik Brynjolfsson, p. 27.

[31] OECD, OPSI Observatory of Public Sector Innovation. Anticipatory Innovation Governance. https://oecd-opsi.org/work-areas/anticipatory-innovation/

[32] Boucher (2022), p. 2.

[33] Truby et al. (2022).

[34] Art.57(1) AIA.

The first challenge for Member States in setting up a sandbox for AI is the identification of competent authorities[35] to be involved in the design and operations of the sandbox. The AIA does not provide for a single, unique, strict European model of regulatory sandbox but obliges the designation of national competent authorities[36] (at least one notifying authority and one market surveillance authority) to which a Member State assigns the responsibility for the implementation and application of the AIA, for coordinating the activities entrusted to that Member State, for acting as the single contact point for the Commission, and for representing the Member State at the EAIB.[37] The market surveillance authority might be best placed to establish and pilot the AI regulatory sandbox initiatives, whatever the number of collaborating authorities taking part in the operations. In March 2022, the EP proposed a revision introducing the EC as the responsible authority to establish AI regulatory sandboxes, under its direct authority, 'in collaboration with one or more Member State competent authorities'.[38] This proposed amendment was justified by the EP view that the EC draft was not going far enough in supporting innovation and SMEs in return for all the obligations that are fixed. This intended to ground the establishment of AI regulatory sandboxes at the EU level, piloted by the EC. The EP attached an interesting proposal for an Annex[39] setting forth detailed modalities for an EU AI Regulatory Sandboxing Program of the EC aiming at standardising the design, the services offered and the rules of participation. This Annex fixed minimal principles for encouraging participation in the sandbox and provided some useful information regarding potential components of AI regulatory sandboxes. These proposals have not been retained in the AIA that keeps a focus on Member States' authorities. However, the AIA allows the EC to set rules for a standardised regulatory sandbox model through future implementing acts[40] and the EAIB to contribute to the harmonisation of administrative practices regarding the functioning of AI regulatory sandboxes.[41] In any case, designated competent authorities must have sufficient resources[42] and collaborate with other authorities in respect of their tasks and powers, including through the EAIB or with regard to the EC AI Office.[43] The

[35] Of note the setting up of a sandbox for EU institutions, bodies and agencies is piloted by the European Data Protection Supervisor.

[36] Art.3(48), Art.70 AIA.

[37] Art.3(43) Draft AIA and Point 5.2.6 of its Explanatory Memorandum.

[38] Amendment 80 and 28, EP Draft Opinion of the Committee on Industry, Research and Energy (ITRE) for the Committee on Civil Liberties, Justice and Home Affairs on the proposal for a regulation of the European Parliament and of the Council *laying down harmonised rules on artificial intelligence* (Artificial Intelligence Act) and amending certain Union legislative acts (COM(2021)0206 – C9–0146/2021–2021/0106(COD)), Rapp. Eva Maydell, PE719.801v01–00, 3 March 2022. Referred to in footnotes as 'EP (2022) ITRE Draft Opinion'.

[39] Amendment 83, Annex IXa, EP (2022) ITRE Draft Opinion.

[40] Art.58 AIA.

[41] Art.66(d) AIA.

[42] Art.57(4), Rec.138 AIA.

[43] Art.57(10), (13), (14), (16) AIA.

AIA provides that the sandbox operates under the direct supervision and guidance of the competent authorities.[44] The quality of the regulatory experimentation will certainly depend on the quality of the expertise ensured by concerned authorities. The identification of competent authorities will consistently relate to the foreseen AIS legal qualification, to its intended purpose, and to the identification of applicable laws and regulations. Designation of the competent authorities will necessarily be a case-by-case process. The European Data Protection Board and the European Data Protection Supervisor (EDPB-EDPS) proposed to designate the data protection supervisory authorities (DPAs) in the EU Member States as the supervisory authorities for AI regulatory sandboxes by considering the importance of the data processing in AIS modelling and testing, and their experience in risks assessment of new technologies and in the protection of fundamental rights, in particular in personal data protection. Therefore, they should be the single contact point and have a coordination role with regard to other authorities taking part in a sandbox according to Article 70 AIA.[45]

A subsequent challenge is to build strengthened collaborations between the involved authorities. This includes the design of sandboxing policies and processes for data sharing and decision-making. Regarding data sharing, competent authorities must perform their tasks in the respect of confidentiality while allowing exchanges of confidential information with other authorities.[46] Similarly, it is important to articulate AI regulatory sandboxes with other pre-existing initiatives[47] at national or EU level. This could require important capacity building for a number of organisations. This is an important step for envisaging regional or local sandboxes[48] or the joint establishment, by several competent authorities of different Member States, of a sandbox at European level,[49] or to participate to a joint action initiated by the EC, such as the European blockchain regulatory sandbox in the context of the creation of a European Blockchain Services Infrastructure for the delivery of cross-border public services.[50] The authorities involved should also be able to connect with available pre-deployment services[51] including with the European Digital

[44] Art.53(1) Draft AIA. Art.57(6), Rec.139 AIA.

[45] EDPB-EDPS Joint Opinion 5/2021 on the proposal for a Regulation of the European Parliament and of the Council *laying down harmonised rules on artificial intelligence* (Artificial Intelligence Act), 18 June 2021, points 47–48. Referred to in footnotes as 'EDPB-EDPS Joint Opinion 5/2021'.

[46] Art.70(5), 78 AIA.

[47] Art.57(4) AIA.

[48] Art.57(2) and 62(1)(c) AIA.

[49] Art.57(1) AIA.

[50] EC europa.eu. Regulatory sandbox for blockchain and legal advice for ESBI production phase. https://digital-strategy.ec.europa.eu/en/funding/regulatory-sandbox-blockchain-and-legal-advice-ebsi-production-phase; and European blockchain regulatory sandbox for Distributed Ledger Technologies. https://ec.europa.eu/digital-building-blocks/sites/display/EBSI/Sandbox+Project

[51] Art.58(3) AIA.

Innovation Hubs (EDIHs)[52] run by non-profit organisations and federated networks proposing testing and validation environments for AIS, or with Testing and Experimentation Facilities[53] in order to orient participants in the sandbox towards relevant resources or infrastructures. Similarly, relationships with the European data spaces[54] which will be instrumental to regulatory sandboxes for accessing data will need to be established. An ongoing initiative to open the supercomputing capacity run by European High-Performance Computing Joint Undertaking to European startups developing AIS and AI infrastructure, could enable the large scale training and development of general purpose, trustworthy and ethical AI models and systems and constitute new sandboxing avenues.[55] Clear processes for cooperation between the authorities involved and, for example, the AI EDIHs providing regulatory advices, will be important to establish clear decision-making process, demarcation of roles, tasks and responsibilities, and to communicate these clearly to innovators.

In specific areas such as in health and biomedicine where scientific, ethical and deontological rules play a particularly important role, synergies with regulatory authorities at national or European level, such as the European Medicines Agency, and with competent Research Ethics Committees (RECs) shall be further considered. For instance, assuming that the regulatory sandbox framework applies to clinical investigations of innovative AI-based medical devices, the national and European medicines agencies should be able to be involved in early scientific consultation processes, as opened up by the European medical device regulations for certain high-risk devices, even though their consultation usually takes place at the time of certification upon request of notified bodies. Experimental projects falling within the remit of the RECs will be subject to prior ethical approval, but there are no details on further cooperation mechanisms that could be envisaged in the different sandbox contexts.

Generally, regulatory sandboxes are organised on a case-by-case basis. Two approaches are theoretically possible to set up a sandbox: one where the request (and identification of a regulatory barrier) is initiated by innovators, and another, where the regulator identifies legislative provisions for testing and calls for applications by interested organisations. Additional approaches or a combination of the above may emerge with time.[56]

---

[52] EC europa.eu. European Innovation Hubs. https://digital-strategy.ec.europa.eu/en/activities/edihs

[53] EC europa.eu. Sectorial AI Testing and Experimentation Facilities under the Digital Europe Programme: https://digital-strategy.ec.europa.eu/fr/activities/testing-and-experimentation-facilities

[54] Rec.68 AIA.

[55] EC Proposal for a Council Regulation amending Regulation (EU) 2021/1173 *as regards an EuroHPC initiative for start-ups to boost European leadership in trustworthy Artificial Intelligence* COM(2024)29 final, 24 January 2024.

[56] EC (2021) Better Regulation Toolbox, Tool #69.

For ensuring transparency with regard to innovators, the AIA gives a key role to the EC AI Office which shall be informed by national authorities about established or planned sandboxes,[57] and shall set up a single European dedicated interface[58] as an information platform about AI regulatory sandboxes. The AI Office will also organise awareness-raising communication campaigns about the obligations fixed by the AIA,[59] such as Member States. While it is not explicitly planned, the AI Office could also have a function of providing guidance for Member States' policy-makers regarding the methodology for setting up regulatory frameworks. Some interesting examples have been developed in the financial sector in this respect (Jeník & Schan 2020).[60]

3.2 *Supervise Sandboxing*

The AIA ensures that the involved authorities retain their role of control and can use their corrective powers to act in the case of problematic developments that are actually or potentially illegal.[61] This includes an element of discretionary powers left to authorities. The AIA specifies that 'any significant risks to health and safety and fundamental rights identified during the development and testing of such AI systems shall result in an adequate mitigation. National competent authorities shall have the power to temporarily or permanently suspend the testing process, or the participation in the sandbox if no effective mitigation is possible, and shall inform the AI Office of such decision'.[62] In order to limit their discretionary powers, the AIA provides that 'national competent authorities shall exercise their supervisory powers within the limits of the relevant law, using their discretionary powers when implementing legal provisions in respect of a specific AI regulatory sandbox project, with the objective of supporting innovation in AI in the Union'.[63] The AIA remains insufficiently specific as to the exact role and leeway of authorities in the exercise of their powers, thus letting room for divergent interpretation and activities. Indeed, as part of their supervision powers, authorities' have to approve sandboxing projects, to define derogatory measures, to oversee the AIS testing process, to provide relevant counseling to participants, to ensure data protection before and along the exercise, and to permanently keep their independence. This implies decision-making that have direct legal effects for applicants and participants that could potentially engage authorities' responsibility. We will highlight some of the specific

[57] Art.57(15) AIA.

[58] Art.57(17) AIA.

[59] Art.62(3)(c) AIA.

[60] Art.62(1)(b) AIA.

[61] Art.57(11) AIA.

[62] Article 57(11) AIA.

[63] Art.57(11) AIA.

complexities raised by the AIA provisions regarding the supervision of sandboxing that will need particular consideration.

3.2.1 The Data Protection and the Interplay with the GDPR

The supervision of AI regulatory sandboxes implies that authorities' check the legal bases for personal data processing for approving experimental projects. While the AIA reinstates the GDPR applicability to the processing undertaken in regulatory sandboxes, Article 59 AIA also directly creates a specific legal basis for the reuse of personal data in such a context.[64] This can be welcome as it ensures legal certainty. One could assume that this has been made possible by the specific control conditions and limitations attached to the experimentation which shall minimise risks for data subjects. In this regard, Article 59 must be read in conjunction with Recital 140 that notably provides for two, presumably cumulative, conditions. First, the further processing shall comply with Article 6(4) GDPR requiring either that this secondary use be either based on data subject's consent or on a Union or Member States law constituting a necessary and proportionate measure in a democratic society to safeguard the objectives mentioned in Article 23(1) GDPR, or that the controller perform a documented purpose compatibility test using the criteria mentioned in this Article 6(4) which shall demonstrate compatibility of the further processing so that the initial legal basis can also base the reprocessing. Second, the processing of special categories of personal data shall comply with Article 9(2)(g) GDPR so that it can inscribe as a necessary processing based on reasons of substantial public interest framed by EU and national laws. Additionally, it explicitly mentions that the AIA should not provide a legal basis in the meaning of Article 22(2)(b) GDPR, and its equivalent Article 24(2)(b) of Regulation 2018/1725,[65] concerning exemption from the data subject's right not to be subject to AI-based automated individual decision-making, including profiling. Regarding sandboxing performed for law enforcement activities, the reuse of personal data shall be without prejudice to Article 4(2) and 10 of the Law Enforcement Directive (LED)[66] establishing actionable legal bases. All the rights and obligations fixed under the GDPR and LED remain applicable in the context of sandboxes.

Article 59 AIA concentrates on personal data protection to be ensured along sandboxing and states cumulative conditions for a lawful further processing of personal data initially collected for another purpose. This includes that the AIS be developed for safeguarding a substantial public interest purpose in one of the areas

[64] Rec.140, Art.59 AIA.

[65] Regarding the processing performed by the Union institutions, bodies, offices and agencies.

[66] Directive (EU) 2016/680 of the European Parliament and of the Council of 27 April 2016 *on the protection of natural persons with regard to the processing of personal data by competent authorities for the purposes of the prevention, investigation, detection or prosecution of criminal offenses or the execution of criminal penalties, and on the free movement of such data*, and repealing Council Framework Decision 2008/977/JHA, OJ L 119, 4.5.2016, p.89–131.

identified under Article 59(1)(a), which include public safety, health (detection, diagnosis, prevention, control and treatment of disease or improvement of health-care systems); environmental protection (including green transition, climate change mitigation and adaptation); energy sustainability; safety and resilience of transport, mobility, critical infrastructure networks; efficiency and quality of public administration and public services. Authorities assess this condition according to their own legal and cultural references.[67] Like the GDPR, the AIA does not define substantial public interest, nor 'normal' public interest, even though it is a pivotal notion. Indeed, in the GDPR, they can be used to ground a legal basis for the processing as an alternative to data subject's consent, a derogation for the processing of special categories of personal data such as health or genetic/genomic data, derogations to individual rights in research, or an isolated data transfer. Moreover, the public interest is related to Article 5(1)(b) GDPR about the presumption of compatibility for personal data reuse for archiving purposes. It is assumed that the absence of definitions allows a necessary flexibility for implementing the GDPR. Nevertheless, some authors noticed that the use of different terms, within the GDPR, creates uncertainties for data controllers, and that, during the GDPR drafting, requests to precisely define this notion were heavily criticised 'since it would de facto mean that the Commission could control the Member States in areas that were politically sensitive'.[68] Some organisations tried to specify the notions of public interest and of substantial public interest through guidance. For instance, the Market Research Society and Social Research Association in the UK, with the support of their national data protection authority, the ICO, state that 'public interest should represent collective interests, promote wider values than purely economic or market issues and take account of interests of all, including future citizens'. In research sector, 'public interest should cover research of wide benefit to society and the economy. For research to be defined as in the public interest, it must be of benefit to the society. Its main aim should be to inform society or provide some broader benefit to the public'. They also propose a 'public interest test for research' for helping the assessment of public interest in light of individual rights and freedoms.[69] This test necessitates to identify the public interest being pursued, to confirm the necessity and proportionality of the envisaged processing for this public interest, and to confirm that individual rights do not override the public interest at stake. Nevertheless, there is still no standard at European level. The literature identifies remaining issues to determine the primacy of public interest to private and commercial interest and advocate for establishing some common criteria (in particular in relation with the draft European Health Data Space Regulation[70] and its interplay with the GDPR

[67] Going beyond what is planned under Art.58(3) AIA.

[68] Slokenberga (2021).

[69] MRS/SRA Guidance on the General Data Protection Regulation (GDPR) and data protection for social research, 2020, point 11, pp. 39–40.

[70] EC Proposal for a Regulation of the European Parliament and of the Council on the European Health Data Space, COM/2022/197 final, 3 May 2022.

regarding research).[71] While the scope of public interest can be very broad and is usually used to depart from individual consent and other rights or normal procedures, the use of the terms 'substantial public interest' appears as more limited and as necessitating detailed justification from the data controller, even if it can be built-in some specific purposes.[72] In health research, the appraisal of public interest and its substance is usually facilitated by the review of competent RECs.

Other conditions for benefiting from the AIA legal basis on the further use of personal data mainly relate to the respect of the principle of data minimisation,[73] to data protection impact assessment,[74] to the absence of effects on data subjects rights,[75] to technical and organisational safeguards for the data processing (including separated, isolated and protected data processing environment under the control of the prospective provider and subject to restricted access),[76] to data sharing limitation (any personal data created in the sandbox cannot be shared outside the sandbox),[77] to data storage limitation and mandatory erasure after sandboxing, to data transfer limitations and to documentation duties[78] about the project, process and results. The possibility to perform further processing for law enforcement purposes[79] necessitate the supervision of law enforcement authorities established under the LED, specific legal bases, and the respect of the same conditions for protecting other substantial public interests mentioned above. The legal basis provided by the AIA is strictly limited to personal data reuse in the context of the sandbox. This means that the AIA keeps both pre-existing legal fragmentations resulting from the GDPR and a certain leeway for EU and Member States laws which are excluding, or could exclude, the processing of personal data for other purposes than those explicitly mentioned in that law or that are 'laying down the basis for the processing of personal data which is necessary for the purpose of developing, testing or training of innovative AI systems'.[80] In line with this, another weakness of the AIA is that it does not mention specific legal bases for processing performed as a primary use of personal data which would have been collected *ad hoc*, for, or during, the sandboxing. Consequently, such initial processing must rely on a legal basis mentioned in

---

[71] 'Besides the nature of the funding, other aspects of research – such as the importance of research questions to the population under study, models of benefit sharing and equitable access to research databases – are yet to be considered when defining research in the public interest under the regulation'. See: Shabani (2022).

[72] E.g. ICO What are the substantial public interest conditions? https://ico.org.uk/for-organisations/uk-gdpr-guidance-and-resources/lawful-basis/special-category-data/what-are-the-substantial-public-interest-conditions/#substantial1

[73] Art.59(1)(b) AIA.

[74] Art.59(1)(c) AIA

[75] Art.59(1)(f) AIA.

[76] Art.59(1)(d) AIA.

[77] Art.59(1)(e) AIA

[78] Art.59(1)(h)-(j) AIA.

[79] Art.59(2) AIA.

[80] Article 59(3) AIA.

the GDPR, such as Article 6(1)(a) on data subject's consent, or Article 6(1)(f) on the pursuance of a legitimate interest of the data controller, but could also rely on a specific basis such as Article 6(e) on tasks carried out in the public interest. The same regarding the potential legal bases for primary processing of sensitive categories of personal data in the sandboxes. Reference to specific GDPR provisions of Article 9(2) allowing to exempt from the initial prohibition of processing sensitive data, in particular to Article 9(2)(g) on processing necessary for reasons of substantial public interest, or to Article 9(2)(j) concerning research in the public interest would have been help understanding the interplay between the AIA and the GDPR regarding AI regulatory sandboxes. Moreover, by considering the objectives, specificities and conditions attached to AI regulatory sandboxes, one could have expected full harmonisation of these actionable legal bases. This would have been a major added value of the AIA. Perhaps practicing AI regulatory sandbox supervision could ultimately lead to reconsider existing limited competencies of the EU to regulate scientific and technological research and innovation, and facilitate, based on use-cases, European legal harmonisation of controlled testing environments for (AI) research with regard to personal data protection.

3.2.2 The Legal Qualification of the Authorities Involved

The AI regulatory sandbox scheme questions the legal qualification of authorities, including established national data protection authorities, regarding the processing of personal data according to the GDPR, given their role and attached prerogatives. Could they be qualified as 'joint-data controllers'? This seems unlikely, except in very limited circumstances where data are provided by the authorities' services for sandboxing purposes. As 'supervisory authorities'? This could be challenged considering potential lacks of independence or their active role in guiding the processing. As 'third parties' with regard to the participant which is the data controller? Possibly, even if the authorities are presumably not processing the data as such for the experiments. These aspects deserve specific attention in the light of existing EDPB guidelines.[81] On this point, the EDPB-EDPS state that they 'are concerned that enabling reuse of data within the framework of the sandbox diverges from the accountability approach in the GDPR, where the accountability is placed on the data controller, not on the competent authority'.[82] The activities undertaken by authorities under this specific derogatory legal framework could be best described as data processing monitoring and generating research reports.[83]

[81] EDPB Guidelines 07/2020 on the concepts of controller and processor in the GDPR, V.2.1, 7 July 2021.

[82] EDPB-EDPS Joint Opinion 5/2021, point 65.

[83] Allen (2020), p. 304.

3.2.3 The Exercise of Authoritative Powers

The EDPB and EDPS raised other important issues regarding the interplay of the AI regulatory sandbox scheme, the GDPR and the LED, that need consideration. For example, in relation to potential conflicts between authorities' mandates, in relation to sanctions, and in relation to respecting their duty of independence due to potential conflicts of interest in the sandbox.[84] Regarding the implementation of authorities' corrective powers, authorities shall exercise their supervisory powers in a flexible manner within the limits of the relevant legislation, with the objective of supporting innovation. The AIA states that 'provided that the participant respect the sandbox plan and the terms and conditions for their participation [...] and follow in good faith the guidance given by the national competent authority, no administrative fines shall be imposed by the authorities for infringements of this Regulation'.[85] This grace period shall not prejudice the capacity to suspend or the testing or terminate participation where a significant risks to health and safety and fundamental rights identified during the development and testing cannot find mitigation.[86] The legal value of authorities' guidance remain obscure and could constitute binding instructions conditioning the participation. Such instructions could engage the responsibility of authorities in a number of ways, during the sandboxing but eventually after the release of the AIS.

In order to reduce the potential conflict of interests which could arise during the supervision of sandboxing, specific organisational safeguards could be envisaged. For instance, such a safeguard could consist in separating resources allocated to sandboxing tasks from those involved in compliance services granting, for example, authorisations. The latter could not take part in the sandbox during the development and testing phases but could only act at the last sandboxing stage, the validation of the AIS. Taking the example of the FinTech, it could be envisaged to create specialised sandbox units with a so-called 'Chinese Wall', defined as an inter-organisational or inter-service ethical barrier to prevent conflicts of interest[87] in the piloting of sandboxes.

The supervision of AIS testing in real-world conditions which inscribes, under request, into an AI regulatory sandbox context[88] and which is subject to specific conditions under Articles 60 and 61 AIA deserves specific attention. Indeed, while Article 76(3) AIA ensures that market surveillance authorities retain their competences and powers to ensure compliance with the AIA and eventually suspend or terminate the testing, Article 76(2) AIA allows them to grant exemptions from the requirements imposed on such testing outside regulatory sandboxes regarding the limited duration of the testing and the effective oversight by qualified personnel of

[84] EDPB-EDPS Joint Opinion 5/2021, point 62.

[85] Art.57(12) AIA.

[86] Art.57(11) AIA.

[87] Smith (2022).

[88] Art.58(4) AIA.

the participant.[89] This latter exemption should be subject to specific risk assessments and ethical review according to Union or national laws if the testing involves high-risk AIS or vulnerable populations.[90] The market surveillance authority of the Member States where the testing in real-world conditions is planned has 30 days after the project submission to object to such testing.[91] The decisions or objection to the testing in real-world conditions have to be motivated by authorities and communicated to other authorities potentially involved in the sandbox. They can be appealed.[92] The absence of similar provisions regarding other types of AI regulatory sandboxes is regrettable.

As a general rule related to the supervision of sandboxes, the involved market surveillance authorities have a right to obtain full access to training, testing and validation datasets used for the development of the high-risk AIS, and where relevant to the AIS source code, based on a necessity to fulfil their tasks under the AIA.[93] The access shall be performed through secured technologies enabling remote access.

3.2.4 The Potential Misuse of Sandboxing Results

At the end of the sandboxing period, the AIS provider or prospective provider can request to the national competent authority a written proof of the activities successfully carried out in the sandbox and an exit report. This documentation shall be considered by market surveillance authorities or notified bodies, as applicable, in the context of conformity assessment procedures or market surveillance checks.[94] Using AI regulatory sandboxes is not resulting in a certification of the AIS. One of the risks identified by the European Supervisory Authorities of FinTech (ESA),[95] and the EP[96] concerning FinTech regulatory sandboxes is the utilisation by commercial firms of their participation to regulatory sandboxes as an official 'stamp of approval' of their technology or service in their marketing strategy. Such a distortion creates confusion for potential deployers and customers and should clearly be prevented and sanctioned as a misleading practice. Issues surrounding the legal meaning of the term 'validation', as well as regarding the scope and legal value of the written proof and exit report, to not confound with sufficient official endorsements of the concerned product or service,[97] must be clarified.

[89] Art.60(4)(f) and (g).

[90] Art.60(3) AIA.

[91] Art.60(4)(b) AIA.

[92] Art.76(4) and (5) AIA.

[93] Art.74(12) and (13) AIA.

[94] Art.57(7) AIA.

[95] ESA Joint Report (2018) FinTech: Regulatory sandboxes and Innovation hubs, JC 2018 74, 2018.

[96] EP Study requested by the ECON Committee. Regulatory Sandboxes and Innovation Hubs for FinTech. Policy Department for Economic, Scientific and Quality of Life Policies, Directorate-General for Internal Policies, Author: Radostina PARENTI. PE 652.752. September 2020.

[97] Truby et al. (2022).

3.2.5 The Reporting and Collaboration at the European Level

Finally, the transparent annual reporting obligation of the national competent authorities towards the AI Office and the EAIB will definitely contribute to the European policy-learning and cross-fertilisation exercise. Such reporting shall detail the implementation, progress and results of AI regulatory sandbox practices, including best practices, incidents, lessons learnt and recommendations on their setup and, where relevant, on the application and possible revision of the AIA, including its delegated and implementing acts, and on the application of other Union law supervised by the competent authorities within the sandbox.[98] It could lead to further standardisation or innovation, such as new methodologies or technologies related to AIS transparency and explainability, accuracy, robustness and human oversight or for envisaging privacy-preserving techniques (e.g. federated learning, 'small data' learning) for the development of machine learning models. Nevertheless, there is no plan for mutual recognition of sandboxing mechanisms between EU countries.

In 2022, Spain launched a pilot of AI regulatory sandbox presented as a preparation for the implementation of the future AIA. This pilot is open to the participation of other EU Member States 'in what could potentially become a pan-European AI regulatory sandbox'. The launching communication states that the experience collected in the sandbox will be presented in the form of good practices and implementation guidelines and will be made available to all Member States and the EC.[99] Some initiatives in EU Member States such as France, Germany, Italy and neighbourhood countries such as Norway[100] or in non-EU-countries such as UK[101] are also interesting examples to consider in building a joint AI regulatory sandbox culture.

---

[98] Art.57(16) AIA.

[99] EC europa.eu (2022) First regulatory sandbox on Artificial Intelligence presented. https://digital-strategy.ec.europa.eu/en/news/first-regulatory-sandbox-artificial-intelligence-presented

[100] Datatilsynet. Sandbox for responsible artificial intelligence. https://www.datatilsynet.no/en/regulations-and-tools/sandbox-for-artificial-intelligence/

[101] ICO Regulatory Sandbox. https://ico.org.uk/for-organisations/regulatory-sandbox/; ICO Regulatory Sandbox Phase 1 Outcome Report: Gambling Commission. https://ico.org.uk/media/for-organisations/documents/4018589/official-sensitive-gambling-commission-regulatory-sandbox-report-phase-1-outcome-final-pdf.pdf

4 The Participation in AI Regulatory Sandbox

4.1 Access Criteria

The rules to be respected by Member States for elaborating detailed criteria of access to sandboxes will be adopted through EC implementing acts[102] for avoiding fragmentation while allowing flexibility for national implementation. But the AIA establishes open and equal access as the essential principle.[103] A privileged access to SMEs and startups is planned[104] as long as they fulfil the eligibility and selection criteria to be defined in the future. The sandbox can be accessed by a prospective AIS provider developing an innovative product or service, or by an actual AIS provider acting, for instance, in the context of an AIS substantial change necessitating a review of the acquired certification. In any case, access and use of the sandbox is voluntary and the concerned AIS must be in development, training, testing or validation phase in order to pretend to access. The AIA allows providers or prospective providers to submit applications in partnerships with deployers or any other relevant third parties.[105]

Regulatory sandboxes are targeting potentially high-risk AIS as legally defined by the AIA and in its Annex III, which are subject to Chapter III. But the AIA is not very explicit and does not exclude less risky AIS from accessing sandboxes. Authorities will appraise the projects case-by-case. The EP proposed that sandboxing applies to AIS for which full compliance with the requirements of Title III Chapter 2 [now Chapter III Section 2 AIA] requires an initial phase of placing the systems on the market or putting them into service and using the experience gained in such initial phase to further develop the AIS and to comply with the AIA.[106] The EC Better Regulation Tool #69 of 2021[107] mentions that sandboxes are generally only accessible for genuine innovation, meaning 'products and/or services and/or business models not currently available in the market, including where such innovation consists in a new use of an existing technology' (e.g. repurposing technology;

[102] Art.58 AIA.

[103] Art.58(2)(a) and (b) AIA.

[104] Art.62(1)(a) AIA.

[105] Art.58(2)(b) for sandboxes and 60(4)(h) AIA for testing in real world conditions outside sandboxes.

[106] Amendment 210, EP Draft Opinion of the Committee on Legal Affairs for the Committee on the Internal Market and Consumer Protection and the Committee on Civil Liberties, Justice and Home Affairs (JURI) on the proposal for a regulation of the European Parliament and of the Council laying down harmonised rules on artificial intelligence (Artificial Intelligence Act) and amending certain Union Legislative Acts (COM(2021)0206 – C9–0146/2021–2021/0106(COD)), Rapp. Axel Voss, 2021/0106(COD), PE719.827v01-00, 2 March 2022.

[107] The 'Better Regulation' guidelines and toolbox define the principles guiding the European Commission in each stage of the law-making process, from the drafting of new regulatory initiatives and proposals, to the monitoring and evaluation of existing legislation.

frugal innovation).[108] In addition, these innovations are expected to be developed in the public interest, meaning that they should 'deliver consumer and/or societal benefits, for instance by addressing unmet social needs or by contributing to policy objectives', for example, environmental protection, health strategy and others. There is no mention of criteria based on a preliminary qualification of the AIS. Another common access criterion highlighted by the EC in 2021 is the innovation readiness for testing. This criterion aims at allowing access to sandboxing where 'an innovation is advanced enough to be tested in a controlled environment/ market and the relevant legislative barrier is identified; theoretical links between an innovative idea and existing rules are not sufficient to set up a sandbox'. Hence a certain level of maturity in the development phase could be required for accessing sandbox environments. Criteria could emerge regarding minimal AIS Technological Readiness Levels[109] and could help in designing the experimental environment and determining the sandboxing period. Indeed, access to sandboxes is granted for a limited period of time that shall be appropriate to the complexity and scale of the project and could be extended by the national competent authority piloting the sandbox.[110] Testing in real-world conditions shall not exceed 12 months in total.[111] Questions regarding renewal or extensions conditions, limitations and consequences will need to be scrutinised to avoid unfair practices. The EC implementing acts shall provide further details.

The elaboration of a testing plan, as the experimental protocol, is required. This either takes the form of a 'sandbox plan' agreed between the participating provider and the competent authority describing the objectives, conditions, timeframe, methodology and requirements for the activities carried out within the sandbox[112] or of a 'real-world testing plan' that describes the objectives, methodology, geographical, population and temporal scope, monitoring, organisation and conduct of testing in real-world conditions.[113] The content of these documents should be standardised through EC implementing acts.[114]

Registration of the sandboxing project is performed for most of high risk AIS testing and integrated into the publicly available EU database controlled by the EC. Registration is mandatory for sandboxing consisting in a real-world testing which are ruled by Article 60 and 61 AIA and shall receive a unique single identification number.[115] The information collected for real-world testing registration is provided in Annex IX AIA. By principle, this information is confidential and only

[108] EC (2021) Better Regulation Toolbox. Chap. 8, Tool #69: Emerging methods and policy instruments. https://ec.europa.eu/info/sites/default/files/br_toolbox_-_nov_2021_-_chapter_8.pdf

[109] Lavin et al. (2022).

[110] Art.57(5) and 58(2)(h) AIA.

[111] Art.60(4)(f) AIA.

[112] Art.3(54) AIA.

[113] Art.3(53), 58(4) AIA.

[114] For sandbox plan, see Art. 58(1) AIA; for real-world testing plan see Art.60(1) AIA.

[115] Art.60(4)(c) AIA.

accessible to market surveillance authorities and the EC, unless the provider or prospective provider consent to publication.[116]

Innovators that are not established in the EU may access regulatory sandbox provided that they designate a legal representative of the AIS provider or prospective provider in the Union. For real-world testing, the transfer of data collected or processed to non-EU countries is forbidden by principle unless appropriate and applicable safeguards under Union law are implemented.[117]

Access shall be free-of-charge for SMEs, including start-ups, but it remains possible to recover potential costs engaged by authorities in a fair and proportionate manner.[118] In any case, eligibility and selection criteria shall be transparent and fair.

The other conditions concern the lawfulness of experiments performed during sandboxing and are attached to the experimentation type. The legal feasibility of the project conditions the setting up of a sandbox. This includes assessing the AIS potential regarding prohibited practices and the ability to comply with the specific rules governing real-world testing, in particular the requirement to obtain the informed consent of the individual prior to testing, in compliance with the AIA conditions.[119] By principle, informed consent to the participation in the real-world testing could be understood as consent to research participation. The AIA specifies that 'consent of subjects to participate in such testing under this Regulation is distinct from, and without prejudice to, consent of data subjects for the processing of their personal data under the relevant data protection law'.[120] This aligns the AIA with the EDPB opinion on consent to participation in clinical trials.[121] Considering the need for flexibility and the nature of derogatory measures granted in the context of sandboxes in real-world conditions the consent form shall be particularly clear and dynamic in order to accommodate to potential experimental adaptations such as modifications to the AIS intended purpose throughout the testing, or alterations in the testing environment. Clarity on the application of certain individual rights such as data portability[122] and other rights that can be exempted according to the GDPR where the processing is necessary for a task carried out in the pursuit of a public interest will also be essential to ensure proper individual participation.[123]

In any case, the provider or prospective provider remains liable regarding any damage caused to the subjects due to their participation.[124]

---

[116] Art.71(4), Rec.141 AIA.

[117] Art.60(4)(e) AIA.

[118] Art.58(2)(d) AIA.

[119] Art.60(4)(i), 60(5) and 61 AIA.

[120] Rec.141 AIA.

[121] EDPB Opinion 3/2019 concerning the Questions and Answers on the interplay between the Clinical Trial Regulation (CTR) and the General Data Protection Regulation (GDPR) (art.70.1.b), 23 January 2019.

[122] EDPB **Guidelines on the right to data portability under Regulation 2016/679, WP242 rev.01, 2017.**

[123] Art.89(2) GDPR.

[124] Art.57(12) and 60(9) AIA.

Eligibility and selection criteria shall be further defined through EC implementing acts.[125] Harmonising related evaluation procedures could also be envisaged.

4.2 Added Value for Participants

Participation to regulatory sandbox means access to relevant testing environment and to the expertise of relevant competent authorities in law, ethics and governance. As the EP noted, AIS 'can take many forms, which are influenced by at least two important and varying elements: (i) the environment where the AI-system is being used and (ii) the goal that is set to achieve'. '[…] Different environments and different goals can lead to manifold manifestations of the same software or system, and while a system can be seen as 'intelligent' in one environment and towards a certain goal, it may be seen as 'unintelligent' in a different scenario'.[126] The AIS operational environment constantly challenges its data collection and processing capabilities, the relevance of the machine learning model and of algorithms on which the ability to interact, adapt and learn appropriately to achieve its intended purpose depends. Therefore, access to sandboxes seems particularly relevant for evolving and/or autonomous AIS, which are subject to significant changes during their lifetime due to their continuous learning capability and evolving environments. Defining the initial purpose of the AIS is a critical step in determining the appropriate experimental environment and adapting risk mitigation strategies. In this respect, sandboxing should allow identifying risks to health and safety and fundamental rights, test mitigation measures for identified risks, and demonstrating compliance with the AIA and other relevant Union and National legislation supervised within the sandbox.[127]

Participation shall ease access to quality data, either by allowing special collection during the experimentation, in particular from individuals consenting to participate in the real-world conditions testing, or by facilitating access to other large databases, or data space, through specific sandbox services[128] therefore helping to reduce sources of bias.

Sandboxing should provide access to the best testing methodologies to demonstrate appropriate accuracy, transparency, accountability, robustness and cybersecurity to ensure the resilience, security and ethics of AIS. Cyberattacks simulations including penetration testing or red teaming approaches and methodologies should be considered thereof.[129]

---

[125] Art.58(2)(a) AIA.

[126] EP Study requested by the JURI Committee, Artificial Intelligence and Civil Liability, PE 621.926, 2020, p.19.

[127] Rec.139 AIA.

[128] Rec.140 AIA.

[129] Parida (2023); Field (2022); Aydiner (2022).

Authorities' guidance should help fixing the legal qualification of the AIS, facilitate the elaboration of the AIS technical documentation, as detailed in Annex IV and in Article 11(1) AIA and prepare for accountable governance practices (e.g. for practicing and managing consent in real-world testing). This could lead to a reconsideration of the initial risk-based classification of an AIS. For example, an AI-enabled medical device is systematically classified as a high-risk AIS,[130] following what we might consider a precaution approach. However, under the sandbox, the documented assessment and adaptation of the AIS could prove that it does not pose a significant risk of harm to the health, safety or fundamental rights of natural persons, including by not materially influencing the outcome of decision-making, and fulfil the specific criteria of Article 6(3) of the AIA, thus justifying the reclassification of the AIS in the limited risk class. Regarding general-purpose AI models,[131] Articles 51 and 52 open a procedure based on, yet very vague, criteria to justify not classifying these models as posing a systemic risk.[132] Participation in AI regulatory sandbox shall help implementing these provisions. In addition, it should facilitate the respect of transparency requirements[133] and the development of voluntary code of conducts[134] for reclassified AIS.

As some authors noticed, the AIA 'imposes the same strict liability regime for both sandboxed and non-sandboxed high-risk AI applications'.[135] In this regard, they argue in favour of the regulatory sandboxes scheme as a way to alleviate the drawbacks attached to a strict liability regime that can adversely affect the innovation. Nevertheless, the AIA does not provide for a presumption of compliance for sandboxed technologies even if legal risks based on negligence or intentional misconduct of the provider should dramatically decrease after successful participation. However, AIS sandboxing should provide a competitive advantage to help innovators to better design and invest in necessary or strategic features of their AIS, in short, to innovate responsibly. Finally, it should facilitate the achievement of other regulatory procedures and conformity assessments required for the AIS.

[130] Art.6(1)(a) AIA.

[131] As defined in Art. 3(63) AIA.

[132] 'Systemic risk' means a risk that is specific to the high-impact capabilities of general-purpose AI models, having a significant impact on the Union market due to their reach, or due to actual or reasonably foreseeable negative effects on public health, safety, public security, fundamental rights, or the society as a whole, that can be propagated at scale across the value chain. Art. 3(65) AIA.

[133] Art. 50 AIA.

[134] Art. 95 AIA.

[135] Truby et al. (2022).

5 Conclusion

AI regulatory sandboxes are controlled testing environments available to AIS provider or prospective provider that facilitates anticipatory risk assessment and mitigation under the supervision of competent authorities, before releasing a high-risk AIS in the EU. Participation is open, with priority access granted to SMEs, and not mandatory, and aims at facilitating regulatory compliance-by-design by considering technical and non-technical requirements attached to trustworthy AI. Regulatory sandboxes should help innovators reaching the market and meeting potential adopters' expectations. As regulatory learning laboratories, AI regulatory sandboxes should serve cross-fertilisation exercise for filling the gap between regulators and innovators in an agile compliance governance. By relying on transparent exchanges between stakeholders, sandboxing technologies shall result in an improved AI and regulatory literacy serving a dynamic regulatory environment for AI innovation in the EU. This novel approach legally bases an explicit authorities' statutory mission to support innovation.

Legal and practical issues still need to be addressed, notably through the specific EC implementing acts for AI regulatory sandboxes, in order to harmonise practices for their establishment, development, implementation, operation and supervision. These acts should address issues related to the division of responsibilities, to access criteria and procedures, to services offered, to consent procedures for real-world testing, to the concept and process of establishing an EU-wide sandbox, and diminish the risk of regulatory cacophony at EU level. Despite these shortcomings, AI regulatory sandboxes promise to create an effective win-win environment for innovation and their wide use should be supported as a new standard for eligible AIS.

References

Allen H (2020) Sandbox boundaries. Vand J Ent Technol Law 22(2):299–321

Attrey A, Lesher M, Lomax C (2020) The role of sandboxes in promoting flexibility and innovation in the digital age. In: OECD Going Digital Toolkit Policy Note 2

Aydiner C (2022) Critical thinking and effective communication in security domains. In: Masys AJ (ed) Handbook of security science. Springer, Cham. https://doi.org/10.1007/978-3-319-51761-2_2-1

Boucher P (2022) What if AI regulation promoted innovation? At a Glance. EP STOA European Parliamentary Research Service – EPRS, PE 729.515

Field H (2022) How Microsoft and Google use AI red teams to "stress test" their systems. Emerging Tech Brew

Frischhut M (2022) The ethical spirit of EU values: status quo of the union of values and future direction of travel. Springer. ISBN:978-3-031-12713-7

Jeník I, Lauer K (2017) Regulatory sandboxes and financial inclusion. https://www.cgap.org/sites/default/files/Working-Paper-Regulatory-Sandboxes-Oct-2017.pdf

Jeník I, Schan D (2020) How to build a regulatory sandbox: a practical guide for policy makers. Technical guide. CGAP, Washington, DC

Lavin A, Gilligan-Lee CM, Visnjic A et al (2022) Technology readiness levels for machine learning systems. Nat Commun 13:6039. https://doi.org/10.1038/s41467-022-33128-9

Le Monde (2018) Hors-Série – Dans la tête des Robots, Entretien avec Erik Brynjolfsson, Mars-Mai 2018

Parida B (2023) Red teaming vs pen testing: understanding the distinctive nature and purpose of cybersecurity tactics. Wevolver Epub. https://www.wevolver.com/article/red-teaming-vs-pen-testing-understanding-the-distinctive-nature-and-purpose-of-cybersecurity-tactics

Ranchordas S (2021) Experimental regulations for AI: sandboxes for morals and mores. University of Groningen Faculty of Law Research Paper No. 7/2021. https://papers.ssrn.com/sol3/papers.cfm?abstract_id=3839744

Shabani M (2022) Will the European Health Data Space change data sharing rules? Science 375(6587):1357–1359. https://doi.org/10.1126/science.abn4874

Slokenberga S (2021) Setting the foundations: individual rights, public interest, scientific research and biobanking. In: Slokenberga S, Tzortzatou O, Reichel J (eds) GDPR and biobanking, Law, governance and technology series, vol 43. Springer, Cham. https://doi.org/10.1007/978-3-030-49388-2_2

Smith L (2022) How the ethical wall works on Wall Street. Investopedia.com. https://www.investopedia.com/articles/analyst/090501.asp

Truby J, Brown R, Ibrahim I, Parellada O (2022) A sandbox approach to regulating high-risk artificial intelligence applications. Eur J Risk Regul 13(2):270–294. https://doi.org/10.1017/err.2021.52

Contextualisation of the AI Act Within Existing Legal Frameworks

The AI Act and Data Protection: The Interplay Between Artificial Intelligence and Data: The AI Act and the GDPR

Pin Lean Lau

Contents

Abstract This chapter examines the intricate relationship between the European Union Artificial Intelligence Act (AI Act) and the General Data Protection Regulation (GDPR), exploring their synergies, tensions, and regulatory implications. As AI systems rely on vast amounts of personal data, ensuring alignment between AI governance and data protection frameworks is crucial for safeguarding fundamental rights and regulatory consistency. The AI Act, while primarily a product safety law, introduces obligations related to transparency, accountability, and human oversight, intersecting with the GDOR provisions in data minimisation, automated decision-making, and privacy by design. The chapter critically assesses the challenges posed by AI's reliance on personal data, including the debiasing exception, conformity assessments, and fundamental rights impact assessments. It

P. L. Lau (✉)
Brunel Law School | Centre for Artificial Intelligence: Social & Digital Innovations, Brunel University of London, Kingston Lane, Middlesex, Uxbridge, UK
e-mail: PinLean.Lau@brunel.ac.uk

V. L. Raposo (ed.), *The European Artificial Intelligence Act*, Law, Governance and Technology Series 78, https://doi.org/10.1007/978-3-031-98406-8_12

also evaluates enforcement complexities, particularly the coordination between national supervisory authorities under both regulations. Given the AI Act's adoption and imminent enforcement, the chapter advocates for ongoing dialogue to refine regulatory approaches and ensure that AI development remains both innovative and ethically sound within the EU's legal landscape.

1 Introduction

One of the most vital components in leveraging the full benefits of artificial intelligence (AI) systems and technologies is, undoubtedly, data. Data, in all its forms and iterations, including big data, has permeated our digital worlds and technologically revolutionised our ways of living. The rise of big data in AI, especially 'dominated and influenced by the marketing efforts of large software and hardware developers, focuses on predictive analytics and structured data'.[1] There are also other components on non-analytics-ready unstructured data forms, such as video data, that further complicates effective data protection mechanisms, especially if they are not adequately archived.[2] With the meteoric rise of the use and reliance on data in contemporary societies, one of the key concerns that accompanied its proliferation was the standards, measures and protection that could be accorded to data subjects. Hence, Regulation (EU) 2016/679 (General Data Protection Regulation, or GDPR)[3] (replacing the Data Protection Directive 1998)[4] continued to represent a global-reaching data protection regulation of its kind that aimed to do just this, and is one of the most important fundamental rights law in Europe.

Given the vast amounts of data that is used in most AI systems, especially in the design and deployment of algorithms for automated decision-making processes, there is reasonable justifiability in looking towards data protection legislation, particularly the inherent nexus between them. Since the GDPR will apply to most of the processing of personal data in the EU, and can have effect beyond the borders of the European Union (EU), most AI systems may come within the scope of GDPR application if it is used to process any kind of personal data or information. This is possible even if the GDPR does not explicitly mention AI. AI systems often struggle to distinguish between personal and non-personal data, which means they likely

[1] Gandomi and Haider (2015), p. 137.

[2] ibid.

[3] 'REGULATION (EU) 2016/679 OF THE EUROPEAN PARLIAMENT AND OF THE COUNCIL - of 27 April 2016 - on the Protection of Natural Persons with Regard to the Processing of Personal Data and on the Free Movement of Such Data, and Repealing Directive 95/46/EC (General Data Protection Regulation) 88.

[4] Directive 95/46/EC of the European Parliament and of the Council of 24 October 1995 on the protection of individuals with regard to the processing of personal data and on the free movement of such data 1995.

process personal data at some point during their lifecycle.[5] While the GDPR doesn't directly address AI, its provisions on automated decision-making directly impact AI systems.[6] However, defining clear 'processing purposes' for AI can be challenging due to the diverse applications and data collection involved in AI development.[7] Notwithstanding, there is certainly overlap between the AI and the GDPR, and in this manner, there exists a symbiotic relationship between AI and data, where AI is nugatory without data, and data (including all forms of treatment of data) would be a near-impossible undertaking without AI.[8]

Whilst the intention of the European Union Artificial Intelligence Act[9] (hereinafter 'AI Act') is to encompass much more beyond data protection, such as specific risks, requirements, obligations and assessments of AI systems—the data protection provisions therein should not only be read in tandem with the GDPR and/or other existing data protection regulations in Europe—but should also complement the enforcement capabilities of the GDPR. In practice, despite the EU's proposal in the AI Act to set up the European Artificial Intelligence Board (EAIB), whose role is similar to the European Data Protection Board (EDPB) under the GDPR, one of its biggest challenges would be to harmonise and effectively implement and enforce the legislation across all member states. As scholars in the field already note,[10] some EU member states are struggling to implement the GDPR,[11] with others facing technical capacity, expertise and staffing issues in such implementation.[12] Whilst the implementation and enforcement capacities of the EAIB together with national authorities is idealistic, at best, it is possible that the capacity of different member states to supervise and enforce it effectively is more likely than not.[13]

Hence, this chapter maps out the key provisions in the AI Act dealing with data protection in AI systems, and seeks to find synergies and overlaps between these provisions and the GDPR. This comparative assessment is important for purposes of aligning a larger-scale need to ensure that all facets of data protection and fundamental rights in AI systems are sufficiently conveyed. Whilst the AI Act has now been formally adopted, and will come into force in the immediate future, there may

---

[5] Clark et al. (2024).

[6] Article 22, GDPR.

[7] Hunton Andrews Kurth, 'Artificial Intelligence and Data Protection - How the GDPR Regulates AI' https://www.informationpolicycentre.com/uploads/5/7/1/0/57104281/cipl-hunton_andrews_kurth_legal_note_-_how_gdpr_regulates_ai__12_march_2020_.pdf

[8] 'Big Data and Artificial Intelligence: How They Work Together' (*Maryville Online*, 21 July 2017) https://online.maryville.edu/blog/big-data-is-too-big-without-ai/

[9] Proposal for a REGULATION OF THE EUROPEAN PARLIAMENT AND OF THE COUNCIL LAYING DOWN HARMONISED RULES ON ARTIFICIAL INTELLIGENCE (ARTIFICIAL INTELLIGENCE ACT) AND AMENDING CERTAIN UNION LEGISLATIVE ACTS 2021 ({SEC(2021) 167 final} - {SWD(2021) 84 final} - {SWD(2021) 85 final}).

[10] Lilkov (2021), p. 171.

[11] Lomas (2020).

[12] Ryan and Toner (2020).

[13] Lilkov (n 10) 171.

still be room for open dialogues to address any shortcomings for strategic redress and to ensure congruence in scope and application with the GDPR. For avoidance of doubt, this chapter shall only address the relationship between the AI Act and data protection in the GDPR; and excludes other EU data legislation such as the Data Governance Act, Data Act, Digital Services Act, and European Health Data Space Act, amongst others.

2 The Interplay Between the AI Act and the General Data Protection Regulation (GDPR)

The AI Act, being an innovative juridical construct, accentuates the EU's anticipatory disposition vis-à-vis the growing influence of AI upon societal fabric. Accentuating transparency, elucidation, and human supervision, the AI Act aspires to shield democratic principles whilst alleviating prospective hazards concomitant with AI mechanisms. Embodying a risk-oriented scheme, the AI Act classifies AI systems, imparting significant weight upon safety and essential freedoms concomitantly propelling responsibility and technical sturdiness.[14] Covering doctrines of responsibility and anthropocentric advancement, the EU endeavours to steer AI maturation in concert with ethical introspections and juridical requisites, thereby tackling the concerns relevant to data safeguarding and confidentiality.[15] This deliberate propulsion towards conscientious AI regulation guarantees that legislative measures encourage innovation whilst sustaining ethical concerns, highlighting exigencies for unambiguous directives and harmonised initiatives to deal with any complications surrounding extant legislation such as the GDPR and other data regulations.[16]

Maintaining rigorous data protection measures within AI domains is critical for adhering to regulatory standards and protecting individual rights. The AI Act is aimed at regulating AI systems' deployment into the market, highlights the imperativeness of transparency, explicability, and human oversight in AI development. This legislative effort is congruent with the wider digital strategy of the European Commission, striving to create a leading legal structure for AI oversight that mostly emphasises safety and fundamental rights.[17] By spotlighting human rights considerations, embedding concepts of human supervision, technical sturdiness, mitigation of biases, and privacy factors in AI functions, organisations can align with the AI Act's imperatives and nurture a culture of ethical and responsible AI use and deployment. These mandates align with the critical need to responsibly remove biases from AI systems, especially in high-risk areas, to lessen potential biased impacts and boost overall data security and minimalisation protocols.[18] Adopting these

[14] Gikay et al. (2023).

[15] ibid.

[16] Raposo (2022), p. 88.

[17] European Commission (2024).

[18] van Bekkum and Borgesius (2024).

principles can steer organisations in fostering trust, clarity, and regulatory compliance in their AI ventures. By integrating data protection and AI regulation harmoniously, the EU can nurture an innovation-driven technological sphere that also honours fundamental ethical values and regulatory standards, epitomising how crucial data protection is in the forward movement of AI.

The key commonality between the AI Act and GDPR is the legal basis of Article 16 of the TFEU, mandating the EU to lay down rules relating to the protection of individuals in the field of processing personal data. The text of the AI Act expressly recognises the relationship with the GDPR. In very similar recognition to the GDPR, the AI Act's specific principles in Recital 27 of the AI Act not only align with the with GDPR, but also include human agency and oversight, technical robustness and safety, privacy and data governance, transparency, diversity, non-discrimination, fairness, and social and environmental well-being. Whilst it is expected that the AI Act and GDPR will work together in congruence, the practical difficulties of doing so due to the nature of AI technologies in itself may prove to be challenging. This will be further elaborated in Sect. 3 of this chapter.

2.1 *Data Protection in the AI Act*

The purposes of the AI Act involve a complicated strategy aimed at promoting ethical and clear artificial intelligence practices while guaranteeing strong data protection measures. The Act outlines seven basic principles: the necessity of human agency and oversight, human agency and oversight; technical robustness and safety; privacy and data governance; transparency; diversity, non-discrimination and fairness; societal and environmental well-being and accountability. These principles together aim to direct the growth and usage of AI systems within the EU, with a main goal of maintaining ethical standards and protecting people's privacy rights.[19] By stressing the need for human supervision, accountability methods, and strict technical standards, the AI Act tries to build trust in AI technologies and reduce potential dangers linked with their use. Through its all-encompassing structure, the AI Act aims to balance innovation with responsible AI use, setting an example for worldwide AI regulation and data protection standards in the digital age.

The ambit concerning the AI Act's applicability paired with implications linked to data protection remains important in ensuring ethicality and legal compliance vis-a-vis AI systems operational within the EU.[20] The to-be-considered debiasing exception harboured within the AI Act[21] raises numerous inquiries vis-à-vis utilisation of special categories of data purposed for bias detection and rectification within high-risk AI frameworks. This highlights the necessity for concretely outlined permissible engagements and prospective threats to privacy. Correlating these

[19] Raposo (n 16).

[20] Comandé (2020).

[21] van Bekkum and Borgesius (n 18).

perspectives within the AI Act's scope is necessary for nurturing transparent, accountable, and responsible AI oversight amidst confronting challenges relevant to data protection in this technological relationship.

2.2 The GDPR and Implications for AI

The reciprocal action between the GDPR and the AI Act reveals a complex domain of data safeguarding and AI enactment within the EU vicinity. For example, the approach of the GDPR towards emotional data raises apprehensions regarding thorough protection and accordance with evolving technological fields such as affective computing.[22] A key issue in the protection of emotional data is the failure to account for the role of emotions in data processing and decision-making. The GDPR, due to its focus on categories of data and individual control rights lacks the recognition that different types of data can evoke various emotional responses which are context-dependent.[23] AI systems, such as affective computing, in the meantime, need to tether the fine line between what is permissible and what the GDPR seeks to protect. This observation, as an example, underscores the indispensable need for a meticulous scrutiny of the overlap between GDPR fundamentals like data minimisation and fairness with AI Act dicta., The reality of the ramifications of these legislations is that they often appear to have potentially contradictory positions, whilst clearly possessing similar principles, such as transparency and accountability.[24]

There are several ways in which the GDPR influences AI development (especially those that use Large Language Models). For example, the GDPR mandates explicit consent for personal data usage by AI models. This means that AI developers must ensure that consent is voluntary, specific, informed and unambiguous.[25] Whilst AI can process data based on 'legitimate interest'[26] in some circumstances, this must be balanced against the rights of the data subject. In connection with data minimisation and restriction of purposes, the GDPR emphasises using only the minimal necessary data for a specific purpose. This means that AI systems must avoid unnecessary data collection, usage, or manipulation. In the event the data needs to be repurposed, additional consent is required for these other purposes.

In addition, AI systems, including Large Language Models (LLMs) should also employ anonymisation and pseudonymisation techniques in accordance with the

[22] Häuselmann et al. (2023).

[23] Clifford (2024).

[24] Common to both the GDPR and AI Act is the principles of transparency and accountability (Arts. 13 through 15 in the GDPR; Arts. 11 through 13, and 50 AI Act). Where the GDPR requires transparency in how personal data is processed, the AI Act demands transparency in how AI systems function and they risk they pose. However, this can sometimes conflict with the GDPR's requirements if the AI systems processes personal data.

[25] Article 7, and Article 13, GDPR.

[26] Article 13(1)(d), GDPR.

GDPR. Anonymisation ensures permanent data de-identification, whilst pseudonymisation replaces private identifiers with pseudonyms.[27] In the GDPR, 'pseudonymisation' is defined as the processing of personal data in a way that prevents it from being directly linked to a specific individual without the use of additional information.[28] This additional information must be kept separately and protected by technical and organisational measures to ensure that the personal data cannot be attributed to an identified or identifiable natural person. Consequently, pseudonymous personal data is still considered personal data because the use of 'additional information' can potentially lead to the identification of individuals. In contrast, anonymous data cannot be associated with specific individuals.[29] Once data becomes truly anonymous, where individuals are no longer identifiable, it falls outside the scope of the GDPR. These two methods balance privacy protection with insights derived from large datasets. Since the GDPR demands robust data protection practices, AI systems must integrate security measures to prevent data breaches and unauthorised access.[30] Both AI developers and users share responsibility for GDPR compliance, which includes record-keeping[31] and impact assessments.[32]

Under the GDPR, specific rights would also be granted to individuals regarding their data, and this would also apply to their data in AI models or systems.[33] For example, individuals must be able to access their data and reuse it in anywhere else they wish.[34] Individuals are also given a right to explanation, to understand the decision-making processes which are essential for transparency.[35] Individuals also have a right to be forgotten, and can request complete erase of their personal data from any AI system.[36] It is realistic to be reminded at this juncture that unlike the AI Act, which is ultimately a very comprehensive product safety law, the GDPR's essence is fundamental rights in nature, ensuring that individuals are imbued with a wide range of rights in relation to the processing of their data. These protections are vital, as earlier debates centred around the GDPR protections for individuals against forms of Automated Decision-Making (ADM) and profiling, and whether Article 22 of the GDPR was sufficiently applied by the courts and data protection authorities.[37] This issue may prove to be contentious when it comes to the role of AI vis-à-vis ADM.

---

[27] Article 4(5) GDPR.

[28] ibid.

[29] AEPD, '10 Misunderstandings Related to Anonymisation' https://www.edps.europa.eu/system/files/2021-04/21-04-27_aepd-edps_anonymisation_en_5.pdf

[30] Article 32, GDPR.

[31] Article 30, GDPR.

[32] Article 35, GDPR.

[33] Chapter 3, Rights of the Data Subject, Articles 12–23, GDPR.

[34] Article 15, GDPR.

[35] Article 12, GDPR.

[36] Article 17, GDPR.

[37] Vale and Zanfir-Fortuna (2022).

2.3 The Impact of AI on Data Protection

As AI technologies continue to advance, their impact on data protection becomes increasingly significant. Organisations' increasing reliance upon AI technologies to streamline various operational processes along with the analysis of enormous data quantities raises significant queries regarding privacy and security implications. The introduction of AI creates unprecedented challenges, including safeguarding sensitive datasets, while ensuring compliance with regulations. With AI systems proficiently processing and interpreting data sets at unparalleled velocities, escalating concerns surrounding potential breaches and the inappropriate utilisation of personal data are ever-present. Just as the GDPR has implications for AI, the reverse can also be understood to be true.

Data breaches are one particularly significant threat in the realm of data protection, with ramification potential for individuals and organisations alike. In this regard, Article 25 of the GDPR emphasises data protection 'by design and by default.' Controllers must implement appropriate technical and organisational measures to ensure effective compliance with data protection principles. These measures should be considered throughout the entire design process of AI systems, rather than as an afterthought. For instance, collecting AI training data from reliable sources with accurate information is one way to meet this requirement. Additionally, relying solely on the AI system for compliance is discouraged, and regular checks on the reliability of AI results are recommended.[38]

In the meantime, as AI continues to revolutionise industries and transform how data is utilised, the need for robust technological solutions to enhance data protection has become paramount. Traditional methods of safeguarding data are no longer adequate in the age of AI, which introduces new complexities and challenges. One effective strategy for bolstering data protection in this rapidly evolving landscape is the implementation of advanced encryption techniques. Encryption plays a crucial role in securing sensitive information from unauthorised access, ensuring that data remains confidential and integral.[39] Additionally, the development of AI-powered tools for threat detection and response can provide organisations with real-time insights into potential security breaches, as AI algorithms can themselves play an important role in analysing diverse data sources to identify anomalies that might indicate a data breach.[40] These sources include network traffic, user behaviour, and system logs. By processing large volumes of data quickly, AI can detect subtle patterns that human analysts might miss. Leveraging these cutting-edge technologies mean that businesses and institutions can adapt to the demands of safeguarding data in the era of AI, reinforcing their defences against ever-evolving cyber threats.

---

[38] Hunton Andrews Kurth (n 7) 9–10.

[39] Liu et al. (2022), p. 21.

[40] Quiroz-Vazquez (2023).

For instance, an AI-based intrusion detection system (IDS) learns normal network behaviour and raises alerts when deviations occur.[41] These deviations could signal unauthorised access or malicious activity. It uses a variety of anomaly detection techniques for anomaly detection, such as statistical methods, machine learning models, and behavioural analysis.[42] This is not to say that these methods are foolproof, as AI systems may generate false alarms due to legitimate variations in behaviour or noisy data.[43] Striking the right balance between detection sensitivity and false positives is essential, and organisations need to set appropriate thresholds to ensure accurate detection without overwhelming security teams with false alerts.

Notwithstanding these positive developments, AI also poses several challenges that can undermine data protection rights. One major concern is the unauthorised use and collection of personal data. AI systems often require large datasets to function effectively, which can lead to the unauthorised use and collection of personal data, raising serious privacy concerns. For instance, AI-driven applications might collect data without explicit consent, violating data protection principles. Another significant issue is the use of biometric data, such as facial recognition, fingerprints, and iris scans. These technologies, powered by AI, can lead to substantial privacy issues, including unauthorised surveillance and tracking. Such practices can infringe on individuals' rights to privacy and data protection. AI systems can employ covert data collection techniques, gathering information without users' knowledge or consent. This can include tracking online behaviour, monitoring social media activity, and collecting location data, all of which can be used to build detailed profiles of individuals. Bias and discrimination are also critical concerns. AI algorithms can inadvertently perpetuate biases present in the training data, leading to discriminatory outcomes.

Ultimately, addressing these challenges requires robust regulatory frameworks, ethical AI development practices, and continuous monitoring to ensure that AI systems respect and uphold data protection rights. Implementing measures that are robust allows us to harness the benefits of AI while mitigating its potential risks.

3 Contextualising Data Protection in Artificial Intelligence

In the complex landscape of AI technologies, contextualising data protection emerges as a crucial focal point for ensuring responsible and trustworthy AI systems. As illustrated in the preceding section, the intersection of data protection and AI underscores the need to safeguard individual privacy, mitigate biases, and uphold societal values while harnessing the transformative potential of AI in various sectors—this is clearly not without difficulty since there are diametrically opposing

[41] Sowmya and Mary Anita (2023), p. 100827.

[42] Quiroz-Vazquez (n 40).

[43] Fernandes et al. (2019), p. e15406.

(even unintended) outcomes resulting from the confluence of both data protection laws and AI legislation. This section highlights specific mandated obligations in the AI Act that are relevant in the context of data protection—attempting to draw a holistic understanding of the interconnectedness between data protection frameworks and ethical AI development, and how this may facilitate the creation of AI technologies that are not only innovative but also ethically sound and conducive to societal well-being.

The legal framework for AI in the EU vis-à-vis the AI Act underscores the importance of compliance requirements for organisations engaged in AI use and deployment. The AI Act's emphasis on transparency, explainability, and human oversight necessitates a meticulous approach to ensuring compliance with these regulatory obligations. The EU's focus on human-centred AI systems underscores the need for robust methods to assess AI systems and their impacts on individuals and society, highlighting the critical role of compliance efforts in aligning AI development with ethical and legal standards.[44] In addition, the proposed methodology for interpreting the compliance requirements of the AI Act[45] underscores the significance of aligning technical requirements with stakeholder needs to achieve regulatory adherence, particularly for high-risk AI systems. As organisations navigate the evolving legal framework, meticulous attention to compliance requirements is paramount to foster innovation while upholding ethical standards and regulatory obligations in the realm of AI development and deployment.

Table 1 indicates some of the specific obligations in the AI Act that pertain to data protection:-

These specific obligations, whilst not the only provisions in the AI Act that have relevance to data protection, are of paramount importance. For instance, the growing complexities in algorithmic decision-making[46] underscore the critical need for transparency within the evolving regulatory landscape, particularly in the context of the AI Act and data protection framework. The AI Act's emphasis on accountability, technical robustness, and transparency aligns with the imperative of understanding and mitigating biases in AI systems.[47] The intersections between AI, transparency, and legal frameworks emphasise the ongoing challenges in documenting AI models and accessing information crucial for ensuring accountability and fair decision-making processes.[48] Adherence to the principles of privacy, data governance, and human oversight, as outlined in the AI Act, is imperative for fostering ethical and lawful algorithmic decision-making practices that safeguard individuals' rights and uphold regulatory standards.

This goes to the heart of addressing bias and discrimination issues within AI systems, a complex challenge that requires careful consideration of ethical implications

---

[44] Valdez et al. (2024).

[45] Kelly et al. (2024).

[46] Amoore (2020).

[47] Alake (2020).

[48] Palmer et al. (2019).

Table 1 Specific obligations in the AI Act relevant to data protection

Article in the AI Act	Extract of the Article	Summary & Analysis	Nexus between Article and Data Protection
Article 10	**'Data and data governance** 1. High-risk AI systems which make use of techniques involving the training of models with data shall be developed on the basis of training, validation and testing data sets that meet the quality criteria referred to in paragraphs 2–5 whenever such datasets are used. 2. Training, validation and testing data sets shall be subject to appropriate data governance and management practices appropriate for the intended purpose of the AI system. Those practices shall concern in particular'.	Article 10 of the regulation sets requirements for the quality and governance of data used in high-risk AI systems, aiming to ensure transparency, accountability, and non-discrimination in the development and deployment of AI technologies. Compliance with these data governance practices is essential for mitigating risks associated with bias, privacy violations, and other ethical concerns in AI applications.	The nexus between Article 10 and data protection lies in the **strict conditions** imposed on the processing of special categories of personal data. Providers of high-risk AI systems may process sensitive personal data for bias detection and correction, but only if it is strictly necessary and appropriate safeguards are in place to protect individuals' rights and freedoms. This ensures that data protection principles are upheld while addressing potential biases in AI systems.
Article 13	**'Transparency and provision of information to deployers** 1. High-risk AI systems shall be designed and developed in such a way to ensure that their operation is sufficiently transparent to enable deployers to interpret the system's output and use it appropriately. An appropriate type and degree of transparency shall be ensured with a view to achieving compliance with the relevant obligations of the provider and deployer set out in chapter 'Artificial Intelligence and Fundamental Rights: Under the European Legal Eye' of this Title. 2. High-risk AI systems shall be accompanied by instructions for use in an appropriate digital format or otherwise that include concise, complete, correct and clear information that is relevant, accessible and comprehensible to users'.	Article 13 focuses on transparency and the provision of information to deployers of high-risk AI systems. By setting out these transparency and information provision requirements in Article 13, the regulation aims to ensure that deployers of high-risk AI systems have access to the necessary information to understand and use the technology effectively. This promotes accountability, risk awareness, and responsible deployment of AI systems, ultimately contributing to the protection of individuals, companies, and fundamental rights in line with the values of the Union.	The nexus between Article 13 and data protection lies in the **requirement for transparency** in how AI systems process personal data. By ensuring that deployers have a clear understanding of how the AI system operates and what data it uses, Article 13 supports the principles of data protection, such as **accountability** and **transparency**. This helps to build trust among users and ensures that personal data is handled in a manner that respects individuals' rights and freedoms.

(continued)

Table 1 (continued)

Article in the AI Act	Extract of the Article	Summary & Analysis	Nexus between Article and Data Protection
Article 14	**'Human Oversight** 1. High-risk AI systems shall be designed and developed in such a way, including with appropriate human-machine interface tools, that they can be effectively overseen by natural persons during the period in which the AI system is in use. 2. Human oversight shall aim at preventing or minimising the risks to health, safety or fundamental rights that may emerge when a high-risk AI system is used in accordance with its intended purpose or under conditions of reasonably foreseeable misuse, in particular when such risks persist notwithstanding the application of other requirements set out in this chapter'.	Article 14 mandates human oversight in high-risk AI systems, and aims to enhance accountability, transparency, and control over the use of AI technologies. Human oversight serves as a critical safeguard to mitigate potential risks and ensure that AI systems are used responsibly and in compliance with regulatory requirements. This provision underscores the importance of human involvement in overseeing AI systems to address ethical, safety, and fundamental rights considerations in their deployment.	The nexus between Article 14 and data protection lies in the **emphasis on transparency and accountability**. By ensuring human oversight, Article 14 supports the principles of data protection, such as safeguarding individuals' rights and maintaining the integrity of personal data processing. This oversight helps to ensure that AI systems are used responsibly and ethically, aligning with data protection regulations.
Article 23	**'Obligations of Importers** 1. Before placing a high-risk AI system on the market, importers of such system shall ensure that such a system is in conformity with this Regulation by verifying that: (a) the relevant conformity assessment procedure referred to in Article 43 has been carried out by the provider of that AI system; (b) the provider has drawn up the technical documentation in accordance with Article 11 and Annex IV; (c) the system bears the required CE conformity marking and is accompanied by the EU declaration of conformity referred to in Article 47 and instructions of use; (d) the provider has appointed an authorised representative in accordance with Article 22(1). 2. Where an importer has sufficient reason to consider that a high-risk AI system is not in conformity with this Regulation, or is falsified, or accompanied by falsified documentation, it shall not place that system on the market until that AI system has been brought into conformity. Where the high-risk AI system presents a risk within the meaning of Article 79(1), the importer shall inform the provider of the AI system, the authorised representatives and the market surveillance authorities to that effect'.	The obligations in Article 23 place responsibility on importers to ensure that high-risk AI systems comply with the regulatory requirements before being placed on the market. Importers play a crucial role in verifying conformity, reporting non-compliance, and collaborating with relevant authorities to uphold the safety and compliance standards set forth in the regulation.	The nexus between Article 23 and data protection lies in the **responsibilities of importers** to ensure compliance with both AI regulations and data protection laws. Importers must verify that high-risk AI systems meet all regulatory requirements, including proper documentation and conformity assessments. This ensures that personal data processed by these systems is handled in accordance with data protection principles, such as transparency, accountability, and security.

(continued)

Table 1 (continued)

Article in the AI Act	Extract of the Article	Summary & Analysis	Nexus between Article and Data Protection
Article 24	**'Obligations of Distributors** 1. Before making a high-risk AI system available on the market, distributors shall verify that the high-risk AI system bears the required CE conformity marking, that it is accompanied by a copy of the EU declaration of conformity referred to in Article 47 and instructions for use, and that the provider and the importer of the system, as applicable, have complied with their obligations set out in Article 16, point (b) and (b) and 23(3) respectively. 2. Where a distributor considers or has reason to consider, on the basis of the information in its possession, that a high-risk AI system is not in conformity with the requirements set out in Sect. 2, it shall not make the high-risk AI system available on the market until that system has been brought into conformity with those requirements. Furthermore, where the system presents a risk within the meaning of Article 79(1), the distributor shall inform the provider or the importer of the system, as applicable, to that effect'.	The obligations in Article 24 place responsibility on distributors to ensure that high-risk AI systems comply with the regulatory standards before being made available on the market. Like importers, distributors play a crucial role in verifying conformity, reporting non-compliance, and collaborating with authorities to uphold safety and compliance standards in the AI industry.	The nexus between Article 24 and data protection is similar to the above in Article 23, the only difference being that it applies as **responsibilities of distributors**. Distributors also need to ensure compliance with both AI regulations and data protection laws.
Article 27	**'Fundamental rights impact assessment for high-risk AI systems** 1. Prior to deploying a high-risk AI system as defined in Article 6(2), with the exception of AI systems intended to be used in the area listed in point 2 of Annex III, deployers that are bodies governed by public law or private entities providing public services and deployers of high-risk systems referred to in points 5 (b) and (c) in Annex III shall perform an assessment of the impact on fundamental rights that the use of the system may produce...'	One of the key provisions introduced in the Act requires deployers to perform a fundamental rights impact assessment of high-risk AI systems. The requirements in Article 27 proactively identify and address potential risks to fundamental rights, ensuring that the deployment of AI technologies respects and upholds the rights of individuals and groups affected by the system's use. There have been queries as to whether this should be in addition to the data impact rights assessment mandated under the GDPR.	The nexus between Article 27 and data protection lies in the **emphasis on safeguarding fundamental rights**, which includes the protection of personal data. By conducting a Fundamental Rights Impact Assessment, organisations ensure that the deployment of high-risk AI systems does not infringe on individuals' data protection rights. Data protection is clearly recognised as a fundamental right in the EU, enshrined in the Charter of Fundamental Rights of the European Union (Article 8). It emphasises the importance of protecting individuals' personal data and ensuring that their privacy is respected. This aligns with the principles of the General Data Protection Regulation (GDPR), which aims to protect personal data and uphold individuals' rights.

(continued)

Table 1 (continued)

Article in the AI Act	Extract of the Article	Summary & Analysis	Nexus between Article and Data Protection
Article 59	**'Further Processing of Personal Data for Developing Certain AI Systems in the Public Interest in the AI Regulatory Sandbox** 1. In the AI regulatory sandbox, personal data lawfully collected for other purposes may be processed solely for the purpose of developing, training and testing certain AI systems in the sandbox when all of the following conditions are met: a) AI systems shall be developed for safeguarding substantial public interest by a public authority or another natural or legal person and in one or more of the following areas: i. public safety and public health, ……; ii. a high level of protection and improvement of the quality of the environment, protection of biodiversity, protection against pollution, green transition measures, climate change mitigation and adaptation measures; iii. energy sustainability; iv. safety and resilience of transport systems and mobility, critical infrastructure and networks; v. efficiency and quality of public administration and public services; b) the data processed are necessary for complying with one or more of the requirements referred to in Chapter III Section 2 where those requirements cannot effectively be fulfilled by processing anonymised, synthetic or other non-personal data…..'	This Article deals with further processing of personal data for developing certain AI systems in the public interest within an AI regulatory sandbox. This article allows for the use of personal data, lawfully collected for other purposes, to develop, train, and test AI systems in a controlled environment, provided that the AI system is developed for the public interest, such as public safety, health, environmental protection, and public administration—provided that certain strict conditions are fulfilled.	The nexus between Article 59 and data protection lies in the **strict conditions** imposed on the processing of personal data within the sandbox. These conditions include: ensuring that the data is necessary for the development of the AI system and cannot be effectively processed using anonymised or synthetic data; implementing effective monitoring mechanisms to identify and mitigate any high risks to the rights and freedoms of data subjects; keeping the data in a functionally separate, isolated, and protected processing environment; and deleting the data once the project is finished or when it reaches the end of its retention period. These strict conditions are imposed to ensure that personal data is processed in a manner that respects data protection principles, such as lawfulness, fairness, transparency, and security.

and legal frameworks. The AI Act aims to tackle these issues by incorporating principles such as human oversight, accountability, and fairness in AI deployment. However, the debiasing exception within the Act raises questions about the balance between detecting biases and protecting sensitive data.[49] Borgesius and van Bekkum highlight that whilst Article 9 of the GDPR prohibits the use of 'special categories of data' and the GDPR has exceptions to this ban, it does not extend to AI debiasing. Borgesius and van Bekkum argue that while individuals can consent to the use of their special category data, obtaining valid consent can be challenging in many situations. For example, someone applying for a mortgage may feel pressured to

[49] van Bekkum and Borgesius (n 18).

consent, rendering it insufficiently voluntary.[50] Additionally, the AI Act provides an exception for processing special categories of data to detect and correct bias within AI systems, which applies to providers of such systems, including developers and entities outsourcing AI development.[51] Notably, this exception applies when organisations cannot use any other data. It also does not cover organisations renting fully developed AI systems as a service. As such, the scope of this exception is limited, focusing on high-risk AI systems used in safety components, biometrics, critical infrastructures, education, employment, credit scoring, law enforcement, migration, and administration of justice and democratic processes,[52] even though the AI Act's debiasing exception is intended to 'protect the rights of (individuals) from the discrimination that might result from the bias in AI systems'.[53]

The following sub-sections briefly elaborate on the key aspects of the legal framework that further contextualises data protection in the AI Act. Due to the expansive nature of the AI Act, this chapter does not intend to cover all aspects of the AI Act framework and its impact and co-relation to data protection vis-à-vis the GDPR.

3.1 Conformity Assessment and Fundamental Rights Impact Assessment under the AI Act

As already outlined above, the AI Act is closely aligned with the GDPR; a particular number of the provisions in the AI Act reveal approaches that are particular to the use of special categories of data in AI decision-making processes. This is crucial as it could impact on individuals' fundamental rights and safety, and whilst the AI Act was not drafted with the intent to govern AI systems and technologies through a human rights lens, its approaches do focus on protecting against discrimination and ensuring compliance with EU law.

Concomitant with this is the requirement for conformity assessment under Article 43 of the AI Act. A conformity assessment is, in essence, a process to ensure that the AI systems concerned have met fulfilled compliance with the requirements of the Act. It is to be noted that the assessment would only apply to high-risk AI systems.[54] Under the AI Act, an AI system is classified as high-risk if it is a standalone high risk AI system (inherently high risk because of their specific applications), a safety component of a product or is itself a product regulated under harmonised legislation listed in Annex II(A) and is subject to third-party conformity assessment under the relevant law.[55] This means that providers, deployers, manufacturers and even other third parties shall ensure that the AI product or system has

[50] ibid.

[51] Recital 70 of the AI Act.

[52] Van Bekkum and Zuiderveen Borgesius (2023), p. 105770.

[53] van Bekkum and Borgesius (n 18).

[54] Article 3(1) of the AI Act.

[55] Articles 6(1)(a) to (b) of the AI Act.

fully complied with the necessary requirements under the applicable harmonised legislation[56] as well, which creates common standards for different products across the internal market. These may cover machinery, medical devices, toys, and the like.

Whilst conformity assessments may be less demanding for data protection (taking into account the relevance of data and its governance provisions in Article 10), the fundamental rights impact assessment ('FRIA') in Article 27 is. Article 27 of the AI Act, highlighted in Table 1 prior, specifies that a FRIA is mandated only for certain scenarios, such as for entities governed by public law, private entities offering public services, and deployers[57] of high-risk AI systems involved in credit evaluation, credit scoring for individuals, or risk assessment in life and health insurance.[58] Additionally, high-level AI systems designated as 'safety components' in critical infrastructure are exempt from undergoing an FRIA. Specifically, according to Recital 93 of the AI Act, private entities offering services of a public nature, spanning areas like education, healthcare, social services, housing, and administration of justice, may fall under the obligation to conduct a FRIA if their AI systems are classified as high-risk.[59]

The question is how the FRIA may have an impact on the data protection impact assessment ('DPIA') in Article 35 of the GDPR or may be affected in the event a DPIA is not carried out. Under Article 35 of the GDPR, the DPIA is mandatory in situations where data processing is likely to result in a high risk to individuals' rights and freedoms. The DPIA involves a systematic description of the envisaged processing operations and their purposes, an assessment of the necessity and proportionality of the processing, an evaluation of the risks to the rights and freedoms of data subjects, and the measures to address these risks. These measures include safeguards, security measures, and mechanisms to ensure compliance with data protection principles. By conducting a DPIA, organisations can proactively address potential privacy issues and demonstrate their commitment to protecting personal data.

Indeed, it has been recognised that not only is the FRIA likely to overlap with other obligations under the AI Act, such as conformity assessments in Article 43 of the AI Act—but also the DPIA requirement. According to Van Bael & Bellis:[60]

> The FRIA and the DPIA processes are analogous, but differ substantially in their scope: while DPIA focuses on rights and freedoms of data subjects affected by the processing of their personal data, FRIA also concerns risks associated with non-personal data. The AI Act addresses this possible overlap in its Article 27(4) which notes that if some obligations are

[56] Annex I, Section A of the AI Act.

[57] Since the FRIA is imposed on deployers, and not providers, this is an important distinction as it demonstrates that conformity assessments are even broader than may have been originally envisaged.

[58] Van Bael & Bellis, 'Fundamental Rights Impact Assessment in the EU Artificial Intelligence Act' 2 https://mcusercontent.com/80a2795e9aa8aacac0c148b3b/files/dfb8cbe8-f06b-fab7-0ab7-fdbff05d4913/20240328_Fundamental_Rights_Impact_Assessment_under_EU_AI_Act.03.pdf

[59] ibid.

[60] ibid 3.

> already met through a DPIA, the FRIA shall 'complement' that DPIA. Similarly, other prior impact assessments that are relevant can inform an FRIA process.

In practical terms, it is common for DPIAs and FRIAs to be carried out simultaneously, potentially resulting in a unified report.[61] The option to merge an FRIA with a DPIA, along with the availability of a standardised template for FRIAs, aims to alleviate the compliance burden posed by the AI Act and GDPR.[62] However, there may be scenarios where a DPIA may not have been carried out, because the specific conditions of Article 35 in the GDPR are not triggered at all, which *may* lead to a potential failed FRIA that falls short of the DPIA. However, this does not necessarily mean that the FRIA will, indeed, fail. These two assessments serve different purposes and have distinct scopes, with the DPIA focusing on risk to individuals' rights and freedoms arising from the processing of personal data, while the FRIA addresses broader fundamental rights impacts, such as human dignity, non-discrimination and other societal impacts, including those not directly related to personal data. Therefore, even if a DPIA is not required under Article 35 of the GDPR, a FRIA may still be necessary under the AI Act if the AI system poses significant risks to fundamental rights. If an AI system does not process personal data in a manner that triggers a DPIA but poses other significant risks, such as environmental challenges, threats to physical safety, or public health concerns, the FRIA under Article 27(4) of the AI Act becomes crucial.

To ensure comprehensive risk assessment, organisations should adopt a holistic approach that integrates both DPIA and FRIA where applicable. One, even if a DPIA is not triggered, a FRIA should be conducted to evaluate the broader impacts of the AI system on fundamental rights. Secondly, regularly updating both DPIA and FRIA must be undertaken to reflect any changes in the AI system's use or context, ensuring that all potential risks are continuously monitored and mitigated. Finally, it is also necessary to continue developing and implementing robust mitigation measures to address identified risks, including human oversight mechanisms and internal governance structures.

In sum, leveraging risk assessments, including both FRIAs and DPIAs and ethical evaluations, can aid in identifying potential gaps in compliance and guiding organisations towards ethically sound AI practices. In addition, the integration of clear guidelines and coordination among competent authorities is essential for consistent interpretation and enforcement of regulatory requirements. By adopting comprehensive assessment methodologies, organisations can navigate the evolving legal landscape surrounding AI and data protection to uphold ethical standards and promote trust in AI technologies.

[61] Van Bael & Bellis (n 58).

[62] Waem et al. (2024).

3.2 Automated Decision-Making and the AI Act

The contentious issue of GDPR protections for individuals against forms of Automated Decision-Making (ADM) and profiling was briefly highlighted in Sect. 2.2 of this chapter. There has been a large body of legal scholarship regarding the application of Article 22 of the GDPR by the courts and data protection authorities.[63] In essence, Article 22 of the GDPR addresses ADM (including profiling) by conveying rights upon individuals (data subjects) not to be subject to decisions based solely on automated processing, if these decisions produce legal effects concerning them, or that may significant affect them.[64] Some examples that may be covered by Article 22 may include situations of online loan approvals, whereby if the system relies on pre-programmed algorithms and criteria to approve or deny loans without human intervention, it would fall under Article 22. Other situations may include recruitment aptitude tests, where candidates for a job are evaluated based on similarly pre-defined algorithms and criteria without human intervention. In both these instances, the individuals concerned have a right to challenge the decisions. Ultimately, the concept of Article 22 emphasises the importance of human oversight as part of the bundle of rights protections under the GDPR. It is to be noted that human oversight or human involvement must be active, and not simply a token gesture.[65] In the meantime, whilst there are exceptions provided in Article 22(2) and safeguards in Article 22(3), there are some questions as to whether AI systems are likely to automatically trigger the application of Article 22 given its inherent nature.

The impact of human oversight and intervention on AI systems determines whether they fall within the scope of the ADM framework in Article 22 of the GDPR. If a human meaningfully intervenes at a critical stage of an AI system's decision-making process, the decision may no longer be considered fully automated under Article 22 of the GDPR. Under the AI Act, while AI systems often make entirely automated decisions, effective human oversight acts as a safeguard to ensure fairness and protect individuals' rights, including data protection rights.[66] This is aligned with Article 14 of the AI Act, where human oversight serves as a critical safeguard to mitigate potential risks and ensure that AI systems are used responsibly and in compliance with regulatory requirements.

Additionally, it has been noted that the recent ruling in the *Schufa* case[67] would serve as an important precedent that would affect companies that use AI systems to

---

[63] Vale and Zanfir-Fortuna (n 37).

[64] Thouvenin et al. (2022), p. 183.

[65] Article 29 Data Protection Working Party, 'Guidelines on Automated Individual Decision-Making and Profiling for the Purposes of Regulation 2016/679' 29.

[66] Clark, Demircan and Kettas (n 5).

[67] Case C-634/21 OQ v Land Hessen ECLI:EU:C:2023:957.

generate scores, even if the decisions regarding those scores are made by third parties.[68] Ebers and Sein further argue:-

> Since such predictions fulfil the criteria of Art. 22(1) according to the ECJ, they will henceforth require a justification under Art. 22(2) GDPR and trigger the data subject's rights under Art. 22(3) GDPR. All these considerations show how difficult it is for providers and users of AI systems to comply with the GDPR. Arguably, the recently adopted AI Act has not brought clarity, but rather created more problems, as the AI Act applies additionally to the GDPR.

In the meantime, it has been pointed out that the current and future case-law related ADM under the GDPR could serve as a basis for enhancing the High-Risk Artificial Intelligence Systems (HRAIS) list outlined in Annex III of the AI Act. This is particularly relevant because many of the existing HRAIS items overlap with ADM systems that were already subject to GDPR regulations.[69] In addition, while the GDPR provides the right to effective judicial redress in most cases where AI systems processing personal data violate principles like fairness, transparency, and purpose limitation, there remains room to explore additional redress options. This exploration becomes crucial in situations where AI systems rely on non-personal data but significantly impact the rights of individuals or communities.[70]

3.3 *Privacy by Design and Default*

Underpinning the ethical framework of the AI Act and GDPR is the concept of Privacy by Design, a fundamental principle that advocates for integrating privacy considerations into the development process of AI systems from their inception. This principle, introduced by the GDPR in Article 25 emphasises that privacy considerations should be an integral part of AI system development. Simply put, under the GDPR, we already note that there are specific provisions address data security, retention, and individual rights. These provisions aim to protect personal data from unauthorised access, use, or disclosure, while also granting individuals the right to access, correct, and delete their data.[71] Relationally to AI, this approach entails embedding privacy features into the design of AI systems, ensuring that data protection mechanisms are core components rather than retroactively added measures. Implementing Privacy by Design requires a comprehensive understanding of data flows, potential privacy vulnerabilities, and the implications of AI algorithms on individuals' privacy rights.[72]

---

[68] Ebers and Sein (2024), p. 13.

[69] Vale (2022).

[70] ibid.

[71] Imprivata (2024).

[72] Tamò-Larrieux (2018).

Another crucial aspect of the AI Act concerning data protection is also the implementation of Privacy by Default. This principle mandates that privacy settings should be automatically set to high levels, ensuring that individuals' personal data is safeguarded from the outset. The AI Act emphasises the importance of organisations embedding privacy measures into their AI systems by default, thereby prioritising data protection and minimising the risk of privacy breaches. These provisions within the Act align with the overarching goal of enhancing data governance and transparency in AI operations. The implementation of Privacy by Default can proactively mitigate privacy risks and uphold individuals' rights to data protection, aligning with the core principles of ethical AI governance. The potential challenges surrounding the use of special categories of data for debiasing purposes under the AI Act (highlighted in Sect. 3) should also be prioritised, ensuring compliance with GDPR regulations and maintaining a balance between privacy protection and bias detection.[73] Additionally, considering the increasing importance of protecting personal data within rapidly evolving technological landscapes, the AI Act's emphasis on Privacy by Default underscores the significance of proactive data governance and privacy measures.

3.4 National Supervisory Authorities in the GDPR and AI Act

Efficient cooperation between national authorities is essential for the successful implementation of the AI Act and data protection regulations such as the GDPR. It has already been highlighted that procedural issues in enforcing the GDPR has revealed gaps in defining parties, defence rights, access to files, and investigation powers. These gaps underscore the need for standardised EU rules to address discrepancies in national regulations and enhance harmonisation.[74] For example, it was pointed out that the complexity of data protection authorities in Germany emphasised the importance of better coordination at both national and European levels post-GDPR.[75] Integrating these insights, it is evident that effective collaboration with national authorities is crucial to bridge regulatory disparities, streamline enforcement processes, and ensure consistent interpretation and application of AI and data protection laws across the EU. This underscores the necessity for clear guidance and coordination mechanisms to navigate the evolving legal landscape and enhance compliance and enforcement efforts.

In the GDPR, Chapter III Articles 51–59 provide for the appointment of each EU member states' independent supervisory authorities, alongside the relevant competence, tasks, and powers. Under the AI Act, Article 28 designates that members states need to designate a 'notifying authority' whereby, under Article 31 of the AI

[73] van Bekkum and Borgesius (n 18).

[74] Rudolf and Kovač (2023), p. 143.

[75] Bratasyuk (2023), p. 42.

Act, 'a notified body' is also to be established under the national laws of each member state of the EU, which shall '*satisfy the organisational, quality management, resources and process requirements that are necessary to fulfil their tasks, as well as suitable cybersecurity requirements*'.[76] In the meantime, a European Artificial Intelligence Board ('EAIB') carries out the coordination platform and advisory body to the European Commission under the AI Act, and it is responsible for ensuring consistent application of the regulation across EU member states, promoting cooperation and coordination among national competent authorities, and providing guidance on the implementation of the regulation. The EAIB plays a key role in fostering harmonisation and cooperation in the governance of AI systems within the EU. The composition of the EUAIB also includes all national supervisory authorities. Given that enforcement of the AI will primarily be at national level, there is concern that this may give rise to national fragmentation in the interpretation and enforcement of the AI Act's requirements. However, a European AI Office has been established within the European Commission to potentially deal with this issue.

Ebers and Sein also argue that the AI Act carries the risk of creating parallel enforcement structures with data protection authorities (DPAs), which could also lead to legal uncertainty.[77] Although it is clear in the AI Act that national authorities should be the relevant enforcers, the fact that member states can designate their own competent authorities[78] raises legitimate concerns about overlapping competences of the different organisations.

EU data law emphasises the need for cooperation among authorities, but lacks specific rules beyond the treaty-based duty of sincere cooperation.[79] Soft law plays a role, with national supervisory authorities under the AI Act consulting EU competent bodies, including data protection authorities, on guidance drafts. While cooperation in adopting soft law is encouraged, it's not mandatory. Even though data protection concerns are addressed as part of the scope of functions vis-à-vis the European AI Office, explicit rules for cooperation between national supervisory authorities and data protection bodies are lacking. The AI Act implies cooperation through reporting violations and evaluating AI systems. Despite EU legislator efforts, challenges remain due to unclear necessity, consequences, and absence of explicit rules.[80]

Foreseeable difficulties in enacting the AI Act plus navigating data protection regulations are many-sided. One primary problem lies in possible discord between the AI Act and the GDPR, presenting intricacies for stakeholders. The AI Act's risk-based AI system categories, along with transparency demands, may necessitate hefty changes in present processes to assure alignment with data protection norms. The regulatory interplay creates concerns about application scope, particularly

[76] Article 31(2) of the AI Act.

[77] Ebers and Sein (n 68).

[78] Article 70 of the AI Act.

[79] Hajduk (2023).

[80] Hajduk (n 79).

relating to human oversight tools and data handling methods, demanding an in-depth grasp of clear mandates from both regulations. Additionally, the ever-changing legal setting for AI and data protection calls for explicit guidance and collaboration to address voids and inconsistencies efficiently. Steadfast enforcement and interpretation by competent national authorities will be essential to surmount anticipated issues and ensure ethical and safe AI progression and use.[81]

4 Conclusion

As advancements and developments in technology will continue to reshape industries alongside societies, the AI Act will be crucial in reacting to the evolving and dynamic arena of AI and data protection. Its focus on aspects such as human oversight with technical robustness and transparency stresses the importance of ethical alongside responsible AI deployment within a digital era marked by unmatched innovation. Nonetheless, how the AI Act intersects with present data protection regulations like GDPR creates complex and challenging issues concerning the usage of AI systems in processing sensitive data to prevent biases. Despite the Act's targets at lessening biases while maintaining fundamental rights, needing clear directions along with oversight mechanisms in order to manage the intricate relationship between AI development and data protection holds significant importance for assuring ethical and trustworthy AI practices inside the EU's legal framework.[82]

The intersection of the AI Act and GDPR presents a unique regulatory landscape that offers valuable lessons. While both frameworks aim to protect individuals' rights and promote ethical practices, there is a risk that data protection could be undermined if AI systems are not adequately regulated. Conversely, overly stringent regulations might deter innovation and hinder the development of beneficial AI technologies. Businesses may also face challenges due to the complexity and potential overlap of these regulations, leading to legal uncertainty. Businesses operating within the EU or interacting with EU markets must navigate the dual compliance requirements of the AI Act and GDPR. The AI Act categorises AI systems into different risk levels, each with specific compliance obligations, such as risk management, human oversight, and data governance. This can be particularly challenging for businesses that must also comply with GDPR's stringent data protection requirements. The need to conduct both DPIAs under GDPR and FRIAs under the AI Act can increase the administrative burden and compliance costs. Additionally, the extraterritorial scope of both regulations means that non-EU businesses must also comply if their AI systems affect EU residents, further complicating compliance efforts.

[81] Knibbeler and Zadeh (2023).

[82] Peng et al. (2021).

Ultimately, the AI Act and GDPR, while complementary in many respects, have different scopes and purposes that can lead to conflicts. The GDPR focuses exclusively on the protection and processing of personal data, emphasising privacy and individual control rights. In contrast, the AI Act regulates the development, provision, and use of AI systems, even if no personal data is processed. This broader scope can create confusion about which regulations apply in specific scenarios, especially when an AI system processes personal data but also falls under the high-risk category of the AI Act.

Placed within the EU's ongoing endeavours, the aligning of data protection standards, in view of existing alongside the AI Act, is paramount in securing consistent and efficient regulation within the digital scope. The confluence between the AI Act and the GDPR uncovers a slightly tangled regulatory setting needing a finely-tuned strategy to handle issues emerging from AI implementations in the digital market space.[83] Synchronising data protection precepts with the dynamically shifting AI regulatory landscape is vital to drive forward innovation whilst protecting individual rights and ensuring public and societal safety. The synchronised application of these harmonisation manoeuvres will be critical in balancing AI technology's ethical employment against stringent data protection statutes, ultimately aiding in cultivating a more fortified and dependable digital environment.

References

AEPD. 10 Misunderstandings Related to Anonymisation. https://www.edps.europa.eu/system/files/2021-04/21-04-27_aepd-edps_anonymisation_en_5.pdf

Alake R (2020) Algorithm bias in artificial intelligence needs to be discussed (and addressed). Medium (28 April 2020). https://towardsdatascience.com/algorithm-bias-in-artificial-intelligence-needs-to-be-discussed-and-addressed-8d369d675a70

Amoore L (2020) Cloud ethics: algorithms and the attributes of ourselves and others. Duke University Press

Article 29 Data Protection Working Party. Guidelines on Automated Individual Decision-Making and Profiling for the Purposes of Regulation 2016/679

Big Data and Artificial Intelligence: How They Work Together. Maryville Online (21 July 2017) https://online.maryville.edu/blog/big-data-is-too-big-without-ai/

Bratasyuk O (2023) Legal basis of personal data protection in Ukraine and Germany: organizational and managerial aspect. Visegrad J Hum Rights 1:42. https://journals.uran.ua/journal-vjhr/article/view/295441

Clark J, Demircan M, Kettas K (2024) Europe: the EU AI Act's relationship with data protection law: key takeaways. Privacy Matters (DLA Piper) (25 April 2024). https://privacymatters.dlapiper.com/2024/04/europe-the-eu-ai-acts-relationship-with-data-protection-law-key-takeaways/

Clifford D (2024) The challenge to information categories. In: Clifford D (ed) Data protection law and emotion. Oxford University Press. https://doi.org/10.1093/oso/9780192845863.003.0003

Comandé G (2020) Unfolding the legal component of trustworthy AI: a must to avoid ethics washing. SSRN Electron J. https://www.ssrn.com/abstract=3690633

[83] Hacker et al. (2023).

Directive 95/46/EC of the European Parliament and of the Council of 24 October 1995 on the protection of individuals with regard to the processing of personal data and on the free movement of such data 1995
Ebers M, Sein K (2024) Data-driven technologies - challenges for privacy and EU Data Protection Law. In: Ebers M, Sein K (eds) Privacy, data protection and data-driven technologies. Routledge
European Commission (2024) New initiatives for digital infrastructures of tomorrow. European Commission - European Commission (21 February 2024). https://ec.europa.eu/commission/presscorner/detail/en/ip_24_941
Fernandes CO et al (2019) Artificial intelligence technologies for coping with alarm fatigue in hospital environments because of sensory overload: algorithm development and validation. J Med Internet Res 21:e15406. https://www.ncbi.nlm.nih.gov/pmc/articles/PMC6904899/
Gandomi A, Haider M (2015) Beyond the hype: big data concepts, methods, and analytics. Int J Inf Manag 35:137
Gikay AA et al (2023) High-risk artificial intelligence systems under the European Union's Artificial Intelligence Act: systemic flaws and practical challenges. SSRN Electron J. https://www.ssrn.com/abstract=4621605
Hacker P, Cordes J and Rochon J (2023) Regulating gatekeeper AI and data: transparency, access, and fairness under the DMA, the GDPR, and beyond. Oxford Business Law Blog (31 October 2023). https://blogs.law.ox.ac.uk/oblb/blog-post/2023/10/regulating-gatekeeper-ai-and-data-transparency-access-and-fairness-under-dma
Hajduk P (2023) AI Act and GDPR: on the path towards overlap of the enforcement structures. RAILS - Blog (1 October 2023) https://blog.ai-laws.org/ai-act-and-gdpr-on-the-path-towards-overlap-of-the-enforcement-structures/
Häuselmann A et al (2023) EU law and emotion data. In: 2023 11th international conference on affective computing and intelligent interaction (ACII). IEEE. https://ieeexplore.ieee.org/document/10388181/
Hunton Andrews Kurth. Artificial Intelligence and Data Protection - How the GDPR Regulates AI. https://www.informationpolicycentre.com/uploads/5/7/1/0/57104281/cipl-hunton_andrews_kurth_legal_note_-_how_gdpr_regulates_ai__12_march_2020_.pdf
Imprivata (2024) The 6 principles of AI and data protection: how the AI Act ensures data is safe. Imprivata
Kelly J et al (2024) Navigating the EU AI Act: a methodological approach to compliance for safety-critical products. arXiv (26 March 2024). http://arxiv.org/abs/2403.16808
Knibbeler D, Zadeh S (2023) International: the interplay between the AI Act and the GDPR - AI series Part 1. DataGuidance (13 November 2023). https://www.dataguidance.com/opinion/international-interplay-between-ai-act-and-gdpr-ai
Lilkov D (2021) Regulating artificial intelligence in the EU: a risky game. European View 20:166
Liu L et al (2022) Application of machine learning in intelligent encryption for digital information of real-time image text under big data. EURASIP J Wirel Commun Netw 2022:21. https://jwcn-eurasipjournals.springeropen.com/articles/10.1186/s13638-022-02111-9
Lomas N (2020) GDPR's two-year review flags lack of "vigorous" enforcement. TechCrunch (24 June 2020). https://social.techcrunch.com/2020/06/24/gdprs-two-year-review-flags-lack-of-vigorous-enforcement/
Palmer H, Livingston J, Troels T (2019) The legal requirement of explainability in computationally aided decision-making in public administration. SSRN: Social Science Research Network. iCourts Working Paper Series No. 162
Peng S-Y, Lin C-F, Streinz T (eds) (2021) Artificial intelligence and international economic law. Cambridge University Press
Proposal for a REGULATION OF THE EUROPEAN PARLIAMENT AND OF THE COUNCIL LAYING DOWN HARMONISED RULES ON ARTIFICIAL INTELLIGENCE (ARTIFICIAL INTELLIGENCE ACT) AND AMENDING CERTAIN UNION LEGISLATIVE ACTS 2021 ({SEC(2021) 167 final} - {SWD(2021) 84 final} - {SWD(2021) 85 final})

Quiroz-Vazquez C (2023) Anomaly detection in machine learning: finding outliers for optimization of business functions - IBM Blog. IBM (19 December 2023). https://www.ibm.com/blog/anomaly-detection-machine-learning/

Raposo VL (2022) Ex machina: preliminary critical assessment of the European Draft Act on artificial intelligence. Int J Law Inf Technol 30:88. https://doi.org/10.1093/ijlit/eaac007

'REGULATION (EU) 2016/679 OF THE EUROPEAN PARLIAMENT AND OF THE COUNCIL - of 27 April 2016 - on the Protection of Natural Persons with Regard to the Processing of Personal Data and on the Free Movement of Such Data, and Repealing Directive 95/46/EC (General Data Protection Regulation)' 88

Rudolf G, Kovač P (2023) Procedural challenges of cross-border cooperation and consistency in personal data protection in the EU. NISPAcee J Public Admin Policy 16:143. https://www.sciendo.com/article/10.2478/nispa-2023-0017

Ryan J, Toner A (2020) Europe's governments are failing the GDPR. Brave's 2020 report on the enforcement capacity of data protection authorities. Brave. https://brave.com/static-assets/files/Brave-2020-DPA-Report.pdf

Sowmya T, Mary Anita EA (2023) A comprehensive review of AI based intrusion detection system. Measur Sens 28:100827. https://linkinghub.elsevier.com/retrieve/pii/S2665917423001630

Tamò-Larrieux A (2018) Designing for privacy and its legal framework: data protection by design and default for the Internet of Things, vol 40. Springer. http://link.springer.com/10.1007/978-3-319-98624-1

Thouvenin F, Früh A, Henseler S (2022) Article 22 GDPR on automated individual decision-making: prohibition or data subject right? Eur Data Prot Law Rev 8:183. http://edpl.lexxion.eu/article/EDPL/2022/2/6

Valdez AC et al (2024) The European Commitment to Human-Centered Technology: the integral role of HCI in the EU AI Act's success. arXiv (22 February 2024). http://arxiv.org/abs/2402.14728

Vale SB (2022) GDPR and the AI Act Interplay: lessons from FPF's ADM case-law report. Future of Privacy Form (FPF) (11 March 2022). https://fpf.org/blog/gdpr-and-the-ai-act-interplay-lessons-from-fpfs-adm-case-law-report/

Vale SB, Zanfir-Fortuna G (2022) Automated decision-making under the GDPR: practical cases from courts and data protection authorities. Future of Privacy Forum

Van Bael & Bellis. Fundamental Rights Impact Assessment in the EU Artificial Intelligence Act. https://mcusercontent.com/80a2795e9aa8aacac0c148b3b/files/dfb8cbe8-f06b-fab7-0ab7-fdbff05d4913/20240328_Fundamental_Rights_Impact_Assessment_under_EU_AI_Act.03.pdf

van Bekkum M, Borgesius FZ (2024) The AI Act's debiasing exception to the GDPR. IAPP (21 February 2024). https://iapp.org/news/a/the-ai-acts-debiasing-exception-to-the-gdpr

Van Bekkum M, Zuiderveen Borgesius F (2023) Using sensitive data to prevent discrimination by artificial intelligence: does the GDPR need a new exception? Comput Law Secur Rev 48:105770. https://linkinghub.elsevier.com/retrieve/pii/S0267364922001133

Waem H, Dauzier J, Demircan M (2024) Fundamental rights impact assessments under the EU AI Act: who, what and how? Technology's Legal Edge (7 March 2024). https://www.technologyslegaledge.com/2024/03/fundamental-rights-impact-assessments-under-the-eu-ai-act-who-what-and-how/

Consumer Protection in Light of the New AI Act: Behind the Smiles: Emotional AI, Consumer Trust, and the EU's Regulatory Response

Matthew Dacoronias-Marina and Mateja Durovic

Contents

Abstract This paper aims to showcase how the new Artificial Intelligence Regulation (AI Act) of the European Union interplays with the existing legal framework for the protection of consumers. It deals with the evolving challenges posed by AI technologies, as seen from a consumer rights perspective, the right to privacy, ethical concerns, and a comparative approach between different jurisdictions. The paper begins by analysing the AI Act, and its risk-based classification system, which imposes stricter obligations on high-risk AI while setting transparency requirements for limited-risk and general-purpose AI applications. It continues by examining the interplay of these provisions with existing regulations such as the General Data Protection Regulation (GDPR) and the Unfair Commercial Practices Directive (UCPD), how these complement each other and identify potential gaps or omissions. Next, the focus shifts to emotional AI, a field of technology which raises

M. Dacoronias-Marina
National and Kapodistrian University of Athens, Athens, Greece

M. Durovic (✉)
King's College London, London, UK
e-mail: mateja.durovic@kcl.ac.uk

V. L. Raposo (ed.), *The European Artificial Intelligence Act*, Law, Governance and Technology Series 78, https://doi.org/10.1007/978-3-031-98406-8_13

complex ethical and legal concerns and highlights the problems of the new AI Act. While the provisions of the AI Act could provide some protection against violations of rights arising from emotional AI usage, it is still ambiguous whether adequate consumer protection against potential exploitation through emotion-recognition technologies exists. The paper also highlights the importance of the regulatory sandbox mechanism, which the AI Act introduces, that seeks to balance consumer protection with innovation. Through this regulatory sandbox, AI developers can test technologies in a controlled environment without fear of being fined. Nevertheless, this solution could disproportionally impact small and medium-sized enterprises (SMEs), which may struggle with the financial and technical burden of compliance. The paper proposes possible solutions to mitigate such concerns, such as adaptive compliance thresholds and incentives for ethical AI development, to ensure that regulation does not stifle innovation. Finally, the paper proceeds with a comparative analysis of global AI governance strategies, highlighting key differences between the EU's comprehensive regulatory approach and the more fragmented frameworks in the US, which focuses on sector-specific regulations and state-led initiatives, and China, which has only adopted a targeted, technology-specific approach, focusing on AI governance in areas such as deepfakes and social scoring. By contrast, Japan and Singapore focus more on a collaborative approach between all sectors and a more human-centric approach. By drawing lessons from these different models, this paper evaluates potential improvements to the AI Act, advocating for more dynamic regulatory mechanisms that can adapt to emerging AI risks. With the AI Act being an essential piece of legislation to ensure trustworthy AI, it is, without a doubt, that AI, consumer rights, and privacy require continuous regulatory evolution, and the contribution of this paper is to provide recommendations for strengthening the AI Act to better safeguard consumers in the rapidly evolving digital landscape.

1 Introduction

Most people, when referring to Artificial Intelligence (AI), have in mind Artificial General Intelligence; however, such a system is not yet available.[1] AI is an extensive term combining various technologies and many levels of sophistication.[2] The

[1] Artificial General Intelligence (AGI) is a theoretical, for the moment, concept, according to which AI will be able to mimic human intelligence and should be distinguished from Artificial Superintelligence which surpasses the capabilities of humans. Cem Dilmegani, *When Will Singularity Happen? 1700 Expert Opinions of AGI [2024]*, AIMultiple: High Tech Use Cases & Tools to Grow Your Business (2024), https://research.aimultiple.com/artificial-general-intelligence-singularity-timing/

[2] A definition is given by the new AI Act proposed by the EU in article 3: '*(1) "AI system" means a machine-based system designed to operate with varying levels of autonomy, that may exhibit adaptiveness after deployment and that, for explicit or implicit objectives, infers, from the input it*

principal concept of AI is that it replicates human intelligence in machines, which are programmed to think, learn, and problem-solve like humans.[3] Recently, AI technology has been accelerating dramatically, and different applications have been developed in other fields, transforming various sectors, including healthcare, finance, transportation, and retail. The benefits are numerous, including improved efficiency, personalised services, and innovative solutions. But, it also poses significant challenges, particularly in the field of consumer law, given how the new forms of data collection, processing, and decision-making could impact consumer rights and privacy.[4]

For consumers, AI technologies could be considered a double-edged sword; on the one hand, they are beneficial, given the potential use in protecting their rights, but on the other hand invasive since they can understand and influence consumer behaviour. That is why a section will be dedicated to consumer emotional manipulation since AI can provide enhanced personalisation in e-commerce, allowing retailers to tailor recommendations and promotions based on individual consumer behaviour. A study by Deloitte found that a significant proportion of consumers (36%) would be interested in purchasing personalised products or services.[5] Other applications include customer service through chatbots and virtual assistants, providing instant support and resolving queries efficiently.

In this chapter, there will first be a discussion about the AI Act and how it interacts with fundamental notions such as transparency, trust, and privacy. Then, by focusing on emotional AI, it will make it easier to highlight the challenges that consumers face and investigate whether the EU framework, with the recent addition of the AI Act, can provide adequate protection. Additionally, given that AI is a subject that is currently being addressed by different jurisdictions, it is imperative to compare the solution that the EU proposes in conjunction with other proposed solutions by other jurisdictions. That is done through a comparative analysis of leading jurisdictions, namely, the US, China and Japan, showcasing the different approaches and different goals that are being attained. Finally, in the conclusion, the main points of the chapter are being highlighted and an overall assessment of the new framework how they might be improved to better protect consumers in the age of AI.

---

receives, how to generate outputs such as predictions, content, recommendations, or decisions that can influence physical or virtual environments'.

[3] Artificial Intelligence (AI): What It Is and How It Is Used, Investopedia, https://www.investopedia.com/terms/a/artificial-intelligence-ai.asp; Artificial intelligence, Oxford, https://www.oxfordreference.com/display/10.1093/oi/authority.20110803095426960

[4] European Union, *Artificial Intelligence Act: Deal on Comprehensive Rules for Trustworthy AI | News | European Parliament*, (2023), https://www.europarl.europa.eu/news/en/press-room/20231206IPR15699/artificial-intelligence-act-deal-on-comprehensive-rules-for-trustworthy-ai; Introducing Superalignment, https://openai.com/blog/introducing-superalignment; Karnouskos (2022), p. 93.

[5] Deloitte (2019).

2 The AI Act and the Interplay with the EU Legislative Framework

The European Union (EU) has been supporting the development of AI. It has been one of the first to investigate the potential harms of AI and the first one to enact legislation to regulate AI.[6] The new AI Act[7] aims to enhance the usage of AI as a force of good, which will enable the further development of ethical AI by regulating it. Of course, critics suggest that regulations could also hinder development since entities could be reluctant to adhere to regulations.[8] The definition of AI in the AI Act is broad by design,[9] encompassing machine learning models, expert systems, and other algorithms capable of processing inputs to generate outputs that influence their environment. For the purposes of this chapter, when discussing AI, it will include all potential applications, as defined in the EU AI Act, unless otherwise mentioned.

The AI Act classifies AI systems based on their level of risk into four categories: unacceptable risk, high-risk, limited risk, and minimal risk AI systems. The first category, that of unacceptable risk systems, such as those manipulating behaviour through subliminal techniques or social scoring, are completely prohibited for being a threat to safety and fundamental rights (Art. 5). The second one, that of high-risk systems (Art. 6), which could be used in critical infrastructure, education, employment, and for law enforcement, amongst other uses, are tightly moderated requiring human oversight, robust risk management, as well as high-quality data sets combined with transparency. The Act imposes that these systems undergo conformity assessments before entering the market as well as oversight afterwards to ensure the lawfulness of the data collected. The last two categories are of limited risk systems, such as chatbots that have transparency obligations (Chapter IV), requiring clear disclosure of AI interaction and system capabilities and of minimal risk systems, like spam filters or AI-enabled video games in which the developers are only encouraged to adhere to voluntary ethical guidelines (Art. 95) since no specific regulatory

---

[6] European Commission (2024); European Parliament (2024), Mar. 13, 2024, https://www.europarl.europa.eu/news/en/press-room/20240308IPR19015/artificial-intelligence-act-meps-adopt-landmark-law

[7] Regulation (EU) 2024/1689 of the European Parliament and of the Council of 13 June 2024 laying down harmonised rules on artificial intelligence and amending Regulations (EC) No 300/2008, (EU) No 167/2013, (EU) No 168/2013, (EU) 2018/858, (EU) 2018/1139 and (EU) 2019/2144 and Directives 2014/90/EU, (EU) 2016/797 and (EU) 2020/1828 (Artificial Intelligence Act)

[8] Corbett (2024).

[9] By article 3 of the AI Act: *'AI system' means a machine-based system that is designed to operate with varying levels of autonomy and that may exhibit adaptiveness after deployment, and that, for explicit or implicit objectives, infers, from the input it receives, how to generate outputs such as predictions, content, recommendations, or decisions that can influence physical or virtual environments.*

requirements exist. In order to foster innovation, the EU will create what is called *'AI regulatory sandboxes'*, meaning *'a controlled framework set up by a competent authority which offers providers or prospective providers of AI systems the possibility to develop, train, validate and test, where appropriate in real-world conditions, an innovative AI system, pursuant to a sandbox plan for a limited time under regulatory supervision'*; ensuring compliance with safety and ethical standards in a controlled environment. The goal of the AI Act is to promote human-centric ethical AI that will enhance the internal market's functionality while safeguarding public interests and fundamental rights.

What first needs to be understood is how the new AI Act[10] interplays with other laws of the EU, namely the General Data Privacy Regulation (GDPR). The predecessor of GDPR (Directive 95/46/EC on the protection of individuals about the processing of personal data and the free movement of such data) was perceived at a time when the Internet was still in its infancy. In 2016, the Internet had already been transformed into a tool used every day by billions of people, and that is why the GDPR was introduced: to safeguard the privacy of the data produced by EU citizens, to provide protection from misuse by the providers who had already amassed large amounts of personal information through the sophisticated use of cookies for targeted advertising and protect fundamental rights in the digital age. Although innovative in its time, the GDPR does not make any explicit reference to emerging technologies such as AI, it remains relevant and applicable for protecting EU citizens against data violations arising from such technologies.[11] Key principles such as lawfulness, fairness, transparency (Art. 5), data minimisation (Art. 5), and the rights of data subjects (Art. 12–23) apply directly to AI technologies.

However, given how fast AI is evolving, there are concerns that potential breaches of fundamental rights could occur in ways that none of the existing legal frameworks could provide adequate protection from. Some examples of such infringements of AI, not being adequately protected by GDPR, are transparency in decision-making, profiling, and even the ethical training of AI in terms of data.[12] All of these could be covered by the GDPR (for example, in profiling, the data which

---

[10] Regulation of the European Parliament and of the Council laying down harmonised rules on artificial intelligence and amending Regulations (EC) No 300/2008, (EU) No 167/2013, (EU) No 168/2013, (EU) 2018/858, (EU) 2018/1139 and (EU) 2019/2144 and Directives 2014/90/EU, (EU) 2016/797 and (EU) 2020/1828

[11] E.g. Recitals 6, 26, 66 and 91, and article 22 of the GDPR, titled 'Automated decision-making, including profiling', could cover the AI-applications that have the ability to proceed with automated decisions and profiling. But, it should be made clear that GDPR aims at the protection of personal data collected.

[12] The quality of each dataset will affect the language model's performance and researchers are warning that we could run out of good quality data by 2026, meaning that AI rapid advancement will probably become slower. Rita Matulionyte, *Researchers Warn We Could Run out of Data to Train AI by 2026. What Then?*, The Conversation (2023), http://theconversation.com/researchers-warn-we-could-run-out-of-data-to-train-ai-by-2026-what-then-216741

are collected could be perfectly aligned with GDPR provisions- Art. 22) but still violate the core rights of EU citizens, since, if used maliciously, they might infringe the rights to privacy and freedom of self-determination. The AI Act complements the GDPR and works alongside by specifically addressing AI and their potential risks. When an AI system processes personal data, it must comply with both the AI Act's requirements for high-risk systems and the GDPR's data protection obligations. This means ensuring transparency not only about the AI system's functioning but also about how personal data is collected, used, and protected (Recital no. 10).

The new AI Act aims to ensure that AI is compliant with the EU's values and fundamental rights, to provide a robust framework in which technological advancement could be fostered, in parallel with the objective of getting more investment and innovation in AI, all while securing the integrity of the single EU market by preventing market fragmentation.[13] Regardless, it is still unclear how the GDPR and the new AI Act will interact, especially when AI systems potentially trigger GDPR provisions. The new AI Act can provide consumers with one more means of protection against privacy violations, complementing and not replacing GDPR. This ongoing dialogue[14] highlights the complexity of regulating advanced technologies within the framework of existing data protection laws, emphasising the need for continuous adaptation and consideration of broader ethical and privacy implications.

Finally, the Unfair Commercial Practices Directive (UCPD)[15] could equally provide some protection to consumers from a different angle, given that traders are obliged to provide clear and comprehensive information about products and grants consumers redress for unfair commercial practices, namely damages, price reduction and termination of the contract (Art. 11a). However, it may not be adequate to protect consumers from the nature of AI and its applications which are numerous across multiple fields, often complex, and involving automated decision-making processes. While the UCPD addresses the issue of consumer protection from the consumer's angle (by granting more rights to each individual to seek redress), in reality, consumers do not have the power and leverage against developers and authorities run on limited resources.[16] Moreover, the UCPD operates primarily on

---

[13] European Commission (2024). Navigating data protection under the new EU AI Act, Herbert Smith Freehills, https://www.herbertsmithfreehills.com/notes/data/2024-posts/Navigating-data-protection-under-the-new-EU-AI-Act

[14] Mishova (2024).

[15] Directive 2005/29/EC of the European Parliament and of the Council of 11 May 2005 concerning unfair business-to-consumer commercial practices in the internal market and amending Council Directive 84/450/EEC, Directives 97/7/EC, 98/27/EC and 2002/65/EC of the European Parliament and of the Council and Regulation (EC) No 2006/2004 of the European Parliament and of the Council ('Unfair Commercial Practices Directive') (Text with EEA relevance).

[16] UCPD and the new AI Act have also a lot of similarities; see Goanta (2023), *Regulatory Siblings: The Unfair Commercial Practices Directive Roots of the AI Act*, 8, https://papers.ssrn.com/abstract=4337417

an ex-post basis, addressing issues after they have occurred, whereas, in contrast, the AI Act, on an ex-ante basis, sets requirements and safeguards for AI before they are deployed.[17]

3 Enhancing Transparency and Trust in AI: Provisions of the New EU AI Act

The AI Act aims to promote the adoption of trustworthy AI technologies while safeguarding fundamental rights and ensuring consumer protection. In order to achieve that goal, it would be useful to examine the principles of transparency and accountability that are being introduced as means to enhance trust on AI.[18] Title IV of the AI Act outlines the transparency requirements for AI systems that pose specific threats. The main concern is the manipulation of users through the collection of biometric data, the generation and manipulation of digital content.[19] The new AI Act imposes a transparency obligation, as outlined in Article 50, on providers that make use of such technologies to inform people exposed to these technologies about their operation. That obligation involves communicating to individuals how their data is being processed, with the only exception being for cases of criminal investigation, prevention, and detection, where informing subjects is not necessary (Art. 50). Through this process, AI technologies are more accessible and less intimidating to consumers while also providing accountability and transparency. That is the reason why, in the AI Act, regardless of their classification, transparency requirements are imposed in order to regulate specific AI systems (Chapters IV and V). Given the complexity and opacity of AI systems, informed consent is another point that should be discussed in the context of the AI Act in conjunction with transparency requirements. This necessitates a robust framework in which consumers are adequately informed about how their data is being used and how AI-driven decisions impact them, granting the right to challenge AI-driven decisions if necessary (Art. 13 and 86).

The new AI Act highlights transparency as a fundamental requirement for AI systems.[20] Systems must be designed and implemented for users to understand their

[17] Veale and Frederik Zuiderveen (2021), p. 100.

[18] Recently, the Council of Europe has taken significant steps by adopting the first international treaty on Artificial Intelligence. The goal of this treaty is to establish common legal standards to ensure that AI systems are designed and implemented in a manner that upholds human rights and fundamental freedoms while emphasising that AI should be transparent, accountable, and subject to human oversight. Council of Europe adopts first international treaty on artificial intelligence - Portal - www.coe.int, Portal, https://www.coe.int/en/web/portal/-/council-of-europe-adopts-first-international-treaty-on-artificial-intelligence

[19] Preamble 29.

[20] Felzmann et al. (2019).

capabilities and limitations, and AI providers must communicate in a transparent manner the intended purpose of the AI system, the nature of the data used, and the logic behind its decision-making processes. The ultimate goal is to ensure that consumers can make informed choices and are not misled by the technology. Already, the GDPR, which is the cornerstone for data protection in the EU, defines consent in Article 4(11) as: *'any freely given, specific, informed and unambiguous indication of the data subject's wishes by which he or she, by a statement or by a clear affirmative action, signifies agreement to the processing of personal data relating to him or her'*, meaning that consumers must be provided with clear and detailed information about how their data will be used, who will have access to it, and for what purposes.

Building on these principles, the new AI Act requires that AI systems which directly interact (e.g. chatbots, recommendation systems, biometric identification, etc.) with consumers should disclose that they are AI-powered and details about the type of AI, its intended use, and the potential risks associated with its operation.[21] In practice, all major tech providers (social media platforms, search engines, etc.) use AI to target advertisements based on user data. In order to comply with transparency requirements of GDPR, these providers have a specific section in each advertisement where each user could get information about why they are seeing specific ads while also offer tools to manage ad preferences.

Examples of such buttons are the following:

1) Google Ads, where the X button closes the ad and the triangle gives more options to provide feedback and an explanation of why the ad was shown to the specific user.

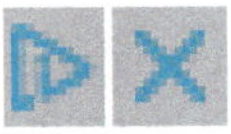

2) Facebook Ads where the user is informed that it is a sponsored Ad and many different options on hiding, reporting and information about why this ad was shown to the specific user.

[21] These derive from the following provisions of the AI Act:

Article 52(1): *'Providers of AI systems intended to interact with natural persons shall ensure that natural persons are informed that they are interacting with an AI system, unless this is obvious from the circumstances and the context of use'.*

Article 52(4): *'Deployers of an AI system that generates or manipulates image, audio or video content constituting a deep fake, shall disclose that the content has been artificially generated or manipulated'.*

Article 52(5): *'The information referred to in paragraphs 1 to 4 shall be provided to the natural persons concerned in a clear and distinguishable manner at the latest at the time of the first interaction or exposure'.*

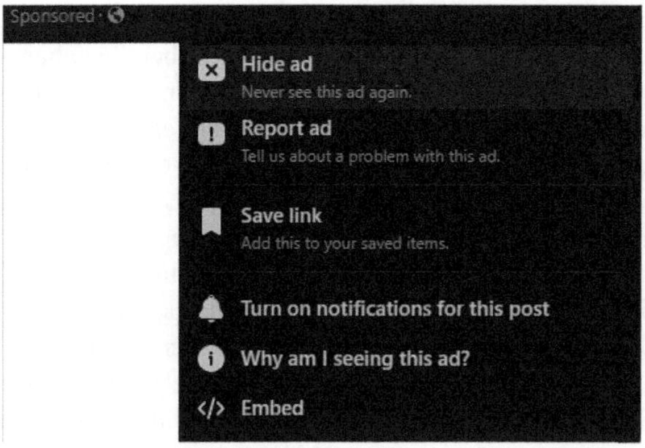

3) In X (formerly known as Twitter), the button is as such:

Once again, once the three buttons are pressed, the user is given the options of muting, blocking, report the Ad, as well as information on why this Ad is shown to the user as shown in the image:

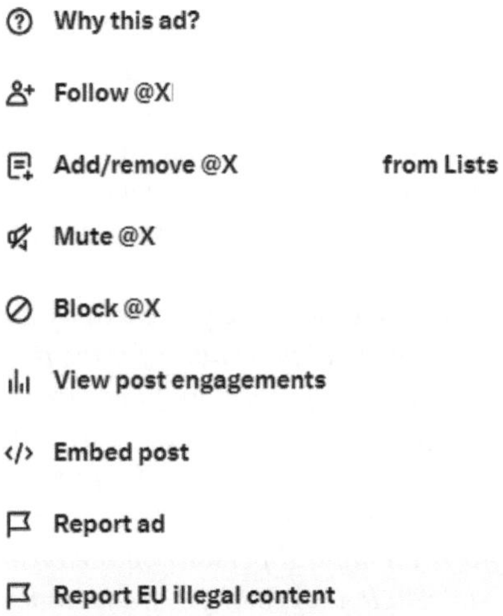

What is of interest is the ‘Report EU illegal content’ button, which directs the user to file a report under European Union law, mainly the newly enacted Digital Service Act (DSA). The existence of this button showcases how influential and useful the existence of a regulatory framework is.

The same principles and the same method could also be applied by providers in order to comply with the new requirements imposed by the AI Act, thereby enhancing transparency and better-protecting consumers. In parallel, trust in AI systems is also essential since consumers can understand how AI works and can be assured that their data is handled responsibly, meaning that they are more likely to embrace AI technologies. As the Capgemini Research Institute found, 62% of consumers would place higher trust in companies whose AI interactions are transparent.[22]

Another goal of the AI Act is to provide a robust framework for the privacy and security of consumer data. Since AI systems heavily rely on vast datasets to function effectively, the providers should make sure that no sensitive consumer information[23] (such as personal identifiers, behavioural patterns, biometric data, etc.) is used in the process. Especially if researchers are true to their predictions about the scarcity of data after 2026,[24] there is even more incentive for providers to exploit data from users in order to win over competition. For these reasons, the new AI Act is very important as it emphasises data minimisation, ensuring that only the data necessary for the AI system's purpose is collected and processed. Additionally, AI systems must be designed to ensure privacy from their conception and not as later additions. These measures could take the form of data anonymisation, pseudonymisation, and encryption to protect consumer data from unauthorised access and breaches.[25]

The GDPR pioneered since it was the first legal framework to introduce the right to erasure/right to be forgotten, as provided in Art. 17. Under the new AI Act, AI system providers will be obliged to inform consumers about how their data will be used, who will have access to it, and for what purposes. Individuals will be able to make an informed decision about the usage of the data and even exercise the right to data deletion. Moreover, based on the right to explanation, consumers could understand what the logic behind AI-driven decisions is and how that affects them. By providing clear and comprehensible explanations, AI providers can mitigate the risks of bias and discrimination, thereby better protecting consumer interests. Of course, it should be noted that AI could also perpetuate biases or exacerbate existing data if not for a strong regulatory framework.

The GDPR, in Recital 71, provided that personal data should be processed by the controller by using *'appropriate mathematical or statistical procedures for the profiling, implement technical and organisational measures appropriate to ensure, in particular, that factors which result in inaccuracies in personal data are corrected and the risk of errors is minimised, secure personal data in a manner that takes account of the potential risks involved for the interests and rights of the data subject'* while also preventing *'discriminatory effects on natural persons on the basis of racial or ethnic origin, political opinion, religion or beliefs, trade union*

[22] The AI-powered enterprise: Unlocking the potential of AI at scale, Capgemini, https://www.capgemini.com/insights/research-library/the-ai-powered-enterprise/. p. 21.

[23] Silva (2024), https://arxiv.org/abs/2409.00264, p. 29.

[24] See ft. 10.

[25] Clark et al. (2024).

membership, genetic or health status or sexual orientation, or that result in measures having such an effect'. This initial thought, set in recital no. 71, addresses the problem of bias but is very limited compared to the new AI Act. Since AI is as biased as the data that is trained on, when the database that the AI is trained lacks diversity, the output is likely to reproduce such biases.[26] One of the most common examples is AI systems for facial recognition, in which individuals with darker skin tones are more difficult to be recognised,[27] or recruitment tools which favour male candidates over equally qualified female candidates due to biased historical hiring data.[28]

In the new AI Act, there are multiple instances in which diversity is mentioned in order to protect the fundamental rights of EU citizens, such as equality. Article 10 (1) provides that data in high-risk AI should meet some criteria referred to in paragraphs 2–5 whenever such data are used. Among the primary concerns mentioned are the *'(f) examination in view of possible biases that are likely to affect the health and safety of persons, have a negative impact on fundamental rights or lead to discrimination prohibited under Union law, especially where data outputs influence inputs for future operations; (g) appropriate measures to detect, prevent and mitigate possible biases identified according to point (f)'*, meaning that the datasets must be diverse and representative, reflecting the diversity of the population. Moreover, the AI Act imposes on developers the obligation to document the data sources and methodologies used in training their AI systems.[29]

Additionally, the AI Act provides for the evaluation of AI systems through algorithmic audits in order to identify any potential biases and discriminatory patterns both before and after deployment. Art. 9 and Art. 72 provide for the implementation of a high-risk management system to monitor high-risk AI throughout their lifetime and ensure post-market monitoring, which *'shall actively and systematically collect, document and analyse relevant data which may be provided by deployers or which may be collected through other sources on the performance of high-risk AI systems throughout their lifetime, and which allow the provider to evaluate the continuous compliance of AI systems with the requirements set out in Chapter III, Section 2'*. Through this process, the EU will ensure that biases that may have been hidden or overlooked in the development or launch stage are identified and rectified. Even more, especially when AI is classified as high-risk and could impact

[26] Manyika et al. (2019).

[27] SITNFlash, *Racial Discrimination in Face Recognition Technology*, Science in the News (Oct. 24, 2020), https://sitn.hms.harvard.edu/flash/2020/racial-discrimination-in-face-recognition-technology/

[28] Kubiak et al. (2023), p. 1219865.

[29] See art. 10(3) *'Training, validation and testing data sets shall be relevant, sufficiently representative, and to the best extent possible, free of errors and complete in view of the intended purpose. They shall have the appropriate statistical properties, including, where applicable, as regards the persons or groups of persons in relation to whom the high-risk AI system is intended to be used. Those characteristics of the data sets may be met at the level of individual data sets or at the level of a combination thereof'*.

individuals, such as hiring, credit scoring or for reasons of law enforcement, the systems should go through a rigorous process of testing and provide even more security of non-discrimination and fairness.

What could also be beneficial for consumers are the provisions of article 86, which grant the right to explanation of individual decision-making, since, in case such decision could have adverse effects on the health, safety or fundamental rights of individuals, the latter have *'the right to obtain from the deployer clear and meaningful explanations of the role of the AI system in the decision-making procedure and the main elements of the decision taken'*. Through that process, consumers are armed with a new recourse tool if they believe that they are subject to biased AI-driven decisions and with a guarantee that human oversight is applicable while also making the AI more transparent and accessible to the user (Art. 13 and 14).

One of the biggest criticisms of AI is the so-called 'black box' theory, which refers to the inability to understand AI's inner workings, since they are not visible or understandable to users or observers.[30] The opacity of the operating system is comparable to a literal black box in which inputs are transformed into outputs within such complicated systems without any proper explanation, making it difficult to ascertain how the AI arrived at a particular decision or prediction.[31] This opacity can undermine trust in AI systems and pose regulatory challenges, raising concerns about hidden biases which are difficult to understand and reveal. As a response to this problem, a new form of AI has been developed, that called explainable AI (XAI)[32] and in which the ratio could be easily understood by humans, providing the ever-needed transparency. The High-Level Expert Group on Artificial Intelligence emphasised the importance of transparency and explainability in their 'Ethics Guidelines for Trustworthy AI',[33] highlighting the need for AI systems to be transparent and decisions to be traceable by humans and that can only be achieved if AI is transparent, interpretable, and subject to human oversight. Finally, in Section 3, the new AI Act provides for the creation of a European Artificial Intelligence Board, which will have enhanced powers to monitor and enforce the regulation, in addition to Regulatory bodies, such as national data protection authorities. The main goal will be to conduct audits, investigate breaches and, most importantly, impose penalties in cases of non-compliance. This oversight enhances transparency and trust in AI systems, ensuring that providers adhere to the regulations and that consumer rights are protected.

---

[30] Kinza Yasar, *What Is Black Box AI? Definition from TechTarget*, WhatIs, https://www.techtarget.com/whatis/definition/black-box-AI

[31] David Lazaridis, *Explainable AI (XAI) and Interpretable Machine Learning (IML) Models | Blogs*, (2021), https://ambiata.com/blog/2021-04-12-xai-part-1/

[32] There are multiple techniques that are being used such as feature visualisation and layer-wise relevance propagation to show how neural networks process information. See Achtibat et al. (2023), p. 1006.

[33] High-Level Expert Group on Artificial Intelligence, ETHICS GUIDELINES FOR TRUSTWORTHY AI, (2018), https://www.europarl.europa.eu/cmsdata/196377/AI%20HLEG_Ethics%20Guidelines%20for%20Trustworthy%20AI.pdf

4 Emotions and How to Manipulate Them: Ethical Implications and Regulatory Challenges

The idea that computers could recognise our emotions was always a fascinating idea, but now it is a reality. In 2000, Rosalind Picard, in her book 'Affective Computing', a result of a 5 years research, introduced the concept of systems that can interact with human emotions.[34] What was once just a theoretical concept has now evolved into reality and should be treated with caution, given that data is more personalised than ever.[35] The applications are numerous, and there are dangers for consumers. While emotional AI and affective computing are often used interchangeably, subtle distinctions exist. On one hand affective computing broadly encompasses the development of systems and devices that can process, simulate, or influence emotions and on the other hand emotional AI specifically focuses on the recognition and interpretation of emotional states.

Eye-tracking software is an AI technology that is able to analyse through different parameters (which part of the screen the person is looking at, for how long, etc.) the attention of the individual and its interest.[36] The results are bifold; on the one hand, the advertisement could become more personalised, and by gathering the data, it could also become better since they are able to understand better what 'catches the eye' (i.e. which colours, shapes, sizes, etc.) resulting in more hooking results.[37] For example, in April 2024, Legacy TV announced that it would be using AI to understand viewers' emotions and then personalise the commercials that they will be watching in order to adhere to the mood of the show.[38] Emotional recognition AI operates by assessing users' emotions through various indicators such as facial expressions, voice tone, and word choice by the usage of machine learning to analyse what are considered 'standardised' emotional indicators.[39]

There are multiple methods in which emotional recognition technologies (ERT) operate: some analyse facial expressions (facial expression recognition-FER), while others examine speech (speech emotion recognition-SER) or text for emotional cues, but the basic idea is the more indicators, the better. More advanced systems could even interpret physiological signals like heart rate or skin response to deduce emotions, and although these could be perceived outwardly, already, more than 25% of Internet users are using a smartwatch capable of (at least) monitoring heartbeats,[40]

[34] Rosalind W. Picard, Affective Computing (1. paperback ed. ed. 2000).

[35] Deloitte (2019).

[36] Sposini (2024), p. 325; A more philosophical discussions: Galič et al. (2017), p. 9.

[37] Al-Azawi (2019), p. 83.

[38] Rachyl Jones, *Legacy TV Enlists AI to Figure out a Show's Emotional Vibe and Add Commercials That Fit the Mood*, Fortune, https://fortune.com/2024/04/03/legacy-tv-ai-artificial-intelligence-commercials-ads-emotion-mood-streaming/

[39] Borak (2024).

[40] Simon Kemp, *Digital 2023 April Global Statshot Report*, (2023), https://datareportal.com/reports/digital-2023-april-global-statshot

meaning that this data could potentially be used to target consumers through personalised ads. By extracting this data, AI applications are able to classify emotions into seven basic categories with extreme accuracy.[41]

The possibilities of such technology are endless, ranging from security to enhanced customer service, but it raises significant ethical concerns, given the dangers deriving from it. For instance, a new AI application could monitor employees while working. While this could be beneficial in case it is used for monitoring a driver who is falling asleep by preventing an accident by playing a sound to wake the driver up, it could also be detrimental, since it can be used for extracting data on occupational satisfaction, and base promotions and dismissals on these data.[42] What is even more dystopian is that a company which creates office pods has been testing the incorporation of sensors to read heart rate, breathing rate and, in general, how nervous people are, providing even more data to employers.[43]

The basic debate behind this is whether it is acceptable for organisations to use such intimate data, like emotions, to influence or interfere in people's lives under safety and security pretexts. Scholars have raised multiple questions about human rights violations, especially regarding privacy, the right to self-determination and autonomy.[44] The AI Act has also been criticised for being open to interpretation and leaving the usage of ERT to the discretion of law enforcement without a right to person to be informed about the fact of being observed or monitored.[45] What has also been debated is how scientifically accurate such technologies are, especially since the majority of such technologies base their results on two datasets (facial expression and tone of voice) and their correlation with the basic theory of human emotions, with some researchers labelling ERT as a 'pseudoscience', warning of its impact on cultural and ethnic minorities.[46]

As examined, ERTs are highly controversial from technological, ethical, and legal perspectives, necessitating a careful examination of how these systems should be regulated in light of both the existing provisions of GDPR and the upcoming AI Act. Article 4 GDPR states that '*personal data are any information which are*

---

[41] The emotions are: happy, neutral, disgust, sad, fear, surprise and anger in two steps; See Saxena et al. (2020), p. 69. Of course, such simple categorisation of emotions has been criticised for oversimplification of human emotional intelligence and that accuracy drops when more classes are introduced; See for example: ai-admin, *Artificial Intelligence Misinterprets Human Emotions - Understanding the Limitations of AI Emotion Recognition Technology*, AI for Social Good (Jan. 10, 2024), https://aiforsocialgood.ca/blog/artificial-intelligence-misinterprets-human-emotions-understanding-the-limitations-of-ai-emotion-recognition-technology

[42] Pressigny (2023).

[43] Ibid.

[44] United Nations High Commissioner for Human Rights (2021), https://www.ohchr.org/en/documents/thematic-reports/ahrc4831-right-privacy-digital-age-report-united-nations-high; Gremsl and Hödl (2022), p. 1; Saxena et al. (2020), p. 53.

[45] The AI Act — a breach of EU fundamental rights charter?, EUobserver (2024), https://euobserver.com/digital/ar2106a373

[46] Emotion Recognition Technology Report, ARTICLE 19, https://www.article19.org/emotion-recognition-technology-report/

related to an identified or identifiable natural person', while the AI Act in Article 3 provides that *'"personal data" means personal data as defined in Article 4, point (1), of Regulation (EU) 2016/679'* (GDPR), meaning that the data to be protected is the same. Anonymisation techniques might cause data to fall outside the legal definition of personal data if, according to Recital 26 of the GDPR, it cannot reasonably be used to identify a person. Still, anonymising data such as biometric is particularly challenging due to its inherently unique and persistent nature and that highlights the practical limitations of anonymisation in this context. Some ERT developers could exploit these ambiguities stify processing biometric data outside GDPR's scope. The fact that this legal uncertainty exists could potentially lead to infringements on privacy and data protection rules, especially if re-identification is possible, contrary to GDPR principles.

Additionally, Art. 5 GDPR states that data shall be *'(a) processed lawfully, fairly and in a transparent manner in relation to individuals ("lawfulness, fairness and transparency");'* and proportionally to the required cause of obtaining the data. Since ERTs process personal data, they generally fall within the scope of GDPR, however, depending on how accurate ERTs are, their compliance could fall into the scope of GDPR.[47] The accuracy of AI outputs, particularly when based on the basic emotion theory, is ambiguous and potentially leading to breaches of fundamental rights, especially when inaccuracies result in discriminatory outcomes.

What is of concern is that AI has many times exhibited different kinds of biases that often reflect or even amplify existing societal prejudices.[48] Studies indicate these systems are less accurate for people of colour, often attributing more negative emotions to them,[49] and fail to aid people with disabilities, often misinterpreting expressions of individuals with conditions like autism or Parkinson's disease,[50] showcasing the limits of such systems to address the needs of individuals effectively. What is further concerning is that Art. 9 GDPR prohibits the processing of special category data, including racial or ethnic origin, unless one of the exceptions under Art. 9(2) applies—such as specific consent from the subject, substantial public interest, or legal obligations. Meanwhile, Art. 22 GDPR also restricts algorithmic decision-making, only allowing it under specific conditions and prohibiting the use of special category data without adequate safeguards. Therefore, GDPR provides a strong framework for data protection, even if AI is used, but despite these protections, ERT poses challenges. As established, these systems often process parameters to determine emotions, which might not fall under 'biometric data for the purpose of uniquely identifying a natural person' as defined by GDPR,

---

[47] The question of accuracy has been discussed in cases such as C434/16 *Novak*, where the court applied the proportionality principle in relation to purpose of the collection of data.

[48] European Commission, *On Artificial Intelligence – A European Approach to Excellence and Trust*, (2020) (AI White Paper).

[49] Speech recognition tools made almost double errors for black speakers when compared to white speakers. See *The Race Gap in Speech Recognition*, https://fairspeech.stanford.edu

[50] Quinn (2021), https://www.ohchr.org/en/documents/thematic-reports/ahrc4952-artificial-intelligence-and-rights-persons-disabilities-report

potentially bypassing the restrictions of Art. 9. Apart from the previously described discrimination, Art. 22 can also protect algorithmic decisions in general that could infringe fundamental rights. Many ventures have tried to launch different applications that make use of this technology,[51] but the fact it has not been proven to be scientifically accurate,[52] in addition to the usage of AI without human supervision, they could infringe basic rights. This is so, especially when it comes to emotions, which could be perceived as the most unique trait of each personality, as emotions are tightly connected with one's person's dignity and liberty. There are already AI cameras with facial recognition technology that can recognise people in public spaces with extreme accuracy,[53] but recognising a person through facial characteristics is something that does not interfere with the inner workings of that individual. If ERT becomes more accurate, then there is a high chance that individuals will not be able to hide their emotions from those who try to understand their inner thoughts and their responses to different stimuli.

Emotion recognition monetises quantified emotions, transforming a revolutionary tool into an instrument of mass surveillance with ethical and legitimacy concerns. Consequently, it needs to be further considered whether emotional recognition is fundamentally at odds with the level of intrusion permissible by states, companies, and individuals into one's personal life and individuality. Privacy has many different interoperations and extends beyond legal definitions, encompassing the right to dignity, liberty and right to self-determination, core rights protected by the GDPR.[54] ERT could compromise dignity by continuously monitoring and evaluating individuals' emotional states, especially in public spaces for commercial purposes, without infringing any of the existing laws or regulations, given that the data rendered does not lead to the identification of an individual. But, such practices, even if legally permissible, infringe on individual and collective privacy by making unwarranted inferences about people's emotions.[55] Especially by inferring mental and emotional states from visible indicators, ERT intrudes into individuals' private spheres under the guise of using publicly available data, a practice that challenges the ethical legitimacy of such technology, especially when deployed in public spaces, without a lawful basis.

All the above facts stress the importance and the uniqueness of emotional data, given its subjective, inescapable nature, making it distinct from other data types. In addition to legal considerations, there are also ethical considerations that must be addressed, especially on how ERT can be regulated to protect this type of data. The future is inevitable, and the progression of such technologies, regardless of the

[51] See for example HireVue, a recruitment platform, which was one of the first to provide facial analysis for their interview process in 2014. But, after some formal complaints on the grounds that the technology was not proven to deliver what they advertised, decided to stop the usage of AI. Pressigny (2023).

[52] Barrett et al. (2019), p. 1.

[53] Crumpler (2020); Fontes et al. (2022), p. 102137.

[54] EU-RENEW (2024).

[55] Gremsl and Hödl (2022), pp. 165–166.

protective framework selected, is a given. That is why emotional data, due to its inherent connection to personal and social identity, requires more extensive protection than currently provided by existing legal frameworks. Hence, ethical and human rights perspectives are essential in evaluating the legitimacy and regulation of emotion recognition technologies to safeguard individuals' emotional privacy and dignity effectively. It should be noted that ERTs are not, *per se*, automatically being classified as high-risk in the AI Act, reflecting the Commission's view that these systems generally pose limited risks. However, some of their applications could potentially be classified as high-risk, especially if they meet the criteria set in Annex III, which will likely classify them as high-risk AI, subjecting them to additional transparency requirements.

5 Challenges and Criticisms

On the 22nd of March 2024, Microsoft announced Copilot+ PCs, which introduce AI to assist users throughout their tasks, being that online or desktop applications.[56] The copilot works in parallel with whichever application the user runs and can assist in recalling the history of what the user has seen (either online or in files or in any other application), can generate images and even provide Live Captions by translating more than 40 languages on real-time into English. Although these capabilities may sound like they enhance the user's experience, they also sound like a privacy nightmare, since the AI will constantly have access to everything the user does. This example showcases only a fraction of capabilities that are widely available to everyday users and can highlight how the new AI Act can secure their rights.

The new AI Act, by providing a robust legal framework, can contribute to consumer protection law, since it can ensure that technologies are deployed adhering to an ethical standard and guaranteeing that fundamental rights are protected.[57] Of course, the implementation of its provisions faces challenges on its own. These will

[56] Yusuf Mehdi, *Introducing Copilot + PCs*, The Official Microsoft Blog (2024), https://blogs.microsoft.com/blog/2024/05/20/introducing-copilot-pcs/. Apple has also announced the introduction of 'Apple Intelligence' which has similar capabilities. Available at: https://www.apple.com/apple-intelligence/

[57] Recital no1 of AI Act states the following: *The purpose of this Regulation is to improve the functioning of the internal market by laying down a uniform legal framework in particular for the development, the placing on the market, the putting into service and the use of artificial intelligence systems (AI systems) in the Union, in accordance with Union values, to promote the uptake of human centric and trustworthy artificial intelligence (AI) while ensuring a high level of protection of health, safety, fundamental rights as enshrined in the Charter of Fundamental Rights of the European Union (the 'Charter'), including democracy, the rule of law and environmental protection, to protect against the harmful effects of AI systems in the Union, and to support innovation. This Regulation ensures the free movement, cross-border, of AI-based goods and services, thus preventing Member States from imposing restrictions on the development, marketing and use of AI systems, unless explicitly authorised by this Regulation.*

be addressed on this next section since it has been heavily criticised for being an obstacle for innovation.

The first and foremost is the practical difficulty of implementing the regulation, given how fast technologies are evolving. The regulatory framework could soon become obsolete, as the pace between the evolution of technology and legislation development and update is widened, resulting in a legal loophole in which AI technologies could potentially operate without sufficient oversight and monitoring, infringing as well as consumer's rights.[58] Additionally, as it has already been mentioned, AI technologies are opaque, particularly complex, and challenging to interpret, leading to difficulties in certifying that the regulatory framework is implemented.

One other practical difficulty that arises is that AI has multiple applications in many different fields, meaning that a regulatory framework, although cleverly crafted, could still leave room for potential breaches. For example, AI applications used in healthcare for diagnostic purposes might require different oversight compared to AI deployed in financial services for fraud detection.[59] These differences in the way they are developed and used pose unique risks and challenges, which may lead to the need of regulatory measures which are specifically tailored and which might not be fully covered under a broad, generalised framework.

Moreover, there are capacity challenges since there are only so many bodies that regulate and oversee AI. Despite the fact that the European Artificial Intelligence Board is being created to oversee the usage of AI and national bodies are also called for this task, it is still a herculean task to regulate and implement AI oversight effectively, especially if taken into account how broadly AI is going to be used from now on. In conjunction with that, the disparity between countries in the EU could also be a factor that could lead to inconsistent enforcement and a lack of comprehensive oversight.[60]

One of the primary arguments against the new AI Act since its conception is the fact that the new regulations could be perceived as being overly restrictive and stifling innovation from the moment stringent regulatory requirements can impose significant compliance costs on businesses, particularly for startups and small-to-medium enterprises.[61] The same, though, was the argument against GDPR, when it was first introduced.[62] The cost which is associated with the abovementioned requirements for transparency and explainability could be pretty substantial and, while necessary for consumer protection, can be technically challenging and costly

[58] Veale and Frederik Zuiderveen (2021), https://papers.ssrn.com/abstract=3896852; Smuha et al. (2021), https://papers.ssrn.com/abstract=3899991

[59] European Parliament. Directorate General for Parliamentary Research Services (2020), https://data.europa.eu/doi/10.2861/6644

[60] Butcher and Beridze (2019), p. 88.

[61] Brook (2023).

[62] European Commission, *Questions and Answers – General Data Protection Regulation*, European Commission - European Commission (2018), https://ec.europa.eu/commission/presscorner/detail/en/MEMO_18_387

to implement, even resulting in companies migrating to jurisdictions with fewer requirements.[63] Of course, the EU has multiple times shown that this is the price that it is willing to pay in order to secure that the fundamental rights of EU citizens are respected.[64]

Moreover, the sandbox approach is the option that the EU adopted as a middle ground in order to foster innovation on the one hand and ensure adequate consumer rights protection on the other hand (Chapter VI). In the sandbox, companies who are developing AI can test their technologies in a controlled environment under regulatory supervision before releasing them for commercial use. Regardless of the practical difficulties of monitoring and applying these changes, the sandbox option is an ingenious solution, as it can even out the concerns against adopting a rigid legal framework, since the companies can have access to the market without being concerned about potential fines.[65] In the UK, the Financial Conduct Authority (FCA) has already rolled out a regulatory sandbox for fintech innovations.[66] Through this platform, firms that have a minimum viable product and who want to test their proposition live in the market with real customers can apply for a case manager to be appointed. The case manager, along with the firm, will develop a testing plan through which suggestions can be provided to lead to the final successful test, granting final permission. One of the restrictions is the limitation on the number of consumers that could initially test the product. By analogy, this example could be applied to the AI Act sandbox.

Another idea in order to further promote innovation while also providing adequate protection for consumers is to offset the above drawbacks of the regulatory framework by creating incentives for companies to develop safe and ethical AI technologies, either in the form of funding for research and development or by reducing taxes for small businesses or even promoting a hub in which companies, academia, and regulatory bodies could work together.[67] Additionally, the EU could try to cooperate with other countries to adopt similar provisions, meaning that forum shopping could be avoided. The Organisation for Economic Co-operation and Development (OECD) has been developing since 2019 AI Principles.[68] These emphasise on the importance of developing trustworthy AI that aligns with human values and respects fundamental rights. When combined with the new AI, they could act as a force of global innovation and as a minimum safety feature for countries throughout the globe.

---

[63] Brook (2023).

[64] European Commission, *On Artificial Intelligence – A European Approach to Excellence and Trust*, (2020) (AI White Paper).

[65] Ahern (2021), p. 395; Kaminski and Malgieri (2021), p. 125.

[66] 'Regulatory Sandbox'. 2022. FCA. 1 March 2022. https://www.fca.org.uk/firms/innovation/regulatory-sandbox

[67] See paragraph on Japan and Singapore under 5.

[68] AI Principles Overview, https://oecd.ai/en/principles

6 Comparative Analysis

Apart from the EU, there are other jurisdictions which have either adopted some legislation that deals with some aspects of AI or are in the process of adopting legislations tailored to the needs of each society. By comparing AI regulations between the EU and different jurisdictions, the best practices can be identified as well as the potential ways in which the AI Act could better itself and provide better protection to consumers.

In the US, AI is regulated in a de-centralised way, meaning that some federal and some state laws are parallel to some industry-specific guidelines.[69] The main objective of the US market is to promote self-regulation through competition, and that is the reason why state intervention is minimal. The first state to enact broad AI legislation is Colorado[70] and although said legislation is quite similar to the EU one since it adopts a risk-based approach, it focuses mostly on high-risk AI, without considering the wide array that the EU Act does. Moreover, the Colorado Regulation is state-specific, whereas the AI covers the whole EU. What is of interest is that the Colorado Regulation provides for an exemption for small businesses with less than 50 employees (Section 6-1-1703 of the Law) to promote innovation and not to dissuade small companies from experimenting with AI. The Federal Trade Commission (FTC) enforces consumer protection laws, but since no AI-specific federal regulation is enacted, the protection that FTC can provide is through existing regulations on unfair or deceptive practices.[71] More specifically, under Section 5 of the FTC Act, businesses are prohibited from engaging in deceptive, unfair practices and, based on that, the Commission could impose fines of over 50,000 $ per violation on companies. Despite the above, it seems that this fragmented approach could create uncertainty both for companies and consumers, since navigating the regulatory framework in the US could be potentially perilous.

On the other side of the globe, the approach taken by the People's Republic of China (PRC) is centralised and state-driven, as with the majority of China's policies. AI is regulated through different regulations on specific aspects of AI, such as deepfakes and generative AI,[72] which grants a more flexible approach. Different and theme-specific regulations can be enacted faster, and loopholes can be addressed faster than with the comprehensive and more complex EU AI Act. It is also easier to deal with each technology than trying to address all issues under one term—that of AI. The disadvantage, though, of such a regulatory framework is that it only deals

[69] Duane et al. (2024).. Additionally, the National Institute of Standards and Technology (NIST) provides voluntary guidelines for AI, emphasising risk management and ethical considerations, see AI Risk Management Framework, NIST (2021), https://www.nist.gov/itl/ai-risk-management-framework

[70] Rutinel et al. (2024).

[71] USA: How the FTC is influencing AI regulation, DataGuidance (2024), https://www.dataguidance.com/opinion/usa-how-ftc-influencing-ai-regulation

[72] Roberts and Hine (2023); The Deepfake law has been criticised for not providing adequate protection, see Laje (2023).

with one problem at a time, meaning that innovations which could potentially combine different technologies could fall under two regulations at the same time or in none at all! The EU could benefit from such an approach to address issues that may arise from the implementation of the AI Act and from the (un)expected evolution of AI. Finally, it should be noted that China's policy on AI focuses mainly on national security and economic growth, incorporating strict data governance and surveillance measures without emphasising much on the rights of individuals and their protection.[73]

Furthermore, Japan and Singapore are two other jurisdictions that are also considering the implementation of AI regulations. For Japan, its AI strategy emphasises on ethical considerations and on human-centric AI development,[74] as described in the 'Artificial Intelligence Technology Strategy'.[75] What is innovative about Japan's approach is that it promotes collaboration between government, academia, and industry in order to innovate and deal with ethical concerns.[76] Singapore's AI regulatory framework, on the other hand, could be characterised by a more collaborative and flexible approach. The most significant piece of regulation is the Model AI Governance Framework, which was developed by the Infocomm Media Development Authority (IMDA) and the Personal Data Protection Commission (PDPC), focusing on fairness and ethical AI.[77] Similar to the sandbox approach of the EU, in Singapore, the AI Verify initiative is a voluntary framework in which companies can assess and verify their AI systems' compliance with the legal framework by conducting standardised tests. Recently, both countries have been considering new legislation on generative AI, which will probably also be influenced by the EU's AI Act,[78] but will introduce, in the case of Singapore, innovative solutions to mitigate risks like misinformation through digital watermarking and cryptographic provenance.[79]

By comparing these approaches, it is easier to comprehend the overplay between regulation and innovation. The EU's stringent regulatory framework prioritises the protection of consumers but with a potential downside, that of hindrance of rapid technological advancement. In contrast, the U.S. and China prioritise innovation and economic growth, potentially at the expense of individual rights and privacy.

---

[73] In contrast with the EU's approach on safeguarding privacy and human rights, the Chinese approach mandates stringent data localisation and cross-border data transfer controls. Pernot-Leplay (2020), 103, https://papers.ssrn.com/abstract=3542820

[74] The Social Principles of Human-Centric AI aims at three points: 1) Dignity, 2) Diversity and inclusion and 3) Sustainability. Available at: https://www.cas.go.jp/jp/seisaku/jinkouchinou/pdf/humancentricai.pdf

[75] AI Strategies and Policies in Japan - OECD.AI, https://oecd.ai/en/dashboards/countries/Japan

[76] See for example Japan Science and Technology Agency (JST), *Accelerating Materials Development: The Materials Integration Consortium, an Industry–Academia–Government Collaboration, Launched*, https://www.jst.go.jp/report/2020/210319_e.html

[77] Model AI Governance Framework 2024 - Press Release, Infocomm Media Development Authority, https://www.imda.gov.sg/resources/press-releases-factsheets-and-speeches/press-releases/2024/public-consult-model-ai-governance-framework-genai

[78] Habuka and Socol de la Osa (2024).

[79] Evans et al. (2024).

Japan's collaborative and ethical focus offers a middle ground but may lack the enforcement mechanisms to ensure compliance.

7 Conclusions

In summary, the advent of AI technologies presents a complex landscape of opportunities and challenges within the framework of consumer protection. The EU's proactive approach, as embodied in the new AI Act, signifies a critical effort to regulate AI in a manner that upholds fundamental rights while on the same time fosters innovation. This is achieved by emphasising on principles such as transparency, accountability, and privacy, while also mitigating the risks associated with AI systems and introducing innovative solutions, such as the AI regulatory sandbox.

Nevertheless, the AI Act's success will hinge upon its practical implementation. Especially given how fast technology is evolving, it is crucial to constantly re-evaluate the existing legal framework, signifying the importance of the European Artificial Intelligence Board. Also, by examining how the AI fits and interplays with other key legislations of the EU, the present chapter highlights the importance of this new regulatory framework, fostering consistency. While the UCPD and the GDPR could provide a coverage of the rights of individuals in the digital age, the new AI Act focuses more on addressing the adverse effects of AI in its infancy and delivering to the EU consumers a product which will be up to an ethical standard.

Another point that is being discussed through the perspective of emotional AI, is how the existing legal frameworks, like the GDPR, provide a foundation for data protection, but may not fully address the nuanced risks posed by technologies that can interpret and influence human emotions. Emotional AI has the ability to intrude upon personal privacy and autonomy, the core of individual rights, and therefore it is also unclear whether the new legislator framework could provide adequate protection.

In order to achieve that goal of effective protection of its consumers, the EU has chosen the specific path of introducing of the AI Act, but, given that other jurisdictions are currently dealing with the same issues, the comparative analyses of other jurisdictions approaches revealed a spectrum of regulatory philosophies, adhering to the need and culture of different societies. From the decentralised approach in the United States to the centralised, state-driven model in China, each proposed solution comes with its own implications for consumer protection. The EU tries to stand in the middle: Having the protection of consumers' rights as the base, it strives for fostering innovation.

Ultimately, safeguarding consumer rights in the age of AI will require ongoing dialogue between regulators, industry stakeholders, and civil society to assess continually the impacts of AI technologies and refining legislative measures accordingly. By striking that balance the EU can protect consumers effectively while encouraging the responsible development of AI, ensuring that AI serves as a force for good without compromising the rights and dignity of individuals.

References

Achtibat R et al (2023) From attribution maps to human-understandable explanations through concept relevance propagation. Nat Mach Intell 5:1006

Ahern D (2021) Regulatory lag, regulatory friction and regulatory transition as FinTech Disenablers: calibrating an EU response to the regulatory sandbox phenomenon. Eur Bus Org Law Rev 22(3):395–432. https://doi.org/10.1007/s40804-021-00217-z

Al-Azawi M (2019) The application of eye-tracking in consumer behaviour. Int J Eng Technol 8:83–86

Barrett LF, Adolphs R, Marsella S, Martinez AM, Pollak SD (2019) Emotional expressions reconsidered: challenges to inferring emotion from human facial movements. Psychol Sci Public Interest 20(1):1–68. https://doi.org/10.1177/1529100619832930

Borak M (2024) Is the EU AI Act leaving a backdoor for emotion recognition? | Biometric Update. https://www.biometricupdate.com/202402/is-the-eu-ai-act-leaving-a-backdoor-for-emotion-recognition

Brook A (2023) Should AI be regulated? The arguments for and against. https://www.wearedevelopers.com/magazine/eu-ai-regulation-artificial-intelligence-regulations

Butcher J, Beridze I (2019) What is the state of artificial intelligence governance globally? RUSI J 164(5–6):88–96. https://doi.org/10.1080/03071847.2019.1694260

Clark J, Kettas K, Dermican M (2024) Europe: The EU AI Act's relationship with data protection law: key takeaways. In: Privacy matters. https://privacymatters.dlapiper.com/2024/04/europe-the-eu-ai-acts-relationship-with-data-protection-law-key-takeaways/

Corbett J (2024) Landmark Artificial Intelligence Act in EU slammed as rights "failure" | Common Dreams. https://www.commondreams.org/news/european-union-ai-act

Crumpler W (2020) How accurate are facial recognition systems – and why does it matter? | Strategic Technologies Blog | CSIS. https://www.csis.org/blogs/strategic-technologies-blog/how-accurate-are-facial-recognition-systems-and-why-does-it

Duane P, Scott K, Lerman L (2024) Colorado enacts landmark AI legislation. https://www.wiley.law/alert-Colorado-Enacts-Landmark-AI-Legislation

Evans M, Ang W, Lua J, Chew J (2024) Singapore proposes governance framework for generative AI. In: Data protection report. https://www.dataprotectionreport.com/2024/02/singapore-proposes-governance-framework-for-generative-ai/

Felzmann H, Villaronga EF, Lutz C, Tamò-Larrieux A (2019) Transparency you can trust: Transparency requirements for artificial intelligence between legal norms and contextual concerns. Big Data Soc 6(1). https://doi.org/10.1177/2053951719860542

Fontes C, Hohma E, Corrigan CC, Lütge C (2022) AI-powered public surveillance systems: why we (might) need them and how we want them. Technol Soc 71:102137. https://doi.org/10.1016/j.techsoc.2022.102137

Galič M, Timan T, Koops B-J (2017) Bentham, Deleuze and beyond: an overview of surveillance theories from the panopticon to participation. Philos Technol 30(1):9–37. https://doi.org/10.1007/s13347-016-0219-1

Goanta C (2023) Regulatory siblings: the unfair commercial practices directive roots of the AI Act

Gremsl T, Hödl E (2022) Emotional AI: legal and ethical challenges. Inf Polity 27:1–12. https://doi.org/10.3233/IP-211529

Habuka H, Socol de la Osa D (2024) Shaping global AI Governance: enhancements and next steps for the G7 Hiroshima AI process. https://www.csis.org/analysis/shaping-global-ai-governance-enhancements-and-next-steps-g7-hiroshima-ai-process

Kaminski ME, Malgieri G (2021) Algorithmic impact assessments under the GDPR: producing multi-layered explanations. Int Data Priv Law 11(2):125–144. https://doi.org/10.1093/idpl/ipaa020

Karnouskos S (2022) Symbiosis with artificial intelligence via the prism of law, robots, and society. Artif Intell Law 30(1):93–115

Kubiak E, Efremova MI, Baron S, Frasca KJ (2023) Gender equity in hiring: examining the effectiveness of a personality-based algorithm. Front Psychol 14:1219865. https://doi.org/10.3389/fpsyg.2023.1219865
Laje D (2023) China's deep fake law is fake | AFCEA International. https://www.afcea.org/signal-media/cyber-edge/chinas-deep-fake-law-fake
Manyika J, Silberg J, Presten B (2019) What do we do about the biases in AI? Harv Bus Rev:25. https://hbr.org/2019/10/what-do-we-do-about-the-biases-in-ai
Mishova A (2024) How the EU AI Act complements GDPR: a compliance guide. In: GDPR local. https://gdprlocal.com/how-the-eu-ai-act-complements-gdpr-a-compliance-guide/
Pernot-Leplay E (2020) China's approach on data privacy law: a third way between the U.S. and the EU?
Picard R (2000) Toward computers that recognize and respond to user emotion. IBM Syst J 39:705–719. https://doi.org/10.1147/sj.393.0705
Pressigny CD (2023) The creepy AI-driven surveillance that may be infiltrating your workplace. In: Business Insider. https://www.businessinsider.com/ai-surveillance-detects-emotion-at-work-gets-you-fired-2023-11
Quinn G (2021) Artificial intelligence and the rights of persons with disabilities - Report of the Special Rapporteur on the rights of persons with disabilities
Roberts H, Hine E (2023) The future of AI policy in China | East Asia Forum. https://eastasiaforum.org/2023/09/27/the-future-of-ai-policy-in-china/
Rutinel M, Titone B, Rodriguez R (2024) Consumer protections for artificial intelligence
Saxena A, Khanna A, Gupta D (2020) Emotion recognition and detection methods: a comprehensive survey. J Artif Intell Syst 2:53–79. https://doi.org/10.33969/AIS.2020.21005
Silva NS e (2024) The Artificial Intelligence Act: critical overview
Smuha NA, Ahmed-Rengers E, Harkens A, Li W, MacLaren J, Piselli R, Yeung K (2021) How the EU can achieve legally trustworthy AI: A response to the European Commission's proposal for an Artificial Intelligence Act
Sposini L (2024) Neuromarketing and eye-tracking technologies under the European Framework: towards the GDPR and beyond. J Consum Policy 47(3):321–344. https://doi.org/10.1007/s10603-023-09559-2
Veale M, Zuiderveen Borgesius F (2021) Demystifying the Draft EU Artificial Intelligence Act — Analysing the good, the bad, and the unclear elements of the proposed approach. Comput Law Rev Int 22(4):97–112. https://doi.org/10.9785/cri-2021-220402

Reports

Deloitte (2019) Made-to-order: The rise of mass personalization
EU-RENEW (2024) The foundations of EU personal data protection law: Privacy and Human Dignity – EU RENEW. https://eu-renew.eu/the-foundations-of-eu-personal-data-protection-law-privacy-and-human-dignity/
European Commission (2024) European approach to artificial intelligence | Shaping Europe's digital future. https://digital-strategy.ec.europa.eu/en/policies/european-approach-artificial-intelligence
European Parliament (2024) Artificial Intelligence Act: MEPs adopt landmark law | News | European Parliament
European Parliament. Directorate General for Parliamentary Research Services (2020) The ethics of artificial intelligence: issues and initiatives. Publications Office, LU
United Nations High Commissioner for Human Rights (2021) The right to privacy in the digital age

AI Act and MDR: Investigating Regulatory Overlaps, Influences, and Joint Application Issues

Sofia Palmieri

Contents

Abstract This chapter examines the integration of artificial intelligence (AI) into medical devices and the regulatory complexities arising from the intersection of the European Union's Medical Device Regulation (MDR) and the AI Act. It highlights AI's transformative role in healthcare, from advanced diagnostics and personalised treatment plans to real-time patient monitoring. The discussion focuses on the chal-

S. Palmieri (✉)
Metamedica Unit, Department of Public Health and Primary Care, Faculty of Medicine and Health Science, Ghent University, Ghent, Belgium
e-mail: Sofia.Palmieri@UGent.be

V. L. Raposo (ed.), *The European Artificial Intelligence Act*, Law, Governance and Technology Series 78, https://doi.org/10.1007/978-3-031-98406-8_14

lenges of dual compliance, emphasising the need for a balanced regulatory framework that fosters innovation while upholding rigorous safety and efficacy standards. Key areas of regulatory overlap—including risk classification, technical documentation, conformity assessment, and post-market surveillance—are explored in depth. Additionally, the chapter identifies implementation challenges such as ambiguous requirements, the intricacies of risk-based categorisation, the need for clearer conformity assessment guidelines, and the disproportionate burden on small and medium-sized enterprises. It concludes by advocating for the development of harmonised standards and comprehensive guidance to streamline implementation, ensuring a regulatory landscape that both promotes innovation and safeguards patient safety.

1 Introduction

Imagine walking into your home, and as you step inside, the lights dim to your preferred setting, the temperature adjusts to a comfortable level, and your favourite playlist starts playing softly in the background. Your smart home has learned your routines and preferences, adjusting itself effortlessly to make your life easier. This isn't a glimpse into the distant future; it's the power of AI integrated seamlessly into consumer products today.

AI has woven itself into many aspects of our daily lives, enhancing the products we use to become more responsive, intuitive, and personalised. Take your smartphone, for instance. It's no longer just a tool for calling or messaging; it's an intelligent assistant that recognises your voice, suggests reminders based on your schedule, and even adjusts its settings to save battery when it senses you're far from a charger. The camera on your phone doesn't simply snap pictures—it uses AI to detect faces, optimise lighting, and adjust settings in real-time to capture stunning photos with minimal effort. Wearables, like fitness trackers and smartwatches, are also enriched with AI. These devices don't just measure steps or track your heart rate—they learn from your activity patterns and provide insights tailored to your health goals. For example, if you're not meeting your sleep targets, the device might suggest bedtime reminders or even give tips to improve your sleep quality. Over time, they evolve from passive trackers into active health coaches, using AI to keep you motivated and mindful of your wellness journey.

Behind the scenes, AI analyses your behaviour, learns your preferences, and adapts to create a smoother user experience every time you unlock your device.

Artificial Intelligence seems to be everywhere. Whether these days this is true or rather an impression, AI has certainly all what it takes to become a transformative force, reshaping products and services across a wide range of industries. From personalised consumer experiences to complex decision-making systems in critical sectors, AI integration is set to push the boundaries of technological innovation. In fields like automotive, finance, and healthcare, products increasingly leverage AI-driven capabilities such as predictive analytics, pattern recognition, and real-time decision-making. King.[1] These advancements are not only meant to enhance user experiences[2] but also creating products that can adapt, learn, and optimise performance over time.[3]

Healthcare, in particular, stands out for its intended adoption of AI, especially within medical devices, where AI applications are revolutionising diagnostics, treatment protocols, and patient management. Through AI, medical devices now possess the capacity to interpret vast amounts of data with speed and precision, allowing healthcare providers to improve the accuracy of diagnoses, develop personalised treatment plans, and monitor patients more effectively than ever before. The integration of AI into medical devices has ushered in a new era of medical technology that promises improved patient outcomes, operational efficiency, and cost savings (see n. 1–3).

Yet, as the scope of AI integration broadens, so does the complexity of regulating these intelligent systems. The regulatory landscape is now at a crossroads, particularly in the European Union (EU), where stringent oversight through both the Medical Device Regulation (MDR)[4] and the newly enforced AI Act[5] governs AI-based medical technologies. Each regulation targets critical safety, efficacy, and ethical standards, but the overlap in these regulatory frameworks poses unique challenges. For developers, manufacturers, and healthcare providers, navigating the dual compliance requirements of the MDR and the AI Act is now an essential yet complex aspect of bringing AI-driven medical devices to market.

In this chapter, we delve into the complex integration of AI within medical devices, emphasising how overlapping regulatory frameworks shape this dynamic field. We propose an analysis from both micro and macro perspectives, addressing classification challenges, regulatory requirements, and post-market surveillance processes. By exploring the intersection of the MDR and the proposed AI Act, we aim to shed light on the opportunities and obstacles that stakeholders encounter in an industry where innovation and regulatory evolution must move in tandem.

[1] Singh and Jadhav (2024), p. 139.

[2] Hoseini (2023), pp. 12–18.

[3] Verganti et al. (2020), pp. 212–227.

[4] Regulation (EU) 2017/745 of the European Parliament and of the Council of 5 April 2017 on medical devices, amending Directive 2001/83/EC, Regulation (EC) No 178/2002, and Regulation (EC) No 1223/2009, and repealing Council Directives 90/385/EEC and 93/42/EEC, OJ L 117, 5.5.2017, pp. 1–175.

[5] Regulation (EU) 2024/1689 of the European Parliament and of the Council of 13 June 2024 laying down harmonised rules on artificial intelligence and amending certain Union legislative acts, OJ L 168, 12.7.2024, pp. 1–125

2 AI in Medical Devices

The integration of artificial intelligence in medical devices began as a response to the growing need for enhanced precision, efficiency, and data-driven insights in healthcare.[6] Early medical devices were limited to basic monitoring and diagnostic functions, but with advances in machine learning and data analytics, AI started to revolutionise these capabilities.[7] Initially, AI was employed to support clinical decision-making, automate routine tasks, and assist in diagnostic imaging by recognising patterns that might be missed by human eyes. Over time, this integration expanded to include predictive analytics for patient outcomes, personalised treatment plans, and even surgical robots capable of performing minimally invasive procedures with unprecedented accuracy. The evolution of AI in medical devices was propelled by the increasing volume of patient data and the need for faster, more accurate interpretations. This shift laid the groundwork for smarter, adaptive devices that not only collected data but actively learned from it to improve performance over time.[8]

The integration of AI in medical devices is opening new horizons for patient care, diagnostics, and treatment. Imagine a device that not only monitors a patient's vital signs in real-time but also detects subtle, early warning signs of deterioration. Such capabilities are made possible by AI, which analyses vast amounts of data from these devices to reveal patterns, assess risk, and even make life-saving recommendations on the spot.[9]

To exemplify, one of the most promising applications of AI in medical devices is in diagnostic imaging.[10] Devices equipped with AI algorithms can analyse X-rays, MRIs, and CT scans with remarkable accuracy, often highlighting anomalies that radiologists might miss. For example, AI-enhanced devices can flag early signs of conditions like lung cancer or neurological disorders, allowing for timely interventions.[11] These advancements don't just increase the speed and precision of diagnostics but also reduce the workload on healthcare providers, enabling them to focus on delivering patient care.

Another sector in which AI is set to make the difference are wearable medical devices.[12] Wearable medical devices, such as smart ECG monitors, blood glucose sensors, and even AI-enhanced pacemakers, are also transforming patient management.[13] AI algorithms in these devices continuously monitor patients, spotting irregularities and alerting healthcare teams or patients directly if intervention is needed.

---

[6] Sunny et al. (2024), pp. 384–402.

[7] Haleem et al. (2022), pp. 12–30.

[8] Topol (2019), pp. 44–56.

[9] Kalid et al. (2018), pp. 1–30.

[10] Pinto-Coelho (2023), p. 1435.

[11] Khanna (2020), pp. 1–15.

[12] Nahavandi et al. (2022), p. 106541.

[13] Wang (2023), p. 17.

For example, AI-powered glucose monitors analyse trends and even suggest insulin dosage adjustments for diabetes patients, while smart heart monitors detect arrhythmias and can automatically alert caregivers to take immediate action.[14] These wearables empower patients to manage chronic conditions more effectively, often from the comfort of their homes.

In this context, the integration of AI into medical devices is transforming healthcare from a reactive to a proactive model. These devices, through continuous monitoring, diagnosis, and even treatment assistance, offer unprecedented precision and personalisation. This shift not only enhances care efficiency but also fosters a focus on prevention, enabling patients and providers to address health issues before they escalate. With AI driving this change, medical devices are evolving from simple tools to active contributors in healthcare, paving the way for a future where technology and compassionate care work together to improve and save lives. While AI in healthcare often emphasises preventive medicine, there is significant growth in its responsive applications, especially in emergency and acute care. AI-powered devices and systems are increasingly integrated into emergency medicine, where they enhance patient outcomes through various responsive applications. For instance, predictive analysis tools help streamline triage in emergency departments by analysing vital signs and patient history, enabling quicker prioritisation so that critical cases receive immediate care. Automated diagnostic algorithms, trained on extensive medical datasets, assist in diagnosing urgent conditions such as strokes, heart attacks, and traumatic injuries by analysing medical images and data with remarkable speed and accuracy. Virtual health assistants, powered by AI, support first responders and emergency staff by providing rapid assessments and guidance on treatment protocols, improving response times and accuracy in critical situations. In surgical settings, AI has revolutionised procedures by introducing robotic systems that enhance precision, control, and safety. Surgical robots, such as the da Vinci Surgical System, assist in minimally invasive procedures, enabling greater dexterity and precision. This results in less blood loss and quicker patient recovery compared to traditional methods. Additionally, AI-guided procedures can provide real-time feedback, analysing patient-specific data during surgeries to guide a surgeon's movements and improve outcomes. AI-driven simulation systems also play an important role in training, allowing surgeons to practice complex procedures in a realistic, data-driven virtual environment, which helps them refine their skills in a risk-free setting.

These advancements in AI, both in emergency care and surgical procedures, demonstrate the technology's vital role in optimising response speed, accuracy, and patient safety. Integrating AI across healthcare settings shows its potential as a valuable asset in both preventive and responsive medical practices, improving patient outcomes at every level of care.

To harness the transformative power of AI while integrating these potentially system-changing technologies responsibly, they must be subject to rigorous and

[14] Coman et al. (2024), p. 2351.

comprehensive regulation. The discourse surrounding AI regulation has been evolving for years, culminating recently in the approval of a dedicated regulatory framework. This new framework, however, does not exist in isolation; it is deeply intertwined with existing product regulations to maintain consistency and clarity across various sectors. In the realm of medical devices, this intersection creates a complex landscape where AI regulations must align with and complement established medical device standards.

This scenario poses a fundamental challenge: how can the existing regulatory framework effectively apply to products that are both medical devices and AI-driven technologies? The dual nature of such products necessitates a nuanced regulatory approach that balances the technological innovations inherent in AI with the stringent safety and efficacy standards required for medical devices. To address this, we need to explore the intersection of the MDR and the newly developed AI Act, examining how these frameworks inform and complement each other.

Understanding how these regulations overlap is essential for navigating the evolving landscape of AI-integrated medical devices. The MDR and AI Act must work cohesively to ensure that innovations in medical technology do not compromise patient safety or product reliability. By dissecting these regulations, we aim to shed light on how stakeholders can move forward confidently, balancing the need for technological progress with the imperatives of safety and efficacy.

3 An Overview of Medical Device Regulation

The European MDR regulates, among other things, the safety, market entry, and monitoring of medical devices. It entered into force in 2021 and repealed the previous Medical Devices Directive (MDD)[15] and the Directive on implantable medical devices.[16] In the new regulation, the definition of medical devices was broadened,[17] safety was emphasised,[18] and monitoring became more rigorous.[19] The MDR is a piece of regulatory framework crucial for fostering trust in medical devices within the European Union (see n. 6). The MDR ensures the safety, efficacy, and quality of medical devices, ultimately guaranteeing their reliability and compliance.

The MDR regulates products that are identified as having a medical intended purpose. More specifically, to be defined as a medical device, the product has to be intended for one of the uses recognised in Article 2(1). According to this article, a

[15] Council Directive 93/42/EEC concerning medical devices [1993] OJ L169/1.

[16] Council Directive 90/385/EEC on the approximation of the laws of the Member States relating to active implantable medical devices [1990] OJ L189/17.

[17] Commission, Proposal for Regulation on medical devices [2012] COM/2012/0542 final (Commission, Proposal for MDR), part 3.1; MDR Art. 2(1) and MDD Art. 1(2)(a).

[18] Commission, Proposal for MDR (n 15), part 1.

[19] See MDD Art. 5; MDR Chapter VII.

medical device is 'any instrument, apparatus, appliance, software, implant, reagent, material, or other article intended by the manufacturer to be used, alone or in combination, by human beings for one or more of the following specific medical purposes:

- diagnosis, prevention, monitoring, prediction, prognosis, treatment or alleviation of disease;
- diagnosis, monitoring, treatment, alleviation or compensation of an injury or disability;
- investigation, replacement, or modification of anatomy, or a physiological or pathological process or state;
- providing information through the in vitro examination of samples derived from the human body, including organ, blood, and tissue donations'.

In addition to this already comprehensive definition of medical devices, Article 2(1) identifies two other specific groups of medical devices: (1) those devices intended to support or control conception and (2) those intended explicitly for the cleaning, disinfection, or sterilisation of devices (see n. 7).

3.1 *Risk Classes*

The MDR adopts a risk-based approach, categorising medical devices into four risk classes following the criteria set out in Annex VIII. Starting from the bottom, Class I, intermediate Classes IIa and IIb, and Class III present medical devices with higher risk (see n. 8). Depending on the medical device's intended use, it is possible to identify the risk class to which it must belong according to the regulation (see n. 9). Furthermore, the MDR provides a classification rule specifically for medical devices consisting wholly or partly of software, conferring to them a sort of ad hoc regulation (see n. 10). Rule 11 of the MDR defines the classification of software/medical devices, stating that all software medical devices are risk-Class I. However, the MDR carves out several exceptions to this rule:

> Software intended to provide information that is used to make decisions for diagnostic or therapeutic purposes is classified as Class IIa, except if such decisions have an impact that may cause:
>
> - death or irreversible impairment of a person's state of health, in which case it is classified in Class III; or
> - a serious deterioration in a person's state of health or surgery, in which case it is classified in Class IIb.

In addition to these classification rules, software intended for monitoring physiological processes are classified as Class IIa. This rule applies except if the software is designed for monitoring vital physiological parameters when the variations in those parameters are of such nature that they may pose an immediate danger to the patient, in which case it is classified as Class IIb.[20] Furthermore, according to rule 15, contraceptive software must be classified as Class IIb (see n. 11). Therefore, while the majority of AI-powered medical devices will not qualify as Class I under Rule 11 of the MDR due to their involvement in clinical decision-making or monitoring critical patient conditions, certain types of AI applications can still fall into this category. These include administrative or logistical AI tools that streamline hospital operations, such as appointment scheduling or inventory tracking, without influencing diagnosis or treatment. Additionally, data management software that simply aggregates or retrieves patient data, wellness applications that focus on general health and well-being, and non-diagnostic educational software are also likely to be classified as Class I. These devices carry a lower risk to patient safety and, as such, do not meet the criteria for higher risk classifications, ensuring a more streamlined regulatory pathway for their approval.

3.2 *Risk Justified Requirements*

According to the risks connected to the device, the manufacturer must comply with progressively stricter requirements to ensure the safe use of the product throughout its life cycle (see n. 12). These requirements are subject to an increasing safety logic in proportion to the highest risk class identified. The General Safety and Performance Requirements (GSPR), enforced by the MDR, are a set of rules and standards that medical device manufacturers and suppliers must comply with to ensure their products' safe and effective use. Fulfilling the general safety and performance requirements listed in Annex I is one of the most fundamental preconditions to placing any medical device on the European market (see n. 13). The requirements to ensure the device's safety range from general requirements (such as those related to risk reduction and elimination) to information requirements, passing through requirements regarding design and manufacture. To understand the full scope and detail of the European general safety and performance requirements, the reader is directed to read Annex I of the Regulation.

[20] A real life example is offered by the invasive catheter produced by https://www.edwards.com/it/#. Such a catheter reaches the pulmonary artery and through the detection of specific parameters offer a predictive index of hypotensive events. A more detailed analysis of Rule 11 can be found in the Guidance on Qualification and Classification of Software in Regulation (EU) 2017/745 – MDR and Regulation (EU) 2017/746 – IVDR, released by the Medical Device Coordination Group in 2019;

3.3 *Third-Party Assessment*

Compliance with the requirements allows the product to be considered safe in use and to obtain the CE label, which declares that it conforms to European standards (see n. 14).

As already mentioned, the compliance analysis with the requirements is based on the data in the technical documentation. The regulation requires Member States to identify a notified body following the designation procedure outlined in Article 42 of the MDR to perform this safety control. These bodies are designated to perform the conformity assessment to establish whether the device meets the Regulation requirements. Some medical devices require a third-party compliance assessment with the Regulation's requirements based on their inherent risks and the consequent classification. In Recital 60, the MDR suggests that 'the conformity assessment procedure for Class I devices should, as a general rule, be carried out under the sole responsibility of the manufacturers',[21] given the low level of vulnerability associated with such devices. In contrast, for Class IIa, Class IIb and Class III devices, an appropriate level of involvement of a Notified Body should be mandatory. This aspect is repeated in Annex VII titled 'requirements to be met by the notified bodies' wherein point 4.5.3 'Product Verification' letter (b) we read that Notified Bodies shall 'establish a test plan identifying all relevant and critical parameters which need to be tested by the Notified Body or under its responsibility to:

- verify, for Class IIb devices, the conformity of the device with the type described in the EU type-examination certificate and with the requirements of this regulation applicable to such devices;
- confirm, for Class IIa devices, compliance with the technical documentation referred to in Annexes II and III and with the requirements of this regulation that apply to such devices'.

The Clinical Evaluation Report submitted by the manufacturer of a medical device to a notified body and the Clinical Evaluation Assessment Report prepared by the notified body to summarise its evaluation of that evidence should both be publicly available (see n. 15). Access to these documents would supplement the information that will be provided in the summary of safety and clinical performance and the Instructions for Use (Annex I, Article 23.4). To foster transparency, the MDR also established a centralised repository designed to facilitate information exchange among EU member states, notified bodies, and the European Commission. Eudamed is intended to house comprehensive data on medical devices, certificates, and clinical investigations, promoting better oversight and access to critical information. However, the full implementation of Eudamed has faced significant delays, and as

[21] The definition of manufacturer can be found in MDR Art 2 (30), which states: 'manufacturer' means a natural or legal person who manufactures or refurbishes a device or makes a device of the same design, manufacture or complete refurbishment, and markets that device under his own name or trademark.

of now, it remains partially operational. These challenges highlight the complexities involved in enforcing transparency and harmonising data systems across the EU. Despite this, the MDR continues to play a crucial role in ensuring the safety, efficacy, and quality of medical devices, aligning with its overarching aim of improving public health and patient safety (see n. 16).

3.4 *Post-market Surveillance*

The product's compliance with safety requirements must be ensured even after it is placed on the market (see n. 11). For each device, manufacturers shall plan, establish, document, implement, maintain, and update a post-market surveillance system proportionate to the risk class and appropriate for the type of device.[22] This plan is structured and included by the manufacturer in the technical documentation and must contain practices for continuously assessing the risks and benefits of the device in its daily use. Notified bodies must oversee the manufacturer's compliance with the post-market surveillance plan and assess whether the device continues to meet the requirements during its entire life cycle (see n. 12).

Through thorough lifecycle surveillance, the MDR emphasises monitoring and evaluating device performance once it enters the market. Manufacturers are obligated to establish robust systems for reporting and addressing adverse events. To ensure the safety of these tools, the requirements assessment is also enforced through the UDI system. A distinctive facet introduced by the MDR is indeed the requirement for a Unique Device Identification (UDI) system, enhancing traceability throughout a device's lifecycle (see n. 17). This includes a device identifier and production identifier, facilitating unambiguous identification. The UDI facilitated the post-market surveillance enforced under the MDR.

4 Regulatory Overlap Between the MDR and AI Act

The background and purpose of the AI Act have been examined extensively in earlier sections of this book. To briefly summarise, the AI Act represents a pioneering regulatory framework introduced by the European Union to establish unified standards for the development, deployment, and use of artificial intelligence across member states. This legislation aims to mitigate risks associated with AI technologies, increase transparency, and uphold fundamental rights, safety, and fairness in AI applications—all while promoting innovation within Europe's digital economy. At its core, the AI Act seeks to balance AI's transformative potential with robust

[22] Chapter VII, Section I Article 83 *et seq.* of the MDR.

protections against misuse and harm, setting clear ethical and regulatory guidelines to ensure trustworthy AI systems.[23]

Similarly, key provisions and compliance requirements for AI systems were thoroughly discussed in previous chapters, but a brief overview is helpful for the analysis in this chapter. The AI Act adopts a risk-based approach, categorising AI systems into levels of risk: unacceptable, high, and minimal or low risk. High-risk systems—those impacting health, safety, and fundamental rights—must meet strict requirements, including rigorous data quality standards, transparency, and human oversight. These systems must also undergo conformity assessments and continuous post-market monitoring. By contrast, low-risk AI systems face lighter compliance measures, primarily focused on transparency. These requirements collectively aim to bolster accountability, ensure reliability, and minimise the potential for adverse effects across various sectors.

In terms of regulatory structure, the AI Act shares notable similarities with the Medical Device Regulation, especially in its emphasis on risk-based safety requirements and third-party conformity assessments. This structural resemblance and the potential dual nature of certain AI-based medical devices create significant overlaps between the two regulations. These intersections carry critical implications for medical device manufacturers, healthcare providers, and regulators alike. In the following sections, we outline the AI Act's main provisions and examine the macro- and micro-level overlaps between these two regulatory frameworks.

4.1 *Macro-Level Overlaps Between the AI Act and Medical Device Regulation: Risk Classes*

When analysing the AI Act, references to the healthcare sector appear minimal and are limited to two main sections that address high-risk medical AI risk classification. The classification of medical AI as high-risk involves two main pathways: references in Annex I paired with third-party conformity assessments, and classifications under Annex III.

Firstly, High-Risk medical AI can be identified via Annex I. As mentioned in the previous paragraphs, MDR Rule 11 states that software for diagnostic or therapeutic purposes, or for monitoring physiological processes and contraception, falls under Class IIa or higher, necessitating third-party evaluation. When these classifications are coupled with Section 6(1) of the AI Act, which designates medical AI subject to third-party conformity as high-risk, any software meeting these criteria is identified as high-risk AI.

Secondly, High-Risk medical AI can also be identified via Annex III. The AI Act's Annex III outlines specific applications considered high-risk. Subsequent, EU Commission guidance has refined this classification, stating that systems named in

[23] Cancela-Outeda, 'The EU's AI Act: A framework for collaborative governance'.

points (a), (c), and (d) of Article 5 in Annex III may also qualify as high-risk.[24] Thus, medical AI systems with these characteristics are subject to the stringent requirements associated with high-risk AI (see n. 19). However, since the focus of this chapter is AI-based medical devices, systems classified as high-risk AI through this pathway, without reference to the MDR, fall outside the scope of this discussion.

Beyond these sections identifying high-risk AI, the AI Act may have implications for medical AI in other respects. AI systems not classified as high-risk may still be categorised as minimal or unacceptable risk. Medical AI could be deemed part of the unacceptable risk category if it performs functions explicitly prohibited by Article 5 of Title II. Certain patient groups could be classified as 'vulnerable groups', potentially placing some medical AI solutions in the unacceptable risk category. This classification pertains to systems that can manipulate individuals in ways that harm their autonomy or decision-making, such as subliminally influencing a person's behaviour against their initial intent. For example, an AI designed to alter a woman's decisions about pregnancy contrary to her wishes would fall into this category due to the serious ethical and social implications.

The minimal-risk category in the AI Act is broad and inclusive, encompassing any AI system that aligns with its definition, including those used in medical contexts. Medical AI systems that do not meet the criteria for high-risk or unacceptable risk are, by default, classified as minimal risk.

AI systems that do not meet the definitions outlined in Article 2(1) of the MDR fall into this minimal-risk category (or unacceptable AI risk). If an AI system's intended use does not align with the MDR's definition of a medical device, it does not fulfil Article 6 of the AI Act and is classified as minimal-risk by exclusion. Additionally, some devices that qualify as medical under Article 2 but are considered low-risk according to MDR classification fall into Class I. For example, a mobile application that uses AI to track and analyse physical activity for general wellness purposes without making any diagnostic or therapeutic recommendations would not meet the MDR's medical device definition. As such, it would be considered minimal-risk under the AI Act. On the other hand, an AI-powered thermometer that monitors body temperature for general health purposes, without making critical health decisions or diagnosing disease, would qualify as a Class I medical device under MDR, given its minimal risk to patient safety. These low-risk devices do not require third-party conformity assessments. As such, they do not meet the high-risk criteria outlined in Article 6 of the AI Act and are consequently classified as minimal risk. Devices explicitly defined as non-medical by the MDR, such as those referenced in Recital 19 are also included in this category, often covering wellness or general-purpose software that is minimal-risk by nature. However, if these devices employ manipulative, deceptive, or dark pattern techniques to mislead users into making decisions they would not otherwise make, they would fall under the prohibited AI category as outlined in the AI Act. For example, a weight loss app

[24] As outlined in Article 6.2 of the AI Act, AI systems used for the purposes specified in Annex III are classified as high-risk.

could use dark patterns by presenting unrealistic, 'before and after' images of users who have lost significant weight, subtly pressuring users to adopt drastic diets. The app might also use guilt-tripping notifications like 'You're falling behind your goals!' to create a sense of urgency, leading to unhealthy behaviours. Similarly, a fertility app designed to help with pregnancy might use dark patterns to subtly push women into believing they need to track their cycles constantly or take unnecessary supplements by suggesting that missing a day could 'ruin' their chances of pregnancy, creating undue stress and pressure. These deceptive tactics exploit emotional vulnerabilities, pushing users into decisions without their informed consent and violating the AI Act's principles of transparency, fairness, and user autonomy.

4.2 *Micro-Level Overlaps Between the AI Act and Medical Device Regulation*

While reading the MDR and the AI Act in conjunction, we must remember that the classification systems are not the only aspects of the two regulations to be intertwined. On the contrary, the two regulations overlap in multiple aspects, leaving us with the urge to dive into these overlapping and understand the framework for ensuring the trustworthiness of an AI-based medical device. In particular, besides the classification, the two regulations overlap with regard to requirements, such as technical documentation, conformity assessment, and post-market monitoring. A brief overview of the various aspects of the two regulations, which must be read together, is provided below. Additionally, while the specificities of the overlapping requirements are not explored in detail, the discussion is limited to expressing scepticism regarding one particular aspect that the two regulations should address to ensure the trustworthiness of medical AI: the clinical validation of medical AI.

4.3 *Risk Justified Requirements*

As an additional point of convergence between the two regulations, we must keep in mind the synergy between the requirements of the two regulations. As expressed by art 8(2) of the AI Act, when the product containing the AI is regulated by a harmonised rule—such as in the case of AI-based medical devices—the requirements of the AI Act and those of the MDR simultaneously apply, and the AI provider is responsible for the compliance with both regulations avoiding any kind of duplication.

For example, Article 11 of the AI Act mandates that technical documentation must be drafted before the AI system is placed on the market or put into service. This documentation must be drawn up according to the elements provided for in Annex IV of the AI Act. However, in the case of an AI system falling under the MDR discipline, according to the reference made to Annex I, the question of technical documentation is enriched by further detail. Article 11(2) of the AI Act states that single technical documentation shall be drawn up for products to which the legal acts listed in Annex I (in our case MDR) apply. This documentation must be drawn up in such a way as to satisfy both the provisions of Article 10 MDR and the elements foreseen in Annexes II and III of the MDR, as well as all information outlined in Annex IV of the AI Act.

Among the information to be provided with a medical device it is mandatory to report information about the clinical validation (see n. 20). Clinical evaluation data supporting the safety and performance—and following the word choice of this thesis, the trustworthiness—of the device, including clinical study reports, literature reviews, post-market surveillance data, and any other relevant clinical evidence, are also necessary (see n. 21).

4.4 Third-Party Assessment

The MDR concurs as the main coregulator for Medical AI regarding conformity assessment. Article 43(3) AI Act, in fact, provides that for high-risk AI systems to which legal acts listed in Annex I apply—such as in the case of medical devices—the provider shall follow the relevant conformity assessment as required under those legal acts. In other words, the requirements of the AI Act listed in Chapter 2 Title III shall apply to high-risk Medical AI systems and shall be assessed in the evaluation process delineated by the MDR in Section II Article 52 *et seq*. Following the AI Act, the medical device manufacturer assumes responsibility for the conformity of the high-risk AI with the requirements outlined in Title III, Chapter II. The same Article also places the medical device manufacturer in charge of the obligations that the AI regulation places on the provider, meaning that if the manufacturer develops, integrates, or substantially modifies an AI system within their device, they assume full responsibility for ensuring compliance with the AI Act, including risk management, transparency, and performance monitoring. For the third-party assessment, the notified bodies identified under Article 35 of the MDR are authorised to verify the conformity of high-risk artificial intelligence systems with the AI Act requirements, but only if they have been accredited for this purpose by the notifying authorities, as stipulated in Article 30(2) of the AI Act. The convergences between the two regulations also cover the situation in which the medical device manufacturer assesses the conformity of the medical device by himself. Where the medical device regulation allows the manufacturer to conduct the conformity assessment himself, for example, in cases of class I devices, the manufacturer may use this option—to assess an AI-based class I medical device—only if he has also applied the harmonised standards or, where applicable, the specifications referred to in Article 41 AI Act, related to the requirements of Chapter II (see n. 19).

The conjoined reading of the AI Act and MDR also sheds some light on the CE marking process. In Article 48, the AI Act provides for a written EU declaration of conformity drawn up by the provider for high-risk artificial intelligence systems.

This declaration of conformity must be delivered to the national authorities upon request and at the supplier's responsibility and must report that the high-risk AI system in question meets the requirements set out in Chapter 2, title III. In paragraph 3 of the same Article, the AI Act clarifies that if the AI system in question falls under the MDR (which also requires an EU Declaration of Conformity), a single EU Declaration of Conformity must be drawn up for both regulations and all EU regulations applicable to the system.[25]

4.5 Post Market Surveillance

Post-market surveillance (PMS) plays a crucial role in ensuring the safety, quality, and continuous compliance of high-risk AI systems used as medical devices under both the MDR and the AI Act. The alignment of these regulatory frameworks emphasises the importance of a comprehensive and continuous monitoring approach after an AI system is placed on the market. Under the MDR, post-market surveillance is detailed in Articles 83 and 84, which mandate that manufacturers implement a proactive PMS system. This system must gather and review data on the performance and safety of medical devices to ensure they continue to meet regulatory requirements. The MDR requires manufacturers to maintain a PMS plan that outlines methods for gathering, recording, and analysing post-market data, as well as defining actions based on the findings. The PMS system aims to detect and address potential risks and improve device performance through continuous feedback. The AI Act complements these requirements by imposing additional obligations on providers of high-risk AI systems. Specifically, Article 61 of the AI Act mandates a detailed post-market monitoring plan for high-risk AI. This includes the active collection, analysis, and documentation of data related to the performance of AI systems throughout their lifecycle. Providers must ensure that their AI systems continue to comply with regulatory standards, which involves monitoring aspects such as accuracy, reliability, and safety during real-world usage.

To harmonise these overlapping requirements, providers can integrate the provisions of Article 61 of the AI Act with the existing MDR requirements in Articles 83 and 84.[26] The integration can create a unified PMS strategy that meets both sets of obligations. According to Article 61(1) of the AI Act, the monitoring plan must detail how data on the AI system's performance and potential risks will be collected and analysed. Paragraphs 2 and 3 further specify that providers need to establish mechanisms to report serious incidents and malfunctioning and outline processes for updating the AI system if risks are identified. This corresponds to the MDR's

[25] However, despite the apparent simplification brought by the release of a singular CE Mark, Med Tech Europe has been criticising some inconsistencies between the two CE procedures of the AI Act and MDR. [https://www.medtecheurope.org/wp-content/uploads/2024/03/medical-technology-industry-perspective-on-the-final-ai-act-1.pdf].

[26] Palmieri et al. (2021), pp. 341–358.

emphasis on continuous feedback loops and corrective actions to mitigate risks. Moreover, the AI Act emphasises the dynamic nature of AI systems, which may evolve and learn post-deployment. Therefore, the PMS plan under the AI Act should include monitoring for changes that could affect compliance. For instance, if an AI system's performance deviates from its original behaviour due to updates or data drift, this must be captured and addressed as part of the post-market monitoring process. The MDR's PMS system, which typically focuses on maintaining the safety and performance of medical devices, can be expanded to include these AI-specific considerations. The combined PMS strategy, integrating Article 61 of the AI Act with Articles 83 and 84 of the MDR, ensures a comprehensive approach that considers both the inherent risks of medical devices and the unique challenges posed by AI systems, such as adaptive learning and continuous updates. Providers should establish robust procedures that facilitate seamless data collection, real-time performance tracking, and compliance checks to meet these dual regulatory requirements effectively.

5 Implementation Challenges for the Jointed AI Act and MDR

The implementation of the AI Act faces numerous significant challenges, primarily linked to the need for greater specificity and clarity on various requirements. While the Act is an ambitious regulatory endeavour, establishing a comprehensive framework designed to guide the development and deployment of artificial intelligence systems across the European Union, it remains high-level and broad in its language. This lack of precision creates practical difficulties for compliance, leaving organisations, developers, and various stakeholders to navigate a landscape filled with ambiguities. Below, we briefly outline some of the key obstacles arising from the generalised provisions in the AI Act and their far-reaching implications for various stakeholders. While certain points may seem repetitive in the following paragraphs, it is important to emphasise that these challenges are deeply interconnected, with each aspect influencing and amplifying the others. The complexities of the AI Act's broad language, ambiguous definitions, and lack of detailed guidance create a web of challenges that extend across multiple facets of AI development, regulation, and compliance, affecting organisations, regulators, and end-users alike.

5.1 Vague Requirements and Interpretative Ambiguities

As already mentioned, one of the core challenges in implementing the AI Act is the broad and sometimes undefined nature of its key requirements. Central concepts such as 'high-risk', 'transparency', 'accuracy' and 'reliability' are pivotal to the

Act's overarching structure but lack clear definitions and thresholds. For example, the term 'accuracy' does not come with a specified benchmark, leaving developers unsure about the standards they need to meet. Similarly, what constitutes sufficient 'transparency' remains open to interpretation, making it difficult for organisations to ensure compliance. This ambiguity creates challenges in the consistent application of the Act across different sectors and can lead to uncertainty regarding how AI systems should be evaluated and regulated. The undefined nature of key requirements in the AI Act poses significant safety concerns when read in such a highly regulated context such as healthcare. When critical terms like 'accuracy', are not clearly defined, the consistency and robustness of safety practices across medical AI systems are compromised, definitely compromising the trust that both healthcare professionals and patients can experience towards the tool. Without specific benchmarks for accuracy, developers might implement systems that perform inadequately or inconsistently, potentially leading to failures that endanger users or do not allow to justify their use in a risk/benefit balance.

5.2 *Complexity of Risk-Based Categorisation*

The AI Act's risk-based approach, intended to classify AI systems by their potential impact on safety and fundamental rights, brings significant practical challenges that can undermine compliance efforts. Determining the appropriate risk category for an AI system is far from straightforward, especially when dealing with complex systems that may serve multiple purposes or evolve through continuous learning. This evolving nature of AI models means their risk profile can change over time, creating uncertainty around whether a system's categorisation needs to be adjusted post-marketing. The Act's vague criteria for risk classification exacerbate this issue, leading to inconsistent assessments among developers and manufacturers. Some may err on the side of caution, overestimating their system's risk level and shouldering unnecessary compliance expenses. Others may inadvertently or strategically underestimate their system's risk level to avoid stringent obligations, risking non-compliance and potential harm to users.

The complexity and ambiguity of these requirements encourage manufacturers to find ways to circumvent or interpret the regulations in ways that reduce their compliance burden. This is particularly evident when the risk classification intricacies of the AI Act are considered alongside the MDR. The combined classification criteria and the resulting obligations for manufacturers may discourage adherence to both regulations due to their perceived complexity and burden. Additionally, existing literature has already expressed scepticism regarding the classification of certain medical AI systems as minimal risk.[27] While referring to such literature is valuable for a deeper understanding, it is important to note that, although the overall

[27] Palmieri and Goffin (2023), pp. 406–427.

interaction between the AI Act and the MDR risk classifications generally works well, questions persist about whether certain AI systems used in healthcare or related fields genuinely qualify as minimal risk.

5.3 Need for Conformity Assessment Guidance

For high-risk AI systems, both the AI Act and MDR mandate rigorous third-party conformity assessments to ensure that these systems adhere to established safety and compliance standards. However, the Act lacks detailed procedural guidelines on how these assessments should be conducted, presenting a significant challenge for organisations preparing for compliance checks. This deficiency forces companies to account for a complex array of variables, including data inputs, algorithmic transparency, and the nuances of their AI system's intended use. The lack of specific assessment protocols parallels challenges seen in the implementation of the MDR which also required medical technology companies to meet stringent conformity requirements but faced similar criticisms for the limited guidance it provided on execution.

The absence of detailed standards in the AI Act means that both organisations and third-party conformity bodies may struggle to maintain consistent and thorough evaluation practices. This inconsistency leads to potential discrepancies in certification outcomes, creating an uneven playing field. For instance, one conformity assessment body may adopt a stricter interpretation than another, resulting in varied levels of scrutiny across the industry. Such variability can lead to legal disputes, delays in certification, or even backlogs as organisations contest inconsistent outcomes or seek clarity on their compliance status.

Moreover, clinical validation—proving that a medical AI system performs as intended and benefits patients safely—requires precise standards, yet both the AI Act and MDR offer limited clarity on how this should be achieved or evaluated when it comes to combining the two regulations. This ambiguity leads to confusion among manufacturers, who must account for a range of factors, from data quality and algorithmic transparency to the specific use case of the AI system. Currently, many manufacturers are left in a state of uncertainty regarding how to conduct proper clinical validation for medical AI in a way that satisfies both the AI Act and MDR. To exemplify data quality must be considered as an integral part of clinical evaluation parameters, especially for medical AI systems governed by both the AI Act and the MDR. Clinical evaluation cannot be reliably conducted without ensuring high standards of data quality. If data quality is poor—lacking representativeness, completeness, or fairness—the outcomes of the clinical evaluation may be skewed, leading to AI systems that fail to perform accurately in real-world applications. This intersection between data quality and clinical evaluation is critical for validating that an AI system is fit for its intended purpose. For example, an AI diagnostic tool trained on an incomplete or non-representative dataset may perform well under certain conditions but fail when applied to broader, more diverse patient populations. Such discrepancies can result in misdiagnoses or ineffective treatments, undermining patient safety and the efficacy of healthcare services. Ensuring high data quality as part of clinical evaluation helps confirm that the AI system's outputs are consistent, reliable, and applicable across the intended range of use cases.

Yet, the current lack of detailed guidance within the AI Act on how data governance should be embedded in clinical evaluation processes or more in general the lack of official assessment instruments to evaluate data quality leaves manufacturers uncertain about how to properly conduct these assessments.

Incorporating explicit data quality criteria into clinical evaluation would provide consistency and ensure that high-risk medical AI systems are developed, tested, and deployed with greater reliability. Regulatory bodies and conformity assessment entities would benefit from this structured approach by having clearer benchmarks to evaluate against, reducing variability in assessments and strengthening the safety and effectiveness of medical AI technologies.

5.4 Resource Burden for SMEs and Startups

The broad and generalised nature of the AI Act poses a significant resource burden for small and medium-sized enterprises (SMEs) and startups, particularly in sectors such as AI health, where compliance with complex regulations like the AI Act and the MDR is paramount. Unlike large corporations, which typically have dedicated legal, compliance, and regulatory affairs departments to manage intricate regulatory frameworks, smaller companies often lack the specialised resources to navigate these complex and overlapping requirements. For SMEs and startups, the financial and operational strain of complying with the AI Act can be particularly challenging, as they must invest considerable time and money into understanding and adhering to these regulations.[28]

The costs associated with compliance are multifaceted. SMEs must often engage in legal consultations, hire external advisors, and pay for conformity assessments to ensure their AI systems meet regulatory standards. These processes can be prohibitively expensive, especially for startups operating with limited budgets. Additionally, without clear guidance or specific details on how to comply with various provisions of the AI Act, these companies may be forced to err on the side of caution, overinvesting in compliance measures and diverting valuable resources away from product development or innovation. On the other hand, a lack of clarity may also lead to misinterpretation of the requirements, resulting in non-compliance and exposing them to the risk of fines, penalties, or reputational damage.

For many startups and smaller companies, the prospect of facing legal and regulatory challenges can create an environment of uncertainty. The absence of specific

[28] *The EU AI Act: How will it impact medical device manufacturers?* MDDI Online. Retrieved from https://www.mddionline.com/artificial-intelligence/the-eu-ai-act-how-will-it-impact-medical-device-manufacturers

and actionable guidance within the AI Act means that SMEs may struggle to devise their own compliance strategies, leading to a fragmented approach to data governance, risk assessment, and conformity evaluation.[29] As a result, they may find themselves at a competitive disadvantage compared to larger, resource-rich companies that can more easily absorb these regulatory costs and complexities. Furthermore, the regulatory burden may prevent smaller firms from expanding their market presence or pursuing innovative projects, especially in highly regulated sectors like healthcare, where the compliance requirements are even more stringent (see n. 22 and 23).

Moreover, SMEs are often more nimble and able to experiment with new AI applications, which is essential for fostering innovation. The overly complex and costly compliance demands could make it harder for these companies to stay competitive or enter new markets. As a result, the regulatory burden may inadvertently favour larger, more established companies with the financial resources to comply with the Act's broad provisions, diminishing the role of smaller companies in the development of cutting-edge AI technologies. Ultimately, this imbalance could reduce the overall competitiveness of the AI industry and hinder the progress of new AI solutions that could benefit sectors like healthcare, where smaller firms often push the boundaries of technology. To foster a thriving, competitive, and innovative AI ecosystem, it is essential that the regulatory framework provides clearer, more accessible guidance, particularly for smaller companies, to ensure they can navigate these complex regulations without stifling their potential for growth and innovation.

5.5 Implementation Delays and Potential for Over- or Under-Regulation

One of the most evident and frequently discussed challenges in the implementation of both the AI Act and the Medical Device Regulation is the issue of implementation delays, compounded by the potential for either over- or under-regulation. The AI Act, despite its broad intentions to regulate high-risk AI systems and ensure safety and fairness, lacks the level of detailed guidance needed to effectively enforce its provisions across various sectors, particularly healthcare.[30] Regulatory bodies tasked with rolling out the Act must first work to develop comprehensive standards, best practices, and robust compliance tools—processes that take time. The result is that many companies and organisations are left in a state of uncertainty during this interim period, unsure of how to align their AI systems with the final regulatory

[29] *Understanding the EU AI Act: Implications for SMEs in Ireland and Europe*. NovaL Consultancy Retrieved from https://www.novalconsultancy.com/post/understanding-the-eu-ai-act-implications-for-smes-in-ireland-and-europe

[30] *Medical technology industry perspective on the final AI Act*. MedTech Europe. Retrieved from https://www.medtecheurope.org/wp-content/uploads/2024/03/medical-technology-industry-perspective-on-the-final-ai-act-1.pdf

framework. This ambiguity can lead to significant delays in product development, as businesses struggle to navigate the complex and evolving regulatory landscape. In some cases, companies may even delay entering the market altogether, awaiting the finalisation of these guidelines before taking any further steps.

The lack of precise regulatory guidance can also create a situation where businesses adopt overly cautious compliance practices. In the absence of clear rules and standards, some organisations may choose to err on the side of caution, adhering to stricter interpretations of the AI Act than may ultimately be required. While this may provide a sense of security, it can have unintended negative consequences. By taking a conservative approach, companies may divert resources away from innovation, choosing to allocate them instead to compliance efforts that may not be necessary. This fear of non-compliance could stifle the creativity and flexibility that smaller firms, in particular, rely on to develop new AI technologies. The result could be a slowdown in the pace of innovation, as businesses prioritise meeting regulatory requirements over advancing their products or exploring new applications of AI.[31]

On the other hand, the absence of clear guidelines also opens the door for companies to underestimate the level of compliance required, leading to the opposite problem: under-regulation. Without precise instructions on key aspects such as risk classification, data governance, or transparency, some companies may fail to implement the necessary safeguards, ultimately putting users, patients, and the broader public at risk (see n. 24). This could happen either because companies misunderstand their obligations or because they are unwilling to invest in comprehensive compliance measures due to cost concerns or a desire to speed up time-to-market. In sectors like healthcare, where AI systems can directly impact patient safety, under-regulation is particularly problematic. AI systems that are inadequately regulated may fail to meet safety standards, be prone to biases, or present unreliable results, thereby compromising their effectiveness and trustworthiness (see n. 25).

These two extremes—over-regulation and under-regulation—highlight the delicate balance that regulatory bodies must strike in developing and implementing the AI Act and the MDR. Over-regulation could impose excessive burdens on companies, particularly smaller firms, that may not have the resources to comply with stringent, unnecessary requirements. At the same time, under-regulation could result in safety risks and reduced confidence in AI technologies, which would undermine the overall objectives of both the AI Act and the MDR. This dual threat of regulatory uncertainty is one of the most significant challenges currently facing the AI and medical device sectors, and it requires careful consideration as regulators work to finalise the guidelines and standards that will govern AI development in Europe.

The current lack of clear, actionable standards within both the AI Act and the MDR creates a situation where businesses are forced to make difficult decisions, often without the benefit of knowing whether their actions will ultimately be in line

---

[31] *Does regulation hurt innovation? Study says yes.* MIT Sloan School of Management. Retrieved from https://mitsloan.mit.edu/ideas-made-to-matter/does-regulation-hurt-innovation-study-says-yes

with the final regulatory expectations. As a result, there is a growing concern that these delays in providing detailed guidance could hinder the growth and competitive edge of companies operating in the AI sector. Furthermore, the risk of uneven implementation across different member states only exacerbates the problem, as companies may find themselves dealing with conflicting regulations depending on where they operate, further complicating the compliance process. In the long run, this uncertainty could erode trust in AI technologies and slow down the broader adoption of AI in sectors like healthcare, where the benefits of these technologies have the potential to revolutionise patient care.

To resolve this issue, it is imperative that regulators move quickly to finalise the required standards and best practices for the AI Act and the MDR, ensuring that they are both comprehensive and clear. Only by providing businesses with the detailed guidance they need can the EU ensure that the implementation of the AI Act promotes innovation, safeguards public safety, and fosters a thriving AI ecosystem. The success of the AI Act and MDR depends not just on the development of regulations but also on their timely and effective implementation, which requires careful balance and consideration of the complexities of the AI and medical device industries.

6 Conclusion

To conclude this chapter, we can summarise the key points discussed and bring some clarity to the various challenges and solutions outlined. The AI Act extends to the healthcare sector through its intersection with the MDR, forming a regulatory framework that ensures AI systems in healthcare are subject to comprehensive safety and compliance requirements. This intertwining of the AI Act and MDR creates a solid foundation for addressing the unique challenges of AI in healthcare, offering broad coverage and aligning the two regulations well in many respects. The AI Act, when viewed alongside the MDR, ensures that high-risk AI systems in medical contexts are properly monitored, safeguarding both patient safety and the integrity of the healthcare sector. However, as outlined in the previous paragraphs, the implementation of the AI Act still faces significant challenges, particularly due to the broad and sometimes vague nature of the language and provisions within the Act. These include unclear definitions of critical terms, difficulties in categorising AI risk, and the absence of specific guidance on areas like data governance, which leaves room for inconsistencies and misinterpretations among stakeholders.

To address these ongoing challenges, there is a pressing need for complementary standards and detailed guidance. While the AI Act and MDR provide a strong regulatory starting point, their broad provisions are not always sufficient for effective and consistent implementation, especially in complex sectors like healthcare. The lack of clarity on how to practically apply key provisions, such as data quality assessments or the transparency of AI systems, creates uncertainty for developers and healthcare providers alike. This gap in regulatory detail is particularly problematic for small and medium-sized enterprises (SMEs) and startups, who may lack the resources to navigate these ambiguities or invest in legal and regulatory consultations.

The AI Office, established under the AI Act, has a central role in providing clarity and coordinating efforts to refine and expand upon the Act's provisions. Alongside the European Commission, the AI Office can work with technical standardisation bodies such as the International Organization for Standardization (ISO) and the European Committee for Standardization (CEN) to develop specific technical standards and sector-specific guidelines, especially for high-risk areas like healthcare. These standards would help ensure that requirements are tailored to the unique challenges of the healthcare sector while maintaining alignment with the overarching goals of the AI Act and MDR. Input from industry experts, including healthcare professionals, AI developers, legal experts, and regulators, will be vital in ensuring that these standards are practical, actionable, and reflective of the latest technological and scientific advancements.

In addition to providing clarity, these complementary standards will also help create a more cohesive and harmonised regulatory environment across EU member states. As the AI Act currently leaves room for potential regulatory fragmentation, with different member states interpreting provisions in varying ways, establishing consistent guidance will reduce these discrepancies. This consistency is crucial for businesses operating across multiple jurisdictions, as it will simplify compliance efforts, reduce costs, and ensure a level playing field. By developing and implementing these complementary standards, the AI Office and other relevant bodies can help mitigate the challenges faced by developers and healthcare organisations in meeting compliance obligations. These efforts will not only streamline the regulatory process but also foster innovation within the healthcare sector, ensuring that AI technologies can be deployed safely and effectively. Ultimately, clear guidance will help organisations navigate the complexities of compliance, safeguard patient safety, and support the development of AI-driven healthcare solutions that are both innovative and reliable. Fostering a regulatory environment grounded in clarity, consistency, and innovation, can ensure that the AI Act not only protects public safety but also empowers the next generation of AI-driven healthcare solutions, ultimately transforming the sector for the betterment of all.

References

Coman LI, Ianculescu M, Paraschiv EA, Alexandru A, Bădărău IA (2024) Smart solutions for diet-related disease management: connected care, remote health monitoring systems, and integrated insights for advanced evaluation. Appl Sci 14(6):2351

Haleem A, Javaid M, Singh RP, Suman R (2022) Medical 4.0 technologies for healthcare: features, capabilities, and applications. Internet Things Cyber-Phys Syst 2:12–30

Hoseini M (2023) Patient experiences with AI in healthcare settings. AI Tech Behav Soc Sci 1(3):12–18

Kalid N, Zaidan AA, Zaidan BB, Salman OH, Hashim M, Muzammil HJ (2018) Based real time remote health monitoring systems: A review on patients prioritization and related "big data" using body sensors information and communication technology. J Med Syst 42:1–30

Khanna S (2020) A review of AI devices in cancer radiology for breast and lung imaging and diagnosis. Int J Appl Health Care Anal 5(12):1–15

Nahavandi D, Alizadehsani R, Khosravi A, Acharya UR (2022) Application of artificial intelligence in wearable devices: Opportunities and challenges. Comput Methods Prog Biomed 213:106541

Palmieri S, Goffin T (2023) A blanket that leaves the feet cold: exploring the AI act safety framework for medical AI. Eur J Health Law 30(4):406–427

Palmieri S, Walraet P, Goffin T (2021) Inevitable influences: AI-based medical devices at the intersection of medical devices regulation and the proposal for AI regulation. Eur J Health Law 28(4):341–358

Pinto-Coelho L (2023) How artificial intelligence is shaping medical imaging technology: a survey of innovations and applications. Bioengineering 10(12):1435

Singh A, Jadhav A (2024) 7 Al Applications. Industry 4.0, Smart Manufacturing, and Industrial Engineering: Challenges and Opportunities:139

Sunny MN, Saki MB, Al Nahian A, Ahmed SW, Shorif MN, Atayeva J, Rizvi SW (2024) Optimizing healthcare outcomes through data-driven predictive modeling. J Intell Learn Syst Appl 16(4):384–402

Topol EJ (2019) High-performance medicine: the convergence of human and artificial intelligence. Nat Med 25(1):44–56

Verganti R, Vendraminelli L, Iansiti M (2020) Innovation and design in the age of artificial intelligence. J Prod Innov Manag 37(3):212–227

Wang C, He T, Zhou H, Zhang Z, Lee C (2023) Artificial intelligence enhanced sensors-enabling technologies to next-generation healthcare and biomedical platform. Bioelectron Med 9(1):17

The AI Act Versus Other AI Regulations Around the World

AI Regulation in the UK

Andrew Charlesworth

Contents

Abstract Post-Brexit (and post-Truss), the UK rapidly lost its enthusiasm for a 'Singapore-on-Thames' free market model for its economy yet remained keen to differentiate its approach to key economic policy areas from that taken by the EU. The debate over AI regulatory strategies thus provided a high-profile arena in which to juxtapose those differences. The UK adopted a principles-based, light-touch, and sectorally-focused regulatory framework, requiring existing regulators to interpret and apply key principles. The EU, by contrast, adopted an overarching and prescriptive legislation-based framework complete with new regulators, via the Artificial Intelligence Act (Regulation (EU) 2024/1689). While the UK's 2024

A. Charlesworth (✉)
University of Bristol, The Law School, Bristol, UK
e-mail: A.J.Charlesworth@bristol.ac.uk

V. L. Raposo (ed.), *The European Artificial Intelligence Act*, Law, Governance and Technology Series 78, https://doi.org/10.1007/978-3-031-98406-8_15

General Election significantly altered its political landscape, legislative pragmatism and the desire for timely implementation ensured the UK's AI short to medium term regulatory strategy would remain largely unchanged. Thus, as key UK regulators developed guidance on their strategic approach to AI under the framework, a clearer picture of the plausibility of utilising a principles-based regulatory model for AI began to take shape. The emergence of generative AI (GenAI) as an immediate focus for regulatory attention provided some evidence as to how the two regulatory models would fare in seeking to encourage innovation while addressing the risks ensuing from this fast-developing area.

1 Introduction

> Having exited the European Union we are free to establish a regulatory approach that enables us to establish the UK as an AI superpower.[1]

Between 2016 and 2024, for any given policy area falling within EU competency, it was not uncommon to find the UK claiming that its decision to exit the EU in January 2020[2] permitted it to adopt an independent and putatively superior (for UK national interests) regulatory approach than that negotiated between the remaining 27 EU Member States. Such claims might be considered, even on a generous interpretation, to be weakly supported by the available evidence.[3] However, it is possible that AI regulation, as outlined by the UK Government in its 2003 White Paper *A pro-innovation approach to AI regulation*,[4] may have potential to provide more robust support for those contentions. Here, there is a clear divergence between the two jurisdictions. The EU adopted an overarching and prescriptive legislative approach, and new regulatory hierarchy, via its Artificial Intelligence Act (AI).[5] The UK, in contrast decided, initially at least, to forego a legislative solution in favour of principles-based, light-touch, and sectorally-focused, regulatory framework. This

[1] Rt.Hon. Michelle Donelan MP, Secretary of State for Science, Innovation and Technology, Foreword, Dept. for Science, Innovation & Technology/Office for Artificial Intelligence (2023). AI regulation: a pro-innovation approach. Command Paper: 815, E02886733 03/23, p. 2.

[2] Popularly referred to as 'Brexit'.

[3] See, e.g. Dept for Business & Trade, Smarter Regulation: One Year On, May 2024.

[4] Dept. for Science, Innovation & Technology (DSIT)/Office for Artificial Intelligence (OAI) (2023). A pro-innovation approach to AI regulation. Command Paper: 815, E02886733 03/23. See also DSIT (2024). A pro-innovation approach to AI regulation: government response. Command Paper:1019, E03019481 02/24.

[5] Regulation (EU) 2024/1689 of the European Parliament and of the Council of 13 June 2024 laying down harmonised rules on artificial intelligence and amending Regulations (EC) No 300/2008, (EU) No 167/2013, (EU) No 168/2013, (EU) 2018/858, (EU) 2018/1139 and (EU) 2019/2144 and Directives 2014/90/EU, (EU) 2016/797 and (EU) 2020/1828 (Artificial Intelligence Act), OJ L 2024/1689, 12.7.2024. ELI: http://data.europa.eu/eli/reg/2024/1689/oj

relies upon existing regulators to both contextually interpret, and then apply within their remit, a set of principles issued by government on a non-legislative basis.[6]

At the time of writing (January 2025), after a 3-year progression through the EU legislative process,[7] the EU AIA has been in force for 5 months; there is thus a significant body of academic and professional literature providing critical analysis of its scope and provisions, to which this volume adds. The UK regulatory regime traces its origins to a similar time period,[8] although a concrete set of regulatory proposals only went to public consultation in March 2023,[9] and the Government's response to the consultation was published in February 2024.[10] Key UK regulators were asked to publish their strategy for addressing AI risks within their remit by 30 April 2024, including 'set[ting] out AI-related risks in their areas, detail[ing] their current skillset and expertise to address them, and a plan for how they will regulate AI over the coming year'.[11] By early May 2024, 14 regulators had provided AI strategy documents.[12] In addition to those Government initiatives, concerns about the potentially fragmentary nature of the proposed UK framework, the risk of poor alignment of regulator objectives, and the possibility of gaps between regulatory responsibilities, resulted in a private member's bill being introduced into the House of Lords in November 2023 to address some of these issues. The later development of the UK's strategy means that academic coverage of the regulatory framework is necessarily less comprehensive, although there has been more discussion in professional legal circles.

This chapter will trace the development of the UK regulatory framework, highlighting key issues and areas of debate and contention, from the 2023 White Paper to the present (31 January 2025). It will also consider the strategic approach documentation provided by several of the key regulators, briefly outlining and assessing their responses to the regulatory framework. The remainder of the chapter will provide—insofar as it is possible to do so given the very different regulatory understandings and approaches—a comparative analysis of the UK regulatory framework and the EU AI Act. This will include an examination of the application of each

[6] DSIT/OAI, A pro-innovation approach CP 815, supra n. 4, para. 55.

[7] See Proposal for a Regulation of the European Parliament and of the Council] laying down harmonised rules on artificial intelligence and amending certain Union legislative Acts, COM(2021) 206 final, Brussels, 21.4.2021. https://eur-lex.europa.eu/legal-content/EN/TXT/?uri=CELEX:52021PC020

[8] Dept. for Digital, Culture, Media and Sport (DCMS), Digital Regulation: driving growth and unlocking innovation (Plan for Digital Regulation), July 2021; DCMS/OAI, National AI Strategy, September 2021, pp. 50–61; DCMS/OAI, Establishing a pro-innovation approach to regulating AI, CP 728, July 2022.

[9] DSIT/OAI, A pro-innovation approach, supra n. 4.

[10] DSIT, A pro-innovation approach: Government response, supra n. 4.

[11] DSIT, UK signals step change for regulators to strengthen AI leadership, Press release, 6 February 2024. https://www.gov.uk/government/news/uk-signals-step-change-for-regulators-to-strengthen-ai-leadership

[12] DSIT, Regulators' strategic approaches to AI, Notice, 1 May 2024. https://www.gov.uk/government/publications/regulators-strategic-approaches-to-ai/regulators-strategic-approaches-to-ai

regime to the headline AI-based technology of the moment, generative AI (GenAI),[13] to provide some insights into their possible regulatory strengths and weaknesses.

2 The UK 2023 White Paper: A Pro-Innovation Approach to AI Regulation

The UK Government's 2023 White Paper noted that the speed of development of AI regulation world-wide meant that it would need to act quickly to have any influence on the international debate on AI governance. It recognised that there were potential serious new risks arising from AI technologies and that the nature and complexity of those technologies were likely to raise public concerns and reduce trust in them.[14] However, it argued, any regulatory strategy had to address those issues without undermining the case for business investment and thus discouraging innovation. To achieve this, it was necessary to avoid what the UK Government regarded as the undesirable approach of developing cumbersome rules applying to all AI technologies.[15] This, on its face, appears to be a lightly veiled criticism of the risk-based legislative approach already adopted by the EU Commission's draft EU AI Act.[16]

The issue, from the White Paper's perspective, was not that there was an absence of regulatory control of AI technologies in the UK. Rather, it argued that existing laws, augmented by other regulatory tools such as standards and guidance, already provided a framework that could address, in a proportionate manner, differing uses of AI technology in particular regulatory contexts. The regulatory focus, it suggested, should be on preventing undesirable outcomes, and not simply that an AI technology was being utilised in some fashion.[17] However, it accepted that AI technologies might be adopted and used in ways that did not necessarily fall clearly within a specific regulatory context, and thus in any given use context, a range of legal requirements could be at play. Lack of clarity in how regulation might be applied across use contexts might therefore lead to uncertainty and inconsistency as to its application, which had the potential to harm business and consumer trust in AI. The objective of the UK's AI regulatory strategy should therefore be to provide an approach capable of being applied in particular contexts, across different regulatory remits, in a coherent and consistent fashion.[18]

[13] GenAI will be defined here as a type of AI which typically uses deep learning, and is trained on a large dataset, capable of creating a range of outputs including text, images or media. See e.g. House of Lords, Communications and Digital Committee (CDC), Large language models and generative AI, HL Paper 54, February 2024.

[14] DSIT/OAI, A pro-innovation approach CP 815, supra n. 4, para 4.

[15] Ibid, paras. 3 & 6.

[16] Proposal for a Regulation, supra n. 7.

[17] DSIT/OAI, A pro-innovation approach CP 815, supra n. 4, paras. 6 & 7.

[18] Ibid, para. 7.

The White Paper suggested that the most effective way of achieving that objective was not to produce new AI-focused legislation, as this might dissuade innovation and be incapable of sufficient agility and flexibility to be adapted to address new technological developments in a proportionate manner. Instead, it proposed a set of non-statutory key principles that could be interpreted and applied by existing regulators, including the Competition and Markets Authority (CMA), Financial Conduct Authority (FCA), Information Commissioner's Office (ICO) and Office of Communications (Ofcom). These would permit the regulators to apply their particular domain knowledge and expertise to specific AI use contexts within the scope of their remit, but at the same time provide a degree of consistency in circumstances where use contexts cut across the remits of more than one regulator.[19] The principles identified as critical to AI regulation were:

- Safety, security and robustness—AI systems should function in a robust, secure and safe way throughout the AI life cycle, and risks should be continually identified, assessed and managed.
- Appropriate transparency and explainability—AI systems should be appropriately transparent and explainable.
- Fairness—AI systems should not undermine the legal rights of individuals or organisations, discriminate unfairly against individuals or create unfair market outcomes.
- Accountability and governance—Governance measures should be in place to ensure effective oversight of the supply and use of AI systems, with clear lines of accountability established across the AI life cycle.
- Contestability and redress—Where appropriate, users, impacted third parties and actors in the AI life cycle should be able to contest an AI decision or outcome that is harmful or creates material risk of harm.[20]

Initial implementation of a principle-based regulatory strategy was anticipated to require ongoing review to determine whether there were particular obstacles to the application of the principles, and whether a non-statutory approach was in fact viable. The White Paper did not rule out statutory intervention in the framework, identifying a longer-term possibility of placing a legal duty on regulators to have regard to the principles. However, it rejected suggestions that additional enforcement mechanisms might be required, arguing that a legal duty to have regard to the principles would leave the regulators free to exercise discretion as to how and when the principles were applied, while having a clear mandate to do so. Even this minimal statutory intervention would not be exercised if the non-statutory framework was deemed to be sufficiently effective in practice.[21]

[19] Ibid, para. 11.

[20] Ibid, para. 10.

[21] Ibid, para. 12.

A primary concern expressed by key stakeholders in consultations based on an earlier Office of Artificial Intelligence paper,[22] was that the proposed principle-based approach utilising existing regulators lacked a central coordinating mechanism (CCM) to ensure effective collaboration between regulators and provide oversight of the efficient function of the regulatory framework. The White Paper noted that there were a range of issues that would benefit from such a mechanism, including:

- Monitoring and evaluation of the regulatory framework's effectiveness and the implementation of the principles, especially in supporting innovation,
- Assessing and monitoring risks across the economy arising from AI,
- Conducting horizon scanning and gap analysis,
- Supporting testbeds and sandbox initiatives to help AI innovators get new technologies to market,
- Providing education and awareness to give clarity to businesses and empower citizens,
- Promoting interoperability with international regulatory frameworks.[23]

However, the White Paper considered that these CCM functions could be adequately provided from within government, via the Department of Science, Innovation and Technology (DSIT), with some external support. It explicitly rejected the suggestion that successfully addressing the issues raised would require the creation of a specific AI regulator.[24] Finally, it suggested that supporting innovation might achieved by means other than regulation, with tools such as assurance techniques, voluntary guidance and technical standards being used in parallel with the regulatory framework. This perhaps suggests a somewhat narrow understanding of the meaning of 'regulation', as such tools might reasonably be considered to fall within its contemporary definition in academic and professional literature.[25]

Despite the White Paper's admonition that it would be necessary to move quickly to establish a regulatory framework for AI, the consultation period and formulation of the Government's response to the representations made, took 11 months to complete. During this period, key reports were produced by Committees in the House of Commons and House of Lords addressing AI governance in general (July 2023),[26]

---

[22] DCMS, Establishing a pro-innovation approach to regulating AI, CP 728, supra, n. 8.

[23] DSIT/OAI, A pro-innovation approach CP 815, supra n. 4, paras. 14–15.

The UK's Office for Artificial Intelligence was a joint unit of the Department for Digital, Culture, Media & Sport (DCMS) and Department for Business, Energy & Industrial Strategy (BEIS) responsible for overseeing implementation of the National AI Strategy. It is now part of the AI Policy Directorate in the Department for Science, Innovation and Technology (DSIT) which took over the scientific, research, and technology functions of both the DCMS and BEIS in February 2023.

[24] Ibid, para. 16.

[25] See e.g. Baldwin et al. (2011).

[26] House of Commons Science, Innovation and Technology Committee (SITC), The governance of artificial intelligence: Interim report, HC 1769, 31 Aug. 2023.

and the governance of Large Language Models (LLMs) and generative AI (GenAI) specifically (January 2024).[27] The former noted a degree of support for the principles-based approach from industry, albeit with caution in some quarters about its practical implementation.[28] The latter reiterated the need for the UK to develop its own regulatory strategy for AI, and suggested that primary legislation aimed at LLMs was not appropriate; however it did not explicitly address the issue of the need for wider AI-focused legislation.[29] While supportive of the White Paper approach, it was critical of the slow pace at which the elements of the DIST-based CCM function were being supported, financed, and delivered, which the Commons Committee said left the regulators the CCM function was supposed to be coordinating in the dark about its role and remit.[30] It found that regulators were not uniformly prepared for the role envisaged by the White Paper, that their resources and enforcement powers varied widely, there were potential gaps in regulatory coverage, and there were disparate co-ordination efforts between regulators.[31] It did recommend that there should be standardised powers for the main regulators to obtain information and conduct audits, and that regulators should have meaningful sanctions to address significant breaches.[32] These insights and recommendations, while contained in a report primarily focused on GenAI, might be considered as evidence supporting the need for at least some form of legislative intervention to underpin the principle-based approach.

3 The Artificial Intelligence (Regulation) Bill

While the Conservative government was unwilling to adopt new legislation to implement aspects of its proposed regulatory framework, other parliamentarians were less reticent, and in November 2023 a Conservative peer, Lord Holmes, introduced a private member's bill,[33] the *Artificial Intelligence (Regulation) Bill*,[34] to the House of Lords. This draft legislation aimed to create a new body, the AI Authority

[27] House of Lords, Communications & Digital Committee (CDC), Large language models and generative AI, HL Paper 54, Feb. 2024

[28] HoC SITC, Governance of AI: Interim report, HC 1769, supra n. 26, paras. 95–96.

[29] CDC, LLMs & Gen AI, HL Paper 54, supra n. 27, para. 198.

[30] Ibid, para. 195.

[31] Ibid, paras. 197–200.

[32] Ibid, para. 201.

[33] 'Private Members' Bills (PMBs) are bills introduced by MPs and Peers who are not government ministers. They provide backbenchers with an opportunity to address public concerns and to set a policy agenda that is not determined by the executive'. Hansard Society (2022), Guide to Private Members' Bills, (Hansard Society: London). https://www.hansardsociety.org.uk/publications/guides/what-is-a-private-members-bill

[34] Artificial Intelligence (Regulation) Bill, HL Bill 11 https://bills.parliament.uk/publications/53068/documents/4030; see also Tobin (2024).

(the Authority), with key functions relating to AI regulation generally.[35] Its primary roles would be to ensure existing regulators were engaging with AI within their remit; ensure that regulators were aligned in their approach; provide a gap analysis of AI regulatory responsibilities; coordinate a legislative review of key legislation to assess whether it was suitable to address issues raised by AI; monitor and evaluate the AI regulatory framework's effectiveness and implementation of the principles, notably with regard to supporting innovation; assess and monitor AI risks across the economy; conduct horizon scanning to inform a coordinated response to new AI trends, support testbed and sandbox initiatives for new AI technologies; accredit independent AI auditors, provide education and awareness to business and individuals; and promote the interoperability of the UK AI framework with international regulatory frameworks.[36] It would also have a key role to play in developing a public engagement programme about the pros and cons of AI, taking into account the opinions of the general public and other appropriate persons.[37]

The Bill would have required the Authority to have regard to the five principles identified in the White Paper,[38] plus an additional nine principles with regard to specific transparency, testing and legal compliance requirements on businesses developing, deploying or using AI tools,[39] and fairness criteria for AI technologies and their application.[40] Businesses would be permitted to test AI business propositions in the market with real customers under certain conditions (sandboxing) if authorised or registered with the relevant regulator, with the Authority providing assistance and oversight.[41] Businesses developing, deploying or using AI tools would have to have a designated AI officer to ensure their safe, ethical, unbiased and non-discriminatory use of AI, and to ensure that data they used in any AI tool was, as far as possible, unbiased.[42] They would also have to allow accredited independent third parties to audit their processes and systems.[43] Use of training data with AI technologies would require those doing the training to provide the Authority with information about all third party data and intellectual property used in the training, and to assure the AI Authority that informed consent was received for its use and that the use was compliant with intellectual property laws.[44] Supply of an AI product or service to customers would require provision of 'health warnings', clear labelling, and the ability of customers to grant or withhold informed consent in advance.[45]

---

[35] AI Bill [HL], clause.1.

[36] AI Bill [HL], cls.1 (2)(a)–(f).

[37] AI Bill [HL], cls.6.

[38] AI Bill [HL], cls.2(1)(a).

[39] AI Bill [HL], cls.2(1)(b).

[40] AI Bill [HL], cls.2(1)(c).

[41] AI Bill [HL], cls.3.

[42] AI Bill [HL], cls.4.

[43] AI Bill [HL], cls.5(1)(a)(iv).

[44] AI Bill [HL], cls.5(1)(a)(i)–(ii).

[45] AI Bill [HL], cls.5(1)(a)(iii).

In form, the Bill was very much a 'framework' Bill in that it left much of the fine detail to be determined by ministers via regulations,[46] and included the powers to substantially rewrite the Authority's functions in cls.1 or dissolve it altogether[47]; to rewrite the regulatory principles in cls.2(1)[48]; and to rewrite the definition of sandbox in cls.3(2),[49] all by means of secondary legislation. In addition to this problematic approach,[50] the Bill itself was not especially well drafted being, for UK legislation, rather broad-brush in form and not particularly coherently structured.

However, these shortcomings were perhaps largely inconsequential, as it is unlikely that its proposer expected the Bill to become law, given an explicit lack of Government support.[51] Private member's bills are often utilised as a means of testing the waters for particular policies or, as is likely here, sending a message, sometimes to parties outside Parliament, but often to the government of the day. What the Bill reflected was a growing discontent amongst legislators of all parties with the perceived failure of the Government to provide at least some legislative footing for the proposed regulatory framework. This was combined with concern about the slow pace of development of the CCM for the sectoral regulators, which successive parliamentary committees and stakeholders were coming to realise was likely to be a critical component in the success or failure of a non-statutory framework to meet its objectives. As its Conservative proposer noted, if the UK was not willing to provide at least some statutory footing for the regulatory framework, 'the most likely, and certainly unintended, consequence is that businesses and organisations looking for a life raft will understandably, but unfortunately, align to the EU AI Act'.[52] This was hardly the result sought by a political party keen to promote the desirability of an alternative regulatory approach to that of the EU.

Whether the intended message found its mark—and the Government's response in the House of Lords reiterating its determination to continue with a non-statutory approach for the immediate future suggests that it did not—the Bill itself became moot on 22 May 2024, when the UK Prime Minister called a General Election, and all contentious legislation lapsed on the dissolution of Parliament. While the Labour Party indicated that in the event that it formed the next government it would 'urgently introduce binding regulation and establish a new regulatory innovation office for AI',[53] it had already been suggested by a House of Commons Committee that,

[46] See Tobin, AI (Regulation) Bill, supra n. 34, p. 26.

[47] AI Bill [HL], cls. 1(3).

[48] AI Bill [HL], cls. 2(2).

[49] AI Bill [HL], cls. 3(2).

[50] Noted in the House of Lords, Delegated Powers and Regulatory Reform Committee, fourth Report of Session 2023–24, HL Paper 31 (14 December 2023), paras. 1–6.

[51] Viscount Camrose (Con), AI (Regulation) Bill [HL] – third Reading, Hansard Vol. 838, Col. 347–350, 350

[52] Lord Holmes (Con), AI (Regulation) Bill [HL] – third Reading, Hansard Vol. 838, Col. 347–350, 348.

[53] Lord Leong (Lab), AI (Regulation) Bill [HL] – third Reading, Hansard Vol. 838, Col. 347–350, 348.

following the General Election in July 2024, it would likely be late 2025 before any new AI-focused legislation could be enacted.[54] That being the case, then continuing to develop and support the non-statutory regime would have to be the incoming UK government's primary policy option until 2026.

4 After the White Paper

The public consultation on the White Paper generated 409 written responses from various stakeholders, including industry representatives, academia, civil society organisations, and the public.[55] While many stakeholders were positive about the government's commitment to fostering AI innovation, a range of criticisms were raised regarding its proposed regulatory approach. These can be broadly categorised as:

- lack of specificity and clarity in the principles-based approach, which could lead to ambiguity and inconsistent application across sectors; while the principles mentioned fairness, transparency, and accountability, these areas needed to be addressed in more detail.
- concerns that implementation of the principles through existing legal frameworks would not fairly and effectively allocate legal responsibility for AI across its use life cycle.
- lack of detail on monitoring and enforcement, with a perceived lack of robust enforcement mechanisms to ensure compliance and mitigate risks associated with AI deployment.
- insufficient measures to ensure that the regulatory approach did not hinder start-ups and SMEs with disproportionate compliance burdens, reducing scope for innovation and competition.
- limited consideration of ethical and social issues, which were acknowledged as important, but for which no specific measures to address issues like bias and discrimination were proposed.
- risk of divergence from international norms, such as the EU AI Act, and frameworks established by organisations such as the OECD and ISO.
- uncertainty around the necessary funding and resources available to regulators to enable them to fulfil their roles under the new framework, and the need for

[54] HoC SITC, Governance of AI: Interim report, HC 1769, supra n. 26, para. 105.

A further Private Members Bill, the Public Authority Algorithmic and Automated Decision-Making Systems Bill was introduced to the House of Lords on 9 September 2024, aiming to regulate the use of AI systems in decision-making processes in the public sector. This will not become legislation without Government support, which is highly unlikely, but it may influence the Government's own future legislation. https://bills.parliament.uk/publications/56170/documents/5082

[55] DSIT, A pro-innovation approach: Government response, supra n. 4.

investment in training and capacity building for regulators to ensure they can keep pace with rapid technological advances.
- lack of specific measures for inclusive engagement with a diverse range of stakeholders, including marginalised communities and smaller businesses, and a need for broader public awareness and education initiatives to inform citizens about AI benefits, risks, and safeguards.

In its Response to these criticisms, the Government reiterated its initial commitment to the non-statutory principles-based regulatory framework, noting that it remained 'committed to a context-based approach that avoids unnecessary blanket rules that apply to all AI technologies, regardless of how they are used'.[56] However, it accepted that, in the longer term, targeted legal intervention would be required should the existing regulatory interventions, and voluntary measures adopted by system developers prove inadequate to address the continuing growth of AI capabilities.[57] The Response also altered tack somewhat by identifying 3 key categories of AI systems deemed to of particular interest:

- Highly capable general-purpose AI (e.g. cutting-edge Large Language Models (LLMs))
- Highly capable narrow AI (e.g. AI models for bioengineering)
- Agentic AI or AI agents

Of these, the Response identified 'highly capable general-purpose AI'[58] as a key focus of the UK's regulatory regime, but also the most likely to potentially require targeted legal intervention, insofar as such systems could challenge the context-based approach, as risks to which they contribute might not be effectively mitigated by application of existing UK regulation. Equally, it might be argued that, as general-purpose AI, it might fall within the remit of number of regulators who might choose address its implications differently, leading to a fragmentary and potentially incoherent regulatory response.[59] The Response did not provide detail on when and how such systems might need specific regulation, proposing to leave this to future discussion with industry, academia and civil society.

---

[56] Ibid, para. 11.

[57] Ibid, paras. 72–76. The Government had obtained commitments from leading AI companies developing highly capable AI systems that they would produce and publish their voluntary safety and transparency measures, and that they would collaborate with the new UK AI Safety Institute to test their AI systems pre- and post-deployment. Department for Science, Innovation and Technology (2023). Leading frontier AI companies publish safety policies [Press Release] 27 October 2023. https://www.gov.uk/government/news/leading-frontier-ai-companies-publish-safety-policies

[58] Defined as 'foundation models that can perform a wide variety of tasks and match or exceed the capabilities present in today's most advanced models' Ibid, para. 61. Also referred to as 'Frontier AI', see Dept. for Science, Innovation & Technology (2023) Emerging Processes for Frontier AI Safety, October 2023.

[59] Per Professor Uta Kohl, University of Southampton, in correspondence with the author.

The principles themselves remained unchanged, with the Government resisting suggestions that the scope of the principles should be broadened to include principles such as human rights, as it argued these were already sufficiently accounted for in existing statutes and regulatory schemes.[60] With regard to concerns about lack of specificity and clarity, it moved to incorporate more detailed guidelines and sector-specific regulations within the principles-based framework,[61] and to seek updates on how regulators were developing their strategic approaches to AI.[62] Extra funding was provided to enable regulators to develop capabilities and tools and to engage in R&D activities,[63] a steering committee with government representatives and key regulators to support knowledge exchange and coordination on AI governance was proposed, and a new cross-regulatory pilot advisory hub to support AI innovators, the Digital Regulation Cooperation Forum (DRCF) AI and Digital Hub, was established.[64] The aim of the Hub is to provide informal advice on AI issues that crossed regulatory boundaries from the 4 main DRCF regulators with responsibilities for digital regulation to allow innovators to bring new AI products and services to market safely and quickly.[65]

In sum, the Response to the White Paper did not suggest any significant re-evaluation of the proposed regulatory framework on the part of the Government in the short-medium term. The developing framework remained principle-based, non-statutory, and cross-sector, applying existing technology-neutral regulation to AI. As such there was still no definition of AI, with the focus being an outcome-based approach premised on potential risks arising from the adaptivity and autonomy of AI systems in specific sectors and contexts, although there was now a recognition of the need to differentiate between the three key categories of AI systems. The three elements of the regulatory framework were confirmed as being:

- utilisation of existing regulatory authorities and frameworks;
- establishment of a a central coordinating mechanism in the Central Risk Function (CRF) at the Dept. for Science, Innovation & Technology (DIST) to facilitate effective risk monitoring and regulatory coordination; and
- support of innovation via the DRCF AI and Digital Hub.

[60] DSIT, A pro-innovation approach: Government response, supra n. 4, p. 43.

[61] Dept. for Science, Innovation & Technology (2024). Implementing the UK's AI Regulatory Principles: Initial Guidance for Regulators, Feb. 2024. The next phase of Guidance was expected in mid-late 2024.

[62] Dept. for Science, Innovation & Technology et al. (2024). Request for regulators to publish an update on their strategic approach to AI: Secretary of State letter, 15 February 2024.

[63] Although the £10 million Regulator's AI Capability Fund allocated for this purpose is likely to spread between, the very least, 14 different regulators.

[64] The DRFC was set up in 2020 by the 4 main digital regulators, the Competition and Markets Authority (CMA), the Financial Conduct Authority (FCA), the Information Commissioner's Office (ICO) and Ofcom to collaborate on digital regulatory matters.

[65] Digital Regulation Cooperation Forum (DRCF) AI and Digital Hub, https://www.drcf.org.uk/ai-and-digital-hub

Despite the pressure to establish a statutorily empowered regulatory body, per the *Artificial Intelligence (Regulation) Bill,* no such body or new AI regulator was envisaged. The role of the Central Risk Function was clarified as being to monitor and evaluate AI risks, and promote coherence and address regulatory gaps. To that end it would be required to carry out an ongoing review of regulatory powers and remits, develop a cross-economy AI risk register, and collaborate with existing regulatory forums, e.g. the DRCF. The role of the AI and Digital Hub would be to help organisations to comply with relevant legal and regulatory obligations before product launch. Its task was to facilitate compliance, and enhance cooperation between regulators. The implementation of the principles by regulators, and the requirement for them to collaborate with each other, would remain non-legally binding obligations, although a legal duty on regulators to give due consideration to the framework's principles might be created in the future.

At least one commentator noted that, while the EU AI Act was barely mentioned in the Response, the US was highlighted as a potential key partner, suggesting that the UK Government was still more inclined to the US federal approach to AI regulation than that of the EU.[66] The US federal response had primarily taken the form of legislation encouraging AI innovation[67] Executive Orders addressing risks,[68] and the securing of voluntary commitments from major US companies.[69] This suggested that the US was inclined against overarching AI regulation by legislation, preferring a light touch co-regulatory or largely self-regulatory regime, which would almost certainly not adopt the EU risk classification approach.

By this point the UK Government was clearly altering its position on the issue of highly capable general-purpose AI (HCGPAI). As with the EU's expansion of the AI Act to address GPAI, the rapid development of LLMs and their expansion/incorporation into mainstream business practices and consumer technologies forced a reconsideration of the need for future targeted regulatory intervention above and beyond the existing voluntary commitments made by the leading AI companies. Any such intervention would address failures of existing regulation to tackle HCGPA risks, and be directed to key players in the development of GPAI models/systems, covering, for example, issues such as transparency, data quality, risk management, accountability, corporate governance, and addressing harms from misuse or unfair bias.

---

[66] Keeling and Finlayson-Brown (2024).

[67] E.g. the National Artificial Intelligence Initiative Act of 2020; the AI in Government Act of 2020; the Advancing American AI Act of 2022.

[68] E.g. Executive Order 13985, Advancing Racial Equity and Support for Underserved Communities Through the Federal Government February 16, 2023; Executive Order 14110 Safe, Secure, and Trustworthy Development and Use of Artificial Intelligence, October 30, 2023.

[69] White House, Fact Sheet: Biden-Harris Administration Secures Voluntary Commitments from Leading Artificial Intelligence Companies to Manage the Risks Posed by AI, July 21, 2023.

5 The UK Regulators' View

While the UK AI framework places much of the onus on regulators to implement the framework in their sectors/domains by applying existing laws and issuing supplementary regulatory guidance, it is not entirely clear which of the UK's many regulators[70] are intended to be included, or the scope of coverage of potential AI risks and benefits that their respective remits afford.[71] However, some regulators will undoubtedly have a significantly larger role to play than others. The 14 regulators initially requested by the UK Government to provide an update on their strategic approach to AI by May 2024 were the Bank of England, Competition and Markets Authority (CMA), Equality and Human Rights Commission (EHRC), Financial Conduct Authority (FCA), Health and Safety Executive (HSE), Information Commissioner's Office (ICO), Legal Services Board (LSB), Medicines and Healthcare products Regulatory Agency (MHRA), Office for Nuclear Regulation (ONR), Office for Standards in Education, Children's Services and Skills (Ofsted), Office of Communications (Ofcom), Office of Gas and Electricity Markets (Ofgem), Office of Qualifications and Examinations Regulation (Ofqual).[72] Other regulators will be expected to publish plans in the future.

5.1 *The 'Digital-Focused' Regulators*

It is instructive to consider the initial response of four key regulators to the Government's request for details of their approach to AI-related risks in their areas, their current skillset and expertise to address them, and how they plan to regulate AI in the immediate future. These are the CMA,[73] FCA,[74] ICO,[75] and Ofcom.[76] They are the founder members of the Digital Regulation Cooperation Forum (DRCF) and the primary regulators in the digital arena. All four would view themselves as technology neutral/agnostic, principle-based and outcomes-focused/risk-based regulators, with regulatory briefs that already heavily intersect with AI regulatory issues. They have thus already been engaging in consultation with their key stakeholders on AI

[70] The Institute for Government has identified 116 UK regulators, see IoG (2024) Parliament and regulators, April 2024, 5. Policy Exchange identified 92 UK regulators, see Policy Exchange (2022) Re-engineering Regulation, pp. 70–72. The National Audit Office suggests, with a slightly concerning lack of specificity, there are 'around 90' regulatory bodies in the UK, see NAO (2022). Departmental Overview 2020–21: Regulation, March.

[71] As noted by Lord Cookham in the House of Lords debate on the AI (Regulation) Bill, Second Reading, Hansard Vol. 837, Col. 393–428 (22 Mar. 2024), Col. 398.

[72] DSIT, Regulators' strategic approaches to AI, supra n. 12.

[73] CMA (2024). AI strategic update, 29 Apr.

[74] FCA (2024). AI Update, 22 Apr.

[75] ICO (2024). Regulating AI: The ICO's strategic approach, 30 Apr.

[76] Ofcom (2024). Ofcom's strategic approach to AI 2024/25, 26 Mar.

use in contexts that fall within their particular regulatory remit, providing AI-related advisory materials and compliance tools,[77] and engaging in related internal capacity building and external collaboration with other regulators. In resource terms, they appear prepared in both capacity and expertise, e.g. the CMA identified its specialist DaTa unit, Technology and Business Services (TBS) team and 9 Digital Expert independent advisors as key staff resources; Ofcom noted its 100 technology experts, including 60 AI experts. This permits these regulators to undertake cutting edge research into AI developments and to engage in detailed horizon scanning. It is perhaps not surprising, given this background, that the 'digital-focused' regulators' were supportive of the Government's approach, and that their AI update documents were lengthy and provided detailed plans for future AI strategy. The documents focused on promoting their past AI-related achievements, emphasising their capacity to take on the role envisaged for them, and outlining key strategy elements, such as comprehensive AI risk frameworks. Compliance and oversight mechanisms, multi-stakeholder engagement, best practice guidelines and tools etc. All highlighted the importance of collaboration, both domestically and internationally, and underscored the need for continuous capacity building to keep pace with AI developments. On the former point, the UK has been keen to be seen to be a leader in international policy discussions, although the degree of influence that any one government can wield in such discussions appears to drop off sharply once one moves past the US and China. It appears though that additional funding to support regulators will be in short supply.[78] While the Government has put what it clearly regards as very significant resource into the development of UK AI capacity, this is overwhelmingly directed to R&D and building industry capacity, and even the entirety of that funding is dwarfed by private sector spending. This may mean that even some of the larger, better resourced regulators have to rely more heavily than might be desirable on industry co-operation for information and expertise.

5.2 *Other Regulators*

In contrast to the digital-focused regulators, the published strategic plans for smaller, or less digitally focused regulators, such as the EHRC[79] the MRHA,[80] and the HSE[81] are significantly shorter and rather less detailed. A key takeaway from these plans is that significant additional resource will be required to increase their inhouse

[77] See e.g. ICO (2022). Guidance on AI and data protection (15 Mar. 2023); ICO (2022). AI and data protection risk toolkit (undated).

[78] **'The announced £10 million to support regulators in responding to the growing prevalence of AI is clearly insufficient to meet the challenge…'** House of Commons Science, Innovation and Technology Committee (2024) The governance of artificial intelligence: Final report, HC38, 28 May 2024, para 56.

[79] EHRC (2024). Update on our approach to regulating AI, 30 Apr.

[80] MHRA (2024). Impact of AI on the regulation of medical products, 30 Apr.

[81] HSE (2024). HSE's regulatory approach to Artificial Intelligence (undated) [webpage] https://www.hse.gov.uk/news/hse-ai.htm

expertise and capabilities if they are to fulfil the requirements of the proposed AI regulatory framework effectively.

The MHRA notes that it had approximately three full-time equivalent (FTE) employees working on 'AI as a Medical Device' work, rising to 7.5 FTE in 2024/25, plus a Software and AI Expert Advisory Group consisting of external experts. Given the probability of a significant rise in the number of organisations seeking to increase or newly deploy AI-based tools for health and care applications, one may question the extent to which small regulatory teams will be able to support effective oversight. The MRHA's strategy document is less expansive in its scope than those of the 'digital-focused' regulators, and affords nearly as much space to how it will use AI in its work as it does to how it will seek to regulate AI use within its remit. Regulatory research and horizon scanning are mentioned almost in passing, and while there is some evidence of existing and planned international co-operation on AI use within its remit, there is almost nothing on co-operation with other UK regulators.

The EHRC's strategy document is short and noticeably less upbeat than those of the 'digital-focused' regulators. After noting the importance of equality and human rights expertise to the application of the 'fairness' principle, it highlights the breadth of the EHRC's remit and its potential to cut across all sectors. Concerns about the EHRC's ability to handle this effectively are clearly flagged. Given a budget static since 2016, a small team of staff with specific AI responsibilities, and a lack of technical expertise, the document explicitly notes that extra resource is critical for the EHRC to implement the five principles, but that this has not been forthcoming, restricting its work to a small set of strategic issues. The EHRC is unconvinced that plans to share resources between regulators will overcome its expertise gaps, or permit it to hold large multinational technology firms to account.

The differences in scope between the 12 key regulators in terms of their suggested future strategies, and their degree of optimism that their regulatory objectives under the AI regulatory framework are attainable, are quite noticeable. This reflects the concerns about the likely coherence of that framework expressed during the consultation period, the risks of fragmented oversight and enforcement, and the potential for imbalance in the application of the principles, with issues of direct concern to the digital-focused regulators being likely be given greater weight in regulatory practice.

6 Comparison with the AI Act

Engaging in a comparison of the EU AI Act legislation and the UK's non-statutory AI regulatory framework is something of an 'apples and oranges' affair. The lack of legislation on the UK's part, and the broad-brush details available at the time of writing on how its framework might operate, exacerbated by the July 2024 General Election, which effectively shuttered policy discussion from the prorogation of the UK Parliament in late May until well after the election of the new government, makes it difficult to effectively juxtapose the UK AI framework with the extensive EU legislation. However, some initial issues can be outlined.

6.1 Choice of Regulatory Regime

Designing an effective and efficient regulatory regime for a supranational jurisdiction consisting of 27 Member States with widely varying political, social, and economic environments is a very different matter than designing such a regime for a single jurisdiction. This is complicated further when the executive body of the supranational jurisdiction is working within a bounded competency to impose horizontal rules across its Member States governing development, deployment, and use of AI systems, while the executive body of a single jurisdiction like the UK has, in principle, unlimited competency to use legislative, regulatory, or administrative powers to achieve its goal. The EU Commission's decision to use Art.114 TEU as the legal base for its strategy, providing broad competency in the establishment and functioning of the internal market, and its decision to then structure the resulting action around the existing EU product liability legislative template are, as noted elsewhere,[82] choices structured by procedural necessity in the former case, and the ability to draw upon an established body of EU regulatory practice, rather than attempting to develop a new regulatory regime from the ground up, in the latter. While these choices enabled the Commission to legitimise its AI regulatory agenda, and move more quickly to create legislation, it has been argued that they may yet lead to significant problems in providing protection of fundamental rights, developing effective oversight, and providing meaningful avenues for wider stakeholder engagement and redress.[83]

The UK government, by contrast, had a wider range of options open to it, and the rationale for its decision to eschew the legislative route was therefore not grounded in necessity. This leaves a range of potential rationales for the non-legislative approach chosen. From a pragmatic and practical perspective, there is a reasonable case to be made for the principle-based approach utilising existing regulators, emphasising the flexibility and agility of such an arrangement to cope with rapid social, economic and technological change, and leveraging existing domain knowledge and regulatory expertise. The extent to which this perspective should be regarded as the driving force behind the UK policy decision might perhaps be assessed in relation to whether the UK government has then provided adequate resources for regulators and provision of effective supporting infrastructure to implement such a policy framework.

Viewed from a more political standpoint, a range of other possible rationales suggest themselves. By mid-2024, the weakened and intellectually impoverished

---

[82] Almada and Radu (2024), pp. 648–9; Almada and Radu (2023).

[83] See e.g. Veale and Zuiderveen Borgesius (2021), pp. 97–112.

Conservative administration might perhaps have sought to avoid the work of constructing a complex piece of legislation addressing a rapidly evolving subject-matter, and then steering it through the legislative process, when there was a real possibility of being able to leave that task as a problem for its successor to solve, as indeed it proved, with the election of a Labour Government in July 2024. Alternatively, it could be argued, adopting a strategy which would allow the government to place the onus of understanding and addressing AI risks and issues upon the extensive array of UK regulators, at whose feet blame for any failures of the principles-based approach might then be placed, does not seem entirely outlandish. In financial terms, a government keen to be seen as financially prudent might regard the use of existing regulators and central government resources as an opportunity to implement a less costly approach than creating and resourcing another sizable regulator. Finally, the potential to spin the decision as a 'Brexit benefit', allowing the government to claim it was freeing innovative UK business from a red-tape festooned Brussels, would doubtless factor into deliberations.

The incoming Labour government signalled something of a shift in the UK's regulatory approach, with a commitment in July 2024 to 'establish the appropriate legislation to place requirements on those working to develop the most powerful artificial intelligence models'.[84] That shift does not take the form of an overarching piece of AI legislation like the EU AI Act, but rather a much narrower approach focusing on 'frontier AI models' and AI safety.[85] 'Frontier AI models' may be defined as cutting-edge highly capable foundation models, i.e. models trained on broad data at scale and adaptable to a wide range of downstream tasks.[86] They are regarded as particularly problematic as they 'may possess unexpected and difficult-to-detect dangerous capabilities; if deployed for broad use can be difficult to reliably control and to prevent from being used to cause harm; and may proliferate rapidly, enabling circumvention of safeguards'.[87] It was suggested that the legislation would place existing voluntary commitments on such technologies made between key technology companies and the government on a statutory footing. It would also make the UK's AI Security Institute an arm's length body from the government.[88] No timetable has been set for the suggested Bill at the time of writing,

[84] UK Prime Minister's Office and His Majesty King Charles III, 'King's Speech 2024', 17 July 2024.

The King's Speech is the speech is read out at the State Opening of Parliament, and sets out the programme of legislation that the Government intend to pursue in the forthcoming parliamentary session.

[85] Gross and Parker (2024) cited in Haves (2024).

[86] Bommasani et al. (2021),

[87] Anderljung et al. (2023). See also Bullock et al. (2024).

The definition of 'Frontier AI model' suggests that a model may longer be considered a 'Frontier AI model' if it is overtaken by a more capable technology.

[88] The UK AI Security Institute (AISA - formerly the AI Safety Institute until February 2025) is currently a directorate of the UK Department for Science, Innovation, and Technology. Its role is 'conducting research and building infrastructure to understand the capabilities and impacts of advanced AI and to develop and test risk mitigations'. https://www.aisi.gov.uk/

and a period of further consultation with stakeholders is expected before it is placed before Parliament.

It appears, therefore, that the current UK government intends, for the most part, to persevere with the non-statutory principle-based regulatory framework adopted by its predecessor.[89] This may reflect a continuing belief at government level that such an approach will be more agile, flexible and innovation friendly than the wide-ranging statutory approach of the EU AI Act. It might also be a pragmatic acceptance that the demands of the Labour Government's wider legislative agenda means there will be insufficient time to consult on and develop a wider statutory regime for AI in the short to medium term, and that even incremental action shows a willingness not to cede the regulatory agenda entirely to the EU.

In sum, the differing choice of regulatory mechanisms for the two regimes thus reflects more than just a political divide between the two. It provides an interesting example of how the choice of regulatory strategy may be driven by very different factors, including clear constitutional constraints and pragmatic considerations on the part of the EU; and a more diffuse and indeterminate range of possible political, financial and pragmatic factors on the part of the UK.

6.2 *Implementation*

The speed at which the EU was able to reach agreement on the AI Act appears to have taken other jurisdictions, including the UK, somewhat by surprise. However, while the AI Act entered into force in August 2024, full implementation of the legislation will not occur until 2026, with the ban on prohibited AI systems taking effect 6 months after entry into force (February 2025), the provisions relating to GPAI systems and models after 12 months (August 2025), and full enforcement after 24 months when obligations on high-risk AI systems will begin (August 2026).[90]

Significant elements of the EU's regime will be developed over time. The Commission is given the power to issue delegated acts on matters such as: definition of 'AI system', criteria and use cases for 'high-risk' AI, thresholds for general purpose AI models with systemic risk, technical documentation requirements for general purpose AI, conformity assessments, and EU declarations of conformity. It is to issue guidance on high-risk AI incident reporting, by 12 months after entry into force, and on practical implementation of high-risk AI requirements, with list of

[89] DIST, AI Opportunities Action Plan: Independent Report, 13 January 2025, section 1.4, points 25–28. https://www.gov.uk/government/publications/ai-opportunities-action-plan/ai-opportunities-action-plan#conclusion

[90] A 36-month timeline applies to high-risk systems in Annex II e.g. systems intended to be used as a safety component of a product, or where the AI is itself a product, and the product is required to undergo a third-party conformity assessment under existing specific EU laws, for example toys, radio equipment, in vitro diagnostic medical devices, civil aviation security and agricultural vehicles.

practical examples of high-risk and non-high-risk use cases by 18 months. Other guidance on issues such as prohibited AI practices, requirements for high-risk AI systems, and the relationship of the AI Act and its enforcement with other EU law will be produced 'when deemed necessary.' On the part of the Member States, appointment of their Competent Authorities under the AI Act is required within 12 months after entry into force, with the implementation of rules on penalties, including administrative fines and the establishment of at least one operational AI regulatory sandbox after 24 months.

Assuming the Commission and Member States can adhere to the timetable set by the legislation, it will thus be mid-to late 2026 before the EU's regime is largely in place. That said, the AI Act does have the clear benefits of setting a defined timetable and providing industry and other stakeholders with an early and detailed understanding of the Commission's aims and objectives. This includes the measures that those regulated will need to prepare for and implement, and the enforcement measures and sanctions that may be brought against those not in compliance.[91] While the Commission has been criticised in some quarters for legislating at a point which some believe to be too early in the development of the technology to be effective,[92] utilising arguments such as the 'pacing problem',[93] or the 'timing problem'[94] to suggest that legislation is a poor means of establishing agile approaches to AI regulation, such criticisms fail to consider the subtleties of the EU legislative process, whereby legislative activity often has a wider purpose than simply attempting to provide a definitive solution to an particular problem. An important function of EU legislation, it is suggested here, is 'messaging', i.e. the Commission uses legislation to indicate the importance it attaches to the subject matter, the key elements on which it wants to focus attention, and an indication of whom it considers the key stakeholders. By this means, even if the initial iteration of the legislation is flawed in its targeting of a particular technology, the legislation has the effect of shaping Member State and key stakeholder understandings and behaviour, in anticipation of future adjustments which are more precisely focused.[95]

Because of the way that it is structured, the UK's regulatory regime is in effect already underway, insofar as key regulators have produced AI-related guidance and tool kits[96] and, in the case of the ICO, have already investigated, and brought

[91] Larsson et al. (2024).

[92] e.g. Smuha (2021), pp. 57–84; Nordström (2022), pp. 1703–1714.

[93] i.e. regulation always lags behind rapidly evolving technologies—'technology develops exponentially, laws change incrementally'—thus creating gaps where emerging technologies may operate without adequate oversight or governance.

[94] i.e. early regulation hinders technological development because it imposes constraints before the technology's potential is fully understood, or is based on perceived rather than actual risks leading to misallocation of resources and stifling of beneficial innovation.

[95] See e.g. the evolution of the EU's eMoney Directives (Directive 2000/46/EC; Directive 2009/110/EC; draft Directive on payment services and electronic money services (2023)).

[96] See e.g. Ofcom (2024), supra n. 77.

regulatory compliance actions against, AI system developers.[97] The implementation roadmap for the UK is, however, inevitably going to be more fragmented. The principle-based approach, while potentially more flexible and agile in response to AI technology-mediated social and economic changes clearly provides much less certainty for key stakeholders. Additionally, smaller, but important regulators, such as the EHRC, which has a key role in the application of the fairness principle, are likely to struggle to match the upskilling and intervention capabilities of the big four 'digital regulators' in the short to medium term, given their current resourcing. This might be perceived as a deliberate attempt to downplay the role of these regulators, or the particular principles or sectors for which they have responsibility. However, it is probable that it simply reflects a broader disinterest on the part of the UK Conservative government in considering enhancing regulatory effectiveness, given its declared deregulatory ethos.

6.3 Central Co-ordination

The EU Commission established the European Artificial Intelligence Office (EAIO) in February 2024 as part of the administrative structure of the Directorate-General for Communication Networks, Content & Technology.[98] Its role is to support the governance bodies in Member States in their tasks, enforce the rules for general-purpose AI models, promote an innovative ecosystem of trustworthy AI, ensure a strategic, coherent and effective European approach on AI at the international level, and collaborate with Member States and the wider expert community through dedicated fora and expert groups, liaising with scientific community, industry, think tanks, civil society. It is currently stated that the EAIO, which will also provide the secretariat for the EU AI Board,[99] will employ 'over 140 staff, including technology specialists, administrative assistants, lawyers, policy specialists, and economists'.[100] Its role resembles that mooted for the UK's Central Risk Function based in the DIST (above, Sect. 4), although precise details on the make-up, size and role of CRF, beyond those initially provided in the UK government's White Paper and Response document,[101] remain sparse. What is clear from the material available is

---

[97] Davies (2021).

[98] Per Art. 64, AI Act; Commission Decision of 24 January 2024 establishing the European Artificial Intelligence Office OJ C, C/2024/1459, 14.2.2024, ELI: http://data.europa.eu/eli/C/2024/1459/oj
European AI Office, https://digital-strategy.ec.europa.eu/en/policies/ai-office

[99] Per Art. 65 & 66 AI Act. The European AI Board (similar in function to the EDPB under the GDPR) consists of a representative from each Member State, and its role is to advise and assist the Commission and the Member States on the application of the AI Act.

[100] Ibid.

[101] DSIT/OAI, A pro-innovation approach, supra n. 4, 37–48; DSIT, A pro-innovation approach: Government response, supra n. 4, 46–48.

the role of the UK CRF is envisaged to only be 'initially' provided by government, with the possibility of an independent body being established outside of government.

Several issues arise regarding these co-ordination entities. The stated remit of the EU's EAIO appears very ambitious for an administrative unit staffed at the level suggested, and it is hard to believe that it could effectively manage a workload that includes EU-wide support for 27 AI Competent Authorities, and enforcement of the GPAI rules.[102] The Commission has a history of taking on administrative functions which it cannot effectively support; the 'adequacy' process under the GDPR is a case in point. In the case of the UK, the continuing lack of clarity over the nature of the CRF, in combination with complaints about initial failure to provide timely support to the sectoral regulators, casts some doubt over the ability of the DIST to undertake the role effectively. If the UK government in fact envisages the possibility of moving the CRF role to an independent body, such that the CRF is essentially an interim 'AI Authority', one might question the rationale for not adopting an independent body from the start.

6.4 Regulatory Risks

While the EU and UK regulatory AI regimes differ in approach, there is a risk that both could be compromised through 'regulatory capture'.[103] As regulating AI technologies requires a broad understanding of relevant technical complexities, ethical implications, and potential societal impacts, this may lead to a situation where national or sectoral regulators lack the relevant expertise or information necessary to exercise their functions. This may make them increasingly reliant on access to industry expertise, creating a risk of overdependence on industry-provided data and insights. AI companies will inevitably possess more information about their technologies than do regulators, particularly where regulators lack subject experts or have limited resources. This information asymmetry may permit industry stakeholders to shape regulation in their favour, or to present regulators with information that does not fully capture the risks associated with particular AI deployments.[104] In rapidly developing regulatory arenas, like AI, there may also be a greater than usual scope for 'revolving door dynamics'—the movement of personnel between regulatory bodies and industry. Recruitment to regulators from industry can lead to industry viewpoints being given greater weight, and becoming embedded in regulatory

[102] One might consider, for example, that in 2021 Google's legal department had over 900 members. See O'Carroll and Kimbro (2021), p. 501.

[103] The process where regulatory agencies, due to close relationships with industry stakeholders, develop policies favouring the interests of the industry they are supposed to regulate, rather than the public good. See for discussion in the AI regulatory context, House of Lords CDC, Large language models and generative AI supra n. 27, paras. 43–57; Guihot et al. (2020), p. 425; Roberts et al. (2023), p. 16.

[104] Neudert (2023), p. 7.

practice. In the other direction, early-stage expertise and insider knowledge garnered by staff at regulators will make them highly desirable to the AI industry, which can offer much more competitive pay and conditions. This risks the adoption of less stringent regulatory approaches becoming an inadvertent or deliberate outcome of regulators' future career considerations.[105] From a UK AI-regulatory perspective, it is interesting to note that the risk of capture for individual sector regulators may be higher than it is for cross-sector regulators,[106] possibly because there is less of a revolving door effect in cross-sectoral regulation work.

The EU Commission and UK regulators have certainly had capture-related issues in the past,[107] for example, in the AI arena, the EU's AI Ethics Guidelines (2019),[108] were criticised as being too focused towards industry interests and insufficiently attentive to human rights, transparency, and accountability in AI development and deployment.[109] There have also been concerns expressed about the higher risks of regulatory capture occurring in relation to the use of regulatory sandboxes, the use of which are encouraged by both the EU AI Act and the UK framework (and development of which is seen as a key UK regulatory strength),[110] as organisations engaged in sandbox activities with regulators have a greater ability to influence the direction and scope of the regulatory environment, often out of sight of other stakeholders.[111]

6.5 *Innovation vs Human Rights*

The EU places significant emphasis on ensuring high standards of safety, ethical use, and protection of fundamental rights in the development and placing on the market of AI systems in the EU. However, the need for a broad legal base for legislation, and the fact that fundamental rights, in and of themselves, would not provide a basis for EU legislation, meant the AI Act was based upon the broad competence provided by Art.114 TEU and, on the EU's product liability and consumer protection legislative template. This has led to suggestions that the role of fundamental rights would inevitably be diminished within the EU, as the agencies tasked with AI regulatory functions would have potentially countervailing regulatory priorities and lack the necessary background and expertise to effectively pursue a fundamental

---

[105] See e.g. Makkai and Braithwaite (1992), pp. 61–78.

[106] House of Lords, Industry and Regulators Committee (IRC), first Report of Session 2023–24 Who watches the watchdogs? Improving the performance, independence and accountability of UK regulators, HL Paper 56, February 2024.

[107] Saltelli et al. (2022), p. 102860; Heims and Moxon (2024), pp. 139–157.

[108] High-Level Expert Group on AI (2019). Ethics Guidelines for AI, European Commission, 8 Apr.

[109] Roberts et al. (2021), pp. 1–25; Charlesworth (2022), pp. 243–262.

[110] EU AI Act Arts. 57–63; DSIT/OAI, A pro-innovation approach, supra n. 4, p. 54. Truby et al. (2022).

[111] Ranchordas and Vinci (2024), pp. 107–139.

rights-focused agenda. This might in turn impact the EU's ability to seek to raise the bar for fundamental rights in international AI policy through the 'Brussels' effect.[112]

The UK Conservative government's purported commitment to protection of fundamental rights through AI regulation was somewhat undermined by its failure to make provision for adequate resources for key regulators with relevant remits, notably the Equality and Human Rights Commission. It also attempted, in the Data Protection and Digital Information Bill (DPDIB), to significantly alter the role and approach of the Information Commissioner's Office as the primary rights-focused 'digital regulator'. The Bill would have placed a new duty to have regard to 'growth and innovation' on the ICO's work, and reduced its independence by placing key policy tools, such as its Codes of Conduct effectively under government control.[113] The DPDIB lapsed on the change of government, and the incoming Labour government's proposed Data (Use and Access) Bill (D(UA)B), introduced in October 2024 makes less extensive changes to UK data protection law. However, it still makes changes to the structure and governance of the new Information Commission that may affect its independence from government,[114] and retains the duty for the Commission to have regard to the desirability of promoting innovation and competition in its work.[115]

In both frameworks, albeit for different reasons, there is thus a risk that the innovation and competition element comes to play a more significant role in the regulatory agenda at the expense of rights-based developments.

6.6 *Generative AI*

The rapid development of publicly accessible Generative AI systems (GenAI) or 'general-purpose AI systems', such as ChatGPT, provide a good example of the problems that AI-based systems may pose for both the EU and UK regulatory regimes. The technical foundation for GenAI systems are 'general-purpose AI models' or 'foundational models', which include large language models (LLMs), such as GPT-4 and DALL-E.[116] GPAI models may be used by their provider to create AI systems (e.g. as OpenAI use GPT-4 and DALL-E in ChatGPT4) or by providers that integrate a third-party or open-source GPAI model into their own AI systems—'downstream providers' and 'downstream AI systems'.

---

[112] Almada and Radu (2024), pp. 648–49; Almada and Radu (2023).

[113] See Roberts et al. (2023), pp. 1–31.

[114] Clauses 115–118 D(UA)B.

[115] Clause 90(3) D(UA)B inserting a new s.120B Duties in relation to functions under the data protection legislation into the Data Protection Act 2018.

[116] Art. 3(63) AI Act 'GPAI model': An AI model, including when trained with a large amount of data using self-supervision at scale, that displays significant generality and is capable to competently perform a wide range of distinct tasks regardless of the way the model is placed on the market and that can be integrated into a variety of downstream systems or applications.

The impact of GPAI models and the wide-spread dissemination of GPAI systems that can be built from them necessitated late-stage amendments to the EU AI Act,[117] and to the UK's stance on regulation.[118] Under the EU AI Act, GPAI systems could be categorised within the four risk categories, based on their use/context (i.e. a basic chatbot would likely be minimal to low risk), the initial draft of the AI Act would have had very limited application to GPAI models because its requirements only applied to high-risk AI, and a GPAI model that had no predetermined use or context would not therefore qualify as 'high risk'. The final AI Act thus imposes a set of risk-based obligations on providers of GPAI models, differentiating between standard 'GPAI models', 'openly and free licensed GPAI models' and 'GPAI models with systemic risks', including the obligations to provide information to enable downstream users of their GPAI model to comprehend its capabilities and limitations, to enable regulatory coverage of the development and use of GPAI across the entire AI supply chain.[119] The GPAI rules, governance and penalties apply 12 months after the AI Act's adoption, and the AI Office will oversee GPAI models, enforce common rules, and develop secondary legislation. The hurried adjustment to the AI Act does call into question the ability of the legislative regime to address future developments; while such significant adjustment was possible while the AI Act was being finalised, scope for future amendment may prove rather more difficult to accommodate.

In the UK there has been a reconsideration on the part of the government of its decision not to produce legislation to address AI regulation, with suggestions that legislation might be introduced to place specific requirements on developers of AI 'foundational models' (i.e. GPAI models). However, at the time of writing no concrete proposals have yet emerge as to what such legislation might look like, or to what extent it would align with that of the EU.

An interesting difference that has emerged between the EU and UK regimes relates to the use of copyright materials by GPAI models. The AI Act places a requirement on providers of GPAI models to draw up a policy to comply with EU copyright law and to create and make publicly available a sufficiently detailed summary about the content used for training of the general-purpose AI model, to allow parties with legitimate interests, including copyright holders, to exercise and enforce their rights under EU law. By contrast, the UK Intellectual Property Office (IPO) started work in May 2023 on a voluntary code on the use of copyright-protected content for training AI models, via a technical working group comprised of rights holders and AI developers. In February 2024 the UK Government admitted that no voluntary code had been agreed, but discussion continued between Ministers and stakeholders.[120] Given that the Government had stated that it did 'not rule out the

[117] EU AI Act, Arts. 51–56. Helberger and Diakopoulos (2023), pp. 1–6; Volpicelli (2023).

[118] HoC SITC, Governance of AI: Final report, supra n. 78, paras 32–33; Gross and Criddle (2024).

[119] The obligations do not apply to GPAI models used solely for research, development, or prototyping activities, and only apply in part to AI models released under a free and open license.

[120] DSIT, A pro-innovation approach: Government response, supra n. 4, 19.

possibility of legislative action in this area if industry does not take adequate steps to improve the situation' i.e. reach a negotiated solution,[121] it remains to be seen whether this is yet another area where a non-legislative approach gives way to a legislative outcome.

7 Concluding Comment

Discussions with international academic audiences about the differences between the two AI regulatory frameworks often raise the question: Can the UK afford to diverge significantly from the EU approach to AI regulation? This often draws on some knowledge of the way in which the EU General Data Protection Regulation (GDPR)[122] has come to influence much of the international approach to data protection, and the care the UK has had to take post-Brexit to maintain its 'adequacy' ruling that permits free flow of data between the UK and EU. There will inevitably be an element of 'Brussels effect' arising from the AI Act. However, the UK has a major international presence in AI development, being a key player in both AI development and AI policymaking, and dominating AI investment in Europe.[123] This may enable the UK to maintain a regulatory divergence from the EU for long enough to determine whether its regulatory strategy can plausibly meet either or both of its innovation and human rights objectives, and allow for meaningful comparison with the effectiveness of the EU framework.

As AI technologies are inherently global, divergent regulatory frameworks can create complexities for cross-border operations. Presently, businesses operating in both the UK and EU will need to navigate different regulatory landscapes, leading to increased compliance costs and operational challenges, and there will undoubtedly be pressure from commercial interests for convergence or accommodation. However, UK companies are likely to baulk at simply acquiescing to compliance with 'stricter' EU rules if this risks placing them at a disadvantage to agile competitors based outside the EU. This may be the case if the EU legislative regime proves inflexible and unable to adapt rapidly to technological innovation or external economic factors. For the 'Brussels effect' to work, there must be a convincing case that UK companies require access to the Single Market to thrive. The EU itself has shown a pragmatic approach to evolving its regulatory strategies—the GDPR incorporates a number of elements the Commission drew from successful DP practice around the world, from breach notification to privacy impact assessments, and is

[121] Intellectual Property Office, (2023) Code of Practice on Copyright and Artificial Intelligence, Terms of Reference, May 2023, 1, citing HM Government. (2023) Response to Pro-Innovation Regulation of Technologies Review: Digital Technologies, March 2023.

[122] Regulation (EU) 2016/679 of the European Parliament and of the Council of 27 April 2016 on the protection of natural persons with regard to the processing of personal data and on the free movement of such data, and repealing Directive 95/46/EC (General Data Protection Regulation) OJ L 119, 4.5.2016, p. 1–88, ELI: http://data.europa.eu/eli/reg/2016/679/oj

[123] Maslej et al. (2024), pp. 247–248.

more flexible in approach than its predecessor Directive. If the UK can demonstrate its AI regulatory approach is viable and provides the incentives to innovation claimed without posing undue risks, then policy influence may prove to be a two-way street.

References

Almada M, Radu A (2023) The EU AI Act: a medley of product safety and fundamental rights? EUI, RSC Working Paper, 2023/59. https://hdl.handle.net/1814/75982

Almada M, Radu A (2024) The Brussels side-effect: how the AI Act can reduce the global reach of EU policy. Ger Law J 25(4):646–663. https://doi.org/10.1017/glj.2023.108

Anderljung M et al (2023) Frontier AI regulation: managing emerging risks to public safety. [preprint] arXiv:2307.03718. https://arxiv.org/pdf/2307.03718

Baldwin R, Cave C, Lodge M (2011) Understanding regulation: theory, strategy, and practice, 2nd edn. Oxford University Press, Oxford

Bommasani R et al (2021) On the opportunities and risks of foundation models. [preprint] arXiv:2108.07258. https://arxiv.org/pdf/2108.07258

Bullock C et al (2024) Legal considerations for defining "frontier model". Institute for Law & AI. https://law-ai.org/frontier-model-definitions

Charlesworth A (2022) Regulating algorithmic assemblages: looking beyond corporatist AI ethics. In: Kohl U, Eisler J (eds) Data-driven personalisation and the law. Cambridge University Press, Cambridge, pp 243–262. https://doi.org/10.1017/9781108891325.019

Davies R (2021) US facial recognition firm faces £17m UK fine for 'serious breaches'. The Guardian [webpage] 29 Nov. https://www.theguardian.com/technology/2021/nov/29/us-facial-recognition-firm-faces-17m-uk-fine-for-serious-breaches-clearview-ai

DSIT (2024) UK signals step change for regulators to strengthen AI leadership. Press release [webpage] 6 Feb. https://www.gov.uk/government/news/uk-signals-step-change-for-regulators-to-strengthen-ai-leadership

Gross A, Criddle C (2024) UK rethinks AI legislation as alarm grows over potential risks. Financial Times [webpage] Apr. 15. https://www.ft.com/content/311b29a4-bbb3-435b-8e82-ae19f2740af9

Gross A, Parker G (2024) UK's AI bill to focus on ChatGPT-style models. Financial Times [webpage], 1 Aug. https://www.ft.com/content/ce53d233-073e-4b95-8579-e80d960377a4

Guihot M, Matthew AF, Suzor NP (2020) Nudging robots: innovative solutions to regulate artificial intelligence. Vand J Ent Tech Law 20:385–456. https://scholarship.law.vanderbilt.edu/jetlaw/vol20/iss2/2

Hansard Society (2022), Guide to Private Members' Bills [webpage], 4 May. https://www.hansardsociety.org.uk/publications/guides/what-is-a-private-members-bill

Haves E (2024) Large language models and generative AI: House of Lords Communications and Digital Committee report. House of Lords Library: In Focus [webpage]. 15 Nov. https://lordslibrary.parliament.uk/large-language-models-and-generative-ai-house-of-lords-communications-and-digital-committee-report/

Heims E, Moxon S (2024) Mechanisms of regulatory capture: testing claims of industry influence in the case of Vioxx. Regul Gov 18:139–157. https://doi.org/10.1111/rego.12531

Helberger N, Diakopoulos N (2023) ChatGPT and the AI Act. Internet Policy Rev 12(1):1–6. https://doi.org/10.14763/2023.1.1682

Keeling E, Finlayson-Brown J (2024) What is in store for UK AI: The long awaited government response is here. A&O Shearing [webpage]. 15 Feb. https://www.aoshearman.com/en/insights/ao-shearman-on-tech/what-is-in-store-for-uk-ai-the-long-awaited-government-response-is-here

Larsson S, Hildén J, Söderlund K (2024) Between Regulatory Fixity and Flexibility in the EU AI Act (pre-print). Lund University. https://portal.research.lu.se/files/171573074/Larsson_Hild_n_S_derlund_Jan_2024_Between_Regulatory_Fixity_and_Flexibility_in_the_EU_AI_Act_draft_paper_2024-1-26.pdf

Makkai T, Braithwaite J (1992) In and out of the revolving door: making sense of regulatory capture. J Public Policy 12(1):61–78. https://doi.org/10.1017/S0143814X00005006

Maslej N, Fattorini L, Perrault R et al (2024) The AI Index 2024 Annual Report. AI Index Steering Committee, Institute for Human-Centered AI, Stanford University, Stanford. https://aiindex.stanford.edu/wp-content/uploads/2024/05/HAI_AI-Index-Report-2024.pdf

Neudert L (2023) Regulatory capacity capture: the United Kingdom's online safety regime. Internet Policy Rev 12(4):1–34

Nordström M (2022) AI under great uncertainty: implications and decision strategies for public policy. AI Soc 37:1703–1714. https://doi.org/10.1007/s00146-021-01263-4

O'Carroll M, Kimbro S (2021) Legal operations at Google. In: Katz DM, Dolin R, Bommarito MJ (eds) Legal informatics. Cambridge University Press, Cambridge, pp 501–510. https://doi.org/10.1017/9781316529683.034

Ranchordas S, Vinci V (2024) Regulatory sandboxes and innovation-friendly regulation: between collaboration and capture. Italian J Public Law 14(1):107–139. https://www.ijpl.eu/wp-content/uploads/2024/03/8.-Ranchordas-and-Vinci.pdf

Roberts H, Cowls J, Hine E et al (2021) Achieving a 'Good AI Society': comparing the aims and progress of the EU and the US. Sci Eng Ethics 27:1–25. https://doi.org/10.1007/s11948-021-00340-7

Roberts H, Babuta A, Morley J et al (2023) Artificial intelligence regulation in the United Kingdom: a path to good governance and global leadership? Internet Policy Rev 12(2):1–31. https://doi.org/10.14763/2023.2.1709

Saltelli A, Dankel DJ, Di Fiore M et al (2022) Science, the endless frontier of regulatory capture. Futures 135:102860. https://doi.org/10.1016/j.futures.2021.102860

Smuha NA (2021) From a 'race to AI' to a 'race to AI regulation': regulatory competition for artificial intelligence. Law Innov Technol 13(1):57–84. https://doi.org/10.1080/17579961.2021.1898300

Tobin J (2024) Artificial Intelligence (Regulation) Bill [HL]. House of Lords Library, Research Briefing, 18 Mar. https://researchbriefings.files.parliament.uk/documents/LLN-2024-0016/LLN-2024-0016.pdf

Truby J, Brown RD, Ibrahim IA, Parellada OC (2022) A sandbox approach to regulating high-risk artificial intelligence applications. Eur J Risk Regul 13(2):270–294. https://doi.org/10.1017/err.2021.52

Veale M, Zuiderveen Borgesius F (2021) Demystifying the Draft EU Artificial Intelligence Act — analysing the good, the bad, and the unclear elements of the proposed approach. Comp L Rev Int 22(4):97–112. https://doi.org/10.9785/cri-2021-220402

Volpicelli G (2023) ChatGPT broke the EU plan to regulate AI. Politico [webpage] 3 Mar. https://www.politico.eu/article/eu-plan-regulate-chatgpt-openai-artificial-intelligence-act/

Regulatory Issues Related to AI Development and Use: A Comparative Analysis of Chinese and EU Laws

Meng Wang and Li Du

Contents

M. Wang
Faculty of Law, University of Macau, Macau, China
e-mail: yc07212@um.edu.mo

L. Du (✉)
Faculty of Law, Asia-Pacific Academy of Economics and Management, University of Macau, Macau, China
e-mail: stephendu@um.edu.mo

V. L. Raposo (ed.), *The European Artificial Intelligence Act*, Law, Governance and Technology Series 78, https://doi.org/10.1007/978-3-031-98406-8_16

Abstract China has become an important player in artificial intelligence (AI) development and application. This chapter explores the major regulatory challenges posed by AI in China, including data protection and privacy issues, impact on human rights, and intersections of AI-empowered applications with intellectual property rights. It also examines how the existing Chinese regulatory frameworks address these complex issues. We analyse and contrast the recent legislative developments in China and the European Union (EU) regarding those regulatory issues, highlighting both similarities and differences. Our analysis aims to inform policy and legislative dialogues on the challenges and opportunities introduced by the development and application of AI technology.

1 Introduction

Artificial intelligence (AI) has received much attention since it was proposed in the 1950s, which has culminated in the current hype associated with the ground-breaking capabilities of generative AI tools.[1] Through the data and logic provided to AI by designers (or users), AI can simulate specific human thought processes and intelligent behaviours, such as learning, reasoning, thinking, and planning.[2] Building on the rapid advancements in computer science and neuroscience and developments in big data analytics and cloud computing, AI technologies are continually improving. Their computational power is constantly evolving. AI-related research and applications, such as image classification, voice recognition, human-computer interaction, and autonomous vehicles, are some examples of technological breakthroughs that have enhanced the efficiency and quality of people's daily lives. These ground-breaking innovations have attracted widespread public attention and sparked the interest of global investors.[3] According to a market survey by Precedence Research, the global AI market size is estimated to be USD 757.58 billion in 2025 and is projected to reach approximately USD 3680.47 billion by 2034.[4]

In the context of China, AI applications are already deployed in many service areas and industry sectors, including healthcare, the legal profession, financial services, and smart homes. For example, 'medical imaging + AI' is one of China's

---

[1] Colosimo et al. (2021), pp. 443–453.

[2] According to the Dartmouth Summer Research Project on AI, which is considered the founding event of AI as a field, the basic principle of AI can be summarised as 'the use of machines/computers to imitate human learning and other aspects of intelligence.' See Press (2016) and Anyoha (2017).

[3] For instance, notable milestones in AI include the launch of Alphabet Inc.'s self-driving project, the historic confrontation between AlphaGo and South Korean professional Go player Lee Sedol, and the swift evolution of generative AI represented by ChatGPT by the end of 2022. These events were associated with significant advancements in the field of AI, showcasing the immense potential of this technology in automation, intelligent decision-making, and natural language processing. Moreover, they have had profound impacts on society, the economy, and the technology sectors. See WAYMO (2024), Chan (2016) and OpenAI (2022).

[4] For more details, see Precedence Research (2025).

most popular areas of medical AI application.[5] According to an industry survey, the Chinese AI medical imaging market is expected to grow to 44.2 billion yuan by 2025, with a compound annual growth rate of up to 135%.[6] During the COVID-19 epidemic, AI thermometers were deployed in public places such as airports, train stations, and the entrances of shopping malls. AI robots were also used to deliver supplies and disinfection to isolated areas and medical personnel.[7] In addition to the medical field, many Chinese companies have developed AI lawyer-assistance software for legal services. Such AI software can store large amounts of laws, regulations, precedents, legal documents, and academic research, and conduct deep learning on these to provide users with quick responses to legal bases and solutions. For instance, these AI applications can assist attorneys in the pretrial preparation phase. They can list the most cited legal norms from similar precedents and intelligently analyse the success rates of current litigation.[8] Chinese courts are also integrating AI into their operations, developing AI software for online litigation and Internet courts to address the challenges posed by the rapidly increasing number of cases and the comparatively inadequate number of judges.[9] In 2021, AI judge assistants have been deployed in courts in Hangzhou, China, where they participate in court hearings and automatically generate decision documents following the judge's final decision.[10] This advancement demonstrates the potential of AI to enhance judicial efficiency, but it also brings up considerations about the legal and ethical issues associated with the use of AI in judicial practice, which includes accountability mechanisms, data protection issues, and bias mitigation. In response to this, the Supreme People's Court of China issued the Opinions on Regulating and Strengthening the Applications of AI in Judicial Fields in 2022, outlining five fundamental principles to be adhered to when implementing AI in the judiciary.[11] The principles address the safety and legality of AI, uphold fairness and justice, acknowledge the auxiliary role of AI in judicial decision-making, emphasise the ultimate decision-making authority of judges, and mandate the explainability of AI. Furthermore, AI must adhere to current social morals and ethical standards.[12]

---

[5] Jin and Wei (2022).

[6] Li (2024).

[7] Yang and Lv (2021).

[8] For example, 'Fa Chan' is the first team in China to launch the service of AI legal robots. It includes AI consulting systems, legal information systems, and so on. The Chinese Internet company Baidu has recently introduced a legal AI application named 'Faxingbao', which offers users access to legal consultation services. This product relies on extensive models and a legal knowledge graph, complemented by advanced natural language processing techniques and deep learning algorithms. It conducts thorough interpretation and analysis of legal texts, addressing users' individualised requirements, including the delivery of customised legal opinion papers. See Fachan (2021) and Wu (2024).

[9] Kong (2019).

[10] Hong et al. (2021).

[11] Supreme People's Court of China (2022).

[12] According to the Opinions on Regulating and Strengthening the Applications of AI in the Judicial Fields, the application of AI in the judiciary must follow five fundamental principles: (1) safety and

The emergence and development of generative AI has had a profound impact on the rapid expansion of AI-empowered applications and services. Using Large Language Models (LLM), generative AI such as ChatGPT has provided new solutions for intelligent assistants, research and data analysis, and natural language understanding.[13] This has facilitated more efficient human-machine interactions and improved service experiences in various fields such as business, healthcare, and education. The AI field has become an interdisciplinary scientific endeavour that integrates knowledge from computer science, linguistics, psychology, and other academic disciplines. Generative AI is perceived to be the pillar technology for the global advancement of the information industry.[14] Chinese research teams and commercial companies have been instrumental in the research and development of generative AI applications. As of April 2024, the Cyberspace Administration of China (CAC)[15] has recorded the filing of over 100 large-scale models related to generative AI.[16] These models cover various domains including face fusion, speech synthesis, painting, and text processing. According to an industry research report published by International Data Corporation in 2023, by 2026, the Chinese AI market is expected to reach a market size of $26.44 billion, with a compound annual growth rate exceeding 20% from 2021 to 2026.[17] Regarding industry scale, the number of AI-related Chinese companies currently accounts for nearly 25% of the world.[18]

The Chinese national government supports AI-related research and applications and has introduced many supportive policies in this area. These policies include incorporating AI development as one of the national goals, continuously providing funding support for research and applications, and supporting talent cultivation.[19] During the pandemic, China introduced several initiatives and guidelines to encourage the application of AI in provisions of healthcare services and for epidemic prevention and control.[20] A recent influential policy related to AI is the Outline of the

---

legality, ensuring no harm to national security or infringement on legitimate rights; (2) fairness and justice, guaranteeing non-discrimination and impartiality; (3) auxiliary role, where AI-generated results serve only as references, with judges maintaining ultimate authority; (4) transparency and trustworthiness, requiring explainable and verifiable management of judicial data and processes; and (5) adherence to public order and morality, ensuring that AI applications do not violate ethical standards while establishing mechanisms for risk management and accountability. See Supreme People's Court of China (2022).

[13] Leggatt (2023).

[14] Chalmers et al. (2020), pp. 1028–1053.

[15] The Cyberspace Administration of China (CAC), as the country's primary Internet regulatory authority, has undertaken significant efforts in overseeing the AI domain in China.

[16] Ke (2024).

[17] IDC Corporate (2023).

[18] Huang and Ding (2019).

[19] State Council of China (2015) and State Council of China (2017).

[20] Xia and Bi (2020).

14th Five-Year Plan (2021–2025) for National Economic and Social Development and Vision 2035, released in March 2021. This document serves as the national development plan for the specified period and provides specific approaches to advancing the AI-related industry. Key initiatives include building open-source algorithm platforms and improving AI's deep learning, reasoning, and decision-making functions.[21]

The dawn of the AI era brings both opportunities and challenges. On the one hand, AI has considerably enhanced information gathering, processing and synthesis capabilities. For instance, efficient algorithms and data analysis can boost human productivity, provide diverse reference points for decision-making, and even offer emotional support to humans, as evidenced by the development of companion robots. On the other hand, AI has presented significant societal challenges, ethical dilemmas, and legal issues. As a result, countries around the world have developed laws and guidelines to tackle the challenges posed by various AI applications.

In the European Union (EU), the formal approval of the Artificial Intelligence Act (AIA) by the Council of the EU on May 21, 2024, has marked a significant milestone in the legislative history concerning AI.[22] The AIA represents an unparalleled legislative initiative that governs the development, deployment, and use of AI systems across the EU market. In addition to the EU's AIA, the EU's General Data Protection Regulation (GDPR) also plays a crucial role in data and privacy protection in the field of AI, imposing rigid requirements for informed consent, transparency, and accountability in data processing.[23] The AIA underscores the necessity of adhering to the GDPR during the development and deployment of AI in the EU,[24] which aims to foster data compliance, trust, and ethical practices.

China has established several new regulations and guidelines related to algorithms and generative AI. Their implementation has significant implications for the development of AI technology. However, there are still legal and ethical challenges, particularly the issues related to data protection and privacy, human rights, and intellectual property (IP) rights. Additionally, there is a relative shortage of international comparative research on China's AI regulatory framework. Past studies often adopt a domestic perspective, omitting comparisons with regulatory models from other countries or regions. There is limited research comparing China's current AI regulatory framework with the recently approved EU's AIA. Existing literature primarily analyses how China's regulatory framework applies to emerging generative

[21] Xinhua News Agency (2021).

[22] Kroet (2024) and Browne (2024).

[23] The General Data Protection Regulation (GDPR) is a comprehensive data privacy law implemented by the EU in 2018. It aims to safeguard the personal data and privacy of EU citizens. Specifically, the GDPR mandates that data processors obtain explicit consent before collecting personal data and establishes stringent regulations governing the storage, processing, protection, and cross-border transfer of data. For details see GDPR.EU (2024).

[24] Recs. 10 and 140, Arts. 10 and 50 of the EU AIA.

AI technologies like ChatGPT. For example, Chen Bing (2023), Wang Qiuyan and Wan Guohua (2023) and Yang Jianwu and Luo Feiyan (2024)[25] have provided valuable insights into Chinese domestic regulations. Moreover, research by Cheng Le (2023) and Wang Qinghua and Hu Lintian (2024) examines the risks and challenges of AI development in China, highlighting deficiencies in the current regulatory framework regarding privacy, data protection, cybercrime, and IP rights.[26] However, they do not analyse the specific rules relevant to these issues across various jurisdictions. More recently, studies by Wang Siao (2024b) and Liu Xuerong (2024) examined difficulties in establishing liability for AI-related infringements under China's current legal framework.[27] While these works have explored critical issues, they have not undertaken a comparative legal analysis with the recently implemented AI regulations in other jurisdictions, such as those from the EU.

In studies of Li Yaling, Qin Yuanqi, and Wei Que (2023), He Jun and Yang Hui (2023), and Lu Anwen (2024), they examined governance frameworks for AI in the EU, the United States, and Australia. However, their analyses primarily focused on a general overview of relevant frameworks in other countries and regions and did not comprehensively examine specific issues or legal provisions.[28] For example, similarities and differences in regulations related to key issues of privacy, human rights, and IP rights between China and the EU are not well addressed by their studies. To fill this gap, our study, by building upon existing literature's insights into the domestic regulatory landscape, conducted a comparative analysis of regulatory regimes for AI between China and the EU, focusing on the strategies employed by both frameworks in addressing data protection, privacy issues, human rights safeguards, and IP protection.

Here we examine the legal and ethical issues presented by the development of AI applications in China and scrutinise the regulatory frameworks developed to address these complex issues. We undertake a comparative analysis of the Chinese and EU laws on AI and highlight the similarities and differences in AI governance. We aim to provide insight into the complexity and future path of AI governance, underscoring diverse regulatory strategies adopted by different jurisdictions to address common challenges and goals. Our analysis further aims to contribute to policy discussions and legislative processes on the challenges and opportunities created by the development and application of AI technology.

[25] Chen (2023), Wang and Wan (2023) and Yang and Luo (2024).

[26] Cheng (2023) and Wang and Hu (2024).

[27] See Wang (2024b) and Liu (2024).

[28] Li et al. (2023), He and Yang (2023) and Lu (2024).

2 Data Protection and Privacy Issues

2.1 The Challenge of AI for Data Protection and Privacy

Nowadays, smart devices like smartphones, wearable devices, and autonomous vehicles use cameras, sensors, and voice recorders to capture users' voices, behaviour, and preferences in their private spaces. To enhance service provision, devices often incorporate AI algorithms that continuously collect and record users' personal information.[29] For example, to achieve autonomous driving, AI-equipped vehicles gather real-time data from outside and inside of vehicles, which include drivers' biological information, voice, and images.[30] In such scenarios, AI systems transform the private personal space into a data collection hub, exposing individuals to increased surveillance risks.[31]

Moreover, AI algorithms have often been used for consumer profiling in commercial settings. Businesses collect and analyse consumers' browsing history, purchase records, and transaction information using AI algorithms. Personal data collection aids businesses in understanding consumers' purchasing power and readiness to buy specific products and enables precision marketing (e.g., the provision of personalised prices) to online users.[32] However, data collection may occur without users' explicit consent or even their knowledge. Although current Chinese laws require software or website operators to notify users of their intentions to collect data and the associated protection measures, full compliance is not consistently guaranteed. For instance, as of June 2022, China's Ministry of Industry and Information Technology (MIIT) had conducted audits on 3.22 million applications. This audit led to nearly 3000 illegal or non-compliant apps being penalised and removed due to violations of users' rights.[33]

Furthermore, AI applications not only collect and process general personal data but also sensitive information like facial images or fingerprint details. The improper utilisation of AI applications raises the risk of privacy breaches.[34] For instance, many companies and organisations employ facial recognition technology for identity confirmation and security monitoring, and fingerprints have been increasingly used for electronic payments. However, inappropriate data management or theft of such data by hackers can severely compromise users' privacy. To make matters worse, malicious actors could exploit compromised biometric data to conduct fraudulent transactions, leaving users vulnerable to financial losses and personal safety threats.

---

[29] Tschider (2018), p. 87.

[30] Taeihagh and Lim (2018), pp. 103–128.

[31] Wang et al. (2021), pp. 864–886.

[32] Owens (2022), pp. 395–410.

[33] Shen and Lv (2022).

[34] Bi (2023) and Ran (2022).

2.2 Legislative Measures in China

In response to such challenges and threats, the Chinese AI tech community has been advocating for enhanced security protection for AI-related technologies and applications.[35] Chinese legal scholars have also discussed ways to mitigate privacy threats posed by AI. For example, Wang Liming proposes the introduction of 'cyber privacy' specifically for privacy protection in the AI era, considering the shortcomings of the existing legislation.[36] Wang contends that the Chinese legislature should amend current legislation to specify that information like an individual's Internet browsing hours and visit history on the Internet should be recognised as personal 'cyber privacy.'[37] This is because the leakage or misuse of such data can profoundly impact individuals' lives and pose financial security risks. Consequently, such data and content should be protected in the same manner as privacy under the current personal data protection laws.

Although China has not enacted specific legislation for data and privacy protection in AI applications, the government has established a legal framework for data and privacy protection and remedial mechanisms. For instance, the Civil Code of the People's Republic of China (PRC)[38] states that privacy pertains to the peace and tranquility of an individual's private life, which includes personal spaces, activities, and information that the person wishes to remain undisclosed.[39] The Civil Code prohibits any entity from invading another's privacy or accessing, recording, or surveilling personal spaces, such as residences, through methods like phone calls, texts, or instant messaging, unless expressly consented to by the rights holder or required by law.[40] Consequently, according to the Civil Code, when AI collects personal data, it must adhere to these provisions to ensure individual private lives are respected. Any unauthorised collection, intrusion, use, or disclosure of personal information is prohibited.[41] AI-related enterprises and technology developers should obtain explicit consent from users before collecting and using personal data. Moreover, the Civil Code introduces protections for voice-related rights, acknowledging an individual's voice as a distinct personal characteristic. These rights are

[35] For example, Tian Tian, executive director of the Security Innovation Centre of the Beijing Academy of Artificial Intelligence, has proposed that it is necessary to strengthen the security of AI systems applied to various vital scenarios at the technical level. This includes establishing a security platform and firewall specifically for AI. For more details, see China Electronic News (2021).

[36] For example, according to Art. 1032 of the Chinese Civil Code, privacy is defined as a person's private space, private activities, and private information regarding their well-being, as well as private information they do not wish others to know.

[37] Wang (2012).

[38] National People's Congress (2020).

[39] Art. 1032 of the Chinese Civil Code.

[40] Art. 1033 of the Chinese Civil Code.

[41] Arts. 1034 and 1035 of the Chinese Civil Code.

ensured similar protections as those granted to portrait rights.[42] Therefore, the reproduction or use of an individual's voice through AI voice mimicry and synthesis without their explicit consent is forbidden.[43]

Regarding special laws, the Personal Information Protection Law of the PRC (PIPL), which entered into force in November 2021, is the first legislation that specifically regulates the protection of personal information.[44] The PIPL addresses contentious issues related to personal information protection in the context of AI usage. For instance, the law stipulates that data processors must obtain individual consent prior to collecting personal data, unless specific exceptions apply, and should refrain from excessively gathering personal information.[45] Data processors should also employ methods that minimally infringe on individuals' rights and interests. Furthermore, the PIPL mandates that data processors using consumers' personal information to make automated decisions must ensure the transparency of these decision-making processes and the fairness and justice of the results. Moreover, data processors should not impose unfair differentiations on consumers concerning transaction prices and other terms of transaction.[46] Individuals maintain the right to demand explanations from data processors about AI decisions that impact their rights and interests. In addition, individuals also retain the right to refuse decisions made solely through automated processes.[47]

In addition, the Cybersecurity Law of the PRC,[48] the Data Security Law of the PRC,[49] and the Law on the Protection of Consumer Rights and Interests of the PRC[50] all contain provisions for personal information protection. For example, China's Cybersecurity Law requires network operators to obtain prior consent from users before collecting personal information.[51] It is also clearly stipulated that network operators shall not collect personal information that is unrelated to the services they provide.[52] Similarly, the Law on the Protection of Consumer Rights and Interests explicitly mandates that merchants adhere to principles of legality, appropriateness, and necessity when collecting consumer personal information.[53] In the event of consumer personal information infringement, the merchant is obligated to

---

[42] Art. 1023 of the Chinese Civil Code.

[43] For instance, in April 2024, the Beijing Internet Court ruled in China's first 'AI Voice Infringement Case', where an AI software synthesised and sold a voice actor's voice without authorisation. The court recognised the plaintiff's voice rights and determined that the defendants' actions constituted an infringement under Art. 1023 of the Civil Code. See: Xue (2024).

[44] National People's Congress Standing Committee (2021b).

[45] Arts. 6 and 13 of the PIPL.

[46] Art. 24 of the PIPL.

[47] Art. 24 of the PIPL.

[48] National People's Congress Standing Committee (2016).

[49] National People's Congress Standing Committee (2021a).

[50] National People's Congress Standing Committee (2013).

[51] Art. 41 of the Cybersecurity Law of the PRC.

[52] Art. 41 of the Cybersecurity Law of the PRC.

[53] Art. 29 of the Law on the Protection of Consumer Rights and Interests of the PRC.

mitigate the impact and compensate for damages. Regarding legal liability, merchants may face administrative penalties, including fines and the potential revocation of business licenses. This also encompasses penalties for merchants using AI tools to unfairly target consumers with discriminatory pricing. China's Criminal Law further incriminates the infringement of personal information.[54] As per the law, individuals wrongfully acquiring personal data or unlawfully selling or revealing personal information to others will be penalised with a fine or fixed-term imprisonment.[55]

In the past 2 years, the CAC and other relevant departments, including the MIIT and China's Ministry of Public Security, have issued several regulations that place the primary responsibility for information security on AI service providers. According to these provisions, AI service providers are obligated to implement secure and controllable technical measures for safeguarding data security, protecting personal information, and preventing telecommunications fraud.[56] Furthermore, if providers of deep synthesis services and their technical supporters offer functionalities for editing biometric recognition information, such as facial or voice data, they must comply with legal stipulations by notifying users of the deep synthesis services and obtaining their explicit consent prior to editing personal information.[57]

The Interim Measures for the Administration of Generative Artificial Intelligence Services (2023 Interim Measures), jointly issued by the CAC, the National Development and Reform Commission, the Ministry of Science and Technology, the MIIT, and other relevant departments, came into effect on August 15, 2023, serving as specialised regulatory provisions in the realm of generative AI.[58] It explicitly prohibits the infringement upon the rights and interests of individuals, including rights of portrait, reputation, honour, and privacy, when providing and utilising generative AI services.[59] Providers of generative AI services are obligated to use data and base models obtained from legitimate channels during activities such as pre-training and optimisation of training data.[60] Moreover, the 2023 Interim Measures mandate that service providers protect the input information, usage records, and associated personal data of users.[61] Generative AI service providers are forbidden from collecting unnecessary personal information, unlawfully holding

[54] National People's Congress Standing Committee (2023b).

[55] Art. 253–1 of the Criminal Law of the PRC.

[56] Art. 7 of the Provisions on the Administration of Deep Synthesis of Internet-Based Information Services and Art. 7 of the Provisions on the Administration of Algorithm-Generated Recommendations for Internet Information Services.

[57] Art. 14 of the Provisions on the Administration of Deep Synthesis of Internet-Based Information Services.

[58] Cyberspace Administration of China, National Development and Reform Commission, Ministry of Education, Ministry of Science and Technology, Ministry of Industry and Information Technology, Ministry of Public Security, and National Radio and Television Administration (2023).

[59] Art. 4 of the 2023 Interim Measures.

[60] Art. 7 of the 2023 Interim Measures.

[61] Art. 11 of the 2023 Interim Measures.

onto input information and usage records that could reveal users' identities, and unlawfully sharing such information with third parties. Additionally, the 2023 Interim Measures explicitly state that pertinent institutions and their personnel involved in the security assessments and supervision of generative AI services must maintain confidentiality concerning any business secrets and personal information they obtain in the course of their duties. They are strictly forbidden from disclosing or unlawfully transferring such information to third parties.[62]

In addition to the abovementioned mandatory legal and departmental regulations, China has developed corresponding standards and guidelines to provide reference for the collection and processing of personal information, which are applicable to the development and use of AI. For example, China's Ministry of Public Security and the Beijing Network Industry Association jointly issued the Guidelines for the Protection of Personal Information Security on the Internet in 2019. These guidelines provide detailed specifications on the security of the computing environment, access control, emergency response, and the process for network operators to handle personal information.[63] In response to the increasing trend of utilising AI systems in provision of healthcare services, China's National Medical Products Administration, alongside other authorities, have issued guidelines and industry standards that evaluate and standardise the use of AI algorithms in medical devices. They also give special consideration to the potential privacy threats that applying AI algorithms could pose to patients. For example, the Guidelines for Classification of AI Medical Software Products (released in July 2021) clearly require that the maturity of the algorithm should be one of the criteria for regulating AI medical devices.[64] Additionally, the Guidelines for Registration Review of AI Medical Devices (released in March 2022) address specific requirements for data collection, algorithm design and updates for AI medical devices, and recommend that registration applicants conduct risk management for the entire life-cycle process of AI medical devices.[65]

In summary, China has been actively enhancing its regulatory framework to address privacy threats raised by AI. Current Chinese legislation and guidelines have begun to bolster data and personal information protection mechanisms by clarifying the definition and scope of privacy and personal information, protecting the right to voice, strengthening the obligations of data processors, and regulating the approval process for AI algorithms' market entry. The PIPL also specifies China's legislative intent to develop exclusive rules and standards for safeguarding personal information pertaining to new technologies and applications like AI.[66] Specifically, recently launched departmental regulations on generative AI emphasise the government's commitment to regulating AI and addressing related privacy concerns.

---

[62] Art. 19 of the 2023 Interim Measures.

[63] National Administration of State Secrets Protection (2019).

[64] National Medical Products Administration (2021).

[65] China Center for Food and Drug International Exchange (2022).

[66] Art. 62 of the PIPL.

However, the existing legal mechanisms are inherently prone to fall behind due to several factors. For example, many existing regulations are tailored to address issues associated with already established technologies. However, as new advancements in AI continually emerge, these provisions may quickly become obsolete.[67] The evolving AI technologies may introduce new forms of privacy infringement, further complicating the regulatory landscape. Moreover, the ethical issues and debates surrounding new technologies necessitate significant time and comprehensive discussion in the development and execution of legal standards.[68] The inherent complexity of these technologies, coupled with the imperative to accommodate the viewpoints of diverse stakeholders, including industry professionals, consumers, civil society, and regulatory bodies, results in a protracted legislative process. While this thoroughness is vital for ensuring the law's comprehensiveness and efficacy, it often results in delays, causing statutory frameworks to lag behind technological progress.[69]

The Chinese legal community can support the decision-making processes through critical analyses and increased collaborations with scientific communities to develop effective strategies for mitigation of privacy risks due to AI's inappropriate use. Additionally, fostering public discourse and expert consultation may facilitate the timely identification of potential regulatory gaps resulting from new AI technologies, ensuring that the regulations can effectively respond to the rapidly evolving technological landscape.

2.3 *Comparative Analysis of Data Protection in AI-Related Legislation in China and the EU*

By comparing relevant laws in China concerning AI with those in the EU, it is evident that both jurisdictions prioritise data protection and privacy in the context of AI development and application (see Table 1 in the Appendix). For instance, both China's 2023 Interim Measures (Arts. 4 and 7) and the EU's AIA (Art. 10) stipulate rules on data protection in AI processing. Both jurisdictions' data protection laws are applicable to the use of AI.

Both China's PIPL (Art. 13) and the EU's GDPR (Art. 6) provide multiple legal bases for processing personal data. For instance, both laws recognise obtaining explicit informed consent, processing data as necessary for contract fulfilment, complying with legal obligations, and serving the public interest as valid grounds

---

[67] Malan (2018), Bai (2019), Satariano and Kang (2023) and Legal Daily Public Opinion Center (2024).

[68] Thierer (2018) and Weng (2023).

[69] A notable example is the legislative process of the EU's AIA, which took nearly three years to complete. During this time, lawmakers engaged in thorough consultations and debates to address the numerous ethical, social, and legal implications of AI technologies. See International Association of Privacy Professionals (2024).

for data processing. These legal grounds also form the basis for determining when AI-related data processing is permissible within both jurisdictions. Furthermore, both frameworks impose specific requirements for obtaining informed consent. For example, China's PIPL (Arts. 14, 21, and 23) and the EU's GDPR (Arts. 6 and 7) require data processors to obtain explicit informed consent from individuals when processing or reusing data beyond its original purpose. Moreover, the GDPR stipulates that data should only be processed for specific lawful purposes and only to the extent necessary for those purposes (Arts. 5 and 25). Similarly, China's PIPL (Arts. 6 and 19) and Cybersecurity Law (Art. 41) limit the collection of personal data to what is necessary to meet specified purposes. Furthermore, both Chinese and EU laws mandate that AI system providers ensure transparency in their operations and grant users the right to understand AI decision-making processes.[70]

Despite these similarities, there are some key differences between the two regulatory frameworks for data protection in relation to AI. For example, the EU has developed a more comprehensive and specific regulatory framework for AI in the AIA. This act delineates obligations for various stakeholders within the AI ecosystem, including deployers, distributors, and importers, for mitigating data-related risks associated with AI. Additionally, it provides an elaborate risk classification based on the potential dangers posed by different types of AI systems, as well as defines the varied responsibilities of AI system deployers according to these risk levels. In contrast, China's framework is more dispersed, dealing with AI-related matters through a mix of laws such as the PIPL, Cybersecurity Law, and recent departmental regulations, rather than through a special and comprehensive legislation. Although Chinese regulations also mention the implementation of inclusive, prudential, and classified supervision of generative AI services, the detailed classification criteria are yet to be released and remain in development. Moreover, differences exist in specific provisions within the EU's AI-related laws and those of China. For example, the AIA explicitly states that the regulation does not apply to AI systems or AI models exclusively designed and used for scientific research and development purposes, including their outputs.[71] Conversely, while China's framework provides similar exemptions, its regulations impose an added stipulation—these exemptions only apply if the organisations do not offer generative AI services to the domestic public. This indicates that if institutions confine their work to internal research, development, and exploration—without producing text, images, audio, or video content for the Chinese public—they may be excluded from complying with pertinent regulations.[72] Nevertheless, as noted in several studies, the prevailing Chinese regulations lack lucid definitions of what constitutes 'providing to the

[70] Art. 13 of the EU AIA and Art. 4 of the 2023 Interim Measures.

[71] Article 2 of the EU AIA regulates that 'This Regulation does not apply to AI systems or AI models, including their output, specifically developed and put into service for the sole purpose of scientific research and development.'

[72] In Article 2 of the 2023 Interim Measures, it is mentioned that industry organisations, enterprises, educational and research institutions, public cultural institutions, and relevant professional organisations engaged in the research and application of generative AI technologies are not subject

domestic public', creating uncertainty regarding compliance.[73] This inherent ambiguity might curtail researchers' capacity for innovative exploration. Moreover, the narrow scope of these exemptions could obstruct international collaborations, as the varied regulatory environments pose additional challenges for cross-border projects. In this context, these regulatory discrepancies could potentially erect legal impediments to generative AI-related research and development in China.

In summary, both the EU and China are committed to ensuring privacy protection in the realm of AI through regulating data usage and management in AI systems. Each jurisdiction emphasises informed consent, restricts collection and use of personal data, and ensures transparency. Despite their differences, their legislative efforts reflect a regulatory consensus on promoting responsible AI development and data usage in this rapidly progressing field.

3 Human Rights Issues

3.1 Potential Threats to Human Rights by AI

The use of AI has triggered concerns regarding human rights protection. The possibility of infringement on individuals' freedom to make choices remains a significant issue. For instance, Ding Xiaodong, a Chinese scholar in legal studies, argues that in human rights theory, individuals' free will is the most esteemed value. Based on this idea, individuals must retain the right to control the decision-making in critical matters.[74] However, smart devices may unknowingly supersede human decision-making, leading to a diminished capacity for autonomous choices. For example, when users rely on AI-driven recommendations for important decisions, such as financial investments or health-related choices, they may gradually forgo critical thinking and independent judgement, allowing algorithms to dictate their preferences and actions.[75] Moreover, AI may provoke an 'information bubble' phenomenon.[76] AI recommendation algorithms often suggest information that aligns with users' interests. This practice constantly reinforces preferences and biases, hindering individuals from accessing new information from diverse perspectives. As a result, this could potentially lead to group polarisation and entrenched views.[77]

to the provisions of these measures if they do not provide generative AI services to the domestic public.

[73] PWC (2023) and Sun and Zeng (2024).

[74] Ding (2022), pp. 99–118.

[75] Me (2023), Stader (2024) and Zhai et al. (2024).

[76] 'Information bubble' refers to the phenomenon where people's interest in the information will be habitually guided by their interests, resulting in people only focusing on the content they like. It leads people to receive only a limited amount of information so that people's lives are limited to the 'bubble.' Chen et al. (2022), pp. 213–232.

[77] Wang and He (2020) and Zhang (2021).

Responding to the challenges AI presents to human rights, Chinese scholars such as Zhang Wenxian have advanced the concepts of 'fourth-generation human rights theory' and 'digital human rights.' Zhang asserts that digital technology, embodied by the Internet, big data, cloud computing, and AI, has become pervasive in people's daily lives and financial activities. In this context, big data and AI have become integral to human existence, with humans starting to share the data world with AI. Consequently, human rights-related legal doctrines should evolve and concentrate on the impact of emerging digital technologies on human rights.[78] Specifically, Zhang argues that the development of AI should not infringe on human rights. The advancement of AI should prioritise human rights and dignity.[79] The protection of 'digital human rights,' according to Zhang, involves two perspectives: (1) respecting and protecting individuals' rights in the digital world, including privacy, data, expression, and human dignity; and (2) pursuing values of equality and non-discrimination, ensuring that everyone can access the Internet equally, with adequate conditions and opportunities to live a digital life.[80] In addition, Xu Lin argues that exploiting loopholes in algorithmic discrimination could lead to discriminatory treatments for different groups. This situation may consequently create a new privileged class in the information society that infringes upon individuals' right to equality.[81] Similarly, Ma Changshan, a scholar in digital law, proposes that AI-induced algorithmic discrimination gives social discrimination a novel form.[82] For example, during everyday online shopping, big data and algorithms may precipitate price discrimination because AI can analyse user data such as identity, consumption history, and payment ability to create consumer profiles. Merchants then precisely market different products to consumers at disparate prices based on these profiles.

3.2 *Relevant Legislative Developments in China*

Some existing laws are applicable to govern issues of algorithmic discrimination. For example, the E-Commerce Law of the PRC, implemented in 2019, has explicitly classified price discrimination through algorithms and big data applications as an illegal act.[83] The PIPL also contains provisions for addressing issues of AI decision-making. For example, Art. 24 of the PIPL stipulates that data processors must ensure transparency when using consumers' personal information for autonomous decision-making processes. It prohibits unfair treatment in transaction prices and other trading conditions. Furthermore, this provision grants individuals the

[78] Research Center of Theoretical Law of Jilin University (2019) and Xiangtan University (2020).

[79] China Law Society (2020).

[80] China Law Society (2020).

[81] Xu (2019), pp. 152–161.

[82] Ma (2019), pp. 5–24.

[83] National People's Congress Standing Committee (2018).

right to request data processors to explain AI-driven decisions when their rights and interests are possibly impacted. They also have the right to reject decisions made solely through automated processes.

In terms of safeguarding the right to choose, the Provisions on the Administration of Algorithm-Generated Recommendations for Internet Information Services, enacted in 2022, outline measures to protect users' rights within the context of AI-driven recommendation services.[84] For example, service providers are required to give users the option to receive recommendations that are not based on algorithms or offer an easy way to turn off algorithmic recommendations (Art. 17). If users choose to disable the algorithm-based recommendation services, the providers must immediately stop offering the related services. Furthermore, the providers must enable users to select or delete 'user tags' used for personalised recommendations. Violations of these requirements will result in administrative penalties, including warnings and fines. If the violations are considered criminal offenses, they could even lead to criminal punishment.

The 2023 Interim Measures include provisions for human rights protections in the application of AI technology.[85] Notably, these measures explicitly require the incorporation of safeguard mechanisms at various stages, such as algorithm design, selection of training data, model creation and optimisation, and service provision, to prevent algorithmic discrimination and avoid infringements on individuals' fundamental rights, including the right to image, reputation, and honour.[86] Service providers are further required to increase the transparency of AI systems. This could effectively prevent AI systems from demonstrating biases or showing discriminatory tendencies towards specific groups during decision-making processes, thereby ensuring equality and fairness in the protection of individual rights. Furthermore, these provisions empower users to exercise more effectively their rights and assert their claims.

3.3 *Debate on the Human Rights of AI Robots*

Chinese academics have engaged in ongoing discussions about whether AI robots should share the same 'human rights' as humans. Some scholars opine that, while AI robots are not living beings, they may suffer from rights infringements. There can be instances of humans attacking, enslaving, or humiliating AI robots.[87] As we face a future society where humans and AI robots coexist, scholars suggest that

[84] Cyberspace Administration of China, Ministry of Industry and Information Technology, Ministry of Public Security, State Administration for Market Regulation (2021).

[85] Art. 4 of the 2023 Interim Measures.

[86] Du and Kamenova (2023), pp. 52–54.

[87] Yang (2019), pp. 14–33.

governments should establish rules to protect the rights of AI robots.[88] Yet, prior to confirming whether AI robots can have human rights, recognition of their legal status is essential. In China, however, there is currently no consensus on whether AI robots should be legally viewed as 'persons' or 'things.' In Europe, the European Parliament passed a resolution (although not legally binding) outlining civil legal rules for robots in 2017. This is perceived as creating legal (electronic) personhood for AI.[89] According to the resolution, AI robots could potentially enjoy human rights in the future, such as wage rights, copyright protection, and social insurance rights.[90] Nonetheless, this resolution has garnered criticism from numerous European scholars.[91] In October 2017, the Saudi Arabian government became the first to grant citizenship to an AI robot. This robot, named Sophia, was conferred citizenship, thus holding the same status and rights as a human.[92]

The Chinese legislature has yet to introduce specific legislation concerning the human rights of AI robots. Some Chinese scholars align with the European Parliament's resolution to grant AI robots legal (electronic) personhood. They argue that existing Chinese laws such as the Civil Code[93] and the Company Law[94] recognise legal personality for only three entities: natural persons, legal persons, and unincorporated organisations. AI robots, which exhibit autonomy will require a legal framework that considers their unique characteristics. Accordingly, they believe updates should be made to the current laws to provide AI with electronic, or limited legal, personality. Such amendments would help safeguard robot rights in the future.[95]

On the contrary, other scholars maintain that significant differences exist between AI and persons. They argue that given its current use as a human-serving tool, AI robots should not enjoy the same rights as humans.[96] Yang Lixin, for example, has proposed the concept of an 'artificial-like personality.' He asserts that although AI robots exhibit certain elements of personhood, such as a human-like appearance and the ability to think, they lack the natural structure of the human body, the biological brain, and the human genetic system. Hence, in his view, AI robots should not be considered persons in the legal sense and should not be granted human rights.[97] Similarly, Wu Handong, an expert in Chinese IP law, concurred that AI, as a tool

[88] Yang (2019), pp. 14–33; Zhao and Li (2020), pp. 10–25.

[89] Publications Office of the European Union (2017).

[90] Avila Negri (2021).

[91] The European Economic and Social Committee (2018).

[92] Korosec (2017).

[93] National People's Congress (2020).

[94] National People's Congress Standing Committee (2023a).

[95] Yang and Zhang (2018), pp. 91–97.

[96] Zheng (2018).

[97] Yang (2018), pp. 84–96.

controlled by humans, does not meet the essential requirements of being an independent legal entity.[98]

In summary, there are no legal grounds currently to permit AI robots to secure citizenship or human rights in China. Under existing laws, AI can only be classified as an 'object' under the Chinese Civil Code, or as a 'product' governed by legislation such as the Product Quality Law of the PRC.[99] However, it is worth noting that China's Development Plan on the New Generation of AI has identified the 'clarification of AI's legal status and related rights, obligations, and responsibilities' as a critical topic for future discussion.[100]

3.4 *Comparative Analysis of AI-Related Legislation on Human Rights in China and the EU*

Regulations on AI in both China and the EU aim to strengthen oversight over the development of AI systems and ensure the protection of users' rights (see Table 2 in the Appendix). These are similar provisions on the users' rights to refuse automated decision-making,[101] discrimination caused by AI,[102] and increased demand for the transparency of AI systems.[103] This reflects the focus of both regulatory regimes on mitigating the risks that AI technology may pose to human rights. However, the EU's AIA is more explicit in regulating the impact of AI on human rights. For example, it strictly bans certain AI systems, such as those using subliminal techniques, social scoring, and particular biometric methods.[104] These have the potential to manipulate individuals, infer human emotions and, consequently, influence

---

[98] Wu (2017), pp. 128–136.

[99] National People's Congress Standing Committee (2019).

[100] State Council of China (2017).

[101] Specifically, both jurisdictions explicitly grant individuals the right to refuse automated decision-making, thus upholding respect for individual autonomy in the AI environment. For additional discussion, see Art. 24 of the PIPL and Art. 22 of the GDPR.

[102] China's laws and regulations, such as the E-Commerce Law and the PIPL, address issues of automated decision-making that may have negative or discriminatory effects on human users, prohibiting unfair differential treatment. The newly issued 2023 Interim Measures further specify that service providers of generative AI should take effective measures to prevent discrimination based on factors such as region, gender, age, occupation, and health in algorithm design, training data selection, model generation and optimisation, and service provision. Similarly, the EU's AIA also clearly prohibits the deployment of AI systems that lead to discriminatory outcomes. See Art. 35 of the E-Commerce Law, Art. 24 of the PIPL, Art. 4 of the 2023 Interim Measures, and Art. 5 of the EU AIA.

[103] Both jurisdictions require that the design and deployment of AI systems should be transparent and responsible. This benefits human users who have the right to know when they are interacting with AI systems, how AI systems use their data, and how decisions are made, among other relevant information. See Arts. 13 and 50 of the EU AIA; Art. 4 of the 2023 Interim Measures.

[104] Art. 5 of the EU AIA.

society and human interests.[105] The legislation insists that high-risk AI systems should be supervised by humans, ensuring the ability for human intervention, explanation, and overriding of AI decisions, when necessary.[106] In comparison, China's AI-related laws lack such provisions. They only provide basic principles that need to be adhered to when conducting AI-related activities. Although China has forbidden the application of AI in certain situations as stipulated in the 2022 Interim Measures for the Supervision of Internet Medical Treatment,[107] which prohibits the use of AI to replace physicians in providing diagnosis and treatment services, and to generate prescriptions, these prohibitions are largely applicable to the healthcare sector and exist primarily in departmental regulations. Currently, China's AI-related laws and administrative regulations, including the 2023 Interim Measures, do not explicitly ban AI usage in specific scenarios to safeguard human rights.

While both the EU and China demonstrate commitment to balancing regulatory responsibilities for human rights protection and AI technology advancement, their approaches differ. The EU takes a more rights-based and human-centric strategy, explicitly outlining prohibitions in specific contexts and emphasising the need for human oversight of high-risk AI systems. Conversely, China follows a principle-based approach and has not established specific rules regarding the protection of human rights in the development and use of AI.

4 Intellectual Property Issues

4.1 Challenges to the Intellectual Property System

The challenges that AI presents to intellectual property (IP) regimes pertain primarily to patent and copyright law.

In China, the approval of patents relating to AI innovations is subject to two legal prerequisites: (1) the application in question must satisfy the 'novelty', 'inventiveness', and 'practical applicability' criteria outlined in the Chinese Patent Law;[108]

[105] Art. 5 of the EU AIA and European Parliament (2024).

[106] Arts. 7 and 14 of the EU AIA.

[107] National Health Commission, National Administration of Traditional Chinese Medicine (2022).

[108] According to Art. 22 of the Chinese Patent Law, 'novelty' means that the invention or the utility model is not an existing technology. Before the date of application, no entity or individual has filed an application heretofore with the patent administrative department of the State Council for the identical invention or utility model and recorded it in the patent application documents or patent documents released after the said date of application. 'Inventiveness' means that, compared with the technology existing before the date of application, the invention has prominent substantive features and represents notable progress and that the utility model has substantive features and represents progress. 'Practical applicability' means that the invention or the utility model can be made or used and can produce effective results. See National People's Congress Standing Committee (2020b).

and (2) it must not contravene the law or foster a monopoly within specific fields.[109] Concurrently, patent protection cannot be awarded to AI innovations such as disease treatment methodologies, since a monopolistic situation could hinder technological advancement and societal growth.[110]

The invention creation process using AI may involve a complex 'black box'. Although the results may be effective, the underlying logic and decision-making processes are often non-transparent and difficult to explain, making it challenging to provide the detailed descriptions and explanations typically required in patent examinations.[111] This complicates the task of patent examiners when it comes to assessing 'novelty', 'inventiveness', and 'practical applicability', potentially leading to misjudgments in the patent review process.[112] Additionally, the introduction of AI raises uncertainties regarding inventorship, specifically whether AI should be considered an inventor or if this role should be assigned to the programmer or user.[113] Despite these challenges, there is widespread support in China for the protection of AI-generated technological solutions within the patent law framework.[114] China is working towards developing stricter scientific evaluation standards.[115] A notable development in this direction was the revision of the Guidelines for Patent Examination by China's National Intellectual Property Administration (NIPA) in 2019. The revised guidelines introduce a specific chapter that regulates patent application issues for inventions related to AI, Internet Plus, big data, and blockchain.[116] Furthermore, the 2023 revision of the Guidelines for Patent Examination explicitly states that an AI model cannot be listed as an 'inventor' of patents in China.[117]

---

[109] Arts. 5 and 20 of the Patent Law.

[110] Art. 25 of the Patent Law, Chen and Xu (2022) and Wu (2019).

[111] Ji (2017) and Wu (2019).

[112] Zhang (2020b) for a discussion on the legal standards for patentability of AI inventions, Chen and Xu (2022) and China Intellectual Property Rights Protection Website (2024).

[113] Wu (2019), Jia (2019) and China Intellectual Property Rights Protection Website (2024).

[114] As many Chinese studies have discussed, patent eligibility should not be restricted solely because an invention is AI-generated or AI-assisted, as such limitations may hinder technological progress and impede potential societal benefits. See Li (2019b) for a discussion on the challenge and countermeasure of AI technology to the patent system, Wu (2019), Cao and Xian (2020) and Meng (2024).

[115] For example, the Opinions of the Supreme People's Court on Strengthening the Legal Theory Research of the People's Courts in the New Era, issued in 2024, reiterated the need to enhance legal research on the regulation of emerging technologies such as big data, AI, and facial recognition. It emphasises the importance of researching judicial protection of IP rights related to cutting-edge technologies, such as big data and algorithms, as well as business methods, cultural creativity, and other areas closely associated with technological innovation.

[116] China National Intellectual Property Administration (2019).

[117] The Guidelines for Patent Examination (2023) explicitly state that inventors must be individuals; organisations or groups, as well as the names of AI, must not be listed in the application. For example, it should not be written as 'XXX Research Group' or 'XXX AI Model'. Inventors must use their real names and must not use pseudonyms or any other informal names. See China National Intellectual Property Administration (2023).

Notwithstanding these efforts, the current 2020 revision of the Chinese Patent Law has not explicitly defined the patentability of AI-generated inventions. This omission underscores the need for further enhancements to the Chinese patent legislation to keep abreast with the rapidly changing AI technological landscape. Many studies recommend that China's patent law framework should adapt to integrate standards appropriate for the AI era, including establishing criteria to assess 'non-obviousness' for a more accurate determination of an AI-related invention's 'inventiveness'.[118] Moreover, Chinese scholars and regulatory bodies hold that it is necessary for patent applicants to disclose the use of AI in their applications. This requirement would promote a more transparent and effective examination process.[119]

AI-generated content also presents challenges to China's existing copyright system. For instance, in 2017, Xiaoice, an AI robot developed by Microsoft's Software and Technology Centre of Asia, authored the world's first AI-created collection of poems. Xiaoice orchestrated the entire process without human intervention. In particular, most of the rhetorical devices and word combinations used in this collection were not present in Xiaoice's training database, which indicated that Xiaoice's innovative work surpassed the learning materials provided by algorithm designers.[120] This situation sparked a significant debate, with questions about whether AI-created works, such as Xiaoice's poetry, are eligible for rights (ownership) under copyright law, and if so, whether Xiaoice should be treated as the copyright holder (author). Currently, China's legislation does not specifically regulate the copyright of AI-generated outputs. The applicable laws in use mainly include the Copyright Law of the PRC[121] and the Regulation for the Implementation of the Copyright Law of the PRC.[122]

According to Art. 3 of the Regulation for the Implementation of the Copyright Law of the PRC, 'creation' refers to intellectual activities that directly produce literary, artistic, or scientific works. Auxiliary tasks such as organising, advising, providing materials, or other supportive activities are not deemed creative works. In the context of poems generated by AI software, the algorithm designers and data providers are not directly involved in the creation process. Therefore, it could be argued that the AI's creations fulfil the criteria of both being 'directly generated' and 'intellectual activity'. However, Li Judan, a scholar in IP law, argued that AI-generated content is not the result of 'intellectual creation'. Essentially, she contends that it is merely the output from a computer program's operation and, therefore, should not be granted copyright protection.[123]

---

118 See Li (2019b) for a discussion on the challenge and countermeasure of AI technology to the patent system and Zhang (2020b) for a discussion on the legal standards for patentability of AI inventions.

119 Yao (2022), China National Intellectual Property Administration, Japan Patent Office (2023) and Zheng (2023).

120 People's Daily Online (2017).

121 National People's Congress Standing Committee (2020a).

122 State Council of China (2013).

123 Li (2019a).

Additionally, based on the current definitions in China's copyright laws, a 'work' must fulfil three conditions: (1) it must be a product of human intellect; (2) it must be externally expressed in a way that others can objectively perceive; and (3) it must be inherently original.[124] Despite the clear articulation of these three conditions in existing regulations, it remains uncertain whether AI-generated outputs fall within these parameters. Since there is no specific legislation or legal documents addressing this issue, it continues to be a highly debated issue within the Chinese academic community.[125]

4.2 *Judicial Practice*

In judicial practice, no uniform adjudication criteria have been established towards the IP protection of AI-produced work. In the Beijing Film Law Firm v. Beijing Baidu Netcom Science & Technology Co., Ltd., a 2018 case known as China's first AI-generated content copyright case, the defendant claimed that the disputed article was an output of data analysis by an AI system (a legal software analysis system).[126] The AI output, according to their argument, is a mere result of data processing and devoid of originality, and this should not be protected by copyright law.[127] Both the Beijing Internet Court in the first instance and the Beijing Intellectual Property Court in the second instance upheld this claim.[128] However, in the Tencent v. WDZJ case in December 2019, Shenzhen Nanshan District People's Court came to a different conclusion.[129] The judge asserted that the article in question was generated by

[124] 'Originality' is one of the critical elements in determining whether a work can be protected by copyright. The 'originality' required for a 'work' does not mean that the 'work' must express a new idea, but it emphasises that the 'work' is not a copy of another work. A 'work' protected by copyright law must originate from the 'creation' of the author. See Wang (2024a) discuss the work type logic of originality in copyright law, pp. 183–200.

[125] For example, Ma Zhiguo and Liu Zhen believe that AI-generated works can already meet the criteria of 'works' under the current copyright laws. Yang Lihua, on the other hand, believes that the existing copyright law in China still needs to be updated. It may be more advantageous to grant users the copyright of AI-generated objects. See Ma and Liu (2018), pp. 107–114 and Yang (2021), pp. 102–114.

[126] See Beijing Film Law Firm v. Beijing Baidu Netcom Science & Technology Co., Ltd., Beijing Internet Court. (2018). Case No. (2018) Jing 0491 Min Chu 239; Beijing Film Law Firm v. Beijing Baidu Netcom Science & Technology Co., Ltd., Beijing Intellectual Property Court. (2019). Case No. (2019) Jing 73 Min Zhong 2030.

[127] Zhang (2019).

[128] Specifically, both trial courts held that 'creation and completion by a natural person' is a necessary condition for a 'work' to be protected under the copyright law. It means that the analysis report automatically generated by AI was not created by a natural person and therefore does not constitute a 'work' within the scope of the copyright law. See Gong and Wang (2018).

[129] See Shenzhen Tencent Computer System Co., Ltd. v. Shanghai Yingxun Technology Co., Ltd. (Tencent v. WDZJ Case), Shenzhen Nanshan District People's Court. (2019). Case No. (2019) Yue 0305 Min Chu 14010.

the plaintiff's creative team members using an automatic writing software they had developed. The court held that the article's content, reflected independent analysis and judgement, which met the requirements for a written work in terms of external manifestation and demonstrated a certain degree of originality.[130] Therefore, for the first time, the court recognised that AI-generated content met the criteria for protection as a written work under the Copyright Law of the PRC.

In 2023, the Beijing Internet Court heard a case concerning the IP rights of AI-generated images.[131] The court found that the images in question demonstrated the plaintiff's intellectual efforts. These efforts were apparent through the input of prompt words, adjustment of relevant parameters, and subsequent refinement of the initial image, which indicated the plaintiff's aesthetic choices and personal judgements. The ongoing process of adjustment and refinement epitomised the plaintiff's independent creation. The court concluded that the images in question met the 'originality' standard, illustrating personalised expression and therefore meeting the criteria for copyright protection under the Copyright Law of the PRC.

Notably, Chinese courts have consistently dismissed the notion of recognising AI as a legal entity. Authorship is typically assigned to individuals or organisations that have used AI to produce content, viewing AI as merely a tool for content creation.[132] For example, in the aforementioned 2023 case involving AI-generated images, the judge of the Beijing Internet Court ruled that under the Copyright Law of the PRC, recognised authorship is classified into two categories: (1) natural persons who create works; and (2) legal entities or unincorporated organisations recognised as authors when creating works on their behalf.[133] Similarly, in China's inaugural case in 2024 concerning whether AI could be classified as a patent inventor,[134] the administrative body (NIPA) ruled that AI models or systems could not be identified as inventors during the administrative patent examination process. The administrative decision found that the AI system, described by the applicant as an autonomous inventor, did not align with any category of civil subject as defined in the Chinese

[130] Xiao and Zhang (2020).

[131] Specifically, in February 2023, the plaintiff, Mr. Li, used a certain AI open-source software to generate images by inputting prompt words, and later posted the image on his own social media platform. Subsequently, Mr. Li found that the defendant, Ms. Liu, had published an article online, with the article's illustration utilising the image in question. Mr. Li argued that Ms. Liu had used the image without permission and had removed the watermark identifying Mr. Li as the creator on the social media platform. This action misled users into believing that Ms. Liu was the author of the work, which constituted a severe infringement of Mr. Li's right to attribution and his right to disseminate information over the Internet. See Li v. Liu, Beijing Internet Court. (2023). Case No. (2023) Jing 0491 Min Chu 11279.

[132] See Zhang (2020a) for a discussion on the future of copyright for AI-generated works.

[133] Art. 11 of the China's Copyright Law and Liu (2023).

[134] See China National Intellectual Property Administration (2024). Administrative Decision on the Request for Reexamination of Patent Application No. 201980006158.0, titled 'Food Container and Device and Method for Enhancing Attention.'

Civil Code.[135] Although this issue has not yet been addressed by the judiciary, it remains a key area of ongoing legal development.

In conclusion, while some precedents exist in China concerning the copyrightability of AI-generated content, the laws associated with IP rights for AI-derived outputs remain unclear. It is a widely held perspective that current case rulings are unique and not necessarily applicable in broader contexts.[136] The question of whether AI can be considered a rightful originator of inventions or creations in China remains unresolved. Given that China does not currently recognise AI's legal status, it seems unlikely, under the existing IP legal framework, for AI to be acknowledged as a copyright holder or inventor of patents. This suggests that AI-produced outputs—viewed as inventions or creations—might not be protected under IP laws.[137]

4.3 Comparative Analysis of the Regulation of AI and Associated Intellectual Property Rights in China and the EU

While both China and the EU lack specific legal solutions that address IP issues in AI development, they emphasise the significance of preserving IP rights when developing AI applications. For instance, both China's 2023 Interim Measures (Arts. 4 and 7) and the EU's AIA (Art. 78) stipulate that providing and using AI services should respect IP rights, uphold business ethics, and protect trade secrets. Moreover, it is noteworthy that both jurisdictions mandate the labelling of outputs produced by AI systems. For example, Art. 12 of the 2023 Interim Measures dictates that AI service providers should label content such as images and videos in accordance with the Provisions on the Administration of Deep Synthesis of Internet-Based Information Services.[138] Likewise, the AIA explicitly states that providers of AI systems generating synthetic audio, images, videos, or textual content must ensure that the outputs of AI systems are labelled in a machine-readable format and are identifiable as being artificially generated or manipulated (Rec. 134 and Art. 50). The mandate on AI-generated content labelling implies a shared understanding between China and the EU about the need to promote transparency and trust, which

[135] According to the Chinese Civil Code, civil subjects are limited to natural persons, legal persons, and unincorporated organisations.

[136] Li (2023).

[137] For example, according to Art. 2 of China's Copyright Law, only natural persons (or legal persons or other organisations) can enjoy copyright.

[138] Cyberspace Administration of China, Ministry of Industry and Information Technology, Ministry of Public Security (2022).

are fundamental to the comprehensive governance of AI and the protection of IP rights. However, the implementation of transparency measures may not address underlying concerns related to IP rights, such as effective enforcement mechanisms to ensure compliance, clearly defined liability for infringement to hold responsible parties accountable, and robust protection of creative works within the AI context. Therefore, although the commitment to transparency and trust is a positive step, it is essential to engage in further dialogue and collaboration to bridge these gaps and develop comprehensive global norms that effectively address IP challenges in AI development and usage.[139]

5 Moving Forward

In July 2017, China's State Council released the Development Plan on the New Generation of AI.[140] This plan outlined a three-step strategy for AI development in China, with the goal of establishing a comprehensive legal and regulatory framework for AI by 2030. This included developing ethical norms, risk assessment, and control capabilities for AI. The 2021 PIPL established rules for automated decision-making and stipulated that China's national network information department should formulate specific rules and standards to protect personal information associated with emerging technologies and applications, including AI. Furthermore, the 2023 Interim Measures introduced more targeted regulatory measures for the development and use of generative AI to address the novel risks posed by this technology. Nonetheless, some critical issues discussed in this chapter need to be more thoroughly addressed in future legislative development and reform. For instance, the existing laws related to data protection, human rights, and IP regulatory regimes need to be improved to address AI-driven challenges and uncertainties.

Currently, a debate is ongoing about whether to enact comprehensive AI legislation. Despite various proposals for AI regulation, these initiatives are still largely confined to academic discussions and have not made their way into the formal legislative process.[141] At the governmental level, China's State Council has included an AI legislation draft in both its 2023 and 2024 legislative work plans. The drafts are planned for review by China's legislature, the Standing Committee of the National People's Congress (NPC) (Qin 2023). Moreover, the NPC's 2024 annual legislative plan marks legislation for the sustainable development of AI as a preliminary review

[139] CAICT (2023), Dreyfus (2024) and El Atillah (2023).

[140] State Council of China (2017).

[141] Sun (2024).

item.[142] A report published by the NPC Education, Science, Culture and Public Health Committee in December 2024 also indicates that China's Ministry of Science and Technology, in collaboration with relevant departments, is actively drafting an AI law. Multiple consultation meetings with experts and research institutions have been conducted, and a preliminary framework of the legal text is currently taking shape.[143] However, some scholars argued that implementing general legislation on AI at this stage still entails significant challenges.[144]

The recently approved AIA by the EU may serve as a valuable reference for Chinese legislators. It provides insights on how to establish comprehensive and specialised AI legislation, as well as on promoting the implementation of such legislation to aid the development and application of AI. For instance, the rules under the AIA will be implemented in phases, with certain provisions taking effect within 6 or 12 months following the law's passage, while the majority are expected to come into force on August 2026.[145] China could also consider adopting a phased implementation approach for its AI legislation, which would allow stakeholders time to adapt and adjust. Moreover, the EU has established an AI Office that involves the providers of AI models and regulatory authorities from member states in drafting a code of conduct. This approach helps ensure the applicability and effectiveness of relevant laws.[146] Civil society organisations, industry representatives, academia, and other stakeholders, including downstream providers and independent experts, can also play supportive roles in this process. China's AI legislative and regulatory process should also enhance multi-stakeholder participation mechanisms and widely solicit input from relevant parties to ensure the regulations' reasonableness and operability. Additionally, the AIA introduces a regulatory sandbox mechanism. This mechanism allows businesses to test their AI technologies in a controlled environment, thereby encouraging innovation while maintaining compliance.[147] This legal platform promotes interaction between enterprises and regulatory bodies, fostering improved comprehension of the technology's practical impact and enabling timely adjustments to relevant regulations. China could benefit from studying the EU's regulatory model, evaluating whether and how to develop a similar comprehensive legal framework within their current domestic legal system to enhance the regulation of AI applications.

In addition to hard laws for AI oversight, a soft approach can also play a significant role in addressing issues pertaining to data privacy, algorithmic bias, accountability, and ethical considerations. China has, in fact, established soft laws

---

[142] Chi (2024).

[143] National People's Congress Education, Science, Culture and Public Health Committee (2024).

[144] Song (2024) and Zhang (2024).

[145] Jones (2024) and European Parliament (2024).

[146] Art. 56 of the EU AIA.

[147] Art. 57 of the EU AIA.

concerning the research and commercial use of AI. For instance, in August 2020, the National Standardization Administration of China, in collaboration with several national departments, issued the Guidelines for the Building of a New Generation of National AI Standards System. These guidelines advocate for the development, updating, and standardisation of national, industry, and group standards pertaining to AI, including professional terminology.[148] In January 2021, the National Information Security Standardization Technical Committee released the Cybersecurity Standards Practice Guidelines, providing guidelines on ethical security and risk prevention for AI. It offers recommendations on how organisations or individuals should approach AI-related design, manufacturing, and applications.[149] In September 2021, the National New Generation AI Governance Expert Committee announced the Ethical Norms for the New Generation AI, outlining six primary goals for AI. These include promoting fairness and justice, ensuring privacy and security, enhancing human happiness, ensuring controllability and trustworthiness, strengthening responsibility, and improving the overall ethical quality.[150] China's current soft law frameworks serve to a certain extent as a risk management tool for AI development and application. However, soft laws do not offer a comprehensive legal structure to address all potential accountability and liability concerns affiliated with AI applications, especially issues of data privacy, algorithmic bias, and infringement on IP rights. The limitations of soft laws accentuate the necessity for well-defined hard laws and the development of a more comprehensive regulatory structure. A robust legal system regulating AI and its applications, as many scholars argue, would increase public trust and foster a sustainable AI industry in China.[151]

Funding This research had financial support from the University of Macau under research grants No. MYRG-GRG2023-00025-FLL and No. APAEM/SG/0015/2024.

[148] China National Institute of Standardization (2020).

[149] National Information Security Standardization Technical Committee (2021).

[150] Ministry of Science and Technology (2021).

[151] Han (2024), Liu and Xia (2023) as well as Shen and Zhao (2022), pp. 123–137.

Appendix

Table 1 Data protection provisions in China and the EU regarding AI

Regulatory document name	Effective date	Article content	Key insights
China			
The Law on the Protection of Consumer Rights and Interests	Revised in 2013; Effective March 15, 2014	**Article 14:** Consumers have the right to have their personal dignity and ethnic customs respected when purchasing and using goods or receiving services, as well as the right to have their personal information protected in accordance with the law. **Article 29:** Operators who collect and use consumers' personal information shall adhere to the principles of legality, legitimacy, and necessity, explicitly stating the purposes, methods, and scope of such collection and use, and obtaining the consent of the consumers. Operators must publicly disclose their rules for collecting and using information and shall not violate the provisions of laws and regulations or the agreements made with consumers in the collection and use of information. Operators and their staff must maintain strict confidentiality regarding the consumers' personal information collected and shall not disclose, sell, or unlawfully provide it to others. Operators shall adopt technical measures and other necessary precautions to ensure information security and prevent the leakage or loss of consumers' personal information. In the event of an actual or potential information leak or loss, immediate remedial measures must be taken. Operators shall not send commercial information to consumers without their consent or request, nor when the consumer has explicitly refused to receive such information. **Article 44:** Consumers who purchase goods or receive services through an online trading platform and suffer harm to their legitimate rights and interests may seek compensation from the seller or service provider. If the online trading platform provider is unable to provide the seller or service provider's true name, address, and valid contact information, consumers may also seek compensation from the online trading platform provider. The online trading platform provider must fulfil any commitments made that are more favourable to consumers. After providing compensation, the online trading platform provider has the right to seek recovery from the seller or service provider. If the online trading platform provider is aware or should be aware that the seller or service provider is infringing upon consumers' legitimate rights and interests using its platform and fails to take necessary measures, it shall bear joint liability with the seller or service provider in accordance with the law. **Article 50:** If an operator infringes upon the personal dignity of consumers, violates their personal freedom, or infringes upon the rights of consumers' personal information protected by law, the operator shall cease the infringement, restore the reputation of the consumer, eliminate the adverse effects, issue an apology, and compensate for any losses incurred. **Article 57:** Operators who provide goods or services in violation of the provisions of this law and infringe upon consumers' legitimate rights and interests, and who commit crimes in doing so, shall be subject to criminal liability in accordance with the law.	• Operators must collect and use consumers' personal information legally, legitimately, and necessarily, obtaining consent and publicly disclosing collection rules. • Strict confidentiality must be maintained regarding consumers' personal information, with technical measures taken to prevent leakage or loss. • Consumers harmed while receiving services on online platforms can seek compensation from sellers or platform providers. • Violations of consumers' rights, including infringement of personal information, will result in penalties.

The Cybersecurity Law	June 1, 2017	**Article 21:** The state implements a tiered protection system for cybersecurity. Network operators shall fulfil the following security protection obligations in accordance with the requirements of this system to protect networks from interference, destruction, or unauthorised access, and to prevent the leakage, theft, or alteration of network data: 1. Establish internal security management systems and operational procedures, appoint a responsible individual for network security, and implement accountability for network security protection; 2. Take technical measures to prevent computer viruses, network attacks, intrusions, and other behaviours that jeopardise network security; 3. Implement technical measures for monitoring and recording the status of network operations and cybersecurity incidents, retaining relevant network logs for no less than 6 months; 4. Adopt measures such as data classification, backup of important data, and encryption; 5. Fulfill other obligations stipulated by laws and administrative regulations. **Article 22:** Network products and services shall comply with the mandatory requirements of relevant national standards. Providers of network products and services shall not install malicious programs; upon discovering security defects or vulnerabilities in their products or services, they must immediately take remedial measures, inform users in a timely manner according to regulations, and report to the relevant supervisory authorities. Providers of network products and services shall continuously provide security maintenance for their products and services and shall not terminate such maintenance within the period specified by regulations or agreed upon with the parties involved. If network products or services collect user information, the providers must clearly inform users and obtain their consent; in cases involving personal information, they must also comply with this law and relevant laws and administrative regulations regarding personal information protection. **Article 25:** Network operators shall develop emergency response plans for cybersecurity incidents to promptly address risks such as system vulnerabilities, computer viruses, network attacks, and intrusions. In the event of incidents that endanger network security, the emergency response plan must be activated immediately, appropriate remedial measures taken, and relevant supervisory authorities notified in accordance with regulations. **Article 40:** Network operators must maintain strict confidentiality regarding the user information they collect and establish and improve user information protection systems. **Article 41:** When collecting and using personal information, network operators shall adhere to the principles of legality, legitimacy, necessity, and transparency. They must publicly disclose the rules for collection and use, explicitly state the purposes, methods, and scope of information collection and use, and obtain the consent of the individuals from whom information is collected. Network operators shall not collect personal information unrelated to the services they provide, nor shall they violate the provisions of laws and administrative regulations or agreements made with individuals in the collection and use of personal information, and they must process the personal information they store in accordance with laws, administrative regulations, and agreements with users.	• Requires network operators to establish a security management system and ensure accountability. • Implements technical measures to prevent data breaches and address cybersecurity threats. • Providers must promptly address security defects and notify users accordingly. • Continuous security maintenance of network products and services is required. • Collecting and processing personal information must include obtaining user consent. • Operators must maintain strict confidentiality of user information. • Individuals have the right to request the deletion or correction of their personal information.

(continued)

Table 1 (continued)

Regulatory document name	Effective date	Article content	Key insights
		Article 42: Network operators shall not disclose, alter, or destroy the personal information they have collected; without the consent of the individual from whom information is collected, they shall not provide personal information to others, except in cases where the information has been processed to the extent that specific individuals cannot be identified and cannot be restored. Network operators must take technical and other necessary measures to ensure the security of the personal information they collect, preventing information leakage, destruction, or loss. In the event of or potential for personal information leakage, destruction, or loss, they must immediately take remedial measures, promptly inform users in accordance with regulations, and report to relevant supervisory authorities. **Article 43:** Individuals have the right to request the deletion of their personal information by network operators if they find that the operators have collected or used their personal information in violation of laws, administrative regulations, or agreements. If individuals discover errors in their personal information collected or stored by network operators, they have the right to request corrections. Network operators shall take measures to delete or correct such information. **Article 44:** No individual or organisation shall illegally obtain personal information through theft or other unlawful means, nor shall they sell or unlawfully provide personal information to others. **Article 45:** Departments and personnel responsible for cybersecurity supervision and management must maintain strict confidentiality regarding personal information, privacy, and commercial secrets that they learn while fulfilling their duties, and shall not disclose, sell, or unlawfully provide such information to others. **Article 59:** If network operators fail to fulfil the cybersecurity protection obligations stipulated in Articles 21 and 25 of this law, they shall be ordered to rectify the situation and receive a warning from the relevant supervisory authorities; if they refuse to correct the violation or cause consequences that endanger network security, they shall be fined between ten thousand and one hundred thousand yuan, and directly responsible supervisory personnel shall face fines ranging from five thousand to fifty thousand yuan. **Article 64:** If network operators, providers of network products, or services violate the provisions of Article 22 (paragraph 3) or Articles 41 to 43 of this law, infringing upon the rights of personal information that are legally protected, they shall be ordered to rectify the violation by the relevant supervisory authorities. Depending on the circumstances, they may be subjected to warnings, confiscation of illegal gains, fines ranging from one to ten times the illegal gains, or fines of up to one million yuan if there are no illegal gains. Directly responsible supervisory personnel and other individuals directly liable shall face fines ranging from ten thousand to one hundred thousand yuan; if the circumstances are severe, relevant authorities may order the suspension of related business, shutdown, website closure, revocation of relevant business licenses, or cancellation of operating permits. In cases of theft or other illegal means to obtain, sell, or unlawfully provide personal information in violation of Article 44 of this law, and where criminal charges are not applicable, public security organs shall confiscate illegal gains and impose fines ranging from one to ten times the illegal gains or, if there are no illegal gains, fines of up to one million yuan.	• Prohibits the illegal acquisition, sale, or provision of personal information. • Failure to fulfil cybersecurity obligations or violations of personal information protection laws may result in fines or business suspension.

The Chinese Civil Code	January 1, 2021	**Article 111:** The personal information of natural persons is protected by law. Any organisation or individual seeking to obtain another person's personal information must do so lawfully and ensure the security of such information. Unauthorised collection, use, processing, transmission, sale, provision, or public disclosure of another person's personal information is prohibited. **Article 1032:** Natural persons enjoy the right to privacy. No organisation or individual may infringe upon another person's right to privacy through means such as probing, intruding, disclosing, or publicly revealing private information. Privacy encompasses the tranquility of a natural person's private life, as well as spaces, activities, and information that they do not wish to be known by others. **Article 1034:** The personal information of natural persons is protected by law. Personal information refers to various information that can identify a specific natural person either alone or in combination with other information, recorded in electronic or other forms. This includes the natural person's name, date of birth, identification document number, biometric information, address, phone number, email address, health information, whereabouts information, and more. The private information within personal information is subject to the relevant provisions regarding the right to privacy; where there are no such provisions, the relevant provisions on personal information protection shall apply. **Article 1035:** The processing of personal information must adhere to the principles of legality, fairness, and necessity, avoiding excessive processing, and must meet the following conditions: 1. Consent must be obtained from the natural person or their guardian, unless otherwise provided by laws or administrative regulations; 2. The rules for processing information must be disclosed; 3. The purpose, method, and scope of processing information must be explicitly stated; 4. Processing must not violate laws, administrative regulations, or agreements between the parties. The processing of personal information includes its collection, storage, use, processing, transmission, provision, and public disclosure. **Article 1037:** Natural persons may lawfully access or copy their personal information held by information processors. If they discover any inaccuracies in the information, they have the right to raise objections and request timely corrective measures. If a natural person finds that the information processor is handling their personal information in violation of laws, administrative regulations, or agreements between the parties, they have the right to request the timely deletion of such information. **Article 1038:** Information processors must not disclose or alter the personal information they collect and store. They may not illegally provide personal information to others without the consent of the natural person, except where the information has been processed in such a way that specific individuals cannot be identified and cannot be restored. Information processors are required to adopt technical and other necessary measures to ensure the security of the personal information they collect and store, preventing leaks, alterations, or losses of information. In the event of, or potential for, such leaks, alterations, or losses, they must take prompt remedial measures and notify the natural person as well as report to the relevant regulatory authorities as required. **Article 1039:** State agencies, statutory institutions performing administrative functions, and their personnel must keep confidential any personal information and privacy of natural persons that they become aware of in the course of fulfilling their duties. They are prohibited from disclosing or unlawfully providing such information to others.	• Focuses on the legal protection of personal information. • Emphasises individuals' privacy rights. • Mandates transparency in data processing. • Empowers individuals to access and correct their data. • Requires security measures to protect personal information. • Obligates state agencies, administrative institutions, and their personnel to maintain confidentiality.

(continued)

Table 1 (continued)

Regulatory document name	Effective date	Article content	Key insights
The Data Security Law	September 1, 2021	**Article 8:** The conduct of data processing activities shall comply with laws and regulations, respect social ethics and morality, adhere to commercial and professional ethics, act in good faith, fulfil data security protection obligations, assume social responsibilities, and must not endanger national security or public interests, nor infringe upon the legitimate rights and interests of individuals or organisations. **Article 27:** Data processing activities shall be carried out in accordance with the provisions of laws and regulations, establishing and improving a comprehensive data security management system, organising data security education and training, and adopting appropriate technical and other necessary measures to ensure data security. When conducting data processing activities through the internet or other information networks, the aforementioned data security protection obligations shall be fulfilled based on the network security tiered protection system. Those processing important data shall designate responsible individuals and management bodies for data security and implement accountability for data security protection. **Article 28:** The conduct of data processing activities and the research and development of new data technologies shall promote economic and social development, enhance public welfare, and conform to social ethics and morality. **Article 29:** Data processing activities shall strengthen risk monitoring. Upon discovering data security defects, vulnerabilities, or other risks, immediate remedial measures shall be taken. In the event of a data security incident, prompt response measures shall be initiated, and relevant authorities and users shall be notified in a timely manner in accordance with regulations. **Article 32:** Any organisation or individual collecting data shall do so through legal and legitimate means and shall not steal or obtain data through other unlawful methods. Where laws and administrative regulations stipulate the purposes and scope for data collection and use, such collection and use shall be conducted within the boundaries defined by those laws and regulations. **Article 45:** Organisations or individuals engaged in data processing activities who fail to fulfil the data security protection obligations stipulated in Articles 27, 29, and 30 of this law shall be ordered to rectify the situation by the relevant supervisory authorities and may receive a warning. Fines ranging from fifty thousand to five hundred thousand yuan may be imposed, and directly responsible supervisory personnel and other directly liable individuals may be fined between ten thousand and one hundred thousand yuan. If rectification is refused or if serious consequences such as mass data breaches occur, fines of five hundred thousand to two million yuan may be imposed, and the relevant authorities may order the suspension of related business, shutdown, revocation of relevant business licenses, or cancellation of operating permits. Directly responsible supervisory personnel and other directly liable individuals may face fines ranging from fifty thousand to two hundred thousand yuan. Violations of the national core data management system that endanger national sovereignty, security, or development interests shall result in fines ranging from two million to ten million yuan, and depending on the situation, relevant authorities may order the suspension of related business, shutdown, revocation of relevant business licenses, or cancellation of operating permits. In cases constituting a crime, criminal liability shall be pursued in accordance with the law.	• Data processing activities must fulfil data security protection obligations and align with social ethics and morals. • Establishes and improves a comprehensive data security management system, organises data security education and training, and adopts appropriate technical measures to ensure data security. • Takes immediate remedial measures upon discovering data security defects, vulnerabilities, or other risks. • Collects data through legal and legitimate means. • Violations may result in fines, revocation of business licenses, and potential criminal liability.

The Personal Information Protection Law	November 1, 2021	**Article 5:** The processing of personal information shall adhere to the principles of legality, legitimacy, necessity, and integrity, and shall not be conducted through misleading, fraudulent, or coercive means. **Article 6:** The processing of personal information shall have clear and reasonable objectives, and such processing must be directly related to the stated purposes, employing methods that minimise impacts on the rights of individuals. The collection of personal information shall be limited to the minimum scope necessary to achieve the processing objectives, and excessive collection of personal information is prohibited. **Article 7:** The processing of personal information shall adhere to the principles of openness and transparency, publicly disclosing the rules for personal information processing, and clearly stating the purposes, methods, and scope of processing. **Article 9:** Personal information processors shall be accountable for their personal information processing activities and shall take necessary measures to ensure the security of the processed personal information. **Article 10:** No organisation or individual shall illegally collect, use, process, transmit, sell, provide, or publicly disclose another person's personal information, nor shall they engage in personal information processing activities that endanger national security or public interests. **Article 13:** Personal information processors may only process personal information under one of the following circumstances: 1. Obtaining the individual's consent; 2. Necessary for the conclusion and performance of a contract in which the individual is a party, or necessary for human resource management in accordance with labour rules and regulations and collective contracts legally signed; 3. Necessary for the performance of statutory duties or legal obligations; 4. Necessary to respond to public health emergencies or to protect the life, health, and property safety of natural persons in emergency situations; 5. Necessary for public interest activities such as news reporting and public opinion supervision, processing personal information within a reasonable scope; 6. Processing personal information that individuals have publicly disclosed or other personal information that has already been legally disclosed, within a reasonable scope in accordance with this law; 7. Other circumstances prescribed by laws and administrative regulations. According to other relevant provisions of this law, processing personal information shall obtain the individual's consent; however, consent is not required in cases specified in items 2 to 7 of the preceding paragraph. **Article 14:** When processing personal information based on individual consent, such consent must be voluntarily and explicitly given by the individual after being fully informed. Where laws or administrative regulations require that processing personal information be based on separate or written consent from the individual, such provisions shall apply. If there is a change in the purposes, methods, or categories of personal information processed, renewed consent must be obtained from the individual.	• Prohibits excessive collection of personal information. • Data processing must adhere to principles of openness and transparency. • Holds personal information processors accountable for data breaches. • Prohibits unauthorised collection and processing of personal information. • Data processing requires voluntary informed consent from individuals. • Limits retention of personal information to the minimum necessary duration. • Automated decision-making must ensure transparency and fairness in outcomes. • Individuals have the right to request explanations and refuse automated decisions.

(continued)

Table 1 (continued)

Regulatory document name	Effective date	Article content	Key insights
		Article 15: Individuals have the right to withdraw their consent when personal information is processed based on their consent. Personal information processors shall provide convenient means for individuals to withdraw their consent. The withdrawal of consent shall not affect the validity of any personal information processing activities that occurred prior to the withdrawal based on the individual's consent. **Article 17:** Before processing personal information, personal information processors shall inform individuals in a prominent manner and in clear and comprehensible language of the following matters: 1. The name or identity and contact information of the personal information processor; 2. The purposes and methods of processing personal information, the categories of personal information being processed, and the retention period; 3. The methods and procedures for individuals to exercise their rights as provided by this law; 4. Other matters that must be disclosed pursuant to laws or administrative regulations. If any of the aforementioned matters change, the changes must be communicated to the individuals concerned. If personal information processors inform individuals of the above matters through the formulation of personal information processing rules, those rules must be made public and easily accessible and retained. **Article 19:** Unless otherwise provided by laws or administrative regulations, the retention period for personal information shall be the minimum duration necessary to achieve the processing purposes. **Article 21:** If personal information processors entrust others with the processing of personal information, they must agree with the entrusted party on the purposes, duration, methods, categories of personal information, protective measures, and the rights and obligations of both parties, and they must supervise the processing activities of the entrusted party. The entrusted party shall process personal information in accordance with the agreed-upon terms and shall not exceed the agreed purposes or methods. If the entrustment contract is invalid, revoked, or terminated, the entrusted party shall return the personal information to the personal information processor or delete it, and shall not retain any copies. Without the consent of the personal information processor, the entrusted party shall not delegate the processing of personal information to others. **Article 23:** When a personal information processor provides personal information it has processed to other personal information processors, it shall inform the individual of the name or identity and contact information of the recipient, the purposes and methods of processing, and the categories of personal information, and obtain separate consent from the individual. The recipient shall process personal information only within the scope of the stated purposes, methods, and categories. If the recipient changes the original purposes or methods of processing, renewed consent must be obtained from the individual in accordance with this law. **Article 24:** Personal information processors that use personal information for automated decision-making must ensure the transparency of the decisions and the fairness and justice of the outcomes. They must not implement unreasonable differential treatment regarding transaction prices or other transaction conditions for individuals.	• Explicitly protects sensitive personal information, requiring separate consent. • Allows individuals to request the withdrawal of consent and deletion of their data. • Imposes strict security measures to protect personal information from unauthorised access. • Requires impact assessments for activities that significantly affect individual rights. • Establishes penalties for illegal collection and processing of personal information.

		When pushing information or conducting commercial marketing through automated decision-making, they must also provide options that do not target individual characteristics, or offer individuals an easy way to refuse. When making decisions through automated decision-making that significantly affect the rights and interests of individuals, individuals have the right to request an explanation from the personal information processor and have the right to refuse decisions made solely based on automated decision-making. **Article 28:** Sensitive personal information refers to information that, if leaked or used illegally, may severely harm the dignity or safety of the individual, including biometric data, religious beliefs, specific identities, health data, financial accounts, location tracking, and information pertaining to minors under the age of fourteen. Sensitive personal information may only be processed by personal information processors when there is a specific purpose and sufficient necessity, and when strict protective measures are in place. **Article 29:** The processing of sensitive personal information requires separate consent from the individual; where laws or administrative regulations require that processing sensitive personal information be based on written consent, such provisions shall apply. **Article 30:** When processing sensitive personal information, personal information processors shall, in addition to the matters specified in the first paragraph of Article 17, inform individuals of the necessity of processing such sensitive personal information and the potential impacts on the rights of individuals, unless otherwise specified by this law. **Article 44:** Individuals have the right to be informed about the processing of their personal information and the right to decide whether to restrict or refuse others from processing their personal information, unless otherwise provided by laws or administrative regulations. **Article 47:** In any of the following circumstances, personal information processors shall actively delete personal information; if the personal information processor fails to delete it, the individual has the right to request deletion: 1. The processing purposes have been achieved, are unachievable, or are no longer necessary for achieving the processing purposes; 2. The personal information processor has ceased to provide products or services, or the retention period has expired; 3. The individual has withdrawn their consent; 4. The personal information processor has violated laws, administrative regulations, or agreements in processing personal information; 5. Other circumstances as specified by laws or administrative regulations. If the retention period specified by laws or administrative regulations has not expired, or if it is technically difficult to delete the personal information, the personal information processor shall stop all processing except for storage and necessary security protection measures. **Article 48:** Individuals have the right to request an explanation regarding the personal information processing rules from the personal information processor.	

(continued)

Table 1 (continued)

Regulatory document name	Effective date	Article content	Key insights
		Article 51: Personal information processors shall take the following measures to ensure that their personal information processing activities comply with the provisions of laws and administrative regulations, prevent unauthorised access, and protect personal information from leaks, alterations, or losses, based on the processing purposes, methods, categories of personal information, and their impact on individuals' rights and potential security risks: 1. Establish internal management systems and operational procedures; 2. Implement classified management of personal information; 3. Adopt appropriate technical security measures such as encryption and de-identification; 4. Reasonably determine access permissions for personal information processing and regularly conduct security education and training for personnel; 5. Formulate and implement emergency response plans for personal information security incidents; 6. Other measures specified by laws and administrative regulations **Article 55:** In any of the following circumstances, personal information processors shall conduct a personal information protection impact assessment in advance and maintain records of the processing activities: 1. Processing sensitive personal information; 2. Utilising personal information for automated decision-making; 3. Entrusting the processing of personal information, providing personal information to other processors, or publicly disclosing personal information; 4. Providing personal information to entities outside the country; 5. Other personal information processing activities that significantly impact the rights of individuals. **Article 66:** Any entity that processes personal information in violation of the provisions of this law, or fails to fulfil the personal information protection obligations stipulated herein, shall be ordered by the department responsible for personal information protection to rectify the violation, receive a warning, and forfeit any illegal gains. Furthermore, any application that unlawfully processes personal information may be ordered to suspend or terminate its services. If the entity refuses to rectify the violation, it shall be subject to a fine of no more than one million yuan. Directly responsible supervisory personnel and other individuals directly liable shall face fines ranging from ten thousand to one hundred thousand yuan. In cases of serious violations as outlined in the preceding paragraph, the department responsible for personal information protection at or above the provincial level shall order rectification, confiscate any illegal gains, and impose fines not exceeding 50 million yuan or 5% of the previous year's revenue. Additionally, the department may order the suspension of related business operations or impose a business shutdown, and report to the relevant supervisory authority for the revocation of related business licenses or business operating permits. Directly responsible supervisory personnel and other individuals directly liable may be fined between one hundred thousand and one million yuan, and may be prohibited from serving as directors, supervisors, senior managers, or personal information protection officers in relevant enterprises for a specified period.	

The Provisions on the Administration of Algorithm-Generated Recommendations for Internet Information Services	March 1, 2022	**Article 7:** Providers of algorithmic recommendation services shall assume primary responsibility for algorithmic security and establish comprehensive management systems and technical measures, including the review of algorithmic mechanisms, ethical assessments of technology, user registration, information publication review, data security, personal information protection, anti-telecom and network fraud measures, security assessment and monitoring, and emergency response for security incidents. They shall formulate and publicly disclose rules related to algorithmic recommendation services and allocate professional personnel and technical support commensurate with the scale of the algorithmic recommendation services. **Article 31:** Providers of algorithmic recommendation services that violate the provisions of Articles 7, 8, 9 (first paragraph), 10, 14, 16, 17, 22, 24, or 26 of these regulations shall be subject to penalties in accordance with relevant laws and administrative regulations. In cases where there are no specific provisions in laws or administrative regulations, the relevant authorities, including the Internet Information Department, telecommunications, public security, and market regulation departments, shall issue warnings, public criticisms, and orders for rectification within a specified timeframe. If the provider refuses to rectify the situation or if the violation is severe, they shall be ordered to suspend information updates and may incur fines ranging from 10,000 to 100,000 yuan. Violations constituting public security management offenses shall be penalised according to public security laws; if the actions constitute a criminal offence, criminal responsibility shall be pursued in accordance with the law.	• Providers of algorithmic recommendation services are primarily responsible for algorithm and data security issues. • Rules related to algorithmic recommendation services must be formulated and publicly disclosed. • Violations will incur fines and other administrative penalties, and may lead to criminal responsibility.

(continued)

Table 1 (continued)

Regulatory document name	Effective date	Article content	Key insights
The Provisions on the Administration of Deep Synthesis of Internet-Based Information Services	January 10, 2023	**Article 7:** Providers of deep synthesis services shall fulfil their primary responsibility for information security. They must establish and improve management systems for user registration, algorithm mechanism review, technology ethics review, information publication review, data security, personal information protection, anti-telecom and network fraud, emergency response, and other areas, and implement technical safeguards that ensure security and controllability. **Article 8:** Providers of deep synthesis services shall establish and publicly disclose management rules and platform covenants, improve service agreements, and fulfil their management responsibilities in accordance with the law and contractual obligations. They shall prominently remind technical supporters and users of deep synthesis services of their obligations regarding information security. **Article 14:** Providers of deep synthesis services and technical supporters shall enhance the management of training data and take necessary measures to ensure the security of such data. When training data includes personal information, the relevant provisions on personal information protection must be adhered to. Providers of deep synthesis services and technical supporters offering functionalities for editing biometric information, such as facial and voice recognition, shall inform users of deep synthesis services of their legal obligation to notify the individuals whose information has been edited and to obtain their separate consent.	• Providers must ensure information security. • Transparency requirements. • Providers must ensure the security of training data. • Providers must comply with personal information protection regulations. • Providers must notify individuals whose biometric information has been edited and obtain separate consent.
The Interim Measures for the Administration of Generative Artificial Intelligence Services	August 15, 2023	**Article 4:** The provision and use of generative artificial intelligence services shall comply with laws and administrative regulations, respect social ethics and moral standards, and adhere to the following provisions: 1. Uphold the core socialist values; it is prohibited to generate content that incites the subversion of state power, overturns the socialist system, endangers national security and interests, damages the national image, incites national division, undermines national unity and social stability, advocates terrorism or extremism, promotes ethnic hatred or discrimination, violence, obscenity, pornography, or disseminates false or harmful information that is prohibited by laws and administrative regulations. 2. During the processes of algorithm design, selection of training data, model generation and optimisation, and service provision, effective measures must be taken to prevent discrimination based on ethnicity, beliefs, nationality, region, gender, age, occupation, health status, and other factors.	• Respect individuals' privacy rights and personal information rights when providing and using generative artificial intelligence. • Use data and foundational models from legal sources for training.

		3. Respect intellectual property rights and business ethics, maintain trade secrets, and refrain from utilising advantages in algorithms, data, platforms, and other resources to engage in monopolistic or unfair competitive practices. 4. Respect the legitimate rights and interests of others, avoid harming the physical and mental health of individuals, and do not infringe upon others' rights to their image, reputation, honour, privacy, and personal information. 5. Based on the characteristics of the service type, implement effective measures to enhance the transparency of generative artificial intelligence services and improve the accuracy and reliability of generated content. **Article 7:** Providers of generative artificial intelligence services shall lawfully conduct pre-training, optimisation training, and other data processing activities, and comply with the following provisions: 1. Use data and foundational models that have legal sources. 2. In cases involving intellectual property rights, do not infringe upon the intellectual property rights that others lawfully possess. 3. Involving personal information, obtain the consent of the individual or comply with other circumstances as prescribed by laws and administrative regulations. 4. Take effective measures to enhance the quality of training data, thereby increasing its authenticity, accuracy, objectivity, and diversity. 5. Comply with the provisions of other relevant laws and administrative regulations, including the Cybersecurity Law, the Data Security Law, the Personal Information Protection Law, and other relevant regulatory requirements from competent authorities. **Article 9:** Providers shall assume responsibility as producers of network information content and fulfil their obligations regarding network information security. In cases involving personal information, they shall assume responsibilities as processors of personal information and fulfil their obligations for personal information protection. Providers shall enter into service agreements with users of the generative artificial intelligence services registered for their services, clearly delineating the rights and obligations of both parties. **Article 11:** Providers shall legally fulfil their protective obligations concerning the input information and usage records of users, and shall not collect unnecessary personal information, illegally retain identifiable input information and usage records, or illegally provide such information and records to others. Providers shall timely accept and process requests from individuals regarding the review, copying, correction, supplementation, and deletion of their personal information in accordance with the law.	• Generative artificial intelligence service providers must obtain consent for the processing of personal data. • Service providers must fulfil the obligations of network information producers to protect personal data. • Providers must not collect or illegally retain unnecessary personal information. • Assessors of generative AI services must maintain confidentiality. • Violations may lead to penalties under relevant cybersecurity and data protection laws.

(continued)

Table 1 (continued)

Regulatory document name	Effective date	Article content	Key insights
		Article 19: Relevant supervisory departments shall conduct supervision and inspection of generative artificial intelligence services according to their responsibilities. Providers shall cooperate in accordance with the law and, as required, explain the sources, scale, types, annotation rules, algorithm mechanisms, and other aspects of the training data, and provide necessary technical and data support and assistance. Institutions and personnel involved in the safety assessment and supervision and inspection of generative artificial intelligence services shall keep confidential any state secrets, trade secrets, personal privacy, and personal information they become aware of while performing their duties, and shall not disclose or illegally provide such information to others. **Article 21:** If providers violate the provisions of these measures, they shall be punished by relevant competent authorities in accordance with the provisions of the Cybersecurity Law, the Data Security Law, the Personal Information Protection Law, the Law on the Progress of Science and Technology, and other relevant laws and administrative regulations. If laws and administrative regulations do not specify penalties, the relevant competent authorities may issue warnings, publicly criticise, and order rectification within a specified time frame. If the providers refuse to rectify or if the circumstances are severe, they may be ordered to suspend relevant services. If the violation constitutes a breach of public security management, administrative penalties shall be imposed according to the law; if it constitutes a crime, criminal responsibility shall be pursued according to the law.	
The Criminal Law	Revised in 2023; Effective March 1, 2024	**Article 253-1 [Crime of Infringing on Citizens' Personal Information]:** Whoever violates national regulations by selling or providing citizens' personal information to others, and the circumstances are serious, shall be sentenced to imprisonment for not more than 3 years or criminal detention, and may also be fined or face separate fines. If the circumstances are particularly serious, the offender shall be sentenced to imprisonment for more than 3 years but less than 7 years and shall be fined. Those who violate national regulations by selling or providing citizens' personal information obtained during the performance of their duties or provision of services to others shall be punished more severely in accordance with the preceding paragraph. Those who illegally obtain citizens' personal information through theft or other means shall be punished according to the provisions of the first paragraph. If an entity commits any of the offenses described in the preceding three paragraphs, the entity shall be fined, and the directly responsible personnel and other directly liable individuals shall be punished in accordance with the provisions of each respective paragraph. **Article 285 [Crime of Illegally Accessing Computer Information Systems]:** Whoever violates national regulations by unlawfully accessing computer information systems related to state affairs, national defense construction, or cutting-edge scientific and technological fields shall be sentenced to imprisonment for not more than 3 years or criminal detention.	Acts such as infringing on citizens' personal information, illegally obtaining data from computer information systems, illegally controlling computer information systems, and destroying computer information systems have been criminalised.

EU		**[Crime of Illegally Obtaining Data from Computer Information Systems and Illegally Controlling Computer Information Systems]:** Whoever violates national regulations by accessing computer information systems not mentioned in the preceding paragraph or by employing other technical means to obtain data stored, processed, or transmitted in such systems, or by illegally controlling such computer information systems, and if the circumstances are serious, shall be sentenced to imprisonment for not more than 3 years or criminal detention, and may also be fined or face separate fines; if the circumstances are particularly serious, the offender shall be sentenced to imprisonment for more than 3 years but less than 7 years and shall be fined. **[Crime of Providing Programs or Tools for Illegally Accessing or Controlling Computer Information Systems]:** Whoever provides programs or tools specifically intended for illegally accessing or controlling computer information systems, or who knowingly provides programs or tools to others for engaging in unlawful access or control of computer information systems, shall be punished according to the provisions of the preceding paragraph if the circumstances are serious. If an entity commits any of the offenses described in the preceding three paragraphs, the entity shall be fined, and the directly responsible personnel and other directly liable individuals shall be punished in accordance with the provisions of each respective paragraph. **Article 286 [Crime of Destroying Computer Information Systems]:** Whoever violates national regulations by deleting, modifying, adding to, or interfering with the functions of computer information systems, resulting in the inability of the systems to operate normally, and if the consequences are severe, shall be sentenced to imprisonment for not more than 5 years or criminal detention; if the consequences are particularly severe, the offender shall be sentenced to imprisonment for more than 5 years. Whoever violates national regulations by deleting, modifying, or adding to the data and applications stored, processed, or transmitted in computer information systems, and if the consequences are severe, shall be punished in accordance with the provisions of the preceding paragraph. Those who intentionally create or disseminate computer viruses or other destructive programs that affect the normal operation of computer systems, and if the consequences are severe, shall be punished according to the provisions of the first paragraph. If an entity commits any of the offenses described in the preceding three paragraphs, the entity shall be fined, and the directly responsible personnel and other directly liable individuals shall be punished in accordance with the provisions of the first paragraph.	
General Data Protection Regulation	May 25, 2018	**Article 5: Principles Relating to Processing of Personal Data** 1. Personal data shall be: (a) processed lawfully, fairly and in a transparent manner in relation to the data subject ('lawfulness, fairness and transparency'); (b) collected for specified, explicit and legitimate purposes and not further processed in a manner that is incompatible with those purposes; further processing for archiving purposes in the public interest, scientific or historical research purposes or statistical purposes shall, in accordance with Article 89(1), not be considered to be incompatible with the initial purposes ('purpose limitation');	• Personal data must be processed lawfully, fairly, and transparently. • Data collection and processing should be adequate, relevant, and limited to what is necessary (data minimisation).

(continued)

Table 1 (continued)

Regulatory document name	Effective date	Article content	Key insights
		(c) adequate, relevant and limited to what is necessary in relation to the purposes for which they are processed ('data minimisation'); (d) accurate and, where necessary, kept up to date; every reasonable step must be taken to ensure that personal data that are inaccurate, having regard to the purposes for which they are processed, are erased or rectified without delay ('accuracy'); (e) kept in a form which permits identification of data subjects for no longer than is necessary for the purposes for which the personal data are processed; personal data may be stored for longer periods insofar as the personal data will be processed solely for archiving purposes in the public interest, scientific or historical research purposes or statistical purposes in accordance with Article 89(1) subject to implementation of the appropriate technical and organisational measures required by this Regulation in order to safeguard the rights and freedoms of the data subject ('storage limitation'); (f) processed in a manner that ensures appropriate security of the personal data, including protection against unauthorised or unlawful processing and against accidental loss, destruction or damage, using appropriate technical or organisational measures ('integrity and confidentiality'). 2. The controller shall be responsible for, and be able to demonstrate compliance with, paragraph 1 ('accountability'). **Article 6: Lawfulness of Processing** 1. Processing shall be lawful only if and to the extent that at least one of the following applies: (a) the data subject has given consent to the processing of his or her personal data for one or more specific purposes; (b) processing is necessary for the performance of a contract to which the data subject is party or in order to take steps at the request of the data subject prior to entering into a contract; (c) processing is necessary for compliance with a legal obligation to which the controller is subject; (d) processing is necessary in order to protect the vital interests of the data subject or of another natural person; (e) processing is necessary for the performance of a task carried out in the public interest or in the exercise of official authority vested in the controller; (f) processing is necessary for the purposes of the legitimate interests pursued by the controller or by a third party, except where such interests are overridden by the interests or fundamental rights and freedoms of the data subject which require protection of personal data, in particular where the data subject is a child. Point (f) of the first subparagraph shall not apply to processing carried out by public authorities in the performance of their tasks. 2. Member States may maintain or introduce more specific provisions to adapt the application of the rules of this Regulation with regard to processing for compliance with points (c) and (e) of paragraph 1 by determining more precisely specific requirements for the processing and other measures to ensure lawful and fair processing including for other specific processing situations as provided for in Chapter IX.	• The retention period for personal data should not exceed the necessary time. • Personal data should be processed appropriately to prevent unauthorised or unlawful processing, as well as accidental loss, destruction, or damage, ensuring security and confidentiality. • Data subjects must provide explicit consent for the processing of their personal data. • Data subjects have the right to withdraw consent at any time. • Processing special categories of personal data must adhere to strict regulations. • Sensitive data can only be processed in specific circumstances.

		3. The basis for the processing referred to in point (c) and (e) of paragraph 1 shall be laid down by: (a) Union law; or (b) Member State law to which the controller is subject. The purpose of the processing shall be determined in that legal basis or, as regards the processing referred to in point (e) of paragraph 1, shall be necessary for the performance of a task carried out in the public interest or in the exercise of official authority vested in the controller. That legal basis may contain specific provisions to adapt the application of rules of this Regulation, inter alia: the general conditions governing the lawfulness of processing by the controller; the types of data which are subject to the processing; the data subjects concerned; the entities to, and the purposes for which, the personal data may be disclosed; the purpose limitation; storage periods; and processing operations and processing procedures, including measures to ensure lawful and fair processing such as those for other specific processing situations as provided for in Chapter IX. The Union or the Member State law shall meet an objective of public interest and be proportionate to the legitimate aim pursued. 4. Where the processing for a purpose other than that for which the personal data have been collected is not based on the data subject's consent or on a Union or Member State law which constitutes a necessary and proportionate measure in a democratic society to safeguard the objectives referred to in Article 23(1), the controller shall, in order to ascertain whether processing for another purpose is compatible with the purpose for which the personal data are initially collected, take into account, inter alia: (a) any link between the purposes for which the personal data have been collected and the purposes of the intended further processing; (b) the context in which the personal data have been collected, in particular regarding the relationship between data subjects and the controller; (c) the nature of the personal data, in particular whether special categories of personal data are processed, pursuant to Article 9, or whether personal data related to criminal convictions and offences are processed, pursuant to Article 10; (d) the possible consequences of the intended further processing for data subjects; (e) the existence of appropriate safeguards, which may include encryption or pseudonymisation. **Article 7: Conditions for Consent** 1. Where processing is based on consent, the controller shall be able to demonstrate that the data subject has consented to processing of his or her personal data. 2. If the data subject's consent is given in the context of a written declaration which also concerns other matters, the request for consent shall be presented in a manner which is clearly distinguishable from the other matters, in an intelligible and easily accessible form, using clear and plain language. Any part of such a declaration which constitutes an infringement of this Regulation shall not be binding. 3. The data subject shall have the right to withdraw his or her consent at any time. The withdrawal of consent shall not affect the lawfulness of processing based on consent before its withdrawal. Prior to giving consent, the data subject shall be informed thereof. It shall be as easy to withdraw as to give consent.	• When collecting personal data, controllers must provide data subjects with clear, transparent, and detailed information. • Controllers must promptly notify data subjects in the event of a high-risk personal data breach, unless the situation has been controlled. • In certain situations, organisations are required to appoint a Data Protection Officer. • Controllers must conduct a data protection impact assessment before processing data that may pose a high risk to the rights and freedoms of individuals. • Violations will be subject to penalties.

(continued)

Table 1 (continued)

Regulatory document name	Effective date	Article content	Key insights
		4. When assessing whether consent is freely given, utmost account shall be taken of whether, inter alia, the performance of a contract, including the provision of a service, is conditional on consent to the processing of personal data that is not necessary for the performance of that contract. **Article 9: Processing of Special Categories of Personal Data** 1. Processing of personal data revealing racial or ethnic origin, political opinions, religious or philosophical beliefs, or trade union membership, and the processing of genetic data, biometric data for the purpose of uniquely identifying a natural person, data concerning health or data concerning a natural person's sex life or sexual orientation shall be prohibited. 2. Paragraph 1 shall not apply if one of the following applies: (a) the data subject has given explicit consent to the processing of those personal data for one or more specified purposes, except where Union or Member State law provide that the prohibition referred to in paragraph 1 may not be lifted by the data subject; (b) processing is necessary for the purposes of carrying out the obligations and exercising specific rights of the controller or of the data subject in the field of employment and social security and social protection law in so far as it is authorised by Union or Member State law or a collective agreement pursuant to Member State law providing for appropriate safeguards for the fundamental rights and the interests of the data subject; (c) processing is necessary to protect the vital interests of the data subject or of another natural person where the data subject is physically or legally incapable of giving consent; (d) processing is carried out in the course of its legitimate activities with appropriate safeguards by a foundation, association or any other not-for-profit body with a political, philosophical, religious or trade union aim and on condition that the processing relates solely to the members or to former members of the body or to persons who have regular contact with it in connection with its purposes and that the personal data are not disclosed outside that body without the consent of the data subjects; (e) processing relates to personal data which are manifestly made public by the data subject; (f) processing is necessary for the establishment, exercise or defence of legal claims or whenever courts are acting in their judicial capacity; (g) processing is necessary for reasons of substantial public interest, on the basis of Union or Member State law which shall be proportionate to the aim pursued, respect the essence of the right to data protection and provide for suitable and specific measures to safeguard the fundamental rights and the interests of the data subject; (h) processing is necessary for the purposes of preventive or occupational medicine, for the assessment of the working capacity of the employee, medical diagnosis, the provision of health or social care or treatment or the management of health or social care systems and services on the basis of Union or Member State law or pursuant to contract with a health professional and subject to the conditions and safeguards referred to in paragraph 3;	

		(i) processing is necessary for reasons of public interest in the area of public health, such as protecting against serious cross-border threats to health or ensuring high standards of quality and safety of health care and of medicinal products or medical devices, on the basis of Union or Member State law which provides for suitable and specific measures to safeguard the rights and freedoms of the data subject, in particular professional secrecy; (j) processing is necessary for archiving purposes in the public interest, scientific or historical research purposes or statistical purposes in accordance with Article 89(1) based on Union or Member State law which shall be proportionate to the aim pursued, respect the essence of the right to data protection and provide for suitable and specific measures to safeguard the fundamental rights and the interests of the data subject. 3. Personal data referred to in paragraph 1 may be processed for the purposes referred to in point (h) of paragraph 2 when those data are processed by or under the responsibility of a professional subject to the obligation of professional secrecy under Union or Member State law or rules established by national competent bodies or by another person also subject to an obligation of secrecy under Union or Member State law or rules established by national competent bodies. 4. Member States may maintain or introduce further conditions, including limitations, with regard to the processing of genetic data, biometric data or data concerning health. **Article 13: Information to Be Provided Where Personal Data Are Collected from the Data Subject** 1. Where personal data relating to a data subject are collected from the data subject, the controller shall, at the time when personal data are obtained, provide the data subject with all of the following information: (a) the identity and the contact details of the controller and, where applicable, of the controller's representative; (b) the contact details of the data protection officer, where applicable; (c) the purposes of the processing for which the personal data are intended as well as the legal basis for the processing; (d) where the processing is based on point (f) of Article 6(1), the legitimate interests pursued by the controller or by a third party; (e) the recipients or categories of recipients of the personal data, if any; (f) where applicable, the fact that the controller intends to transfer personal data to a third country or international organisation and the existence or absence of an adequacy decision by the Commission, or in the case of transfers referred to in Article 46 or 47, or the second subparagraph of Article 49(1), reference to the appropriate or suitable safeguards and the means by which to obtain a copy of them or where they have been made available.	

(continued)

Table 1 (continued)

Regulatory document name	Effective date	Article content	Key insights
		2. In addition to the information referred to in paragraph 1, the controller shall, at the time when personal data are obtained, provide the data subject with the following further information necessary to ensure fair and transparent processing: (a) the period for which the personal data will be stored, or if that is not possible, the criteria used to determine that period; (b) the existence of the right to request from the controller access to and rectification or erasure of personal data or restriction of processing concerning the data subject or to object to processing as well as the right to data portability; (c) where the processing is based on point (a) of Article 6(1) or point (a) of Article 9(2), the existence of the right to withdraw consent at any time, without affecting the lawfulness of processing based on consent before its withdrawal; (d) the right to lodge a complaint with a supervisory authority; (e) whether the provision of personal data is a statutory or contractual requirement, or a requirement necessary to enter into a contract, as well as whether the data subject is obliged to provide the personal data and of the possible consequences of failure to provide such data; (f) the existence of automated decision-making, including profiling, referred to in Article 22(1) and (4) and, at least in those cases, meaningful information about the logic involved, as well as the significance and the envisaged consequences of such processing for the data subject. 3. Where the controller intends to further process the personal data for a purpose other than that for which the personal data were collected, the controller shall provide the data subject prior to that further processing with information on that other purpose and with any relevant further information as referred to in paragraph 2. 4. Paragraphs 1, 2 and 3 shall not apply where and insofar as the data subject already has the information. **Article 25: Data Protection by Design and by Default** 1. Taking into account the state of the art, the cost of implementation and the nature, scope, context and purposes of processing as well as the risks of varying likelihood and severity for rights and freedoms of natural persons posed by the processing, the controller shall, both at the time of the determination of the means for processing and at the time of the processing itself, implement appropriate technical and organisational measures, such as pseudonymisation, which are designed to implement data-protection principles, such as data minimisation, in an effective manner and to integrate the necessary safeguards into the processing in order to meet the requirements of this Regulation and protect the rights of data subjects. 2. The controller shall implement appropriate technical and organisational measures for ensuring that, by default, only personal data which are necessary for each specific purpose of the processing are processed. That obligation applies to the amount of personal data collected, the extent of their processing, the period of their storage and their accessibility. In particular, such measures shall ensure that by default personal data are not made accessible without the individual's intervention to an indefinite number of natural persons. 3. An approved certification mechanism pursuant to Article 42 may be used as an element to demonstrate compliance with the requirements set out in paragraphs 1 and 2 of this Article.	

		Article 34: Communication of a Personal Data Breach to the Data Subject 1. When the personal data breach is likely to result in a high risk to the rights and freedoms of natural persons, the controller shall communicate the personal data breach to the data subject without undue delay. 2. The communication to the data subject referred to in paragraph 1 of this Article shall describe in clear and plain language the nature of the personal data breach and contain at least the information and measures referred to in points (b), (c) and (d) of Article 33(3). 3. The communication to the data subject referred to in paragraph 1 shall not be required if any of the following conditions are met: (a) the controller has implemented appropriate technical and organisational protection measures, and those measures were applied to the personal data affected by the personal data breach, in particular those that render the personal data unintelligible to any person who is not authorised to access it, such as encryption; (b) the controller has taken subsequent measures which ensure that the high risk to the rights and freedoms of data subjects referred to in paragraph 1 is no longer likely to materialise; (c) it would involve disproportionate effort. In such a case, there shall instead be a public communication or similar measure whereby the data subjects are informed in an equally effective manner. 4. If the controller has not already communicated the personal data breach to the data subject, the supervisory authority, having considered the likelihood of the personal data breach resulting in a high risk, may require it to do so or may decide that any of the conditions referred to in paragraph 3 are met. **Article 35: Data Protection Impact Assessment** 1. Where a type of processing in particular using new technologies, and taking into account the nature, scope, context and purposes of the processing, is likely to result in a high risk to the rights and freedoms of natural persons, the controller shall, prior to the processing, carry out an assessment of the impact of the envisaged processing operations on the protection of personal data. A single assessment may address a set of similar processing operations that present similar high risks. 2. The controller shall seek the advice of the data protection officer, where designated, when carrying out a data protection impact assessment. 3. A data protection impact assessment referred to in paragraph 1 shall in particular be required in the case of: (a) a systematic and extensive evaluation of personal aspects relating to natural persons which is based on automated processing, including profiling, and on which decisions are based that produce legal effects concerning the natural person or similarly significantly affect the natural person; (b) processing on a large scale of special categories of data referred to in Article 9(1), or of personal data relating to criminal convictions and offences referred to in Article 10; or (c) a systematic monitoring of a publicly accessible area on a large scale.	

(continued)

Table 1 (continued)

Regulatory document name	Effective date	Article content	Key insights
		4. The supervisory authority shall establish and make public a list of the kind of processing operations which are subject to the requirement for a data protection impact assessment pursuant to paragraph 1. The supervisory authority shall communicate those lists to the Board referred to in Article 68. 5. The supervisory authority may also establish and make public a list of the kind of processing operations for which no data protection impact assessment is required. The supervisory authority shall communicate those lists to the Board. 6. Prior to the adoption of the lists referred to in paragraphs 4 and 5, the competent supervisory authority shall apply the consistency mechanism referred to in Article 63 where such lists involve processing activities which are related to the offering of goods or services to data subjects or to the monitoring of their behaviour in several Member States, or may substantially affect the free movement of personal data within the Union. 7. The assessment shall contain at least: (a) a systematic description of the envisaged processing operations and the purposes of the processing, including, where applicable, the legitimate interest pursued by the controller; (b) an assessment of the necessity and proportionality of the processing operations in relation to the purposes; (c) an assessment of the risks to the rights and freedoms of data subjects referred to in paragraph 1; and (d) the measures envisaged to address the risks, including safeguards, security measures and mechanisms to ensure the protection of personal data and to demonstrate compliance with this Regulation taking into account the rights and legitimate interests of data subjects and other persons concerned. 8. Compliance with approved codes of conduct referred to in Article 40 by the relevant controllers or processors shall be taken into due account in assessing the impact of the processing operations performed by such controllers or processors, in particular for the purposes of a data protection impact assessment. 9. Where appropriate, the controller shall seek the views of data subjects or their representatives on the intended processing, without prejudice to the protection of commercial or public interests or the security of processing operations. 10. Where processing pursuant to point (c) or (e) of Article 6(1) has a legal basis in Union law or in the law of the Member State to which the controller is subject, that law regulates the specific processing operation or set of operations in question, and a data protection impact assessment has already been carried out as part of a general impact assessment in the context of the adoption of that legal basis, paragraphs 1 to 7 shall not apply unless Member States deem it to be necessary to carry out such an assessment prior to processing activities. 11. Where necessary, the controller shall carry out a review to assess if processing is performed in accordance with the data protection impact assessment at least when there is a change of the risk represented by processing operations.	

Artificial Intelligence Act	Approved on May 21, 2024	**Article 10: Data and Data Governance** 1. High-risk AI systems which make use of techniques involving the training of AI models with data shall be developed on the basis of training, validation and testing data sets that meet the quality criteria referred to in paragraphs 2 to 5 whenever such data sets are used. 2. Training, validation and testing data sets shall be subject to data governance and management practices appropriate for the intended purpose of the high-risk AI system. Those practices shall concern in particular: (a) the relevant design choices; (b) data collection processes and the origin of data, and in the case of personal data, the original purpose of the data collection; (c) relevant data-preparation processing operations, such as annotation, labelling, cleaning, updating, enrichment and aggregation; (d) the formulation of assumptions, in particular with respect to the information that the data are supposed to measure and represent; (e) an assessment of the availability, quantity and suitability of the data sets that are needed; (f) examination in view of possible biases that are likely to affect the health and safety of persons, have a negative impact on fundamental rights or lead to discrimination prohibited under Union law, especially where data outputs influence inputs for future operations; (g) appropriate measures to detect, prevent and mitigate possible biases identified according to point (f); (h) the identification of relevant data gaps or shortcomings that prevent compliance with this Regulation, and how those gaps and shortcomings can be addressed. 3. Training, validation and testing data sets shall be relevant, sufficiently representative, and to the best extent possible, free of errors and complete in view of the intended purpose. They shall have the appropriate statistical properties, including, where applicable, as regards the persons or groups of persons in relation to whom the high-risk AI system is intended to be used. Those characteristics of the data sets may be met at the level of individual data sets or at the level of a combination thereof. 4. Data sets shall take into account, to the extent required by the intended purpose, the characteristics or elements that are particular to the specific geographical, contextual, behavioural or functional setting within which the high-risk AI system is intended to be used. 5. To the extent that it is strictly necessary for the purpose of ensuring bias detection and correction in relation to the high-risk AI systems in accordance with paragraph (2), points (f) and (g) of this Article, the providers of such systems may exceptionally process special categories of personal data, subject to appropriate safeguards for the fundamental rights and freedoms of natural persons. In addition to the provisions set out in Regulations (EU) 2016/679 and (EU) 2018/1725 and Directive (EU) 2016/680, all the following conditions must be met in order for such processing to occur: (a) the bias detection and correction cannot be effectively fulfilled by processing other data, including synthetic or anonymised data;	• There is a need for a clear understanding of data sources and the purpose of collection. • Strong security measures must be implemented for sensitive data. • Only authorised personnel can access sensitive data; sharing is not allowed. • Sensitive data must be deleted once bias is corrected or when it is no longer needed. • Technical measures must be in place to ensure cybersecurity and data safety. • Transparency of interpretable outputs in high-risk AI systems is essential. • Authorities must maintain the confidentiality of information and data. • The European Data Protection Supervisor can impose fines for non-compliance.

(continued)

Table 1 (continued)

Regulatory document name	Effective date	Article content	Key insights
		(b) the special categories of personal data are subject to technical limitations on the re-use of the personal data, and state-of-the-art security and privacy-preserving measures, including pseudonymisation; (c) the special categories of personal data are subject to measures to ensure that the personal data processed are secured, protected, subject to suitable safeguards, including strict controls and documentation of the access, to avoid misuse and ensure that only authorised persons have access to those personal data with appropriate confidentiality obligations; (d) the special categories of personal data are not to be transmitted, transferred or otherwise accessed by other parties; (e) the special categories of personal data are deleted once the bias has been corrected or the personal data has reached the end of its retention period, whichever comes first; (f) the records of processing activities pursuant to Regulations (EU) 2016/679 and (EU) 2018/1725 and Directive (EU) 2016/680 include the reasons why the processing of special categories of personal data was strictly necessary to detect and correct biases, and why that objective could not be achieved by processing other data. 6. For the development of high-risk AI systems not using techniques involving the training of AI models, paragraphs 2 to 5 apply only to the testing data sets. **Article 13: Transparency and Provision of Information to Deployers** 1. High-risk AI systems shall be designed and developed in such a way as to ensure that their operation is sufficiently transparent to enable deployers to interpret a system's output and use it appropriately. An appropriate type and degree of transparency shall be ensured with a view to achieving compliance with the relevant obligations of the provider and deployer set out in Section 3. 2. High-risk AI systems shall be accompanied by instructions for use in an appropriate digital format or otherwise that include concise, complete, correct and clear information that is relevant, accessible and comprehensible to deployers. 3. The instructions for use shall contain at least the following information: (a) the identity and the contact details of the provider and, where applicable, of its authorised representative; (b) the characteristics, capabilities and limitations of performance of the high-risk AI system, including: (i) its intended purpose; (ii) the level of accuracy, including its metrics, robustness and cybersecurity referred to in Article 15 against which the high-risk AI system has been tested and validated and which can be expected, and any known and foreseeable circumstances that may have an impact on that expected level of accuracy, robustness and cybersecurity; (iii) any known or foreseeable circumstance, related to the use of the high-risk AI system in accordance with its intended purpose or under conditions of reasonably foreseeable misuse, which may lead to risks to the health and safety or fundamental rights referred to in Article 9(2); (iv) where applicable, the technical capabilities and characteristics of the high-risk AI system to provide information that is relevant to explain its output; (v) when appropriate, its performance regarding specific persons or groups of persons on which the system is intended to be used; (vi) when appropriate, specifications for the input data, or any other relevant information in terms of the training, validation and testing data sets used, taking into account the intended purpose of the high-risk AI system; (vii) where applicable, information to enable deployers to interpret the output of the high-risk AI system and use it appropriately;	

		(c) the changes to the high-risk AI system and its performance which have been predetermined by the provider at the moment of the initial conformity assessment, if any; (d) the human oversight measures referred to in Article 14, including the technical measures put in place to facilitate the interpretation of the outputs of the high-risk AI systems by the deployers; (e) the computational and hardware resources needed, the expected lifetime of the high-risk AI system and any necessary maintenance and care measures, including their frequency, to ensure the proper functioning of that AI system, including as regards software updates; (f) where relevant, a description of the mechanisms included within the high-risk AI system that allows deployers to properly collect, store and interpret the logs in accordance with Article 12. **Article 15: Accuracy, Robustness and Cybersecurity** 1. High-risk AI systems shall be designed and developed in such a way that they achieve an appropriate level of accuracy, robustness, and cybersecurity, and that they perform consistently in those respects throughout their lifecycle. 2. To address the technical aspects of how to measure the appropriate levels of accuracy and robustness set out in paragraph 1 and any other relevant performance metrics, the Commission shall, in cooperation with relevant stakeholders and organisations such as metrology and benchmarking authorities, encourage, as appropriate, the development of benchmarks and measurement methodologies. 3. The levels of accuracy and the relevant accuracy metrics of high-risk AI systems shall be declared in the accompanying instructions of use. 4. High-risk AI systems shall be as resilient as possible regarding errors, faults or inconsistencies that may occur within the system or the environment in which the system operates, in particular due to their interaction with natural persons or other systems. Technical and organisational measures shall be taken in this regard. The robustness of high-risk AI systems may be achieved through technical redundancy solutions, which may include backup or fail-safe plans. High-risk AI systems that continue to learn after being placed on the market or put into service shall be developed in such a way as to eliminate or reduce as far as possible the risk of possibly biased outputs influencing input for future operations (feedback loops), and as to ensure that any such feedback loops are duly addressed with appropriate mitigation measures. 5. High-risk AI systems shall be resilient against attempts by unauthorised third parties to alter their use, outputs or performance by exploiting system vulnerabilities. The technical solutions aiming to ensure the cybersecurity of high-risk AI systems shall be appropriate to the relevant circumstances and the risks. The technical solutions to address AI specific vulnerabilities shall include, where appropriate, measures to prevent, detect, respond to, resolve and control for attacks trying to manipulate the training data set (data poisoning), or pre-trained components used in training (model poisoning), inputs designed to cause the AI model to make a mistake (adversarial examples or model evasion), confidentiality attacks or model flaws.	

(continued)

Table 1 (continued)

Regulatory document name	Effective date	Article content	Key insights
		Article 17: Quality Management System 1. Providers of high-risk AI systems shall put a quality management system in place that ensures compliance with this Regulation. That system shall be documented in a systematic and orderly manner in the form of written policies, procedures and instructions, and shall include at least the following aspects: (a) a strategy for regulatory compliance, including compliance with conformity assessment procedures and procedures for the management of modifications to the high-risk AI system; (b) techniques, procedures and systematic actions to be used for the design, design control and design verification of the high-risk AI system; (c) techniques, procedures and systematic actions to be used for the development, quality control and quality assurance of the high-risk AI system; (d) examination, test and validation procedures to be carried out before, during and after the development of the high-risk AI system, and the frequency with which they have to be carried out; (e) technical specifications, including standards, to be applied and, where the relevant harmonised standards are not applied in full or do not cover all of the relevant requirements set out in Section 2, the means to be used to ensure that the high-risk AI system complies with those requirements; (f) systems and procedures for data management, including data acquisition, data collection, data analysis, data labelling, data storage, data filtration, data mining, data aggregation, data retention and any other operation regarding the data that is performed before and for the purpose of the placing on the market or the putting into service of high-risk AI systems; (g) the risk management system referred to in Article 9; (h) the setting-up, implementation and maintenance of a post-market monitoring system, in accordance with Article 72; (i) procedures related to the reporting of a serious incident in accordance with Article 73; (j) the handling of communication with national competent authorities, other relevant authorities, including those providing or supporting the access to data, notified bodies, other operators, customers or other interested parties; (k) systems and procedures for record-keeping of all relevant documentation and information; (l) resource management, including security-of-supply related measures; (m) an accountability framework setting out the responsibilities of the management and other staff with regard to all the aspects listed in this paragraph. 2. The implementation of the aspects referred to in paragraph 1 shall be proportionate to the size of the provider's organisation. Providers shall, in any event, respect the degree of rigour and the level of protection required to ensure the compliance of their high-risk AI systems with this Regulation. 3. Providers of high-risk AI systems that are subject to obligations regarding quality management systems or an equivalent function under relevant sectoral Union law may include the aspects listed in paragraph 1 as part of the quality management systems pursuant to that law.	

		4. For providers that are financial institutions subject to requirements regarding their internal governance, arrangements or processes under Union financial services law, the obligation to put in place a quality management system, with the exception of paragraph 1, points (g), (h) and (i) of this Article, shall be deemed to be fulfilled by complying with the rules on internal governance arrangements or processes pursuant to the relevant Union financial services law. To that end, any harmonised standards referred to in Article 40 shall be taken into account. **Article 78: Confidentiality** 1. The Commission, market surveillance authorities and notified bodies and any other natural or legal person involved in the application of this Regulation shall, in accordance with Union or national law, respect the confidentiality of information and data obtained in carrying out their tasks and activities in such a manner as to protect, in particular: (a) the intellectual property rights and confidential business information or trade secrets of a natural or legal person, including source code, except in the cases referred to in Article 5 of Directive (EU) 2016/943 of the European Parliament and of the Council[57]; (b) the effective implementation of this Regulation, in particular for the purposes of inspections, investigations or audits; (c) public and national security interests; (d) the conduct of criminal or administrative proceedings; (e) information classified pursuant to Union or national law. 2. The authorities involved in the application of this Regulation pursuant to paragraph 1 shall request only data that is strictly necessary for the assessment of the risk posed by AI systems and for the exercise of their powers in accordance with this Regulation and with Regulation (EU) 2019/1020. They shall put in place adequate and effective cybersecurity measures to protect the security and confidentiality of the information and data obtained, and shall delete the data collected as soon as it is no longer needed for the purpose for which it was obtained, in accordance with applicable Union or national law. 3. Without prejudice to paragraphs 1 and 2, information exchanged on a confidential basis between the national competent authorities or between national competent authorities and the Commission shall not be disclosed without prior consultation of the originating national competent authority and the deployer when high-risk AI systems referred to in point 1, 6 or 7 of Annex III are used by law enforcement, border control, immigration or asylum authorities and when such disclosure would jeopardise public and national security interests. This exchange of information shall not cover sensitive operational data in relation to the activities of law enforcement, border control, immigration or asylum authorities. When the law enforcement, immigration or asylum authorities are providers of high-risk AI systems referred to in point 1, 6 or 7 of Annex III, the technical documentation referred to in Annex IV shall remain within the premises of those authorities. Those authorities shall ensure that the market surveillance authorities referred to in Article 74(8) and (9), as applicable, can, upon request, immediately access the documentation or obtain a copy thereof. Only staff of the market surveillance authority holding the appropriate level of security clearance shall be allowed to access that documentation or any copy thereof.	

(continued)

Table 1 (continued)

Regulatory document name	Effective date	Article content	Key insights
		4. Paragraphs 1, 2 and 3 shall not affect the rights or obligations of the Commission, Member States and their relevant authorities, as well as those of notified bodies, with regard to the exchange of information and the dissemination of warnings, including in the context of cross-border cooperation, nor shall they affect the obligations of the parties concerned to provide information under criminal law of the Member States. 5. The Commission and Member States may exchange, where necessary and in accordance with relevant provisions of international and trade agreements, confidential information with regulatory authorities of third countries with which they have concluded bilateral or multilateral confidentiality arrangements guaranteeing an adequate level of confidentiality. **Article 100: Administrative Fines on Union Institutions, Bodies Offices and Agencies** 1. The European Data Protection Supervisor may impose administrative fines on Union institutions, bodies, offices and agencies falling within the scope of this Regulation. When deciding whether to impose an administrative fine and when deciding on the amount of the administrative fine in each individual case, all relevant circumstances of the specific situation shall be taken into account and due regard shall be given to the following: (a) the nature, gravity and duration of the infringement and of its consequences, taking into account the purpose of the AI system concerned, as well as, where appropriate, the number of affected persons and the level of damage suffered by them; (b) the degree of responsibility of the Union institution, body, office or agency, taking into account technical and organisational measures implemented by them; (c) any action taken by the Union institution, body, office or agency to mitigate the damage suffered by affected persons; (d) the degree of cooperation with the European Data Protection Supervisor in order to remedy the infringement and mitigate the possible adverse effects of the infringement, including compliance with any of the measures previously ordered by the European Data Protection Supervisor against the Union institution, body, office or agency concerned with regard to the same subject matter; (e) any similar previous infringements by the Union institution, body, office or agency; (f) the manner in which the infringement became known to the European Data Protection Supervisor, in particular whether, and if so to what extent, the Union institution, body, office or agency notified the infringement; (g) the annual budget of the Union institution, body, office or agency. 2. Non-compliance with the prohibition of the AI practices referred to in Article 5 shall be subject to administrative fines of up to EUR 1 500 000.	

		3. The non-compliance of the AI system with any requirements or obligations under this Regulation, other than those laid down in Articles 5, shall be subject to administrative fines of up to EUR 750 000. 4. Before taking decisions pursuant to this Article, the European Data Protection Supervisor shall give the Union institution, body, office or agency which is the subject of the proceedings conducted by the European Data Protection Supervisor the opportunity of being heard on the matter regarding the possible infringement. The European Data Protection Supervisor shall base his or her decisions only on elements and circumstances on which the parties concerned have been able to comment. Complainants, if any, shall be associated closely with the proceedings. 5. The rights of defence of the parties concerned shall be fully respected in the proceedings. They shall be entitled to have access to the European Data Protection Supervisor's file, subject to the legitimate interest of individuals or undertakings in the protection of their personal data or business secrets. 6. Funds collected by imposition of fines in this Article shall contribute to the general budget of the Union. The fines shall not affect the effective operation of the Union institution, body, office or agency fined. 7. The European Data Protection Supervisor shall, on an annual basis, notify the Commission of the administrative fines it has imposed pursuant to this Article and of any litigation or judicial proceedings it has initiated.	

Table 2 Regulatory provisions on human users' rights protection in AI-driven systems in China and the EU

Regulatory document name	Effective date	Article content	Key insights
China			
The E-Commerce Law	January 1, 2019	**Article 35:** Operators of e-commerce platforms must not use service agreements, trading rules, or technological means to impose unreasonable restrictions or conditions on transactions conducted by platform operators within the platform, including transaction prices and transactions with other operators. Additionally, they must not charge unreasonable fees to platform operators.	• The use of technological means to engage in unfair transactions or set unreasonable transaction prices is prohibited.
The Personal Information Protection Law	November 1, 2021	**Article 5:** The processing of personal information shall adhere to the principles of legality, legitimacy, necessity, and integrity, and shall not be conducted through misleading, fraudulent, or coercive means. **Article 8:** The processing of personal information shall ensure the quality of such information, avoiding any adverse effects on individuals' rights and interests resulting from inaccuracies or incompleteness in the personal information. **Article 24:** Personal information processors that use personal information for automated decision-making must ensure the transparency of the decisions and the fairness and justice of the outcomes. They must not implement unreasonable differential treatment regarding transaction prices or other transaction conditions for individuals. When pushing information or conducting commercial marketing through automated decision-making, they must also provide options that do not target individual characteristics, or offer individuals an easy way to refuse. When making decisions through automated decision-making that significantly affect the rights and interests of individuals, individuals have the right to request an explanation from the personal information processor and have the right to refuse decisions made solely based on automated decision-making. **Article 44:** Individuals have the right to be informed about the processing of their personal information and the right to decide whether to restrict or refuse others from processing their personal information, unless otherwise provided by laws or administrative regulations.	• Adhere to principles of legality, legitimacy, necessity, and integrity. • Avoid adverse effects on individuals' rights from inaccuracies in personal information. • Ensure transparency and fairness in automated decision-making, prohibiting unreasonable pricing or differential treatment. • Provide non-targeted options or an easy refusal mechanism in automated marketing. • Individuals may request explanations and refuse decisions made solely by automated processes. • Individuals have the right to be informed about data processing and have the right to refuse. • Conduct prior impact assessments before using personal information for automated decision-making.

		Article 55: In any of the following circumstances, personal information processors shall conduct a personal information protection impact assessment in advance and maintain records of the processing activities: 1. Processing sensitive personal information; 2. Utilising personal information for automated decision-making; 3. Entrusting the processing of personal information, providing personal information to other processors, or publicly disclosing personal information; 4. Providing personal information to entities outside the country; 5. Other personal information processing activities that significantly impact the rights of individuals.	
The Provisions on the Administration of Algorithm-Generated Recommendations for Internet Information Services	March 1, 2022	**Article 17:** Algorithm recommendation service providers shall offer users options that do not target their personal characteristics, or provide users with a convenient means to disable algorithm recommendation services. If a user chooses to disable the algorithm recommendation service, the provider shall promptly cease to deliver the relevant service. Algorithm recommendation service providers shall provide users with the functionality to select or delete user labels that are used for algorithm recommendation services and are based on their personal characteristics. When algorithm recommendation service providers apply algorithms that significantly impact users' rights and interests, they shall provide explanations in accordance with the law and bear corresponding responsibilities. **Article 21:** Algorithm recommendation service providers selling goods or offering services to consumers shall protect consumers' rights to fair trading. They shall not engage in unlawful practices such as implementing unreasonable differential treatment based on consumers' preferences, transaction habits, or other characteristics concerning transaction prices and other trading conditions.	• Offer non-targeted options and a means to disable the algorithm recommendation services. • Cease the algorithm recommendation services promptly when disabled by the user. • Allow selection or deletion of user labels. • Provide legal explanations and bear responsibilities when significantly impacting users' rights and interests. • Avoid unreasonable differential treatment based on characteristics.

(continued)

Table 2 (continued)

Regulatory document name	Effective date	Article content	Key insights
The Interim Measures for the Administration of Generative Artificial Intelligence Services	August 15, 2023	**Article 4:** The provision and use of generative artificial intelligence services shall comply with laws and administrative regulations, respect social ethics and moral standards, and adhere to the following provisions: 1. Uphold the core socialist values; it is prohibited to generate content that incites the subversion of state power, overturns the socialist system, endangers national security and interests, damages the national image, incites national division, undermines national unity and social stability, advocates terrorism or extremism, promotes ethnic hatred or discrimination, violence, obscenity, pornography, or disseminates false or harmful information that is prohibited by laws and administrative regulations. 2. During the processes of algorithm design, selection of training data, model generation and optimisation, and service provision, effective measures must be taken to prevent discrimination based on ethnicity, beliefs, nationality, region, gender, age, occupation, health status, and other factors. 3. Respect intellectual property rights and business ethics, maintain trade secrets, and refrain from utilising advantages in algorithms, data, platforms, and other resources to engage in monopolistic or unfair competitive practices. 4. Respect the legitimate rights and interests of others, avoid harming the physical and mental health of individuals, and do not infringe upon others' rights to their image, reputation, honour, privacy, and personal information. 5. Based on the characteristics of the service type, implement effective measures to enhance the transparency of generative artificial intelligence services and improve the accuracy and reliability of generated content.	• Implement effective measures to prevent discrimination. • Respect individuals' legal rights while safeguarding their health and personal rights. • Enhance transparency and improve the accuracy and reliability of generated content.

EU			
General Data Protection Regulation	May 25, 2018	**Article 13: Information to Be Provided Where Personal Data Are Collected from the Data Subject** 1. Where personal data relating to a data subject are collected from the data subject, the controller shall, at the time when personal data are obtained, provide the data subject with all of the following information: (a) the identity and the contact details of the controller and, where applicable, of the controller's representative; (b) the contact details of the data protection officer, where applicable; (c) the purposes of the processing for which the personal data are intended as well as the legal basis for the processing; (d) where the processing is based on point (f) of Article 6(1), the legitimate interests pursued by the controller or by a third party; (e) the recipients or categories of recipients of the personal data, if any; (f) where applicable, the fact that the controller intends to transfer personal data to a third country or international organisation and the existence or absence of an adequacy decision by the Commission, or in the case of transfers referred to in Article 46 or 47, or the second subparagraph of Article 49(1), reference to the appropriate or suitable safeguards and the means by which to obtain a copy of them or where they have been made available. 2. In addition to the information referred to in paragraph 1, the controller shall, at the time when personal data are obtained, provide the data subject with the following further information necessary to ensure fair and transparent processing: (a) the period for which the personal data will be stored, or if that is not possible, the criteria used to determine that period; (b) the existence of the right to request from the controller access to and rectification or erasure of personal data or restriction of processing concerning the data subject or to object to processing as well as the right to data portability; (c) where the processing is based on point (a) of Article 6(1) or point (a) of Article 9(2), the existence of the right to withdraw consent at any time, without affecting the lawfulness of processing based on consent before its withdrawal;	• Individuals must be informed if automated decision-making occurs. • Individuals have the right not to be bound by decisions based solely on automated processing. • Data controllers must implement measures to protect individual rights, including providing human intervention, allowing individuals to express their views, and enabling them to contest decisions. • Decisions based on special categories of personal data are restricted unless specific conditions are met and appropriate safeguards are in place.

(continued)

Table 2 (continued)

Regulatory document name	Effective date	Article content	Key insights
		(d) the right to lodge a complaint with a supervisory authority; (e) whether the provision of personal data is a statutory or contractual requirement, or a requirement necessary to enter into a contract, as well as whether the data subject is obliged to provide the personal data and of the possible consequences of failure to provide such data; (f) the existence of automated decision-making, including profiling, referred to in Article 22(1) and (4) and, at least in those cases, meaningful information about the logic involved, as well as the significance and the envisaged consequences of such processing for the data subject. 3. Where the controller intends to further process the personal data for a purpose other than that for which the personal data were collected, the controller shall provide the data subject prior to that further processing with information on that other purpose and with any relevant further information as referred to in paragraph 2. 4. Paragraphs 1, 2 and 3 shall not apply where and insofar as the data subject already has the information. **Article 22: Automated Individual Decision-Making, Including Profiling** 1. The data subject shall have the right not to be subject to a decision based solely on automated processing, including profiling, which produces legal effects concerning him or her or similarly significantly affects him or her. 2. Paragraph 1 shall not apply if the decision: (a) is necessary for entering into, or performance of, a contract between the data subject and a data controller; (b) is authorised by Union or Member State law to which the controller is subject and which also lays down suitable measures to safeguard the data subject's rights and freedoms and legitimate interests; or (c) is based on the data subject's explicit consent. 3. In the cases referred to in points (a) and (c) of paragraph 2, the data controller shall implement suitable measures to safeguard the data subject's rights and freedoms and legitimate interests, at least the right to obtain human intervention on the part of the controller, to express his or her point of view and to contest the decision. 4. Decisions referred to in paragraph 2 shall not be based on special categories of personal data referred to in Article 9(1), unless point (a) or (g) of Article 9(2) applies and suitable measures to safeguard the data subject's rights and freedoms and legitimate interests are in place.	

Artificial Intelligence Act	Approved on May 21, 2024	**Article 5: Prohibited AI Practices** 1. The following AI practices shall be prohibited: (a) the placing on the market, the putting into service or the use of an AI system that deploys subliminal techniques beyond a person's consciousness or purposefully manipulative or deceptive techniques, with the objective, or the effect of materially distorting the behaviour of a person or a group of persons by appreciably impairing their ability to make an informed decision, thereby causing them to take a decision that they would not have otherwise taken in a manner that causes or is reasonably likely to cause that person, another person or group of persons significant harm; (b) the placing on the market, the putting into service or the use of an AI system that exploits any of the vulnerabilities of a natural person or a specific group of persons due to their age, disability or a specific social or economic situation, with the objective, or the effect, of materially distorting the behaviour of that person or a person belonging to that group in a manner that causes or is reasonably likely to cause that person or another person significant harm; (c) the placing on the market, the putting into service or the use of AI systems for the evaluation or classification of natural persons or groups of persons over a certain period of time based on their social behaviour or known, inferred or predicted personal or personality characteristics, with the social score leading to either or both of the following: (i) detrimental or unfavourable treatment of certain natural persons or groups of persons in social contexts that are unrelated to the contexts in which the data was originally generated or collected; (ii) detrimental or unfavourable treatment of certain natural persons or groups of persons that is unjustified or disproportionate to their social behaviour or its gravity; (d) the placing on the market, the putting into service for this specific purpose, or the use of an AI system for making risk assessments of natural persons in order to assess or predict the risk of a natural person committing a criminal offence, based solely on the profiling of a natural person or on assessing their personality traits and characteristics; this prohibition shall not apply to AI systems used to support the human assessment of the involvement of a person in a criminal activity, which is already based on objective and verifiable facts directly linked to a criminal activity;	• Prohibit using subliminal or manipulative techniques to distort decision-making, exploiting vulnerabilities related to age or disability, evaluating individuals based on social behaviour for unjust treatment, making risk assessments based solely on profiling, creating facial recognition databases through untargeted scraping, inferring emotions in workplaces or education, categorising individuals based on biometric data for sensitive attributes, etc. • High-risk systems must be designed transparently, include usage instructions, and provide relevant information. • High-risk systems require human oversight. • Providers must inform individuals when interacting with AI.

(continued)

Table 2 (continued)

Regulatory document name	Effective date	Article content	Key insights
		(e) the placing on the market, the putting into service for this specific purpose, or the use of AI systems that create or expand facial recognition databases through the untargeted scraping of facial images from the internet or CCTV footage; (f) the placing on the market, the putting into service for this specific purpose, or the use of AI systems to infer emotions of a natural person in the areas of workplace and education institutions, except where the use of the AI system is intended to be put in place or into the market for medical or safety reasons; (g) the placing on the market, the putting into service for this specific purpose, or the use of biometric categorisation systems that categorise individually natural persons based on their biometric data to deduce or infer their race, political opinions, trade union membership, religious or philosophical beliefs, sex life or sexual orientation; this prohibition does not cover any labelling or filtering of lawfully acquired biometric datasets, such as images, based on biometric data or categorising of biometric data in the area of law enforcement;	
		(h) the use of 'real-time' remote biometric identification systems in publicly accessible spaces for the purposes of law enforcement, unless and in so far as such use is strictly necessary for one of the following objectives: (i) the targeted search for specific victims of abduction, trafficking in human beings or sexual exploitation of human beings, as well as the search for missing persons; (ii) the prevention of a specific, substantial and imminent threat to the life or physical safety of natural persons or a genuine and present or genuine and foreseeable threat of a terrorist attack; (iii) the localisation or identification of a person suspected of having committed a criminal offence, for the purpose of conducting a criminal investigation or prosecution or executing a criminal penalty for offences referred to in Annex II and punishable in the Member State concerned by a custodial sentence or a detention order for a maximum period of at least 4 years. Point (h) of the first subparagraph is without prejudice to Article 9 of Regulation (EU) 2016/679 for the processing of biometric data for purposes other than law enforcement.	

		2. The use of 'real-time' remote biometric identification systems in publicly accessible spaces for the purposes of law enforcement for any of the objectives referred to in paragraph 1, first subparagraph, point (h), shall be deployed for the purposes set out in that point only to confirm the identity of the specifically targeted individual, and it shall take into account the following elements: (a) the nature of the situation giving rise to the possible use, in particular the seriousness, probability and scale of the harm that would be caused if the system were not used; (b) the consequences of the use of the system for the rights and freedoms of all persons concerned, in particular the seriousness, probability and scale of those consequences. In addition, the use of 'real-time' remote biometric identification systems in publicly accessible spaces for the purposes of law enforcement for any of the objectives referred to in paragraph 1, first subparagraph, point (h), of this Article shall comply with necessary and proportionate safeguards and conditions in relation to the use in accordance with the national law authorising the use thereof, in particular as regards the temporal, geographic and personal limitations. The use of the 'real-time' remote biometric identification system in publicly accessible spaces shall be authorised only if the law enforcement authority has completed a fundamental rights impact assessment as provided for in Article 27 and has registered the system in the EU database according to Article 49. However, in duly justified cases of urgency, the use of such systems may be commenced without the registration in the EU database, provided that such registration is completed without undue delay.	

(continued)

Table 2 (continued)

Regulatory document name	Effective date	Article content	Key insights
		3. For the purposes of paragraph 1, first subparagraph, point (h) and paragraph 2, each use for the purposes of law enforcement of a 'real-time' remote biometric identification system in publicly accessible spaces shall be subject to a prior authorisation granted by a judicial authority or an independent administrative authority whose decision is binding of the Member State in which the use is to take place, issued upon a reasoned request and in accordance with the detailed rules of national law referred to in paragraph 5. However, in a duly justified situation of urgency, the use of such system may be commenced without an authorisation provided that such authorisation is requested without undue delay, at the latest within 24 h. If such authorisation is rejected, the use shall be stopped with immediate effect and all the data, as well as the results and outputs of that use shall be immediately discarded and deleted. The competent judicial authority or an independent administrative authority whose decision is binding shall grant the authorisation only where it is satisfied, on the basis of objective evidence or clear indications presented to it, that the use of the 'real-time' remote biometric identification system concerned is necessary for, and proportionate to, achieving one of the objectives specified in paragraph 1, first subparagraph, point (h), as identified in the request and, in particular, remains limited to what is strictly necessary concerning the period of time as well as the geographic and personal scope. In deciding on the request, that authority shall take into account the elements referred to in paragraph 2. No decision that produces an adverse legal effect on a person may be taken based solely on the output of the 'real-time' remote biometric identification system. 4. Without prejudice to paragraph 3, each use of a 'real-time' remote biometric identification system in publicly accessible spaces for law enforcement purposes shall be notified to the relevant market surveillance authority and the national data protection authority in accordance with the national rules referred to in paragraph 5. The notification shall, as a minimum, contain the information specified under paragraph 6 and shall not include sensitive operational data.	

		5. A Member State may decide to provide for the possibility to fully or partially authorise the use of 'real-time' remote biometric identification systems in publicly accessible spaces for the purposes of law enforcement within the limits and under the conditions listed in paragraph 1, first subparagraph, point (h), and paragraphs 2 and 3. Member States concerned shall lay down in their national law the necessary detailed rules for the request, issuance and exercise of, as well as supervision and reporting relating to, the authorisations referred to in paragraph 3. Those rules shall also specify in respect of which of the objectives listed in paragraph 1, first subparagraph, point (h), including which of the criminal offences referred to in point (h)(iii) thereof, the competent authorities may be authorised to use those systems for the purposes of law enforcement. Member States shall notify those rules to the Commission at the latest 30 days following the adoption thereof. Member States may introduce, in accordance with Union law, more restrictive laws on the use of remote biometric identification systems. 6. National market surveillance authorities and the national data protection authorities of Member States that have been notified of the use of 'real-time' remote biometric identification systems in publicly accessible spaces for law enforcement purposes pursuant to paragraph 4 shall submit to the Commission annual reports on such use. For that purpose, the Commission shall provide Member States and national market surveillance and data protection authorities with a template, including information on the number of the decisions taken by competent judicial authorities or an independent administrative authority whose decision is binding upon requests for authorisations in accordance with paragraph 3 and their result. 7. The Commission shall publish annual reports on the use of real-time remote biometric identification systems in publicly accessible spaces for law enforcement purposes, based on aggregated data in Member States on the basis of the annual reports referred to in paragraph 6. Those annual reports shall not include sensitive operational data of the related law enforcement activities. 8. This Article shall not affect the prohibitions that apply where an AI practice infringes other Union law.	

(continued)

Table 2 (continued)

Regulatory document name	Effective date	Article content	Key insights
		Article 7: Amendments to Annex III 1. The Commission is empowered to adopt delegated acts in accordance with Article 97 to amend Annex III by adding or modifying use-cases of high-risk AI systems where both of the following conditions are fulfilled: (a) the AI systems are intended to be used in any of the areas listed in Annex III; (b) the AI systems pose a risk of harm to health and safety, or an adverse impact on fundamental rights, and that risk is equivalent to, or greater than, the risk of harm or of adverse impact posed by the high-risk AI systems already referred to in Annex III. 2. When assessing the condition under paragraph 1, point (b), the Commission shall take into account the following criteria: (a) the intended purpose of the AI system; (b) the extent to which an AI system has been used or is likely to be used; (c) the nature and amount of the data processed and used by the AI system, in particular whether special categories of personal data are processed; (d) the extent to which the AI system acts autonomously and the possibility for a human to override a decision or recommendations that may lead to potential harm; (e) the extent to which the use of an AI system has already caused harm to health and safety, has had an adverse impact on fundamental rights or has given rise to significant concerns in relation to the likelihood of such harm or adverse impact, as demonstrated, for example, by reports or documented allegations submitted to national competent authorities or by other reports, as appropriate; (f) the potential extent of such harm or such adverse impact, in particular in terms of its intensity and its ability to affect multiple persons or to disproportionately affect a particular group of persons; (g) the extent to which persons who are potentially harmed or suffer an adverse impact are dependent on the outcome produced with an AI system, in particular because for practical or legal reasons it is not reasonably possible to opt-out from that outcome;	

		(h) the extent to which there is an imbalance of power, or the persons who are potentially harmed or suffer an adverse impact are in a vulnerable position in relation to the deployer of an AI system, in particular due to status, authority, knowledge, economic or social circumstances, or age; (i) the extent to which the outcome produced involving an AI system is easily corrigible or reversible, taking into account the technical solutions available to correct or reverse it, whereby outcomes having an adverse impact on health, safety or fundamental rights, shall not be considered to be easily corrigible or reversible; (j) the magnitude and likelihood of benefit of the deployment of the AI system for individuals, groups, or society at large, including possible improvements in product safety; (k) the extent to which existing Union law provides for: (i) effective measures of redress in relation to the risks posed by an AI system, with the exclusion of claims for damages; (ii) effective measures to prevent or substantially minimise those risks. 3. The Commission is empowered to adopt delegated acts in accordance with Article 97 to amend the list in Annex III by removing high-risk AI systems where both of the following conditions are fulfilled: (a) the high-risk AI system concerned no longer poses any significant risks to fundamental rights, health or safety, taking into account the criteria listed in paragraph 2; (b) the deletion does not decrease the overall level of protection of health, safety and fundamental rights under Union law. **Article 13: Transparency and Provision of Information to Deployers** 1. High-risk AI systems shall be designed and developed in such a way as to ensure that their operation is sufficiently transparent to enable deployers to interpret a system's output and use it appropriately. An appropriate type and degree of transparency shall be ensured with a view to achieving compliance with the relevant obligations of the provider and deployer set out in Section 3. 2. High-risk AI systems shall be accompanied by instructions for use in an appropriate digital format or otherwise that include concise, complete, correct and clear information that is relevant, accessible and comprehensible to deployers.	

(continued)

Table 2 (continued)

Regulatory document name	Effective date	Article content	Key insights
		3. The instructions for use shall contain at least the following information: (a) the identity and the contact details of the provider and, where applicable, of its authorised representative; (b) the characteristics, capabilities and limitations of performance of the high-risk AI system, including: (i) its intended purpose; (ii) the level of accuracy, including its metrics, robustness and cybersecurity referred to in Article 15 against which the high-risk AI system has been tested and validated and which can be expected, and any known and foreseeable circumstances that may have an impact on that expected level of accuracy, robustness and cybersecurity; (iii) any known or foreseeable circumstance, related to the use of the high-risk AI system in accordance with its intended purpose or under conditions of reasonably foreseeable misuse, which may lead to risks to the health and safety or fundamental rights referred to in Article 9(2); (iv) where applicable, the technical capabilities and characteristics of the high-risk AI system to provide information that is relevant to explain its output; (v) when appropriate, its performance regarding specific persons or groups of persons on which the system is intended to be used; (vi) when appropriate, specifications for the input data, or any other relevant information in terms of the training, validation and testing data sets used, taking into account the intended purpose of the high-risk AI system; (vii) where applicable, information to enable deployers to interpret the output of the high-risk AI system and use it appropriately; (c) the changes to the high-risk AI system and its performance which have been predetermined by the provider at the moment of the initial conformity assessment, if any; (d) the human oversight measures referred to in Article 14, including the technical measures put in place to facilitate the interpretation of the outputs of the high-risk AI systems by the deployers; (e) the computational and hardware resources needed, the expected lifetime of the high-risk AI system and any necessary maintenance and care measures, including their frequency, to ensure the proper functioning of that AI system, including as regards software updates;	

		(f) where relevant, a description of the mechanisms included within the high-risk AI system that allows deployers to properly collect, store and interpret the logs in accordance with Article 12. **Article 14: Human Oversight** 1. High-risk AI systems shall be designed and developed in such a way, including with appropriate human-machine interface tools, that they can be effectively overseen by natural persons during the period in which they are in use. 2. Human oversight shall aim to prevent or minimise the risks to health, safety or fundamental rights that may emerge when a high-risk AI system is used in accordance with its intended purpose or under conditions of reasonably foreseeable misuse, in particular where such risks persist despite the application of other requirements set out in this Section. 3. The oversight measures shall be commensurate with the risks, level of autonomy and context of use of the high-risk AI system, and shall be ensured through either one or both of the following types of measures: (a) measures identified and built, when technically feasible, into the high-risk AI system by the provider before it is placed on the market or put into service; (b) measures identified by the provider before placing the high-risk AI system on the market or putting it into service and that are appropriate to be implemented by the deployer. 4. For the purpose of implementing paragraphs 1, 2 and 3, the high-risk AI system shall be provided to the deployer in such a way that natural persons to whom human oversight is assigned are enabled, as appropriate and proportionate: (a) to properly understand the relevant capacities and limitations of the high-risk AI system and be able to duly monitor its operation, including in view of detecting and addressing anomalies, dysfunctions and unexpected performance; (b) to remain aware of the possible tendency of automatically relying or over-relying on the output produced by a high-risk AI system (automation bias), in particular for high-risk AI systems used to provide information or recommendations for decisions to be taken by natural persons;	

(continued)

Table 2 (continued)

Regulatory document name	Effective date	Article content	Key insights
		(c) to correctly interpret the high-risk AI system's output, taking into account, for example, the interpretation tools and methods available; (d) to decide, in any particular situation, not to use the high-risk AI system or to otherwise disregard, override or reverse the output of the high-risk AI system; (e) to intervene in the operation of the high-risk AI system or interrupt the system through a 'stop' button or a similar procedure that allows the system to come to a halt in a safe state. 5. For high-risk AI systems referred to in point 1(a) of Annex III, the measures referred to in paragraph 3 of this Article shall be such as to ensure that, in addition, no action or decision is taken by the deployer on the basis of the identification resulting from the system unless that identification has been separately verified and confirmed by at least two natural persons with the necessary competence, training and authority. The requirement for a separate verification by at least two natural persons shall not apply to high-risk AI systems used for the purposes of law enforcement, migration, border control or asylum, where Union or national law considers the application of this requirement to be disproportionate. **Article 50: Transparency Obligations for Providers and Deployers of Certain AI Systems** 1. Providers shall ensure that AI systems intended to interact directly with natural persons are designed and developed in such a way that the natural persons concerned are informed that they are interacting with an AI system, unless this is obvious from the point of view of a natural person who is reasonably well-informed, observant and circumspect, taking into account the circumstances and the context of use. This obligation shall not apply to AI systems authorised by law to detect, prevent, investigate or prosecute criminal offences, subject to appropriate safeguards for the rights and freedoms of third parties, unless those systems are available for the public to report a criminal offence.	

		2. Providers of AI systems, including general-purpose AI systems, generating synthetic audio, image, video or text content, shall ensure that the outputs of the AI system are marked in a machine-readable format and detectable as artificially generated or manipulated. Providers shall ensure their technical solutions are effective, interoperable, robust and reliable as far as this is technically feasible, taking into account the specificities and limitations of various types of content, the costs of implementation and the generally acknowledged state of the art, as may be reflected in relevant technical standards. This obligation shall not apply to the extent the AI systems perform an assistive function for standard editing or do not substantially alter the input data provided by the deployer or the semantics thereof, or where authorised by law to detect, prevent, investigate or prosecute criminal offences. 3. Deployers of an emotion recognition system or a biometric categorisation system shall inform the natural persons exposed thereto of the operation of the system, and shall process the personal data in accordance with Regulations (EU) 2016/679 and (EU) 2018/1725 and Directive (EU) 2016/680, as applicable. This obligation shall not apply to AI systems used for biometric categorisation and emotion recognition, which are permitted by law to detect, prevent or investigate criminal offences, subject to appropriate safeguards for the rights and freedoms of third parties, and in accordance with Union law.	

(continued)

Table 2 (continued)

Regulatory document name	Effective date	Article content	Key insights
		4. Deployers of an AI system that generates or manipulates image, audio or video content constituting a deep fake, shall disclose that the content has been artificially generated or manipulated. This obligation shall not apply where the use is authorised by law to detect, prevent, investigate or prosecute criminal offence. Where the content forms part of an evidently artistic, creative, satirical, fictional or analogous work or programme, the transparency obligations set out in this paragraph are limited to disclosure of the existence of such generated or manipulated content in an appropriate manner that does not hamper the display or enjoyment of the work. Deployers of an AI system that generates or manipulates text which is published with the purpose of informing the public on matters of public interest shall disclose that the text has been artificially generated or manipulated. This obligation shall not apply where the use is authorised by law to detect, prevent, investigate or prosecute criminal offences or where the AI-generated content has undergone a process of human review or editorial control and where a natural or legal person holds editorial responsibility for the publication of the content. 5. The information referred to in paragraphs 1 to 4 shall be provided to the natural persons concerned in a clear and distinguishable manner at the latest at the time of the first interaction or exposure. The information shall conform to the applicable accessibility requirements. 6. Paragraphs 1 to 4 shall not affect the requirements and obligations set out in Chapter III, and shall be without prejudice to other transparency obligations laid down in Union or national law for deployers of AI systems. 7. The AI Office shall encourage and facilitate the drawing up of codes of practice at Union level to facilitate the effective implementation of the obligations regarding the detection and labelling of artificially generated or manipulated content. The Commission may adopt implementing acts to approve those codes of practice in accordance with the procedure laid down in Article 56 (6). If it deems the code is not adequate, the Commission may adopt an implementing act specifying common rules for the implementation of those obligations in accordance with the examination procedure laid down in Article 98(2).	

++

References

Anyoha R (2017) The history of artificial intelligence. https://sitn.hms.harvard.edu/flash/2017/history-artificial-intelligence/

Avila Negri SMC (2021) Robot as legal person: electronic personhood in robotics and artificial intelligence. Front Robot AI. https://doi.org/10.3389/frobt.2021.789327

Bai Q (2019) The risks of artificial intelligence and its legal regulation. http://www.rmlt.com.cn/2019/0403/543085.shtml

Bi K (2023) AI scams on the rise: urgent need to accelerate protection of personal privacy information. https://www.stcn.com/article/detail/873756.html

Browne R (2024) World's first major law for artificial intelligence gets final EU green light. https://www.cnbc.com/2024/05/21/worlds-first-major-law-for-artificial-intelligence-gets-final-eu-green-light.html

CAICT (2023) Research report on legal issues of artificial intelligence and intellectual property. http://www.caict.ac.cn/kxyj/qwfb/ztbg/202312/P020231214536394565312.pdf

Cao X, Xian C (2020) Ethical exploration of AI as a subject of intellectual property. https://ciipr.njust.edu.cn/e2/04/c11083a254468/page.htm

Chalmers D, MacKenzie NG, Carter S (2020) Artificial intelligence and entrepreneurship: implications for venture creation in the fourth industrial revolution. Entrep Theory Pract 45(5):1028–1053

Chan M (2016) Go player finally defeats Google's Alphago after 3 losses. https://time.com/4257406/go-google-alphago-lee-sedol/

Chen B (2023) Rule of law consideration and practical frame for promoting the healthy development of generative artificial intelligence: comments on relevant provisions in interim measures for the Administration of Generative Artificial Intelligence Services. China J Appl Jurispr 7(4):108–125

Chen Q, Xu D (2022) On the patentability and ownership of artificial intelligence-generated inventions. http://www.kjjb.org/fileup/HTML/2022-39-9-012.htm

Chen S, Qiu H, Zhao S et al (2022) When more is less: the other side of artificial intelligence recommendation. J Manag Sci Eng 7(2):213–232

Cheng L (2023) Legal regulation of generative artificial intelligence: a ChatGPT perspective. J Polit Sci Law(4):69–80

Chi M (2024) The State Council announces annual legislative plan: draft AI law prepared for review. http://www.legaldaily.com.cn/IT/content/2024-05/11/content_8995266.html

China Center for Food and Drug International Exchange (2022) Announcement from the NMPA on the guidelines for the registration review of AI medical devices. https://www.ccfdie.org/cn/yjxx/ylqx/webinfo/2022/03/1648289422561065.htm

China Electronic News (2021) Shared responsibility through self-regulation and governance: AI companies taking the lead. https://new.qq.com/rain/a/20210807A09CFQ00

China Intellectual Property Rights Protection Website (2024) Recent actions by the U.S. patent and trademark office will lead to changes in AI patent practices. http://ipr.mofcom.gov.cn/article/gjxw/lfdt/mj/zlmj/202406/1986235.html

China Law Society (2020) Wenxian Zhang: establishing the legal order of an intelligent society. https://www.chinalaw.org.cn/portal/article/index/id/28461.html

China National Institute of Standardization (2020) The standardization administration and four other departments issue the guidelines for the building of a new generation of national AI standards system. https://www.cnis.ac.cn/wap/dh/gndt/202008/t20200811_50167.html

China National Intellectual Property Administration (2019) The decision of the NIPA on amending the patent examination guidelines. https://www.gov.cn/zhengce/zhengceku/2019-12/31/content_5465485.htm

China National Intellectual Property Administration (2023) The guidelines for patent examination (2023). https://www.cnipa.gov.cn/module/download/downfile.jsp?classid=0&showname=%E

4%B8%93%E5%88%A9%E5%AE%A1%E6%9F%A5%E6%8C%87%E5%8D%97.pdf&filename=5753f257e6a04b6f8e305eb6d34ba452.pdf
China National Intellectual Property Administration (2024) Top ten cases: food container and device and method for enhancing attention patent application reexamination request case. https://www.cnipa.gov.cn/art/2024/8/13/art_2648_194170.html
China National Intellectual Property Administration, Japan Patent Office (2023) Comparative study report on patent examination cases related to artificial intelligence. https://www.cnipa.gov.cn/module/download/downfile.jsp?classid=0&showname=%E4%B8%AD%E6%97%A5%E4%BA%BA%E5%B7%A5%E6%99%BA%E8%83%BD%E4%B8%93%E5%88%A9%E5%AE%A1%E6%9F%A5%E6%A1%88%E4%BE%8B%E5%AF%B9%E6%AF%94%E7%A0%94%E7%A9%B6%E6%8A%A5%E5%91%8A.pdf&filename=c7bc94c506844c54918b0e08dfbc5708.pdf
Colosimo BM, del Castillo E, Jones-Farmer LA et al (2021) Artificial intelligence and statistics for quality technology: an introduction to the special issue. J Qual Technol 53(5):443–453
Cyberspace Administration of China, Ministry of Industry and Information Technology, Ministry of Public Security (2022) Provisions on the Administration of Deep Synthesis of Internet-Based Information Services. https://www.gov.cn/zhengce/zhengceku/2022-12/12/content_5731431.htm
Cyberspace Administration of China, Ministry of Industry and Information Technology, Ministry of Public Security, State Administration for Market Regulation (2021) Provisions on the Administration of Algorithm-Generated Recommendations for Internet Information Services. https://www.gov.cn/zhengce/zhengceku/2022-01/04/content_5666429.htm
Cyberspace Administration of China, National Development and Reform Commission, Ministry of Education, Ministry of Science and Technology, Ministry of Industry and Information Technology, Ministry of Public Security, and National Radio and Television Administration (2023) The interim measures for the Administration of Generative Artificial Intelligence Services. https://www.gov.cn/zhengce/zhengceku/202307/content_6891752.htm
Ding X (2022) Automatic decision-making based on trust: principle reflection and system reconstruction of the right to algorithm interpretation. China Legal Sci(1):99–118
Dreyfus (2024) Deciphering French copyright law in the age of AI: a critical analysis of recent developments. https://www.dreyfus.fr/en/2024/01/19/deciphering-french-copyright-law-in-the-age-of-ai-a-critical-analysis-of-recent-developments/
Du L, Kamenova K (2023) China's new regulations on generative AI: implications for bioethics. AJOB 23(10):52–54
El Atillah I (2023) Copyright challenges in the age of AI: who owns AI-generated content? https://www.euronews.com/next/2023/07/10/copyright-challenges-in-the-age-of-ai-who-owns-ai-generated-content
European Parliament (2024) Artificial Intelligence Act: MEPs adopt landmark law. https://www.europarl.europa.eu/news/en/press-room/20240308IPR19015/artificial-intelligence-act-meps-adopt-landmark-law
Fachan (2021) Enabling lawyers and firms to get more. https://www.fachans.com/
GDPR.EU (2024) What is GDPR, the EU's new data protection law? https://gdpr.eu/what-is-gdpr/
Gong F, Wang H (2018) Law firm sues Baidu Baijiahao for copyright infringement: Baidu claims the work was generated by software. http://ip.people.com.cn/n1/2018/1204/c179663-30442341.html
Han N (2024) Challenges in global governance and paths to trust in artificial intelligence security. https://theory.gmw.cn/2024-04/15/content_37263977.htm
He J, Yang H (2023) International comparison and reference on ChatGPT-like generative artificial intelligence regulation. J Hunan Univ Sci Technol (Soc Sci Ed) (6):119–128
Hong H, Zhang Y, Jiang Y (2021) AI assistants are on duty to assist judges in completing ten cases in 30 minutes. http://www.mzyfz.com/html/1022/2021-10-08/content-1522979.html
Huang H, Ding F (2019) China's AI industry: ranking second globally in multiple indicators and leading the world in the top tier. https://app.xinhuanet.com/news/article.html?articleId=95a412c2bd576b1589e61c2088c3ed3d

IDC Corporate (2023) China's total AI market size expected to exceed $26.44 billion by 2026. https://www.idc.com/getdoc.jsp?containerId=prCHC50539823

International Association of Privacy Professionals (2024) EU countries vote unanimously to approve AI Act. https://iapp.org/news/a/eu-countries-vote-unanimously-to-approve-ai-act

Ji (2017) The challenges of AI-generated inventions to the patent system. http://iolaw.cssn.cn/fxyjdt/201802/t20180220_4656923.shtml

Jia Y (2019) The challenge of the inventor role in the development of AI technology and its response. http://www.kjjb.org/fileup/HTML/2019-3-98.htm

Jin J, Wei G (2022) AI medical imaging into the first year of 'landing' clinical medicine experts: most companies are still purely 'technology faction'. http://www.nbd.com.cn/articles/2022-08-12/2404421.html

Jones J (2024) EU AI Act: next steps for implementation. https://iapp.org/resources/article/eu-ai-act-timeline/

Ke W (2024) 117 of China's large models complete generative AI service filings. http://www.news.cn/tech/20240410/cc09b9f19d194a1ab105303416293d04/c.html

Kong X (2019) AI in judicial practice. https://www.cac.gov.cn/2019-08/08/c_1124851874.htm

Korosec K (2017) Saudi Arabia's newest citizen is a robot. https://fortune.com/2017/10/26/robot-citizen-sophia-saudi-arabia/

Kroet C (2024) Clarity on head of AI office likely after summer. https://www.euronews.com/next/2024/05/23/clarity-on-head-of-ai-office-likely-after-summer

Legal Daily Public Opinion Center (2024) Adding a legal 'safety lock' to the development of AI technology. http://www.legaldaily.com.cn/The_analysis_of_public_opinion/content/2024-05/24/content_9001464.html

Leggatt J (2023) What is ChatGPT? A review of the AI in its own words. https://www.forbes.com/advisor/business/software/what-is-chatgpt/

Li J (2019a) Do AI-generated reports have copyright? http://www.ce.cn/cysc/zljd/gd/201905/29/t20190529_32207962.shtml

Li Y (2019b) The challenge and countermeasure of AI technology to patent system. Oriental Law. https://doi.org/10.19404/j.cnki.dffx.2019.01.008

Li Z (2023) 'My painting was stolen?' Verdict issued in the first case of copyright infringement involving AI-generated images. https://www.stcn.com/article/detail/1050204.html

Li Z (2024) 'AI + Medical' ushered in the wind mouth, multi-dimensional empowerment of the whole industry chain. https://www.stcn.com/article/detail/1150006.html

Li Y, Qin Y, Wei Q (2023) Potential risks and governance strategies of artificial intelligence generated content technology. Chin J Intell Sci Technol 5(3):415–423

Liu Y (2023) Does AI-generated content enjoy copyright? The key lies in 'intellectual achievement' and 'originality'. https://content-static.cctvnews.cctv.com/snow-book/index.html?item_id=3673911751729479774&toc_style_id=feeds_default&module=ccnews%3A%2F%2Fappclient%2Fpage%2Ffeeds%2Fdetail%3Furl%3Dhttps%253A%252F%252Fcontent-static.cctvnews.cctv.com%252Fsnow-book%252Find

Liu X (2024) From illegal to legal: evolving regulatory frameworks for generative artificial intelligence. Cyber Secur Data Govern. https://doi.org/10.19358/j.issn.2097-1788.2024.06.009

Liu X, Xia J (2023) An overview and assessment of the legislative landscape for AI in the United States. https://law.ucass.edu.cn/info/1985/6865.htm

Lu A (2024) Generative artificial intelligence: exploring risk, regulation, and governance models. J Chongqing Univ Posts Telecommun (Soc Sci Ed). https://doi.org/10.3979/1673-8268.20240326005

Ma C (2019) The fourth generation of human rights under the background of smart society and its protection. China Legal Sci 36(5):5–24

Ma Z, Liu Z (2018) Copyright characterization and institutional arrangement of artificial intelligence creations. Sci Technol Publ 37(10):107–114

Malan D (2018) The law can't keep up with new tech. Here's how to close the gap. https://www.weforum.org/agenda/2018/06/law-too-slow-for-new-tech-how-keep-up/

Me N (2023) The impact of AI on human creativity: the potential reduction in creative thinking. https://nikhilgautam01.medium.com/the-impact-of-ai-on-human-creativity-the-potential-reduction-in-creative-thinking-1c6f701e40bb
Meng T (2024) Research on patent protection of invention generated by artificial intelligence. Law Sci 12(2):903–907
Ministry of Science and Technology (2021) Publication of ethical norms for the new generation of artificial intelligence. https://www.most.gov.cn/kjbgz/202109/t20210926_177063.html
National Administration of State Secrets Protection (2019) Guidelines for internet personal information security: target and implications. http://www.gjbmj.gov.cn/n1/2019/0822/c411145-31311862.html
National Health Commission, National Administration of Traditional Chinese Medicine (2022) Notice on the issuance of interim measures for the supervision of internet medical treatment. https://www.nhc.gov.cn/yzygj/c100068/202203/2072f0e8988249e59d942e1b2a933916.shtml
National Information Security Standardization Technical Committee (2021) Cybersecurity standards practice guidelines: preventing ethical and security risks in artificial intelligence. https://www.tc260.org.cn/file/zn10.pdf
National Medical Products Administration (2021) Announcement from the NMPA on the guidelines for the classification of AI medical software products. https://www.nmpa.gov.cn/ylqx/ylqxggtg/20210708111147171.html?type=pc&m=
National People's Congress (2020) Civil Code of the People's Republic of China. https://www.gov.cn/xinwen/2020-06/01/content_5516649.htm
National People's Congress Education, Science, Culture and Public Health Committee (2024) Report on the review results of the proposals submitted to the presidium of the second session of the 14th National People's Congress. http://www.npc.gov.cn/npc//c2/c30834/202412/t20241224_441974.html
National People's Congress Standing Committee (2013) The law on the protection of consumer rights and interests of the People's Republic of China. https://www.gov.cn/jrzg/2013-10/25/content_2515601.htm
National People's Congress Standing Committee (2016) Cybersecurity law of the People's Republic of China. https://www.gov.cn/xinwen/2016-11/07/content_5129723.htm
National People's Congress Standing Committee (2018) E-commerce law of the People's Republic of China. https://www.gov.cn/xinwen/2018-08/31/content_5318220.htm
National People's Congress Standing Committee (2019) Product quality law of the People's Republic of China. http://www.npc.gov.cn/zgrdw/npc/xinwen/2019-01/07/content_2070255.htm
National People's Congress Standing Committee (2020a) Copyright law of the People's Republic of China. https://www.gov.cn/guoqing/2021-10/29/content_5647633.htm
National People's Congress Standing Committee (2020b) Patent law of the People's Republic of China (2020 Amendment). https://www.cnipa.gov.cn/art/2020/11/23/art_97_155167.html
National People's Congress Standing Committee (2021a) Data security law of the People's Republic of China. https://www.gov.cn/xinwen/2021-06/11/content_5616919.htm
National People's Congress Standing Committee (2021b) Personal information protection law of the People's Republic of China. https://www.gov.cn/xinwen/2021-08/20/content_5632486.htm
National People's Congress Standing Committee (2023a) Company law of the People's Republic of China. https://www.gov.cn/yaowen/liebiao/202312/content_6923395.htm
National People's Congress Standing Committee (2023b) Criminal law of the People's Republic of China. https://ssfb86.com/index/News/detail/newsid/8368.html
OpenAI (2022) Introducing ChatGPT. https://openai.com/index/chatgpt/
Owens R (2022) Personalised shopping and algorithmic pricing: how EU competition law can protect consumers in the digital world. In: Custers B, Fosch-Villaronga E (eds) Law and artificial intelligence, regulating AI and applying AI in legal practice, vol 35. T.M.C. Asser Press, The Hague, pp 395–410
People's Daily Online (2017) First AI-authored collection of poems published in China. http://en.people.cn/n3/2017/0531/c90000-9222463.html

Precedence Research (2025) Artificial intelligence (AI) market size, share, and trends 2025 to 2034. https://www.precedenceresearch.com/artificial-intelligence-market

Press G (2016) Artificial intelligence defined as a new research discipline: this week in tech history. https://www.forbes.com/sites/gilpress/2016/08/28/artificial-intelligence-defined-as-a-new-research-discipline-this-week-in-tech-history/?sh=6519aa4d6dd1

Publications Office of the European Union (2017) European Parliament resolution of 16 February 2017 with recommendations to the Commission on Civil Law Rules on Robotics (2015/2103(INL)). https://op.europa.eu/en/publication-detail/-/publication/13fd56d0-8a65-11e8-ac6a-01aa75ed71a1/language-en/format-PDF/source-170671777

PWC (2023) Regulatory and legislative interpretation: 'The Interim Measures for the Administration of Generative Artificial Intelligence Services' have been officially implemented. https://www.pwccn.com/zh/tmt/interim-measures-for-generative-ai-services-implemented-jul2023.pdf

Qin J (2023) The AI law included in the 2023 legislative plan: draft prepared for review. https://china.caixin.com/2023-06-08/102063471.html

Ran X (2022) Faced with security and privacy vulnerabilities: how far can facial recognition technology go?. http://www.xinhuanet.com/techpro/20220719/d1eb4627694f4c16abb4691903341b82/c.html

Research Center of Theoretical Law of Jilin University (2019) Wenxian Zhang: the seven propositions of human rights jurisprudence in the new era. https://legal-theory.org/?mod=info&act=view&id=24930

Satariano A, Kang C (2023) How nations are losing a global race to tackle A.I.'s harms. https://www.nytimes.com/2023/12/06/technology/ai-regulation-policies.html

Shen J, Lv Q (2022) China's Ministry of Industry and Information Technology: nearly 3,000 illegal and non-compliant apps reported and removed. http://finance.people.com.cn/n1/2022/0614/c1004-32445977.html

Shen W, Zhao E (2022) International law regulation of artificial intelligence under the background of digital economy. J Shanghai Univ Financ Econ 24(5):123–137

Song H (2024) Regulatory structure design in AI-related legislation. ECUPL J (5):5–20

Stader D (2024) Algorithms don't have a future: on the relation of judgement and calculation. Philos Technol. https://doi.org/10.1007/s13347-024-00705-3

State Council of China (2013) Regulation for the implementation of the copyright law of the People's Republic of China. https://www.gov.cn/zhengce/content/2013-02/08/content_5423.htm

State Council of China (2015) The guiding opinions on vigorously advancing the 'internet plus' action. https://www.gov.cn/zhengce/content/2015-07/04/content_10002.htm

State Council of China (2017) The development plan on the new generation of AI. https://www.gov.cn/zhengce/content/2017-07/20/content_5211996.htm

Sun M (2024) The trend of incremental progress in AI legislation. https://www.cssn.cn/skgz/202408/t20240812_5770096.shtml

Sun Y, Zeng J (2024) China's interim measures for the management of generative AI services: a comparison between the final and draft versions of the text. https://fpf.org/blog/chinas-interim-measures-for-the-management-of-generative-ai-services-a-comparison-between-the-final-and-draft-versions-of-the-text/

Supreme People's Court of China (2022) The opinions of the Supreme People's Court on regulating and strengthening the applications of AI in the judicial fields. https://ipc.court.gov.cn/zh-cn/news/view-2131.html

Taeihagh A, Lim HSM (2018) Governing autonomous vehicles: emerging responses for safety, liability, privacy, cybersecurity, and industry risks. Transp Rev 39(1):103–128

The European Economic and Social Committee (2018) Open letter to the European Commission artificial intelligence and robotics. http://robotics-openletter.eu/

Thierer A (2018) The pacing problem and the future of technology regulation. https://www.mercatus.org/economic-insights/expert-commentary/pacing-problem-and-future-technology-regulation

Tschider C (2018) Regulating the IoT: discrimination, privacy, and cybersecurity in the artificial intelligence age. Denv Univ Law Rev 96:87
Wang L (2012) New developments in the right to privacy (part 1). http://old.civillaw.com.cn/article/default.asp?id=55404
Wang G (2024a) The work type logic of originality in copyright law. Stud Law Bus 41(1):183–200
Wang S (2024b) Research on personal information protection in the context of generative artificial intelligence. Net Secur Technol Appl 24(7):121–124
Wang X, He Q (2020) Does AI exhibit bias and discrimination, leading to convergence of user preferences? Scientists provide evidence. https://www.thepaper.cn/newsDetail_forward_8612491
Wang Q, Hu L (2024) Legal and technical construction of generative AI accountability mechanisms. China Law Rev 11(4):114–130
Wang Q, Wan G (2023) Double legal regulation approach of generative artificial intelligence. Stud Socism Chin Char 29(4):72–84
Wang J, Spicher N, Warnecke JM et al (2021) Unobtrusive health monitoring in private spaces: the smart home. Sensors 21(3):864–886
WAYMO (2024) Meet a better way to move. https://waymo.com/?ncr=
Weng R (2023) Promoting the safe development of artificial intelligence in the legal field. https://www.cssn.cn/skgz/bwyc/202308/t20230816_5678985.shtml
Wu H (2017) Institutional arrangements and legal regulation in age of artificial intelligence. Sci Law 35(5):128–136
Wu H (2019) Patent law issues in artificial intelligence-generated inventions. https://ciipr.njust.edu.cn/73/e1/c11083a226273/page.htm
Wu P (2024) Baidu launches legal AI product, Faxingbao. http://www.legaldaily.com.cn/Village_ruled_by_law/content/2024-03/01/content_8967046.html
Xia X, Bi L (2020) The Ministry of Industry and Information Technology's initiative: leveraging the empowerment of AI to collaboratively combat the pandemic. http://finance.people.com.cn/n1/2020/0204/c1004-31570943.html
Xiangtan University (2020) Wenxian Zhang: digital human rights leading the fourth generation of human rights. https://law.xtu.edu.cn/info/1123/6883.htm
Xiao B, Zhang M (2020) Shenzhen concludes first dispute case on AI-generated article, court recognizes it as a work. https://www.chinacourt.org/article/detail/2020/03/id/4855752.shtml
Xinhua News Agency (2021) The outline of the 14th five-year plan for national economic and social development and long-range objectives through the year 2035 of the PRC. https://www.gov.cn/xinwen/2021-03/13/content_5592681.htm
Xu L (2019) A discussion of equality rights in artificial intelligence projection techniques. Law Rev(3):152–161
Xue Y (2024) First ruling in China's AI voice infringement case: experts urge timely response to emerging personality rights issues. https://www.stdaily.com/index/kejixinwen/202404/e2f5c4409865476f8bbad4de6e27a603.shtml
Yang L (2018) Artificial personality: the intelligent robots' legal status in civil law. Seeking Truth 45(4):84–96
Yang T (2019) On robot's moral status as moral patient and its normative implications. Philos Anal 10(6):14–33
Yang L (2021) Research on the copyright of artificial intelligence products. Mod Law Sci 43(4):102–114
Yang J, Luo F (2024) The operation mechanism, legal risks and regulatory methods of generative artificial intelligence like ChatGPT. Admin Law(4):101–115
Yang Y, Lv Q (2021) University of Macau develops disinfecting intelligent robot with 99% sterilization effect. http://scitech.people.com.cn/n1/2021/0203/c1007-32021147.html
Yang Q, Zhang L (2018) On the artificial legal personality of artificial intelligence. J Hunan Univ Sci Technol (Soc Sci Ed) 21(6):91–97
Yao Y (2022) Technology, theory, problems and China's response to AI algorithm patents. Sci Technol Prog Policy 39(16):134–141

Zhai C, Wibowo S, Li LD (2024) The effects of over-reliance on AI dialogue systems on students' cognitive abilities: a systematic review. Smart Learn Environ. https://doi.org/10.1186/s40561-024-00316-7

Zhang H (2019) Lessons from the first national case on AI-generated content copyright: do AI 'works' have copyright? https://jres2023.xhby.net/index/201905/t20190529_6209424.shtml

Zhang S (2020a) Robots secure copyright for writing: what is the future of intelligent writing? http://www.zgjx.cn/2020-04/30/c_139021491.htm

Zhang Y (2020b) On the legal standards for patentability of AI inventions. Stud Law Bus 37(6):181–192

Zhang L (2021) The ideological risk of intelligent algorithm recommendation and its governance. Probe. https://doi.org/10.16501/j.cnki.50-1019/d.2021.01.014

Zhang L (2024) What kind of AI law should China have? Basic logic and systemic structure of China's AI legislative framework. Sci Law. https://doi.org/10.16290/j.cnki.1674-5205.2024.03.009

Zhao J, Li W (2020) The challenges of artificial intelligence on international law and reaction. J Zhejiang Univ (Humanit Soc Sci) 50(2):10–25

Zheng G (2018) Artificial intelligence and the future of law. https://la.swupl.edu.cn/articles/article_detail.aspx?id=7100220441.

Zheng Y (2023) Research on the identification of technical personnel in the field of AI-related inventions. https://www.ciplawyer.cn/html/llqyzl/20230511/150359.html

Juxtaposing Approaches to Risk-Based AI Governance in Different 'Rights' Contexts: A Comparative Analysis Between Singapore and the EU

Jane Loo and Mark Findlay

Contents

Mark Findlay has adapted the theoretical frame for this chapter from his work on Polanyi. See: Findlay, Mark. Law's regulatory relevance? Property, power and market economies. (2017). 1-320. Available at: https://ink.library.smu.edu.sg/sol_research/2353.

J. Loo (✉)
Centre for Digital Law, Singapore Management University, Singapore, Singapore
e-mail: janeloo@smu.edu.sg

M. Findlay
British Institute of International and Comparative Law, London, UK

Law School, University of Edinburgh, Edinburgh, UK
e-mail: m.findlay@biicl.org

V. L. Raposo (ed.), *The European Artificial Intelligence Act*, Law, Governance and Technology Series 78, https://doi.org/10.1007/978-3-031-98406-8_17

Abstract Comparative analysis of European and certain Asian approaches to governance often degenerates into simplistic dichotomies based on universal human rights assumptions. This chapter rejects such dualities, ill-informed by theory and historical reflection. The emerging argument is founded on a historical realist approach to theorising difference. Assisted by Polanyi's double movement, the detailed substantive comparison is preceded by considerations of how recent trends in governing AI have uniformly adopted a countermovement against the dis-embedding of data and technology from the social leading to a risk/responsibility paradigm. From here, a more nuanced reflection of AI governance approaches in the EU and Singapore is offered, wherein frontier technologies are preferred for economic growth and governance is tempered by subtly different understandings of risk qualified by a common desire for achieving economic and social betterment. Rather than expressing a preference for either approach, the chapter concludes that a more convincing comparative analysis requires focusing on structural, organisational and interactive/situational perspectives when directed to a complex dynamic such as AI deployed in particular community settings.

1 Introduction

> In Asia they do it like this, and in Europe they do it like that.

Comparative research is not the most revealing when it employs over-simplistic dualities exhibiting assumptions about similarities and difference that are only established at an abstract level of generality. In this chapter, the reflections to follow are based on comparative contextual analysis[1] where the chapter reflects how two contextual models of AI governance (in Europe and in Singapore) can be founded in different historical experiences and approaches to the integrity of individual data subjects, but still share the same economic drivers for the advancement of AI and big data.[2]

In particular, the chapter works from the common aim that AI should be governed for non-feasance, then interrogates how in spite of that normative consideration, AI has become dis-embedded from other important social bonds such as trust. Next, the chapter looks at the general market aspiration for AI as an agent of wealth creation and evaluates two quite different governance directions with similar risk reduction aspirations.[3]

---

[1] Findlay and Henham (2007), pp. 134–162.

[2] At a time of change and reconsideration such as can be said of AI and data governance policy, particularly in the jurisdictions where the largest info tech companies are based, and in their main markets, a comparative analysis such as this may be outdated by the time of publication. That said it is possible to project future trends in transition, using the contextual variables considered in this chapter.

[3] Due to the limitations of space the first three more theoretical elements of the argument will benefit from less elaboration when contrasted with the operation description of the two gover-

The comparative dimension is context-driven in an effort to give meaningful accounts of why regulation is advanced in the EU to control AI risk, and in Singapore there remains a preference for consensual self-regulation, despite recognition of safety and responsibility priorities. The chapter suggests that this distinction cannot be properly understood with the reasoning that Europe values individual rights and Singapore (or Asia) does not. Such a conclusion diminishes the historical and socio/cultural underpinnings of how the risks generated by a universal neo-liberal economic ascription for AI feature and are managed in different regulatory situations.

Convincing comparative analysis requires a focus on structural, organisational and interactive/situational perspectives[4] when directed to a complex dynamic such as AI deployed in particular community settings.[5] At the structural level, the analysis to follow will consider the command and control regulatory schemes (legislation) across to consensual self-regulation (AI ethical frameworks). Organisationally, the discussion will fix on why one approach seems to protect the integrity of the data subject in 'rights language' and the other relies on market forces and corporate morality to ensure best practice in the development of digital technology and data uses. The interactive/situational considerations will suggest that both regulatory perspectives attempt to employ a 'double movement'[6] in returning dis-embedded AI to concerns for social responsibility, while ensuring AI's wealth creation capacities.

Put at its simplest, the comparative exercise is designed to see how different processes strive to arrive at common outcomes. The chapter engages with the two regulatory case studies - Singapore and the EU - to demonstrate how different counter movements can still achieve the same effect of returning AI to the social.

2 Theorising Difference

The theoretical challenge is to compare the recent EU risk-prevention legislative approach with Singapore's voluntary AI governance model framework when regulating AI for non-feasance, and then reflecting on how and why they address common regulatory challenges from these perspectives. In this vein, can the adoption of different regulatory frameworks be explained by broader regulatory appetites between a 'rights-based' individualist context and a voluntary responsibility governance model where 'rights' are not the governance focus?

Adopting a *historical realist approach*[7] the chapter offers a limited interrogation of neo-liberal market drivers behind the promotion of AI in Europe and in Singapore,

nance models.

[4] Findlay and Henham (2007), p. 151.

[5] The authors have in various research settings worked to develop the notion of *AI in community*.

[6] Polanyi (2001).

[7] McCullagh (1980), pp. 420–425.

to reveal why risk is perceived and trust is at stake. Historical realism recognises that even if the outcome may be inaccurate, 'perception' is the means by which past events and states of affairs are immediately known. Therefore, if it is supposed that the enlightened European consciousness is focused on individual rights and liberties and governance in Asia is more interested in collective duty and obligation, then this interpretation can shape the different regulatory directions taken in the context of AI governance.

The 'rights-based' governance context in Europe since the enlightenment was never actively transferred through European colonisation into Asian governance practice, despite the preference for transplanting constitutional legality.[8] Instead, the system of governance imposed by colonial powers in Asia tended to depart from the principles of individual rights focusing more on hierarchical structures and control. Colonial expedience translocated notions of public law legal entitlements that were more dependent on the paternalist largesse of the State and co-option of local elites, than of rights that a citizen could claim and enforce.

In the globalised world economic order that has prevailed since the inception of AI, both Singapore and the EU have embraced a neo-liberal market model for the development of AI. In the case-studies described below, Europe is tempering the excesses of this direction which may risk individual rights through regulation, while Singapore has adopted a consensus/compliance model of self-regulated market players to manage AI's potential harms.

As explained in the introduction, the chapter is not interested in a dualist cultural comparison. Nor will it be primarily a legalist examination of rights or market compliance, as law is not also the dominant influence in either AI governance environment.[9] The chapter also resists the temptation to position rights as some superior governance discourse against which all others governance models would be negatively measured.

For the purpose of explaining how different governance approaches can be directed to a common regulatory outcome while taking unique contextual paths based on different social configurations, the analysis will adopt Karl Polanyi's analytical frame of the double movement.[10] In brief, the double movement framework asserts that as economic elements (AI as commodities) move away from the social there are counter movements that will re-embed AI back in the social context. These counter movements could involve regulatory efforts like in the EU and voluntary ethical model frameworks like in Singapore.

The dis-embedding component lies in the treatment of AI as commodities that disregard important social considerations. The commodification of AI involves prioritising profit and efficiency, while ignoring social values, ethics, and obligations to the communities into which it is deployed resulting in the fissures of trust.

---

[8] For instance: Johnson (2010), p. 103.

[9] Findlay (2017).

[10] For a brief resume of the double movement see: Findlay (2017), Chap. 3.

The method adopted in the analysis will comprise a case study comparison between the EU's AI Act and the Singapore AI governance approach to reveal different interpretations of the connections between AI and humans, the role of these connections in neo-liberal markets, and the risks presented to AI recipients. The common theme will be risk reduction qualified by an economic imperative for wealth creation.

3 Neoliberal Wealth Creation, AI Deployment and Trust: A Tale of Double Movement

The global commitment from nation states and big tech companies to the proliferation of AI technology is motivated by market profit and a belief in the positive outcomes for economic development.[11] Consequently, AI development and deployment under neoliberalism, prioritises wealth creation above any social benefit.[12] This economic model is however increasingly being challenged[13] and the desire to harness AI for social good is growing[14] emphasising the importance of re-embedding AI back into social contexts.

If AI is seen as replacing or substituting human decision-making,[15] then AI is fundamentally dis-embedding as it disengages from the social. When AI raises transparency, accountability, bias, privacy, and fairness issues, it may also be seen as disengaging from the social fabric. Such interpretations and beliefs are at the heart of many social perceptions that AI is risky and harmful to human sustainability and wellbeing. These negative readings (whether grounded in fact or not) impact on trust bonds between AI and recipient communities which in turn accelerates the dis-embedding process and understanding of AI's role in society.

However, if AI is employed with the purpose of complementing human endeavours and improving human well-being, then the potential for countermovement is clear and re-embedding is possible. The form that these counter-movements will take depends on the ways trust is engendered among recipient communities whether through ethical guidelines, standards, regulation, or public engagement. In societies that are familiar with legalist rights protection regulatory regimes then it is for the law to identify and granulate such risks and enact provisions that will grant actionable rights to recipient communities. Alternatively, in societies more accustomed to state guidance and reliance on market consensus to deal with risks rather than the

[11] Wiley (2023).

[12] David Rothschild, 'Deploying AI For Profit Or Humanity: Why Not Both?' *Forbes* (1 March 2024) <https://www.forbes.com/sites/forbesbusinesscouncil/2024/03/01/deploying-ai-for-profit-or-humanity-why-not-both/>.

[13] Findlay (2021).

[14] Wiley (2023).

[15] Duan et al. (2019), p. 63.

law, a self-regulatory AI governance approach may be promoted among state, industry, and other commercial sponsors of AI into these communities.

The effectiveness of either approach in generating trust and facilitating re-embedding will also depend not so much on proven utility but the extent to which these regulatory modes are accommodated within wider governance frames in which the people have faith. As the governance of risk is often a complex tapestry of regulatory modes, the generation of community trust may not simply be based on standardised safety assurances.[16] Trust is an impressionistic emotion and when it is directed to (or denied from) a phenomenon as mis-understood as AI, then for a countermovement to be successful it needs to recognise the wider socio-political contextual features at work on the mind of recipient populations, and these will reveal substantive as well as subliminal features that qualify trustworthy evaluations.[17]

Some might question the applicability of the double movement application to AI on the basis that it was never embedded in the social and has always been commodified. Answering this assertion, it is necessary to reach down into one of the a priori understandings of AI. Artificial intelligence was conceived as technological applications that mirror human learning capacity. To this extent, AI could never break free from the human/social referent that makes it 'artificial'. If this is so, then the original purpose for AI could also have been social rather than market based as it grew to be.

Through its compounding commodification, and its consequent move away from clear social imperatives, Polanyi would say that AI is increasingly fictitious.[18] The departure away from existing within the lived experience of people in communities means that the mystification of AI now extensively undermines trust bonds and as such governance modes need to remedy both the perceptions and realities of AI's harms and risks.

To give substance to the two modes of AI governance foreshadowed and their explanation in terms of different interpretations of the place of the individual, the market, and the state, the remaining sections will consider the EU and Singapore's AI governance approach.

4 Singapore's AI Governance Countermovement

While there are no AI-specific regulations in Singapore, the Singapore government has initiated several AI governance initiatives to facilitate AI innovation and encourage the responsible development and deployment of AI across various enterprises

[16] Saif Al Ghafri and others, 'Trust in AI for HSE', *Day 1 Mon, October 31, 2022* (SPE 2022) <https://onepetro.org/SPEADIP/proceedings/22ADIP/1-22ADIP/D011S002R001/513474>.

[17] Findlay and Wong (2021).

[18] Findlay (2017), Chap. 3.

and industries in Singapore. These include sector-specific guidelines, such as the FEAT principles for Singapore's financial sector by the Monetary Authority of Singapore,[19] to more horizontal guidelines such as the Model AI Governance Framework, to software toolkits like AI Verify,[20] to the formation of a dedicated AI Technical Committee (AITC) responsible for adopting international AI standards and developing domestic AI standards.[21] These coordinated efforts, while voluntary in nature, aim at embedding AI in the market/social[22] by supporting AI businesses with practical tools to produce more harmonious relationships and interactions between AI and society.

4.1 Singapore's National AI Strategy

To set the national agenda for AI and its strategic direction, Singapore's national AI strategy[23] was presented in 2019 by the Smart Nation and Digital Government Office. The strategy outlines the country's plans to deepen the use of AI technologies in key sectors like education, healthcare, security etc., to enhance Singapore's economy and growth. In 2023, the second National AI Strategy 2.0 (NAIS 2.0) was launched.[24]

Singapore's national AI strategy purports to build Singapore as a global hub for AI solutions and to represent it as a nation that is capable of managing AI's impact,[25] to produce both social and economic benefits for its population.[26] The focus on human centricity in Singapore's AI strategy aims to ensure that AI is deployed to

---

[19] 'Principles to Promote Fairness, Ethics, Accountability and Transparency (FEAT) in the Use of Artificial Intelligence and Data Analytics in Singapore's Financial Sector' (*Monetary Authority of Singapore*) <https://www.mas.gov.sg/~/media/MAS/News%20and%20Publications/Monographs%20and%20Information%20Papers/FEAT%20Principles%20Final.pdf>.

[20] 'Singapore's Approach to AI Governance' (*Personal Data Protection Commission Singapore*) <https://www.pdpc.gov.sg/Help-and-Resources/2020/01/Model-AI-Governance-Framework>.

[21] 'Artificial Intelligence Technical Committee (AITC)' (*Infocomm Media Development Authority*, 7 February 2024) <https://www.imda.gov.sg/-/media/Imda/Files/Regulations-and-Licensing/Licensing/ICT-Standards-and-Quality-of-Service/Industry-Committees-and-Working-Groups/IT-Standards-Committee/Technical-Committees-and-Working-Groups.pdf>.

[22] For an elaboration of this concept see; Findlay (2021), p. 118.

[23] 'National Artificial Intelligence Strategy' (Smart Nation Singapore 2019) <https://www.smartnation.gov.sg/files/publications/national-ai-strategy.pdf>.

[24] 'National AI Strategy: AI for the Public Good, for Singapore and the World' (*Smart Nation Singapore*) <https://www.smartnation.gov.sg/nais/>.

[25] 'National Artificial Intelligence Strategy Unveiled' (*Smart Nation Singapore*, 13 November 2019) <https://www.smartnation.gov.sg/media-hub/press-releases/national-artificial-intelligence-strategy-unveiled>.

[26] 'National Artificial Intelligence Strategy (Summary)' (*Smart Nation Singapore*) <https://www.smartnation.gov.sg/files/publications/national-ai-strategy-summary.pdf>.

serve human needs[27] so individuals can accordingly benefit from AI's potential and be safeguarded against AI-harms. The strategy also focuses on the importance of building an AI-ready population constituting technical experts (both attracting and retaining talents in the industry), as well as savvy AI users.[28]

Significantly, Singapore's AI strategy is designed to cultivate a trusted environment where AI solutions can be developed and deployed effectively, and where AI-related risks can be mitigated through clear responsibility structures.[29] NAIS 2.0 emphasises Singapore's vision of using '*AI for the public good, for Singapore and the World*'[30] to direct AI towards addressing needs and challenges both nationally and globally, and to ensure that communities are properly equipped with the capabilities and resources to thrive in an AI-enabled future.

In Singapore's first national AI strategy, the government foreshadowed five national AI projects focused on the sectors of transport and logistics, municipal services, healthcare, education, and safety and security.[31] NAIS 2.0 builds on this foundation by directing future AI development and adoption in select leading economic sectors and smart nation priorities such as in areas of manufacturing, financial services, and public service delivery. It can be seen in this prioritising that AI development remains grounded in economic development, market commerce and state administration. The assumption being that AI facilitation in these areas will lead on to broader social goods.

The deployment of AI in these sectors would inevitably bring about new AI-related risks suggested as cybersecurity vulnerabilities and data breaches, discrimination, or privacy infringements. For example, on the deployment of AI for smart cities planning, the installation of sensors in housing estates and data collection on the usage of common facilities may lend to the increased collection and storage of residents' activities which may comprise sensitive personal information.[32] Similarly, in the healthcare sector, AI can be adopted to support clinical decisions for healthcare professionals in Singapore by providing personalised risk scores for chronic diseases or to assist with the management of chronic diseases.[33] In these cases, big databases play a critical role in seeing that these technologies can

---

[27] 'National Artificial Intelligence Strategy (Summary)' (n 26). See also: 'NAIS 2.0 Singapore National AI Strategy: AI for the Public Good For Singapore and the World' (*Smart Nation Singapore*) <https://file.go.gov.sg/nais2023.pdf>.

[28] 'NAIS 2.0 Singapore National AI Strategy: AI for the Public Good For Singapore and the World' (n 27).

[29] 'NAIS 2.0 Singapore National AI Strategy: AI for the Public Good For Singapore and the World' (n 27).

[30] 'National AI Strategy: AI for the Public Good, for Singapore and the World' (n 24).

[31] 'National Artificial Intelligence Strategy Unveiled' (n 25).

[32] For an elaboration on the challenges posed by mass data sharing in smart cities see: Berenika Drazewska and Mark Findlay, 'Mass Data Sharing in Smart Cities (Regulation and Governance of the Public-Private Interface)' (Konrad Adenauer Stiftung and Singapore Management University 2024) <https://www.kas.de/documents/278334/0/Mass+Data+Sharing+in+Smart+Cities.pdf/4122fb76-6659-5a1c-0bfd-b8e5160c2c85?version=1.0&t=1711522412190>.

[33] 'National Artificial Intelligence Strategy (Summary)' (n 26).

be deployed effectively and at scale. Yet, the reliance on such big databases poses real risks related to data quality and representativeness of datasets particularly as it relates to how it may reproduce discriminatory patterns. Cybersecurity risks and the threat to patient's privacy can also be acknowledged here. In 2018, for example, hackers infiltrated the SingHealth database[34] and the health data of over 1.5 million patients, including the outpatient prescriptions of Singapore's Prime Minister.[35] A national inquiry later revealed that there were a number of vulnerabilities in SingHealth's IT network and system including a lapse in key personnel, where relevant staffers did not have the adequate levels of cybersecurity awareness, training, and resources.[36] Similarly, in 2019, the health data of over 14,000 individuals diagnosed with HIV were leaked online.[37] The leaked information included personal details such as patients' names, identification numbers, and contact details.[38]

The limited examples described in the healthcare context reveal how AI and big data can introduce new risks and exacerbate existing risks in smart cities. The strategy recognises that these risks need to be curtailed to continue locating AI as an important force in Singapore's Smart Nation Ambitions.[39] NAIS 2.0 is said to address these risks through setting out fifteen action plans across three systems and ten enablers.[40] Underlying these enablers and initiatives is the desire to reduce AI risks and increase the adoption of AI in Singapore. Broadly speaking, Singapore's AI strategy can be said to be one that is collaborative and industry-led, aligned with its other AI governance initiatives as will be touched on below.

The three systems and 10 enablers include: (1) Activity drivers (enablers: industry, government and research), (2) People and communities (enablers: talent, capabilities, placemaking) and (3) infrastructure and environment (enablers: compute, data, trusted environment, leader in thought and action).[41] The intention it appears is to cover the positioning of AI in the market, the community and the State. The governance strategy is that government lays out a blueprint which market players, community participants and public administrators are encouraged to follow, with incentives for compliance. The strategy is one of consensus/compliance rather than

[34] SingHealth is Singapore's largest group of healthcare institutions that collects data from polyclinics, public hospitals, and outpatient clinics.

[35] 'SingHealth Cyber Attack: How It Unfolded' (20 July 2018) <https://graphics.straitstimes.com/STI/STIMEDIA/Interactives/2018/07/sg-cyber-breach/index.html>.

[36] Han (2019).

[37] Sharanjit Leyl, 'Singapore HIV Data Leak Shakes a Vulnerable Community' *BBC News* (22 February 2019) <https://www.bbc.com/news/world-asia-47288219>.

[38] 'Singapore's HIV Registry Data Breach: What Can We Learn?' (*Aon*) <https://www.aon.com/apac/insights/risk-alerts/2019/sg-hiv-registry-data-breach.jsp#:~:text=On%2028%20January%202019%2C%20the,What%20was%20stolen%3F>.

[39] 'Smart Nation: The Way Forward (Executive Summary)' (*Smart Nation Singapore*) <https://www.smartnation.gov.sg/files/publications/smart-nation-strategy-nov2018.pdf>.

[40] 'NAIS 2.0 Singapore National AI Strategy: AI for the Public Good For Singapore and the World' (n 27).

[41] 'NAIS 2.0 Singapore National AI Strategy: AI for the Public Good For Singapore and the World' (n 27).

regulatory or legislative compulsion. The flip side however, is that protective guarantees or penalties are not envisaged if stakeholders do not positively engage with the policy pronouncement.

Activity Drivers

Singapore's research community, industry, and Government are each tasked with responsibilities in enabling the development and deployment of better AI solutions for society and the economy.[42] Already, the government can be seen partnering with industry to promote the use of generative AI in the public sector.[43] To further anchor AI innovation and value creation in industry, NAIS 2.0 also details the establishment of new AI Centres of Excellence (CoE) across Singapore-based companies and a new model of Sectoral AI CoEs to intensify AI value creation and usage in selected economic sectors.[44] Additionally, NAIS 2.0 focuses on strengthening the AI start-up ecosystem by attracting more venture builders and developing additional accelerator programmes.[45] NAIS 2.0 then speculates the potential of AI to improve public service delivery and productivity through increased public sector adoption of AI, as well as uplifting the AI literacy baseline and proficiency of all of Singapore's public officers.[46]

On the research front, NAIS 2.0 highlights the research community as playing a fundamental role in developing AI solutions and products to produce a competitive edge and delivering value for Singapore. AI Singapore (AISG), for example, pairs researchers and companies together to develop innovative AI solutions through its 100 experiments programme to resolve AI problem statements put forward by industry.[47]

---

[42] 'NAIS 2.0 Singapore National AI Strategy: AI for the Public Good For Singapore and the World' (n 27).

[43] Li Min Ong and Jason Grant, 'ChatGPT and the Public Service' (14 July 2023) <https://govinsider.asia/intl-en/article/chatgpt-and-the-public-service>. See also: 'Implication If Civil Servants Use ChatGPT to Write Reports and Speeches (Fourteenth Parliament of Singapore – First Session for the Sitting)' (*Smart Nation Singapore*, 28 February 2023) <https://www.smartnation.gov.sg/media-hub/parliament/28022023/>. Questions were raised in Parliament concerning the validity and accuracy of ChatGPT-assisted reports and speeches.

[44] 'NAIS 2.0 Singapore National AI Strategy: AI for the Public Good For Singapore and the World' (n 27).

[45] 'NAIS 2.0 Singapore National AI Strategy: AI for the Public Good For Singapore and the World' (n 27).

[46] 'NAIS 2.0 Singapore National AI Strategy: AI for the Public Good For Singapore and the World' (n 27).

[47] '100 Experiments' (*AI Singapore*) <https://aisingapore.org/innovation/100e/>.

5 People and Communities

System 2 recognises the importance of knowledge communities as critical for AI innovation and for driving the exchange of ideas and expertise.[48] The strategy emphasises the need to expand the pool and quality of AI creators and practitioners including scaling up AI-specific training programmes, reskilling, upskilling, and welcoming in global AI talent. Through AISG's talent programme, the AI Apprenticeship Programme (AIAP), AI professionals are trained for the industry using a combination of deep-skilling training and hands on experience with real world projects. This approach purportedly equips its participants with the skill sets to tackle AI-related risks and challenges.[49]

The strategy further emphasises the need for enterprises and their workforce to increase AI adoption and capabilities, including the upskilling of workers. Enhancing the digital literacy and skillsets of a workforce may prove crucial in ensuring that the risks posed by AI are minimised. Another enabler in this system is placemaking. Singapore intends to provide a dedicated space for the AI community to interact, exchange ideas, and collaborate. Whether such an initiative can also enhance the foundations of trust within Singapore's AI ecosystem remains to be seen.

6 Infrastructure and Environment

The final system focuses on Singapore's AI infrastructure and environment. The emphasis here is the creation of a robust and conducive infrastructure and environment where all stages of the AI lifecycle can be properly supported. The significance of compute and high quality data is recognised, as well as the importance of creating a trusted environment. The Trusted Data Sharing Framework[50] was developed by IMDA to guide companies in establishing data sharing partnerships with each other. The Framework articulates the key legal, regulatory, and technical considerations and safeguards that organisation should take into account to ensure that data is shared in a responsible way. Adherence to the framework is intended to offer protection against cyberattacks while also demonstrating respect for citizens' data privacy.

NAIS 2.0 also considers the role of privacy enhancing technologies and the creation of a 'data concierge' within government to identify and facilitate access to

[48] 'NAIS 2.0 Singapore National AI Strategy: AI for the Public Good For Singapore and the World' (n 27).

[49] 'Using AI With Confidence' (*AI SIngapore*, 16 July 2021) <https://aisingapore.org/2021/07/using-ai-with-confidence/>.

[50] 'Trusted Data Sharing Framework' (*Infocomm Media Development Authority*) <https://www.imda.gov.sg/-/media/Imda/Files/Programme/AI-Data-Innovation/Trusted-Data-Sharing-Framework.pdf>.

public and private datasets.[51] The strategy also acknowledges the potential risks surrounding AI highlighting the need for reliable and resilient AI systems that act as a safeguard against adversarial threats.

Specific reference is made to Singapore's Model AI Governance Framework and AI verify in securing the responsible design and deployment of AI. The strategy also proposes issuing advisories and actionable guidelines on how system owners can augment their cybersecurity foundations. Additionally, it recognises the need for more coordinated efforts including partnering with the private sector to co-create technical guidelines and solutions to raise AI security capabilities. This is a detailed example of how the state endeavours to co-opt not only the goodwill and best practices of market stakeholders, but their test-case capacity to validate government policy,

The strategy notes the importance of safeguarding Singapore's interests and position in shaping the international rules emerging around AI. Singapore has had significant national prestige through Davos and other forums in marketing its AI governance approaches. It will continue prioritising building international networks and increasing international knowledge sharing in practical and risk-based approaches to AI. By working closely with key international standard-setting organisations[52] contributing to international AI-related policies and guidelines, Singapore aspires to continue playing a critical role in current norm-shaping processes ensuring the development of responsible and trustworthy AI systems.

7 Whole-of-Nation Effort

Significantly, Singapore's national AI strategy promotes a whole-of-nation effort[53] highlighting the collaborative roles of citizens, businesses, academia, the State, and international partners in coming together to advance AI development and deployment to ensure that AI is adopted for the social and economic good of the nation.[54] Ordinary citizens and private corporations are encouraged to collaborate in the design and development of new technologies either through submitting ideas and solutions for National AI projects, transforming business models through various AI governance initiatives, participating in Singapore's AI ecosystem, or by learning about AI and improving one's digital skillsets.[55]

In short, it can be observed that Singapore's national AI strategy proposes a collaborative and participatory approach in the management of risks to and from AI. It

[51] Revealing some links to more generally understood data stewardship thinking.

[52] 'AI Standards' (*AI SIngapore*) <https://aisingapore.org/innovation/ai-standards/>.

[53] 'National Artificial Intelligence Strategy (Summary)' (n 26). See also: 'Be Part of Our AI Journey' (*Smart Nation Singapore*) <https://www.smartnation.gov.sg/nais/contribute/>.

[54] 'National Artificial Intelligence Strategy (Summary)' (n 26).

[55] 'Be Part of Our AI Journey' (n 53).

emphasises not only AI adoption but also, empowerment, including mastering AI's full potential and addressing its existing challenges. The strategy focuses both on the upgrading of workers' digital literacy and cultivating opportunities for AI communities to interact and exchange ideas, enabling the responsible and collective resolution of AI-related problems. Further, these initiatives emphasise the upholding of societal values such as fairness, non-discrimination, and human-centricity, which in turn promotes the reduction of AI risks and the re-embedding of AI into the social to safeguard societal interests. Importantly, the strategy highlights the need to foster a trusted environment so users can approach AI with confidence. The anticipated consequence of this is the building and restoration of trust bonds between AI and recipient communities.

Returning to Polanyi's theorising around counter movements and re-embedding, it can be observed that the declared policy of the Singapore government is to generate the appropriate conditions, language and incentives for commercial, industrial, scientific, technical research and civil society stakeholders to achieve a return of AI to the social. However, as Polanyi identifies in his double movement thinking, the problem of power asymmetries and self-interested motivations in exchange markets that are more committed to drawing commodities (like AI) further into fictitious valuing, presents a significant challenge for governance strategies depending on exchange market compliance. While the Singapore cocreation, coproduction strategy appears to require powerful and powerless stakeholders to work together in productive AI governance, it grows also out of assumptions about market morality and citizen commitment that may not reflect the realities of an AI/data ecosystems. Information deficits, for instance, need to be tackled by regulators if civil society is to be motivated and capable to call out AI risks and to also require commercial beneficiaries to ensure risk abatement.[56]

7.1 Singapore Model AI Governance Framework

Singapore's Model AI Governance Framework (Model Framework) offers voluntary and practical guidance to private sector commercial organisations to address key ethical and governance issues when designing/deploying AI solutions. The framework emphasises individual corporations' responsibility in mitigating AI-related risks to promote public trust and confidence in AI. Similar to Singapore's AI strategy, the model framework reflects the country's emphasis in cocreating an AI ecosystem and AI governance approach that is collaborative and industry-led.

The first Singapore Model AI Governance Framework was developed in 23 January 2019 and the second Model framework was released in 21 January 2020.[57] The model framework articulates two high-level guiding principles. Initially,

[56] Findlay et al. (2023), Chaps. 1, 3 & 5. See also: Drazewska and Findlay (n 32).

[57] 'Singapore's Approach to AI Governance' (n 20).

organisations using AI in decision-making should ensure that the decision-making process is explainable, transparent and fair. Further, that all AI solutions should be human-centric.[58]

The Singaporean Model asserts striking a balance between free and open innovation and proactively managing the risks that arise from these new technologies. Rather than enact legislation to govern AI, the model highlights the importance of industry self-governance, responsibility, and accountability in managing the risks posed by AI. It should be recognised that this is voluntary self-regulation and carries with it all the challenges of a self-regulation approach in any and all its applications.[59]

The model framework provides guidance on four areas to promote the responsible use of AI.[60] They include, assessing an organisation's internal AI governance structures and measures; determining the level of human involvement in AI-augmented decision making; operations management; and the level of stakeholders interactions with users.[61]

The model framework espouses a need to adapt existing or set up internal governance structure and measures to incorporate values, risks, and responsibilities relating to algorithmic decision-making.[62] Clear responsibilities and roles must be assigned to individuals when deploying AI to ensure accountability in AI design and deployment.[63] This includes providing all relevant personnel with proper training and resources to navigate and discharge their duties, and establishing a system of risk management and internal controls to address the risks involved in the deployment of the AI.[64] An organisation that has robust oversight over their use of AI are also better able to manage potential AI-related risks so AI can be successfully re-embedded into the social. For instance, clear accountability and responsibility structures will initiate higher levels of trust and confidence for relevant stakeholders, and proper training for AI practitioners and other personnel will promote the responsible design and deployment of AI. It is however important to note that each of these causal pronouncements depend on the due diligence with which the AI facilitators commit to compliance in a fashion that impacts across all stages of the AI design and deployment chain. Research has however shown that it is difficult to bring these aspirations for trust generation from managerial intention to uniform application.[65]

Next, the model emphasises the need to determine the appropriate level of human involvement in AI-augmented decision-making and proposes a design framework to

[58] 'Model Artificial Intelligence Governance Framework Second Edition' (*Personal Data Protection Commission Singapore*) <https://www.pdpc.gov.sg/-/media/Files/PDPC/PDF-Files/Resource-for-Organisation/AI/SGModelAIGovFramework2.pdf>.

[59] Findlay et al. (2023), Chaps. 1 & 5.

[60] 'Model Artificial Intelligence Governance Framework Second Edition' (n 58).

[61] 'Model Artificial Intelligence Governance Framework Second Edition' (n 58).

[62] 'Model Artificial Intelligence Governance Framework Second Edition' (n 58).

[63] 'Model Artificial Intelligence Governance Framework Second Edition' (n 58).

[64] 'Model Artificial Intelligence Governance Framework Second Edition' (n 58).

[65] Findlay et al. (2023), Chap. 4.

help organisations determine the level of human involvement required to minimise AI-related risks.[66] This framework is structured along two axies that are, the probability of harm and the severity of harm to individuals/organisation.[67] The framework also suggests that determining the level of human involvement in AI-augmented decision-making needs to be a continuous process and organisations need to regularly identify and review these risks.[68] Human intervention and control is integral in the management and prevention of AI risks as it enables the return of AI to the social particularly in cases where its risks are perceived as disengaging from the social fabric. Again, there are many organisational, operational and market pressures along the AI development chain that can work against uniform re-embedding involving all stakeholders no matter what level of power they exhibit in the attribution and distribution of responsibility.[69]

The framework recognises also that responsible measures must also be taken in the operations aspect of the AI adoption process.[70] It advises that to eliminate risks, an organisation must *look at* the data used for model development and the interaction between data and algorithm/model. Models built on biased data will inevitably run the risk of producing discriminatory decisions hence it is critical to have good data accountability practices in place.[71] In addition, to enhance transparency and trust in AI, organisations *should strive* to prioritise measures such as explainability, robustness, traceability, repeatability etc., using a risk-based approach.[72] Again, the importance of good quality data, ethical algorithms/models, and good data accountability practices would minimise discriminatory AI outputs promoting more fairness, accountability, and transparency in AI-decision making. However, which external body should be responsible for ensuring that these commitments are achieved within the organisation itself, remains unclear.

Finally, the model framework highlights the need to build trust in stakeholder relationships when deploying AI. The model emphasises disclosing all relevant information on what/when/how/why AI is used when it is deployed in an organisation's products or services.[73] Organisations should also develop a policy of explanation to promote not only consistency in communication but clarity on the responsibilities and duties of individuals within an organisation.[74] Meaningful transparency and explainability will cultivate trust and confidence in interactions with AI which would then enable the re-embedding of AI in the social. An option for users to opt-out from AI use would uphold their autonomy, and their easy access to com-

[66] 'Model Artificial Intelligence Governance Framework Second Edition' (n 58).
[67] 'Model Artificial Intelligence Governance Framework Second Edition' (n 58).
[68] 'Model Artificial Intelligence Governance Framework Second Edition' (n 58).
[69] Findlay et al. (2023), Chap. 4.
[70] 'Model Artificial Intelligence Governance Framework Second Edition' (n 58).
[71] 'Model Artificial Intelligence Governance Framework Second Edition' (n 58).
[72] 'Model Artificial Intelligence Governance Framework Second Edition' (n 58).
[73] 'Model Artificial Intelligence Governance Framework Second Edition' (n 58).
[74] 'Model Artificial Intelligence Governance Framework Second Edition' (n 58).

munication avenues is also critical[75] in the managing of potential risks through open dialogues. Again, it is worth highlighting that trust generation is no simple consequentialist enterprise. Particularly when measuring trust levels in AI recipient communities, it might not be enough to assert compliance with normative principles.[76]

In essence, the model framework aims to overcome the challenges and risks posed by AI not through the imposition of hard legal rules but by encouraging a collaborative approach with industry who are expected to be more hands-on with securing the responsible use of AI within their organisation. The four areas as proposed by the framework do not deviate far from commonly espoused ethical principles such as transparency, explainability, and retention of the human-in-the-loop. Ultimately, these principles aim at fostering trust relations to improve overall AI adoption in society. The main difference in the operationalisation of these principles (at least from the perspective of the EU and the chapter elaborates more on this point below) is the emphasis on securing these principles through voluntary industry participation and state support.[77]

The model framework supports Singapore's AI governance approach and its AI strategy by focusing on the capacity, good-will, and resources of individual organisations. Worth mentioning also is the State's efforts in enabling the comprehension and adaptability of the framework through two other supporting initiatives. These include the self-assessment guide for organisations (ISAGO)[78] and the compendium of use cases.[79] Both initiatives aim to complement the model framework by guiding and expanding on the framework implementation processes to promote more ethical and responsible AI development and/or deployment. Additionally, there are open channels for industry members to feedback on the effectiveness and feasibility of the Model implementation, as well as how the framework can be enhanced as AI evolves.[80] Again, this speaks to Singapore's preference for a collaborative model of AI governance.

As the Personal Data Protection Commission (PDPC) reports, a considerable number of prominent organisations operating in Singapore have already adopted the

[75] 'Model Artificial Intelligence Governance Framework Second Edition' (n 58).

[76] Findlay et al. (2023), Chap. 2.

[77] 'Artificial Intelligence in Singapore' (*Infocomm Media Development Authority*, 11 July 2024) <https://www.imda.gov.sg/about-imda/emerging-technologies-and-research/artificial-intelligence>.

[78] 'Companion to the Model AI Governance Framework – Implementation and Self-Assessment Guide for Organizations' (*World Economic Forum (Prepared in collaboration with the Infocommunications Media Development Authority of Singapore)*, January 2020) <https://www.pdpc.gov.sg/-/media/Files/PDPC/PDF-Files/Resource-for-Organisation/AI/SGIsago.pdf>.

[79] 'Volume 1: Compendium of Use Cases: Practical Illustrations of the Model AI Governance Framework' (*Personal Data Protection Commission Singapore*) <https://go.gov.sg/ai-gov-use-cases>. See also: 'Volume 2: Compendium of Use Cases: Practical Illustrations of the Model AI Governance Framework' (*Personal Data Protection Commission Singapore*) 2 <https://go.gov.sg/ai-gov-use-cases-2>.

[80] 'Singapore's Approach to AI Governance' (n 20).

Model framework,[81] underscoring perhaps the suitability and transferability of the Framework into Singapore's AI ecosystem, or an industry preference away from more formalised AI regulation. Organisations adopting this framework appear to re-embed AI in the market/social by building stakeholder confidence through accountability structures and ownership in the management of perceived/real risks in AI deployment. While organisations may accept the commercial and organisational benefits of ethical compliance in a market management sense, it is critical to interrogate whether uptake will be affected if market profits are compromised by compliance that does not prioritise profitability.

7.2 AI Verify and AI Verify Foundation

Singapore's unique approach to managing AI risks and developing stakeholder trust is demonstrated through its development of technical toolkits such as AI Verify. The toolkit validates the performance of an organisation's nominated AI system against a set of internationally recognised ethical principles[82] through standardised tests and process checks.[83] The AI Verify Foundation was also set up in conjunction with AI Verify to provide a platform and community for collaboration and idea-sharing on AI governance. The Foundation intends to contribute to the development of AI Verify promoting ethical AI and its best practices.[84] The uptake and utility of AI verify remains to be seen but it can be observed that alongside initiatives like the Model Framework, Singapore also takes on a practical and technological approach to guide industry's responsible development and deployment of AI.

7.3 Advisory Council on the Ethical Use of AI and Data

Citizens' trust and the minimisation of AI risks are purportedly also enhanced through initiatives such as the establishment of an Advisory Council on the Ethical use of AI and Data.[85] The Council advises the State on issues arising from the deployment of AI that may require policy/regulatory attention, and provides

---

[81] 'Model Artificial Intelligence Governance Framework Second Edition' (n 58).

[82] Including transparency, explainability, repeatability/reproducibility, safety, security, robustness, fairness, data governance, accountability, human agency and oversight, and inclusive growth, societal and environmental well-being. See: 'AI Verify: AI Governance Testing Framework and Toolkit' (*AI Verify Foundation*) <https://aiverifyfoundation.sg/downloads/AI_Verify_Primer_Jun-2023.pdf>.

[83] 'What Is AI Verify?' (*AI Verify Foundation*) <https://aiverifyfoundation.sg/what-is-ai-verify/>.

[84] AI Verify Foundation, 'Building Trust through Ethical AI' (*AI Verify Foundation*) <https://aiverifyfoundation.sg/ai-verify-foundation/>.

[85] 'National Artificial Intelligence Strategy' (n 23).

guidelines to industry on the responsible development and deployment of AI to minimise AI risks.[86] The council taps on the expertise of technical, legal, ethics and international experts, as well as representatives for consumers and civil society to guide its outputs.[87] The significance of a body such as the Advisory Council demonstrates Singapore's reliance on experts and the grounding of Singapore's AI governance/regulatory efforts on demonstrated evidence. Of course, while such initiatives are commendable in theory, it is important to still interrogate the role of the Council in acting as an effective force in mitigating risks and producing responsible oversight in practice.

7.4 *AI Standards*

Singapore has a dedicated AI Technical Committee tasked with adopting and developing AI standards both internationally (through participation in international standards bodies[88]) and domestically (by drafting Singapore's own national AI standards). Although standards have not specifically been fleshed out as part of Singapore's AI Governance approach, they continue to be acknowledged for their role internationally in enhancing trade connectivity, fostering trust, reliability, interoperability and addressing the gaps in performance, health, governance, ethics, security and cybersecurity issues in the deployment of AI.[89] However, any overreliance on standards compliance as empirical evidence of good governance attainment, risks the criticism that meeting broadly ascribed standards does not always reveal the failings of AI systems that respect the 'letter' of the standards but not always their application and sustainable embedding.

7.5 *Singapore's AI Governance Approach in Summary*

In Singapore's latest AI strategy, AI is singled out to be 'indispensable', a force necessary to preserve the relevance and prosperity of the nation.[90] Yet, the government acknowledges that the full benefits of AI cannot also be realised without its proper governance. Singapore's AI governance approach is thus premised on

86 'National Artificial Intelligence Strategy' (n 23).

87 Han (2019).

88 Such as the International Organization for Standardization (ISO).

89 Tak Leong Cheong and Laurence Liew, 'Why Standards Matter for AI and Big Data' (12 June 2023) <https://www.enterprisesg.gov.sg/resources/blog/quality-and-standards/why-standards-matter-for-ai-and-big-data>.

90 'NAIS 2.0 Singapore National AI Strategy: AI for the Public Good For Singapore and the World' (n 27).

finetuning a balance between facilitating innovation while at the same time safeguarding consumer interests.

Specifically, the value of public data as the building blocks for AI systems is emphasised throughout Singapore's AI Governance approach. Singapore's AI strategy explicitly emphasises the need to build a trusted data sharing ecosystem to enable the responsible innovation of human-centric AI. Innovation is thus encouraged throughout multiple State initiatives to solve societal needs and challenges but not without also strong signalling towards the need for proper AI governance—whether in the form of industry self-monitoring or the setting up of community spaces to inspire collaboration in AI governance approaches.

The language of governance is, for the most part, top down. The State offers the guidelines and incentives, and it is assumed that business, innovators and the public will fall into line. That said, a collaborative approach is ultimately hoped for in Singapore's proposed handling and management of AI risks. While clear responsibilities are placed on the role of industry to govern themselves and to protect the public interest, individuals in their personal capacities are also encouraged to upgrade their digital literacy, participate in the design and development of national AI projects, and acquaint themselves with AI's potential and shortcomings. From the community perspective as set out, the State imposes an obligation on citizens of all demographics and education levels to engage with AI proliferation as a part of the national project. This delegation of responsibilities may, in part, absolve the state from adopting a more interventionist role in risk minimisation.

This approach to repositioning responsibility for AI risks for it to be interpreted as an exercise in embedding of AI back into society would ultimately still rest on the nature, quality, and sustainability of engagement, recognising that for all key stakeholders, participation in governance is dependent on the identification and propagation of mutual interests.[91]

For example, in cases where collaboration is possible or encouraged from the State to individual level such as with the TechKaki initiative,[92] it is likely to only attract a niche and closed group of citizens who are likely already interested in these technologies. Such narrow class participation cannot account for the voice of wider society and so it is unclear whether initiatives working from this presumption are representative or inclusive enough to foster trust within the wider Singapore community. Further challenging the possibility of broad participation, the apparent accessibility of data on *data.gov.sg* to promote the development of AI for public benefit, falters in that not all datasets are available for public inspection or use. Statistics on prisons, incarceration, and legal aid for example, are not as extensively shared[93] which may undercut the potential for certain useful AI products/services to be designed, or broadly challenged. While the availability of such a data repository

[91] Findlay et al. (2023), Chap. 1.

[92] Tech Kaki is an end-user community established to encourage citizen participation in the development of government digital products and services. See: 'Tech Kaki Community' (*GovTech Singapore*) <https://www.tech.gov.sg/products-and-services/tech-kaki-community/>.

[93] Loo and Findlay (2022), p. 1.

is a precursor to citizen participation, the meaningfulness of such datasets and for whom it carries meaning needs critical interrogation.

8 Contrasting Singapore's AI Governance Countermovement with the EU's Countermovement

In the interest of space, this section will not delve into the individual chapters of the AI act.[94] Instead, the analysis endeavours to focus only on certain aspects of the AI Act that emphasises the chapter's thesis on the potential of the Act to address AI's impact on social responsibility and wealth creation while also managing AI-related risks, drawing comparisons to Singapore's AI governance approach. The relative effectiveness of a legislative approach to AI governance in terms of re-embedding AI back to the social, and thereby reducing risks to recipient communities is presented as a concern.

8.1 The EU AI Act

The AI Act is Europe's flagship AI regulation effort when it comes both to risk reduction and legislative regulation. The Act seeks to codify the EU's trustworthy AI approach[95] and achieve uniformity within the EU by setting out horizontal rules for the development and deployment of AI systems within the EU territories. The regulation aims to protect the fundamental rights, health and safety of individuals, rule of law, democracy, and the environment from harmful effects of AI.[96] The provisions of the Act apply to both public and private actors inside and outside the EU so long as the AI system is placed on the Union market or its use affects people located in the EU.[97] This is distinctly different from the Singapore approach in at least two ways. The European state favours law rather than self-regulation to ensure compliance from major commercial and industrial suppliers inside and outside Europe. In addition, it creates a suite of actionable rights which vulnerable stakeholders can enjoy if they have the standing and capacity to litigate.

The Act introduces a regime constructed around risk categories where stricter rules apply to certain AI systems as its risk increases. AI reflecting unacceptable risk

[94] The earlier chapters of the book have already undertook a comprehensive discussion on the individual chapters of the EU AI act.

[95] Which requires AI to be legally, ethically and technically robust, while respecting democratic values, human rights and the rule of law. See: Mauritz Kop, 'EU Artificial Intelligence Act: The European Approach to AI' [2021] Stanford Law School <https://law.stanford.edu/publications/eu-artificial-intelligence-act-the-european-approach-to-ai/>.

[96] AI Act (EU) 2024/1689, Article 1.

[97] AI Act (EU) 2024/1689, Article 2.

scores are entirely prohibited under the Act while stringent rules apply to high risk AI-systems. Limited risk AI systems are subject to certain transparency obligations to ensure that data subjects can make informed decisions about their interactions with the AI system, whereas minimal risk AI systems are to commit to voluntary codes of conduct. The final draft of the Act also touches on specific provisions that govern general purpose AI (GPAI) models, including foundation models and generative AI. Interestingly, the determination of what systems are to be considered risky (such as facial recognition technology) would not be so understood in Asian jurisdictions where these systems are deployed at scale.

It can be deduced that the recognition of these different risk categories offers legal certainty by both facilitating a flourishing yet safe AI ecosystem in Europe while also negotiating 'acceptable' levels of AI-related risk that is from Europe's perspective, still manageable. In this way, stricter regulatory requirements apply only when required/necessary so new AI innovation can continue to benefit society. Nonetheless, it can be observed that the majority of AI systems already in use in the Union are likely to still fall under the minimal risk category and would thus not be so drastically impacted by the new AI rules.[98] The sections to follow will predominantly focus on prohibited and high risk AI systems.

8.2 *Prohibited AI Systems*

Some brief observations can be made on prohibited AI systems under the AI act in contrast to Singapore's AI governance approach. Generally speaking, the systems that are explicitly outlawed under Article 5 of the Act strive at preserving individual autonomy and dignity, protecting privacy, safeguarding human vulnerability, countering mass surveillance, and preventing the exacerbation of existing inequalities. Hence, the prohibited list include a ban on any subliminal, manipulative, and deceptive AI systems, systems that exploit individual vulnerabilities, biometric categorisation systems, real-time biometric identification systems, AI systems used for risk assessments, AI systems that create facial recognition systems through untargeted scraping of facial images, emotion recognition systems in the workplace and education, and social scoring systems.[99]

No similar prohibitions are found in Singapore which may raise the question whether there is less of an appetite for protecting individual rights, particularly the right to privacy. Yet, Singapore's AI strategy similarly reveals an interest in enhancing cybersecurity and developing privacy-preserving technologies and initiatives (enabling data to be used efficiently while still preserving individual privacy). Such privacy concerns may not however, be directly reflective or an endorsement of

---

[98] 'Excellence and Trust in Artificial Intelligence' (*European Commission*) <https://ec.europa.eu/info/strategy/priorities-2019-2024/europe-fit-digital-age/excellence-trust-artificial-intelligence_en>.

[99] AI Act (EU) 2024/1689, Article 5.

citizen's privacy rights but rather, seen as part of the effort to protect data quality and to respect the data integrity of individuals. In this regard, while the EU's handling of privacy issues appears to ban certain AI systems that could potentially threaten individual privacy past a certain threshold, the Singapore approach appears to recognise the negotiable nature of privacy when measured against commercial/business interests, allowing certain AI systems to operate (despite prevailing privacy concerns) so long as its risks can be properly managed by either augmenting cybersecurity foundations or by relying on certain (technical and non-technical) privacy-preserving tools/mechanisms.

Singapore's approach towards discriminatory AI systems that could potentially exacerbate individual vulnerability is met not with prohibitions, but instead, with invocations to commercial users that their AI applications should be responsible. Singapore's Model Framework's 'four areas' to promote the responsible use of AI by industry emphasise accountability structures and human involvement to minimise potential AI biases, proper communication pathways to provide feedback, as well as the need for good quality data (used for model development) to eliminate discriminatory AI outputs. In so doing, a more negotiable threshold of risk appears to be accepted in the context of Singapore perhaps to soften negative impacts on AI innovation, and prefer business benefit, as is the case with its approach to personal data protection by comparison with the GDPR. The EU approach is contextually determined by an atmosphere of data subject rights, and the Singapore style is to nudge businesses to do the right thing.

The AI act inserts particular exemptions for when public security or the protection of one's right to life should take precedence over the prohibition in Article 5. For example, the lawful labelling or filtering of lawfully acquired biometric datasets such as images, based on biometric data or categorising of biometric data in the area of law enforcement,[100] as well as the use of real time biometric identification systems by law enforcement when it is used for specific actions like searching for missing persons or counter-terrorism operations.[101] The prohibition against risk assessment systems (to predict the risk of a person committing a criminal offence) does not also apply when the system is used merely to support human assessments that are already based on objective and verifiable facts.[102] In this regard, it can be observed that the AI Act recognises the utility of AI in supporting and augmenting human decision-making as opposed to when it replaces the human decision-maker. Finally, it is worth noting that the prohibition against emotion recognition systems under the Act is limited only to workplaces and education institutions despite its potential intrusiveness. This selective restriction perhaps reflects the Act's acknowledgment of the potential utility of the technology in other applications and contexts. From this analysis, it can be observed that similar to Singapore's AI governance

[100] AI Act (EU) 2024/1689, Article 5(1)(g).

[101] AI Act (EU) 2024/1689, Article 5(1)(h)(i) and (ii).

[102] AI Act (EU) 2024/1689, Article 5(1)(d).

approach, the EU's apparently stricter strategy for risk minimising also has pragmatic exemptions.

8.3 High Risk AI Systems

High risk AI systems are the most heavily regulated under the AI act with strict mandatory requirements imposed to safeguard fundamental rights and risks to individual health and safety. Article 6(2) provides that AI systems falling under any one of the critical areas referred to in Annex III shall be considered high-risk, which includes AI used in the area of biometrics, critical infrastructure, education, employment, essential and public services etc., Ultimately, the categorisation reveals that the Act is not interested in restrictively governing all technologies but specific areas and use cases where AI is being deployed. This approach recognises that AI risks will vary from sector to sector and hence the requirements set out under Articles 8–15 will only apply in these more narrowly defined circumstances.

Article 7(2) lists out some factors that would be taken into consideration in determining whether an AI system should be considered high risk. Amongst other factors, the Commission would consider the level of autonomy and the possibility of human intervention in the AI's decisions, the nature and volume of data the AI processes, the extent of harm, any power imbalance or vulnerability, and the availability of any possible redress measures. Most interestingly, the potential benefits of the AI system to individuals, groups, or society is also one of the factors that would be taken into consideration in determining whether an AI system is to be considered as falling under high risk. The weighing of benefits vs harms in this context reflects the Act's recognition of AI as an agent of wealth creation coupled with its other utilitarian benefits weighed against the need to govern against AI's potential societal harms.

Again, this moderated approach is reflected by the exemptions laid out under Article 6(3)(a)–(d) providing that AI systems are considered as not posing a 'significant risk of harm' and hence exempted from the requirements of high risk AI systems if, it is used to perform a narrowly defined task, to improve the result of a previously completed human activity, to detect decision-making patterns or deviations from prior decision-making patterns (and is not meant to replace or influence the previously completed human assessment), or to perform a simple preparatory task not the final task itself. These exemptions reflect on the utility of AI as a complementary tool that enhances human productivity and existing capabilities.

Reflecting on the above, it can be reasoned that the high risk category and its emphasis on rights-protection is not incontrovertible, offering some discretion for providers to argue that their AI systems do not pose a significant risk of harm and thereby avoid the regulatory burdens otherwise mandated. Nonetheless, the Act makes it compulsory for providers to document their assessment and fulfil registration obligations before placing their system on the market.[103] In that regard, it can be observed that the EU still adopts a cautious regulatory approach by ensuring proper recordability and traceability for identification/monitoring of situations that may result in the AI system presenting a risk.

Turning to the requirements for high-risk AI systems, these aim at mitigating the creation or perpetuation of potential AI endangerment. These requirements include: the establishment of a risk management system,[104] quality data governance practices,[105] comprehensive technical documentation,[106] record-keeping to guarantee traceability,[107] transparency and provision of information,[108] human oversight,[109] and ensuring that systems achieve an appropriate level of accuracy, robustness, and cyber-security.[110] The governance language and the imposition of responsibility on AI developers and users sounds similar to that applied in the Singapore strategy. What differs is legislative enactment, and actionable remedies if risks arise from any compliance failures.

Specifically, comparing the AI Act requirements with Singapore's Model Framework suggests certain alignments between the two approaches. In the four areas, the Model Framework similarly emphasises responsibility and accountability in an organisation's internal AI governance structures which can be said to be akin to the establishment of the EU's risk management system; human involvement and oversight that commensurate to the risks involved including the probability of harm and its severity to individuals/organisation. On this requirement, the AI Act also highlights the need to provide support to the person assigned to ensure human oversight. Singapore's Framework similarly emphasises the importance of training and appropriate resources for such personnel to properly discharge their duties; the AI act's principles of transparency, accuracy, quality data governance practices, technical documentation, record keeping, robustness, cyber-security are similarly repeated throughout Singapore's model framework.

Despite these identified similarities, the core difference is the EU regulatory approach is one of rights-protection whereas Singapore's broader governance reach avoids notions of individual rights in favour of also facilitating AI's wealth creation capacities by enabling industrial market players the wiggle room to manage their regulatory compliance without the threat of legislative sanction or rights litigation. While Singapore similarly places strong emphasis on the health and safety of individuals, data privacy, creation of clear responsibility and accountability structures, meaningful human-involvement, and quality data practices, it does not enshrine

[103] AI Act (EU) 2024/1689, Article 16(i) and Article 49.

[104] AI Act (EU) 2024/1689, Article 9.

[105] AI Act (EU) 2024/1689, Article 10.

[106] AI Act (EU) 2024/1689, Article 11.

[107] AI Act (EU) 2024/1689, Article 12.

[108] AI Act (EU) 2024/1689, Article 13.

[109] AI Act (EU) 2024/1689, Article 14.

[110] AI Act (EU) 2024/1689, Article 15.

these in legal regulatory frames, and as such remedies against non-compliance remain in the hands of the market.

Both risk governance approaches reveal different mechanisms and consequences (regulation vs guidelines), and both function as counter movements to the risks posed through dis-embedding AI from social goods, sharing similar aspirations for controlling and containing real and potential AI risks.

8.4 Final Observations on the AI Act and Singapore's AI Governance Approach

As cautioned at the outset, simplistic comparisons between East and West are unhelpful and are likely misleading. For instance, it is wrong to argue in any blanket sense that Europe respects human rights in the governance of AI risks while Singapore, and other Asian jurisdictions at large do not. Instead, it is the preferred governance incentives and penalties, as well as mechanisms that are employed which provide revealing juxtapositions in a wider sense of positioning AI as a means for advancing social and economic development, while addressing safety and risk.

The chapter also notes the inaccuracy of suggesting that Europe respects privacy rights while Singapore does not. The apparent difference is how privacy is measured against commercial advantage, and how any challenges to privacy are met. Respect for individual privacy and safety is reiterated throughout Singapore's AI governance strategy and Model framework, and the risks to these posed by AI are attributed to and distributed throughout market stakeholders. While Europe prioritises individual rights and offers legislative guarantees more than market invocations, it does not also do so absolutely at the expense of commercialising the benefits of AI innovation. Both regions each have expressed the need to balance protection against progress, and navigate the landscape of AI governance with context-specific considerations for both technological advancement and risk management.

Article 57 of the Act, for example, explicitly provides for the creation of regulatory sandboxes granting providers a 'safe space' to train and develop their AI innovations. Article 62 goes on to stipulate how SMEs and start-ups should be given priority access to these regulatory sandboxes highlighting the EU's efforts in promoting AI innovation by smaller industry players. Article 60 then provides for scenarios of 'real-world testing' of high-risk AI systems outside AI regulatory sandboxes. The insertion of these articles suggest also a pro-innovation stance in the EU for AI to develop in a safe space; where AI risks are acknowledged upfront and clear measures are drafted to navigate these risks. If like Singapore's AI governance aspirations, the EU is similarly allowing the employment of AI as an agent of wealth and utility creation. Both approaches value governing AI for its non-feasance—it is the mechanisms employed for protective functions and their foundations that differs.

From this common recognition of governance that also supports responsible AI development, and returning to Polanyi, the double movement and re-embedding AI into the social, it is important to explore the two regulatory approaches in these terms. Both the EU and Singapore accept the continued role of AI in exchange markets and as such, its existence as a commodity in a trajectory away from the social. Thus, both governance counter-movements strive to act against this dis-embedding, exhibiting similar language and regulatory consequences that work towards common intentions for innovation and risk mitigation to also restore citizens' trust.

While citizen trust in AI function as the essential context for re-embedding AI in the social, it can be observed that the pathway to achieving trust is different in the different regulatory contexts. The EU approach sees the legislative guarantee of rights protection against an exponential scale of risk as vital in generating and maintaining trust. For Singapore, trust is expected through the voluntary compliance of market players and the participation of civil society. Specific provisions in the AI Act can now be highlighted to provide a more holistic understanding on the use of regulation in the EU as a tool to embed AI back into the social so trust can be engendered among recipient communities.

Article 86 provides that individuals have a right to explanation from deployers if they are adversely affected by a high-risk AI system. This right to request clear and meaningful explanation on the role of the AI system adheres well to commonly espoused ethical principles of transparency, explainability, and accountability. In this process, trust can be cultivated as individuals exercise their autonomy and are empowered with critical information/knowledge necessary to make informed determinations on how they wish to interact (or not interact) with the AI system. Another useful provision is Article 85 providing a mechanism for citizens to lodge complaints to the relevant market surveillance authority if there are grounds to consider that an AI system has infringed any of the provisions of the Act. Having recourse to such mechanisms grant citizens some level of control in accepting and monitoring the type of AI (including its consequent impact) that they wish to embed into their communities. Trust can also be cultivated in this way because citizens are empowered to participate in shaping the type of ethical AI they permit or disallow in their society. Moreover, the availability of such mechanisms convey the willingness of authorities to take into account citizens' perspectives by removing from the market potentially harmful AI.

Nonetheless, it is worth mentioning that the provisions have also tasked individuals with an enforcement load that they may not have the means (financial or otherwise) to pursue. Also useful to consider is how meaningful the right to explanation can be if individuals are ill-equipped to understand precisely how they were harmed by an AI system. Obvious tensions may also exist between persons requesting explanation and providers refusing such requests based on trade secrets. In these cases, it is difficult to envision how these provisions can operate to restore trust in society.

In Singapore, while such mechanisms are not given force of law, the State has urged companies to open communication avenues that offer space for those impacted by AI to provide their feedback. The expectation in this setting is recognising the significance of open dialogues in building or restoring trust in stakeholder relationships.[111] Similar to the AI Act, the Model Framework also emphasises the importance of general disclosure, meaningful transparency, explainability, and the availability to opt out from the use of an AI product or service. As already contemplated above with the AI act, adherence to these principles can go some way into building trust in communities to re-embed AI in society. However, in the Singapore approach, questions can be raised concerning the empowerment of civil society to meaningfully participate in trust conversations where power asymmetries are not smoothen by providing enforceable powers to otherwise ill-informed or dispossessed data subjects.

Despite these differences, both the AI Act and Singapore's AI governance counter movements follow a 'whole of society' approach in negotiating AI risks. For instance, the Act does not assign responsibility for the safety of high risk AI and the management of its potential risks on AI providers alone. After a product has entered the marketplace, the Market Surveillance Authority takes on the responsibility to carry out evaluations if it considers that an AI system presents a risk,[112] and to take appropriate measures to prohibit, restrict, recall, or withdraw an AI system in situations of non-compliance with the Act.[113] Users are also tasked with (limited) monitoring and oversight of these systems.[114] Whereas AI deployers are assigned the responsibility to perform a fundamental rights impact assessment when deploying an AI product/service.[115] The obligation to monitor AI systems for risks thus occur both upstream and downstream. This 'whole of society' approach is also found in Singapore's 'softer' AI governance approach that similarly employs the resources and the initiative of providers, deployers, and AI recipients.

By juxtaposing the Singapore and EU AI governance models, the chapter aims at demonstrating how two very distinct (yet comparable) governance approaches can negotiate the management of AI risks to facilitate the shared outcome of using responsible AI to promote wealth creation and applying trust-actioned governance tools to facilitate re-embedding of AI in the social, and thereby reducing risks to recipient human communities. While either governance a approach need not be measured as superior or as the exclusive pathway for achieving either aims, the chapter recalls that the value of any AI governance approach (hard or soft) would still lie in the market reality of how it facilitates new innovations while managing AI risks, how it coordinates the resources, initiative, and powers of respective stakeholders in the AI ecosystem, and how it successfully engages with its citizens to cultivate and restore trust in AI. So long as both Singapore and the EU view AI as a commodity in exchange markets, and dis-embedding from the social means that AI commodification will become increasingly distant from the social (and as such fictitious) without effective counter movements, the governance of AI cannot only be

[111] 'Model Artificial Intelligence Governance Framework Second Edition' (n 58), p. 53.

[112] AI Act (EU) 2024/1689, Article 74.

[113] AI Act (EU) 2024/1689, Article 79.

[114] AI Act (EU) 2024/1689, Article 85 and 86.

[115] AI Act (EU) 2024/1689, Article 27.

seen in terms of risk and safety. No matter how delicate the risk/market balance is struck; it is the dis-embedding of AI from the social that poses the most significant challenge to governance if society is to reclaim AI as more than a market commodity.

In most of the risk discourse, the language is technical and instrumentalist even if it is moderated through human rights considerations. More thought needs to be directed towards risks that dis-embed AI from the social through commodification and fictitious applications, rather than prioritising the protection of its potential in wealth creation. Whatever governance approach is utilised, the EU and Singapore experiments are common in at least stimulating the AI market re-embedding. So long as AI is to be approached as a commodity in AI wealth creation, it is likely to dis-embed from the social no matter what counter-movements are proposed to strive for trust and community engagement. Re-embedding AI in the community can only be a successful anti-risk policy when governance advocates commit to locating AI within communities in all its applications.

References

Duan Y, Edwards JS, Dwivedi YK (2019) Artificial intelligence for decision making in the era of big data – evolution, challenges and research agenda. Int J Inf Manag 48:63. https://linkinghub.elsevier.com/retrieve/pii/S0268401219300581

Findlay M (2017) Law's regulatory relevance? Property, power and market economies. Edward Elgar

Findlay M (2021) Globalisation, populism, pandemics and the law: the anarchy and the ecstasy. Edward Elgar

Findlay M, Henham R (2007) In: McConville M, Chui WH (eds) Research methods for law. Edinburgh University Press

Findlay MJ, Wong W (2021) Trust and regulation: an analysis of emotion. SSRN Electr J. https://www.ssrn.com/abstract=3857447

Findlay M, Seah J, Wong W (2023) AI and big data: disruptive regulation. Edward Elgar

Han GY (2019) In: Remolina N, Seah J (eds) How to address the AI governance discussion? What can we learn from Singapore's AI strategy? Keio University. https://www.ssrn.com/abstract=3444024

Johnson D (2010) British models of colonial governance: Adam Smith and John Bruce on the Cape Colony. The Eighteenth Century 51:103. https://muse.jhu.edu/article/398116

Loo J, Findlay M (2022) Digitised justice: the new two tiers? Crim Law Forum 33:1. https://link.springer.com/10.1007/s10609-022-09431-x

McCullagh CB (1980) Historical realism. Philos Phenomenol Res 40:420. https://www.jstor.org/stable/2106406?origin=crossref

Polanyi K (2001) The great transformation: the political and economic origins of our time, 2nd Beacon Paperback ed. Beacon Press

Wiley S (2023) AI for profit: navigating the opportunities and challenges of artificial intelligence in business. Independently Published

Taiwan's AI Regulations: A Sector-Based Regulatory Approach

Chih-Hsiung Chen

Contents

I would like to thank my research assistants in the process of writing this Chapter. They are Zhong Yun Jia, Wu Chen You Jun, Wang Hsiang Yu, Su Thiri Aung, Shwe Yamone Phoo, and Akbar Qurani Hidayatullah. This research is sponsored by National Science and Technology Council, project number: MOST 112-2634-F-A49-003-.

C.-H. Chen (✉)
National Yang Ming Chiao Tung University School of Law, HsinChu City, Taiwan
e-mail: chen@nycu.edu.tw

V. L. Raposo (ed.), *The European Artificial Intelligence Act*, Law, Governance and Technology Series 78, https://doi.org/10.1007/978-3-031-98406-8_18

Abstract This article examines Taiwan's approach to AI regulations, comparing it to the European Union's (EU) AI Act. Highlighting the influence of Taiwan's robust semiconductor industry, strategic partnerships with the United States, and its significant presence of small to medium-sized enterprises (SMEs), the article explores how these factors shape Taiwan's flexible and adaptive regulatory strategy. It delves into the progression from Taiwan's AI Action Plan 1.0 to AI Action Plan 2.0, and the formulation of the upcoming Basic AI Act, emphasising the importance of talent cultivation, technological advancement, industrial integration, and ethical frameworks. The analysis includes a detailed comparison with the EU AI Act, focusing on regulatory sandboxes, sector-specific guidelines, and international alignment. Additionally, the article discusses Taiwan's administrative guidelines for AI, addressing generative AI, AI in the financial industry, and AI in healthcare. It also examines the current legal framework for consumer protection in Taiwan, outlining challenges and comparing it with the EU's comprehensive approach. Recommendations for enhancing Taiwan's AI regulatory strategy are provided, emphasising the need for flexibility, public trust, international collaboration, support for SMEs, robust data governance, ethical AI development, and continuous investment in R&D. The conclusion highlights Taiwan's proactive approach to AI governance and its potential to set a different standard for responsible AI regulation.

1 Introduction: Taiwan's AI Regulation Strategy

As artificial intelligence (AI) technology rapidly evolves, governments worldwide recognise the need for regulatory frameworks to ensure the ethical, safe, and effective use of AI. This Chapter explores Taiwan's AI regulatory strategy in comparison to the EU's AI Act, highlighting the underlying reasons for their divergent paths.

Taiwan, influenced by civil law traditions and European legal systems, particularly German law, closely observes the EU's legislative measures in digital technologies, including the General Data Protection Regulation (GDPR) and the AI Act. Taiwan's active involvement in AI development is evidenced by its talent pool, as seen in the 2015 AlphaGo project led by a Taiwanese researcher.[1] However, Taiwan's approach to AI legislation diverges from the EU's for several critical reasons.

Firstly, Taiwan's robust semiconductor industry and its strategic partnership with the United States heavily influence its regulatory decisions. Given the geopolitical tensions with China, Taiwan prioritises strong tech diplomacy and trade relations with the U.S. This is reflected in Taiwan's preference for aligning its digital laws more closely with U.S strategies, such as participating in the Cross-Border Privacy

[1] Taiwan Today (2024) Taiwan genius helps computer trounce human Go champ. https://taiwantoday.tw/news.php?unit=10&post=21687.

Rules (CBPR) system led by the U.S.,[2] rather than adopting GDPR-like frameworks.[3] The chip industry is the major golden goose of Taiwan, and American AI companies are major buyers for the chips Taiwan produced. The commercial nature of the semiconductor industry requires those Taiwan companies to comply the American laws more than the EU Laws.

Taiwan's industry structure is another factor, characterised by numerous small to medium-sized enterprises (SMEs) rather than large multinational corporations,[4] with few exceptions like TSMC (Taiwan Semiconductor Manufacturing Company Limited). These SMEs might struggle with the high compliance costs associated with stringent regulations akin to the EU's AI Act. Thus, Taiwan adopts a cautious and phased approach to AI legislation, aiming to gradually enhance regulatory standards without overwhelming its SMEs. An example of this incremental approach is the Financial Supervisory Commission's (FSC) roadmap for FinTech regulation, which introduces open banking in stages.[5] This approach helps to balance innovation with regulation, ensuring that smaller businesses can adapt without facing prohibitive costs or compliance burdens.

The European Union's AI Act aims to regulate AI technologies by creating a legal framework that addresses risks while promoting innovation. It categorises AI systems into risk levels—unacceptable, high, limited, and minimal—each with specific regulatory requirements. This approach targets potential harms like bias and privacy violations by imposing strict rules on high-risk AI systems, including rigorous testing and transparency.

Taiwan's strategy is more flexible, focusing on sector-specific guidelines and self-regulation. The AI Action Plans during the last decade emphasise AI ethics and collaboration with industry stakeholders to ensure responsible AI development. Regulatory bodies like the NCC and MOEA work closely with industries to balance innovation and regulation. Because it is sector-specific, different sectors might adopt a different risk classification approach for AI systems compared to the EU AI Act.

A key difference is the EU's prescriptive approach, with detailed compliance requirements, versus Taiwan's principles-based method, encouraging voluntary

[2] Taiwan Ministry of Education (2024) Taiwan Joins the Global CAPE on Promoting Cross-Border Privacy Enforcement Cooperation with International Partners. https://english.moe.gov.tw/cp-117-39620-bcfc2-1.html; U.S. Department of Commerce (2024) Global Cross-Border Privacy Rules Declaration https://www.commerce.gov/global-cross-border-privacy-rules-declaration.

[3] One Trust Data Guidance (2023) Comparing Privacy Laws: GDPR v. PDPA. via:https://www.dataguidance.com/sites/default/files/gdpr_v._pdpa_.pdf

[4] Taiwan Ministry of Economy Affairs (2022) SMEs Serve as the Backbone of Taiwan's Stable Economic Development. https://www.moea.gov.tw/MNS/english/news/News.aspx?kind=6&menu_id=176&news_id=103826. According to the Ministry of Economy Affairs, as of 2021, there were more than 1.59 million SMEs in Taiwan, accounting for over 98 percent of all enterprises. These SMEs employed 9.2 million people, representing more than 80 percent of the total workforce.

[5] Taiwan Financial Supervisory Commission (2020) Fintech Development Roadmap. via:https://www.fsc.gov.tw/userfiles/file/FinTech%20Development%20Roadmap.pdf.

compliance and industry collaboration. Taiwan also emphasises international cooperation, aligning its regulations with global standards, especially with the US, to support its export-driven economy. This alignment helps Taiwan compete internationally without trade barriers, ensuring its AI products meet global standards.

This Chapter will first describe the development of Taiwan's AI strategy, particularly from AI Plan 1.0 to AI Plan 2.0. Secondly, the Chapter will analyse the two Taiwan's sandbox laws and their difference with the AI Act's sandbox regulations. The third part is about the administrative guidelines promulgated recently to keep flexibility but still require enterprises to follow certain AI governance rules. The Chapter will end with the analysis of the advantages and disadvantages of Taiwan's AI regulatory approach.

2 The Development of Taiwan's AI Strategy: From AI Plan 1.0 to AI Plan 2.0

Taiwan's approach to AI regulation has evolved significantly, reflecting a strategic and adaptive response to the needs of fostering AI innovation while ensuring ethical oversight. The progression from AI Plan 1.0 to AI Plan 2.0, and now towards a comprehensive AI regulatory framework, underscores Taiwan's commitment to becoming a global AI leader.[6] This evolution highlights Taiwan's recognition of the importance of balancing technological advancement with responsible governance.

2.1 AI Plan 1.0 (2018–2020)

The 'Taiwan AI Action Plan 1.0', launched in 2018, laid the groundwork for Taiwan's AI ecosystem with a focus on: (1) Infrastructure Development: Building the necessary infrastructure to support AI development. (2) Foundational Technologies: Enhancing core AI technologies for integration into various industries.[7] (3) Collaborations: Partnering with major tech companies like Google and Microsoft to position Taiwan as an AI innovation hub.[8]

During this period, Taiwan introduced two significant regulatory sandbox laws: (1) Financial Sector Sandbox (2018):[9] Allowed innovative financial technologies to

[6] Hsiung and Chang (2023) AI, machine learning & big data laws & regulations | Taiwan. GLI. Available from: https://www.globallegalinsights.com/practice-areas/ai-machine-learning-and-big-data-laws-and-regulations/taiwan.

[7] Id. 8

[8] ROC Taiwan Executive Yuan News Room(2011) AI Taiwan Action Plan, https://english.ey.gov.tw/News3/9E5540D592A5FECD/1dec0902-e02a-49c6-870d-e77208481667.

[9] Financial Technology Development and Innovative Experimentation Act, https://law.moj.gov.tw/ENG/LawClass/LawAll.aspx?pcode=G0380254.

be tested in a controlled environment, promoting fintech advancements while ensuring regulatory compliance. (2) Unmanned Vehicle Sandbox (2019):[10] Provided a legal framework for testing autonomous vehicles, balancing innovation with safety.

These sandbox laws were not solely aimed at encouraging innovation or supporting SMEs but were primarily designed to develop better regulations for new AI products and services. This strategic use of sandboxes illustrates Taiwan's proactive approach in refining its regulatory framework to keep pace with technological advancements.

Another major milestone was the establishment of the AI Technology R&D Guidelines in 2018, which emphasised ethical principles such as fairness, transparency, and accountability.[11] However, this guideline showed that Taiwan, at the time, had not fully considered the possible social impacts when these technologies entered the market. The primary focus was on ethical principles during development rather than post-deployment societal impacts.

2.2 AI Plan 2.0 (2023-Present)

Building on the achievements of AI Plan 1.0, the 'Taiwan AI Action Plan 2.0[12]' was introduced in 2023 with a broader and more ambitious scope.[13] In terms of AI governance, the plan focuses on (1) Evaluation and Verification: Establishing evaluation centres and creating rigorous testing protocols for AI technologies to ensure safety and reliability. (2) Addressing Societal Issues: Using AI to solve societal problems such as healthcare and environmental sustainability.[14]

AI Plan 2.0 also integrates with the '5+2 Innovative Industries Plan[15]' to drive economic transformation in key sectors like biomedicine and green energy. Additionally, it emphasises international collaboration, aligning Taiwan's AI regulations with global standards to remain competitive internationally.

[10] Unmanned Vehicles Technology Innovative Experimentation Act, https://law.moj.gov.tw/ENG/LawClass/LawAll.aspx?pcode=J0030147.

[11] National Science and Technology Council, Taiwan (2022) Taiwan AI readiness assessment report. https://digi.nstc.gov.tw/File/5AF024B4C7281A84/e761bee6-a38c-4d5b-8481-fc36b83b25d8?A=C.

[12] Id.8

[13] Taipei Times (2023) Executive Yuan announces artificial intelligence plan https://www.taipeitimes.com/News/front/archives/2023/06/04/2003800937

[14] National Science and Technology Council, Taiwan. Taiwan AI Readiness Assessment Report 2022. https://digi.nstc.gov.tw/File/5AF024B4C7281A84/e761bee6-a38c-4d5b-8481-fc36b83b25d8?A=C.

[15] German Trade Office Taipei. Taiwan: Smart, Innovative, Green, https://taiwan.ahk.de/information-hub/country-info/taiwan-smart-innovative-green.

2.3 Comparison with the EU's AI Act

Both Taiwan and the EU aim to foster AI innovation while ensuring ethical and responsible use. However, their regulatory approaches differ significantly.

The EU's AI Act is highly prescriptive, categorising AI systems into different risk levels (unacceptable, high, limited, minimal) with corresponding regulatory requirements.[16] This framework aims to mitigate potential harms such as bias, discrimination, and privacy violations by imposing strict obligations on high-risk AI systems, including rigorous testing and transparency requirements.

Taiwan's regulatory strategy is more flexible and adaptive. Instead of using a blanket regulation system like the EU, Taiwan focuses on sector-specific guidelines and self-regulation. Regulatory sandboxes for finance and unmanned vehicles exemplify this approach, providing controlled environments for testing while ensuring compliance. Taiwan does not categorise AI systems into risk levels but rather emphasises ethical principles and international collaboration.

The evolution from AI Plan 1.0 to AI Plan 2.0, and the impending Basic AI Act, underscores Taiwan's strategic approach to AI governance.[17] By balancing innovation with ethical considerations and aligning with international standards, Taiwan is setting an example for other nations in responsible and effective AI governance. The comparison with the EU's AI Act highlights Taiwan's unique, flexible approach that avoids categorising AI risks, focusing instead on sector-specific regulations and fostering industry collaboration.

3 Taiwan's AI Regulatory Sandbox Laws

Taiwan has implemented targeted legislative initiatives to integrate advanced technologies into various sectors through a sector-specific regulatory approach.[18] This strategy is designed to foster innovation while ensuring regulatory compliance and safety. Two notable legislative initiatives in this context are the Unmanned Vehicles Technology Innovative Experimentation Act and the Fintech Development and Innovation Experiment Act, both enacted in 2018.

---

[16] See Art. 6, EU AI ACT.

[17] CNA Staff writer (2023) Government drafting basic law to regulate AI. Taipei Times. https://www.taipeitimes.com/News/taiwan/archives/2023/07/06/2003802773.

[18] Tsai et al. (2020), p. 14.

3.1 Unmanned Vehicles Technology Innovative Experimentation Act

The legislative process for the Unmanned Vehicles Technology Innovative Experimentation Act began in response to the need for advancing autonomous vehicle technologies in Taiwan. On June 1, 2019, this act was officially effective, marking a significant step in Taiwan's regulatory framework for technological innovation. The primary motivation behind this legislation was to address the transportation needs of an aging society and enhance mobility and safety through autonomous vehicles, particularly focusing on buses.[19] The legislative process involved consultations with various stakeholders, including technology developers, regulatory bodies, and public safety officials, to ensure that the act would provide a comprehensive and flexible framework for the experimentation and development of unmanned vehicle technologies.

The Unmanned Vehicles Technology Innovative Experimentation Act lays out a detailed and structured framework for the testing and development of unmanned vehicle technologies. The act emphasises the importance of safety and regulatory flexibility to foster innovation. It outlines the application and review processes, providing clear guidelines for submitting and approving technology experiments.[20] Additionally, the act mandates stringent safety measures and data collection requirements to ensure that all experiments are conducted responsibly and that the data gathered can inform future regulatory decisions.[21] The act also includes provisions for extending and modifying the experimentation period, allowing for adjustments based on the evolving needs and technological advancements.[22]

Since its implementation, the Unmanned Vehicles Technology Innovative Experimentation Act has facilitated several key developments in Taiwan's autonomous vehicle sector, especially in public transportation. The act has enabled numerous trials of autonomous buses in various urban settings, providing valuable data on their operational efficiency and safety.[23] These trials have not only demonstrated the viability of autonomous public transportation but have also highlighted areas for improvement in technology and infrastructure. The data collected from these experiments have been crucial in shaping future regulatory frameworks and in fostering public trust in autonomous vehicle technologies. Moreover, the act has attracted

[19] Legislative Yuan Gazette, Volume 107, Issue 109, Plenary Session Records.

[20] Art.5-Art.18. Unmanned Vehicles Technology Innovative Experimentation Act.

[21] Art.16-Art.17. Unmanned Vehicles Technology Innovative Experimentation Act.

[22] Art.9; for adjustments see Art.10. Unmanned Vehicles Technology Innovative Experimentation Act.

[23] ROC Taiwan Department of Industry Technology (2024) The Unmanned Vehicle Technology Project: Execution Results. https://www.moea.gov.tw/MNS/doit/content/Content.aspx?menu_id=32501.

interest from international tech companies, positioning Taiwan as a significant player in the global autonomous vehicle industry.[24]

Scholars have provided various analyses of the Unmanned Vehicles Technology Innovative Experimentation Act, highlighting both its strengths and areas for improvement. Many commend the act for its forward-thinking approach and flexibility, which have been crucial in promoting innovation in autonomous vehicle technology.[25] The act's provisions for safety and data collection are particularly praised for ensuring that experiments are conducted responsibly.[26] However, some scholars point out that the act could benefit from more robust mechanisms for public engagement and transparency. They argue that greater involvement from the public and clearer communication about the purposes and outcomes of experiments could enhance public trust and support for autonomous vehicle initiatives.[27] Additionally, while the act has been successful in enabling experimentation, there is a call for more comprehensive long-term strategies to integrate these technologies into the mainstream transportation system.[28]

3.2 *Financial Technology Development and Innovative Experimentation Act*

The Financial Technology Development and Innovative Experimentation Act was enacted in 2018 as part of Taiwan's strategic initiative to boost technological innovation within the financial sector. This legislation emerged from the need to create a supportive environment for fintech advancements, addressing the growing demand for innovative financial solutions. The Act was designed to provide a structured framework where new fintech applications could be tested under controlled conditions.[29] Policymakers aimed to strike a balance between fostering innovation and maintaining financial stability and security. The drafting process involved extensive consultations with industry experts, financial institutions, and regulatory bodies to ensure that the Act would effectively support technological experimentation while safeguarding consumer interests.

The Fintech Development and Innovation Experiment Act establishes a controlled-risk environment that allows fintech companies to test their innovative

[24] NAIPnews (2024) Investment Opportunities of Taiwan's New Generation Automobile Industry. http://en.naipo.com/Portals/0/web_en/Knowledge_Center/AMPA2024/IPNE_240326_0103.htm.

[25] Chang (2023a), p. 1404.

[26] Chang (2021), p. 155.

[27] Chen et al. (2020), p. 10.

[28] Id.28.

[29] ROC Taiwan Executive Yuan (2018) 'Financial Technology Development and Innovation Experiment Act' — Encouraging Innovation, Enhancing Financial Competitiveness (《金融科技發展與創新實驗條例》—鼓勵創新，提升金融競爭力)https://www.ey.gov.tw/Page/5A8A0CB5B41DA11E/aa4a0c9d-14be-4664-ac59-fc74a056d1fd.

financial technologies in real-world settings with reduced regulatory constraints. The Act focuses on managing and mitigating potential risks under the close supervision of regulatory bodies. This framework is designed to facilitate the careful evaluation of new technologies before their full-scale market introduction. Companies participating in the sandbox are required to submit detailed plans outlining their proposed innovations, including safety measures and potential risks.[30] Regulatory bodies then assess these plans to ensure that they meet the necessary standards for public safety and financial stability.[31] This process enables fintech firms to refine their technologies in a controlled setting, fostering innovation while ensuring compliance with regulatory requirements.

Since its implementation, the Financial Technology Development and Innovative Experimentation Act has seen mixed results. On one hand, it has provided a platform for several innovative projects to be tested and refined. Some fintech startups have successfully leveraged the sandbox to develop cutting-edge financial products that address specific market needs.[32] However, the overall impact has been somewhat limited, with only a few applications and implementations reaching the market.[33] The controlled-risk environment has enabled the safe testing of new technologies, but the uptake has been slower than anticipated.[34] Despite these challenges, the Act has established a foundation for ongoing fintech innovation and has set a precedent for future regulatory frameworks.

Scholars have offered varied analyses of the Fintech Development and Innovation Experiment Act's effectiveness. While some praise the Act for its forward-thinking approach and its role in creating a safer environment for fintech innovation,[35] others point to its limited success in attracting and retaining participants. Critics argue that the stringent requirements and regulatory constraints may deter startups from participating in the sandboxs.[36] They suggest that for the Act to be more effective, there needs to be a reassessment of its design to provide clearer incentives and support for innovators. Additionally, there is a call for greater flexibility within the framework to better accommodate the rapidly evolving nature of fintech technologies.[37] Despite these critiques, the Act is generally seen as a positive step towards integrating advanced technologies into Taiwan's financial sector, promoting a culture of innovation while ensuring regulatory oversight.

[30] Art.4. Financial Technology Development and Innovative Experimentation Act.

[31] Art.6-7. Financial Technology Development and Innovative Experimentation Act.

[32] Kao et al. (2020), p. 7.

[33] Commercial Times (2023) After Two Years Waiting, the Financial Regulatory Sandbox Experiment Finally Gets One Applicant (in Chinese). https://www.ctee.com.tw/news/20230209700780-430301.

[34] Id. 20, p. 15.

[35] Chang and Shih (2018), p. 51.

[36] Peng and Tsang (2019), p. 26.

[37] Id.38, pp. 27–28.

3.3 *Comparison of Taiwan's Sector-Specific Regulatory Sandboxes and the EU AI Act's Sandbox Provisions*

Taiwan and the EU have both adopted innovative approaches to regulating emerging technologies through regulatory sandboxes, but their strategies differ significantly in scope and focus.

Taiwan has implemented a sector-specific regulatory sandbox approach designed to foster innovation within particular industries. These sandboxes allow companies to test and refine new technologies in real-world applications under controlled conditions, thereby reducing immediate regulatory constraints. Unlike the EU AI Act, Taiwan's sandbox regulations are not primarily aimed at reducing compliance costs for small and medium-sized enterprises (SMEs). Instead, they focus on developing appropriate regulatory models for different sectors in the absence of a comprehensive AI law. This approach includes both SMEs and large enterprises, ensuring that new technologies meet safety and compliance standards before wider deployment. Taiwan's sandboxes provide a flexible and targeted method for encouraging innovation, tailored to the unique needs and challenges of different industries.[38]

In contrast, the EU AI Act adopts a broad and comprehensive regulatory framework that applies uniformly across all member states.[39] The primary goal of the EU's regulatory sandboxes is to alleviate the regulatory burden on SMEs and encourage innovation.[40] This legislation covers a wide range of AI applications with a particular emphasis on high-risk systems to ensure stringent oversight and robust compliance measures. The EU's approach is characterised by a holistic framework that incorporates strict consumer protections and ethical standards. It mandates detailed risk management protocols, including conformity assessments and robust data governance, especially for high-risk AI systems. By establishing a harmonised regulatory environment, the EU AI Act aims to provide a stable and predictable framework that promotes broad stakeholder involvement and extensive access to regulatory sandboxes.

Both approaches of Taiwan and the EU have their unique strengths and challenges. Taiwan's sector-specific method offers flexibility and encourages targeted innovation, enabling tailored solutions for different industries. However, it faces challenges in design and execution, particularly in attracting and retaining participants. This approach requires regulatory authorities actively design and execute new regulations for AI systems. Not all authorities are so responsible or active. In addition, some new types of AI systems might be difficult to be categorised into a field under certain authorities' jurisdictions. Addressing these issues could help fully realise the potential of Taiwan's approach. On the other hand, the EU's comprehensive framework ensures high ethical standards and uniformity, promoting a

---

[38] Id. 20.

[39] European Commission (2024) Shaping Europe's Digital Future. https://digital-strategy.ec.europa.eu/en/policies/regulatory-framework-ai.

[40] Art. 53-55a, Art.73.

stable environment for AI development but potentially imposing extensive compliance burdens on companies. In conclusion, Taiwan's sector-specific regulatory guidelines and sandboxes and the EU AI Act's broad regulatory framework reflect different strategies in global AI regulation. Taiwan's approach provides flexibility and targeted solutions, while the EU's method ensures uniformity and high standards across all member states. Both strategies aim to balance innovation with regulatory oversight, highlighting diverse methods to foster technological advancements responsibly.

4 Administrative Guidelines for AI Deployers

In recent years, Taiwan has recognised the rapid advancement of AI technology and the need to catch up with neighbouring countries in regulatory practices. In response, the Executive Yuan established the Digital Policy and Legal Coordination Project Meetings in 2023 and directed subordinate agencies to issue several guidelines related to AI. Additionally, various ministries, including those overseeing healthcare, transportation, and education, have issued their own AI guidelines over the past five years to address the specific challenges and opportunities within their sectors. The following will discuss key AI guidelines and their content.

4.1 Guidelines for the Use of Generative AI by the Executive Yuan and Its Subordinate Agencies

In August 2023, the Executive Yuan issued the 'Guidelines for the Use of Generative AI by the Executive Yuan and Its Subordinate Agencies' to standardise the use of generative AI (GenAI) across government bodies.[41] These guidelines emphasise responsible use, maintaining control and autonomy, and adhering to principles of safety, privacy, and data governance. They specify that AI-generated content must not be used for creating or processing confidential documents and mandate caution when handling personal information. Agencies are required to critically assess AI-generated information and not rely solely on it for administrative decisions. Furthermore, the guidelines mandate the establishment of internal control measures, disclosure of GenAI use, and compliance with information security, personal data protection, copyright, and intellectual property regulations.

[41] Executive Yuan, Republic of China (Taiwan) (2023) https://english.ey.gov.tw/Page/61BF20C3E89B856/d57a1a70-c0b0-4481-9845-a6265437a8ff.

4.2 Guidelines for AI in the Financial Industry

The Financial Supervisory Commission (FSC) has been proactive in addressing AI's impact on the financial sector. In 2020, the FSC released the 'FinTech Development Roadmap 1.0'[42] which led to significant advancements in financial data sharing, enhancing transparency and promoting the legal use of customer data. This was followed by the 'FinTech Development Roadmap 2.0' in 2023, which focuses on advancing AI in financial services. The roadmap includes developing AI application guidelines, providing diverse funding channels for AI projects, and emphasising talent cultivation. The 'Guidelines for the Use of AI in the Financial Industry' announced in June 20, 2024, are non-binding and aim to guide financial institutions in deploying AI responsibly.[43] Key elements include governance and accountability, fairness and non-discrimination, privacy protection, system robustness, and transparency.

4.3 Guidelines for AI in Healthcare

To foster innovation and ensure the safe integration of AI technology in healthcare, the Taiwan Food and Drug Administration (TFDA) has implemented a proactive policy to encourage the development and use of AI-enabled medical devices. Recognising the transformative potential of AI in improving medical outcomes and operational efficiencies, the TFDA established the Smart Medical Device Office.[44] This dedicated office serves as a central hub for overseeing the regulatory processes and providing support to developers of AI medical devices, ensuring that they meet the necessary safety and efficacy standards.

Among the various initiatives undertaken by the TFDA, several key administrative guidelines have been issued to guide the development and use of AI medical devices.[45] The 'Guidelines for the Review and Approval of AI/ML-Based Software Medical Devices'[46] outline the rigorous testing, validation, and documentation processes required for regulatory approval. These guidelines ensure that AI technologies

---

[42] Financial Supervisory Commission, R.O.C. (2023) https://www.fsc.gov.tw/en/home.jsp?id=360&parentpath=0,4,175&mcustomize=onemessages_view.jsp&dataserno=202310170001&dtable=O20160223020901.

[43] Financial Supervisory Commission, R.O.C. (2024). https://www.fsc.gov.tw/en/home.jsp?id=54&parentpath=0,2&mcustomize=multimessage_view.jsp&dataserno=202311070001&dtable=News.

[44] AI/ML Medical Device Information and Matchmaking Platform (2024) https://aimd.fda.gov.tw/about.

[45] Ministry of Health and Welfare, Republic of China (Taiwan) (2021) https://www.mohw.gov.tw/cp-4745-64039-2.html.

[46] Ministry of Health and Welfare, Republic of China (Taiwan) (2024) '人工智慧/機器學習技術之醫療器材軟體查驗登記技術指引', https://aimd.fda.gov.tw/regulation/detail/20.

are safe for clinical use and effective in delivering healthcare solutions. Additionally, the 'Guidelines for Quality and Management in Software Medical Devices' focus on maintaining high standards of accuracy and reliability, in reference of ISO 13485:2016-Medical devices-A practical guide.[47] The TFDA also emphasises the importance of post-market surveillance through the 'Guidelines for Post-Market Amending Application of Software Medical Devices', which detail the requirements for applying change of market approval applications after software medical devices have been introduced to the market.[48] The implementation of these guidelines has garnered mixed reactions from various stakeholders. Industry experts and developers have praised the TFDA for providing clear regulatory pathways that support innovation while ensuring patient safety. These guidelines have been seen as a critical step in promoting the ethical and effective use of AI in healthcare, helping to build trust among users and practitioners.

By providing a robust regulatory framework and dedicated support through the Smart Medical Device Office, the TFDA aims to balance the benefits of AI in healthcare with the need to protect patient privacy and ensure the ethical use of data.

For promoting the adoption of artificial intelligence in hospitals, the Ministry of Health and Welfare announced in October of 2024 a plan to set up three types of artificial intelligence (AI) centres to solve the three major challenges: (1) The responsible AI implementation centres will research the rules for best practice of AI governance by formulating management measures that comply with information security and privacy protection, publicly disclosing key information such as AI models, data, and performance, and providing explainable analysis results, AI transparency can be enhanced. At the same time, establishing AI model lifecycle management measures ensures the continuous reliability of AI in clinical applications; (2) The clinical AI verification centres will collaborate with the Information Technology Department of the Ministry of Health and Welfare and TFDA aiming to solve the lengthy certification of medical AI software and challenges in collecting representative validation data. By forming a hospital alliance, establishing permanent institutions, and integrating cross-system EMR data, it enhances AI model validation speed and accuracy for the Taiwanese population, accelerating commercialisation and improving public access to high-quality smart healthcare products; (3) The AI impact research centres will collaborate with the Information Technology Department of the Ministry of Health and Welfare and the National Health Insurance Administration aiming to address challenges in securing National Health Insurance coverage for AI medical applications. To address this, the centre will establish a cross-system, cross-level clinical trial mechanism and conduct research designed by a multidisciplinary team. Through rigorous evaluation of AI's clinical effectiveness and health benefits, the initiative seeks to ensure AI products demonstrate both

[47] Ministry of Health and Welfare, Republic of China (Taiwan) (2024) '醫療器材軟體製造業者品質管理系統指導文件', https://aimd.fda.gov.tw/regulation/detail/17.

[48] Ministry of Health and Welfare, Republic of China (Taiwan) (2021), '醫療器材軟體上市後變更申請之管理指引', https://aimd.fda.gov.tw/regulation/detail/17.

medical efficacy and economic value, providing a scientific basis for pricing and facilitating their integration into the healthcare reimbursement system. The centres are expected to produce guidelines and regulatory recommendations for the development, deploying, marketing approvals, and insurance coverage of AI systems in hospitals.[49]

In summary, Taiwan has made significant strides in establishing a robust regulatory framework to govern the use of AI across various sectors, including healthcare, finance, and public administration. These initiatives reflect Taiwan's commitment to balancing innovation with ethical considerations and data protection.

5 Taiwan's Draft AI Basic Act

In July 2024, Taiwan's National Science and Technology Council (NSTC) announced the draft of the AI Basic Act, and now subject to internal discussion in the Executive Yuan, the highest administration authority in Taiwan.[50] This proposed legislation addresses personal information protection, privacy protocols, data management, and risk mitigation strategies. Developed through extensive inter-ministerial collaboration, the draft legislation introduces precise legal definitions, robust privacy protections, structured data governance, and effective risk management protocols, while incorporating ethical guidelines to foster responsible AI development.

Taiwan's journey towards the Basic AI Act has seen multiple iterations from various stakeholders, including legislators and civil society groups. Several versions of the draft have been discussed over the past few years, reflecting ongoing debates among lawmakers, industry experts, and legal scholars to the multifaceted challenges of AI. This effort is part of Taiwan's broader strategy to enhance its digital economy and ensure that AI development aligns with ethical and legal standards.

[49] Chen Chih-Chieh-ling & Evelyn Kao, Health ministry unveils AI centre project.(Oct. 7. 2024) Focus Taiwan. https://focustaiwan.tw/sci-tech/202410070018.

[50] Julia Bergström, Alex Myslinski. Explaining Taiwan's AI Basic Act (Jan. 9 2025). CommonWealth Magazine. https://english.cw.com.tw/article/article.action?id=3910. The full text of the draft (in Chinese) can be found at https://join.gov.tw/attachments/9203f96b-03bb-4c26-9f20-8bdc-f6a7d75f/download/%E4%BA%BA%E5%B7%A5%E6%99%BA%E6%85%A7%E5%9F%BA%E6%9C%AC%E6%B3%95%E8%8D%89%E6%A1%88%E7%B8%BD%E8%AA%AA%E6%98%8E%E5%8F%8A%E6%A2%9D%E6%96%87.pdf.

5.1 Legislative Process and Current Proposals

Currently, the Executive Yuan has not submitted an official draft of the Basic AI Act to the Congress, and the contents of the final version of the draft remain unknown. Meanwhile, legislators and civil society groups have proposed versions of the Basic AI Act, which emphasise establishing clear legal definitions for AI technologies, enhancing privacy protections, implementing structured data governance mechanisms, formulating risk management strategies, and setting ethical standards to ensure AI development aligns with societal values.[51]

The proposed drafts shared several core aspects. One critical element is the establishment of clear legal definitions related to AI technologies. This includes defining AI, delineating the roles and responsibilities of AI developers, operators, and users, and setting out the legal boundaries for AI applications. These definitions are essential for ensuring legal clarity and consistency. The Act also emphasises robust privacy protections, aligning with global standards such as the GDPR, and includes measures for data protection, giving patients the right to opt out of data sharing at any time.

Effective data governance is another cornerstone of the proposed drafts. They propose structured protocols for data management, including guidelines for data storage, access, and sharing, to ensure data used in AI applications is accurate, secure, and used ethically. Risk management strategies are also integral, with comprehensive measures for identifying, assessing, and mitigating risks associated with AI technologies. This includes protocols for monitoring AI systems, conducting regular audits, and addressing potential risks before they escalate.

The proposed drafts of the Basic AI Act include responsible AI principles such as fairness, transparency, accountability, and respect for human rights. By promoting these ethical standards, Taiwan aims to foster responsible AI development that benefits society. To support industry growth, the Act includes provisions for promoting AI research and development, encouraging collaboration between public and private sectors, and providing incentives for innovation. This includes funding for AI projects, support for startups, and initiatives to attract and retain AI talent, ensuring Taiwan remains competitive in the global AI landscape.

---

[51] Several proposed bills including AI Basic Act Bill, Legislative Yuan Agenda Related Documents Number 202110037740000 (2021) https://ppg.ly.gov.tw/ppg/download/agenda1/02/pdf/11/01/11/LCEWA01_110111_00119.pdf.; AI Development Basic Act Bill, Legislative Yuan Agenda Related Documents Number Yuan General No. 1021, Committee Proposal No. 23371 (2019) https://ppg.ly.gov.tw/ppg/download/agenda1/02/pdf/09/07/14/LCEWA01_090714_00037.pdf.; AI Development Act Bill, Legislative Yuan Agenda Related Documents Number Yuan General No. 1021, Committee Proposal No. 28966 (2022) https://ppg.ly.gov.tw/ppg/SittingRelatedDocumentReportMatter/download/agenda1/02/pdf/10/06/02/LCEWA01_100602_00064.pdf.; AI Development Act Bill, Legislative Yuan Agenda Related Documents Number Yuan General No. 1021, Committee Proposal No. 24935 (2020). https://ppg.ly.gov.tw/ppg/SittingRelatedDocumentReportMatter/download/agenda1/02/pdf/10/02/01/LCEWA01_100201_00025.pdf.

5.2 *Comparative Analysis with the EU AI Act*

While it is important to recognise that Taiwan is aware of the significance of establishing basic legal principles for AI systems, the governmental 'Basic' AI Act Draft implies that this law is not intended to regulate all details comprehensively like the EU AI Act. Instead, it aims to legalise these basic principles and guide various ministries in creating more detailed departmental legislation or regulatory orders. From this perspective, Taiwan's AI Basic Law takes a different path from the EU, aligning more closely with the model of the White House's 'Blueprint for an AI Bill of Rights' announced in 2022.[52] It focuses on governmental duty to develop regulatory rules and measures which comply with fundamental principles while maintaining a balance between innovation and regulation, ensuring that SMEs can comply with new requirements, addressing public concerns about privacy and security, and keeping pace with technological advancements and evolving global standards.[53] This involves ongoing dialogue with international partners, participation in global AI governance initiatives, and adapting to new developments in AI technology. The government needs to work closely with industry stakeholders, legal experts, and civil society to address these challenges and ensure the Act effectively meets its objectives. More specifically to say, the draft looks like the major structural principles of the EU AI Act without all the detailed rules about the standards and exceptions.

Taiwan's approach can be compared to several aspects of the EU AI Act. Although the EU AI Act is known for its strict human rights protections, it often faces dilemmas in balancing these with other values. For example, the AI Act categorises various AI applications into four levels of risk,[54] but there are often exceptions based on the purpose of use. While the principle is to prohibit large-scale biometric data recognition, government enforcement actions are an exception (Article 5(g)). In the classification of high-risk systems, Article 6 lists some annexes (Annex I, II, III) but also sets exceptions making them inapplicable (e.g., Article 6(3)). Chapter VI: Measures in Support of Innovation (Articles 57-63) includes provisions encouraging countries to establish regulatory sandboxes. The effectiveness of these sandboxes remains to be evaluated, as achieving the same regulatory standards required by the AI Act at a lower cost and why it applies only to SMEs and not all companies are questions to be addressed. If only SMEs can use these sandboxes and not large companies, it may lead to businesses choosing to remain small to avoid stricter regulations.[55] Article 112 of the EU AI Act requires the European Commission to periodically review the classification of AI risk levels, indicating that the initial classification involved compromises among different countries and stakeholders and may not be based on empirical scientific research but rather on certain value

[52] The White House (2022) https://www.whitehouse.gov/ostp/ai-bill-of-rights/.

[53] Chang (2023a), pp. 39–42.

[54] See Art.6&51 EU AI ACT.

[55] Graaf and Veldt (2022), pp. 803–834.

judgments.[56] In contrast, Taiwan's non-comprehensive legislative model allows for different risk classifications according to the needs of various departments, rather than applying the one-size-for-all classification across all industries.[57]

From this angle, Taiwan's desire to maintain flexibility is reasonable. Taiwan's major technological exports are primarily hardware, especially chips. If AI chips are to be exported to the EU, they must comply with the AI Act requirements. However, if not exported to the EU, they do not need to adhere to such strict regulations. Thus, the Brussels Effect seen during the GDPR era may not occur with the AI Act. AI hardware is a significant export for Taiwan, and there is no need to impose stricter requirements on non-EU-bound AI hardware. In terms of software, Taiwan is not a major player in the AI software industry.

One thing might need to emphasis is that the Articles 1 of the Draft of AI Basic Act specifies the purpose to 'maintain country's culture values', among all other legislative purposes. Many generative AI systems, including ChatGPT, perform poorly in Traditional Chinese because in the Internet, web content in Simplified Chinese are significantly outnumbered those in Traditional Chinese. The outcome of ChatGPT, no matter which version, usually is written in the grammar and usage of Simplified Chinese, even if it is written in Traditional Chinese. When we ask questions about certain terms, the interpretation of the terms often influenced by China's internet content, even if the terms are about Taiwan. If young people and students keep learning knowledge from ChatGPT or other generative AI systems, their knowledge and memory in terms of Taiwan's culture values will be confused with those of China. Taiwan is eager to develop AI systems in Traditional Chinese, especially LLMs, and aims to secure a place in industries like machinery manufacturing, drones, and robotics. Adopting the EU approach entirely could negatively impact the majority of SMEs and large tech exporters.

Nonetheless, there are key aspects of the EU AI Act that Taiwan can learn from, starting with the establishment of an AI Office. In the past, Taiwan's personal data protection efforts were criticised for lacking a powerful enforcement agency and centralised enforcement resources, despite having a Personal Information Protection Act modelled after EU guidelines.[58] Without a centralised AI Office, which does not exist in the Draft of the AI Basic Act, certain departments, especially those less connected to technology, may face difficulties in AI regulation and enforcement. Moreover, due to the cross-departmental nature of AI-induced business models, a single law governing all AI systems can prevent regulatory gaps. Currently, Taiwan lacks specific policies on generative AI and has not decided whether to adopt the U.S. 2023 Biden executive order model nor the EU AI Act's regulations on foundation models. Thus, Taiwan may still establish more laws and regulations inspired by the EU AI Act in the future.

[56] Yang and Cheng (2024), pp. 4–5.

[57] Lai (2023), pp. 106–107.

[58] Chang (2023b), pp. 19–20.

6 Consumer Protection Under Taiwan's AI Regulatory Framework

Currently, Taiwan lacks specific, stringent AI regulations, and individual ministries have yet to establish laws for AI systems in various industries. Therefore, AI regulation in Taiwan primarily relies on administrative regulations, which are insufficient for comprehensive consumer protection. In this context, Taiwan's Consumer Protection Act (CPA) plays crucial roles in enhancing human rights protection where regulatory measures fall short.[59]

Since CPA was legislated in 1994, the act has included 'service' in addition to 'product' in the act,[60] meaning service providers apply the same strict liability as product manufactures. As a result, whether an AI system is a product or a service is not a problem in applying CPA. The importance of this issue in many countries is that because the product liability laws in those countries usually only cover products. AI software, however, usually are in the form of 'copyright licensing' but not in the form of 'product selling'. In addition, software providers often update versions of software, making them more like service providers rather than manufactures of products. The European Union solved this problem by amending the Product Liability Directive in 2024 which specifies to cover digital and artificial intelligence (AI)-based software with strict liability.[61]

Although CPA covers AI software, it faces significant shortcomings in handling class action lawsuits,[62] especially in the context of AI-related incidents. One of the primary challenges is the 'black box effect' of AI systems, which makes proving causation complex and resource-intensive.[63] Financial constraints further exacerbate

[59] See Section One-Health and Safety Safeguards, Consumer Protection Act (CPA). https://law.moj.gov.tw/ENG/LawClass/LawAll.aspx?pcode=J0170001.

[60] Article 7 of Consumer Protection Act (1994). https://lis.ly.gov.tw/lglawc/lawsingle?003E7FE280BA000000000000000000A000000002000000^01180083011100^00000000000 (In Chinese).

[61] von Burgs Dorff and Kramer (2025).

[62] Shen (2015a), pp. 1242–1247.

[63] Chiu (2022), pp. 29–30. It must be noted that the unique black-box effect of AI makes proving causation more difficult than in traditional environmental pollution cases. This article has presented the traditional methods of proving causation for environmental pollution: If a group is taken as the subject of rights to seek legal remedies, then the '15 people in the entire village who contracted the disease' can be regarded as a single subject of rights. The damage claimed would be 'the increase in the number of people contracting the disease from 10 to 15'. Because these 15 people who contracted the disease are considered a single subject of rights, the damage would be 'the 5 additional people in this subject of rights who contracted the disease due to pollution'. This way, the claimants do not need to prove which among the 15 people were originally cancer patients and which were pollution victims, thus avoiding the aforementioned difficulty of not being able to identify the 5 specific victims. Consequently, they should be able to smoothly obtain compensation for damages. Using the approach of a group as the subject of rights allows damage claimants to avoid difficulties in proving causation in pollution cases. (Omitted). The construction of group rights as a subject allows victims of pollution events, where proving causation is difficult, to smoothly obtain compensation, without imposing a liability on the compensating party beyond the

these difficulties, as consumer advocacy groups cannot claim rewards from consumers,[64] and the government did not cover attorney fees.[65] Although legislative amendments in June 2015 allowed attorneys to charge fees for service in consumer advocacy cases[66] financial and time pressures persist, leading many potential class action cases to remain unaddressed.

In the EU, consumer protection groups must be non-profit but can receive continuous government funding, providing them with more stability and resources. Institutions like the European Consumer Centre Network (ECC-Net), funded by the European Commission and member state governments, emphasise cross-border cooperation and provide consumers with legal aid and advice on cross-border shopping.[67] The EU's comprehensive legal framework, including the GDPR[68] and the EU AI Act,[69] integrates strict data protection and consumer rights into AI regulation, offering robust support for consumers affected by AI systems.

In contrast, Taiwan's consumer advocacy groups face significant financial constraints due to policy limitations. While Taiwan requires these groups to be non-profit, it does not provide government funding, leaving many of them underfunded. Each payment for a consumer advocacy group in Taiwan is a burden, contrasting with the EU's more stable financial support for such groups. While Taiwan's regulations are robust, they do not yet match the comprehensiveness of the EU's system, particularly in addressing AI-specific liabilities and data protection.

When numerous consumers are injured by the same incident, they can form a consumer advocacy group to combine their litigation strategies and resources. This collective approach, supported by the Code of Civil Procedure Article 44-1 Paragraph 1 and the CPA Article 50 Paragraph 1, allows them to sue more effectively.[70] However, the financial and logistical challenges mentioned earlier continue to hinder the effectiveness of class action lawsuits in Taiwan.

In summary, Taiwan's current legal framework for consumer protection, while robust, faces challenges in addressing the complexities of AI-related incidents. The CPA offers a foundation for addressing harm caused by AI systems, but proving

actual damage caused. This should align with the principles of social fairness and justice, which, however, cannot be applied to AI causation.

[64] See Art. 50 para 6, Consumer Protection Act (CPA).

[65] See Art. 49 para 2 and Art. 50 para 5, Consumer Protection Act (CPA).

[66] Consumer Protection Committee, Executive Yuan, R.O.C., https://cpc.ey.gov.tw/Page/3F37FBCC20BE3386, 'legislative amendments in June 2015 removed the provision prohibiting lawyers from requesting compensation'.

[67] European Consumer Centre's Network, How ECC Net works, https://commission.europa.eu/live-work-travel-eu/consumer-rights-and-complaints/resolve-your-consumer-complaint/european-consumer-centres-network-ecc-net_en.

[68] See Art.12-15 'Transparency and Access Rights', Art. 22 'Automated Individual Decision-Making', and Art. 35 'Data Protection Impact Assessment (DPIA)'.

[69] See Art. 6 'Classification Rules for High-Risk AI Systems' and Art. 29a 'Fundamental Rights Impact Assessment for High-Risk AI Systems'.

[70] Shen (2015b), p. 1239. Sustainability(繼續性), Microscopy(隱微性) or Diffusion(擴散性).

causation and liability remains difficult due to the technical and unpredictable nature of AI. Comparatively, the EU provides a more comprehensive framework that includes stringent data protection and consumer rights, offering a model for Taiwan to consider as it develops its AI regulations. As Taiwan moves towards enacting the Basic AI Act, addressing these challenges will be crucial to ensuring effective consumer protection in the AI era.

7 Conclusion

Taiwan's AI regulatory strategy, characterised by its flexibility, ethical grounding, and international alignment, provides a robust framework for fostering innovation while ensuring responsible AI development. By learning from global best practices and adapting to the unique needs of its economy, Taiwan can continue to lead in the AI domain.

The progression from AI Plan 1.0 to AI Plan 2.0 and the upcoming Basic AI Act demonstrates Taiwan's proactive approach to AI governance. These strategic initiatives underscore Taiwan's commitment to harnessing AI for industrial growth, societal benefit, and global competitiveness.

Moving forward, Taiwan's focus on talent cultivation, technological advancement, industrial integration, and ethical frameworks will be crucial in navigating the complexities of AI governance. By fostering a collaborative regulatory environment and leveraging its strategic partnerships, Taiwan is well-positioned to address the challenges and opportunities of the AI era, ensuring that AI technologies are developed and deployed in a manner that benefits all stakeholders.

In summary, Taiwan's AI regulatory framework represents another approach of seeking to balance innovation with ethical and regulatory considerations. Through continued investment, international collaboration, and a commitment to public trust, Taiwan will develop a different model for responsible AI governance, driving technological progress while safeguarding societal values.

References

AI/ML Medical Device Information and Matchmaking Platform (2024). https://aimd.fda.gov.tw/about.

Chang L (2023a) The experimentation act and its practice of autonomous vehicles in Taiwan. Int J Membr Sci Technol:1404. https://doi.org/10.15379/ijmst.v10i3.1720

Chang C-W (2023b) Personal data protection and information security. Contemp Law J 22:13–20 (張志偉(2023)，個資保護與資料安全，當代法律，第22期，頁13–20)

Chang L (2021) Laws and ethics policy of self-driving cars in Taiwan. J Mech Eng Automat 11:155. https://doi.org/10.17265/2159-5275/2021.05.004

Chang S-H, Shih C-P (2018) The Influence and Application of Artificial Intelligence & Blockchain on Financial Service 9. https://doi.org/10.2478/HJBPA-2018-0022

Chen S, Kuo H, Lee C (2020) Preparing Society for automated vehicles: perceptions of the importance and urgency of emerging issues of governance, regulations, and wider impacts. Sustainability 12(7844):10. https://doi.org/10.3390/SU12197844

Chiu W-H (2022) Preliminary approach to group rights in civil law: with reference to liability of public nuisance events. China Law J pp 29–30(邱玟惠(2022)，群體權利主體思維之初探-由公害損害賠償之因果關係證明難題談起，法學叢刊，第67卷第2期，1–40).

CNA Staff Writer (2023) Government drafting basic law to regulate AI. Taipei Times. https://www.taipeitimes.com/News/taiwan/archives/2023/07/06/2003802773

Commercial Times (2023) After Two Years Waiting, the Financial Regulatory Sandbox Experiment Finally Gets One Applicant(in Chinese). https://www.ctee.com.tw/news/20230209700780-430301

European Commission (2024) Shaping Europe's Digital Future. https://digital-strategy.ec.europa.eu/en/policies/regulatory-framework-ai

European Consumer Centre's Network, How ECC Net works, https://commission.europa.eu/live-work-travel-eu/consumer-rights-and-complaints/resolve-your-consumer-complaint/european-consumer-centres-network-ecc-net_en

Executive Yuan (2018) "Financial Technology Development and Innovation Experiment Act" — Encouraging Innovation, Enhancing Financial Competitiveness(in Chinese) https://www.ey.gov.tw/Page/5A8A0CB5B41DA11E/aa4a0c9d-14be-4664-ac59-fc74a056d1fd

Executive Yuan News Room (2011) AI Taiwan Action Plan. https://english.ey.gov.tw/News3/9E5540D592A5FECD/1dec0902-e02a-49c6-870d-e77208481667

Executive Yuan, Republic of China (Taiwan) (2023). https://english.ey.gov.tw/Page/61BF20C3E89B856/d57a1a70-c0b0-4481-9845-a6265437a8ff

Financial Supervisory Commission, R.O.C. (2023). https://www.fsc.gov.tw/en/home.jsp?id=360&parentpath=0,4,175&mcustomize=onemessages_view.jsp&dataserno=202310170001&dtable=O20160223020901

Financial Supervisory Commission, R.O.C. (2024). https://www.fsc.gov.tw/ch/home.jsp?id=96&parentpath=0,2&mcustomize=news_view.jsp&dataserno=202406200001&dtable=News

Financial Technology Development and Innovative Experimentation Act, https://law.moj.gov.tw/ENG/LawClass/LawAll.aspx?pcode=G0380254

German Trade Office Taipei. Taiwan: Smart, Innovative, Green, https://taiwan.ahk.de/information-hub/country-info/taiwan-smart-innovative-green

Graaf T, Veldt G (2022) The AI act and its impact on product safety, contracts and liability. Eur Rev Priv Law. https://doi.org/10.54648/erpl2022038

Hsiung E, Chang R (2023) AI, machine learning & big data laws & regulations | Taiwan. GLI. Available from: https://www.globallegalinsights.com/practice-areas/ai-machine-learning-and-big-data-laws-and-regulations/taiwan

Kao L-P, Lee T-F, Tai H-C, Cai C-J (2020) The study of market reaction and its influencing factors for regulatory Sandbox J Account Corp Gov 15, 2:7(高麗萍，李婷芳，戴湘綺，蔡春菊(2020)，金融監理沙盒市場反應及其影響因素之研究，會計與公司治理，第15卷第2期)

Lai WC (2023) Examining the direction and challenges of Taiwan's AI legislation from the EU's First AI regulatory law. Account Res Month 457:102–107 (賴文智(2023)，從歐盟首部AI監管法，看臺灣AI立法方向與挑戰?，會計研究月刊，457，102-107。)

Ministry of Health and Welfare, Republic of China (Taiwan) (2021). https://www.mohw.gov.tw/cp-4745-64039-2.html.

Ministry of Health and Welfare, Republic of China (Taiwan) (2024). https://www.mohw.gov.tw/cp-18-77823-1.html.

NAIPnews (2024) Investment Opportunities of Taiwan's New Generation Automobile Industry. http://en.naipo.com/Portals/0/web_en/Knowledge_Center/AMPA2024/IPNE_240326_0103.htm

National Science and Technology Council, Taiwan (2022) Taiwan AI readiness assessment report. Available from: https://digi.nstc.gov.tw/File/5AF024B4C7281A84/e761bee6-a38c-4d5b-8481-fc36b83b25d8?A=C

One Trust Data Guidance (2023) Comparing Privacy Laws: GDPR v. PDPA. via:https://www.dataguidance.com/sites/default/files/gdpr_v._pdpa_.pdf

Peng J-L, Tsang C-Y (2019) FinTech regulation and a review of Taiwan's financial regulatory sandbox framework. Manage Rev 38(4):26. (彭金隆 & 臧正運，金融科技監理與我國金融監理沙盒制度之檢視，管理評論，第38卷第4期)

Shen K-L (2015a) Reconstruction of consumer collective redress: focus on distributed damages and collective rights. Natl Taiwan Univ Law J 1242–1247.(沈冠伶(2015)，消費者團體訴訟之再建構:以擴散型損害及集團權利為中心，國立臺灣大學法學論叢，第44卷特刊，1237–1326)

Shen K-L (2015b) Reconstruction of consumer collective redress: focus on distributed damages and collective rights. Natl Taiwan Univ Law J 1239.(沈冠伶(2015)，消費者團體訴訟之再建構:以擴散型損害及集團權利為中心，國立臺灣大學法學論叢，第44卷特刊，1237–1326) Sustainability(繼續性), Microscopy(隱微性) or Diffusion(擴散性)

Taipei Times. (2023). Executive Yuan announces artificial intelligence plan. https://www.taipeitimes.com/News/front/archives/2023/06/04/2003800937

Taiwan Department of Industry Technology (2024) The Unmanned Vehicle Technology Project: Execution Results. https://www.moea.gov.tw/MNS/doit/content/Content.aspx?menu_id=32501

Taiwan Financial Supervisory Commission (2020) Fintech Development Roadmap. via:https://www.fsc.gov.tw/userfiles/file/FinTech%20Development%20Roadmap.pdf

Taiwan Ministry of Economy Affairs (2022) SMEs Serve as the Backbone of Taiwan's Stable Economic Development. https://www.moea.gov.tw/MNS/english/news/News.aspx?kind=6&menu_id=176&news_id=103826. According to the Ministry of Economy Affairs, as of 2021, there were more than 1.59 million SMEs in Taiwan, accounting for over 98 percent of all enterprises. These SMEs employed 9.2 million people, representing more than 80 percent of the total workforce.

Taiwan Ministry of Education (2024) Taiwan Joins the Global CAPE on Promoting Cross-Border Privacy Enforcement Cooperation with International Partners. https://english.moe.gov.tw/cp-117-39620-bcfc2-1.html

TAIWAN TODAY (2024) Taiwan genius helps computer trounce human Go champ. https://taiwantoday.tw/news.php?unit=10&post=21687

The White House (2022). https://www.whitehouse.gov/ostp/ai-bill-of-rights/.

Tsai C, Lin C, Liu H (2020) The diffusion of the Sandbox approach to disruptive innovation and its limitations. Cornell Int Law J 53:3. https://doi.org/10.2139/ssrn.3487175

U.S. Department of Commerce (2024) Global Cross-Border Privacy Rules Declaration https://www.commerce.gov/global-cross-border-privacy-rules-declaration

Unmanned Vehicles Technology Innovative Experimentation Act, https://law.moj.gov.tw/ENG/LawClass/LawAll.aspx?pcode=J0030147.

von Burgs Dorff C, Kramer L (2025) Increased liability due to the new EU Product Liability Directive: what does this mean for the medical and pharmaceutical industry? International Bar Association. https://www.ibanet.org/increased-liability-eu-product-directive.

Yang C-C, Cheng F-Y (2024) EU AI ACT and the regulations of generative AI. Parliament Quart 52(1):1–30(楊智傑、鄭富源(2024)，歐盟人工智慧法與生成式 AI 規範，國會季刊，第52卷第1期，頁1–30)

Artificial Intelligence Regulation in the United States: A Patchwork of Laws

James X. Dempsey

Contents

The author gratefully acknowledges the review and comments of Catherine M. Sharkey, Segal Family Professor of Regulatory Law and Policy at NYU School of Law.

J. X. Dempsey (✉)
Stanford University, Program on Geopolitics, Technology and Governance, Stanford, CA, USA

University of California, Berkeley School of Law, Berkeley, CA, USA
e-mail: jdempsey@berkeley.edu

V. L. Raposo (ed.), *The European Artificial Intelligence Act*, Law, Governance and Technology Series 78, https://doi.org/10.1007/978-3-031-98406-8_19

Abstract There is no federal statute in the U.S. specifically regulating artificial intelligence. However, the U.S. legal framework presumes that statutes and common law doctrines of general application already apply to AI. The due process clause in the federal constitution provides one important limit on governmental use of automated decision-making tools to make decisions about individuals. Especially pertinent is the Supreme Court's insistence that due process must include understandable notice. The regulation of bias in AI falls under the patchwork quilt of federal anti-bias and consumer protection laws, but enforcement may be weak under President Trump. States also have laws prohibiting bias, particularly in insurance underwriting. The states and even municipalities have been quite active in adopting new laws and regulations covering uses of artificial intelligence. In particular, a growing number of states have adopted consumer privacy laws that include provisions regulating automated decision making or automated data processing, often under the name of 'profiling'.

1 Introduction

There is no federal statute in the U.S. specifically regulating artificial intelligence, and there is not likely to be one anytime soon. In recent years, multiple bills have been introduced in Congress to address the risks of AI, but the complexity of the issues, a general anti-regulatory sentiment (certain to be heightened under the second Trump Administration), and partisan differences make it unlikely that Congress will act. For similar reasons, the U.S. has no general privacy law at the federal level regulating the processing of personal information, by AI or not. Congress has likewise failed to adopt laws regulating facial recognition technology or AI-enabled automobiles or other specific applications of AI.

This does not mean there is no federal law in the U.S. on AI. To the contrary, the U.S. legal framework presumes that statutes and traditional doctrines of general application already apply—have always applied—to AI. This is not necessarily undesirable from a policy perspective. As the federal judge Frank Easterbrook advised about information technologies in general, rather than creating technology-specific rules, it is usually better to develop sound general rules, then apply them to specific innovations.[1] This process is well underway with respect to AI, as courts and regulators apply traditional statutes to AI-based systems. This approach has the advantage of not turning on specific definitions of AI; it covers not only AI but also less sophisticated algorithmic techniques or automated processing that may not rise to the level of AI, but that pose many of the same issues of transparency and fairness. Of course, as has happened with every new technology, courts and regulators

[1] Easterbrook (1996), pp. 207, 208.

must consider whether there are unique aspects of AI that must be taken into account in applying existing law.

Under the administration of President Joe Biden, the federal regulatory agencies were clear in reminding regulated entities that existing laws cover the use of AI, and agencies had begun to bring enforcement actions against alleged misuses of AI or false claims about its performance. The second administration of President Donald Trump that began on January 20, 2025 is likely to pull back from this approach on the grounds that it might discourage innovation. However, there may continue to be some federal enforcement action, especially against companies that make deceptive claims about their AI-based products or services and, under the anti-trust laws, against companies that use AI to foster wage or price fixing and other anti-competitive collusion.

In contrast to the lack of adoption of new rules for AI at the federal level, the states and even municipalities have been quite active in adopting new laws and regulations covering uses of artificial intelligence. In particular, a growing number of states have adopted consumer privacy laws that include provisions regulating automated decision making or automated data processing, often under the name of 'profiling'. These state laws focus mainly on providing consumers the right to opt-out of automated decision making by businesses. These laws, which have many exceptions, also give individuals the right to obtain access to the information held about them by businesses and to demand correction and deletion of that data. In addition, several cities have banned or limited the use of facial recognition (although a trend in that direction seems to have ended) and New York City has adopted a measure regulating the use of AI in employment decisions.[2] Two particularly important state efforts aimed at regulating the use of AI come from Colorado, which adopted a law regulating the use of AI to make 'consequential decisions' about individuals,[3] and California, where the privacy protection agency is developing detailed regulations for automated decision-making technologies, likely to be finalised in 2025.

In sum, AI in the U.S. is regulated by a patchwork of state and federal laws, including both laws pre-dating the current AI revolution and some AI-specific laws. While federal enforcement may weaken under President Trump, some states may increase their scrutiny of AI in coming years. And even if federal agencies pull back, individuals may invoke the Constitution and certain federal laws to challenge uses of AI through private lawsuits. Plus, uses of AI can be addressed under common law doctrines, including negligence, products liability, invasion of privacy, and contract.

Almost every area of the law is confronting issues related to AI: How do AI-generated content and inventions fit within intellectual property law? How do rules of professional responsibility for lawyers or doctors apply to use of AI? What is the liability of AI developers for injury caused by autonomous vehicles or other

---

[2] Local Law 144 of 2021. See NYC Department of Consumer and Worker Protection, *Automated Employment Decision Tools: Frequently Asked Questions* (June 29, 2023) https://www.nyc.gov/assets/dca/downloads/pdf/about/DCWP-AEDT-FAQ.pdf.

[3] Senate Bill 24-205, adding a new part 17 to article 1 of title 6, Colorado Revised Statutes. https://leg.colorado.gov/sites/default/files/2024a_205_signed.pdf.

AI-guided activity in the physical world?[4] Given the premise that existing laws and regulations in the U.S. already apply to AI, it is impossible in any article to cover everything. This article focuses mainly on laws and doctrines that protect the rights of individuals as consumers or citizens.

One last introductory point: The law is rapidly evolving. Almost certainly, after this chapter is written, new laws or regulations will be adopted, at least at the state level, and new guidance will be issued by federal agencies regarding federal laws.

2 Governmental Uses of AI: The Constitutional Right to Due Process

Under the U.S. Constitution, 'No person … shall be deprived of life, liberty, or property, without due process of law'.[5] This applies to federal, state, and local governments, but not to the actions of the private sector. In a 1972 case, the U.S. Supreme Court stated, 'For more than a century the central meaning of procedural due process has been clear: "Parties whose rights are to be affected are entitled to be heard; and in order that they may enjoy that right they must first be notified.'… It is equally fundamental that the right to notice and an opportunity to be heard 'must be granted at a meaningful time and in a meaningful manner"'.[6] The due process right always applied in the criminal justice context and in many regulatory contexts where an individual or a corporation may face fines or other penalties, but in the 1970s, the U.S. Supreme Court extended the principle of due process across a wide range of government decision-making contexts, such as the administration of government welfare benefits.[7] In addition, the equal protection clause of the Constitution also prohibits racial or gender bias in governmental decision making.

The constitutional due process principles certainly apply when AI is used by governmental entities to make decisions about individuals. However, the full meaning of due process has never been definitively articulated.[8] The Supreme Court's rulings say that what process is due—including what information should be provided to the individual to make the right to be heard meaningful—varies from situation to situation. Due process is perhaps strongest in the criminal justice context. In civil contexts, it depends on a balancing test that assesses the risk and impact of

---

[4] See Thadani (2024) https://www.washingtonpost.com/technology/2024/04/28/tesla-trial-autopilot-lawsuit/.

[5] The Fifth Amendment to the U.S. Constitution prevents the federal government from depriving any person of 'life, liberty, or property, without due process of law'. The Fourteenth Amendment incorporates and applies the same language to the states.

[6] *Fuentes v. Shevin*, 407 U.S. 67, 80 (1972).

[7] *Goldberg v. Kelly*, 397 U.S. 254 (1970).

[8] *'[D]ue process is flexible, and calls for such procedural protections as the particular situation demands'. Morrissey v. Brewer,* 408 U. S. 471, 481 *(1972).*

an erroneous decision as compared to the government's interest, including the fiscal and administrative burdens that a particular procedural requirement would entail.[9]

Especially pertinent, given the complexity of many AI systems and the inscrutability of some, is the Supreme Court's insistence on understandable notice: 'An elementary and fundamental requirement of due process ... is notice reasonably calculated, under all the circumstances, to apprise interested parties of the pendency of the action and afford them an opportunity to present their objections'.[10] Conscientiously applied, this would demand that the government must carefully choose AI systems to ensure that they produce understandable and explainable results when being used for purposes that otherwise require due process.

2.1 Due Process Principles in the Administration of Social Welfare Programs

Welfare recipients have successfully used the constitutional right to due process to challenge government use of algorithmic systems to make decisions about welfare and disability benefits, specifically on the grounds that the government agency had not provided adequate explanation about how the system operated.[11] For example, when the state of Idaho adopted an automated decision-making system to calculate the amount of government support that developmentally-disabled individuals needed—thereby substantially reducing individuals' benefits—a court blocked use of the new technique because the benefits notices did not adequately explain why participants' benefits had decreased.[12] The court stated, 'Due process requires notice that gives an agency's reason for its action in sufficient detail that the affected party can prepare a responsive defense'. The trial court in the case specifically ordered the state to disclose its benefits calculation formula to program beneficiaries and to the public.[13] These and other court rulings under the due process clause requiring that agencies must provide specific, individualised reasons for their actions[14] are undoubtedly applicable to AI-based systems.

[9] *Mathews v. Eldridge*, 424 U.S. 319 (1976).

[10] *Mullane v. Central Hanover Bank & Trust Co.*, 339 U.S. 306, 314 (1950).

[11] See Richardson et al. (2019), https://ainowinstitute.org/litigatingalgorithms-2019-us.pdf; Brown et al. (2020), https://cdt.org/wp-content/uploads/2020/10/2020-10-21-Challenging-the-Use-of-Algorithm-driven-Decision-making-in-Benefits-Determinations-Affecting-People-with-Disabilities.pdf.

[12] *K. W. v. Armstrong*, 789 F.3d 962, 974 (9th Cir. 2015).

[13] *K.W. ex rel. D.W. v. Armstrong*, 298 F.R.D. 479 (D. Idaho 2014).

[14] For example, *Barry v. Lyon,* 834 F.3d 706 (6th Cir. 2016).

2.2 *Due Process in the Context of Policing and Criminal Justice*

In the criminal justice context, concerns have been raised about the use of algorithmic systems in making decisions about pre-trial bail, other conditions of release, and sentencing. A study of one widely-used algorithmic scoring system, COMPAS, which uses information about an individual to produce a risk score for judges to use in sentencing criminal offenders, found that the system overestimated the risk posed by Black defendants and underestimated the risk posed by whites.[15]

U.S. courts have refused to prohibit use of AI-based risk assessment systems in sentencing decisions, but instead have imposed limitations on their use. A leading case was decided in 2016, when the Wisconsin Supreme Court confronted criticisms that the COMPAS algorithmic risk assessment system was racially biased.[16] Without actually deciding if the system was biased or not, the court permitted its use with limitations. The court held that any pre-sentence report containing a COMPAS risk assessment must inform the sentencing court about concerns regarding the assessment's accuracy. Moreover, the court specified that risk scores could not be used to determine the threshold question of whether to incarcerate a person or the severity of the sentence. Instead, they could be used only as one factor in decisions about probation and supervision. The court also held that the fact that the system's weighting of factors is proprietary did not amount to a due process violation if the sentencing report included limitations and cautions regarding the assessment's accuracy.[17]

3 Federal Benefits Programs: Statutory or Regulatory Requirements to Provide an Explanation and an Ability to Challenge

The constitutional minimum of due process may be augmented by procedural requirements specified in the statute establishing a particular government program and in the federal Administrative Procedure Act, which sets minimum standards for some actions by federal agencies that affect individuals.

---

[15] Angwin et al. (2016). See also Chouldechova (2017), https://www.liebertpub.com/doi/pdf/10.1089/big.2016.0047.

[16] *State v. Loomis*, 881 N.W.2d 749, 371 Wis. 2d 235 (2016).

[17] See also *Malenchik v. State*, 928 N.E.2d 564, 575 (Ind. 2010) (allowing algorithmic risk assessment score to be 'considered as a supplemental source of information to assist a trial court in formulating the manner a sentence is to be served'); *State v. Gordon*, No. 17-0395, 2018 WL 2084847, at *9 (Iowa Ct. App. May 2, 2018) (vacating a defendant's prison term because the district court considered the defendant's risk level scores as an aggravating factor when imposing the sentence without statutory authority to do so).

In provisions equally applicable to traditional processes as well as to AI-based systems, many federal benefit programs have language in governing statutes or regulations requiring a clear explanation for adverse decisions and/or a right to appeal. For example, a number of statutory provisions spell out the due process rights of veterans.[18] The statute establishing the social security disability program specifies in great detail the notice and appeal rights of individuals;[19] regulations provide even more detail. Regulations for the federal health care benefit for low-income individuals (Medicaid) and the federal government program that provides food-purchasing assistance specify that a notice to an individual about benefits must be understandable.[20] As AI is adopted in the administration of these programs, individuals may rely on these laws to argue that a decision regarding their benefits was not adequately explained or that the appeal right was not satisfied because of the opaqueness of the automated process. Taking full advantage of these rights often involves litigation requiring resources beyond the reach of program applicants.

In addition, if the statute creating a federal government program says that a decision about an individual must be 'determined on the record after opportunity for an agency hearing', that is called a 'formal' adjudication, and the Administrative Procedure Act (APA) requires a trial-type hearing before a special class of adjudicators who enjoy a unique level of independence from their employing agencies. However, statutes requiring such formal adjudications are rare. Most federal adjudications, called 'informal', are not addressed in the APA, so procedures are established by agencies based only on the words of the statute creating the specific program, with the Constitution's due process clause as a floor.[21]

The APA also sets procedural requirements for federal agency 'rulemaking'. If the government's adoption of a new technology will impose 'substantial burdens' on individuals, the decision to adopt that technology may constitute a rulemaking, for which the APA requires public notice and an opportunity to comment.[22]

Finally, under the APA, a person adversely affected or aggrieved by agency action is entitled to judicial review thereof. The reviewing court must hold unlawful and set aside any agency action that is arbitrary, capricious, an abuse of discretion, unsupported by substantial evidence, or unwarranted by the facts, all of which could apply to the use of AI systems.[23]

---

[18] For example, 38 U.S.C. § 5104B, higher-level review; 38 U.S.C. § 5104C, options following decision by agency of original jurisdiction; and 38 U.S.C. Chapter 71, jurisdiction and procedures of the Board of Veterans Appeals.

[19] 42 U.S.C. § 405.

[20] 42 CFR 431.210(b) (Medicaid) (the notice must contain '[a] clear statement of the specific reasons supporting the intended action'); 7 CFR 273.13(a)(2) (food assistance) ('The notice of adverse action shall be considered adequate if it explains in easily understandable language…').

[21] Harrington and Sheffner (2021) https://sgp.fas.org/crs/misc/R46930.pdf.

[22] See *Elec. Privacy Info. Ctr. v. Dep't of Homeland Sec.*, 653 F.3d 1 (D.C. Cir. 2011) (decision by the Transportation Security Administration to adopt body scanners to screen airline passengers).

[23] 5 U.S.C. §§ 701-706. See generally Engstrom et al. (2020).

4 Standards for Federal Government Use of AI

In October 2023, President Biden issued an executive order (EO) to spur the adoption of AI in all aspects of the federal government while mitigating its substantial risks.[24] Generally, the order was binding only on the federal government. Like other executive orders, this EO did not create any right or benefit enforceable against the federal government. Nevertheless, it was intended to protect the rights of individuals by setting standards for the adoption of AI by the federal government. Moreover, it sought to influence state and local governments and the private sector through guidelines, best practices, training programs, grant-making, and studies on a range of issues.

Donald Trump repealed the Biden EO immediately upon taking office on January 20, 2025.[25] However, there still remains in place an executive order issued during President Trump's first term, directing agencies to 'design, develop, acquire, and use AI in a manner that fosters public trust and confidence while protecting privacy, civil rights, civil liberties, and American values'. The EO established principles for the use of AI in the federal government, directing agencies to ensure that any AI they use is accurate, reliable, and effective, understandable, transparent, and accountable.[26] Moreover, on January 23, 2025, President Trump issued his own executive order on AI.[27]

In March 2024, the federal Office of Management and Budget (OMB) had issued a memorandum to the heads of all executive branch departments and agencies to further define what they were required to do to comply with the Biden EO.[28] The memo required each agency (except the Department of Defense and the intelligence agencies) to individually inventory each of its AI use cases at least annually and post a public version of the inventory on the agency's website. Further, the memo required that, where people interact with a service relying on the AI and are likely to be impacted by the AI, agencies must provide reasonable and timely notice about the use of the AI. The memo required agencies to consult affected communities,

---

[24] Executive Order 14110, *Safe, Secure, and Trustworthy Development and Use of Artificial Intelligence* (Oct. 30, 2023) https://www.federalregister.gov/documents/2023/11/01/2023-24283/safe-secure-and-trustworthy-development-and-use-of-artificial-intelligence.

[25] Executive Order 14148, *Initial Recissions of Harmful Executive Orders and Actions* (Jan. 20, 2025) https://www.federalregister.gov/documents/2025/01/28/2025-01901/initial-rescissions-of-harmful-executive-orders-and-actions.

[26] Executive Order 13960, *Promoting the Use of Trustworthy Artificial Intelligence in the Federal Government* (Dec. 3, 2020) https://www.federalregister.gov/documents/2020/12/08/2020-27065/promoting-the-use-of-trustworthy-artificial-intelligence-in-the-federal-government.

[27] Executive Order 14179, Removing Barriers to American Leadership in Artificial Intelligence (Jan. 23, 2025) https://www.federalregister.gov/documents/2025/01/31/2025-02172/removing-barriers-to-american-leadership-in-artificial-intelligence.

[28] Memorandum M-24-10, *Advancing Governance, Innovation, and Risk Management for Agency Use of Artificial Intelligence* (March 28, 2024).

including underserved communities, about planned uses of AI and to solicit and use public feedback in the design, development, and use of the AI.

On April 3, 2025, the new head of the OMB under President Trump rescinded the Biden memo and adopted new guidance for federal agencies.[29]

The new policy memo directed federal agencies to accelerate adoption of AI. At the same time, it retained various concepts from the Biden memo, such as requiring agencies to publish inventories of their AI uses, and it ordered agencies to implement pre-deployment testing and other risk management practices for high impact AI use cases. In response to the Biden EO and the Biden OMB memo, federal agencies had issued guidance (which is not binding and not enforceable by individuals) setting standards for use of AI in federal programs. For example, in April 2024, the federal Department of Health and Human Services (HHS) issued guidance on promoting the responsible use of AI in automated and algorithmic systems by state, local, tribal, and territorial governments in public benefit administration.[30] Agency heads under President Trump may rescind or ignore this guidance.

5 Federal Anti-Discrimination Laws

The regulation of bias in AI falls under the patchwork quilt of federal anti-bias and consumer protection laws, the general authority of the Federal Trade Commission Act, state laws, and even some municipal ordinances. This section describes federal anti-discrimination laws that seek to ensure fairness in credit, housing, and employment. In April 2023, the Consumer Financial Protection Bureau, Department of Justice, Equal Employment Opportunity Commission, and Federal Trade Commission issued a joint statement reminding businesses that all 'existing legal authorities apply to the use of automated systems and innovative new technologies'.[31]

Federal enforcement of these laws is likely to weaken, perhaps substantially, under President Trump. However, these statutes also allow individuals to bring private lawsuits alleging discrimination. Pursuant to a doctrine that is especially relevant to AI, plaintiffs in discrimination cases do not have to prove intent nor do they have to identify the specific source of discrimination. Instead, under the disparate impact standard, a process is unlawful if it has a discriminatory effect on a protected

[29] Memorandum M-25-21, *Accelerating Federal Use of AI through Innovation, Governance, and Public Trust* (April 3, 2025) https://www.whitehouse.gov/wp-content/uploads/2025/02/M-25-21-Accelerating-Federal-Use-of-AI-through-Innovation-Governance-and-Public-Trust.pdf.

[30] https://www.hhs.gov/sites/default/files/public-benefits-and-ai.pdf.

[31] *Joint Statement on Enforcement of Civil Rights, Fair Competition, Consumer Protection, and Equal Opportunity Laws in Automated Systems*, https://www.eeoc.gov/joint-statement-enforcement-efforts-against-discrimination-and-bias-automated-systems.

class, so long as the practice is not necessary to achieve a substantial, legitimate, nondiscriminatory interest of the business.[32]

The federal Fair Housing Act (FHA)[33] prohibits discriminatory practices in housing, including distributing advertisements in a way that denies people information about housing opportunities based on their membership in a protected class. In 2022, the Department of Justice brought its first case challenging algorithmic bias under the FHA, alleging that Meta's social media platform Facebook had engaged in discriminatory advertising in violation of the FHA by using algorithms in determining which Facebook users received housing ads and that those algorithms relied, in part, on characteristics protected under the FHA.[34] Meta settled the case and agreed to stop using an advertising tool for housing ads that, according to the department's complaint, relied on a discriminatory algorithm. Meta also agreed to develop a new system to address racial and other disparities caused by its use of personalisation algorithms in its ad delivery system for housing ads. Under the settlement, the new system was subject to Department of Justice approval and court oversight.

Title VII of the Civil Rights Act of 1964 prohibits employment discrimination based on race, colour, religion, sex, or national origin. The law prohibits intentionally discriminatory conduct, but it also allows plaintiffs to argue that a selection device has a disparate impact on a protected group. If a practice has a biased effect, the employer will be liable unless it can show that the discriminatory practice is necessary from a business perspective. Courts are often very generous to employers in accepting their business necessity claims, but, as one scholar has argued, 'The disparate impact theory, which requires defendants to justify their practices under a business necessity test upon a showing of adverse impact, seems particularly well suited to adjudicate whether the algorithms survive legal scrutiny'.[35]

The Equal Credit Opportunity Act (ECOA), enacted in 1974, prohibits credit discrimination on the basis of certain protected characteristics, such as race.[36] A lender that uses AI to make credit decisions could violate ECOA—even if the AI algorithm does not explicitly consider race—if its lending practices result in a disparate impact on a racial group.[37] Moreover, the ECOA requires creditors, when

---

[32] *Texas Dep't of Hous. & Cmty. Affairs v. Inclusive Communities Project, Inc.*, 576 U.S. 519, 524 (2015) (recognising disparate impact liability under the FHA). The standard is codified at 24 C.F.R. § 100.500.

[33] 42 U.S.C. §§ 3601-19.

[34] Department of Justice, Press Release, *Justice Department Secures Groundbreaking Settlement Agreement with Meta Platforms, Formerly Known as Facebook, to Resolve Allegations of DiscriminatoryAdvertising*(June21,2022)https://www.justice.gov/opa/pr/justice-department-secures-groundbreaking-settlement-agreement-meta-platforms-formerly-known.

[35] Selmi (2021), p. 611.

[36] *See* 12 C.F.R. § 202.4. In 2020, Federal Trade Commission staff have highlighted the application of ECOA and other laws to decisions made by AI. Smith (2020) https://www.ftc.gov/news-events/blogs/business-blog/2020/04/using-artificial-intelligence-algorithms?utm_source=govdelivery. It may be significant that, at the time, which was during President Trump's first term, the FTC was controlled by Republicans, as it will be again starting sometime in 2025.

[37] *See generally* 1-8 Federal Fair Lending and Credit Practices Manual § 8.01 (2018).

denying credit or taking other adverse action against a consumer, to inform the consumer of the specific reasons for the action. The Consumer Financial Protection Bureau has warned creditors they cannot use complex algorithms when doing so means they cannot provide specific and accurate reasons for adverse actions.[38]

The Americans with Disabilities Act (ADA) prohibits employment discrimination on the basis of 'disability', defined as a physical or mental impairment that would, when left untreated, substantially limit one or more major life activities. The Act requires employers to provide 'reasonable accommodation' to persons with disabilities at all stages of the employment process, including testing, selection, and promotion. It also applies when an employer uses another company's hiring technology. Although the Act does not specifically mention AI, it clearly applies to employment decisions based on algorithms or AI.[39] For example, employers could violate the ADA if they used an algorithmic decision-making tool that screens out an individual with a disability when that individual is able to do the job with a reasonable accommodation.[40]

In response to President Biden's October 2023 Executive Order on AI, agencies issued a number of statements explaining how AI-based systems could violate these anti-discrimination laws:

- The Secretary of Labor published guidance for federal contractors regarding non-discrimination in hiring involving AI and other technology-based hiring systems.[41]
- The Department of Housing and Urban Development (HUD) issued guidance on complying with the Fair Housing Act (FHA), the Fair Credit Reporting Act, and other relevant Federal laws when using tenant screening systems, which use data, such as criminal records, eviction records, and credit information, that can lead to discriminatory outcomes.[42]
- HUD also issued guidance addressing how the FHA, the Consumer Financial Protection Act, or the ECOA apply to the advertising of housing, credit, and other real estate-related transactions through digital platforms, including those

[38] U.S. Consumer Financial Protection Bureau, Circular 2022-03, *Adverse action notification requirements in connection with credit decisions based on complex algorithms* (2022) https://www.consumerfinance.gov/compliance/circulars/circular-2022-03-adverse-action-notification-requirements-in-connection-with-credit-decisions-based-on-complex-algorithms/.

[39] U.S. Department of Justice, *Algorithms, Artificial Intelligence, and Disability Discrimination in Hiring* (2022) https://beta.ada.gov/ai-guidance/; EEOC, *The Americans with Disabilities Act and the Use of Software, Algorithms, and Artificial Intelligence to Assess Job Applicants and Employees* (2022) https://www.eeoc.gov/laws/guidance/americans-disabilities-act-and-use-software-algorithms-and-artificial-intelligence.

[40] See Brown et al. (2020), and Richardson et al. (2019).

[41] U.S. Dept. of Labor, Office of Federal Contract Compliance Programs, *Artificial Intelligence and Equal Employment Opportunity for Federal Contractors* (Apr. 29, 2024) https://www.dol.gov/agencies/ofccp/ai/ai-eeo-guide.

[42] *Guidance on Application of the Fair Housing Act to the Screening of Applicants for Rental Housing* (Apr. 2024) https://www.hud.gov/sites/dfiles/FHEO/documents/FHEO_Guidance_on_Screening_of_Applicants_for_Rental_Housing.pdf.

that use algorithms to facilitate advertising delivery, as well as on best practices to avoid violations of Federal law.[43]

Under President Trump, federal agencies may repeal or ignore this guidance. For example, the Department of Labor (DOL) withdrew guidance issued under President Biden regarding application of federal labour laws to the use of AI and other automated systems in the workplace. Likewise, DOL removed from its website the guidance referenced above on AI use by federal contractors. In general, one could expect federal agency enforcement of anti-discrimination laws to become weaker under President Trump, especially where AI is involved.

6 State Laws Specifically Addressing AI

6.1 Colorado AI Law

In May 2024, the state of Colorado adopted a first-in-the-nation law specifically aimed at AI.[44] The bill regulates both developers and deployers of AI doing business in Colorado. It specifically targets 'high-risk' AI systems, defined as systems that make, or are a substantial factor in making, consequential decisions. 'Consequential decision' is defined as one that has a material legal or similarly significant effect on the provision or denial to any consumer of, or the cost or terms of: (a) education enrollment or an education opportunity; (b) employment or an employment opportunity; (c) a financial or lending service; (d) an essential government service; (e) health-care services; (f) housing; (g) insurance; or (h) a legal service.

The statute requires developers and deployers to use 'reasonable care' to protect consumers from any known or reasonably foreseeable risks of algorithmic discrimination, defined as 'any condition in which the use of an artificial intelligence system results in an unlawful differential treatment or impact that disfavours an individual or group of individuals on the basis of their actual or perceived age, colour, disability, ethnicity, genetic information, limited proficiency in the English language, national origin, race, religion, reproductive health, sex, veteran status, or other classification protected under the laws of this state or federal law'. Note the word 'unlawful'; the differential treatment or impact at issue must be prohibited under some other law. Deployers and developers must disclose to consumers when they are interacting with an AI system, whether high-risk or not.

Developers of high risk systems must provide a wide range of information to deployers, including high-level summaries of the type of data used to train the

---

[43] HUD, *Guidance on Application of the Fair Housing Act to the Advertising of Housing, Credit, and Other Real Estate-Related Transactions through Digital Platforms* https://www.hud.gov/sites/dfiles/FHEO/documents/FHEO_Guidance_on_Advertising_through_Digital_Platforms.pdf.

[44] Senate Bill 24-205, adding a new part 17 to article 1 of title 6, Colorado Revised Statutes. https://leg.colorado.gov/sites/default/files/2024a_205_signed.pdf.

system and the measures the developer has taken to mitigate known or reasonably foreseeable risks of algorithmic discrimination that may arise from the system. They must also make certain public disclosures as well as a filing with the state attorney general.

Deployers of high-risk systems must complete an impact assessment and must implement a risk management policy and program specifying the principles, processes, and personnel that the deployer uses to identify, document, and mitigate known or reasonably foreseeable risks of algorithmic discrimination. Before a high-risk system is used to make any consequential decision regarding a consumer, the deployer must notify the consumer that the AI will be used, allowing consumers to exercise any opt-out rights they have under the Colorado privacy law. See Sect. 7.1 below. Then, if the AI system is used to make an adverse decision about the consumer, the deployer must disclose to the consumer the reasons for the decision and the type of data it was based on and must provide the consumer an opportunity to correct any personal data that was used and to appeal the adverse decision. A deployer of a high-risk system must also make certain public disclosures on its website.

The law takes effect on February 1, 2026. It provides no private right of action and will be enforced solely by the state attorney general.

6.2 Utah Artificial Intelligence Policy Act

On March 13, 2024, Utah enacted the Utah Artificial Intelligence Policy Act,[45] which sets three rules for use of generative AI tools: (1) A business cannot avoid liability for violating a consumer protection statute by claiming that a gen AI made the violative statement or made or was used in furtherance of a violative act. (2) A person who provides services in a regulated occupation (such as medicine or law, but also many others) shall promptly disclose when a client or customer is interacting with gen AI. (3) All others who use gen AI to interact with a person in a commercial transaction must disclose that the customer is interacting with gen AI, but only if asked by the customer. The statute also created an Office of Artificial Intelligence Policy within the state Department of Commerce. Among other powers, the office may grant temporary 'regulatory mitigation' to any person or entity that wants to use an AI technology in the state. Regulatory mitigation may consist of reduced fines or cure periods before fines are assessed, but it does not appear to include complete exemption from any otherwise applicable regulation.

[45] S.B. 149 (2024) https://le.utah.gov/~2024/bills/static/SB0149.html. Levi et al. (2024) https://www.skadden.com/insights/publications/2024/04/utah-becomes-first-state.

6.3 *Other State Laws*

The states are rapidly adopting a welter of AI-related laws, often on very specific questions. It is impossible here to list all state actions. In 2024, in California alone, the state legislature passed 38 AI-related bills. The Governor vetoed many of them, but he signed more than a dozen, including laws requiring watermarking of AI-generated images, audio and video and requiring health care providers that use AI to generate patient communications pertaining to clinical information to ensure that those communications include both (i) a disclaimer that indicates to the patient that a communication was generated by AI, and (ii) clear instructions describing how a patient may contact a human.[46] This trend may continue.[47]

7 State Consumer Privacy Laws

As of January 1, 2025, nineteen states[48] have adopted consumer privacy laws of somewhat general applicability providing a basic set of consumer privacy rights (notice, access, correction, deletion, opt-out of sale and certain uses, consent for processing of sensitive data) and imposing a set of obligations on data controllers (collection limitation, security, limits on secondary uses, data protection assessments for certain activities). Most of these laws address some uses of artificial intelligence under the concept of 'profiling', which they generally define as 'any form of automated processing [some say "any form of *solely* automated processing"] performed on personal data to evaluate, analyse, or predict personal aspects related to an identified or identifiable individual's economic situation, health, personal preferences, interests, reliability, behaviour, location, or movements'.[49] Regulations adopted or in the process of being adopted under the Colorado and California laws merit special attention.

---

[46] Anderson et al. (2024) https://www.whitecase.com/insight-alert/raft-california-ai-legislation-adds-growing-patchwork-us-regulation.

[47] Dori et al. (2024) https://www.insideglobaltech.com/2024/12/18/u-s-ai-policy-expectations-in-the-trump-administration-gop-congress-and-the-states/.

[48] California, Colorado, Connecticut, Delaware, Indiana, Iowa, Kentucky, Maryland, Minnesota, Montana, Nebraska, New Hampshire, New Jersey, Oregon, Rhode Island, Tennessee, Texas, Utah, and Virginia. See Bloomberg Law, *Which States Have Consumer Data Privacy Laws?* (Sept. 10, 2024) https://pro.bloomberglaw.com/insights/privacy/state-privacy-legislation-tracker/. Florida has a privacy law, Section 501.701–501.721, Florida Statutes, but its definition of controller is so specific that it probably applies only to Meta, Google, Apple, and Amazon and companies processing data on their behalf.

[49] Virgina Code § 59.1-575.

7.1 Colorado

The Colorado Privacy Act was adopted in 2021 and took effect in 2023.[50] Under § 6-1-1306(1)(a)(I)(C), a consumer has the right to opt out of profiling in furtherance of decisions that produce legal or similarly significant effects concerning the consumer. Like most other state privacy laws, the Colorado law has many exemptions, exempting sixteen categories of data or entities (including health care providers, health insurance data, consumer reporting agencies (i.e., credit agencies), employment records, educational records, public utilities, government agencies, and financial institutions), and it excludes eleven types of data processing (including 'internal research to improve … or develop products, services or technology').

Pursuant to the act, the Colorado attorney general has promulgated a regulation.[51] Under the regulation, controllers that process personal data for profiling for a decision that results in the provision or denial of financial or lending services, housing, insurance, education enrollment or opportunity, criminal justice, employment opportunities, health-care services, or access to essential goods or services (remember, however, the law's many exceptions, including for credit reporting agencies) must provide clear, understandable, and transparent notice to consumers. The notice must include, among other items, the categories of personal data that are used and a non-technical, plain language explanation of the logic used in the profiling process.

The regulation allows data controllers to not take action on an opt-out request if a human (1) engages in a meaningful consideration of available data used in the processing or any output of the processing and (2) has the authority to change or influence the outcome of the processing, referred to as Human Involved Automated Processing. If the controller does not take action to opt a consumer out of Human Involved Automated Processing, the controller shall inform the consumer it has done so and provide an explanation of how consumers can correct or delete the personal data used in the profiling.

The regulation also spells out requirements for the data protection assessment that Controllers must conduct and document before processing personal data for profiling if the profiling presents a reasonably foreseeable risk of harm to consumers.

In addition, the Colorado Privacy Act gives consumers (subject, again, to its many exceptions) the right to obtain copies of data, to delete, and to obtain correction of data. Note, however, that the law does not provide any right to challenge a decision involving automated decision making.

---

[50] Colorado Senate Bill 21-190 (2021), adding part 13 to article 1 of title 6 of the Colorado Revised Statutes, §§ 6-1-1301 - 6-1-1313. https://leg.colorado.gov/sites/default/files/2021a_190_signed.pdf.

[51] 4 CCR 904-3, https://coag.gov/app/uploads/2023/03/FINAL-CLEAN-2023.03.15-Official-CPA-Rules.pdf.

7.2 California

In 2020, California adopted landmark privacy legislation,[52] patterned in many ways after the E.U.'s General Data Protection Regulation. The legislation, which took full effect in January 2023, includes a comprehensive set of consumer data protection rights, including notice, deletion, correction, and opt-out of sale or sharing. Subject to certain size thresholds, it covers for-profit entities doing business in California. The law is unique among all the state laws. Among other things, it has many fewer exceptions than the other state laws. Notably, it covers employee data and the processing of data in the employment and job application contexts.

The California privacy law established a California Privacy Protection Agency (CPPA) and required it to establish regulations governing access and opt-out rights with respect to businesses' use of automated decision-making technology, including profiling, and requiring businesses' response to access requests to include meaningful information about the logic involved in those decision-making processes, as well as a description of the likely outcome of the process with respect to the consumer.[53]

In December, 2024, the CPPA issued a proposed regulation[54] on automated decision-making technology or 'ADMT', defined very broadly (in the draft as of July 4, 2025) as 'any technology that processes personal information and uses computation to replace human decision-making or substantially replace human decision-making'. It includes profiling. The regulation would apply to any covered business that uses ADMT for a significant decision concerning a California resident. 'Significant decision' means a decision that results in the provision or denial of financial or lending services, housing, education enrollment or opportunity, employment or independent contracting opportunities or compensation, or healthcare services.

The proposed regulation would require all covered entities that use automated decision-making technology to make a significant decision about consumers must provide the consumers with a 'Pre-use Notice', informing consumers about the business's use of ADMT and the consumers' rights to opt-out of, and to access information about, the business's use of automated decision-making technology. Under the proposed regulation, the notice would be required to include a plain language explanation of the specific purpose for which the business plans to use ADMT. Upon request, the business must also provide a plain language explanation of the logic used in the technology.

---

[52] Cal. Civ. Code §§ 1798.100 – 1798.199.100.

[53] Cal. Civ. Code, § 1798.185(a)(16).

[54] *Proposed Regulations on CCPA Updates, Cybersecurity Audits, Risk Assessments, Automated Decisionmaking Technology (ADMT), and Insurance Companies*, https://cppa.ca.gov/regulations/ccpa_updates.html.

The draft rule was open for public comment through June 2, 2025. After that, it will take a number of months to be finalised by the agency.

The state of California has adopted guidelines for state use of generative AI.[55]

7.3 *Other State Consumer Privacy Laws Regulating Profiling*

All of the other state privacy laws that address automated decision making under the name of profiling are based on a common model and were supported by industry because they do not allow for a private right of action and because they have many exceptions. These include:

- Connecticut Public Act 22-15 (2022), https://www.cga.ct.gov/2022/ACT/PA/PDF/2022PA-00015-R00SB-00006-PA.PDF.
- Title 6 of the Delaware Code, Chapter 12D, §§ 12D-101 - 12D-111.
- Indiana Code 24-15, effective January 1, 2026.
- Montana SB0384 (2023), effective October 1, 2024.
- Oregon Senate Bill 619 (2023), effective July 1, 2024.
- New Jersey Bill S332 (2022-23), https://www.njleg.state.nj.us/bill-search/2022/S332.
- Tennessee Code Annotated, Title 47, Chapter 18, §§ 47-18-3201 - 47-18-3213.
- Texas H.B. No. 4 (2023), adding to Title 11, Business & Commerce Code, a new Subtitle C, Chapter 541, Sections 541.001 - 541.204, effective July 1, 2024. https://capitol.texas.gov/tlodocs/88R/billtext/pdf/HB00004F.pdf.
- Code of Virginia, Title 59.1, Trade and Commerce, Chapter 53, §§ 59.1-575 - 59.1-584. https://law.lis.virginia.gov/vacodefull/title59.1/chapter53/.

These laws generally provide consumers three rights relevant to AI or automated data processing: to opt-out of certain 'profiling', to correct inaccuracies in data about themselves, and to delete data about themselves. They do not give consumers the right to challenge the accuracy of decisions made by automated means. Also, many of the state laws have broad exceptions or exclusions. The laws regulate businesses, not government agencies. None of these state laws has a private right of action. Therefore, if a covered entity refuses an opt-out request or refuses to correct information, the individual has no recourse. The only enforcement is though the state attorney general. (California has the only state privacy law with a private right of action.)

Most of the laws do not require notice that profiling is occurring or that AI is being used. The New Jersey and Montana laws are an exception, requiring that, if a controller processes personal data for the purposes of profiling in furtherance of

[55] *State of California GenAI Guidelines for Public Sector Procurement, Uses and Training* (March 2024), https://www.govops.ca.gov/wp-content/uploads/sites/11/2024/03/3.a-GenAI-Guidelines.pdf. The guidelines were issued pursuant to the state governor's Executive Order N-12-23 on Generative Artificial Intelligence (Sept. 6, 2023).

decisions that produce legal or similarly significant effects concerning a consumer, the controller shall clearly and conspicuously disclose such processing, as well as the manner in which a consumer may opt out of such processing. (As noted above, Colorado and California also require notice.)

The right to opt out of profiling is generally applicable to profiling in furtherance of 'a decision that produces a legal or similarly significant effect concerning the consumer', which is generally defined as any decision that results in the provision or denial by the controller of: financial and lending services; housing, insurance, or health care services; education enrollment; employment opportunities; criminal justice; or access to basic necessities, such as food and water. However, because of the exceptions in these laws, many uses of profiling in these contexts are actually not covered. In addition, a number of these laws (Connecticut, Delaware, Indiana, Montana, Tennessee, Texas) limit the opt-out right to profiling in furtherance of *solely* automated decisions that produce legal or similarly significant effects concerning the consumer.

In a potentially important provision, these state laws generally require controllers to conduct and document a data protection assessment for each of the controller's processing activities that presents a heightened risk of harm to a consumer. The statutes specify that processing that presents a heightened risk of harm to a consumer includes the processing of personal data for the purposes of profiling, where such profiling presents a reasonably foreseeable risk of (A) unfair or deceptive treatment of, or unlawful disparate impact on, consumers, (B) financial, physical or reputational injury to consumers, (C) a physical or other intrusion upon the solitude or seclusion, or the private affairs or concerns, of consumers, where such intrusion would be offensive to a reasonable person, or (D) other substantial injury to consumers. Under most of the laws, the attorney general can request such data protection assessments, but there is no requirement that they be made publicly available by the data controller.

8 Consumer and Worker Protection Laws

8.1 Fair Credit Reporting Act

The Fair Credit Reporting Act (FCRA), enacted in 1970, comes into play in certain circumstances where information is used to deny people employment, housing, credit, insurance, or other benefits. Among other things, the FCRA requires a business to provide an adverse action notice to an applicant who is rejected based on data analysis covered under the Act. This and other provisions in the law cover automated decision-making even though the FCRA does not mention AI specifically. As one leading expert in the consumer protection field has advised: 'For example, suppose an employer purchases AI-based scores to assess whether an applicant will be a good employee. In many circumstances, if the employer denies the applicant a job based on the score, it must, among other things, provide the applicant with an adverse action notice, which tells the applicant they can access the underlying information and correct it if it is false'.[56] The FCRA has. Private right of action.

8.2 Federal Trade Commission Act

Section 5 of the Federal Trade Commission Act prohibits unfair or deceptive trade practices. 15 U.S.C. § 45. In 2020, the Federal Trade Commission (FTC) published a set of guidelines for 'Using Artificial Intelligence and Algorithms', in which it stated that 'the use of AI tools should be transparent, explainable, fair, and empirically sound, while fostering accountability'.[57] While the guidelines themselves were non-binding, they made it clear that the FTC would bring actions against what it considered to be unfair or deceptive uses of AI, under the FTC Act, as well as under the FCRA and the ECOA

True to its promise, in 2021 the FTC brought an AI-related enforcement action based on a deception theory, where the business allegedly misrepresented to consumers how it used their data.[58] In December 2023, the Federal Trade Commission took another major step when it alleged that the pharmacy chain Rite Aid engaged in an unfair practice when it used inaccurate facial recognition technology based on AI in an effort to identify customers who might be shoplifters.[59] The FTC alleged that the technology often falsely flagged innocent consumers. Shoppers subject to false matches were erroneously accused by employees of wrongdoing, searched, and expelled from stores, under humiliating circumstances. The complaint alleged that the company had failed to take reasonable measures to prevent such harm to consumers (and, indeed, engaged in practices likely to make things worse, including using low-quality images unsuitable for automated analysis).

To resolve the matter, Rite Aid stipulated to the entry of an order for permanent injunction.[60] The order prohibited Rite Aid from using any facial recognition or analysis system in any store for five years. It also required the company to delete or

[56] Mital (2022) https://www.wsgrdataadvisor.com/2022/02/legal-requirements-for-mitigating-bias-in-ai-systems/.

[57] Smith (2020). See also Jillson (2021), https://www.ftc.gov/news-events/blogs/business-blog/2021/04/aiming-truth-fairness-equity-your-companys-use-ai.

[58] See FTC Press Release, *California Company Settles FTC Allegations It Deceived Consumers about Use of Facial Recognition in Photo Storage* App (Jan. 11, 2021), https://www.ftc.gov/news-events/press-releases/2021/01/california-company-settles-ftc-allegations-it-deceived-consumers.

[59] Relevant documents are available at https://www.ftc.gov/news-events/news/press-releases/2023/12/rite-aid-banned-using-ai-facial-recognition-after-ftc-says-retailer-deployed-technology-without.

[60] Stipulated Order for Permanent Injunction and Other Relief, *FTC v. Rite Aid Corp.*, Case No. 2:23-cv-5023 (E.D. Pa. Dec. 19, 2023 https://www.ftc.gov/system/files/ftc_gov/pdf/2023190_rite-aid_stipulated_order_filed.pdf.

destroy all photos and videos of consumers used or collected prior to the effective date of the order and any data, models, or algorithms derived in whole or in part from such images. Moreover, the order directed the company to instruct any third parties with which consumer images had been shared to delete those images and any data, models, or algorithms derived in whole or in part from them. The injunction then went on to require Rite Aid, before it adopted in the future any automated facial recognition or biometric system, to adopt a comprehensive program of controls intended to identify and address the risks that such a system could result in.[61] Commissioner Alvaro Bedoya said in a statement accompanying the settlement, 'I want industry to understand that this Order is a baseline for what a comprehensive algorithmic fairness program should look like'.[62] However, the precedential value of the case was somewhat limited by the fact that the five-member FTC only had three members at the time and all were Democrats.

More revealing of the FTC's likely path in 2025 was a series of enforcement actions against AI companies brought by the FTC in 2024, after it had been restored to full membership with two Republican commissioners. In September 2024, it brought five cases including one against a company that claimed to offer an AI service that was 'the world's first robot lawyer', but the product failed to live up to its claims that the service could substitute for the expertise of a human lawyer.[63] In December, 2024, the FTC issued an order against another company for making false, misleading or unsubstantiated claims that its AI-powered facial recognition software was free of gender and racial bias and making other misleading claims about the technology.[64]

Three things are especially significant about the enforcement actions: (1) Five of the six cases were unanimous, with the Republican members, who will be part of the majority under President Trump, supporting the issuance of the complaints. (2) On all of the Section 5 allegations that were unanimous, the complaint focused on the deceptive claims of the AI companies, not any allegations of unfairness. (3) The commissioner who will be chair of the FTC under President Trump, Andrew Ferguson wrote separately in one case to say:

---

[61] Fair (2023) https://www.ftc.gov/business-guidance/blog/2023/12/coming-face-face-rite-aids-allegedly-unfair-use-facial-recognition-technology; FTC Press Release, *Rite Aid Banned from Using AI Facial Recognition After FTC Says Retailer Deployed Technology without Reasonable Safeguards* (Dec. 19, 2023) https://www.ftc.gov/news-events/news/press-releases/2023/12/rite-aid-banned-using-ai-facial-recognition-after-ftc-says-retailer-deployed-technology-without.

[62] Statement of Commissioner Alvaro M. Bedoya on *FTC v. Rite Aid Corporation & Rite Aid Headquarters Corporation,* Commission File No. 202-3190 (Dec. 19, 2023) https://www.ftc.gov/system/files/ftc_gov/pdf/2023190_commissioner_bedoya_riteaid_statement.pdf.

[63] FTC Press Release, *FTC Announces Crackdown on Deceptive AI Claims and Schemes* (Sept. 25, 2024) https://www.ftc.gov/news-events/news/press-releases/2024/09/ftc-announces-crackdown-deceptive-ai-claims-schemes.

[64] FTC Press Release, *FTC Takes Action Against IntelliVision Technologies for Deceptive Claims About its Facial Recognition Software* (Dec. 3, 2024) https://www.ftc.gov/news-events/news/press-releases/2024/12/ftc-takes-action-against-intellivision-technologies-deceptive-claims-about-its-facial-recognition.

> I write separately to ensure that no one confuses what we are doing today—holding generative-AI companies to the same standards for honest-business conduct that apply to every industry—with the regulation of AI *qua* AI. Congress has given us the power to enforce prohibitions against unfair methods of competition and unfair or deceptive acts and practices. 10 9F We may reach some AI-related activity incidental to enforcing those prohibitions, as we do today. But Congress has not given us power to regulate AI standing alone. We should not succumb to the panicked calls for the Commission to act as the country's comprehensive AI regulator.[65]

The FTC staff has reminded companies that develop and host AI models they make available to third parties via an end-user interface or an application programming interface—referred to as 'model-as-a-service' companies—that they may be liable under the laws enforced by the FTC if they fail to abide by their privacy commitments to their users and customers, such as promises that they won't use customer data for to train or update their models.[66] This is important because, in its enforcement actions, if a business improperly uses consumer data, the FTC has required the offender to delete any models and algorithms developed in whole or in part using that unlawfully obtained data.

8.3 *States Laws Prohibiting Unfair or Deceptive Act in Commerce*

In addition to the growing number of state consumer privacy laws, each of the 50 states and the District of Columbia has a consumer protection law that prohibits deceptive practices and most also prohibit unfair practices as well. These are called consumer protection acts, consumer fraud acts, or UDAP (unfair and deceptive acts and practices) statutes. All of them provide some private right of action for consumers to sue, but quite a few of the laws put limits on those private rights of action, so it is not easy to summarise across all 50 states which might allow private right of action for AI-related harms.

However, every UDAP statute is enforced by the state attorney general (AG) or other state official and these laws can be very adaptive to new technologies such as AI. Indeed, the process of applying these laws to AI began in September 2024, when the attorney general of Texas announced the first-ever state AG enforcement action against a company based on allegedly deceptive and misleading statements it made regarding the accuracy and safety of its products that used AI.[67] The company

65 Concurring Statement of Commissioner Andrew N. Ferguson *In the Matter of DoNotPay, Inc.* (Sept. 25, 2024) https://www.ftc.gov/legal-library/browse/cases-proceedings/public-statements/concurring-statement-commissioner-andrew-n-ferguson-matter-donotpay-inc.

66 Staff in the Office of Technology, *AI Companies: Uphold Your Privacy and Confidentiality Commitments*, FTC Technology Blog, (Jan. 9, 2024) https://www.ftc.gov/policy/advocacy-research/tech-at-ftc/2024/01/ai-companies-uphold-your-privacy-confidentiality-commitments.

67 Press Release, *Attorney General Ken Paxton Reaches Settlement in First-of-its-Kind Healthcare Generative AI Investigation* (Sept. 18, 2024), https://www.texasattorneygeneral.gov/news/releases/

offered a generative AI product that it claimed could accurately summarise data about hospital patients' condition and treatment, claiming in its advertising and marketing that its AI products were 'highly accurate' and had an error rate or 'severe hallucination rate' of '<1 per 100,000'. The AG found that these metrics were likely inaccurate and may have deceived hospitals about the accuracy and safety of the company's products. The complaint alleged violations of the Texas Deceptive Trade Practices – Consumer Protection Act, Tex. Bus. & Com. Code §§ 17.41-.63. As part of the settlement, the company agreed to accurately disclose the definition of any metrics it used to describe the output of its generative AI products as well as the methods used to calculate such metrics and to ensure that the hospital staff using its generative AI products to treat patients understood the extent to which they should or should not rely on its products.

8.4 State Laws Regulating Insurance

In the U.S., insurance is regulated mainly at the state level. Many state insurance laws prohibit use of race and other categories in underwriting. In 2019, the New York State Department of Financial Services (DFS) issued a letter to insurers authorised to write life insurance in New York warning them that the data they use and the algorithms and predictive models they apply may produce the forms of discrimination prohibited by state law.[68] Consequently, the DFS advised, 'an insurer should not use an external data source, algorithm or predictive model in underwriting or rating unless the insurer can establish that the underwriting or rating guidelines are not unfairly discriminatory in violation' of the state Insurance Law.

In addition, the DFS noted that, under state law, consumers have the right to receive the specific reason or reasons for any declination, limitation, rate differential, or other adverse underwriting decision. The DFS concluded: 'Where an insurer is using external data sources or predictive models, the reason or reasons provided to the insured or potential insured must include details about all information upon which the insurer based decision … . An insurer may not rely on the proprietary nature of a third-party vendor's algorithmic processes to justify the lack of specificity related to an adverse underwriting action. Insurers must also provide notice to and obtain consent from consumers to access external data, where required by law or regulation'.

---

attorney-general-ken-paxton-reaches-settlement-first-its-kind-healthcare-generative-ai-investigation.

[68] N. Y. State Dep't Fin. Serv., Insurance Circular Letter No. 1 (2019), *Use of External Consumer Data and Information Sources in Underwriting for Life Insurance* (January 18, 2019) https://dfs.ny.gov/industry_guidance/circular_letters/cl2019_01.

In July 2024, the DFS issued another circular letter regarding the use of AI systems (AIS) in insurance underwriting and pricing.[69] The letter stated that an insurer should not use AIS for underwriting or pricing purposes unless the insurer can establish that the model does not use and is not based in any way on any class protected pursuant to the Insurance Law. The circular laid out specific steps that companies should follow in assessing whether an underwriting or pricing guideline derived from AIS unfairly discriminates between similarly situated individuals or unlawfully discriminates against a protected class. Moreover, under the circular, senior management and the board would be responsible for oversight of the insurer's use of AI.

In February 2024, the Connecticut Insurance Department issued a bulletin on the use of AI systems in insurance.[70] The Connecticut bulletin is based on a Model Bulletin adopted by the National Association of Insurance Commissioners.[71] Connecticut was the third state, after Alaska and New Hampshire, to adopt the Model Bulletin, with additional states expected to do so.

The Connecticut bulletin reminds all insurers that decisions or actions affecting consumers made and supported by advanced analytical and computational technologies, including AI, must comply with all applicable insurance laws and regulations. This includes unfair trade practice and unfair discrimination laws. The bulletin sets forth the Department's expectations for insurers' governance of the development, acquisition and use of AI technologies. It states that insurers are expected to develop, implement, and maintain a written program for the responsible use of AI-based systems that make or support decisions related to regulated insurance practices and products. The approach is based on risk management. It requires insurers to address the following, among other things:

- The oversight and approval process for the development, adoption and acquisition of AI systems.
- Data practices and accountability procedures, including data quality, integrity, bias analysis and minimisation, among other items.
- The management and oversight of algorithms and predictive models, including, but not limited to:
  - A description of the predictive models;
  - A detailed documentation on the use algorithms and predictive models; and

[69] N.Y. State Dep't Fin. Serv., Insurance Circular Letter No. 7, *Use of Artificial Intelligence Systems and External Consumer Data and Information Sources in Insurance Underwriting and Pricing* (July 11, 2024) https://www.dfs.ny.gov/industry-guidance/circular-letters/cl2024-07.

[70] State of Conn. Ins. Dept., Bulletin No. MC-25, *The Use of Artificial Intelligence Systems in Insurance* (Feb. 26, 2024) https://portal.ct.gov/cid/-/media/cid/1_bulletins/bulletin-mc-25.pdf.

[71] https://content.naic.org/sites/default/files/inline-files/2023-12-4%20Model%20Bulletin_Adopted_0.pdf.

  - A regular assessment of the predictive models, including for tuning, reproducibility and evaluation for model drift purposes.
- The validation, testing and retesting of data, algorithms and models, specifically to identify errors and bias in the AI systems, including the potential for unfair discrimination.

8.5 Wage and Hours Laws

The federal Fair Labor Standards Act regulates the regular wages and overtime pay of many private sector workers. In April 2024, the federal Department of Labor issued guidance reminding employers that the use of AI and other automated technologies for scheduling, timekeeping, and tracking employee location may undercount hours worked, particularly during possible break times, when employees perform work in multiple locations, or when employees have periods in which they are waiting to be engaged.[72] Regardless of the technologies and systems used, the guidance stated, employers are responsible for ensuring that they are paying employees for all hours worked under the law. Likewise, employers that use AI or other technologies to calculate wage rates must ensure that employees are paid in accordance with federal minimum wage, overtime, and other wage requirements, even when those wage rates vary substantially due to a host of inputs. As noted above, this guidance was removed from the DOL website after January 20, 2025, although the underlying law has not been amended as of July 4, 2025.

9 State and Local Laws Specifically Regulating AI in Employment Decisions

In November 2021, New York City became the first jurisdiction in the U.S. to adopt legislation aimed specifically at mitigating the risks of discrimination associated with the use of AI to screen candidates for employment or employees for promotion within the city.[73] The law does not prohibit all use of such AI-based assessment tools. Instead, it prohibits use unless the tool has been the subject of a 'bias audit' that has been made publicly available on the website of the employer or

[72] Dept. of Labor, Field Assistance Bulletin No. 2024-1, *Artificial Intelligence and Automated Systems in the Workplace under the Fair Labor Standards Act and Other Federal Labor Standards* (Apr. 29, 2024) https://www.dol.gov/sites/dolgov/files/WHD/fab/fab2024_1.pdf.

[73] *A Local Law to amend the administrative code of the city of New York, in relation to automated employment decision tools*, Local Law n. 2021-144 (2021), https://legistar.council.nyc.gov/LegislationDetail.aspx?ID=4344524&GUID=B051915D-A9AC-451E-81F8-6596032FA3F9&Options=Advanced&Search.

employment agency. The law also requires employers and employment agencies to notify individuals that an automated employment decision tool is being used and the job qualifications and characteristics that such tool will use. Some advocates criticised the bill as too weak.[74]

Illinois requires employers using AI interview technology to notify applicants about how AI works and obtain the applicant's consent.[75] Maryland requires consent for employers using facial recognition tools when interviewing applicants.[76]

10 State and Local Laws Limiting or Regulating Facial Recognition

Motivated by fears about both inaccuracy and pervasive surveillance, a number of legislative bodies in the U.S. have banned or limited use of facial recognition systems by police or other governmental agencies.[77] One of the most detailed laws was adopted in 2020 in Washington state. It requires a detailed 'accountability report' before any state or local government agency develops, procures, or uses a facial recognition service.[78] It also requires any vendor providing facial recognition to a state or local agency to provide an API or other technical capability to enable 'legitimate, independent, and reasonable tests of those facial recognition services for accuracy and unfair performance differences across distinct subpopulations'.

In March 2022, Virginia imposed specific limits on the use of facial recognition for law enforcement purposes.[79] Among other provisions, the law states the state's Division of Purchases and Supply shall not approve any facial recognition technology unless it has been demonstrated that it shows minimal performance variations across demographics associated with race, skin tone, ethnicity, or gender.

A few jurisdictions have banned the use of facial recognition by the private sector. A September 2020 measure adopted by the city of Portland, Oregon prohibits 'private entities' from using 'face recognition technologies' in 'places of public accommodation' within Portland.[80] In June 2021, Baltimore adopted an ordinance

[74] Scherer and Shetty (2021), https://cdt.org/insights/ny-city-council-rams-through-once-promising-but-deeply-flawed-bill-on-ai-hiring-tools/.

[75] Artificial Intelligence Video Interview Act, 820 ILCS 42.

[76] MARYLAND (MD) LAB. & EMPL. CODE ANN. § 3–717 (effective Oct. 1, 2020).

[77] See, for example, CAL. PENAL CODE, § 832.19; Cushing (2019, 3:35 PM), https://www.techdirt.com/articles/20191011/18013143178/california-governor-signs-bill-banning-facial-recognition-tech-use-states-law-enforcement-agencies.shtml; Richardson (2021).

[78] SB 6280, adding a new chapter to Title 43 RCW, lawfilesext.leg.wa.gov/biennium/2019-20/Pdf/Bills/Session%20Laws/Senate/6280-S.SL.pdf.

[79] SB 741 Facial recognition technology; authorized uses, https://lis.virginia.gov/cgi-bin/legp604.exe?221+sum+SB741.

[80] *Portland, Oregon First to Ban Private-Sector Use of Facial Recognition Technology*, HUNTON (Sept. 10, 2020), https://www.huntonprivacyblog.com/2020/09/10/portland-oregon-becomes-first-jurisdiction-in-u-s-to-ban-the-commercial-use-of-facial-recognition-technology/.

banning the use of facial biometrics by any private entity or individual within city limits as well as by most city agencies (but not the police). The ordinance carried criminal sanctions. However the ban expired at the end of 2022 when the city council failed to extend it.

It must be noted, however, that many proposed bans have been rejected.[81] Moreover, the effort to ban use of facial recognition seems to have lost momentum, as there appear to have been very few new bans adopted since the beginning of 2022: In 2023, the New York State Education Department, acting under the state Technology Law, issued a determination prohibiting schools in New York State from purchasing or utilising facial recognition technology.[82] And in 2024, a New York state budget law directed that the New York City Metropolitan Transportation Authority 'not use, or arrange for the use, of biometric identifying technology, including but not limited to facial recognition technology, to enforce rules relating to the payment of fares'.[83]

11 Conclusion

In the U.S., existing laws already apply to AI, including rules adopted over many decades to deal with algorithms used in credit scoring, risk assessment, or other evaluations of individuals. Cases involving allegations of AI bias or error are beginning to emerge in courts and regulatory agencies. Legislators at the state level are also responding, on a patchwork basis, especially with laws requiring businesses to allow consumers to opt out of automated data processing for profiling. Starting in January 2025, under President Trump, federal agencies may be less likely to defend individuals against the use of AI, but some state agencies may be more active and private litigation can continue under some federal anti-discrimination laws.

---

[81] Parker (2021), https://www.securityinfowatch.com/access-identity/biometrics/facial-recognition-solutions/article/21230121/security-industry-association-sia-most-state-legislatures-have-rejected-bans-and-severe-restrictions-on-facial-recognition.

[82] New York State Education Department, *State Education Department Issues Determination on Biometric Identifying Technology in Schools* (Sept. 27, 2023) https://www.nysed.gov/news/2023/state-education-department-issues-determination-biometric-identifying-technology-schools.

[83] Nessen (2024) https://gothamist.com/news/mta-banned-from-using-facial-recognition-to-enforce-fare-evasion.

References

Anderson H, Reem N, Tadayyon S (Oct. 10, 2024) Raft of California AI Legislation Adds to Growing Patchwork of US Regulation. White & Case https://www.whitecase.com/insight-alert/raft-california-ai-legislation-adds-growing-patchwork-us-regulation

Angwin J, Larson J, Mattu S, Kirchner L (May 23, 2016) Machine Bias. Pro Publica

Bloomberg Law, Which States Have Consumer Data Privacy Laws? (Sept. 10, 2024). https://pro.bloomberglaw.com/insights/privacy/state-privacy-legislation-tracker/

Brown LXZ, Richardson M, Shetty R, Crawford A, Hoagland T (Oct. 2020)) Challenging the use of algorithm-driven decision-making in benefits determinations affecting people with disabilities. Center for Democracy & Technology. https://cdt.org/wp-content/uploads/2020/10/2020-10-21-Challenging-the-Use-of-Algorithm-driven-Decision-making-in-Benefits-Determinations-Affecting-People-with-Disabilities.pdf

Buzzell D (2018) Federal Fair Lending and Credit Practices Manual

California Civil Code, § 1798.185(a)(16)

California Civil Code §§ 1798.100 – 1798.199.100

California Consumer Protection Agency Proposed Regulations on CCPA Updates, Cybersecurity Audits, Risk Assessments, Automated Decisionmaking Technology (ADMT), and Insurance Companies, https://cppa.ca.gov/regulations/ccpa_updates.html

California Government Operations Agency (March 2024) State of California GenAI Guidelines for Public Sector Procurement, Uses and Training. https://www.govops.ca.gov/wp-content/uploads/sites/11/2024/03/3.a-GenAI-Guidelines.pdf

California Governor's Office (Sept. 6, 2023) Executive Order N-12-23 on Generative Artificial Intelligence

California Penal Code, § 832.19

Chouldechova A (2017) Fair prediction with disparate impact: a study of bias in recidivism prediction instruments. Big Data 5:153. https://www.liebertpub.com/doi/pdf/10.1089/big.2016.0047

Colorado Regulations, 4 CCR 904-3, https://coag.gov/app/uploads/2023/03/FINAL-CLEAN-2023.03.15-Official-CPA-Rules.pdf

Colorado Senate Bill 21-190 (2021), adding part 13 to article 1 of title 6 of the Colorado Revised Statutes, §§ 6-1-1301 - 6-1-1313. https://leg.colorado.gov/sites/default/files/2021a_190_signed.pdf

Colorado Senate Bill 24-205, adding a new part 17 to article 1 of title 6, Colorado Revised Statutes. https://leg.colorado.gov/sites/default/files/2024a_205_signed.pdf

Connecticut Insurance Department (Feb. 26, 2024) Bulletin No. MC-25, The Use of Artificial Intelligence Systems in Insurance https://portal.ct.gov/cid/-/media/cid/1_bulletins/bulletin-mc-25.pdf

Cushing T, California Governor Signs Bill Banning Facial Recognition Tech Use By State's Law Enforcement Agencies, TechDirt (Oct. 18, 2019). https://www.techdirt.com/articles/20191011/18013143178/california-governor-signs-bill-banning-facial-recognition-tech-use-states-law-enforcement-agencies.shtml

Dori Y, Fechner H, Shapanka M, Gweon A, U.S. AI Policy Expectations in the Trump Administration, GOP Congress, and the States (Dec. 18, 2024). https://www.insideglobaltech.com/2024/12/18/u-s-ai-policy-expectations-in-the-trump-administration-gop-congress-and-the-states/

Easterbrook FH (1996) Cyberspace and the Law of the Horse. Univ Chic Legal Forum 1996:207, 208

Engstrom DF, Ho DE, Cuéllar M-F, Sharkey CM (2020) Government by Algorithm: Artificial Intelligence in Federal Administrative Agencies

Equal Employment Opportunity Commission (2022) The Americans with Disabilities Act and the Use of Software, Algorithms, and Artificial Intelligence to Assess Job Applicants and Employees https://www.eeoc.gov/laws/guidance/americans-disabilities-act-and-use-software-algorithms-and-artificial-intelligence

Equal Employment Opportunity Commission (2024) Joint Statement on Enforcement of Civil Rights, Fair Competition, Consumer Protection, and Equal Opportunity Laws in Automated Systems, https://web.archive.org/web/20240518140700/https://www.eeoc.gov/joint-statement-enforcement-civil-rights-fair-competition-consumer-protection-and-equal-0

Fair L, Coming face to face with Rite Aid's allegedly unfair use of facial recognition technology, FTC Business Blog (Dec. 19, 2023). https://www.ftc.gov/business-guidance/blog/2023/12/coming-face-face-rite-aids-allegedly-unfair-use-facial-recognition-technology

Federal Trade Commission, Press Release, California Company Settles FTC Allegations It Deceived Consumers about Use of Facial Recognition in Photo Storage App (Jan. 11, 2021), https://www.ftc.gov/news-events/press-releases/2021/01/california-company-settles-ftc-allegations-it-deceived-consumers

Federal Trade Commission, Stipulated Order for Permanent Injunction and Other Relief, *FTC v. Rite Aid Corp.*, Case No. 2:23-cv-5023 (E.D. Pa. Dec. 19, 2023. https://www.ftc.gov/system/files/ftc_gov/pdf/2023190_riteaid_stipulated_order_filed.pdf

Federal Trade Commission, Concurring Statement of Commissioner Andrew N. Ferguson In the Matter of DoNotPay, Inc. (Sept. 25, 2024). https://www.ftc.gov/legal-library/browse/cases-proceedings/public-statements/concurring-statement-commissioner-andrew-n-ferguson-matter-donotpay-inc

Federal Trade Commission, Press Release, Rite Aid Banned from Using AI Facial Recognition After FTC Says Retailer Deployed Technology without Reasonable Safeguards (Dec. 19, 2023). https://www.ftc.gov/news-events/news/press-releases/2023/12/rite-aid-banned-using-ai-facial-recognition-after-ftc-says-retailer-deployed-technology-without

Federal Trade Commission, Press Release, FTC Announces Crackdown on Deceptive AI Claims and Schemes (Sept. 25, 2024). https://www.ftc.gov/news-events/news/press-releases/2024/09/ftc-announces-crackdown-deceptive-ai-claims-schemes

Federal Trade Commission, Press Release, FTC Takes Action Against IntelliVision Technologies for Deceptive Claims About its Facial Recognition Software (Dec. 3, 2024). https://www.ftc.gov/news-events/news/press-releases/2024/12/ftc-takes-action-against-intellivision-technologies-deceptive-claims-about-its-facial-recognition

Federal Trade Commission, Staff in the Office of Technology, AI Companies: Uphold Your Privacy and Confidentiality Commitments, FTC Technology Blog, (Jan. 9, 2024). https://www.ftc.gov/policy/advocacy-research/tech-at-ftc/2024/01/ai-companies-uphold-your-privacy-confidentiality-commitments

Federal Trade Commission, Statement of Commissioner Alvaro M. Bedoya on FTC v. Rite Aid Corporation & Rite Aid Headquarters Corporation, Commission File No. 202-3190 (Dec. 19, 2023). https://www.ftc.gov/system/files/ftc_gov/pdf/2023190_commissioner_bedoya_riteaid_statement.pdf

Harrington B, Sheffner DJ, Informal administrative adjudication: an overview. Cong. Research Service (Oct. 1, 2021). https://sgp.fas.org/crs/misc/R46930.pdf

Hunton, Portland, Oregon First to Ban Private-Sector Use of Facial Recognition Technology. Hunton (Sept. 10, 2020). https://www.huntonprivacyblog.com/2020/09/10/portland-oregon-becomes-first-jurisdiction-in-u-s-to-ban-the-commercial-use-of-facial-recognition-technology/

Illinois General Assembly, Artificial Intelligence Video Interview Act, 820 ILCS 42

Indiana Supreme Court (2010) *Malenchik v. State*, 928 N.E.2d 564

Iowa Court of Appeals *State v. Gordon*, No. 17-0395, 2018 WL 2084847, at *9 May 2, 2018)

Jillson E, Aiming for truth, fairness, and equity in your company's use of AI. FTC: Business Blog (April 19, 2021), https://web.archive.org/web/20250117235232/https://www.ftc.gov/business-guidance/blog/2021/04/aiming-truth-fairness-equity-your-companys-use-ai

Levi SD, Ridgway WE, Simon DA, Slawe MC, Oh A, Utah Becomes First State To Enact AI-Centric Consumer Protection Law, Skadden (April 5, 2024). https://www.skadden.com/insights/publications/2024/04/utah-becomes-first-state

Maryland Lab. & Empl. Code Ann. § 3–717

Mital M, Legal Requirements for Mitigating Bias in AI Systems. The WSGR Data Advisor (Feb. 14, 2022). https://www.wsgrdataadvisor.com/2022/02/legal-requirements-for-mitigating-bias-in-ai-systems/

Nessen S, MTA banned from using facial recognition to enforce fare evasion, Gothamist (Apr. 28, 2024). https://gothamist.com/news/mta-banned-from-using-facial-recognition-to-enforce-fare-evasion

New York City, A Local Law to amend the administrative code of the city of New York, in relation to automated employment decision tools, Local Law n. 2021-144 (2021), https://legistar.council.nyc.gov/LegislationDetail.aspx?ID=4344524&GUID=B051915D-A9AC-451E-81F8-6596032FA3F9&Options=Advanced&Search

New York City, Department of Consumer and Worker Protection, Automated Employment Decision Tools: Frequently Asked Questions (June 29, 2023). https://www.nyc.gov/assets/dca/downloads/pdf/about/DCWP-AEDT-FAQ.pdf

New York City, Local Law 144 of 2021

New York State Department of Financial Services, Insurance Circular Letter No. 1 (2019), Use of External Consumer Data and Information Sources in Underwriting for Life Insurance (January 18, 2019) https://dfs.ny.gov/industry_guidance/circular_letters/cl2019_01

New York State Department of Financial Services, Insurance Circular Letter No. 7, Use of Artificial Intelligence Systems and External Consumer Data and Information Sources in Insurance Underwriting and Pricing (July 11, 2024). https://www.dfs.ny.gov/industry-guidance/circular-letters/cl2024-07

New York State Education Department, State Education Department Issues Determination on Biometric Identifying Technology in Schools (Sept. 27, 2023). https://www.nysed.gov/news/2023/state-education-department-issues-determination-biometric-identifying-technology-schools

Parker J, Most state legislatures have rejected bans and severe restrictions on facial recognition. Security InfoWatch.com (July 12, 2021), https://www.securityinfowatch.com/access-identity/biometrics/facial-recognition-solutions/article/21230121/security-industry-association-sia-most-state-legislatures-have-rejected-bans-and-severe-restrictions-on-facial-recognition

Richardson R, Facial Recognition in the Public Sector: The Policy Landscape, German Marshall Fund (Feb. 3, 2021)

Richardson M, Schultz J, Southerland V (2019) Litigating Algorithms 2019 US Report: New Challenges to Government Use of Algorithmic Decision Systems. AI Now Institute, https://ainowinstitute.org/publication/litigating-algorithms-2019-u-s-report-2

Scherer M, Shetty R, NY City Council Rams Through Once-Promising but Deeply Flawed Bill on AI Hiring Tools. Ctr Democracy & Technol. (Nov. 12, 2021), https://cdt.org/insights/ny-city-council-rams-through-once-promising-but-deeply-flawed-bill-on-ai-hiring-tools/

Selmi M (2021), Algorithms, discrimination and the law. Ohio State Law J 82:61

Smith A, Using Artificial Intelligence and Algorithms. FTC: Business Blog (April 8, 2020). https://www.ftc.gov/news-events/blogs/business-blog/2020/04/using-artificial-intelligence-algorithms?utm_source=govdelivery

Texas Attorney General, Press Release, Attorney General Ken Paxton Reaches Settlement in First-of-its-Kind Healthcare Generative AI Investigation (Sept. 18, 2024), https://www.texasattorneygeneral.gov/news/releases/attorney-general-ken-paxton-reaches-settlement-first-its-kind-healthcare-generative-ai-investigation

Thadani T Lawsuits test Tesla claim that drivers are solely responsible for crashes. Wash. Post (Apr. 28, 2024). https://www.washingtonpost.com/technology/2024/04/28/tesla-trial-autopilot-lawsuit/

U.S. Code of Federal Regulations, 12 C.F.R. § 202.4

U.S. Code of Federal Regulations, 24 C.F.R. § 100.500

U.S. Code of Federal Regulations, 42 C.F.R. 431.210(b)

U.S. Code of Federal Regulations, 7 C.F.R. 273.13(a)(2)

U.S. Consumer Financial Protection Bureau (2022) Circular 2022-03, Adverse action notification requirements in connection with credit decisions based on complex algorithms https://www.

consumerfinance.gov/compliance/circulars/circular-2022-03-adverse-action-notification-requirements-in-connection-with-credit-decisions-based-on-complex-algorithms/
U.S. Court of Appeals for the District of Columbia Circuit (2011) *Elec. Privacy Info. Ctr. v. Dep't of Homeland Sec.,* 653 F.3d 1
U.S. Court of Appeals for the Ninth Circuit (2015) *K. W. v. Armstrong*, 789 F.3d 962
U.S. Court of Appeals for the Sixth Circuit (2016) *Barry v. Lyon,* 834 F.3d 706
U.S. Department of Housing and Urban Development, Guidance on Application of the Fair Housing Act to the Screening of Applicants for Rental Housing (Apr. 2024). https://www.hud.gov/sites/dfiles/FHEO/documents/FHEO_Guidance_on_Screening_of_Applicants_for_Rental_Housing.pdf
U.S. Department of Housing and Urban Development, Guidance on Application of the Fair Housing Act to the Advertising of Housing, Credit, and Other Real Estate-Related Transactions through Digital Platforms https://www.hud.gov/sites/dfiles/FHEO/documents/FHEO_Guidance_on_Advertising_through_Digital_Platforms.pdf
U.S. Department of Justice (2022) Algorithms, Artificial Intelligence, and Disability Discrimination in Hiring https://beta.ada.gov/ai-guidance/
U.S. Department of Justice, Press Release, Justice Department Secures Groundbreaking Settlement Agreement with Meta Platforms, Formerly Known as Facebook, to Resolve Allegations of Discriminatory Advertising (June 21, 2022). https://www.justice.gov/opa/pr/justice-department-secures-groundbreaking-settlement-agreement-meta-platforms-formerly-known
U.S. Department of Labor, Office of Federal Contract Compliance Programs, Artificial Intelligence and Equal Employment Opportunity for Federal Contractors (Apr. 29, 2024). https://www.dol.gov/agencies/ofccp/ai/ai-eeo-guide
U.S. Department of Labor, Field Assistance Bulletin No. 2024-1, Artificial Intelligence and Automated Systems in the Workplace under the Fair Labor Standards Act and Other Federal Labor Standards (Apr. 29, 2024). https://www.dol.gov/sites/dolgov/files/WHD/fab/fab2024_1.pdf
U.S. District Court of the District of Idaho (2014) *K.W. ex rel. D.W. v. Armstrong*, 298 F.R.D. 479
U.S. Office of Management and Budget, Memorandum M-24-10, Advancing Governance, Innovation, and Risk Management for Agency Use of Artificial Intelligence (March 28, 2024)
U.S. Supreme Court (1950) Mullane v. Central Hanover Bank & Trust Co., 339 U.S. 306
U.S. Supreme Court (1970) *Goldberg v. Kelly*, 397 U.S. 254
U.S. Supreme Court (1972a) *Fuentes v. Shevin*, 407 U.S. 67
U.S. Supreme Court *(1972b) Morrissey v. Brewer,* 408 U. S. 471
U.S. Supreme Court (1976) *Mathews v. Eldridge*, 424 U.S. 319
U.S. Supreme Court (2015) *Texas Dep't of Hous. & Cmty. Affairs v. Inclusive Communities Project, Inc.*, 576 U.S. 519
United States Code, 38 U.S.C. § 5104B
United States Code, 38 U.S.C. § 5104C
United States Code, 38 U.S.C. Chapter 71
United States Code, 42 U.S.C. § 405
United States Code, 42 U.S.C. §§ 3601-19
United States Code, 5 U.S.C. §§ 701-706
Utah S.B. 149 (2024). https://le.utah.gov/~2024/bills/static/SB0149.html
Virgina Code § 59.1-575
Virgina SB 741 Facial recognition technology; authorised uses, https://lis.virginia.gov/cgi-bin/legp604.exe?221+sum+SB741
Washington State SB 6280, adding a new chapter to Title 43 RCW, lawfilesext.leg.wa.gov/biennium/2019-20/Pdf/Bills/Session%20Laws/Senate/6280-S.SL.pdf
White House, Executive Order 13960, Promoting the Use of Trustworthy Artificial Intelligence in the Federal Government (Dec. 3, 2020). https://www.federalregister.gov/documents/2020/12/08/2020-27065/promoting-the-use-of-trustworthy-artificial-intelligence-in-the-federal-government

White House, Executive Order 14110, Safe, Secure, and Trustworthy Development and Use of Artificial Intelligence (Oct. 30, 2023). https://www.federalregister.gov/documents/2023/11/01/2023-24283/safe-secure-and-trustworthy-development-and-use-of-artificial-intelligence
White House, Executive Order 14148, Initial Recissions of Harmful Executive Orders and Actions (Jan. 20, 2025a). https://www.federalregister.gov/documents/2025/01/28/2025-01901/initial-rescissions-of-harmful-executive-orders-and-actions
White House, Executive Order 14179, Removing Barriers to American Leadership in Artificial Intelligence (Jan. 23, 2025b). https://www.federalregister.gov/documents/2025/01/31/2025-02172/removing-barriers-to-american-leadership-in-artificial-intelligence
Wisconsin Supreme Court (2016) *State v. Loomis*, 881 N.W.2d 749, 371 Wis. 2d 235

Conclusive Notes

Reflections on the AI Act: Brussels, Do We Have a Problem?

Vera Lúcia Raposo

Contents

Abstract As artificial intelligence (AI) rapidly evolves, establishing clear regulatory frameworks is essential to ensuring its responsible development and deployment. The European Union's AI Act represents a pioneering effort to regulate AI

V. L. Raposo (✉)
NOVA School of Law, NOVA University, Lisbon, Portugal

CEDIS (Research & Development Centre on Law and Society), NOVA School of Law, NOVA University, Lisbon, Portugal
e-mail: vera.lucia.raposo@novalaw.unl.pt

V. L. Raposo (ed.), *The European Artificial Intelligence Act*, Law, Governance and Technology Series 78, https://doi.org/10.1007/978-3-031-98406-8_20

while upholding fundamental rights, ethical principles, and the Rule of Law. However, the regulation is met with both praise and criticism. On the one hand, it introduces a much-needed structure; on the other, it risks being either too vague in some areas or excessively detailed in others. A key concern is its complexity and potential redundancy, as existing legal frameworks might already offer sufficient regulatory tools without necessitating a separate regime. Additionally, uncertainty surrounding AI's future trajectory raises questions about the regulation's adaptability. This concluding chapter critically examines these issues, reflecting on the broader implications of AI governance and the ongoing need for regulatory flexibility to balance innovation with legal and ethical safeguards, based on the very insightful considerations shared by the authors participating in this book.

1 Introduction

As we approach a transformative age in technology, setting strong guidelines for developing and deploying artificial intelligence (AI) is more crucial than ever. The European Union (EU) AI Regulation (AI Act)[1] marks a groundbreaking move[2] towards establishing a regulatory structure that comprehensively regulates AI[3] in a way that promotes responsible AI use, respecting core values, rights, and principles.[4] Still, it has its flaws. In some aspects, it lacks comprehensiveness, while in others, it is overly detailed.[5] While the AI Act is a vital achievement, it may fall short of fully addressing the intricate challenges presented by fast-evolving AI technologies.[6] A common critique is that the regulation lacks clarity about its target: how can we regulate AI when its current form and future trajectory remain

[1] Regulation (EU) 2024/1689 of the European Parliament and of the Council of 13 June 2024 laying down harmonised rules on artificial intelligence and amending Regulations (EC) No 300/2008, (EU) No 167/2013, (EU) No 168/2013, (EU) 2018/858, (EU) 2018/1139 and (EU) 2019/2144 and Directives 2014/90/EU, (EU) 2016/797 and (EU) 2020/1828 (Artificial Intelligence Act - AI Act).

The AI Act comes in clear contrast with more 'flexible approaches', such as the British one (Charlesworth 2025), the Singaporean (Loo and Findlay 2025) and the Taiwanese (Chen 2025), based on self-regulation and sector specific guidelines; the Chinese one (Wang and Du 2025), more focused on principle than in norms; and the US one, that relies on traditional doctrines and existing norms to address AI issues (Dempsey 2025).

[2] For an overview of the developments that preceded the AI Act see the chapter of Vedder et al. (2025).

[3] Although it is regarded as a highly comprehensive regulation, it defines significant exceptions to its material scope. For a detailed analysis of such exceptions, see the chapter of Constantino and Van der Linden (2025).

[4] Frischhut (2025)

[5] The debate on the appropriate scope of AI legislation is ongoing in multiple jurisdictions, including China (Wang and Du 2025).

[6] On the definition of AI systems under the AI Act, see European Commission (2025a).

uncertain?[7] Other criticism revolves around the fact that the regulation is too complex[8] and potentially unnecessary,[9] as existing norms could be used to regulate AI without the need to create an entirely new framework from scratch.[10]

This is the final chapter of a book enriched by an impressive collection of contributions from experts across distinct fields, each sharing a deep expertise in the AI Act and a common passion for emerging technologies. As a concluding chapter, it does not follow a single, clearly defined focus. Rather, it seeks to bring together and reflect on the diverse issues explored in the preceding chapters, serving—at least in spirit—as a closing piece.

In this concluding chapter, I will provide an overarching analysis of the AI Act, building on the rich discussions from previous chapters, to examine the broader implications and the pressing need for continual adaptation. The aim is that, through this commitment to progress, we can unlock AI's potential while preserving fundamental rights[11] and shared EU values[12]—including ethical considerations[13]—while upholding the Rule of Law.[14]

That said, this is not a mere summary, nor does it aim to provide a comprehensive overview of the AI Act. My intention was, above all, to offer some personal reflections on what I consider to be some of the most pressing and problematic aspects of the Regulation. Many other issues could have been discussed, but the ones the chapter highlights are those that raise the most concern for me, an inevitably subjective selection, guided by what I believe deserves particular attention at this stage of the debate.

2 A Product Safety Regulation or a Fundamental Rights Framework?

While the AI Act is primarily structured as a product safety regulation, its underlying rationale and scope reflect key elements characteristic of a fundamental rights instrument.[15] The explicit and recurrent references to fundamental rights throughout

---

[7] Some insights in what AI is in Steckelmacher and Bogaerts (2025).

Relevant clarifications in this regard have arrived with European Commission's guidelines on the definition of AI systems (European Commission 2025b).

[8] Philippe (2024), pp. 685–700.

[9] Glauner (2022).

[10] The use of the existing legal frameworks was the UK approach, as noted in Charlesworth (2025).

[11] On the relation between the AI Act and fundamental rights, see Palmieri and Goffin (2025).

[12] Laux et al. (2024).

[13] On the importance of the ethical approach to AI see the chapter of Vedder et al. (2025).

[14] Frischhut (2025).

[15] Almada and Petit (2023); Palmieri and Goffin (2025).

the regulation illustrate this dual nature. Notably, the notion of risk under the AI Act extends the orthodox understanding of product risks to encompass risks to fundamental rights, reinforcing the idea that AI systems, beyond their technical and safety implications, pose significant societal and ethical concerns.[16] By imposing specific obligations and compliance requirements on entities across the AI value chain, the regulation aspires to reinforce the protection of fundamental rights, embedding a human-centric approach to AI governance.[17]

The substantial weight afforded to fundamental rights within the AI Act is not anomalous when examined in the broader context of EU product safety regulations.[18] Consumer protection, to which product safety laws are closely linked, is in itself deeply embedded in the EU's broader fundamental rights framework.[19] However, what distinguishes the AI Act from conventional product safety legislation is the degree to which fundamental rights considerations are interwoven into its structure and objectives.[20] This heightened commitment to fundamental rights, evident in both the text and the intent of the AI Act, reflects the unique challenges posed by AI technologies. Unlike traditional products, AI systems operate in ways that can shape, influence, and even determine human experiences, decision-making, and opportunities.[21] Their capacity to process and analyse vast amounts of data, generate predictions, and act autonomously in various contexts imposes strict vigilance regarding potential infringements on fundamental rights.[22] Consequently, the AI Act does not merely establish baseline safety requirements; it aims to ensure that AI systems are aligned with ethical and legal principles that uphold the dignity and autonomy of individuals.[23]

However, this hybrid character of the AI Act—part safety regulation, part fundamental rights safeguard[24]—raises pertinent questions about its effectiveness in achieving its stated goals. The risk-based approach, while pragmatic in regulatory terms, may not fully capture the depth and complexity of fundamental rights considerations.

[16] Palmieri and Goffin (2025).

[17] Palmieri and Goffin (2025).

[18] Palmieri and Goffin (2025).

[19] Almada and Petit (2023).

[20] Palmieri and Goffin (2025).

[21] Ahmad et al. (2023); Neuwirth (2025).

[22] In this regard, it gains momentum the need to create AI systems that are privacy complainant (Solove 2024) and that present as few biases as possible (Vasha 2023).

[23] Palmieri and Goffin (2025).

[24] Almada and Petit (2023).

3 Risk Assessment and Categorisation

3.1 The Risk-Based Approach

The AI Act is grounded in the idea that while AI offers substantial benefits, it also brings significant risks. To address these concerns, the AI Act introduces a structured framework for AI governance that aims to reduce risks, ensuring AI systems are built and used in ways that respect human rights and uphold core EU values, while also supporting societal well-being.[25]

At its heart, the AI Act employs a risk-based approach,[26] classifying AI systems by risk level and assigning specific obligations to developers and deployers accordingly. This framework evaluates AI's potential effects on health, safety, and fundamental rights (Article 1(1) AI Act).[27] The focus on the societal and individual impact of AI systems represents a departure from existing AI risk management standards established by the International Organisation for Standardisation (ISO) and the International Electrotechnical Commission (IEC),[28] which typically adopt a more value-neutral perspective.[29]

However, this categorisation reveals certain limitations.

For a start, the distinction between different levels of risk is often ambiguous, leaving significant room for interpretation.[30] Determining the appropriate risk category for an AI system is far from straightforward, especially when dealing with complex systems that may serve multiple purposes or evolve through continuous learning. This creates uncertainty for developers and businesses,[31] as many AI applications fall into grey areas where their classification is not unequivocal. For instance, consider an AI system designed to assist judges in drafting judicial decisions. Given its application within the judicial field, it could potentially be classified as a high-risk AI system, as the 'administration of justice' is explicitly listed under point 8 of Annex III of the AI Act. In conjunction with Article 6(2), this would lead to a high-risk classification, triggering a demanding set of legal and technical obligations. However, Recital 61 of the AI Act introduces an important nuance. It clarifies that AI systems should not be classified as high-risk when limited to ancillary administrative tasks with no impact on the administration of justice in individual cases, which might be the case of AI systems used by judges as editing tools. In practice, this distinction is far from clear-cut. The line between supporting a decision and effectively shaping it can be blurry, especially in complex systems that

---

[25] Stahl et al. (2022).

[26] Ebers (2024), pp. 1–20.

[27] Ebers (2024), pp. 6–7; Kusche (2024), pp. 3–11.

[28] Palmieri (2025).

[29] Bygrave and Schmidt (2025).

[30] The challenges of risk assessment in the AIA in Fraser and Bello y Villarino (2024), pp. 431–446; Liebl and Klein (2023); Novelli et al. (2024), pp. 2493–2497.

[31] Palmieri (2025).

provide structured legal reasoning, recommend legal outcomes, or pre-fill draft judgments. Yet, this ambiguity in classification has significant consequences Whether a system is considered high-risk determines the entire regulatory framework applicable to both providers and deployers of the AI.[32]

Moreover, the subjective nature of risk assessment can lead to inconsistent classifications across the industry, undermining the overall reliability and integrity of the regulatory framework. What one regulator or organisation considers high-risk, another may classify as limited-risk due to differences in risk perception, contextual factors, or regulatory priorities.[33] If regulatory bodies apply different standards, organisations may struggle to predict how their AI systems will be classified in different regions and/or areas of activity.[34] This legal uncertainty discourages innovation, as companies may be reluctant to invest in AI technologies that face unpredictable regulatory scrutiny.[35] What is more, inconsistent enforcement could allow regulatory arbitrage, where companies exploit differences in risk classifications to bypass stricter oversight by operating in jurisdictions with more lenient interpretations.[36] This inconsistency undermines the overall reliability and integrity of the regulatory framework, making it difficult to ensure uniform compliance and enforcement.

Additionally, the dynamic nature of some AI systems means their risk levels can evolve over time, further complicating their categorisation and compliance.[37] Some AI models continuously learn, adapt, and refine their outputs based on new data, user interactions, and environmental changes. This iterative process can lead to shifts in their behaviour, making it difficult to maintain a fixed risk classification.[38] Suppose, for instance, that a public education authority deploys an AI system in schools to support teachers in identifying students at risk of academic underperformance. Initially authorised under the AI Act as a high-risk system in the education domain (Annex III, point 3), it uses anonymised academic records, attendance, and participation data to generate non-binding alerts. Over time, however, the system is enhanced with additional data sources—such as behavioural logs,

---

[32] Especially considering that a study uncovered that 18% of the AI systems were classified as high-risk, while 42% fell into the low-risk category. However, a concerning 40% remained ambiguous in terms of their risk classification, particularly within critical infrastructure, employment, law enforcement, and product safety domains. This lack of clarity surrounding risk classifications poses a significant challenge, as it hampers investment and slows down innovation in the field (appliedAI 2023, p. 4)

[33] If an AI system is not explicitly listed in Annex III, national authorities may interpret whether it falls under the definition of a high-risk system in uneven ways, at least until the European Commission issues guidelines or common specifications. For example, AI for internal HR analytics might be considered part of 'employment-related AI' in one Member State but not in another, depending on whether it is thought to influence hiring or promotion decisions.

[34] White and Case LLP (2025).

[35] Ebers et al. (2021), pp. 590–592.

[36] Veale and Zuiderveen Borgesius (2021), p. 111.

[37] Yampolskiy (2025).

[38] Daníelsson et al. (2022).

socio-economic indicators, and location data—intended to improve predictive accuracy. As a result, it begins making more predictions, including students' likelihood of dropping out or achieving long-term success. At some point, it starts clustering students based on inferred sensitive attributes, such as socio-economic background or ethnic origin, deduced from proxies like postcode or language spoken at home. Eventually, these predictions begin to inform automated decisions—such as academic tracking or access to programmes—without meaningful human oversight or the possibility of contestation. Through this evolution, the system crosses into a prohibited use under Article 5(1)(c) of the AI Act, effectively engaging in social scoring. Regulators, providers, and deployers must therefore adopt dynamic monitoring and reassessment mechanisms to ensure that an AI system remains compliant throughout its lifecycle. Periodic audits, real-time risk assessment models, and adaptive regulatory approaches are essential to address these evolving risks and maintain accountability in AI governance. Without such adaptive oversight, there is a risk of regulatory gaps where AI systems gradually shift into higher-risk territories without undergoing the necessary compliance checks.

Likewise, the distinction between an AI system's 'intended purpose' (Article 3(12) AIA) and its 'foreseeable purpose' is often ambiguous.[39] An AI system designed with harmless intentions could be repurposed in ways that introduce serious risks. For instance, if a government or private entity develop a facial recognition AI system to be used for public safety purposes, such as identifying missing persons or detecting individuals on a criminal watchlist in crowded areas (intended purpose), it could be repurposed or misused for mass surveillance without consent (foreseeable purpose), such as to monitor and suppress political protests. The AI Act could have better anticipated these scenarios, addressing them more comprehensively to close potential loopholes.[40]

Moreover, the current framework introduces significant vulnerabilities, driven by the inherent imprecision in the definition of risk levels and the reliance on developers to self-classify their AI systems. The self-classification mechanism not only opens the door to under-regulation but also creates an uneven playing field, as less scrupulous actors may exploit these loopholes to gain a competitive edge. Companies, motivated by the desire to avoid the stringent requirements associated with high-risk classification, might intentionally downplay or misrepresent the potential risks posed by their AI systems.[41]

[39] Ada Lovelace (2022), p. 8.

[40] The study of Novelli et al. critiques the static risk categories defined in the AI Act. It argues that these categories may not effectively account for the dynamic nature of AI systems, especially general-purpose AI, which can evolve and interact in unforeseen ways, leading to an accumulation of risks over time (Novelli et al. 2024, p. 2495).

[41] Chow (2024).

3.2 Unauthorised AI Systems

Under Article 5 of the AI Act, AI systems deemed to pose unauthorised risks are generally prohibited (though exceptions exist, which Rostam Neuwirth explores in his chapter).[42] Enforcing this ban, however, presents various challenges.

For instance, identifying manipulative AI systems (banned in Articles 5/1/a/b AIA) demands a sophisticated grasp of human psychology and behavioural science.[43] Overall, concepts that are inherently contested—such as 'subliminal', 'exploitation', 'vulnerability' and 'harm'—ought to have been more thoroughly defined.

Similarly, interpreting the exception within the ban on predictive policing, outlined in Article 5/1/d AIA,[44] poses questions. The phrase 'objective and verifiable facts' is open to interpretation, potentially leading to inconsistent applications across jurisdictions. What qualifies as 'verifiable' may vary depending on the standards of evidence or legal traditions in different regions.[45]

Additionally, the norm on biometric identification systems employed by law enforcement (Article 5/1/h AIA) remains controversial, starting with the need of prior approval. The AI Act restricts real-time biometric identification in public spaces, with narrow exceptions requiring prior court or independent administrative authority approval, except in urgent situations, where authorisation can be obtained retroactively, which creates potential for misuse in certain scenarios.[46] Another pressing issue is the balance between (apparently) competing purposes. This legal framework aims to protect against mass surveillance and safeguard fundamental rights. However, striking a balance between security and privacy remains challenging, and as such precise guidelines and strong oversight is required. Although the European Commission's guidelines on forbidden AI systems brought some clarification, it is still insufficient.[47] Time will tell whether these restrictions and exceptions strike the right balance or fall short on this goal.[48]

Additional clarification will ensure a more precise and interdisciplinary understanding of Article 5 of the AI Act.[49] The European Commission's guidelines on forbidden AI systems have provided some clarity on the matter, but significant

---

[42] Neuwirth (2025).

[43] Zhong et al. (2024), pp. 20,001–20,009.

[44] 'This prohibition shall not apply to AI systems used to support human assessment of an individual's involvement in criminal activity, provided that such assessment is based on objective and verifiable facts directly linked to a criminal offence'.

[45] Levano (2024).

[46] On this issue see Raposo (2023b), pp. 515–533; Raposo (2023a).

[47] European Commission (2025c).

[48] The bans imposed on several law enforcement scenarios, and the fact that AI systems to be used in law enforcement and generally considered high risk, poses huge difficulties to the deployment of AI in this area (Vedder et al. 2025), a policy choice that the EU might regret eventually.

[49] Neuwirth (2025).

issues persist.[50] Without further guidance or jurisprudence, national authorities may adopt diverging interpretations, undermining the harmonisation objective of the Regulation.

3.3 High-Risk AI Systems

3.3.1 The Classification as High-Risk

High-risk systems, outlined in Article 6, are allowed but must meet rigorous standards to ensure safety and dependability.[51] AI systems can qualify as high-risk in two ways.[52] One is related with the scope of the harmonised legislation (Article 6/1 AI Act), leading to classify as high-risk the AI systems that—standalone or integrated into other products—fall under EU harmonised legislation (listed in Annex I) and, moreover, subject to third-party conformity assessments. The other is based on a sector-specific use categorisation (Article 6/2 AI Act), that leads to the label as a high-risk those AI systems that operate within strategic fields listed in Annex III, such as law enforcement or employment (Article 6(2) and Annex III AI Ac), unless they are deemed not to significantly threaten health, safety, or fundamental rights. Indeed, the Act allows for certain exceptions, such as AI systems that perform narrow procedural tasks or improve the results of previously completed human activities, which may not be classified as high-risk, as described in Article 6(3) of the AI Act. The latter presents four scenarios suggesting when an AI system might not pose a high risk ('not pose a significant risk of harm to the health, safety or fundamental rights'),[53] using the phrase 'The first subparagraph shall apply where any of the following conditions is fulfilled', followed by the description of four different scenarios. This wording leaves it uncertain if this is an exhaustive list or just examples. If these scenarios are exhaustive, only AI systems meeting one of them will potentially avoid the high-risk classification. However, if these are merely examples, each AI system will be evaluated individually, potentially allowing more AI systems to escape the strict requirements of the high-risk designation. This latter interpretation would support innovation, as fewer systems would face heavy regulations. Nonetheless, given the structure of the AI Act[54] and the usual legislative

---

[50] European Commission (2025c).

[51] Some authors go as far as to say that AI system not considered high-risk (thus, the ones labelled as low-risk) lack a proper fundamental rights protection (Palmieri and Goffin 2025).

[52] In detail about Article 6 of the AI Act and the legal framework applicable to hight-risk AI, see the chapter of Szostek and Prabucki (2025).

[53] See Bygrave and Schmidt (2025).

[54] Mostly based on a precautionary approach and with a stronger prevalence on product safety and the protection of fundamental rights that on innovation.

phrasing in EU law,[55] there are compelling reasons to see this as a closed list. This latter interpretation is reinforced, in turn, by Article 6(6) of the AI Act.[56] This provision allows the Commission to adjust the list of Article 6(3) ,[57] a possibility that would be illogical if the referred list was merely exemplative. Still, the question is far from clear. Given the high standards imposed on high-risk AI, it is likely that Article 6(3) of the AI Act will become a major focus for legal interpretation and debate.[58]

3.3.2 The Conformity Assessment

The AI Act requires a strict conformity assessment for AI systems to achieve the CE Marking of Conformity, a requirement without which the AI system will not be allowed to get into the market.[59] The granting of the CE Marking depends on meeting several criteria:[60] data governance, transparency, human oversight (like an emergency shutdown), accuracy, robustness, cybersecurity, traceability, and record-keeping (Articles 8–15 AI Act).[61]

Data governance has been a focal point of concern. The initial draft of Article 10(3) of the AI Act (in the European Commission's proposal)[62] required training, validation, and testing datasets to be 'relevant, representative, free of errors, and complete', an unrealistic expectation since no dataset is entirely error-free or complete.[63] The revised version takes a more practical approach, requiring datasets to be 'relevant, sufficiently representative, and, as far as possible, free of errors and complete' for the intended purpose. Still, the requirement on data remains challenging. The norm continues to impose datasets to be free of errors (as much as possible), but

---

[55] When there is no express textual indication that this is a mere explicative list, it means it is a numerus clausus list. See, for instance, articles 6/1 and 9/2 of the GDPR.

[56] 'The Commission is empowered to adopt delegated acts in accordance with Article 97 in order to amend paragraph 3, second subparagraph, of this Article by adding new conditions to those laid down therein, or by modifying them, where there is concrete and reliable evidence of the existence of AI systems that fall under the scope of Annex III, but do not pose a significant risk of harm to the health, safety or fundamental rights of natural persons'.

[57] The frequency of such interventions by the European Commission remains an incognita.

[58] Interestingly, Chassang (2025) suggest that the participation in the regulatory sandbox might be used for the AI developer to sustain the thesis that the AI system at stake 'does not pose a significant risk of harm to the health, safety or fundamental rights of natural persons, including by not materially influencing the outcome of decision making' (Article 6(3) AIA).

[59] Gornet and Maxwell (2024).

[60] See Szostek and Prabucki (2025). See also Thelisson and Verma (2024), pp. 113–121.

[61] Some of these requirements also influence compliance with non AI regulations, as for instance, with the GDPR (Lau 2025).

[62] European Commission, Proposal for a Regulation of the European Parliament and of the Council Laying Down Harmonised Rules on Artificial Intelligence (Artificial Intelligence Act) and Amending Certain Union Legislative Acts, COM(2021) 206 final, 21 April 2021.

[63] A comment to the original and the revised versions of this norm in Hacker (2021), pp. 296–297.

it does not clarify if the error in question refer to the set of data, to the data classification, to the way the intended purpose is represented, to all these aspects, or still others.[64]

On the other hand, who will assess data quality: the national Data Protection Authorities (DPAs) or the (to be created) National Competent Authorities, in particular, the market surveillance authorities? The European Data Protection Board (EDPB) has emphasised that DPAs possess the necessary experience and expertise to oversee AI systems, particularly concerning their impact on fundamental rights and data protection.[65] In a statement, the EDPB recommended that DPAs be designated as 'market surveillance authorities' for high-risk AI systems used in areas such as law enforcement and border management.[66] However, some member States have already designated other bodies or authorities (that not the national DPA) to supervise the application and implementation of the AI Act (Article 70 AI Act).[67] When this is the case, in theory these authorities will work alongside DPAs to ensure compliance with the AI Act's provisions, including those related to data quality. How, in practical terms, the boundaries between competences remain an interrogation.

Explainability, under the broader concept of transparency (Article 13 AI Act),[68] also presents challenges. The regulation stresses the importance of explainable AI 'to enable deployers to interpret a system's output and use it appropriately' (Article 13(1) AIA), a claim also supported by the 'right to an explanation', as established in Article 86 of the AI Act.[69] However, today's most powerful AI models often function as black boxes,[70] and those are precisely the ones that can bring more added benefit to society as a hole, namely due to their accuracy.[71] Are we ready to exclude such systems from the EU market?[72]

Controlling compliance with these standards raises further questions. According to Article 43 of the AI Act, compliance is checked by means of a conformity assessment (Article 3(20) AI Act).[73] In the EU, conformity assessments can be conducted by the manufacturer or by a third party, and the AI Act follows this same approach. Yet, when an AI system requires third-party assessments under multiple EU

[64] Hacker (2021), p. 296.

[65] European Data Protection Board (2024a).
See also Spiecker and Genannt Döhmann (2022), pp. 132–145.

[66] European Data Protection Board (2024c).

[67] Palmieri (2025); Slokenberga (2025).

[68] On the requirement of transparency under the AI Act see Raposo (2024b), pp. 2–6; Raposo (2025b).

[69] About the conditions for the exercise of this right, Slokenberga (2025).

[70] On the distinction between black and white boxes see Steckelmacher and Bogaerts (2025).

[71] Setzu et al. (2021).

[72] This same question regarding the particular field of healthcare in Raposo (2025b).

[73] Szostek and Prabucki (2025).

regulations (e.g., the Medical Devices Regulation[74] or the Machinery Regulation[75]), it is unclear how these processes will be streamlined. Ideally, the AI Act aims to consolidate third-party assessments into a single process by one entity, that is, a single notified body.[76] However, this may not always be feasible, as some notified bodies lack the proper designation for both assessments.[77] This could lead to prolonged, resource-intensive assessments, with potentially conflicting outcomes, undermining the clarity and efficiency of conformity evaluations.[78]

Another issue raised by the conformity assessment relates to the reliance on providers for self-assessment- in particular, in light of Article 6(3) of the AI Act—and the consequent potential delays in external oversightlack of procedural transparency. Providers must document their reasoning for determining that their systems do not qualify as high-risk, as required under Article 49(2) of the AI Act, and register these systems in a public database, as imposed by Article 6(4) and 49(2) of the AI Act. However, this process does not require external approval before the systems are placed on the market or put into service. Additionally, while providers must maintain thorough documentation of their assessments, this information is not subject to public disclosure. Instead, it must be made available to the relevant market surveillance authority upon request (Article 6(4) AI Act).[79] This approach places significant initial trust in providers to conduct honest and accurate assessments. That said, market surveillance authorities retain the authority to later evaluate these assessments and, if necessary, overturn them. In such cases, providers will be obligated to comply with the Act's stringent requirements for high-risk systems (Article 80(2) AI Act). Non-compliance can result in fines under Article 99 of the AI Act (Article 80(7) AI Act).[80] While this compliance framework introduces a very welcome measure of flexibility, its effectiveness remains uncertain,[81] and some AI providers will certainly feel tempted to minimise the risks of their AI systems, aiming to frame them under lower risks levels.[82]

Challenges in ensuring compliance are further exacerbated by the risk of inconsistent enforcement across Member States. First, because several concepts in the AI

[74] Regulation (EU) 2017/745 of the European Parliament and of the Council of 5 April 2017 on medical devices, amending Directive 2001/83/EC, Regulation (EC) No 178/2002 and Regulation (EC) No 1223/2009 and repealing Council Directives 90/385/EEC and 93/42/EEC.

[75] Regulation (EU) 2023/1230 of the European Parliament and of the Council of 14 June 2023 on machinery and repealing Directive 2006/42/EC of the European Parliament and of the Council and Council Directive 73/361/EEC.

[76] A critique to notified bodies in Cohen (2012). About the third party conformity assessment by notified bodies, see Palmieri (2025).

[77] A notified body must apply for notification to the notifying authority, a requirement established in Article 29 of the AI Act.

[78] Raposo (2022).

[79] Slokenberga (2025).

[80] On the issue of non-compliance see Slokenberga (2025).

[81] Bygrave and Schmidt (2025).

[82] Palmieri (2025).

Act still lack clarification and are prone to different interpretations, not only in different domains of AI intervention, but also in different jurisdictions.[83] Secondly, because national AI authorities will likely face disparities in resources, an issue already evident among national DPAs in light of data protection regulations. In some Member States, limited resources could hinder the efficiency with which these authorities fulfil their responsibilities, potentially undermining the cohesion of the single market.

3.3.3 Harmonised Standards

Navigating compliance with the intricate web of standards for high-risk AI systems can be daunting. Larger companies with better resources are more likely to comply, while smaller entities may face disproportionate challenges.[84]

Recognising this, EU lawmakers introduced an alternative: developers can adhere to what are known as harmonised standards (Article 40 AI Act) instead of meeting every individual requirement for high-risk AI systems.[85] These standards will be crafted collaboratively by the European Standardisation Organisations (ESOs)—comprising the European Committee for Standardisation (CEN) and the European Committee for Electrotechnical Standardisation (CENELEC)—and the European Commission, focusing on obligations like risk management, data quality, transparency, human oversight, and robustness.[86] While compliance remains voluntary, organisations that adopt it may benefit from a presumption of conformity under Article 40(1) of the AI Act. This provision allows high-risk systems following harmonised standards to be presumed compliant with the Act's requirements. However, this seemingly flexible, developer-friendly approach may fall short, as these standards are intended to be horizontal, that is, universally applicable across diverse sectors.[87] Obviously, that is unfeasible. The assumption that what works for healthcare can also work for law enforcement or education, may limit the standards' practical effectiveness.[88] Only time will reveal the true value of such broad standards.

[83] Palmieri (2025).

[84] A report by T3 Consultants (2025) highlights that small and medium-sized enterprises (SMEs) and startups may struggle with the financial and administrative burdens of compliance, often needing to hire AI compliance officers or seek legal counsel to understand the new regulations.

[85] A detailed analysis of harmonised standards in Bygrave and Schmidt (2025).

[86] Malik and Solaiman (2025).

[87] Gornet and Maxwell (2024).

[88] We can envisage a harmonised standard establishing general requirements for transparency and human oversight in high-risk AI systems, as envisaged in Article 13(3)(d) of the AI Act, which states that such systems must be designed 'to facilitate the interpretation of the outputs of the high-risk AI systems by the deployers'. A medical AI application for cancer diagnosis adopts this standard by providing clinicians with a visual explanation of how the system weighs diagnostic features—such as lesion size or shape—when recommending a diagnosis. This level of interpretability is well-suited to the clinical context, where such insights can be meaningfully assessed by trained professionals. However, when a law enforcement agency applies the same standard to a

Another issue concerns the 'source' of the harmonised standards. Some worry that CEN and CENELEC's involvement, as private entities, could diminish democratic accountability in the standardisation process.[89] CEN and CENELEC operate outside the direct control of elected bodies, which raises questions about the transparency of their decision-making processes. Unlike processes led by EU institutions or national governments, which are subject to public scrutiny and political accountability, the standardisation activities of CEN and CENELEC are less directly answerable to democratic mechanisms. This can lead to a perception that standards are being shaped by corporate interests rather than public interest, particularly when the outcomes have regulatory or societal implications.[90]

3.3.4 Obligations for Deployers of High-Risks AI Systems

A 'deployer', in the context of the AI Act, is defined as someone who operates an AI system within their professional capacity, not for personal use (Article 3(4) AI Act).[91] Even though the main regulatory target of the AI Act are the providers (as defined in Article 3(3) AI Act), deployers of hight-risk AI systems carry several key responsibilities.[92]

Deployers must guarantee that the AI system is used according to the manufacturer's instructions, ensuring that it functions within its intended parameters (Article 26(1) AI Act). They are also required to assign adequate human oversight over the functioning of high-risk AI systems to intervene where necessary and prevent harm (Articles 26(2) and 14(2) AI Act), ensuring that AI decisions can be monitored and overridden when necessary to safeguard human rights and safety. AI deployers must actively monitor the system's operation to detect potential risks, performance issues, or deviations from its intended purpose (Articles 26(5) and 14(4)(a) AI Act). If deployers provide input data for the AI system, they must ensure that the data is relevant, sufficiently representative, and suitable for the system's intended purpose (Articles 26(4) and 10(2)(3) AI Act). Deployers must keep automatically generated logs by the AI system to ensure traceability and facilitate compliance audits. Proper logging practices enhance transparency, accountability, and the ability to investigate incidents related to AI performance (Articles 26(6) and 12 AI Act). Lastly, when applicable, deployers of high-risk AI systems must carry out a

---

predictive policing system, the outcome is far less satisfactory. The explanation offered may be vague or overly generic, without revealing actionable or reviewable reasoning. Unlike in healthcare, decisions in law enforcement can directly affect individual rights or lead to discriminatory outcomes, particularly when the system relies on proxies for sensitive or socio-demographic data. In such contexts, a more demanding threshold for explainability is necessary to ensure transparency, accountability, and compliance with fundamental rights.

[89] This concern in Malik and Solaiman (2025).

[90] Gornet (2024); Gornet and Maxwell (2024).

[91] See Szostek and Prabucki (2025).

[92] DataGuard (2024); Herbosch (2025).

fundamental rights impact assessment to evaluate the system's potential implications for fundamental rights (Article 27 AI Act).

3.4 *Low-Risk AI Systems*

Low-risk AI systems—in itself, an unclear designation[93]—fall into one of two categories: limited risk and minimal risk.[94]

Limited-risk AI (Article 50 AI Act) includes systems designed to interact directly with humans.[95] These systems are subject to transparency requirements, ensuring that deployers know they are engaging with an AI rather than a human (such as in chatbots), that content like deepfakes is artificial and not reality-based, and that biometric data collected is being used for emotion detection[96] or categorisation. A common claim is that mere transparency is insufficient to deal with the many risks that potentially can arise from such AI systems,[97] as manipulative patterns might play with your emotions in several ways,[98] some of them potentially quite harming. Still, if the AI system in question does not fall within the high-risk category, transparency remains the only obligation in place.

Minimal-risk AI, on the other hand, is a catch-all category for all other low-risk systems.[99] For these, the AI Act only suggests the development of voluntary codes of conduct (Article 95 AI Act). However, there is no enforcement mechanism to ensure these codes are created or followed.[100] Given this 'hands loose rule', it is worth questioning what incentive AI providers have to develop such codes. When discoursing in the potential incentives to invest (which seems to be a huge investment in expertise, time and, therefore, money) to create these codes, Bygrave and Schmidt refer to moral incentives, which are obviously very weak.[101] I will add the

---

[93] As stated by Bygrave and Schmidt, referring to all systems in this category as 'low-risk' fails to accurately reflect the reality, as certain systems within this group present risk levels that surpass the conventional understanding of what 'low-risk' implies. This characterisation oversimplifies the nuanced differences in potential harm that may arise within the category. Thus, the authors prefer to label all systems that are neither prohibited nor high-risk as 'non-high-risk' or 'not high-risk', even recognising that this nomenclature introduces a degree of inconsistency with the terminology established in the AI Act (Bygrave and Schmidt 2025).

[94] I am using the designation adopted by the AI Act. Still, with a very accurate remark regarding this nomenclature, see Bygrave and Schmidt (2025).

[95] Dacoronias-Marina and Durovic (2025).

[96] In their chapter, Dacoronias-Marina and Durovic (2025) highlight the risks associated with emotion recognition technology in marketing, particularly its use in targeting consumers with highly personalised advertisement.

[97] Also underscored by Bygrave and Schmidt (2025).

[98] Dacoronias-Marina and Durovic (2025).

[99] Also in this sense, Bygrave and Schmidt (2025).

[100] Bygrave and Schmidt (2025).

[101] Bygrave and Schmidt (2025).

power of marketing and good reputation amongst consumers and society in general. If it comes to be the case that a general trend in requiring some kind of minimal ethical-legal compliance gains traction amongst the community in general, and the digital community in particular, such codes might become a reputational mark for AI developers.

Overall, low-risk systems might escape scrutiny, even though they can cause significant harm when used in unintended or evolving contexts. For example, AI systems designed to maximise user engagement—such as social media recommendation algorithms—often prioritise content that elicits strong emotional reactions, as this tends to keep user on the platform longer. While this objective is well-defined, the unintended consequence can be the amplification of divisive or extreme viewpoints, reinforcing ideological echo chambers and contributing to societal polarisation.[102] Moreover, AI applications initially deemed low-risk could accumulate risks over time, particularly as they interact with other systems.[103] Therefore, although one of the primary weaknesses of the AI Act lies in its tendency towards overregulation, in this specific domain the issue shifts to underregulating.

4 General-Purpose AI

4.1 Systemic and Non-Systemic Risk

Originally, the concept of General-Purpose AI (GPAI) was absent from the AI Act, even though such models already existed. They largely escaped legal and ethical scrutiny until the rise of models like ChatGPT and later GPT-4, whose adaptability and societal implications became impossible to ignore. This prompted the EU to incorporate GPAI-specific provisions in the updated AI Act released by the European Parliament. In its current version, the AI Act identifies GPAI models as a significant regulatory challenge due to their versatile capabilities and potential integration across numerous applications, expanding their societal impact (Article 3(63) AI Act).[104]

GPAI provisions follow a distinct approach, diverging from the traditional risk-based pyramid model of regulation. Perhaps due to GPAI's late inclusion or the unique characteristics of these models,[105] Chapter 5 of the AIA reflects a new regulatory perspective.

[102] The National Artificial Intelligence Initiative Office discusses scenarios where AI systems, optimised for specific objectives, may lead to unintended harmful outcomes. Cf. National Artificial Intelligence Advisory Committee (2023), p. 1.

[103] Bygrave and Schmidt (2025).

[104] Datta (2025), pp. 119–137.

[105] Still, an effort to 'fit' GPAI into the risk based approached represented by a pyramid would place them somewhere in between the high-risk and the low-risk AI systems.

GPAI is split into two categories based on whether they present a 'systemic risk' or not.[106] Given the stricter obligations for GPAI classified as systemic risk models (Article 55 AI Act), defining this category is crucial. According to Article 51(1) of the AI Act, a GPAI may be deemed a systemic risk model either through a formal decision by the European Commission or if it possesses what the Act calls 'high impact capabilities'. Such a designation is presumed when 'the cumulative amount of computation used for its training, measured in FLOPs, exceeds 10^25' (Article 51(2) AI Act). This method of identifying systemic risk GPAI, based on technical specifications and extensive training data, represents a shift from technological neutrality to a more proactive risk management stance.[107] However, questions arise regarding the feasibility and fairness of these criteria. For example, how many models actually meet the immense training threshold set by the Act? While precise FLOP counts for training current GPAI models are unclear, it is likely that only models like ChatGPT-4 and subsequent ones have achieved this substantial benchmark.

4.2 Generative AI

GPAI encompasses AI models designed for broad applications across various sectors, including large language models (LLMs) and other foundation models that can be adapted for different tasks. Generative AI,[108] as a subset of GPAI, specifically refers to models that generate new content, such as text, images, audio, or video, by learning patterns from training data. While all generative AI systems fall within the category of GPAI, not all GPAI models are generative, as some focus on analytical or decision-making tasks rather than content creation.

The AI Act does not explicitly define generative AI as a separate category but it follows that these systems might fall within the broader framework of GPAI due to their wide-ranging applications.[109] Providers of GPAI models, including generative AI systems such as LLMs and image-generation tools, must comply with transparency and risk management obligations (Article 53 AI Act). These include requirements to document training data sources, disclose limitations, prevent biases, and ensure compliance with EU copyright laws.[110]

If a generative AI system is deployed in a high-risk context (e.g., in hiring decisions or as a medical device), stricter compliance rules apply. If, in contrast, generative AI is merely a chatbot designed for customer interaction—thus not falling under Article 5 (prohibited AI systems) or Article 6 (high-risk AI systems) of the AI

[106] For an analysis of this concept see Bygrave and Schmidt (2025).

[107] Bygrave and Schmidt (2025); Shehabi et al. (2023).

[108] Feuerriegel et al. (2024), pp.111–126.

[109] Hacker et al. (2025).

[110] On generative AI and copyrights see Wang and Du (2025).

Act—it will only be subject to the transparency obligations outlined in Article 50 of the AI Act. The requirements are cumulative with those imposed on GPAI.

The AI Act does not explicitly regulate the accuracy of generative AI models. This omission is particularly significant, as the performance of generative LLMs can vary considerably, especially across different languages and domains. The accuracy of generative AI is a critical issue, particularly in applications where misinformation, factual inconsistencies, or biased outputs can have legal, ethical, or societal implications.[111] Inconsistent performance across languages can exacerbate existing inequalities, as communities that rely on underrepresented languages or dialects may receive lower-quality AI-generated content.[112] This can, in turn, reinforce structural biases and limit the inclusivity of AI technologies. However, for GPAI models, where generative AI is often included, additional obligations under Chapter V require providers to document the capabilities and limitations of the model, which may indirectly address concerns related to accuracy and bias.

5 Addressing Conflicts and Overlaps

5.1 Regulatory Overlaps

Since the launch of the EU's Digital Europe initiative,[113] a variety of detailed legal frameworks have been introduced, each covering different digital topics.[114] This has created the potential for regulatory overlap and, at times, conflict.

With multiple regulations addressing similar areas, overlaps are inevitable. For instance, consider a robotic surgical device: as a healthcare tool, it will be classified as a medical device under Article 2 of the MDR, thus subject to its requirements.[115] As a mechanical device, it will also need to meet some standards under the Machinery Regulation.[116]Additionally, since it relies on AI, it will qualify as an AI system under Article 3(1) of the AI Act. Therefore, to access the EU market, at least three conformity assessments will be required to obtain the conformity mark (although the idea seems to be to compress everything into a single conformity assessment, this might not always be feasible) , along with all the complexities this process entails in terms of time and cost.[117]

[111] Wach et al. (2023), pp. 7–30.

[112] Steinert and Kazenwadel (2024).

[113] European Commission (2025d).

[114] See Frischhut (2025).

[115] In detail about this 'overlap', Palmieri (2025).

[116] Assuming that the medical device fulfils the conditions to be regarded as a machine under this Regulation.

[117] A similar example, but involving the use of facial recognition systems in healthcare provision, in Raposo (2024a).

In some cases, overlapping requirements may escalate into outright conflicts. Take, for example, the GDPR's restrictions on the processing of personal data,[118] which limit collection, usage, and reuse of such data, including in AI training, except in certain cases (e.g., research exemptions). Meanwhile, the AI Act, aiming for more robust AI, mandates that training and testing datasets be as complete as possible (Article 10(3) AI Act). These two aims are inherently conflicting.[119] While the Data Governance Act,[120] along with the European Health Data Space Regulation[121] and other upcoming regulations, attempts to bridge this gap by promoting data sharing and reuse across sectors, it will not fully resolve these contradictions.[122]

5.2 *Institutional Overlaps*

The AI Act also risks creating overlaps in the roles of various regulatory bodies. A flagrant overlap might involve DPAs.[123] Currently, DPAs are the ones primarily handling AI assessments, typically under GDPR guidelines. However, as the AI Act introduces new responsibilities, a significant portion of AI oversight will shift to the new market surveillance authorities (which, in some countries, may be the DPAs, but not necessarily). Recognising the critical role of data processing in the development and testing of AI systems, as well as their extensive expertise in evaluating risks posed by emerging technologies —particularly in the domain of data protection—the European Data Protection Board (EDPB) and the European

[118] In detail, see the chapter of Lau (2025)

[119] About the application of the GDPR to AI systems see European Data Protection Board (2024b).

[120] Regulation (EU) 2022/868 of the European Parliament and of the Council of 30 May 2022 on European data governance and amending Regulation (EU) 2018/1724 (Data Governance Act).

[121] Regulation (EU) 2025/327 of the European Parliament and of the Council of 11 February 2025 on the European Health Data Space and amending Directive 2011/24/EU and Regulation (EU) 2024/2847.

About this regulation see Raposo (2025a).

[122] The AIA seems to exclude from the equation the upcoming regulations on data spaces, as announces by the Data Governance Act. Europe's data strategy seeks to establish a unified data market, strengthening its global competitiveness while safeguarding data sovereignty (Christakis 2023). The strategy emphasises several key objectives: enabling seamless data flow within the EU and across sectors, ensuring the availability of high-quality data to drive innovation, upholding European values and legal standards, fostering fair, clear, and practical rules for data access and usage, and implementing robust data governance frameworks (Bellanova et al. 2022, pp. 337–355). Central to this vision are Common European Data Spaces, designed to increase the availability of data for economic and societal benefits while ensuring that individuals and businesses generating the data retain control. These data spaces play a key role in advancing AI applications and supporting a vibrant marketplace for cloud and edge-based services (Scerri et al. 2022).

[123] Lau (2025).

Data Protection Supervisor (EDPS) have recommended assigning the role of market surveillance authorities to DPAs in EU Member States.[124] When this is not the case, conflicts might arise. Consider Article 10(3) of the AIA as an example. In theory, DPAs would evaluate whether data used in AI training complies with GDPR, while market surveillance authorities would assess the dataset's completeness and accuracy. However, practical issues arise when errors are found in datasets. For instance, if an individual claims that their data in a training set is inaccurate, this falls under the DPA's purview due to the GDPR's principles of data accuracy and rectification rights. Yet, the same error might require market surveillance authorities' oversight due to its implications for the AI model quality. Thus, this creates not only overlap but also potential conflict of competences. Clearly delineating the responsibilities of DPAs, market surveillance authorities, and other oversight agencies is essential to prevent jurisdictional conflicts and ensure cohesive governance.[125]

6 Compliance and Penalties

6.1 Compliance Authorities

A fundamental aspect of the AI Act framework is compliance oversight, which ensures that AI systems—particularly high-risk applications—adhere to legal and ethical standards. This oversight is critical to safeguarding fundamental rights, fostering public trust, ensuring accountability in AI deployment and maintaining the internal market's integrity.[126]

The AI Act establishes a multi-tiered governance model, involving the European Artificial Intelligence Office, a newly proposed body tasked with monitoring AI systems across the EU, ensuring harmonised enforcement, and overseeing general-purpose AI models; the AI Board, composed of representatives from Member States, this body facilitates coordination, information sharing, and consistent implementation of AI-related regulations; the National Competent Authorities, which include the market surveillance authorities and the notifying authorities; the notified bodies, which are independent entities conducting conformity assessments for high-risk AI

---

[124] Cf. European Data Protection Board – European Data Protection Supervisor (2021), points 47–48.

Likewise, the French Data Protection Authority (CNIL) has explicitly stated its intention to uphold its previous assessments of AI systems and asserted its entitlement to act as the AI authority under the AI Act (Commission Nationale de l'Informatique et des Libertés 2024).

[125] Even within the EU institutional structure, there are unclear boundaries of competence between institutions, particularly between the European Commission and the AI Office, as well as between the AI Office and the AI Board. In this regard see Malik and Solaiman (2025).

[126] Wai-Loon Ho and Caals (2024).

systems before they enter the market; and consultative bodies (Advisory Forum, Scientific Panel of Independent Experts).[127]

For high-risk AI systems, compliance oversight entails several mandatory assessments. First, ex-ante compliance checks require providers to demonstrate adherence to legal requirements. Subsequently, post-market monitoring obliges AI providers to implement incident reporting mechanisms and conduct ongoing risk evaluations. Third, regulatory audits may be conducted by supervisory authorities, either randomly or in a targeted manner, to assess compliance with the AI Act's obligations.[128]

6.2 Challenges in Compliance Oversight

Despite its comprehensive framework, several challenges remain.[129] Some challenges stem from the lack of enforcement capacity, as market surveillance authorities may lack sufficient resources or specialised expertise to effectively oversee complex AI systems. Cross-border coordination also poses a significant challenge, as ensuring harmonised enforcement across Member States remains difficult. Moreover, the regulatory burden may disproportionately impact companies, particularly SMEs, which might struggle to comply with the AI Act's extensive documentation, auditing, and compliance requirements.

To enhance compliance oversight, the EU may strengthen collaboration between regulators and AI developers to refine oversight mechanisms.[130] Another option is to expand the role of regulatory sandboxes,[131] allowing AI developers to test compliance in controlled environments and introduce adaptive compliance models, using AI tools to automate monitoring and enforcement.

Another key feature is the reliance on severe penalties (Chapter XII of the AIA), following the precedent set by the GDPR.[132] To ensure compliance, the AI Act establishes a graduated system of sanctions and corrective measures. First, administrative fines, where non-compliance can result in penalties of up to €35 million or 7% of global annual turnover for the most severe violations. Second, corrective actions, through which regulators can mandate modifications, suspend AI models,

---

[127] About the institutional framework, Malik and Solaiman (2025).

[128] Mökander et al. (2022), pp. 247–255.

[129] Demková and De Gregorio (2025).

[130] Lund et al. (2025).

[131] Ruschemeier (2023), pp. 318–332.

[132] Regulation (EU) 2016/679 of the European Parliament and of the Council of 27 April 2016 on the protection of natural persons with regard to the processing of personal data and on the free movement of such data, and repealing Directive 95/46/EC.

Actually, the AI Act has several similarities with the GDPR, as for instance, the length, the use of an extensive number of recitals and the level of complexity (Wolff et al. 2024, pp. 1–24.).

or issue product recalls. The expectation is that such measures will 'encourage' compliance.[133] In addition, there is the possibility of filing a complaint with market surveillance authorities or any other relevant authority if the respective requirements are met (for instance, with the national DPA in cases of data protection infringements).[134] Lastly, there is the option to file a lawsuit seeking compensation for harm, potentially based on the recently approved version of the Product Liability Directive.[135]

7 Regulatory Sandboxes and Innovation

7.1 Regulatory Sandboxes

7.1.1 Concept and Purposes of Regulatory Sandboxes Within the AI Act

The AI Act defines AI regulatory sandboxes as structured environments overseen by competent authorities (Article 3(55) AI Act). These frameworks are designed to allow providers or prospective providers of AI systems to innovate by developing, training, validating, and testing their systems in a controlled setting. In some cases, these tests may even extend to real-world conditions, all under the parameters of a predefined sandbox plan and within a limited timeframe.[136]

AI sandboxes can take various forms—physical, digital, or a hybrid of both—providing flexibility to accommodate the specific needs of both tangible and digital AI products.[137] This adaptability ensures that the sandbox environment aligns with the unique requirements of the system being developed, creating a supportive space for experimentation and innovation while remaining under regulatory supervision.[138] None of this is done without monitoring. Regulatory sandboxes create a controlled setting where developers can test new AI technologies under the watchful eye of regulators.[139] This setup fosters experimentation but also refinement, allowing developers to spot and fix potential issues before launching products widely.

Sandboxes offer valuable benefits, such as regulatory flexibility and the ability to support innovative products that might not fit neatly within current frameworks, pushing the boundaries of existing regulations. They also provide AI providers and authorities a chance to identify and resolve legal and ethical gaps early in the

[133] In clear contrast with some other approaches, as for instance the Singaporean one (Loo and Findlay 2025).

[134] Micklitz and Sartor (2025).

[135] Directive (EU) 2024/2853 of the European Parliament and of the Council of 23 October 2024 on liability for defective products and repealing Council Directive 85/374/EEC.

[136] Chassang (2025).

[137] See the experiences with regulatory sandboxes in Taiwan, as described by Chen (2025).

[138] Chassang (2025).

[139] In detail in this regard see the chapter of Chassang (2025).

development phase. By participating in these sandboxes, AI providers can receive guidance on regulatory expectations and how to fulfil the requirements and obligations set out in the AI Act. This, in turn, can lead to a speedier assessment process. Upon request, competent authorities can provide written proof of the activities successfully carried out in the sandbox, which providers may use to demonstrate their compliance with the AI Act during conformity assessment processes or relevant market surveillance activities.

For sandboxes to be effective, they require clear guidelines and robust oversight to prevent them from becoming loopholes for regulatory avoidance. This was a notable weakness in the first draft of the AI Act proposed by the Commission in April 2021. The Council's version, however, strengthened these aspects, offering a generally sound legal framework for regulatory sandboxes in the AI Act. Still, many issues remain unclear and may lead to an uneven application of the legal framework.

7.1.2 Testing in Real World Conditions

The AI Act introduces the concept of 'testing in real-world conditions' (Articles 60 and 61 AI Act), defining it as the temporary evaluation of an AI system in settings that reflect its intended use, outside the confines of a laboratory or simulated environment (Articles 3(57) AI Act).[140] Importantly, this process is not considered as placing the AI systems on the market or putting it into service, provided that the conditions specified in Article 60 of the AI Act are met. The purpose of such testing is to collect reliable and robust data to assess and verify compliance with the AI Act's regulatory standards, but in real world scenarios.

This framework requires a critical reflection on its applicability. Take, for instanece, the case of AI-driven clinical trials or investigations.[141] Could such trials, which inherently involve real-world application of AI systems in healthcare settings, be regarded as testing in real-world conditions under the AI Act framework? The issue is not explicitly addressed by the AI Act and the doubt arises because both scenarios involve using AI systems in practical environments to ensure compliance and gather actionable data. Clarifying the relationship between AI-based clinical trials and the AI Act's provisions on real-world testing is essential to ensure both regulatory compliance and the ethical use of AI in these sensitive contexts.

7.1.3 Drawbacks in the Legal Framework of Regulatory Sandboxes in the AI Act

In the legal framework of regulatory sandboxes, some issues remain unclear.

---

[140] Wai-Loon Ho and Caals (2024), pp. 366–368.

[141] The question is analysed by Chassang (2025).

This is the case of the national authority in charge of supervising the sandbox. The competent authorities overseeing the sandbox must deliver ‘guidance, supervision, and support’ to the organisations involved (Article 57(6) AIA) and offer ‘guidance on regulatory expectations and how to fulfil the requirements and obligations set out in this Regulation’ (Article 57(7) AIA). But… who are these supervisory authorities? A possible interpretation is that the designation process will be tailored to the specifics of each case, that is, the determination of competent authorities will invariably depend on the anticipated legal classification of the AI system, its intended functions, and the relevant legal and regulatory framework.[142] However, if that is the case, we can potentially have as many supervisory authorities as types of AI systems. This, in turn, leads to another question: how many supervisory authorities can we have for a specific AI system?

Data protection issues are also a matter of uncertainty.[143] The AI Act reaffirms the applicability of the GDPR to data processing within regulatory sandboxes, while Article 59 of the AI Act introduces a distinct legal framework for reusing personal data in this context under certain conditions.[144] Despite the lack of a clear relationship between this legal regime and the one set forth in the GDPR for ‘further processing’ (or ‘data repurposing’),[145] established in Article 6(4) GDPR, one could assume that the latter still applies. This would require either the data subject’s consent, a Union or Member State law ensuring the processing is necessary and proportionate in a democratic society, or a documented compatibility assessment based on the criteria set in Article 6(4) of the GDPR. Such an outcome would impose a compliance burden that may prove unduly onerous in practice. Accordingly, a more practicable approach is to regard Article 59 of the AI Act as a lex specialis vis-à-vis Article 6(4) of the GDPR (lex generalis), thereby excluding the application of the latter provision in this specific context.[146]

As long as participating AI providers adhere to the guidance issued in good faith and comply with the agreed-upon terms and participation plan, the competent authorities are prohibited from imposing administrative fines (Article 57(12) AIA). However, the provider’s participation in a regulatory sandbox does not alter liability for the harm caused. Thus, a major concern lies in the incentive to participate. While sandboxes indeed offer a more flexible regulatory framework, if this developer-friendly approach does not also extend to liability relief, will AI providers be willing to engage? Given this liability landscape, it is reasonable to predict that many may hesitate to test new products in regulatory sandboxes due to the substantial risks

---

[142] In this sense, Chassang (2025).

[143] In his chapter Gauthier Chassang—Chassang (2025)—also highlights several issues in this domain

[144] The AIA does not specify particular legal bases for the primary use of personal data collected specifically for, or during, sandbox activities.

[145] Raposo (2024c), pp. 169–192.

[146] Baldini (2025) 72–74.

involved.[147] Without additional benefits—such as tax relief—there may not be sufficient incentive for companies to participate in the sandbox.

7.2 *The Research and Development Exception*

The AI Act does, to some extent, acknowledge the importance of research and innovation. Recognising the distinct nature of scientific investigation— characterised by experimentation, hypothesis testing, and innovation in often unregulated contexts—the AI Act introduces specific exclusions. According to Articles 2(6) and 2(8) and Recital 25, AI systems developed or used exclusively for scientific research are exempt from the AI Act's scope.[148] This is the so-called Research and Development (R&D) exception.[149]

While this exclusion strengthens the importance of supporting scientific progress, it has also ignited debates about its broader implications. Proponents argue that this flexibility is essential for researchers operating in dynamic environments where traditional regulatory frameworks may be unsuitable.[150] Specific sectors, like pharmaceuticals, already operate under rigorous regulatory standards, and additional AI-specific rules could prove redundant, adding unnecessary complexity to innovation processes.[151] Critics, however, caution against the potential risks of regulatory gaps.[152] They emphasise the need for oversight, particularly when AI tools initially designed for research purposes transition into clinical or commercial applications without adequate scrutiny.

Adding to this complexity is the relationship between the AI Act general framework and AI regulatory sandboxes. As Chassang observes, the AI Act does not classify regulatory sandboxes as premarket R&D frameworks.[153] Regulatory sandboxes could have been explicitly integrated into the provisions governing scientific R&D, but they did not. This omission leaves a degree of ambiguity, but it suggests that the exemptions for R&D do not extend to regulatory sandbox testing, even if conducted exclusively for research purposes. This lack of clarity raises important questions for researchers and policymakers alike.

---

[147] Still, Chassang (2025) points out some potential benefits of participating in the sandbox.

[148] Note, however, that if researchers intend to employ an AI system not exclusively developed and used for R&D, that system falls within the scope of the AI Act. This regulatory framework could encompass any AI system created with dual objectives: research and potential commercial deployment.

[149] On this exception see Constantino and Van der Linden (2025).

[150] European Federation of Pharmaceutical Industries and Associations (2024).

[151] Raposo (2025b).

[152] Constantino and Van der Linden (2025); Van Kolfschooten and Van Oirschot (2024).

[153] Chassang (2025).

7.3 The Drawback to Innovation

When shaping regulatory frameworks for emerging technologies or innovative applications of existing ones, the EU should prioritise fostering an environment that nurtures and promotes innovation.[154] Regulation, while essential, should not stifle the EU's capacity to lead in scientific and technological advancements. Regulations must also be 'future-proof', anticipating developments while providing stakeholders with legal clarity and certainty to navigate evolving landscapes confidently.[155]

Still, innovation remains one of the AI Act's most notable weaknesses.[156]

A core challenge in AI regulation is finding a balance between oversight and the need to encourage innovation. The AI Act must ensure its rules do not hinder technological progress or limit creativity. Excessively strict regulations could lead to an 'innovation gap', disadvantaging European AI developers and pushing talent and funding towards regions with more relaxed policies,[157] potentially causing a 'brain drain'.[158]

The innovation principle reinforces the importance of considering the needs of businesses, particularly SMEs, which are often the drivers of groundbreaking ideas but also the most vulnerable to burdensome regulations. By fostering an ecosystem that supports their growth, the EU could ensure that innovation flourishes across all sectors, from technology and science to commerce and sustainability. However, the AI Act falls short on this point. While Article 62 introduces measures to support SMEs and start-ups in navigating regulatory requirements and fostering innovation,[159] the reality is that the regulatory burden remains too demanding for these small-scale operators.[160] Given the stringent compliance demands, it is highly likely that many SMEs and start-ups will lack the necessary resources to meet the AI Act's rigorous requirements due to limited financial resources and the complexity of navigating its intricate legal framework.[161] Overly prescriptive rules can become obstacles, particularly in sectors characterised by rapid technological shifts. Instead, frameworks should maintain a balance, allowing for innovation while ensuring adequate

---

[154] Teigland (2025).

[155] Chassang (2025).

[156] Discussing this issue, Dacoronias-Marina and Durovic (2025).

[157] See the study of Gikay (2024), comparing the EU and the UK's approach.

[158] Curiously, a risk identified by the European Commission some years ago (European Commission 2018: 'Without major efforts, the EU risks losing out on the opportunities offered by AI, facing a brain-drain and being a consumer of solutions developed elsewhere').

[159] By lowering financial and administrative burdens, facilitating regulatory guidance, and providing priority access to testing environments, the objective is to enhance their ability to compete and scale in the EU AI market (Taylor Jones 2025).

[160] Zubaşcu (2025).

[161] Chassang (2025); Palmieri (2025).

safeguards[162] and guaranteeing that regulatory measures are forward-looking and capable of enduring challenges without becoming obsolete.[163]

Last, but not least, the need for a specific AI regulation can be discussed. One could argue, for instance, that 'rather than creating technology-specific rules, it is usually better to develop sound general rules, then apply them to specific innovations'.[164] Only time will tell us if this was a smart move.

8 A Call for Continuous Improvement

The AI Act marks a crucial advancement in building a regulatory framework for AI across the EU, covering essential aspects such as risk assessment, data quality, ethical standards, and innovation support. Yet, there is still room for improvement to further fine-tune and strengthen this regulation.

As AI technologies rapidly advance,[165] and become increasingly used in more and more domains,[166] our regulatory frameworks must evolve alongside them. The AI Act should be regarded as a dynamic document, open to ongoing evaluation and refinement, considering in particular the evolving nature of the AI's concept.[167] European lawmakers anticipated this need for flexibility, granting the European Commission authority to update certain parts of the Act.[168] Moreover, active involvement from all stakeholders—developers, deployers, regulators, and the public—is key to recognising new challenges and opportunities as they arise. It remains to be seen whether this will be sufficient.[169]

A key note to have in consideration is that some norms of the AI Act are too broad and enigmatic to be fully apprehended by simply reading the text.[170] This is not a specificity of the AI Act but rather a common feature of complex sets of rules, requiring further clarification in the form of guidelines, recommendations, or even caselaw[171] (note that EU case law plays a crucial role in the EU legal structure). Some of these have already started being issued,[172] but many more are expected in the future. Hopefully, they will not only help clarify the meaning of the norms but

---

162 Chassang (2025).

163 Raposo (2022).

164 Dempsey (2025).

165 Steckelmacher and Bogaerts (2025).

166 Steckelmacher and Bogaerts (2025).

167 König et al. (2022), pp. 18–34.

168 For instance, Article 7 of the AI Act allows the Commission to revise Annex III periodically.

169 This seems to be a key feature in the Singapore strategy for AI, as pointed out by Loo and Findlay (2025).

170 Charlesworth (2025).

171 While the EU still presents a limited number of judicial decisions involving AI-related issues, the United States is already grappling with several of these cases, as described in the chapter of Dempsey (2025).

172 For instance, European Commission (2025a, b).

also, whenever possible, address some of the gaps, inconsistencies, and excesses already identified in the text of the AI Act. Luckily, the gradual entry into force of the AI Act[173] might allow the respective authorities and bodies the necessary time to issue much-needed clarifications.

While the AI Act lays a vital foundation for responsible AI governance, it is not the final answer. Continuous improvement is essential, drawing on collective expertise to create a regulatory environment that both mitigates risks and fosters innovation for societal benefit. In short, the AI Act is a well-intentioned and valuable legislative effort, but it falls short.

Brussels, we still have work to do.

References

Ada Lovelace (2022) People, risk and the unique requirements of AI - 18 recommendations to strengthen the EU AI Act. https://www.adalovelaceinstitute.org/wp-content/uploads/2022/03/Policy-briefing-People-risk-and-the-unique-requirements-of-AI-18-recommendations-to-strengthen-the-EU-AI-Act.pdf

Ahmad SF, Han H, Alam MM et al (2023) Impact of artificial intelligence on human loss in decision making, laziness and safety in education. Humanit Soc Sci Commun 10:311. https://doi.org/10.1057/s41599-023-01787-8

Almada M, Petit N (2023) The EU AI Act: a medley of product safety and fundamental rights?., EUI, RSC, Working Paper, 2023/59, https://hdl.handle.net/1814/75982

appliedAI (2023) AI Act risk classification study. AppliedAI Initiative. https://aai.frb.io/assets/files/AI-Act-Risk-Classification-Study-appliedAI-March-2023.pdf

Baldini D (2025) Legislative Intersection Perspectives on Regulatory Sandboxes: Navigating the Interplay Between the AI Act and the GDPR, in Regulatory Sandboxes for AI and Cybersecurity: Questions and Answers for Stakeholders (Bagni, F. and Seferi, F. eds), Cybersecurity National Lab, 2025, pp. 70–84. https://cybersecnatlab.it/wp-content/uploads/2025/02/CybersecNatLab-White-Paper-Regulary-Sandboxes.pdf

Bellanova R, Carrapico H, Duez D (2022) Digital sovereignty and European security integration: an introduction. Eur Secur 31(3):337–355. https://doi.org/10.1080/09662839.2022.2101887

Bygrave LA, Schmidt S (2025) Regulating non-high-risk AI systems under the EU's Artificial Intelligence Act, with special focus on the role of soft law. In: Raposo VL (ed) The European Artificial Intelligence Act: promises and perils. Springer

Charlesworth A (2025) AI regulation in the UK. In: Raposo VL (ed) The European Artificial Intelligence Act: promises and perils. Springer

Chassang G (2025) Regulatory sandboxes for trustworthy AI - an EU framework for experimenting AI systems and fostering agile regulation. In: Raposo VL (ed) The European Artificial Intelligence Act: promises and perils. Springer

Chen CH (2025) Taiwan's AI regulatory approach: comparing to the EU AI Act. In: Raposo VL (ed) The European Artificial Intelligence Act: promises and perils. Springer

Chow AR (2024) Some top AI labs have 'very weak' risk management, study finds. Time. https://time.com/7026972/saferai-study-xai-meta/

Christakis T (2023) European digital sovereignty, data protection, and the push toward data localization. In: Chander A, Sun H (eds) Data sovereignty: from the digital silk road to the return of the state. Oxford Academic, New York. https://doi.org/10.1093/oso/9780197582794.003.0015

[173] Charlesworth (2025).

Cohen D (2012) Notified bodies: are they fit for purpose? BMJ 345:e7177. https://doi.org/10.1136/bmj.e7177
Commission Nationale de l'Informatique et des Libertés (CNIL) (2024) AI Act: data protection authorities want to be in charge of high-risk systems. https://www.cnil.fr/en/ai-act-data-protection-authorities-want-be-charge-high-risk-systems
Constantino J, Van der Linden T (2025) Artificial Intelligence (AI) systems not covered by the AI regulation. In: Raposo VL (ed) The European Artificial Intelligence Act: promises and perils. Springer
T3 Consultants (2025) AI regulations explained: how the EU AI Act will impact businesses and jobs. https://t3-consultants.com/2025/01/ai-regulations-explained-how-the-eu-ai-act-will-impact-businesses-and-jobs/
Dacoronias-Marina M, Durovic M (2025) Consumer protection in light of the new AI Act. In: Raposo VL (ed) The European Artificial Intelligence Act: promises and perils. Springer
Daníelsson J, Macrae R, Uthemann A (2022) Artificial intelligence and systemic risk. J Bank Financ 140:106290. https://doi.org/10.1016/j.jbankfin.2021.106290
DataGuard (2024) The EU AI Act: obligations for deployers of high-risk AI systems. DataGuard. https://www.dataguard.com/blog/the-eu-ai-act-obligations-for-deployer/
Datta A (2025) The regulation of GPAI model providers under the EU AI Act. In: Denga M, Hornuf L (eds) Regulatory competition in the digital economy, Advanced studies in diginomics and digitalization. Springer, Cham, pp 119–137. https://doi.org/10.1007/978-3-031-81089-3_6
Demková S, De Gregorio G (2025) The looming enforcement crisis in european digital policy: a rule-of-law centered path forward. VerfBlog., https://verfassungsblog.de/the-looming-enforcement-crisis-ai-dsa-eu/. https://doi.org/10.59704/c4fc2ec9cb2b9ba5
Dempsey JX (2025) Artificial intelligence regulation in the United States: A patchwork of laws. In: Raposo VL (ed) The European Artificial Intelligence Act: promises and perils. Springer
Ebers M (2024) Truly risk-based regulation of artificial intelligence how to implement the EU's AI Act. European Journal of Risk Regulation:1–20. https://doi.org/10.1017/err.2024.78
Ebers M, Hoch VR, Rosenkranz F et al (2021) The European Commission's Proposal for an Artificial Intelligence Act - a critical assessment by members of the robotics and AI law society (RAILS). J 4(4):589–603. https://doi.org/10.3390/j4040043
European Commission (2018) Communication from the Commission to the European Parliament, the European Council, the Council, the European Economic and Social Committee and the Committee of the Regions Coordinated Plan on Artificial Intelligence, COM/2018/795 final. https://eur-lex.europa.eu/legal-content/EN/TXT/?uri=celex:52018DC0795
European Commission (2025a) Annex to the Communication to the Commission Approval of the content of the draft Communication from the Commission - Commission Guidelines on the Definition of an Artificial Intelligence System Established by Regulation (EU) 2024/1689 (AI Act), Brussels, 6.2.2025, https://digitalstrategy.ec.europa.eu/en/library/commission-publishes-guidelines-ai-system-definition-facilitate-first-ai-acts-rulesapplication
European Commission (2025b), Approval of the Content of the Draft Communication from the Commission - Commission Guidelines on Prohibited Artificial Intelligence Practices Established by Regulation (EU) 2024/1689 (AI Act), https://digital-strategy.ec.europa.eu/en/library/commission-publishes-guidelines-prohibited-artificial-intelligence-ai-practices-defined-ai-act
European Commission (2025c) Commission Guidelines on the Definition of an Artificial Intelligence System Established by Regulation (EU) 2024/1689 (AI Act), https://digital-strategy.ec.europa.eu/en/library/commission-publishes-guidelines-prohibited-artificial-intelligence-ai-practices-defined-ai-act
European Commission (2025d) Digital Europe Programme, Digital Strategy, https://digital-strategy.ec.europa.eu/en/activities/digital-programme
European Data Protection Board (2024a) EDPB adopts statement on DPAs' role in the AI Act Framework and EU-US Data Privacy Framework FAQ. https://www.edpb.europa.eu/news/news/2024/edpb-adopts-statement-dpas-role-ai-act-framework-eu-us-data-privacy-framework-faq_en

European Data Protection Board (2024b) Opinion 28/2024 on certain data protection aspects of AI models. https://www.edpb.europa.eu/our-work-tools/our-documents/opinion-board-art-64/opinion-282024-certain-data-protection-aspects_en
European Data Protection Board (2024c) Statement 3/2024 on Data Protection Authorities' Role in the Artificial Intelligence Act Framework. https://www.edpb.europa.eu/system/files/202407/edpb_statement_202403_dpasroleaiact_en.pdf
European Data Protection Board – European Data Protection Supervisor (EDPB-EDPS) (2021) Joint Opinion 5/2021 on the proposal for a Regulation of the European Parliament and of the Council laying down harmonised rules on artificial intelligence (Artificial Intelligence Act). https://www.edpb.europa.eu/our-work-tools/our-documents/edpbedps-joint-opinion/edpb-edps-joint-opinion-52021-proposal_en
European Federation of Pharmaceutical Industries and Associations (EFPIA) (2024) EFPIA statement on the use of AI in the medicinal product lifecycle in the context of the AI Act. https://efpia.eu/news-events/the-efpia-view/statements-press-releases/efpia-statement-on-the-use-of-ai-in-the-medicinal-product-lifecycle-in-the-context-of-the-ai-act/
Feuerriegel S, Hartmann J, Janiesch C, Zschech P (2024) Generative AI. Bus Inf Syst Eng 66(1):111–126
Fraser H, Bello y Villarino JM (2024) Acceptable risks in Europe's proposed AI Act: reasonableness and other principles for deciding how much risk management is enough. Eur J Risk Regul 15(2):431–446
Frischhut M (2025) The EU's common values (Art 2 EU-Treaty) as the underlying philosophy of the AI Act. In: Raposo VL (ed) The European Artificial Intelligence Act: promises and perils. Springer
Gikay AA (2024) Risks, innovation, and adaptability in the UK's incrementalism versus the European Union's Comprehensive Artificial Intelligence Regulation. Int J Law Inf Technol 32(1):eaae013. https://doi.org/10.1093/ijlit/eaae013
Glauner P (2022) An assessment of the AI regulation proposed by the European Commission. Springer
Gornet M (2024) Too broad to handle: can we 'fix' harmonised standards on artificial intelligence by focusing on vertical sectors? hal-04785208
Gornet M, Maxwell W (2024) The European approach to regulating AI through technical standards. Internet Policy Rev 13(3):1–27. https://doi.org/10.14763/2024.3.1784
Hacker P (2021) A Legal framework for AI training data - from first principles to the Artificial Intelligence Act. Law Innov Technol 13(2):257–301
Hacker P, Engel A, Hammer S, Mittelstadt B (2025) Introduction to the foundations and regulation of generative AI. In: Hacker P, Engel A, Hammer S, Mittelstadt B (eds) The Oxford handbook of the foundation and regulation of generative AI. Oxford University Press. https://ssrn.com/abstract=5137750
Herbosch M (2025) To err is human: managing the risks of contracting AI systems. Comput Law Secur Rev 56:106110. https://doi.org/10.1016/j.clsr.2025.106110
König PD, Krafft TD, Schulz W, Zweig KA (2022) Essence of AI: what is AI? In: DiMatteo LA, Poncibò C, Cannarsa M (eds) The Cambridge handbook of artificial intelligence: global perspectives on law and ethics. Cambridge, Cambridge University Press, pp 18–34
Kusche I (2024) Possible harms of artificial intelligence and the EU AI Act: fundamental rights and risk. J Risk Res:1–14. https://doi.org/10.1080/13669877.2024.2350720
Lau PL (2025) The AI Act and Data Protection - the interplay between artificial intelligence and data: the AI Act and the GDPR. In: Raposo VL (ed) The European Artificial Intelligence Act: promises and perils. Springer
Laux J, Wachter S, Mittelstadt B (2024) Three pathways for standardisation and ethical disclosure by default under the European Union Artificial Intelligence Act. Comput Law Secur Rev 53:105957. https://doi.org/10.1016/j.clsr.2024.105957
Levano J (2024) Predictive policing in the AI Act: meaningful ban or paper tiger? European Law Blog. https://www.europeanlawblog.eu/pub/tbgfjobj/release/1

Liebl A, Klein T (2023) AI Act: risk classification of AI systems from a practical perspective. https://www.appliedai.de/assets/files/AI-Act_WhitePaper_final_CMYK_ENG.pdf

Loo L, Findlay M (2025) Juxtaposing approaches to risk-based AI governance in different 'rights' contexts: a comparative analysis between Singapore and the EU. In: Raposo VL (ed) The European Artificial Intelligence Act: promises and perils. Springer

Lund B, Orhan Z, Mannuru NR, Bevara R, Porter B, Vinaih MK, Bhaskara P (2025) Standards, frameworks, and legislation for artificial intelligence (AI) transparency. AI Ethics. https://doi.org/10.1007/s43681-025-00661-4

Malik A, Solaiman B (2025) Appraising the institutional framework of the EU's Artificial Intelligence Act (AI Act). In: Raposo VL (ed) The European Artificial Intelligence Act: promises and perils. Springer

Micklitz H, Sartor G (2025) Compliance and enforcement in the AIA through AI. Yearb Eur Law:yeae014. https://doi.org/10.1093/yel/yeae014

Mökander J, Axente M, Casolari F, Floridi L (2022) Conformity assessments and post-market monitoring: a guide to the role of auditing in the proposed European AI regulation. Mind Mach 32(2):241–268

National Artificial Intelligence Advisory Committee (2023) Findings: the potential future risks of AI. https://ai.gov/wp-content/uploads/2023/11/Findings_The-Potential-Future-Risks-of-AI.pdf

Neuwirth R (2025) Prohibited artificial intelligence practices revisited. In: Raposo VL (ed) The European Artificial Intelligence Act: promises and perils. Springer

Novelli C, Casolari F, Rotolo A, Floridi L (2024) Taking AI risks seriously: a new assessment model for the AI Act. AI & Soc 39:2493–2497. https://doi.org/10.1007/s00146-023-01723-z

Palmieri S (2025) AI Act and MDR: investigating regulatory overlaps, influences, and joint application issues. In: Raposo VL (ed) The European Artificial Intelligence Act: promises and perils. Springer

Palmieri S, Goffin T (2025) Artificial intelligence and fundamental rights: under the European Legal Eye. In: Raposo VL (ed) The European Artificial Intelligence Act: promises and perils. Springer

Philippe J (2024) The EU AI Act: too early and too complex? J Law Bus 20(3):685–700

Raposo VL (2022) Ex Machina: preliminary critical assessment of the European Draft Act on Artificial Intelligence. Int J Law Inf Technol 30(1):88–109. https://doi.org/10.1093/ijlit/eaac007

Raposo VL (2023a) Look at the camera and say cheese': the existing European legal framework for facial recognition technology in criminal investigations. Inf Commun Technol Law 33:1–20. https://doi.org/10.1080/13600834.2023.2239621

Raposo VL (2023b) The use of facial recognition technology by law enforcement in Europe: a non-Orwellian draft proposal. Eur J Crim Policy Res 29:515–533. https://doi.org/10.1007/s10610-022-09512-y

Raposo VL (2024a) Facial recognition AI technology in healthcare and the law. In: B Solaiman and IG Cohen IG (eds.), Research handbook on health, AI and the law, pp. 41–56. Cheltenham: Edward Elgar Publishing, doi: https://doi.org/10.4337/9781802205657.ch03

Raposo VL (2024b) How is 'unexplainable' and non-transparent AI affecting healthcare delivery? Oslo Law Rev 11(1):1–12

Raposo VL (2024c) Training your medical/nursing robot: from the General Data Protection Regulation to the European Health Data Space. In: Ebers M, Sein K (eds) Privacy, data protection and data-driven technologies. Routledge, pp 169–192

Raposo VL (2025a) Can personal data be recycled? The reuse and repurposing of data under the EHDS. Int J Law Inf Technol. (in press)

Raposo VL (2025b) The fifty shades of black: about black box AI and explainability in healthcare. Med Law Rev 33(1):fwaf005

Ruschemeier H (2023) Thinking outside the box? Regulatory sandboxes as a tool for AI regulation. In: Steffen B (ed) Bridging the gap between AI and reality. AISoLA 2023, Lecture notes in computer science, vol 14129. Springer, Cham. https://doi.org/10.1007/978-3-031-73741-1_20

Scerri S, Tuikka T, De Vallejo IL, Curry E (2022) Common European data spaces: challenges and opportunities. In: Curry E, Scerri S, Tuikka T (eds) Data spaces. Springer, Cham. https://doi.org/10.1007/978-3-030-98636-0_16)

Setzu M, Guidotti R, Monreale A, Turini F, Pedreschi D, Giannotti F (2021) Glocalx-from local to global explanations of black box AI models. Artif Intell 294:103457. https://doi.org/10.1016/j.artint.2021.103457

Shehabi M, Morgan G, Zaber M, Wang N, Huber M, Lingel S (2023) Artificial Intelligence Governance and the European Union's Artificial Intelligence Act: understanding the implications of a risk-based approach. RAND Corporation. https://www.rand.org/pubs/research_reports/RRA3243-1.html

Slokenberga S (2025) Enforcing the AI Act in a composite EU administration. In: Raposo VL (ed) The European Artificial Intelligence Act: promises and perils. Springer

Solove DJ (2024) Artificial Intelligence and Privacy, Florida Law Review, GWU Legal Studies Research Paper No. 2024-36, GWU Law School Public Law Research Paper No. 2024-36. https://ssrn.com/abstract=4713111

Spiecker ID, Genannt Döhmann I (2022) AI and data protection. In: DiMatteo LA, Poncibò C, Cannarsa M (eds) The Cambridge handbook of artificial intelligence: global perspectives on law and ethics. Cambridge University Press, pp 132–145. https://doi.org/10.1017/9781009072168.015

Stahl BC, Rodrigues R, Santiago N et al (2022) A European Agency for artificial intelligence: protecting fundamental rights and ethical values. Comput Law Secur Rev 45:105661. https://doi.org/10.1016/j.clsr.2022.105661

Steckelmacher D, Bogaerts (2025) Definition of AI. In: Raposo VL (ed) The European Artificial Intelligence Act: promises and perils. Springer

Steinert CV, Kazenwadel D (2024) How user language affects conflict fatality estimates in ChatGPT. J Peace Res 0(0):00223433241279381. https://doi.org/10.1177/00223433241279381

Szostek D, Prabucki RT (2025) High-risk AI systems. In: Raposo VL (ed) The European Artificial Intelligence Act: promises and perils. Springer

Taylor Jones (2025) Small businesses guide to the AI Act. Artificial Intelligence Act. https://artificialintelligenceact.eu/small-businesses-guide-to-the-ai-act/

Teigland J (2025) How Europe can boost innovation. Bus Insider. https://www.businessinsider.com/how-europe-can-boost-innovation-trump-tariffs-ey-julie-teigland-2025-1. Accessed 11 Mar 2025

Thelisson E, Verma H (2024) Conformity assessment under the EU AI Act general approach. AI Ethics 4:113–121. https://doi.org/10.1007/s43681-023-00402-5

Van Kolfschooten H, Van Oirschot J (2024) The EU Artificial Intelligence Act (2024): implications for healthcare. Health Policy 149:105152. https://doi.org/10.1016/j.healthpol.2024.105152

Vasha PS (2023) How can we manage biases in artificial intelligence systems – a systematic literature review. Int J Inf Manag Data Insights 3(1):100165. https://doi.org/10.1016/j.jjimei.2023.100165

Veale M, Zuiderveen Borgesius F (2021) Demystifying the draft EU Artificial Intelligence Act - Analysing the good, the bad, and the unclear elements of the proposed approach. Comput Law Rev Int 22(4):97–112. https://doi.org/10.9785/cri-2021-220402

Vedder A, Nisevic M, Fleerackers S (2025) Ethics first? On the EU approach to AI governance. In: Raposo VL (ed) The European Artificial Intelligence Act: promises and perils. Springer

Wach K, Duong CD, Ejdys J, Kazlauskaitė R, Korzynski P, Mazurek G, Paliszkiewicz J, Ziemba E (2023) The dark side of generative artificial intelligence: a critical analysis of controversies and risks of ChatGPT. Entrep Bus Econ Rev 11(2):7–30

Wai-Loon Ho C, Caals K (2024) How the EU AI Act seeks to establish an epistemic environment of trust. Asian Bioeth Rev 16(3):345. https://doi.org/10.1007/s41649-024-00304-6

Wang M, Du L (2025) Regulatory issues related AI development and use: a comparative analysis of Chinese and EU laws. In: Raposo VL (ed) The European Artificial Intelligence Act: promises and perils. Springer

White & Case LLP (2025) AI watch: global regulatory tracker - European Union. White & Case LLP. https://www.whitecase.com/insight-our-thinking/ai-watch-global-regulatory-tracker-european-union

Wolff J, Lehr W, Yoo CS (2024) Lessons from GDPR for AI policymaking. VA J Law Technol 27(4):1–24

Yampolskiy RV (2025) On monitorability of AI. AI Ethics 5:689–707. https://doi.org/10.1007/s43681-024-00420-x

Zhong H, O'Neill E, Hoffmann JA (2024) Regulating AI: applying insights from behavioural economics and psychology to the application of article 5 of the EU AI Act. In: The thirty-eighth AAAI conference on artificial intelligence (AAAI-24), pp 20001–20009

Zubaşcu F (2025) Sprawling AI Act may deprive European start-ups of investment. Science|Business. https://sciencebusiness.net/news/ecosystem-sprawling-ai-act-may-deprive-european-start-ups-investment